D0321129

THE AMBIENT CENTURY

To Jock,

All the very best wishes
for your birthday – enjoy!

Lots of love

Nwi x Diane

x x   x x x

BY THE SAME AUTHOR

Irish Rock: Roots, Personalities, Directions (O'Brien Press 1987)
The Isle of Noises (St Martin's Press 1990)
The Jimi Hendrix Companion (as contributor) (Schirmer Books 1996)
Rough Guide to Classical Music (as contributor) (Rough Guides 1994/98)
Tangerine Dream – Tangents 1973–1983 (Virgin 1994)

THE AMBIENT CENTURY

FROM MAHLER TO TRANCE – THE EVOLUTION OF SOUND IN THE ELECTRONIC AGE

Mark Prendergast

BLOOMSBURY

For Genie and Natasha

PICTURE CREDITS: courtesy of Angel Records: page 7 *bottom*; Courtesy of Piers Allardyce: page 6 *bottom*; Courtesy of Apple Corps Ltd: page 7 *top left*; Camera Press: page 1 *bottom*; Courtesy of Chrysalis: page 2 *bottom*; Courtesy of Columbia Records: page 3 *bottom right*; Courtesy of ECM Records: page 4 *bottom right*; Courtesy of EMI Records: page 16 *top left*; Courtesy of Yuka Fujii: page 12 *bottom*; Courtesy of Colm Henry: page 13 *top*; Hulton Deutsh: page 1 *top left, top right*, 2 *top left*; Courtesy of Maria Vedder/Atelier Markgraph: page 5 *top left*; Courtesy of Nonsuch: page 4 *top left*, page 5 *bottom right*; Courtesy of Opal Ltd: page 4 *top right*; Courtesy of Reiner Pfisterer: page 15 *top right*; Courtesy of Polydor: page 14 *bottom*; Redferns: page 3 *top left, top right*, 8 *top, bottom right*, 11 *top*, 16 *bottom left, bottom right*; Retna: page 2 *top right*, 7 *top right*, 9 *top, bottom left, bottom right*, 10 *top left*, 13 *bottom right*, 15 *top left*; Rex: page 8 *bottom left*, 16 *top right*; Courtesy of Mark Rusher: page 12 *top right*; Courtesy of Sony: page 11 *bottom left*; Courtesy of Virgin: page 4 *bottom left*, 5 *top right, bottom left*, 10 *bottom*, 12 *top left*, 15 *bottom*; Courtesy of WEA/Warner Music UK Ltd: page 13 *bottom left*; Courtesy of Paul White & Sound on Sound: page 3 *bottom left*.

Every reasonable effort has been made to ascertain and acknowledge the ownership of copyrighted photographs, illustrations and quoted material included in this volume. Any errors that have inadvertently occurred will be corrected in subsequent editions provided notification is sent to the publisher.

First published in Great Britain 2000

Copyright © 2000 by Mark Prendergast
Foreword Copyright © 2000 by Brian Eno

The moral right of the authors have been asserted

Bloomsbury Publishing Plc, 38 Soho Square, London W1V 5DF

A CIP catalogue record for this book is available from the British Library

ISBN 0 7475 4213 9

1 3 5 7 9 10 8 6 4 2

Typeset by Hewer Text Ltd, Edinburgh
Printed in Great Britain by Clays Ltd, St Ives plc

CONTENTS

ACKNOWLEDGEMENTS

MUSIC INDUSTRY

Over the years many lovely people have facilitated my requests for interviews, information and recordings. Here are some of the best: Lisa Agasee, Gill Alice, Mike Alway, Laurence Aston, Lisa Anthony, Nick Austin, Rob Ayling, Emma Bagnall, Mike Barnes, Sophie Beck, John Best, Johnny Black, Ian Blackaby, Anne Boller, Mark Borkowski, Sue Brown, Vicky Bruce, Katharine Burton, Harriet Capaldi, Mick Carpenter, Dave Cawley, Richard Chadwick, Murray Chalmers, Jane Chapman, Barbara Charone, Patrick Crowther, Ted Cummings, James and Jelena Doheny, Emma Duyts, Deborah Edgley, Rachel Edwards, John Ellson, Sara Fécamp, Pete Flatt, Heather Finlay, Andy Garibaldi, Jilly Grafton, Louise Greidinger, Tony Goodwin, Alf Goodrich, Mike Gott, Tara Guha, Florence Halfon, Peter Hall, the late Philip Hall, Pippa Hall, Dave Harper, Mick Houghton, Amy Howard, Katherine Howard, Dorothy Howe, Talia Hull, Ann-Louise Hyde, Gabriel Ibos, Robert Barrs-James, Steve Kalidoski, Sharon Kelly, Debbi Lander, Pete Lawrence, Sarah Lees, Samantha Link, Judy Lipsey, Samantha Lock, Carol Lowry, Gerry Lyseight, Colleen Maloney, Eugene Manzi, Gaylene Martin, Sandra McKay, Alison McNicol, Nigel Molden, Tom Morden, Klaus Mueller, Pat Naylor, Kris Needs, Lee Ellen Newman, Shane O'Neill, Suzanne Parkes, Rob Partridge, Chantal Passamonte, Steve Phillips, Kelly Pike, Caroll Pinkham, Karen Pitchford, Jo Pratt, Andy Prevezer, Paul Reedy, Iain Robinson, Hildegard Schmidt, Steven Sanderson, Chareen Steel, Becky Stevenson, Suzanne Stephens, Anthea and Dominic Norman-Taylor, Rachel Thomas, Caroline Turner, Laurence Verfaillie, Debbie Walker, the late Johnny Waller, Steve Waters, Chris White, Amanda Whitwell, Tony Wilson, Carol Yaple, Rob Young.

EDITORIAL

Much appreciation to the editors of various magazines, newspapers and books who allowed me to explore electronic music through interviews, features and other contributions. Ian and Paul Gilby at *Sound On Sound* deserve special mention for giving me my first important break in the UK during the late 1980s.

Also at *SOS* Paul Ireson for his sterling support during the 1990s. Other important publications like *Blueprint, New Hi-Fi Sound, Zig Zag, Option* (US), *Hi-Fi Review, Record Collector, Music & Musicians International, Lime Lizard, Select, Guitarist, International Musician, Making Music, Attitudes, High Fidelity, New Statesman, Keyboard Player, Classic CD, Observer, Future Music, Independent, Rough Guides, Keyboard* (Japan), *Variant, Keyboard* (US), *Ikon, Mojo* and *UNCUT* deserve credit, as do their respective editors: Deyan Sudjic; Neville Farmer; Don Perretta; Richie Unterberger; Chris Frankland and Malcolm Steward; Peter Doggett and Mark Paytress; Basil Ramsey; Britt Collins; Tony Stewart and David Cavanagh; Neville Martin; Paul Trynka; Paul Colbert; Matthew Manning; Liz Hughes; Boyd Tonkin; Steve Miller; Roger Mills and Neil Evans; Rupert Christiansen; Andy Jones; Nick Coleman; Jonathan Buckley; Brian Jacobs; Malcolm Dickson; Bob Doerschuk; Glyn Brown; Barney Hoskyns; Paul Lester and Allan Jones.

SPECIAL CONTRIBUTIONS

Gerry Kenny (for all those tapes), Lin Barkass (for all her support), Victoria Bevan (musical input to Book One), Julia Snyder (Tangerine connection), Declan Colgan and Simon Hopkins (tireless new-music champions), Regine Moylett (always there), Paul Brown (book finder), Russell Mills, Rodney Breen (early support and photography), Nick Luscombe (DJ stuff),the late Yagnesh Patel (for his singular contribution to Book Four), Nigel Hogan (Mac plus), Os (Altair5), John Lloyd (technical), Gary Jeff (discs), Roger and Bee Eno, Jon Tye, Neil Jones, Catherine Dempsey and Brian Eno. Thanks also to the following musicians for significant interview experiences: Harold Budd, Robert Fripp, the late great Nico, Vini Reilly, David Sylvian, John McLaughlin, Daniel Lanois, Holger Czukay, Robert Wyatt, Michael Nyman, Klaus Schulze, Bill Nelson, Edgar Froese, Michael Brook, Pete Namlook, Sonic Boom and Mixmaster Morris.

PUBLISHING

On the way to winning a contract the following people played crucial roles: Harry Shapiro, Mic Cheetham, Sarah Lazin, the late Diane Cleaver and of course my diligent agent Simon Trewin. Special appreciation goes to Ian Gilby and Michael Nyman for their referrals and also to the Hinrichsen Foundation for their financial assistance. During the lengthy run-up to publication the following deserve just praise: my dear editor Richard Dawes, and, at Blooms-bury, my serene desk editor Helena Drakakis, Mike Jones and Elizabeth

O'Malley for all their patience, but most of all, for his vision and unwavering commitment to the book from start to finish, Matthew Hamilton.

PERSONAL

Liz Booth (for her sustaining belief), Clive Crump and Sue Bill (for their loyalty and love), Holly Robertson, Tim Davies, Mark and Nicky Holmes (and the entire Holmes clan), Mattea Di Gaetano, Penny Seddon (for her cabin retreat), Sally Reeves, Carla Foster, Valerie Webb, Terry and Diana Duggan, Louise and Katharine ffoulkes, Kirk Martin, Sarah and Ian Oliff, David West and Valerie Webb. Also: Yuka Fujii, Louise Gray, Josephine Machon, Kathy Etchingham, Philip Dodd and Mary Talbot. Especial thanks to my loving father William Prendergast, my brother Billy, Marina Capel, Charice Cosmas and my extended family, Beth and Jennifer, in America. Above all, much love and gratitude to my darling wife Genie Cosmas and our fabulous daughter Natasha.

FOREWORD

From a classical perspective the major revolutions in music have been described as changes in the ways composers put notes, chords and instruments together. Such a composition-centred view of musical history leaves out a lot of other types of musical evolution. It doesn't tell you very much about, for example, rock and roll. I recall a conversation I had in the early 70s with a classical composer, who said to me, 'Of course, everything in rock music had happened in classical music before 1832.' 'But it doesn't account for Elvis,' I protested. 'Well,' he replied, 'that wasn't a musical revolution, but a social one.'

One of the many trajectories along which music develops is its social dimension. New forms of music can be new in many different ways, and one of them is what role they are intended to play in a listener's life, or, to put it another way, what use the listener will put them to. The difference between sitting quietly in a chair and only coughing in the spaces between movements, and screaming your head off in a stadium full of hysterical young girls is a real difference. The difference between apprehending the compositional subtleties of a Bach fugue and filling your apartment with Heavy Metal is a real difference. These differences have to do with what social activity the music addresses, what music is thought to be for.

Until recently music was inseparable from the space in which it was performed – including the social space. One very strong movement in the late-nineteenth and twentieth centuries was towards music as an immersive, environmental experience. You see this in Mahler, Debussy, Satie, Varèse and then in Cage, La Monte Young and the Modernists. It's a drift away from narrative and towards landscape, from performed event to sonic space.

But it was recording which really liberated music from the moment of performance and from the performers themselves. Records meant that music could be carried and collected and listened to over and over. They allowed people to take the music home, and to choose when and where and how they would use it.

Recording and electronics also allowed composers to work with impossible perspectives and relationships. Producers and musicians discovered that tiny sounds could be made huge, and huge ones compacted. And, using echoes and reverberations, those sounds could seem to be located in a virtual space which was entirely imaginary. The act of making music becomes the art of creating new sonic locations and creating new timbres, new instruments: the most basic materials of the musical experience.

Another important thread in the story of Ambient music is film soundtracks – music made to support something else, an evocation of a psychological space within which something is intended to happen, a sense of music which presented a climate but left out the action. I was intrigued by the soundtracks that Nino Rota made for the Fellini films – whole albums with two or three themes replayed in different moods. It was like constructing geography and not populating it. The listener, I felt, became the population of a sonic landscape and was free to wander round it.

Perhaps the strangest surprise was watching these threads weaving together in the popular music of the 1980s and 90s. The mantric repetitiveness of 60s experimental music married with 80s sequencer programmes ended up entertaining millions of people in Trance clubs in Ibiza, Goa, Manchester and Tokyo.

This whole complex and interesting story forms the backbone of the mammoth undertaking that is *The Ambient Century*. Here Mark Prendergast has assembled a huge narrative, a long and intricate journey through a hundred years of music, seen through the lens of the Ambient perspective.

Brian Eno, 2000

BOOK ONE

THE ELECTRONIC LANDSCAPE

IT WAS THE summer of 1968. For some a time of student unrest, for others a time of discovery. For the German composer Karlheinz Stockhausen it was a time of intense emotional upheaval. His wife and children had left him. Alone in his house in Kurten, near Cologne, he contemplated his fate. Ideas of suicide crossed his mind. He went on hunger strike and vowed to wait for his family to return. As time passed he began to write down Japanese-style verses like:

> Play a sound,
> Play it for so long,
> Until you feel that you should stop

or

> Play a vibration in the rhythm of the universe,
> Play a vibration in the rhythm of dreaming.

That such words could lead to what Stockhausen termed 'intuitive music' is one of the great fascinations of the twentieth century. Here the composer was getting right inside what it meant to create sound, no longer only concentrating on the external but also the internal processes of becoming aware of what a sound was actually like when first encountered. Or, more accurately, when it was encountered in a different way. Stockhausen played a piano tone after four days of fasting. What he heard changed his life for ever.

John Cage had already opened up the world to the reality of silence. During the late 1940s and early 1950s the guru from the American Midwest had pushed music from Eastern-inspired piano pieces of exquisite calm to nothing at all, expressed most concisely in 4' 33". Here, for that duration of time, any performer of any instrument was required to not-play. The music was everything else heard, the Ambient sounds of whatever environment the 'performance' was happening in. Cage had professed that his favourite music was when everything was still, when nothing was attempted. The very sounds of his everyday environment were 'poetry to his ears'.

This non-purposeful acceptance of extraneous sound as music was symptomatic of the increasing hubbub of twentieth-century urban life, where silence as an experience was very rare. To flash back to the mid–nineteenth century, music was something that was experienced as a singular occurrence – once you'd been to the concert hall and heard the orchestra play the symphony, that was it. Music was live or not at all. There was always the piano, but you had to be musically literate to enjoy it. Or at least know somebody who was.

Then along came the player piano, which could record a composer's performance. But then Edison realized you could record music magnetically and away we went towards the capturing of music on record. By the beginning of the twentieth century even Debussy was putting his music on to the new medium. Add to that the increasing popularity of records, the universality of radio, the rise of the tape recorder, the clatter of mass production, the coming of electronic instruments, the increased demand for cars, the universal spread of television and so on – and by John Cage's time modern noise was indeed deafening. Music didn't need to have to jolt people out of their quiet lethargy. It no longer, as it did in the Romantic music of the early nineteenth century, had to carry the sum of all human emotions. Life was hectic enough without more stormy symphonies. Many opted for quiet.

The twentieth century saw two things occur in music which had never happened before. Firstly, music was deconstructed. Before, Western music was quite rigid. The sonata form of the Classical period had specific rules which had to be adhered to. Of course there were exceptional talents but they were constrained within a chosen form. Then the Romantics started to loosen things. Wagner's grandiose operatic orchestration and Bruckner and Mahler pushed the symphony to its limits so that by the end of the nineteenth century it began to creak under its own weight. Then along came Satie, Debussy and Ravel with a lighter touch. They wrote more accessible melodies in shorter forms which openly embraced modernity and the need to look beyond parochialism to the riches to be found in other cultures such as the Orient. As a boy in New England Charles Ives would hear his bandleader father's experiments in overlapping the sounds of different marching bands playing different tunes. In France, Messiaen would show that sound could possess rich colours if exotic scales were used. Schoenberg and his pupils of the Second Viennese School tore up the rule book on music and rewrote it imposing upon it a destabilizing force known as Serialism.

As old musical ideas begun to be supplanted by new, a second radical change occurred – and this was in the very way music was generated. Composers and musicians began to be fascinated by the nature of individual tones. Serialism, in its dislocative way, had thrown up an interest in the essence of a single sound. The leaders of the post-Second World War avant-garde in Europe, such as Stockhausen, Schaeffer and Varèse, seized on new electronic equipment and began to experiment with tape recorders. New qualities in sound were perceived, new tonalities divorced from any traditional acoustic instruments were realized. De Forest's invention of the valve in the 1920s had made amplification possible. This, coupled with the concept of the sound environment, made for some spectacular results. The work of Varèse and Xenakis in the pointed Philips pavilion at the 1958 World Fair in Brussels became a twentieth-century archetype of progress married to artistic achievement.

Many, feeling the tug of technological evolution, had campaigned for new musical means. Debussy famously wrote of the century of aeroplanes deserving a music of its own. Varèse saw that electronics could free music from the shackles of the past. The conductor Leopold Stokowski saw a future in which music would be generated by hitherto unknown means. But it took time for technology to catch up with ideas. There were many brave and interesting attempts at creating music machines. In the 1920s both the Theremin and Ondes Martenot were valid sources of novel electronic sound. But it wasn't until the tape experiments of Schaeffer and others that it was realized that a device would have to be built to handle all aspects of organizing and creating music. Hence the arrival of the first synthesizer in the US in the early 1950s. But, as with the computers of the period, music synthesis was tied to the laboratory or similar locations. Then Bob Moog took synthesizers out of the lab and made them more compact and portable. Electronic means had become accessible to any musician who wanted them. Stockhausen's prediction in 1955 that new electronic instruments would yield 'what no instrumentalist has ever been capable of' was at last becoming a reality.

The importance to twentieth-century music of atmospheric sound, its timbre and personality – indeed its 'Ambience' – is a measure of how much innovative musical ideas intertwined with technological change. The series of quiet, luscious Hispanic-inflected albums which Miles Davis made in the late 1950s are a case in point. The spirit of Debussy and Iberian composers such as Rodrigo infuses this beautiful work but so too does the already impressive state of studio and recording technology of the time. Multi-track recording and editing at the production console, enhanced by special microphone placement, highlighted qualities in the music that in earlier times would have been buried underneath gramophone crackle and tape hiss. It's true to say that improvements in production and consumption of music allowed quieter, more experimental elements to creep in. Could Ligeti's beautiful *Lux Aeterna* of 1966 have been rendered credibly on old scratchy 78s?

In the nineteenth century symphonies were often loud and raucous affairs that gave the public a visceral jolt through the sheer dynamic of the orchestra. In the twentieth century rock seemed to take over this function. This left composers free to experiment. Wendy (formerly Walter) Carlos transcribed Bach for Moog synthesizer. Iannis Xenakis used mathematics and computers to generate music. Toru Takemitsu fused Debussy with his Oriental sensibility in a reverse image of what had occurred at the beginning of the century. Moreover synthesizers became digital, with the ability to sample other instruments through the new microprocessing technology of silicon chips. By the end of the twentieth century music was capable of being rendered via small personal computers through a veritable treasure-trove of new electronic samplers, effects units and complex software. New music no longer needed to shout loud to impress. It could do so quietly through the beautiful textures of new super sound technology.

The dominance of the computer in music at the end of the twentieth century was made possible by developments in software and miniaturization. In sound labs at prestigious places like the Massachusetts Institute of Technology (MIT) huge advances were made in areas such as acoustic modelling and spontaneous musical response. In the first of these fields researchers are coming close to a perfect replication of the human voice, in itself an echo from Kubrick's prescient film *2001: A Space Odyssey*, where the fictitious HAL 9000 computer could speak. In the latter field computers are being designed to become more musically intelligent, so that they can accompany a human ensemble or instrumentalist.

Important as these things are to the century of sound they would be just aspects of research and development if it weren't for the fidelity of Compact Disc, or CD. The ability of a reflective disc with a diameter of just four and a half inches to communicate music in all its recorded perfection has rendered technological advances audible in the home. With better hi-fi systems the listener can hear the subtleties of Ambient sound whether it be by Satie, Delius, Cage or Eno. Stockhausen has remastered in digital form his entire life's work for presentation on CD. The availability of so much music on the new sound medium has radically changed people's perception of what music is. The combination of constant reissuing of back-catalogue and newer musical hybrids has blurred old prejudices, making it acceptable to like an eclectic mix of styles. At the end of the twentieth century old categories like jazz, pop and classical no longer really applied. Everything was thrown into the sonic soup by virtue of new digital technology. Over a century music had traversed an electronic landscape and now, by virtue of technology, its very texture, its very essence, had become digitally encoded. The search for newer and newer sounds had opened up music to the endless possibilities of Ambient sound. Now, the bleeding heart of electronic progress had, by its very nature, rendered all recorded music, by definition, Ambient.

GUSTAV MAHLER

Though many point to Wagner's awe-inspiring Prelude to Act 3 of *Tristan und Isolde* (1859) as being where modern music begins, its chromatic or uncertain key style and hazy effect presaging a future era, for me Gustav Mahler is the real connection between Romanticism and Modernism. His use of extremely long melodic lines, recurring thematic elements and clear orchestral tones shifted the history of music towards the repetitive conceptual music of the twentieth century. Hence it's not for nothing that Mahler became big news when the recording industry coalesced in the 1960s. His cycle of symphonies seemed tailor-made for continuous listening pleasure.

Most people's entry point to Mahler, born in 1860 in Bohemia, is the achingly beautiful *Adagietto* from *Symphony No. 5* of 1902. And this because of Visconti's mesmeric film *Death In Venice* (1971), which places a fictitious Mahler (played to the hilt by Dirk Bogarde) in a plague-doomed Venice in search of perfect homoerotic love. In truth this limpid masterpiece for harp and strings was a love poem to the real-life composer's future wife, Alma.

Mahler's life was conventional in that he rose through the academic system without fail. He gave his first live performance when only ten and by 1878 had graduated from the Prague and Vienna Conservatories and began conducting to make money. In 1895 he converted from Judaism to Catholicism to become head of the Vienna Opera, then the most prestigious musical appointment in the world. Yet his own music was ridiculed for its ardent sprinkling of cow bells and herd horns, its open-air sound, its use of folk tunes and nursery rhymes. A complete Romantic, Mahler believed he could put everything into his work and every summer retired to a country retreat in the Salzburg Alps to do so.

What is remarkable about Mahler is that through a loosened key structure he created a mysterious language that is full of intense yearning. This was first heard in 1895's *Symphony No. 3*, whose concluding *Adagio*, subtitled 'What Love Tells Me', blueprints the Mahler sound. The lilting shifts of the *Poco Adagio* from 1900's 'Fourth' expands the idea with a subtly understated rhythmic figure. The aforementioned *Adagietto* from the Fifth is a compound of airy lightness and ornate melancholia derived from one of the composer's songs, *Ich Bin Der Welt Abhanden Gekommen* ('I Am Lost To The World'). The *Andante Moderato* from 1904's Sixth is sadness suffused in sound and tragically anticipated the loss, in 1907, of both his job and his young daughter and his being diagnosed as having heart disease. His song-symphony based on Chinese poems, *Das Lied von der Erde* (*Song Of The Earth*) (1909), was a daring way to come to terms with tragedy but the lengthy *Adagio* to his unfinished Tenth (1910) revealed his true despair in a music which gradually dissipates tonality until we hear loud discord. Within a year he was dead.

Mahler is singular among Romantic composers in that a selection of his music can be programmed for performance or playing on CD and the result in both cases is a truly Ambient experience of landscape and emotion. This is particularly fascinating in that his use of incidental sounds would be mirrored by such Ambient House stars as The Orb nearly a century after his death.

LISTENING

Mahler is one of those composers whose work nearly every prominent conductor wants to excel at, and so there are versions and boxed sets galore of his music. Sir Georg Solti on Decca, Bernard Haitink on Philips, Rafael Kubelik on Deutsche Grammophon and Klaus Tennstedt on EMI are the main heavyweights who have recorded all the symphonies. Yet individual works are brought out better by different conductors. My favourites include Bernard Haitink's masterly control of the Fourth's *Poco Adagio* in 1967, Sir John Barbirolli's velvet touch with the Fifth's *Adagietto* in 1969 and Herbert von Karajan's 1975 controlled *Andante* from the Sixth plus his take on 'I Am Lost To The World' with Christa Ludwig, and finally Karl Rickenbacher's sonorous 1989 interpretation of the Tenth's *Adagio*.

ERIK SATIE

The father of modern Ambience and Minimalism, Erik Satie, in the years 1887–93 changed the whole course of musical history with three sets of miniatures titled *Trois Sarabandes*, *Trois Gymnopédies* and *Gnossiennes*. With their clear melodic phrases, exquisite lightness and fresh texture, Satie literally blew away the pomp and rhetoric of the old order. Here was a music of repetition with strong emphasis on chords which seemed simpler and more fitting to a new age. Not only did he influence the likes of Debussy and Ravel but he also impressed figures such as Picasso and Cocteau. In fact all the way through the twentieth century musicians and composers have acknowledged his vision and rebellious modernity.

Satie's life reads like a catalogue of controversy and recklessness. The son of a shipbroker but reared by a stepmother who was also a composer, Satie was born in Honfleur in northern France in 1866. His entry into the Paris Conservatoire in 1879 led to expulsion in 1882 for absenteeism and laziness. Recognized as gifted, he just wouldn't conform. Private piano lessons exasperated teachers as Satie refused to sight-read. A spell in the army in 1886 led to bronchitis.

With his father trying his hand at music publishing, Satie began to write in earnest. *Trois Sarabandes* (1887) was a short set of three dance pieces which used unresolved chords to create a strange floating harmony. A certain tranquillity and slowness of movement, particularly in the first piece, would shape his style and have immediate effect on the writing of Debussy and Ravel. The following year came the revolutionary *Trois Gymnopédies*, three slow pieces lasting together less than ten minutes which gracefully utilized delicate modal harmony and gossamer-like transparency. Satie derived the name from an old Spartan ritual of naked youths dancing around a statue of Apollo. A trip to the Paris Exposition gave him a flavour for the Orient which infected his crowning achievement, the six *Gnossiennes* of 1890–3. In these pieces, named after the Cretan palace of Knossos, Satie incredibly dispatched with bar lines and any kind of formal time signature. In their place on the score were strange instructions like 'be clairvoyant'. Still the ability of these beautifully riveting miniatures to capture a sense of spiritual calm and induce quietude has made them famous the world over.

During this time Satie became a true Montmartre bohemian and official composer of the Rosicrucians, a mystical sect. His *Le fils des étoiles* (*The Son Of The Stars*), written in 1891 for their flamboyant leader, Sar Péladan, was an ambient 'sound decor'. That year Satie also met Debussy, who would remain a friend for twenty-five years. Soon afterwards Satie broke with Péladan and, attired in soft cap, corduroy and goatee, this young anarchist in his mid-twenties involved himself with duels, hard drinking, love affairs and even formed his own church. In 1893 came *Vexations*, an eighteen-note minimalist piece that was scored to be repeated 840 times. During the 1960s John Cage and John Cale would famously perform this in New York. By 1896 Debussy had orchestrated the clever *Trois Gymnopédies*.

Having gone through a substantial legacy with which he bought, among other things, twelve identical velvet suits, Satie moved in 1898 to the Parisian suburb of Arcueil, where he would spend the rest of his life. He considered himself a radical socialist with an interest in the poor. Every day for fifteen years he walked to Montmartre to earn his living as a café and music-hall pianist. Both *Je te Veux* (*I Want You*) and *Poudre d'Or* (*Golden Powder*) from 1900–01 reflect gay Parisian life of the period. He wrote the strange *Trois morceaux en forme de poire* (*Three Pieces In The Shape Of A Pear*) for four-handed piano and enrolled in the Schola Cantorum in 1905 for a diploma course. Though he was outwardly the eccentric, Satie's humour always hid an insecurity about his lack of formal education. In 1908 he graduated with a diploma in fugue and counterpoint. By 1911 both Debussy and Ravel were performing his music to enthusiastic audiences. Satie's music continued to be best in miniature, the serene second part of 1914's *Trois Valses* (*Three Waltzes*) or the *Idyll To Debussy* from the following year's *Avant-dernières pensées* (*Second To Last Thoughts*).

By now an omnipresent Parisian figure with his bowler hat and umbrella, Satie began an association with the poet, playwright and film director Jean Cocteau which would make him famous after the war. In 1917 a huge scandal erupted over *Parade*, a ballet on which Satie worked with Cocteau, Pablo Picasso and Francis Picabia. Full of Satie's piano style, the show included the sounds of pistol shots, a siren and a typewriter. Critics were outraged; Satie insulted them and received a jail sentence and a fine (later quashed). In 1918 came the strange cantata *Socrate* (*Socrates*), which many believe to be the zenith of his search for a 'music of bare bones'. Based on the dialogues of Plato, the piece has a religious plainchant flavour with unadorned, almost free-flowing piano. A year later came *Cinq nocturnes* (*Five Nocturnes*) and in 1920 Satie's famous 'furniture music', background Ambience for boring intervals in concert music. His last scandal came in 1924 with *Relâche* (*Relax*) another ballet with Picabia, with the highly surrealistic René Clair film *Interval* inserted in the middle.

Years of heavy drinking had led to illness. Friends put Satie up in hotels but in 1925 his liver gave out and he died. Afterwards associates like Darius Milhaud found piles of manuscript in his bare rooms in Arcueil – testament to his dedication to a music 'conceived in a spirit of humiliation and renunciation'.

The bizarre titles of Satie's pieces (no less humorous in English), such as *Dreamy Fish*, *Cold Pieces* or *Four Veritable Flabby Pieces For A Dog*, hid a talent which Ravel considered to be one of a genius completely ahead of its time. Satie's very nature blueprinted the free-flowing creative spirit of the twentieth century, his ability to shock coinciding with the true artist's ability to produce timeless creations. His pellucid music is the essence of Ambience.

Satie's interest in symmetrical repetition is the essence of Minimalism. The easy swing and luminous texture can be traced right down to 1990s House music. Edgard Varèse, John Cage and even Brian Eno owe him an enormous debt. During the 1980s his music inspired the New Age movement in America, one famous pianist, George Winston, recording an album of the Frenchman's music for the Windham Hill label. A veritable Neoclassicist, Erik Satie took a great risk. History has served him well.

LISTENING

Erik Satie – Anne Queffélec (Virgin 1988)
Erik Satie: Socrate (Wergo 1991)
Satie: Piano Works – Daniel Varsano and Philippe Entremont (Sony 1992)
Erik Satie: Early Piano Works – Reinbert De Leeuw (Philips Duo 1998)
Piano Dreams – *The Erik Satie Collection* – Pascal Rogé (Decca 1997)

The practical difficulty with Satie's piano music, particularly *Trois Gymnopédies*, is that it is often played too fast. Reinbert De Leuuw's performance over three discs recorded in the late 1970s has never been equalled: it is, exactly as per the composer's instructions, exquisitely slow. The Philips Duo reissue of this recording is simply superb. Wergo's disc of *Socrate* pairs Satie with piano music from his inheritor John Cage. The Queffélec disc combines the *Gnossiennes* with a range of quirky pieces such as *Embryons desséchés* (*Dried Embryos*), *Vieux séquins et vieilles cuirasses* (*Old Sequins And Armour*) and *Sonatine bureaucratique* (*Bureaucratic Sonatina*). The Varsano and Entremont performance recorded in a Paris church in 1979 is the most economical entry point as it combines the best of the early pieces with the café music and the later work, including a sample of the *Nocturnes* of 1919. *Piano Dreams* – *The Erik Satie Collection* (subtitled '25 Hypnotic Tracks') boasts crystalline performances, recorded during the 1980s and 1990s, by the renowned French interpreter Pascal Rogé.

CLAUDE DEBUSSY

For many modern music began with Debussy and the 'voluptuous ambience' of his *Prélude à l'après-midi d'un faune* (*Prelude To The Afternoon Of A Faun*), composed in 1894. Here was an orchestral music that simultaneously rejected the huge symphonic form of German music, the traditional classical exposition of Mozart and reliance on strong melodic development. In their place, over a compact eleven minutes, was a single series of, according to its author, 'discreet' sound events for flute, harp and coloured orchestra. Through his fame, his writings and his uncompromising nature Debussy (even more than Satie and Ravel) was able to raise the flag for total innovation and mesmerically succeed. He once said: 'As there are no precedents I must create anew.' And just as tellingly: 'The century of aeroplanes deserves a music of its own.'

Unlike most schooled musicians, Debussy was a pure artist whose academic ability had little or no bearing on his eventual winding path towards creative brilliance. Born in 1862, he was brought up in Paris and the South of France by a maternal aunt. Initially he dabbled in art before succumbing to the piano at the age of ten. One of his teachers being related to Verlaine, it is certain that the young Debussy met the bohemian poet's hash-smoking friend the poetic genius Rimbaud. By eleven Debussy was studying at the Paris Conservatoire, where his bizarre chordings, strange tonalities and love of improvisation caused disconcertion. Yet by eighteen Tchaikovsky's wealthy patroness wanted him as her household piano teacher. In 1884 he effortlessly won the Prix de Rome and spent the next three years in the Italian capital.

Here Debussy was to live and write music. He met Liszt, whose spatial pedal technique would be discernible in Debussy's later piano scores. Fascinated by Symbolist poetry and the Pre-Raphaelites, he wrote a piece for submission to the Conservatoire called *La Damoiselle élue* (*The Blessed Damozel*), based on a poem by Dante Gabriel Rossetti. Its wistful aspect, use of harp and woodwinds, wave-like motions and shimmering beauty in one unified block of sound caused his teachers to gasp. They considered Debussy to be afflicted with a disease that made him write music that was 'bizarre, incomprehensible and impossible to execute', which they also dubbed 'vague impressionism', thus giving Debussy and his followers in 1887 a perfect moniker to hang their art on.

In the second half of the nineteenth century Paris was awash with the dreamy creations of Impressionism and Symbolist poets and painters. The iridescence of Monet, Manet, Degas and Renoir was paralleled by the darker, more evocative worlds of Baudelaire and Rimbaud and the work of the artists Moreau and Redon. At twenty-five Debussy threw himself into this 'dream within a dream world', hung out in the salon of the poet Mallarmé, read Poe's story 'The Fall of The House of Usher' and Huysmans's brilliantly decadent novel *À rebours* (*Against Nature*), which he described as a 'symphony of odours'. He took up with Gaby Dupont, lived in a garret and went to Bayreuth to hear Wagner, a composer he would later disown. It was Debussy's visit to the Centennial Exposition Universelle of 1889 (celebrating the Revolution) in Paris that sparked the greatest change in him. The start of the Belle Époque with the opening of the Eiffel Tower saw the composer tour the folk-music pavilions to hear the music of Africa, Arabia and Russia and especially the gamelan orchestras of Bali and Southeast Asia. The elusive melodies and harmonies of the latter and the black-keyed scales of traditional Chinese and Irish folk musics turned his head. After that he stated: 'I should prefer the creation of a type of music that has neither motifs nor themes, a more universal music.'

Both *Clair de Lune* (*Moonlight*) and the first of the *Deux arabesques* (*Two Arabesques*) from this period are limpid piano pieces, flush with sensual delight as if the finger-runs, with their changing tempi, are playing a hazy summer reflection. In 1891 Debussy met Erik Satie in Montmartre and the two became lifelong friends. Satie purged Debussy of any liking for German music and spoke famously of a desire for 'music without sauerkraut'.

After two years' work Debussy produced his masterpiece, *Prélude à l'après-midi d'un faune*, based on Mallarmé's erotic poem. At thirty-two he became instantly famous with a work which for many benchmarked an entire century of music. Gossamer-like, this short but intensely beautiful orchestral work glided across the senses, individual tones flowing out, silence slowly alternating with fantastic sonorities, Eastern and exotic timbres and moods hanging within the sound of clarinets, harp, flute and delicate strings. In 1894 no one had heard anything like it. The critics dubbed it superficial and indefinite.

Personally Debussy entered into a period of confusion. He had many affairs and was for a short time engaged. He worked relentlessly on an opera, *Pelléas et Mélisande*, based on a play by the Belgian Symbolist Maeterlinck. His perfectionism meant it took him eight years to complete. He was in London for Oscar Wilde's trial, a writer he admired enormously. Publishers' advances kept him in an extravagant lifestyle. His love of women led to Gaby Dupont's attempted suicide in 1897. By 1899 he had married a Burgundy dressmaker, Rosalie 'Lily' Texier, with Satie as witness, and the same year he produced the allusive *Nocturnes* for orchestra. *Nuages* (*Clouds*), from this set of three pieces, was an exquisite example of Debussy's precious art.

Legal disputes about monies for *Pelléas et Mélisande* dogged the composer, yet he lived and worked in a handsome green study with Chinese cats and ornamental silks. In 1903 came *Estampes* (*Engravings*), three piano pieces full of Spain. In 1904 he met Fauré's former mistress, Emma Bardac, who was married to a rich banker. After Debussy and Emma had an affair on the Channel Isles, Lily shot herself but recovered in hospital. Debussy scandalously refused to see his wife or pay her medical bills. Many friends turned away from him but he poured his turbulent emotions into the symphonic *La Mer* (*The Sea*) (1905), which was also inspired by the world-famous wave paintings of the Japanese artist Hokusai.

Now living in the Bois de Boulogne, Debussy settled down to his last phase: one of domestic bliss, increased fame and growing illness. His new wife, Emma, bore him Chou-Chou, his beloved only daughter, for whom he wrote his famous *Children's Corner* piano suite. Of more import were two sets of *Images* (1905–7), results of what he termed 'experiments with musical chemistry'. In avoiding major and minor tonalities Debussy effortlessly conjured up reflections in water, church bells heard through rustling leaves and the quietude of moonlight. By 1908 Debussy's music was a universal success. His *Iberia* (from *Images*) was considered another tour de force, particularly its slow and dreamlike section with celesta, oboes and bassoon. The Spanish composer Manuel de Falla found it intoxicating. At a later performance Ravel was moved to tears. Tragedy struck in 1909 when Debussy, while in London on a conducting tour, was diagnosed as having cancer.

Still rejecting the music of Mahler and Schoenberg, Debussy survived to write his last great works, the two books of *Préludes* (1909–13), which perfectly elicited his 'music of the play of waters, the play of curves described by changing breezes'. For example, *Des pas sur la neige* (*Footsteps In The Snow*) and *La cathédrale engloutie* (*The Sunken Cathedral*) (the latter after Monet) are perfect interior sound worlds. The composer showed an interest in Hungarian dance and collaborated with the Italian poet Gabriele D'Annunzio on a version of the martyrdom of St Sebastian. Such was his fame that Debussy attracted the likes of W. B. Yeats and Stravinsky to his house for intellectual soirées.

The outbreak of the First World War depressed Debussy greatly. While both Satie and Ravel enlisted, Debussy's illness kept him at home, numbed by morphine. Pouring himself into music, he edited works by Chopin and Bach, as well as writing three chamber sonatas, twelve *Études* (1915) and attempting to finish an opera of Poe's morbid 'The Fall Of The House of Usher'. Radium treatment and two operations did not stem his cancer and in March 1918, as German cannon and Zeppelins bombarded Paris, France's greatest-ever composer expired surrounded by family and friends.

Debussy's critics use words like 'nebulous' to describe his output and it was true that he hated 'musical mathematics' but technically his music was nothing less than brilliant. His use of medieval modes in parallel motion, the whole-tone and pentatonic scales associated with Far Eastern music and folk styles, his strange floating and escaping harmonies and his grasp of instrumental timbre, not forgetting his outspoken writings and predictions, earned him the title 'Father of Modern Music'. Certainly, the high points of twentieth-century electronic music, like Pink Floyd's *Dark Side Of The Moon*, were first envisaged in Debussy's ample imagination.

LISTENING

Debussy In Paris – Alain Lombard (Erato 1990)
Images, Estampes, Masques – Alice Ader (MusiFrance 1991)
Orchestral Music – Bernard Haitink (Phillips/Duo 1991)
La Damoiselle élue – Esa-Pekka Salonen (Sony 1995)
The Complete Works For Piano – Walter Gieseking (EMI 1995)

Bernard Haitink's two-disc set of the *Prélude*, the *Nocturnes*, *Iberia*, *La Mer* and other pieces with the Concertgebouw Amsterdam, from 1976–7, is a stand-out recording. The sway of the orchestra in *Iberia* is staggering. Yet I prefer

Lombard's shimmering 1975 recording of the *Prélude* with the Strasbourg Philharmonic on the *Debussy In Paris* disc, which also includes *La Mer*. Salonen's version of *La Damoiselle élue* is silken perfection, as is his interpretation of *Nuages*. For piano music the undisputed king of versions is Gieseking's, recorded in mono between 1951 and 1955. Full of luminous colour, depth and the breathing pedal so close to Debussy's requirements, this performance was digitally remastered for disc and released in 1995. Those who like their Debussy a little cooler may prefer Alice Ader's renditions of *Images*, *Estampes* and *Masques*.

MAURICE RAVEL

Once described as an 'epicure and connoisseur of instrumental jewellery' by Stravinsky, Ravel stands as the third great French writer of quiet music after Debussy and Satie. The nocturnal stillness and translucent brilliance of his instrumental works, particularly his piano creations, have been overshadowed by the disproportionate attention given to his *Bolero* (1928), whose infectious repetition was only ever an experiment in Ravel's mind, albeit one which influenced the genesis of Minimalism four decades later.

Ravel's life was one dedicated to finding musical perfection. Born in 1875 at Ciboure in the French Pyrenees of Swiss and Basque parentage, he soon moved to Paris, where he would spend the rest of his life. A gifted child, he started learning and playing music at seven, and by the age of twelve was studying harmony. Within two years he was admitted to the Paris Conservatoire, an institution which would occupy sixteen years of his relatively short life. Like Debussy, Ravel was strongly influenced by the Exposition Universelle of 1889, where he encountered Spanish music, the gamelan and Russian dance. An early short piece, *Habanera* (1895), reflected his deep interest in repetitive ideas and Spanish idioms.

Influenced and befriended by Satie, the young Ravel was a typical bohemian who loved the writings of Baudelaire, Rimbaud, Verlaine and Edgar Allan Poe; the paintings of Van Gogh, Cézanne and Whistler; and the music of Chopin, Wagner and Debussy. In 1899 he created *Pavane pour une infante défunte* (*Pavane For A Dead Princess*) which, according to the composer, was 'a slow dance that a young Princess might have danced in bygone days at the Spanish court'. This is his all-time classic, a piece of melodic genius for piano which lasts barely six minutes but stays in the mind for ever. The subtlety and grace of its musical flow, its irregular use of time, its unexpected turns into new territory and beautiful resolution make it one of the great cut-off points between excessive Romanticism and twentieth-century modernism. Its publication in 1900, when Ravel was only twenty-five, made him famous but also confirmed the new dawn heralded by Satie and Debussy.

The next five years would be taken up trying to achieve the prestigious Prix de Rome, an award which jealous committee members refused the young genius because of his outright flouting of convention. In 1905 there was so much outcry at Ravel's failed fourth attempt that heads rolled at the Conservatoire and Fauré, Ravel's teacher, became its director. The same year Ravel finished *Sonatine* and *Miroirs* (*Mirrors*), which again display a precise understanding of short-form and the ability of music – particularly the latter with its sections *Une barque sur l'océan* (*A Boat On The Ocean*) and *La vallée des cloches* (*The Valley Of Bells*) – to conjure up a sense of place. This faculty would be broadened in *Rapsodie espagnole* (*Spanish Rhapsody*) three years later, a fifteen-minute work for two pianos which many consider to be unrivalled as a musical portrait of Spain. Its soft 'Prelude Of The Night' is four minutes of pure Ambient meditation.

Before the outbreak of war in 1914, Ravel was extremely creative. In 1908 came his *Gaspard de la nuit* (*Gaspard Of The Night*), a three-part piano piece inspired by some strange prose poetry, which many consider to be very difficult to play. Its middle section, *Le Gibet* (*The Gibbet*), involves a hypnotic tolling bell figure which conveys the swaying movement of the sunburnt corpse depicted in Aloysius Bertrand's writing. In 1910 came *Ma mère l'oye* (*Mother Goose*), a children's piece which reflected Ravel's search for simplicity. Its opening section, *Pavane de la belle au bois dormant* (*Pavane For The Sleeping Beauty*), is a masterpiece of stillness. During the next four years Ravel wrote waltzes, a ballet, met Stravinsky and executed the short (one minute fifteen seconds) *Prelude*, another exquisite delicacy.

Too short to be accepted into the army, Ravel was eventually accepted by the airforce, as a driver in the transport corps. He was by all accounts a brave contributor to the war effort, but was discharged in 1916 because of dysentery. His dedication to lost friends, *Le Tombeau de Couperin* (*The Tomb Of Couperin*) (1917), is full of the wistful solitude which characterizes nearly all of Ravel's work. By the time of Debussy's death in 1918 he was France's foremost composer but bad memories of the Paris Conservatoire made him refuse the Legion of Honour two years later. After this he left Paris and did much orchestration, including works by Chopin, Satie and even Debussy. In 1928, the year of *Bolero*, he toured the US and Canada on condition that he was provided with the best French wines and cigarettes. He was also awarded an honorary degree by Oxford University. By the 1930s he had succumbed to depression, due mainly to insomnia he had picked up during the war. Nevertheless he enjoyed Parisian jazz clubs, but in 1932, after a car smash, he developed a rare brain disease which eventually robbed him of his talent to write, read or even remember music. Fearing further mental disintegration, he risked a dangerous brain operation in the winter of 1937 from which he died.

An absolute perfectionist and dandy, Ravel would shut himself up for months in order to attain what he called 'a ripened conception'. Only to be seen on long, thought-filled walks across Paris in the early hours of the morning, he was extremely self-critical and once stated: 'I can be occupied for years without writing a single note.' It is said that, once finished, a Ravel composition needed not one jot of correction. In eliminating the superfluous in search of clarity, in 'feeling intensely' what he wrote, Ravel ended his life dissatisfied. In the end he stated: 'I have written very little . . . I've said nothing, I have still everything to say.' An extremely private man though he was, Ravel wrote highly communicative music which remains essential listening for anyone wishing to understand the arc of twentieth-century music.

His art, which grows more luminous on repeated listening, reveals an interest in folk and jazz modes. Ravel derived his parallel chordings from Satie and, as in jazz, mixed time signatures. His expanded key concepts gave his music the impressive breadth of his beloved Symbolist poetry, while his themes, both natural and pictorial, were the stuff of the ardent enthusiast of post-Impressionism. Yet he also loved the baroque keyboardists, whose structuring elements led to his innovative inelastic movement, which in turn greatly influenced Ligeti and, more importantly, Terry Riley and the whole Minimalist revolution of the 1960s.

LISTENING

Complete Piano Works – Philippe Entremont (Sony 1994)
Piano Works – Vlado Perlemuter (Nimbus 1996)
Intégrale de l'Oeuvre Pour Piano Vols. 1 and 2 –
    Begona Uriarte (Wergo 1988 1989)
Orchestral Works – Jean Martinon (EMI 1999)

Those looking for an antique sound that Ravel would surely have appreciated should try the Perlemuter. The pianist was a confidant of the composer who studied with him and in 1929 played the whole piano oeuvre live. The disc also gives the text that inspired *Gaspard de la nuit*. The Wergo discs are pristinely presented with unusual pieces, *Vol. 2* including *Rapsodie espagnole* as well as *Bolero* in a version for two pianos. Yet in terms of enunciation and that sensuous saturated piano sound, the Entremont, recorded in 1974, excels. This is a brilliant disc which includes the sublime *Pavane pour une infante défunte*. Conductor Jean Martinon made Ravel's orchestral music famous after the Second World War. His two-disc set, recorded in 1974, includes a vast slew of music from the *Pavane* right up to *Bolero* – here in one of its most bewitching versions.

FREDERICK DELIUS

One only has to hear pieces like the *Irmelin Prelude, A Song Before Sunrise, Sea Drift, Summer Night On The River* and *On Hearing The First Cuckoo In Spring* to gain an insight into the twilight world of Frederick Delius. The ethereal music of Frederick Delius was the closest England came to Debussy's vision. Modal scales and block-like parallel motion were there in evidence yet there is a Romantic rapture and unsettling movement to Delius's music which links it to the great works of Mahler and even Wagner. Simultaneously looking back and forward, Delius had the gift of creating a music of great tranquillity.

Born in Yorkshire in 1862 to a prosperous German merchant, Delius emigrated to Florida in the 1880s to run an orange plantation and was inspired to begin composing by hearing labourers singing American folk songs. After returning to Europe, he studied from the age of twenty-four at Leipzig Conservatory, where he met the Norwegian composer Grieg. A move to Paris led to a riotous life of sex and alcohol in the company of innovative painters and writers. He eventually married a painter, Jelka Rosen, and settled down in 1897 to a life of composition in a beautiful house at Grez-sur-Loing, near Fontainebleau.

Here Delius wrote with great vigour, producing operas, choral works, string quartets and concertos – the usual varied output of a gifted composer. But his genius lies in shorter, quieter moments, which began with the 1898 nocturne *Paris: The Song Of A Great City*. With *Brigg Fair* (1907) and *In A Summer Garden* (1908) he honed his rhapsodic bucolic writing, but it was in *On Hearing The First Cuckoo In Spring* (1912) that his ability to perfectly capture melancholy shone. Over seven minutes Delius used a small orchestra of strings, woodwinds and horns to capture the emotions of spring, of sunlight seen on green vales, nature unfolding its opulence, nostalgia heard through folk melody and the simple tune of the evening cuckoo. Though he said he disliked England, its rural hush dapples through the sensuous hue of this work to create a true Ambient masterpiece.

Delius had contracted syphilis as a young man in Paris and, as a result, in his later years became paralysed and blind, although his appalling condition did not stop him dictating his fantastic musical visions for posterity. He died in 1934.

LISTENING

Beecham Conducts Delius (EMI 1987)

This disc contains fabulous versions of the orchestral poems to nature, in readings both subtle and luminous by Delius's greatest champion, Sir Thomas Beecham, at the helm of the Royal Philharmonic in the late 1950s and early 60s.

CHARLES GRIFFES

Tragically, just as his music was gaining recognition in his native land, Charles Tomlinson Griffes was to die at the age of thirty-five of pneumonia and pleurisy.

The most significant American Impressionist of his day, Griffes wrote the elegiac and fantasy-sprinkled *The Pleasure-Dome Of Kubla Khan* (1912–9), which absorbed all the colour and flow of his idol Debussy. Born in New York in 1884, Griffes studied in Berlin for four years before returning home to become a teacher at twenty-three. A man of reverie, he nevertheless supported the more primal music of Stravinsky and Schoenberg while revelling in the ornate sounds of Ravel, Debussy and the Far East. His dreamy woodwind orchestrations and use of wide intervals gave his music an opulent texture as evinced by the suitably 'foggy' *Pleasure-Dome*, a piece inspired by Coleridge's opium-induced poem. *Three Tone Pictures: The Lake At Evening, The Vale Of Dreams*, and *The Night Winds* (1912), *The White Peacock* (1916) *and Poem For Flute And Orchestra* (1918) are visionary soundscapes whose smooth Ambience (aided by a craftsman's attention to the nuances of celesta and harp) was years ahead of its time.

LISTENING

The Musical Fantasies of Charles Griffes (with Deems Taylor) – Gerard Schwarz, Seattle Symphony Orchestra (Delos 1990)

This exemplary performance of Griffes by Schwarz and the Seattle Symphony makes one wonder and revel.

The Kairn of Koridwen – Emil De Cou (Koch 1994)

Derived from the Druidic legend of The Sanctuary of the Goddess of the Moon, this work was written in 1916 to accompany a dance-drama and is fifty-five minutes of pure dream music for horns, flute, celesta, harp and piano.

CHARLES IVES

The son of a American Civil War bandleader who set out to break the musical rules, Charles Ives became simultaneously an American folk hero and a millionaire philanthropist who was the first to provide life insurance for widows and orphans. In his quest for a music of utopian transcendence he arrived at Ambient music with the 1906 compositions *The Unanswered Question* and *Central Park In The Dark*, where superimpositions and discrepant sounds created environmental music years before Cage explored the area.

   Ives was a New Englander, born in Danbury, Connecticut in 1874. He played organ in the local church and drums in his father George's marching band. Ives Senior taught his son to ignore rules and think of pure sound – of what it would be like to hear two bands together playing different tunes; or splitting up a band into quarters and standing in the middle of the town square to hear the effect; playing a popular tune in two different keys; or exploring 'microtones'. From this experience George Ives took ideas that would later, through his son, be fundamental to Minimal and Ambient music. He even built a quarter-tone piano to play tone clusters and reproduce the sound of peeling bells.

Charles Ives went to study at Yale in 1894 and after four years realized that he would never make a living with the kind of innovative music he wished to write. At twenty-four he entered the insurance business and at thirty-five he founded his own firm, all the time composing furiously. His music was multi-tonal with a great degree of freedom in the areas of rhythm and key, full of cluster chords with allusions to American hymns and folk song. He didn't even use regular bar lines or key signatures. Much of his work contains dissonant or inharmonious chords. Working in isolation in his spare time and holidays, he produced music that most people found incomprehensible and unplayable. Scripts piled up in a Connecticut barn.

It is said that Mahler was so impressed with Ives's work that he took a copy of his *Symphony No. 3* back with him to Vienna in 1911 with the intention of conducting it. Alas Mahler died and the manuscript was lost until the late 1940s. Ives composed pieces for chimes and church bells, small brass en-sembles, marching bands, hundreds of songs, and of course there are the orchestral works. Of these, *Hymn* (for strings) from 1904, *Central Park In The Dark* and *The Unanswered Question* (both for chamber ensemble) from 1906 and the two extravagant creations *Three Places In New England* (for orchestra) and *Concord Sonata* (for piano) from 1903 to 1915 all contain the sublime stillness of Ambience.

Having only rarely heard his own music and then only when he hired musicians to play it, Ives felt a growing frustration which brought on a heart attack in 1918. During the 1920s he published some of his own music and writings on the same. In 1930 he withdrew from business, but the huge, beautiful *Concord Sonata* had made an impact. His music was conducted in Europe, Webern doing him the honours in Vienna. He spent a long time travelling, savouring his belated success.

In 1939 Ives became the most important living American composer when the *Concord Sonata* received its debut in New York. In 1947 he became an American hero when he was offered the Pulitzer Prize for his *Symphony No. 3*, but the ever-tetchy composer declined the award. By 1948 Bernstein was conducting Ives's music with the New York Philharmonic and at eighty the composer died a happy man.

Ives's contribution to the history of twentieth-century music has never been in any doubt, inspiring both the likes of Schoenberg and Boulez to venture into unknown areas. The radical style of his works has often upset critics, certain pieces of music being intentionally impossible to play in order to push the sensibilities of its interpreters. His double life as businessman and composer probably held back commercial exploitation of his music but it is in his influence on the development of Ambience and Minimalism that he has been neglected. His use of microtones and cluster chords had a direct influence on Minimalism while his multi-dimensional music, as heard in *Three Places In New England* and the haunting seven-minute *Central Park In The Dark*, where a brass band breaks in on the eerie quiet to crescendo like *A Day In The Life* from The Beatles' *Sgt. Pepper* album and then disappears back into the musical hue, is the very essence of sound-field multi-track recordings of the 1960s. Above all, Ives realized that sound created a charged atmosphere and not a body of rules which dictated what certain instruments should play and be played.

LISTENING

Concord Sonata – Herbert Henck (Wergo 1988)

This work is Ives's beautiful tribute to writers and thinkers Emerson, Hawthorne, the Alcotts and Thoreau, leading lights of the New England movement Transcendentalism between 1840 and 1860. The piece is mostly stately piano but is assisted by flute and viola, and one can hear traces of Debussy and the future Keith Jarrett. Brilliant use is made of cluster chords.

Symphony No. 2 – Leonard Bernstein, New York Philharmonic (Deutsche Grammophon 1990)

An excellent introductory disc with Bernstein conducting which also includes the essential *Hymn*, *Central Park In The Dark* and *The Unanswered Question*.

IBERIAN SOUNDS

The cool effect of music emanating from Spanish and Portuguese sensibilities has certainly coloured the development of Ambient music. During the late nineteenth century Spanish music was altered for the better by the influence of French musical Impressionism. Over the successive century its growing stature affected other musics, notably the sound of Miles Davis and various composers' approaches to acoustic guitar.

Many point to Felipe Pedrell, a teacher in Madrid, as being the source of this influence. He taught both Manuel de Falla and Isaac Albéniz to overcome compositional problems by absorbing folk melodies into a wider Impressionistic style. A Catalonian, Isaac Albéniz was the first to have success in this technique. Born in 1860, he made his debut on piano in Barcelona at the age of four. Gifted and wayward, he travelled all over the US, South America and Eastern Europe before meeting Debussy and Ravel in the Paris of the 1890s. Thence he retired to Nice to write *Iberia* between 1906 and 1909. Considered a masterpiece, this series of twelve piano pieces conjures up the peninsula in terms of subtlety and nuance.

Though Albéniz died in France in 1909, his work would influence Manuel de Falla, who was born in Cadiz in 1876 and would become Spain's first great Modernist. This came about after Falla had spent seven years in Paris, as an excellent graduate of the Madrid Conservatoire, on a musical voyage of discovery that took in the circles of Ravel and Debussy. His *Cuatro Piezas Españolas* (*Four Spanish Pieces*) of 1914 culminated his stay and paid homage to Albéniz, but were more spare and forward-looking than the earlier composer's work. After that Falla returned to Spain to finish his more exotic *Noches en los jardines de España* (*Nights In The Gardens Of Spain*) (1911–16), a three-part set à la Debussy of symphonic impressions of the beauties of Granada and Cordoba. A friend of the anti-fascist writer Lorca, he nevertheless lasted out the Spanish Civil War. Finding the Franco regime distasteful, he emigrated in 1939 to Argentina, where he conducted and finished a guitar and piano tribute to Debussy and Pedrell. He died there in 1946.

Heitor Villa-Lobos is considered one of the greatest writers for the acoustic guitar. His ability to conjure up a twilight stillness which glows through slow cascades of guitar ambience is one of the finest achievements of twentieth-century music. This was made possible by his invention of the *choros*, a new type of compositional technique meshing Brazilian music with Indian and popular tunes.

Villa-Lobos was born in Rio de Janeiro in 1887. He received no formal education and, incredibly, taught himself every available instrument. He played in street bands, travelled Brazil in search of folklore and accompanied silent films. His first *Choros* (1920), for guitar, brought him fame. The pianist Artur Rubinstein discovered Villa-Lobos in 1923, just as he had finished his enigmatically beautiful *Popular Brazilian Suite For Guitar*. He was sent to Paris, where even Varèse praised his eclectic modernism.

During the 1930s he was given control of Brazil's musical education and wrote fusion music in the form of the *Bachianas Brasileiras*, a series of nine Baroque-Brazilian suites modelled on Bach, written for all manner of instruments and reflecting aspects of musical Impressionism and Minimalism. The limpid lyrical song from *No. 5* (1938), for voice and cellos, became his most famous piece. Though he was criticized for the large number (some say thousands) of his works, many for slushy flutes and orchestra, Villa-Lobos's guitar pieces remain brilliant distillations. His *Five Preludes For Guitar* (1940) are superlative, immediately instilling a contemplative mood in the listener. Though Villa-Lobos died in 1959, Finnish guitarist Timo Korhonen has recently said: 'The technical inventiveness which his guitar works display, their use of harmonics, their dynamic and emotional climaxes are unsurpassed in guitar literature. They are one at the same time, the bread and butter, the crown jewels, the Mount Everest of the guitarist's repertoire!'

Another Hispanic composer for guitar who deserves mention is Joaquin

Rodrigo, who was born in Valencia, Spain, in 1901. Blinded by diphtheria at the age of three, he nevertheless showed a tremendous interest in music from the age of eight and entered Valencia's Conservatoire at sixteen. After studying in Madrid he went to Paris, where he worked hard as a composer in the 1920s and 30s. He and his wife Vicky travelled between Germany, Spain and France before returning to Spain in 1939 at the end of the Spanish Civil War and the beginning of the Second World War. With them they carried the score for the *Concierto de Aranjuez* (*The Aranjuez Concerto*), destined to become one of the twentieth century's greatest classics.

This piece, with its flamenco guitar wedged against horns and strings, clarinets, oboes and flutes, is pure Ambience in three movements – wafting between Impressionism and a sort of strident Minimalism. When premiered in 1940, it made Rodrigo Spain's leading composer after Falla. He became a professor at Madrid University in 1946 and composed a total of some 170 pieces. Though much of his output is saccharine and simplistic, both *Seville Fantasy* (1952) and *Royal Dance* (ballet featuring guitar, 1954) are notable. During the 1950s and 60s Rodrigo wrote for the guitarist Andrés Segovia but it was the release of the recording of the *Concierto de Aranjuez* by Miles Davis in 1960 that made him a star. By emphasizing its slow part alongside Davis's characteristic pinched trumpet delivery plus sound use of rhythmic patterns by orchestrator Gil Evans, this version showed just how clever Rodrigo's writing really was. The composer has also had a profound influence on the guitar music of John McLaughlin. Having lived throughout, and contributed so much to, the twentieth century, Rodrigo died peacefully in Madrid in 1999.

LISTENING

Albéniz, Falla and Rodrigo are celebrated on several EMI CD collections, the first two in versions from the 1950s and 60s, the latter in orchestral works recorded in 1995 in Mexico. An essential recording is Miles Davis's *Sketches Of Spain* (Columbia, 1960), which also contains work by Falla. For Villa-Lobos, Timo Korhonen's *Complete Works For Guitar* on Ondine are superb. *Volume 2* (1995), containing the *Preludes*, *Bachianas Brasileiras No. 5*, the *Brazilian Suite* and *Choros No. 1*, is outstanding.

WILLIAM DUDDELL

Often credited with inventing the first electronic instrument, although Thomas Edison's 1877 tin-foil phonograph had precedence, William Duddell kick-started electronic music as we know it today. His Singing Arc allied to a keyboard generated actual music during the early 1900s. Like Marconi, he was interested in wireless telegraphy and the possibilities presented by alternating current.

Duddell, born in 1872, was an outstanding electro-physicist who had been privately educated in the UK and France and had risen quickly through the prestigious City & Guilds Schools via scholarships. His reputation was such that when new electric 'arc' lamps, which were being fitted in turn-of-the-century London, began to play up he was called in to solve the problem. These lamps whistled quite loudly and Duddell explained the problem by demonstrating the effects of fluctuating current. As a result of rigging up a demonstration for lectures, he invented in 1899 the Singing Arc, which could generate musical notes by way of a keyboard which interrupted oscillations in a circuit. It played tones but with little diversity.

Although he happened upon electronic music through science, Duddell deserved recognition and was duly made a Fellow of the Royal Society in 1913, four years before his early death.

THADDEUS CAHILL

The Canadian businessman Thaddeus Cahill will for ever be remembered for the invention of the giant Telharmonium, which weighed 200 tons, measured sixty feet across and cost the New England Electric Music Company the staggering sum of $200,000 in 1906. With the Telharmonium Cahill exploited to the hilt Edison's ideas in telecommunications and recording. This colossus of a machine used banks of whirring, rotating electromagnetic generators to create electrical impulses which, through a keyboard and various other controls, were sent down wires to a series of telephone receivers fitted with acoustic horns. In the days before amplification and speakers the Telharmonium was indeed an innovation, quite loud and with a huge harmonic range from which the player could mix different frequencies. In some ways it was the first great synthesizer and Cahill's later ideas of generating its music to homes throughout the US prefigured both Muzak and on-line computer-accessed music.

Alternatively called an Electric Music Plant or Dynamophone, Cahill's invention dates from 1895 and was patented in 1897. His desire was to 'produce the notes and chords of a musical composition with any timbre desired'. Three machines were built, an important demonstration in Massachusetts and New York City provoking prominent Italian composer, pianist and intellectual Ferruccio Busoni to write a rapturous approval in his 1907 paper 'Sketch Of A New Aesthetic Of Music'. In this he disowned all past music and saw the Telharmonium as a gateway to 'unlimited tonal material . . . abstract sounds . . . new concepts of harmony'. Busoni wanted 'pure invention and sentiment in tone colours' and saw the Telharmonium as allowing musicians to rhapsodically 'follow the line of the rainbow and vie with the clouds in breaking sunbeams'.

As the only early commercial non-valve electronic instrument ever made, it was indeed a breakthrough. Its image of the keyboard surrounded by loads of wires and electronics established the futuristic look for all time. Cahill developed a further instrument between 1908 and 1911. By that time he wanted to pump 'Telharmony' into hotels, theatres, restaurants and houses via the telephone system and have a Telharmonium in every city. The problem was, it jammed the existing phone system. And anyway its sheer bulk and cost were prohibitive. In retrospect it is clear that the increasing popularity of radio killed off the idea. But, with its harmonic versatility, its characteristically noisy gear shifts (its rotating magnets anticipated the Hammond organ) and its ability to synthesize to a very high standard of sound production, the Telharmonium was the first true classic of electronic music production.

LEE DE FOREST

One of the most significant inventors of the twentieth century, Lee De Forest made a contribution to electronic and Ambient music that is still being felt today. Not only did he invent the valve, which allowed for amplification and much-improved sound quality, but he also made significant contributions to recording technology. Many believe that his role in developing computers, telephone, radio, microphone, TV and other communications was so crucial that it was only eclipsed in 1947 with the coming of the transistor.

An interesting man, whose life reads like a film script (he actually died in Hollywood in 1961), De Forest suffered ostracism as a child and litigation and bankruptcy several times as an adult. Thrice married, he never got the Nobel Prize he so richly deserved but lived to see his best innovations, bought from him for a song, turned into multimillion-dollar corporate profits. A rugged individualist in the American tradition, De Forest was a great showman who in 1910 broadcast Enrico Caruso singing from the Met in New York to prove the worth of his innovation.

In 1894 a German scientist named Herz realized that electromagnetic waves travelled through the air at the speed of light. In 1899 the part Italian part Irish Marconi was transmitting these waves using wireless telegraphy across the English channel. In 1904 an Englishman, Ambrose Fleming, developed the diode, a glass tube through which a current could pass. De Forest's genius was in synthesizing these innovations together. In 1906 he introduced the idea of a triode into Fleming's so-called vacuum tube in order to control the flow of electric current, hence the name thermionic valve or simply valve.

De Forest had grown up in Alabama among black children as his minister father taught at a segregated college. Made to feel isolated by whites and confused, he lost himself in inventions. After working his way through Yale, he emerged with a brilliant PhD in electronic communications in 1899. After a time working for Western Electronics in Chicago he formed his own company in 1902 and in 1907 patented his new 'valve' system under the name Audion Tube for amplification purposes.

A contradiction in terms, De Forest never tired of demonstrating his invention, yet by 1912 he had lost two companies. Though bad at business, he was a dazzling innovator. By that year he had developed a circular feedback system using his tubes plus a much higher-definition amplification system by arranging transfer of signals from one valve to another. In 1913 he was experimenting with magnetic-wire recording for possible use in film and in the 1920s developed Phonofilm, an optical recording system which transformed sound waves into pulses of light. This was initially ridiculed by the motion-picture industry but later modified and widely applied.

It is said that an Audion Piano based on beat frequencies, began in 1915 but never completed, prefigured the Ondes Martenot and Armand Givelet's electronic organ, both invented in 1928. During his life De Forest applied for 300 patents and eventually his valve amplification system became much prized in the recording industry. Even innovative Ambient Techno musicians of the 1990s praised valve equipment for its warmth and depth of sound. Today specialist high-fidelity companies will supply complete valve-driven sound systems for hundreds of thousands of pounds.

LUIGI RUSSOLO

The Italian Luigi Russolo was the youngest of the Milanese Futurists who allied themselves to 'a new form of beauty' as outlined by the rich artistic entrepreneur and writer Filippo Marinetti in 1909 in terms of 'violent electric moons' and 'the chatter of propellers'. Though the Futurists have often been seen as extremist Modernists who hastened the path of young Italy towards Fascism, it is important to point out Russolo's contribution to both electronic and Ambient music.

As a painter, Russolo was one of the first to explore synaesthesia, or sensory confusion. Works like *Perfume* and *Music* (1909–11) attempt to convey odour and sound through kaleidoscopic colour and can be seen as preludes to the more intense psychedelic sensibility of the 1960s. In 1913 he published his now famous 'Art Of Noises' manifesto in which he outlined the need for a new music based on a wider acceptability of sound. He wrote: 'We are now satiated with Beethoven and Wagner. We find more enjoyment in the combination of noises of trams, carriages and crowds.' He was fascinated with the actual gradations of pitch of all sounds and recognized that 'noise' is only different from musical sound in terms of the latter's purposive arrangement.

Incredibly, he saw, well before the coming of real electronic music in the 1950s, that gradations up and down the chromatic scale could be achieved by

seemingly non-musical devices. So convinced was he of his vision that he
enlisted the help of the percussionist Uno Piatti in building 'noise machines'
(*intonarumori*), which looked like big wooden boxes with megaphone horns and
handles, to produce the desired effect. The result was a series of rustling,
burbling and detonating sounds. Unveiled during a Futurist concert with
Marinetti in Milan in 1914, they were highly successful.

In addition Russolo developed keyboard noise generators called *psofarmoni*
and also in 1914 he performed a series of concerts at the Coliseum in London.
His compositions had strange titles like *A Meeting Of Motorcars And Aeroplanes*
and *The Awakening Of The Great City*. His interests in acoustics and sound, his
illumination of the importance of environmental and artificially produced noise
and randomness make him a visionary forerunner of Pierre Schaeffer's *musique
concrète* ('concrete' or 'real sound' music) as well as the sonic explorations of
Stockhausen, Cage and even Brian Eno.

LEON THEREMIN

The Russian Leon Theremin (born Lev Termen) has passed into legend, not
only for his invention of his ingenious ether-wave instrument the Theremin,
operated by the movement of hands in the air, but because of his extraordinary
life and the subsequent uptake of his instrument by pop and rock groups of the
1960s. Certainly his invention was the first of the pioneering electronic devices
to hit the top of the charts on both sides of the Atlantic – firstly on The Beach
Boys' 'Good Vibrations' single of 1966 and secondly in 1969 on Led Zeppelin's
second album, where its siren-like sound filled in the stuttering guitar masonry
of what has become one of rock's greatest creations, 'Whole Lotta Love'.

Theremin was born in St Petersburg in 1896. In his teens he showed a
pronounced interest in both physics and music. He studied the first at Petrograd
University, the second at the city's Musical Institute. In 1919, some years after St
Petersburg was renamed Leningrad, he became Director of the Laboratory of
Electrical Oscillations in its Physico-Technical Institute. His interest in radio
engineering made him dream of uniting electronics and music. In August 1920
he demonstrated his remarkable Aetherphon at the All-Union Electrical
Congress. The method of sound creation was through the interaction of
two radio frequencies, one fixed and the other variable. The method of playing
was by movement of the hands near an aerial, volume being controlled by a
pedal. Quality of sound, or timbre, came from a variety of filters operated by a
simple switch.

By 1923 Theremin had refined the Aetherphon into the Thereminvox,
which still had an aerial but also a ring for the left hand which controlled
volume, looked compact but impressive. The right hand could make pitch
changes and even produce chords, but neither hand actually needed to touch

the 'space-controlled' device. It looked like magic, and the Soviet leader Lenin was impressed. Early models used earphones and cardboard horns but by the mid-1920s the loudspeaker had been invented and thus the device was now a full electronic instrument. Theremin's friend Clara Rockmore, a classical violinist, became its leading virtuoso. Though it was monophonic (capable of playing only one note at a time), the Thereminvox had an impressive three-octave range. As envoys of the new socialist Russia Theremin and Rockmore toured throughout Europe between 1923 and 1927.

In the latter year they arrived in the US, where Theremin quickly patented the device. Changing his name from Lev Termen to Professor Leon Theremin, he settled down to a decade of celebrity. He struck a deal with RCA in 1928 for the manufacture of what he now called the Theremin. In 1929, after he had developed a four-octave keyboard model, RCA emblazoned its advertising with the logo: 'Not a radio. Not a phonograph. Not like anything you have ever heard or seen!' Though the Theremin was eagerly taken up by musicians and composers, the general public stayed away and sales of the instrument never exceeded the hundreds. In 1930 Theremin even created a cylindrical finger-board version which looked like a cello.

Though the Theremin was used in symphonic music in Leningrad in the mid-1920s, it wasn't until Joseph Schillinger's *1st Airphonic Suite*, performed in Ohio in 1929, that it really entered the concert repertoire. Edgard Varèse's important *Ecuatorial* (1934) called for two Theremins. In New York the instrument was often used in dance and music halls, and in 1932 there was even a 'Theremin Electrical Symphony' in which sixteen of the dream-weaving boxes performed at the city's Carnegie Hall. Though composers like Charles Ives and Aaron Copland would work for the instrument, and the radical conductor Leopold Stokowski would champion its application, it was in the world of the cinema that it really took off. One can hear it evoking the delirium of a drunken writer in Billy Wilder's film *Lost Weekend* of the mid-1940s, or the strangeness of alien contact on the soundtracks of classic sci-fi movies like *The Day The Earth Stood Still* (1951), *It Came From Outer Space* (1953) and *Forbidden Planet* (1956).

All this time Theremin's life had gone through turmoil. His marriage to a black entertainer in New York broke a taboo in a still-segregated America. A return to Russia in 1938 led to his being kidnapped by the KGB. Seen as a defector in Stalin's eyes, he was sent to work in the mines for his pains. Eventually he was transferred to the KGB's espionage centre and spent the Cold War developing sophisticated surveillance equipment.

Between 1954 and 1966 the famous Robert Moog generated five more versions of the Theremin. He increased the octave range and applied the ideas to the experimental music of John Cage, most notably in *Variations V* (1965), where dancers trigger music generated by antennae. Subsequently the music of The Beach Boys would fix the Theremin in the public imagination for ever, 'Good Vibrations' becoming a staple in advertising jingles, television and film.

In 1988 contemporary Ambient guru Brian Eno included a new Theremin track, 'For Her Atoms', performed by Theremin's granddaughter Lydia, on his album *Music For Films 3*. At the time Professor of Electronic Musical Instruments at the University of Moscow, Theremin himself approved the track before its release in the West.

In the era of glasnost Theremin was able to return to New York in the early 1990s and reunite with Clara Rockmore and once again demonstrate the instrument. Though imitations calling themselves strange names like the Ethonium and Croix Sonore have come and gone in its wake, no other instrument has captured the imagination like the Theremin. From its truly Ambient use by Jimmy Page on Led Zeppelin's 1973 US tour to its reapplication in Ambient electronica of the 1990s it has become a true archetype of musical innovation. Theremin himself died in Moscow in 1993, apparently a contented man.

MAURICE MARTENOT

Like Theremin, Maurice Martenot lent his name to an electronic device which would become one of the most abiding musical inventions of the twentieth century. Its quivering, bewitching sound became the centrepiece of Olivier Messiaen's masterful Ambient movement of his luminous *Turangalîla-symphonie* (*Turangalila Symphony*) of 1946–8. In fact the instrument was so successful that it has become a permanent part of French musical life. Its unmistakable dreamy sound has been heard on over 1,000 film soundtracks.

Martenot was born in Paris in 1898. His standard middle-class education included classes in cello, composition and piano at the Conservatoire. An interest in exotic sounds, particularly those of the Far East, led him to invent the '*ondes musicales*' (musical waves), later known as the Ondes Martenot. After meeting Theremin in 1923 and being impressed by the possibilities of the 'ether-wave instrument', Martenot developed his own. He premiered it in Paris in April 1928 as soloist in the forgotten *Symphonic Poem* by Levidis. Within a year the prescient Edgard Varèse was using it to produce synthetic sounds in his *Amériques*. Martenot was on his way to fame and fortune.

Like the Theremin, the Ondes Martenot used the principle of two swaying vibrations produced by radio valves of different frequencies whose interaction produced sound. The early version of 1928 was in two pieces: the right-hand side used a pull wire, the left contained the timbral, volume and harmonic controls. Quickly Martenot unified these functions into a single unit and developed a ribbon and ring device which stretched across a guide keyboard and altered the pitch. By the early 1930s he had refined an excellent keyboard capable of microtonal changes, with slide and vibrational qualities aided by the ribbon. Amplification could be varied, and included the use of the '*palme*' or floral-shaped speaker covered with resonating strings. In adding this feature to the various tone colours and filtering provided by the left-hand controls, Martenot developed one of the most versatile electronic instruments of the pre-synthesizer era.

With his sister Gillette he played over 1,000 Ondes Martenot concerts, including the 1938 Paris Exposition, when eight of his instruments played in unison. He founded at Neuilly a school specializing in the Art of the Martenot which eventually had branches at most French music schools. Naturally enough, he became the leading exponent of the instrument at the Paris Conservatoire in the late 1940s.

The list of composers who have used the Ondes Martenot is large. Varèse substituted it for the Theremins he used in his 1934 *Ecuatorial*, while Messiaen very eagerly used six in his *Fêtes des belles eaux* (*Feasts Of The Beautiful Waters*) of 1937. Pierre Boulez advocated its properties, played it and even wrote a quartet for Ondes Martenots in 1945–6.

Ravel, Samuel Barber, Darius Milhaud and Satie devotee Arthur Honegger all contributed to the instrument's repertoire, the last-named stating in 1951 that it had both 'power and speed of utterance'. The seven-octave keyboard range and other qualities of the Ondes Martenot have been likened to the human voice. But though its popularity in France has never waned – it is used in theatres and by young French composers to this day – it was always viewed as very much a French invention and property. Martenot himself died in 1980 having significantly opened up electronic and Ambient music for the twentieth century. His legacy can best be heard in the exquisite reverie 'The Garden Of Sleeping Love' from Messiaen's *Turangalila Symphony*.

JORG MAGER

Often dubbed the father of German electronic music, Jorg Mager was born in 1880 and began his career as an organist. He worked briefly as a school teacher but fascination with microtones – the tones between the keys of a piano which are usually heard in folk and ethnic music, particularly that of India – led him to the invention of instruments and specifically to the application of microtones to keyboards. In doing so between 1921 and 1930 he contributed enormously to the advent of the synthesizer.

In 1911 he succeeded in constructing a quarter-tone harmonium, thus producing keyboard sounds that previously could only be heard on a violin. After the First World War he studied electronics in Berlin and worked with the Lorenz firm in creating the Elektrophon in 1921. This was a monophonic musical device based on the frequency screech produced by radio. It was very much a contraption but was upgraded in 1923 to the Sphaerophon (meaning 'the voice of the spheres'). Tapping into the old idea that ether conveyed sound, Mager demonstrated the Sphaerophon in 1926 at Donaueschingen to considerable interest. Sound was generated using feedback and controlled with a complicated dial and lever system.

In 1927 came Mager's Kaleidophon, a keyboard device which could be tuned at will, was touch sensitive and capable of changes in timbre and vibrato. Though no examples survive, Mager was obviously a genius, years ahead of his time. A successful demonstration at Frankfurt led to the offer of a castle at Darmstadt where he could develop his instrument, and here he founded the Electro-Acoustic Music Society in 1929. He continued to refine the Sphaerophon, which, with the addition of two small keyboards and a pedal board, had by this time become the Klaviatursphaerophon.

Mager's research resulted in the Partiturophon in 1930–1, a multi-voiced five-keyboard device with pedal board and extras, which could play scored music. He made it produce thunder sounds for performances of Wagner's operatic *Ring* cycle at Bayreuth in 1931 and the following year he provided microtonal music for thirty performances of Goethe's *Faust*. Mager's fame was in the ascendant as offers of concerts and film-score commissions flooded in. But when Hitler came to power in 1933 his work was doomed. Considered a decadent artist, he eventually lost his castle and died in isolation in 1939. The war destroyed all his ingenious inventions yet he is remembered precisely for his visionary courage. Mager wanted the Partiturophon to be available in every home and dreamed of an Omnitonium, an instrument that could play every possible sound in any tuning. Only today is that possible, so far ahead of its time was Mager's imagination.

FRIEDRICH TRAUTWEIN AND OSKAR SALA

The Trautonium, invented in Berlin in 1930, is still considered today one of the most versatile and interesting of the early electronic instruments. The fact that it could produce sounds far more complex than the piano meant that a wide variety of applications were found for it. From producing the manifold background shrieks and screeches in Alfred Hitchcock's film *The Birds* (1963) to its adoption by the German Ambient guru Pete Namlook in the 1990s, the Trautonium has played a key role in the development of electronic and atmospheric music.

The instrument was developed not only by its originator, Friedrich Trautwein, but also by the composer Paul Hindemith and the inventor and musician Oskar Sala. Firstly, Trautwein, who was born in 1888. An electrical engineer, a lawyer, a doctor of physics and Professor of Musical Acoustics at the Berlin Academy of Music, he was interested in expanding electronic sound and developing an instrument with more harmonic possibilities than the Theremin. To this end he worked with the composer Hindemith at Berlin's Experimental Radio Centre and by 1930 had produced the Trautonium.

Early versions sound fascinating. Radio-tube fluctuations produced electronic pulses which were amplified through a speaker. A pulsating neon light, with the help of a number of dials, controlled tone. A taught wire stretched across a strip of metal akin to a guitar fretboard produced notes when held against it, but electronically in that a circuit was completed. The volume of this monophonic device was controlled by a pedal, its three-octave range altered by means of a switch. Hindemith, who in the 1920s had campaigned for 'Everyday Music' and more presciently 'House Music', in the spirit of Satie, saw the Trautonium as a great step forward. He wrote a *Trautonium Trio* in 1930 and a celebrated *Concerto For Trautonium And Strings* in 1931.

Trautwein wrote a manual for his invention in 1936 and after the Second World War developed an amplified harpsichord and electronic bells. He established a school for recording engineers which became part of the Schumann Conservatory in the 1950s. Trautwein died in 1956, having done much to spread the teaching and knowledge of electronic music through papers, lectures and numerous articles in magazines. He was particularly interested in 'listening' and how sound is identified and understood.

The Trautonium was enhanced by his pupil Oskar Sala. Born in 1910 in Thuringia, Sala was a brilliant composition student at the Berlin Academy, where he met Trautwein. At nineteen Sala became a virtuoso on the instrument, performing Hindemith's pieces in concert. After the latter left Germany (to live in Turkey, then the UK and finally the US) Trautwein saw the potential in Sala's ideas and supported him. By 1935 Sala had come up with the Radio Trautonium, with two wire and metal boards controlled by metal tongues and an array of knobs and levers. It looked for all the world like some weird organ. A concert version, independent of radio technology, was also produced and used. Between 1949 and 1952 Sala discovered circuitry that could enormously expand the tonal ability of the Radio Trautonium and produce subharmonic rows and chords. By being able to play the tones between the notes on a piano, the new Mixturtrautonium could get nearer to natural and unnatural sounds. The instrument was patented in the US, Germany and France, and subsequently further generators were added.

In 1958 Sala set up his own studio and by the 1960s he also had a workshop for producing independent film music. His most famous score was for Hitchcock's *The Birds*, among 300 other films. Sala composed many pieces for the Trautonium, including *Electronic Impression* (1987) and *Fantasy For Mixturtrautonium* (1988). In that year three professors at a Berlin postal college refined a micro-electronic version of the instrument.

Sala has been neglected, probably because he stayed in Germany throughout Hitler's Third Reich. But the beauty of his refinements to Trautwein's original invention cannot be denied. He lent it great variety of pitch and tone colour as well as spring-based pressure-sensitive liquid resistors which give the player a real hands-on feel. Between 1990 and 1995 the Frankfurt Ambient Techno star Pete Namlook recognized Sala's contribution by remastering an entire CD of

Trautonium music played by Sala titled *My Fascinating Instrument* (Fax). At the time Namlook was outspoken about the brilliance of the Trautonium: 'I did a lot of programming work on it, producing subharmonic chords. Compared to today's synthesizers it has the best interface for monophonic sounds. You can create every tone, and with direct attack and tremolo, with a move of the finger. It is strange that modern synthesizer companies, still thinking of the piano and the even-tempered scale, cannot even compete with technology of the 30s. With Sala and the Trautonium you get the intensity which only a musician playing with his hands, feet and whole body can produce.'

ARNOLD SCHOENBERG

At first there may seem to be no connection between Schoenberg and Ambient and electronic music. Why should someone who wrote difficult, almost unlistenable atonal and 'Serial' works have anything to do with velvety, atmospheric Ambience? Well, taught by Mahler and himself the chief mentor to John Cage, Schoenberg was responsible for taking German Romanticism and breaking it in two. By abandoning key signatures and eventually the 'even-tempered' (do-re-mi-fa-so-la-ti-do) scale he caused a revolution which echoed down through the twentieth century and was singular in shaping Stockhausen's electronic inventions. Moreover, as noted by the German social philosopher and musicologist Theodor Adorno, Schoenberg's objective rigour led to a music and system which could rely on itself; and it was in this way that it opened up the creative space for Minimalism and the Ambience which followed it.

Schoenberg, born in 1874, was a mostly self-taught Viennese shoemaker's son who started on violin when eight but in his teens left composition lessons for a bank job. Further lessons never deflected him from his famous maxim: 'Genius learns only from itself, talent chiefly from others.' His early brooding music caused scandals in Vienna yet two pieces which surfaced in 1902, *Verklärte Nacht* (*Transfigured Night*) and *Pelleas und Melisande* (also the subject of an opera by Debussy) have all the flavour of Romantic longing. After marriage and a stint in a Berlin theatre he returned to Vienna and a poverty-stricken life of teaching and painting. Mahler helped him with his music and saw Schoenberg move towards extreme musical unrest or dissonance, causing howls of indignation along the way. In 1908, during a marriage crisis, he dispensed with structured tonality for random key signatures. The string quartets he wrote in this style caused riots.

After Mahler's death Schoenberg became famous for a new type of spoken music theatre with *Pierrot Lunaire* (1912). During the First World War he was stationed in Vienna and formed the Society for Private Music. Over eight years he wrote no music but invented Serialism – a new compositional tool which used all twelve tones of the octave which, individually, could be written only once as part of the row or series. Tone rows could only be transformed in mirrored or inverted form. This rigorous system had precedents in baroque and classical music, particularly Bach's *Fugues*, but in Schoenberg's hands it led to the abandonment of recognizable melodies. This technique allowed him to blue-print emotional methods of creating film music, as was evidenced in the 1930 *Accompaniment To A Film Score*.

Having lost his wife in the 1920s, Schoenberg remarried and was settling down to a good professorship at the Berlin Academy when the Nazis came to power. As usual he flew in the face of conservatism, emphasized his Jewish heritage and fled to the US, where he taught at the University of California in Los Angeles. Though he hated the commercialization of Hollywood, he met producer Irving Thalberg in 1935 to discuss the scoring of the MGM film *The Good Earth*. The composer disliked Thalberg's musical ignorance and de-manded a huge fee of $50,000 plus complete control over actors and the musical score. Unsurprisingly, the deal fell through. Schoenberg was un-wavering in his adherence to his inventions. He once said 'The laws of nature manifested in a man of genius are but the laws of the future.' After problems with his heart he died in 1951 at the age of seventy-six, having rewritten the history of music.

LISTENING

Schoenberg is more famous for his ideas than for the music itself. Tunes and melodies were always subservient to form and concept. *Verklärte Nacht* (*Trans-figured Night*) (1902), a poetic string sextet, is considered erotic. The atonalities of his *String Quartet No. 2* (1908) have been described as eerie while the sound-colour section 'Summer Morning By A Lake' from 1909's *Five Orchestral Pieces* is regarded as a high point of tranquil music. Yet the best introduction to his sound-world is the post-Romanticism of *Pelleas und Melisande* (1902), where, during a single movement lasting nearly fifty minutes, Schoenberg's restless, endlessly shifting writing takes on a strange Ambient character. Recommended is the recording by Christopher Eschenbach and the Houston Symphony Orchestra (Koch 1995).

ALBAN BERG AND ANTON WEBERN

Of the dozens of pupils who surrounded Arnold Schoenberg in the Vienna of the early twentieth century it was Alban Berg and Anton Webern who became famous. In fact the trio made up the so-called Second Viennese School, whose visionary commitment to the revolutionary Twelve-Tone system was seen as important as that of Haydn, Mozart and Beethoven (the First Viennese School) to classical music more than a century earlier. Both composers are important to the development of electronic and Ambient music in their refinement and development of Schoenbergian technique.

Berg, born in 1885, was a typical Viennese bourgeois who swung between shy introspection and intense sensuality. His life was littered with affairs. In 1904, when he met Schoenberg, the nineteen-year-old Berg swore lifelong musical fidelity. He formally studied with the older composer for six years and wrote about and propagated Schoenberg's theories up to his death. Berg's music incorporated classical structures, Romantic melodic fragments from Mahler and Wagner, folk tunes and suchlike. He suffered from bad asthma and depression and was obsessively interested in numerology. Though he was famous for applying austere atonality and Twelve-Tone ideas to opera (*Wozzeck*, 1921), his instrumental works such as the *Lyric Suite* (1925–6) and his *Violin Concerto* (1935) contain aspects of incredible beauty and quietude. Berg died in 1935, at the age of fifty, from an infected insect bite, his mentor in exile in the US, his own music decried as decadent by the rising Nazi regime. Yet in his ability to make Schoenberg's ideas flow and float, Berg made the forbidding Twelve-Tone system accessible.

In contrast to Berg, his fellow-Austrian Anton Webern, born two years earlier in 1883, was fiercely academic. He reduced Schoenberg's ideas to such economy that most of his music could fit on two compact discs. One famous work, his *Symphony* (1928), lasts for only ten minutes, its score taking up only a couple of pages. While at Vienna University Webern began studying, at the age of twenty-one, with Schoenberg and spent seven years in the most intense exploration of the new musical ideas. *Passacaglia* (1908) would be his longest piece, at eighteen minutes, and sounded like compacted Mahler. The following year's *Five Movements For String Quartet* laid out his style – concise with extreme contrasts between the climactic and brooding near silence. In between conducting jobs he fiercely supported Schoenberg, helping run his Society for Private Music from 1918.

After the First World War he settled in suburban Vienna, worked as a conductor and from 1923 refined and analysed the Twelve-Tone process into near invisibility. Schoenberg was to comment on his technique: 'Every glance is a poem, every sigh is a novel.' Webern developed Schoenberg's 'tone-colour melody' ideal to an extreme where each tone was played by a different instrument. In his world sound became the most desirable thing, with every-thing else – pitch, timbre, rhythm – being subsumed to the Serial technique. Even silence was strictly measurable. He remained in an Austria under Nazi occupation, his family having tenuous links with the party but his music banned as 'cultural bolshevism'. He worked as a proofreader but retreated to his daughter's house near Salzburg during the Allied bombings of 1945. There he was accidentally shot dead by an American sentry for lighting a cigar on his porch during curfew. In post-war music Webern's total Serialism technique was to have a profound influence on the course of electronic music for it mapped out a concrete direction for the ground-breaking innovations of Karlheinz Stockhausen and Pierre Boulez.

LEOPOLD STOKOWSKI

The conductor who stands out most as a musical thinker, Leopold Stokowski was unique in the way he used the musical establishment to champion completely new ideas in sound deployment, electronic music and Ambience. The first to champion novel electrical instruments in the concert hall and the first to seize on the recorded medium and become a star, Stokowski was first and foremost a radical who turned every opportunity into a moment of confrontation.

Coming from Irish and Polish parentage in London certainly helped shape his unconventional vision. Born in 1882, he was the youngest-ever entrant, at thirteen, to the Royal College of Music, where his gift for violin and keyboards led to a fellowship at eighteen in composition, organ music and theory. By the age of twenty-one he had also gained a degree from Oxford and up to 1908 he played the organ at churches in London and New York as well as pursuing additional studies in Munich, Paris and Berlin. He preferred to turn his remarkable abilities outward rather than pursue an academic career and readily accepted US citizenship in 1915, three years after being appointed conductor of the Philadelphia Orchestra.

His leadership there between 1912 and 1936 profoundly affected American music in all sorts of ways. In 1917 he became the first conducting and recording star, having signed to what would become the RCA Victor label. Stokowski well understood that sound in the broadest sense was the way forward in the twentieth century and that old ways of confining music or limiting its appeal had to be ditched if progress was to be made. He shocked audiences by championing the new over the old. His support of Varèse's disquietening sonic blast *Amériques* in 1926 caused a storm. When the four-octave Theremin arrived in 1929 Stokowski wrote the classic lines: 'Soon we shall have entirely new methods of tone production by electrical means. Thus will begin a new era in music.' He used the instrument's strangely pitched sounds to enhance orchestral tone.

Having ditched the conductor's baton for a new expressivity using his hands, Stokowski then experimented with orchestral design, changing things around to enliven sound – an innovation which would inspire Stockhausen. He would go on to champion the likes of Schoenberg, Berg and Webern, verbally attacking the audience if they refused the new music a chance to breathe. In 1932, at a meeting of the Acoustical Society in the US, he set out his stall in no uncertain terms. New forms of communication like radio and records were paramount. The synthesis of sounds in electronic music was the way forward. 'Musical notation cannot by any means express all the possibilities of sound. In time the musician will create directly into Tone, not on paper. Any frequency, any duration, any intensity or combinations of harmony or rhythm.'

This call for a pure electronic music would shape much of the twentieth century's musical search. The lush, deep tone of the Philadelphia Orchestra in the concert hall, coupled with its recorded legacy, radically changed the public's attitudes to records and neglected music. Stokowski championed Mahler in new, luminous versions and his extensive research into acoustics and electronics improved studio sound quality in the US, Germany and Holland.

Thrice married (the last time to heiress Gloria Vanderbilt in 1945), Stokowski led various American orchestras up to 1972. He certainly influenced how the American public considered such mavericks as Charles Ives, and the tall, charismatic figure, with his interest in Asian music, his penchant for changing a score if it suited him, his ability to conduct from memory alone, his interest in music and film innovation and, above all, his dedication to new sounds, became a crucial bridge between the classical world and the modern. Still dreaming about conducting some new music on his hundredth birthday, he died quietly in Hampshire, England in 1977, five years short of his century.

EDGARD VARÈSE

Beloved of musicians as diverse as Frank Zappa and Stockhausen, Edgard Varèse was one of the twentieth century's great mavericks. In his search for a music of 'beautiful parabolic and hyperbolic curves' Varèse, as early as 1916, was demanding 'new instruments and new technical means' through which to realize 'the organized sounds' of his imagination. He felt that composers and musicians should be able to satisfy every dictate of musical thought and believed that 'electronics could free music'. His life would be a search and a realization of this ideal.

Of Franco-Italian parentage, Varèse was born in Paris in 1883 but moved to Turin with his family while young. He studied harmony and had penned an opera by the age of eleven, but a talent for maths and science led him to study those subjects at Turin University. After returning to Paris in the early 1900s Varèse studied at the Schola Cantorum and the Conservatoire. It was not long before this bright young man attracted the interest of Debussy and Satie and their milieu, which included the poet Apollinaire and the writer Jean Cocteau. Yet Varèse was more interested in the radical ideas of Ferruccio Busoni after reading the latter's 1907 paper 'Sketch For A New Aesthetic Of Music' and went to Berlin in 1909 to meet the man. There he was stimulated by the Italian's theories of 'free music' and the possibility of musical tones beyond the normal scale (microtonality).

Working as a conductor, Varèse divided his time between Berlin and Paris. In 1913 he met the inventor René Bertrand but the following year he was conscripted into the French Army. His war service was short and after being discharged on grounds of illness he emigrated to the US. His arrival in New York in December 1915 had the aura of an evangelist coming to transform the New World. He immediately organized an Orchestra for New Music but there were no audiences. He pleaded in the *New York Telegraph* for 'new technical means' and by 1921 had set up the International Composers' Guild for the dissemination of new sounds. Over six years dozens of works from all over the world were performed for the first time, including those of the Second Viennese School.

In Varèse's mind sounds that had been heard were old hat. He wrote in an American journal in 1922 that 'speed and synthesis are characteristics of our own epoch'. But since equipment didn't exist to create the new sounds he reasoned he had to invent new sonorities with existing instruments. His flow of compositions through the 1920s and 30s confused many, but Varèse found a willing ally in the conductor Leopold Stokowski. Works like *Amériques* (1921), *Hyperprism* (1923), *Intégrales* (1924) and *Ionisation* (1931) were all takes on the urban landscape, using percussion and strange instrumental combinations to convey, through 'beams of sound', a 'music of the fourth dimension'. Varèse's use of sound blocks and extreme rhythmic changes made his music a challenge and often caused uproar in audiences. Only the short four-minute *Density 21.5* for flute could be said to have Ambient properties.

Of more interest was his direct involvement in electronics. In the late 1920s he approached Bell Telephone for the use of a laboratory to research into possible instruments but no funds were available. In 1927 his friend Bertrand had invented the Dynaphone, a dial-operated monophonic oscillation device like the Theremin, and this was showcased in several European cities. The following year Varèse returned to Paris in order to build a studio to develop the instrument and other ideas. Interestingly, he wrote that the studio contained a complete record collection of 'all races, all cultures', so the world's music might have been available for electronic sampling. But in the 1930s Western electronic engineers, although sympathetic to Varèse's aims, were unable to find the finances. His 1933 application to the Guggenheim Foundation for a grant to research into new scales and frequency ranges with the improved Dynaphone was similarly rebuffed. Frustrated, he experimented by playing records backwards, predating later musical trends by over half a century.

In 1934 Varèse came up with *Ecuatorial*, a twelve-minute piece for voices, instrumental ensemble and two Theremins. This Mayan-inspired piece later used two Ondes Martenots to convey the gleaming haze of the ancient Central American civilization. Varèse continued to experiment with the idea of 'new harmonic splendours' and the possibilities inherent in 'sound projection' at his home in New York. One project began in 1935 but never realized was *Space* – an extremely ambitious global musical link-up in which music would be relayed from every capital city via radio. Given the economic climate of the times, it's no surprise that there was little support for the idea, which was nevertheless fifty years ahead of Live Aid.

After the Second World War Varèse lectured at the new summer school in Darmstadt, a hotbed of new musical ideas. He received the gift of a tape recorder in 1953 and used it to build up a library of sounds. Around this time he received an appreciative visit from the French avant-gardist Pierre Boulez. In 1954 came *Déserts*, a work based on the far-flung open spaces of America and the inner spiritual emptiness of twentieth-century life. In three parts, the piece compounds orchestral passages with taped factory sounds, ship sirens, motors. Finished in Pierre Schaeffer's Paris studio, the work used found sounds, or *musique concrète*, in a novel way. Its debut in the Champs-Élysées in 1954 caused outrage. Yet it was the first piece of its kind to be broadcast on French Radio and the first to be put out in stereo. Later that year Stockhausen was proud to be involved in a live concert of *Déserts* in Hamburg. Varèse would spend seven years refining the piece. A planned cinematic accompaniment was never realized but Varèse did finally perfect *Déserts* in 1961 at Otto Luening's Columbia-Princeton Electronic Music Center in New York.

Varèse's finest achievement was his *Poème electronique* for the Philips pavilion at the Brussels World Fair of 1958. The futuristic pavilion was co-designed by Le Corbusier and the architect-composer Iannis Xenakis and has become a strident historical symbol of post-war modernism. Invited to Eindhoven by Philips, Varèse was provided with a special sound laboratory with the latest equipment and the finest engineers available. There he realized a piece for eleven-channel tape which was relayed through 425 speakers. Sound projection was organized so that the chorus of bells, piano, organs, pulse-generated drums, continuous rhythm and an electronically treated girl's voice could be heard from any angle. Through the use of tape looping, the eight-minute piece could be heard continuously but it was strangely different each time the sequence repeated. This effect was enhanced by an array of coloured lights which projected images in synchronization with the music. In a flash of creative genius, Varèse had invented environmental Ambience. It's estimated that two million people had experienced *Poème electronique* by the end of 1958.

That year Stockhausen met Varèse in New York and declared him 'the father figure of electronic music'. By demanding 'twentieth-century instruments for twentieth-century music', Varèse was practically applying Debussy's dream of a new music. In his writings Varèse precisely predicted the rise of synthesizers and the role of sampling equipment in creating new sounds. His tragedy was that he was too far ahead of his time, without the tools or the finance to realize his dreams. His legacy is more to other musicians than to listeners. What is striking is that his ideas for light and colour projection, his use of records and the sound environment of *Poème electronique* were a blueprint for Ambient Techno Music of the 1990s. On the death of this pioneer in 1965, Stockhausen affirmed both his artistic and human greatness.

LISTENING

Selections of Varèse's music appears on discs from Sony, Decca and Erato featuring interpretations by Pierre Boulez, Zubin Mehta and Kent Nagano respectively. Boulez, who made a name for himself conducting Varèse with the New York Philharmonic in the 1970s, is heard doing a fine version of *Density 21.5* on the Sony disc from 1990. Kent Nagano, with the National Orchestra of France, conducts two volumes of Varèse (Vol. 1: 1920–1927, Vol. 2: 1925–1958) on Erato (1993, 1996). He is a smooth translator of the composer's intentions and the second disc contains fine versions of *Ecuatorial*, *Déserts* and the unfinished *Nocturnal* from 1961. A disc version of *Poème electronique* should be made available.

PERCY GRAINGER

The memory of the idiosyncratic Australian pianist Percy Grainger is tinged with contrasting views. Some say he wished for the widest communication between peoples, their music and ideals. Others have accused him of racial purity in his obsession with Nordic mythology and Scandinavia. What isn't in dispute is his early interest in Ambient music and his willingness to experiment with electronics.

Born in Melbourne in 1882, he was giving concerts at the age of ten and at thirteen entered the Hoch Conservatory in Frankfurt, where he excelled in piano and composition. He settled in London in 1901 and immediately began to experiment with alternating metres and free rhythms in *Train Music*. Inspired by the sounds of flowing water, he had already written the Ambient *Bush Music* in 1900. A 1903 study period in Berlin with the ultra-radical Busoni strengthened his avantism. In 1907 he wrote the orchestral *Sea Song Sketch*, which incorporated the sound of lapping waves.

He also became a famous world-touring pianist, admired by Grieg and Delius. In 1906 Grainger had endorsed the wax cylinder as a principal device for collecting disappearing folk songs and by 1910 he had recorded some 500 from all over the British Isles. In 1914 he went to the US and, like Ives, played in army marching bands. He became an American citizen in 1918. In the 1920s he collected hundreds of Danish folk tunes and in 1928 married his Nordic princess, the Swedish artist and poet Ella Storm in an over-the-top ceremony at the Hollywood Bowl.

During the 1930s Grainger divided his time between experiments with 'Free Music' – a music without recourse to traditional notation, pattern or symmetry – and his ethnomusicological museum in Melbourne. Already embodied in the form of a 1907 string quartet, his Free Music principles were applied in 1935–6 to music for arrays of Theremins, the score consisting of a mass of curves and zigzags. Despite having raised money to aid his adoptive country during the Second World War, Grainger died in isolation in New York in 1961. Even his wish to have his skeleton exhumed and displayed at his Melbourne museum was ignored. Only recently has reappraisal begun of his contribution to experimental music. In his 400 or so works (many of them attributed folk settings) Grainger certainly had an ear for sounds way beyond the confines of tradition, and composed pieces for nonsense syllables, improvised ensembles, guitars, mallet instruments, bells and glasses. He also wrote articles supporting his musical experiments, for he understood that electronics, both in recording and dissemination, were the future.

OLIVIER MESSIAEN

Influenced by Satie and Debussy, Olivier Messiaen became the pivotal French composer of the century through a process of osmosis. By absorbing a variety of musics – ancient Greek, the gamelan of Indonesia, Hindu chant, medieval plainsong, Aztec and Inca pipe music and the music of Japan – and applying these to the work of Schoenberg, Berg and Webern, Messiaen broke through into public consciousness with a new dreamlike style that affected everybody who heard it. Seizing on such instruments as the Ondes Martenot, Messiaen became a beacon for electronic iconoclasts such as Stockhausen, Boulez and Xenakis, all of whom he taught. By pushing Western scales and notation beyond the instrumental into the realm of natural birdsong he laid the groundwork for environmental Ambience. His concentration in 1950 on the importance of the elements of a single musical note is said to have shaped the century of sound.

The son of literary parents, Messiaen was born in Avignon in 1908. Brought up a strict Catholic, he taught himself the piano and was writing his first compositions at the age of seven. He entered the Paris Conservatoire at eleven and stayed there for over a decade, studying everything and winning all the academic competitions. Privately he worked on Eastern scales and rhythms. A series of *Preludes*, from as early as 1929, took what Debussy and the group Les Six (followers of Satie) had done and placed it in the context of new modes. These were short scales lifted from the Twelve-Tone row of Schoenberg, which gave the music a rich, shimmering quality.

A virtuoso of the organ, Messiaen was appointed organist of the Trinity Church, Paris in 1931 – a post he held for over five decades. This church would also be his postal address until his death. He married a violinist, Claire Delbos, in 1932 and by 1936 he was teaching at both the Schola Cantorum and École Normale de Musique, at the latter as a professor. More important was his founding of 'Young France' the same year, a loose group passionately committed to fostering new French music. Very much in that spirit was Messiaen's embracing of the electro-acoustic instrument the Ondes Martenot. His *Fêtes des belles eaux* (*Feasts Of The Beautiful Waters*) (1937) was written for six Ondes Martenots and showed spirited commitment towards the idea of electronic music. The hazy quality of the Ondes Martenot appealed to Messiaen and was what he was looking for outside Western music. *Two Odes In Tones* (1938) refined the experiment and the Ondes Martenot would fruitfully crop up in later works.

The coming of the Second World War saw Messiaen conscripted to the medical corps but he was captured by the Nazis and interned at a camp at Gorlitz on the Polish border. Driven on by hunger and cold, he wrote music to suit what he envisioned as 'the end of time'. Pulled along by his faith, he saw things in terms of angels at the moment of the apocalypse, swords of fire, superhuman colours and bursts of stars. *Quatuor pour la fin du temps* (*Quartet For The End Of Time*), written to save his life and the lives of three other French musicians, was first performed in front of 5,000 prisoners in 1941 and instantly became a twentieth-century classic. Fluttering clarinet and ethereal, open-ended piano tones made the forty-five-minute piece float along in a manner not previously heard. In truth it had as much to do with Indian music as it did with the Western tradition. In Messiaen's imagination it was designed to bring the listener closer to space, to the infinite. Hence it is one of the great Ambient pieces of the last century.

Luckily Messiaen was out of the camp by 1942 and back in Paris. He was quickly appointed a professor at the Conservatoire and taught there diligently until 1978. In 1944 he laid out his musical means, in particular the use of archaic eight-note scales, in the publication *Techniques Of My Musical Language*. He then fell in love with the violinist Yvonne Loriod, although since he was bound by Catholic marriage vows, he poured this new-found sensuality into his music. He still wrote for the Ondes Martenot and after a trip to the US conceived the powerful *Turangalîla-symphonie* (*Turangalila Symphony*) (1946–8), the title of which comes from the ancient Indian Sanskrit and means 'life-cycle symphony'. In this work sprawling over ten movements, the continuous piano line, strange Varèse-style block percussion and sparkling use of vibraphone, glockenspiel and Ondes Martenot made it sound quite unique. The very soft, very tender section 'The Garden Of Sleeping Love' floats along, Messiaen finding such a delicacy of balance between piano and Ondes Martenot that the piece easily transcends its initial Hollywood-style character. He is certainly the master musician of Martenot's instrument.

During the late 1940s Messiaen's analysis classes at the Paris Conservatoire became legendary. He was beginning to absorb more and more music, looking simultaneously back in history and beyond mere music into other realms of sound. Xenakis, Boulez, Stockhausen and the revolutionary Irish composer Sean O'Riada were all attracted to his expansive teaching style. For a long time Messiaen had been thinking about the relationship between numbers, colours and music and was wholly interested in 'synaesthetic' vision, the kind of sensory confusion which occurs naturally in a tiny number of people but is more often brought about by hallucinogenic drugs. The idea of hearing smells and tasting sounds would, of course, become a major reality for musicians of the psychedelic era and here again Messiaen was decades ahead of his time. In 1949 he composed *Modes de valeurs et d'intensités* (*Modes Of Values And Intensities*), which he unveiled at Darmstadt that year. This piano piece, made up of rhythmic cells, concentrated on the individual note, giving particular prominence to its length, loudness, tone colour and pitch. The single sound was the idea of total Serialism, where everything that could be notated was introduced, and in 1951 Stockhausen was inspired to write *Kreuzspiel* (*Crossplay*), which introduced his mature style.

Messiaen set to work at the studios of ORTF (Radio France) with his pupil Pierre Henry on a concrete-music piece titled *Timbres-durées* (*Sound Durations*). Yet he was dissatisfied with the state of electronic music and wanted more flexibility and expansiveness. For this he turned to birdsong and travelled rural France transposing and listening. His *Catalogue d'oiseaux* (*Catalogue Of Birds*) (1956–8) was thirteen piano pieces which ingeniously utilized Greek and Indian rhythms in tandem with exotic bird cries. His first wife died in 1959 and he married Yvonne Loriod in 1962, the same year he visited Japan. Inspired by his visit, he wrote *7 Haikai* for piano and orchestra based on the ancient Japanese poem form.

By now laden with academic honours, Messiaen again visited the US and came back filled with inspired visions of the Rocky Mountains in Utah. Written between 1971 and 1974 and over one and a half hours long, *Des canyons aux étoiles* (*From The Canyons To The Stars*) is a huge, sprawling work for a forty-musician triple ensemble. Here the sounds of Africa, Asia, Java and Bali are offset by the twinkling electronic sounds of vibraphone and Ondes Martenot. The sparkling effect, like glinting stars on a clear light, a glowing, shifting and uncertain musical landscape, are definitive Messiaen. This fragmentary work is a journey in sound – through the desert, hearing the golden–yellow oriole birds, through Bryce Canyon and upwards to the morning star of Aldebaran and the song of the woodthrush.

The next decade would be spent writing devotional music. The opera *St Francis Of Assisi*, written between 1975 and 1983, was full of static sound. Messiaen also spent much time composing organ works. In 1984 he visited Israel and annotated several species of rare birdsong. Two years later he received France's Legion of Honour. Though known as a mystic with a huge and imaginative love of God, Messiaen had a robust faith which allowed him to experiment in areas where many would be merely cautious. His encouragement of Boulez and Stockhausen helped to shape twentieth-century electronic music while his own sweet, shimmering sound gave the best form for successive developments in Ambient music. His individuality and lack of a Schoenbergian ego probably diminished his popular appeal, but his spirited innovations and embracing of new instruments and cultures influenced many. His death in 1992 was mourned by a nation to which he had given so much.

LISTENING

Quatuor pour la fin du temps (*Quartet For The End Of Time*) (Delos 1987) is a richly satisfying disc featuring Chamber Music Northwest. The *Turangalîla-symphonie* (*Turangalila Symphony*) and *Des canyons aux étoiles* (*From The Canyons To The Stars*) are available on two double-disc sets: the first (Sony 1986) with Esa-Pekka Salonen conducting and Paul Crossley (piano), the second (Auvidis 1994) with the great Satie interpreter Reinbert De Leeuw conducting various ensembles. The latter interestingly replaces the original mix of vibraphone and Ondes Martenot with wind and sand machines. These are long pieces, but suitable excerpts are available on Sony's excellent 1993 compilation *To The Edge Of Dream*.

PAUL BOWLES

The influence of the American author and composer Paul Bowles on Ambient music has only recently been acknowledged as musicians like Bill Laswell and Nicky Skopelitis sculpt resonantly atmospheric soundscapes to Bowles's chilling tales of the Sahara. This only son of a New York suburban dentist fled the cruelty of his father at the end of the 1920s with only $24 in his pocket. After arriving in Paris he was to meet Jean Cocteau and the artist Joan Miró. He had started piano lessons as early as five and now studied with the great teacher Nadia Boulanger. An early ambition to be a poet was crushed by the American writer Gertrude Stein.

During the 1930s and 40s, while Bowles was being supported and tutored by the composers Aaron Copland and Virgil Thompson, he wrote light, feathery, burlesque-influenced pieces. This work comprises fourteen compositions for piano and orchestra, three operas, four ballets, twelve film scores and various pieces for voice and Broadway. It is said that his best work was music for a 1950s production of Tennessee Williams's play *Sweet Bird Of Youth*, starring Paul Newman. Bowles's worldwide best-selling novel *The Sheltering Sky* brought him out of conventionality and into the world of innovative literature. Exiled in Tangier, he became a magnet for Beat poets and writers like William Burroughs, free-jazz explorers like Ornette Coleman, The Rolling Stones, Brion Gysin and the aforementioned Laswell.

Bowles's grant from the Rockefeller Foundation in 1959 led to 25,000 miles of travel and it was he who set up recordings of the Master Musicians of Jajouka, in Morocco, for both Brian Jones and Ornette Coleman, thus allowing true ethnic music to filter into Western consciousness. Of his own music, the *Six Preludes For Piano* (1945) mark his zenith, capturing all the delicacy of musical Impressionism while being suffused with much of the melancholy of his prose.

LISTENING

Black Star At The Point Of Darkness (Psalmody Sub Rosa 1991) features Bowles's own recordings of Moroccan music, some stories and an exemplary rendition of the *Six Preludes For Piano* by Jean-Luc Fafchamps. *An American In Paris* (Koch 1995) is a live Radio France production of various songs, piano pieces and concerto and is better for the sleeve notes than the music. *Baptism Of Solitude* (Meta 1995) is where Bowles's drained prose and oblique look at North African life meets 1990s electronica in a perfect Ambient symbiosis.

PIERRE SCHAEFFER AND PIERRE HENRY

Two of the first people to experiment successfully with tape technology, Frenchmen Pierre Schaeffer and Pierre Henry changed world perceptions at the end of the 1940s and the beginning of the 1950s with innovations in *musique concrète*, a style of composition which relied on compiling and editing existing sounds. Philosopher and essayist Schaeffer acknowledged that recorded sound would 'upset music for ever' and that music of the past was 'abstract and symbolic' while music of the future would be 'concrete'. Working in the studio of Radio France's Club d'Essai (Experimental Club), Schaeffer in particular would attract the attentions of many musicians keen to investigate the new idea, including Stockhausen, Varèse and Boulez. Both directly and indirectly the French duo's work would ripple through a half-century of Ambient music, sampling techniques of the 1990s being just one example of their fertile legacy.

Schaeffer came from a musical background and was born in Nancy in 1910. Yet his interest was science. After attending a polytechnic he became a communications engineer in Strasbourg and in 1936 a technician at Radio-diffusion France. His interests in philosophy led him to the Armenian mystic Gurdjieff, while his wish to subvert drove him to create the Club d'Essai to explore electronic music in 1943. Schaeffer's interest was in everyday sounds, whether produced by a train, a crowd or a tinkling piano, and the turning of them into 'sound objects'. For this he had to turn to disc recordings and manipulate a panoply of turntables to get vari-speed movements or jump-cuts. Though commonplace in the Rap and Techno worlds of the late twentieth century, this technique was unheard of in 1948 when Schaeffer broadcast on Radio France his collection of five pieces known in English as *Concert Of Noises*. Notable among these was his edit of train sounds, the famous *Étude aux chemins de fer* (*Railways Study*).

The time-consuming method of making experimental collages on disc from other discs would soon be forsaken for the new technology of tape, but not before Schaeffer made *Symphonie pour un homme seul* (*Symphony For A Man Alone*), a twenty-two-minute piece made in conjunction with Pierre Henry, a young musician who had come to Radio France's Paris studio from the Conservatoire in 1949. Using a variety of natural, musical and noise sources, the duo successfully conjured up sounds of the human body in twelve short movements. Premiered live in 1950, the work signalled the arrival of electronic music in France.

The following year Schaeffer founded the Research Group for Concrete Music and would here investigate with Henry the possibilities of tape – what could be done with editing, multi-tracking, fading, backwards editing, tape loops and various echo and delay effects. Schaeffer was fascinated with the microphone, with what sounds, intentional or accidental, could be captured on tape. In 1952 he wrote a book called *In Search Of Concrete Music*, which outlined his aesthetic.

Schaeffer's interest in sound went beyond music. His interest was the systematic analysis of all sounds to build up a new understanding of how various art forms collide and meld into one. He was bored by Serial music and was infuriated when Boulez brought Stockhausen to his Paris studio in the early 1950s and the young German spent much time breaking down a single sound rather than classifying the various sounds and noises Schaeffer had given him. Moreover Schaeffer wasn't interested in making his own sounds whereas Stockhausen was. In 1958 Schaeffer broadened the Research Group's investigations to include many areas based on musical perceptions. Within two years he had set up a similar lab for visual research. Having lost interest in concrete music, he then turned his attention to science-fiction novels, though he was made a Professor of Electronic Music at the Paris Conservatoire in 1968.

Meanwhile Pierre Henry voyaged deeper into the area. Henry, born in Paris in 1927, studied at the Conservatoire under Nadia Boulanger and Messiaen for ten years from the age of ten. Studying everything from birdsong to rhythm, he had an early interest in 'noise' and was a gifted drummer. From the early 1950s to 1958 he headed Schaeffer's Research Group. One of his early disc recordings was called *The Well-Tempered Microphone*. He extensively analysed sounds and what occurred to them under tape manipulations. *Vocalise* (1952) is an impressive manipulation of the sound 'ah'. He used prepared piano and created notation for concrete music. In addition to composing for the cinema and the stage, he created in 1958 his own electronic studio, where he merged both concrete and synthetic sound.

During the 1960s Henry's work became more complex: *The Voyage* for tape was nearly an hour long and based on the *Tibetan Book Of The Dead*. He wrote an electro-acoustic mass for Liverpool Cathedral in 1968 and a lengthy twelve-track tape piece, *The Apocalypse Of Joan Of Arc*, in the same year. Henry's most bizarre project was *Ceremony* (1969), a mass written in collaboration with a progressive British rock group of the time, Spooky Tooth. In 1971 he experimented further with his *Setting Of Music For Cortex Art*, an audiovisual concept which transformed brainwaves into sound and light projections. Two years later he electronicized various Beethoven symphonies in *The Tenth*.

The fundamental point about Schaeffer and Henry is that they brought electronic music to France and demonstrated the potential of the new technology. Their legacy can clearly be seen in the work of Stockhausen and The Orb but such artists as Ireland's Roger Doyle, who made convincing concrete-music records between the 1970s and the 1990s, and America's Tortoise have pushed Schaeffer and Henry's ideas into a new dimension.

JOHN CAGE

Through a constellation of musics John Cage became the guru of twentieth-century Ambient composition. Deriving inspiration from Erik Satie, Charles Ives and then Arnold Schoenberg, Cage did more than anybody else before him to isolate the quality of sound. In his quest for the ultimate sound he arrived at silence. In his mind there was no difference between noise, sound and silence – all were poetry to his ears. His presence throughout the twentieth century initiated much experiment in the fields of electronic music, mixed-media, total Serialism (where an attempt is made to measure everything in music) and environmental music. He was a beacon to talents as diverse as Pierre Boulez, Stockhausen, La Monte Young, David Tudor, The Velvet Underground, Brian Eno and many more. Above all he opened huge causeways for the dissemination of Ambient music. In 1989 he said: 'People will often opt for quiet sounds. The awful presence of intention in music makes the non–intentional Ambient sound more useful. It is more possible to live affirmatively if you find environmental sound beautiful.'

Cage's almost mythic fame has led many to believe that his aesthetic arrived in a flash of inspiration, fully formed. This was not the case. Born in Los Angeles in 1912, he was the son of an engineer and inventor. He took piano lessons in Santa Monica from an early age. A family friend, Fannie Dilon, later tutored him in the art of birdsong transcription. His first media appearance was a radio concert at the age of twelve and by fourteen he was obsessed with nineteenth–century piano styles, particularly that of Edward Grieg. The Norwegian composer had written a series of short *Lyric Pieces* for the instrument, some lasting minutes, others mere seconds, which greatly impressed Cage. At sixteen he graduated from high school in Los Angeles with the highest of grades and entered Pomona College, in his native California, to study for the priesthood.

There he began to write poetry, though a yearning for travel led him to persuade his parents to send him to Europe, where he studied music and painting in Berlin and Paris. In the latter he worked for an architect and practised hard on piano, even studying Bach. Journeys around Italy and Spain ended in Cage experimenting with mathematical music but the American depression forced his return after eighteen months to help his parents. Back in

California, he lectured and cooked for a living. Thereafter he went to New York to study composition and theory with Adolf Weiss.

Back in California in 1933, Cage enrolled in the New School for Social Research run by Henry Cowell. Already inspired by Varèse, Cage was to gain much from Cowell, a man whose book *New Musical Resources* (1919) Cage had read with enthusiasm. Cowell was a radical who supported Ives and who, from 1912 to 1929, had experimented with the piano in terms of tone clusters and new tunings. He had also worked with the Thereminvox and was interested in extending Western music to embrace elements of Eastern and Far Eastern musics. Certainly Cage's ideas for the 'prepared piano' came from here. In 1934 Cage married Xenia, the daughter of an Alaskan orthodox priest; the same year he invented the water gong, an instrument to be used for underwater ballets! Yet for Cage his most significant experience of that year was meeting Arnold Schoenberg.

From 1934 until 1937 Cage took music lessons with Schoenberg in California. Initially the Viennese inventor of Serialism said that his would-be pupil couldn't afford his fees. The ever-charming Cage admitted that he had no money but pledged to devote his life to music, and Schoenberg took him on. Already writing in the serial style, Cage had great difficulty mastering harmony or chordal progression. Schoenberg felt that his student was beating his head against a brick wall. One day the composer sent Cage to the blackboard in order to answer a musical problem. When Cage found one, Schoenberg demanded another. When Cage answered this, Schoenberg demanded another, and then another. Frustrated, Cage asked, 'Why?' To which Schoenberg requested an underlying principle. This questioning of what music actually was would stay with Cage for the rest of his life. He worshipped Schoenberg's ingenuity and the latter said famously of Cage that he was much 'more than a musician but an inventor – of genius'.

As a composer and accompanist at dance classes at the Cornish School in Seattle, Cage realized that his experience with Schoenberg had made him see that listeners could actively choose what to listen to at the point of listening. In 1937 he wrote a brilliant lecture titled 'The Future Of Music (Credo)', which he delivered at the school. This predicted the rise of electronic music: 'Through the aid of electrical instruments we will reach a music which will make available all sounds that can be heard.' Cage talked of any sounds or noises being capable of electrical reproduction 'within or beyond the reach of the imagination'. In his mind electronics opened up 'the entire field of sound, the entire field of time where no rhythm would be beyond the composer's earth'. Significantly he saw conventional use of inventions like the Theremin as being redundant, and looked instead to possibilities in radio, disc and film technology. These were explored in a series of radical pieces called *Imaginary Landscapes* (1939–52). *No. 1* (1939) featured vari-speed turntables playing RCA test recordings. *No. 2* (1942) featured sounds produced by amplifying wire coil. *No. 3*, from the same year, included audio-frequency oscillators, amplified contact mikes and vari-speed turntables, while *No. 4* (1951) featured twelve radio sets being continuously retuned. For the last of the series, *Imaginary Landscape No. 5* (1952), Cage, with the help of Earle Brown and Bebe Barron, collaged forty-two jazz records into a huge tape mix.

The early electronic pieces mentioned above featured much percussion. Cage was fascinated with percussion, particularly that of the Javanese gamelan. In 1938 he found that by inserting everyday objects like pieces of rubber and paper, parts of broken dolls, bolts, screws, bits of felt and so on between the strings of a piano he could make it sound like a percussion ensemble. Thus was invented the 'prepared piano'. That year he first used it on *Bacchanale* and it would crop up again and again in pieces right up to the mid-1950s. Classic examples include the 1943 *She Is Asleep* (duet with voice), the Orientally flavoured *Perilous Night* (1944) and the Indian-influenced *Sonatas And Interludes* (1949).

Cage continued to work with percussion with Lou Harrison in California in 1939. The following year he invented 'Living Room Music' for any percussion instruments found in a normal living room. During the early 1940s Cage accepted a post with the Hungarian László Moholy-Nagy (who had already done many electronic sound experiments at the Bauhaus) at the Chicago School of Design, teaching electronic music. But it was in 1942, on his arrival in New York, that the final piece of the jigsaw would slot into place. At the home of Max Ernst, Cage and his wife Xenia met two other founders of the Surrealist movement in painting, André Breton and Marcel Duchamp. As early as 1913 Duchamp had written a piece of music using 'chance' as a compositional tool. Cage and he immediately clicked and would in the future play many chess games together. Later during the same gathering Cage would meet the Irish-American choreographer Merce Cunningham. Their relationship would blossom, Cage becoming musical director of the Merce Cunningham Dance Company until 1968 and living openly with Cunningham from 1947 after divorcing his wife in 1945.

If the dance context was fertile for Cage's fervent experimentalism, New York gave him more opportunities. He studied Zen Buddhism in 1946–7, and its calming aspect is apparent in the contemplative *Nocturne* (for violin and piano). In 1948 Cage hit his zenith as a composer. During a year when he organized an Erik Satie festival at Black Mountain College came two seven-minute piano pieces, *Dream* and *In A Landscape*, whose lack of adornment echoes Satie but whose drift reflects Cage's growing Zen orientation. As his scores became more colourful and graphic, he spent nine months tossing coins, as outlined by the Chinese oracle the *I Ching*, to create charts for his forty-six-minute piano piece *Music Of Changes*, written in 1951 for David Tudor, a Philadelphian new musician who was involved in presenting all of Cage's works up to 1970.

By 1952 Cage was pursuing many directions at once. First, through the Magnetic Tape Music Project with Morton Feldman, Christian Wolff and Earle Brown, he came to be seen as America's most radical electronic experimenter.

Secondly, at Black Mountain College he staged the first 'happening' in the form of *Theatre Piece*, where Cunningham's dancers, images by artist Robert Rauschenberg and David Tudor's generated sounds confused and mesmerized an audience. Thirdly, his use of 'chance operations' continued with the ambitious *Williams Mix* for 600 collaged LP records written out over 192 pages of script derived from the *I Ching*. Yet it was the performance of 4′ 33″ at Woodstock, in New York State, which revealed Cage as an Ambient visionary. In a performance delivered to a stupefied audience, Tudor raised the lid of the piano, sat there for the duration specified by the title of the piece and then closed the lid. The music was whatever sound the audience heard in the immediate vicinity. Cage had taken the Hindu philosophy of music to quieten the mind to its ultimate destination – *silence*. But in so doing he made everybody realize that such a thing didn't really exist. He would go on to say: 'The music I prefer is what we hear if we are just quiet.' For such aphorisms as 'I have nothing to say but saying it, that is poetry' Cage would become infamous. A piano composition of that year, *Waiting*, was full of silence.

From that time on Cage caused uproar wherever he went. A European tour with Tudor provoked consternation. Pierre Boulez, with whom Cage had corresponded, was baffled by the American's latest ideas. A 1958 retrospective of his work in New York enraged the audience with the random directions of the music, or non-music. (Some compared the hostile reaction to the riotous scenes which greeted Stravinsky's multi-rhythmic *Rite Of Spring* in 1913.) The same year he went to Darmstadt, where he criticized Stockhausen's eleventh *Klavierstück* (*Piano Piece*) for its lack of 'indeterminacy' and responded with the first of his anarchic *Variations* series, which from that time until 1978 were presented by means of all manner of electro-acoustic devices with the barest hint of direction. *Variations 5* (1965) used Theremins and dancers to trigger sound, while *Variations 8* (1978) was merely a title, with no music or recording whatsoever.

'Indeterminacy' Cage saw as beyond chance, with almost nothing of the outcome being predictable. Luciano Berio invited Cage to Milan to work up the 'indeterminate' *Fontana Mix*, named after Cage's landlady in an electronic studio. Over four months Cage used transparent sheets, drawings and graphs all superimposed in order to create three different recordings of hissing and gurglings, feedback and Cathy Berberian singing multi-lingual vowels and consonants in a number of different musical styles.

During the 1960s Cage became a hero of the times. As Professor of Advanced Studies at the University of Connecticut he had academic clout while his soft-spoken, humorous persona and mental brilliance made him shine wherever he went. Stockhausen, who always admired him, felt Cage was 'spiritually very consequent'. Such pieces as *Cartridge Music* (for turntable cartridges and other media) and 'HPSCHD' (for harpsichords, tapes, images and computer generated permutations courtesy of Lejaren Hiller), written in 1960 and 1968 respectively, were electronic landmarks demonstrating an acute mind looking forward into the multi-media future. From 1952 to 1967 Cage wrote five pieces for the electronic Carillon, a neglected keyboard device developed in the US to replace the sound of belfry bells. In 1969 he created *Cheap Imitation*, which uses Satie's *Socrate* for a new transparently Ambient composition. A lover of Satie, Cage (who had already performed the French composer's *Vexations* over two days in New York in 1963) played Satie's 'furniture music' at a University of California performance, also in 1969. Two more versions of *Cheap Imitation*, for up to ninety-five players and for violin solo would be penned in 1972 and 1977 respectively. Satie would also crop up in 1978's *Letter To Erik Satie* and 1979's *J. Joyce, M. Duchamp, E. Satie: An Alphabet*.

Cage's listed works total more than 330. His series of books from *Silence* (1961) onwards would go on to influence generations of musicians. An adept at mushroom farming, chess and literature, Cage was a true Renaissance man of the electronic age. By working in so many media he showed that the fundamental precepts of Schoenberg and Debussy could be used to finally unyoke twentieth-century music from the past. His use of 'sound lines' taken at random from text, starting in the late 1960s with James Joyce's *Finnegans Wake*, were a revolutionary step towards a new vocal language. By objectifying art and eliminating purpose he raised the ideal of music composition to a new spiritual plane. He said once: 'I don't actually hear music before I write it. I write it in order to hear it.' Full of paradoxes, he never owned any records and preferred the everyday noises outside his Manhattan apartment to anything else. When he died in 1992, at the age of seventy-nine, Cage's hovering presence over the twentieth century was duly recognized. To him the essence of music was sound, the essence of making sounds was to 'wake people up to the very life they are living'.

LISTENING

Works For Piano And Prepared Piano Vol. 1 – Joshua Pierce (Wergo 1986/88)
Works For Piano And Prepared Piano Vol. 2 – Joshua Pierce/Dorothy Jonas (Wergo 1988)
Music Of Changes (for David Tudor) – Herbert Henck (Wergo 1988)
The Perilous Night/Four Walls – Margaret Leng Tan (New Albion 1991)
Cheap Imitation – Herbert Henck (Wergo 1991)
A Chance Operation – Various (Koch 1993)
In A Landscape – Stephen Drury (Catalyst 1994)

Wergo has done a comprehensive cycle of recordings through its Edition John Cage. *Vol. 1* covers 1943–52 and includes *She Is Asleep*, the beautiful *In A Landscape* and *Waiting*. *Vol. 2* (1944–58) features *Dream*, *The Perilous Night* and *Nocturne*, among other pieces. *Music Of Changes*, recorded in Bremen in 1982, contains some superlative sleeve notes by the performer, Herbert Henck. His version of *Cheap Imitation* is backed with Satie's *Socrate*, from which it is derived.

Leng Tang is a Cage scholar and was a close associate; her *Four Walls* is the first recording of a 1944 piece influenced by Indian time-cycles. *A Chance Operation* is a John Cage tribute, with all proceeds going to Gay Men's Health Crisis. In more than 183 tracks on two discs, which are supposed to be randomly played so that there is never a repeated sequence, old friends like Christian Wolff, Earle Brown, Meredith Monk, John Cale and David Tudor, along with the likes of Laurie Anderson, the Kronos Quartet and Frank Zappa, pay homage to the composer. Anderson's dulcet tones and soft electronic backing are used to good effect on Cage's *Cunningham Stories* text. Cage pieces and new material in the spirit of Cage are mixed and matched. Ryuichi Sakamoto performs his own electronic Haiku while Frank Zappa produces himself performing *4' 33"*. Completists should look out for the reissue of *Voices And Instruments*, a 1976 recording of Robert Wyatt performing *In A Landscape* in a very quiet piano style, produced by Brian Eno. The 1994 Catalyst disc was specifically recorded to enhance the Ambient nature of Cage's oeuvre and includes thoughtful piano explorations by Stephen Drury of both *In A Landscape* and *Dream*.

OTTO LUENING AND VLADIMIR USSACHEVSKY

An American and a Russian, Otto Luening and Vladimir Ussachevsky, were credited with the first public performance of tape music in the US, when, in 1952, they used Ampex tape recorders to manipulate a variety of musical sound sources. This odd pair went on to pioneer studio music in the form of their Columbia-Princeton Electronic Music Center in New York in 1959. Housing the first rather cumbersome RCA synthesizer, this allowed composers such as Varèse and Milton Babbitt to freely experiment in the realm of purely artificial sound.

Born in 1911 and raised in the Russian Orthodox church by an army officer in Manchuria, Vladimir Ussachevsky arrived in America in 1930. His interests in timbre, or sound quality, and musical structure and rhythm were refined by studies at Pomona College in California and Eastman School of Music in Rochester, New York. In 1947 he began teaching at Columbia University, a job he held until 1980. When Columbia received a gift of an Ampex tape recorder in 1951, Ussachevsky began experimentally recording violin, piano, vocal and clarinet sounds on the machine. This resulted in a series of short sound studies, *Transposition*, *Reverberation*, *Experiment*, *Composition* and *Underwater Waltz*, which emphasized tape's versatility. The likes of Cage's teacher Henry Cowell appreciated the freshness of the idea and Ussachevsky was soon joined by Otto Luening, a flautist with a bent for experiment who also taught at Columbia.

Luening was born in Milwaukee in 1900. He had a fairly traditional musical education, attending music academy in Munich, and the Conservatoires of Paris and Zurich. The latter experience was important for Luening, for there between 1918 and 1920 he studied with Busoni, who instilled in him the quest for radicalism. By now an able flautist, he returned to America to teach in various colleges in Arizona and Vermont. He arrived at Columbia in the mid-1940s and stayed there until the late 60s. His meeting with Ussachevsky in 1952 was pivotal. Luening was also keen on the idea of tape music and the duo spent many months in various houses, including those of Cowell and the conductor Toscanini, working up new pieces.

News spread and Stokowski was prepared to direct a performance of their tape music at the Museum of Modern Art in late 1952. Amid unprecedented publicity, the pair unveiled *Sonic Contours*, *Invention*, *Low Speed* and *Fantasy In Space*. All revealed the full versatility of tape for the first time and how it would alter for ever the idea of orchestral music. Ussachevsky, who wrote the first piece, leaned more towards pure experimentation, while Luening was a neoclassicist who favoured an integration of old and new. Purchase of a tape machine resulted in joint creations, the most important being the fourteen-minute *A Poem For Cycles And Bells*, which deftly melded orchestral sounds and tape manipulations.

In the mid-1950s the pair received a Rockefeller Scholarship to research into electronic resources in the US and Europe. A tour of nearly two months brought them into contact with all the important studio wizards of the time: Pierre Schaeffer in Paris, Herbert Eimert at WDR in Cologne, where Stockhausen worked, and Luciano Berio in Milan, among others. Yet in America comparable facilities did not exist. Except for isolated commercial research carried out by companies, there was no US studio nor studio network which allowed proper exploration of the field by musicians and composers. On their return they were allowed to set up a lab at Columbia University. In 1956 Ussachevsky produced *Piece For Tape Recorder*, a five-and-a-half-minute work in which gong, cymbal and piano sounds were manipulated and flushed against environmental sounds. Luening also produced Ambient music for a version of *King Lear* by Orson Welles.

The same year RCA unveiled its first synthesizer. Ussachevsky and Milton Babbitt were keen to get their hands on it. After much to-ing and fro-ing, Rockefeller again stumped up the cash, some $180,000, for the purchase of an RCA MK1 synthesizer and the building of a permanent facility at Columbia with Milton Babbitt also involved. Babbitt, who taught at Princeton and whose interest was in the refinement of Serial music, believed wholeheartedly in the new technology. He once said that 'any recording is electronic music'. With the cumbersome RCA synthesizer (now at MK2 stage), which used what looked like a series of typewriters to create punched cards using the numbered coding system of alternate 1s and 0s, Babbitt painstakingly built up his compositions with the help of tape and noise and tone generators. Such pieces as *Ensembles For Synthesizer* (1962–4) and *Philomel* (where a girl's voices mutates into that of a nightingale) are considered landmarks of the Columbia-Princeton synthesizer lab.

Meanwhile Ussachevsky and Luening busied themselves with such creations as *Concerted Piece* (1960), which further integrated tape experiment, electronics and orchestra. Ussachevsky continued further into sonic exploration with *Of Wood And Brass* (1965), which includes clever transformations of a Korean gong, but by the latter part of the decade he was obsessed with computer music. In this area Ussachevsky worked hard to synthesize new sound and form links between keyboard and computer in order to make easier the musician's job of controlling complex systems. He also wrote music for film and television. He died in New York in 1990. As for Luening, he somehow returned to his neoclassical and late-Romantic predilections, penning large-scale symphonies and small-scale chamber works with the flute as a mainstay. No matter, for the two men's electronic and Ambient excursions of the early to mid-1950s were to change forever the direction of American music.

KARLHEINZ STOCKHAUSEN

One of the most significant figures in twentieth-century music, Karlheinz Stockhausen was the first composer to realize the dream of 'pure' electronic music. His inventions of the 1950s catapulted him to world fame where he became the spokesman of the post-war avant-garde. As the 1960s dawned Stockhausen's brand of open and improvised music became associated with hippiedom – he was often criticized for his association with the likes of The Grateful Dead and his Zen Buddhist-influenced musings. Yet here was one of the most acute and rigorous minds in modern composition acknowledging the musicality of the new psychedelia. His *Gesang der Jünglinge* (*Song Of The Youths*) and *Hymnen* (*Anthems*) both affected The Beatles. Stockhausen was a friend of John Lennon, and the German's influence can be heard on the group's extraordinary single 'Strawberry Fields Forever', the 'Revolution 9' collage (on *The White Album*) and on the 1967 album *Sgt. Pepper's Lonely Hearts Club Band*, the cover of which features a photographic tribute to Stockhausen. One of the foremost exponents of live electronic music, Stockhausen pursued an endless quest for new sounds, leading to the growth of World Music. In the 1990s his opinion was still being sought by Techno and Ambient musicians as to the validity of their work.

Stockhausen's strange and tragic upbringing undoubtedly forged his hugely resilient and workaholic character. Born in 1928 in the mining town of Mödrath, near Cologne, to a schoolteacher father and pianist mother, Stockhausen was to endure a succession of moves as a child. These, coupled with numerous pregnancies, caused the mental breakdown of his mother, Gertrud, who was institutionalized in 1932. Within a year Stockhausen's younger brother was dead and soon after Karlheinz found himself in the cathedral town of Altenberg. Still, travelling circuses and improvised theatre peppered his early years and he started on piano when only three. He listened avidly to both radio and records, this fascination with sound leading to a damaged right ear when he put it too close to a transformer. His father's links with the Nazis and remarriage led to Stockhausen fleeing home, first working as a cobbler, then attending teacher-training college at Xanten when only fifteen.

There he studied the oboe, violin and piano, but then the coming of the war saw the college turned into a hospital. Stockhausen became a stretcher-bearer, witnessed many horrors and came within an inch of his life on more than one occasion. His survival he put down to his Catholic faith: 'I knew for certain that God was shining up there and looking at me and he gave me so much light.' Worse was to follow. At the end of the war in 1945 Stockhausen learned that his father had been denounced and virtually murdered at the front, while his mother had perished in a gas chamber as early as 1941. Now seventeen, he was an orphan.

The theatre, forestry and farming were some of the varied activities Stock-hausen involved himself in before going to Cologne to study music. There he played jazz for black GIs and after more study was admitted to the Music School in 1948. In addition he studied philosophy, musicology and the history of language at Cologne University. He wrote literature which was praised by Hermann Hesse and met the pianist Doris Andreae, who was to become his first wife. During the later part of his studies he went on the road with the conjuror Adrion and played piano in a 'magic chamber art' show. His first compositions, *Chöre für Doris* (*Choruses For Doris*) and *Chorale*, both written in 1950, were incredibly accomplished. The latter was inspired by Schoenberg and displayed a virtuosic use of lengthy silences and volume cadences. Both undoubtedly reflect the bleak North Rhine landscape of Stockhausen's childhood.

Nineteen fifty-one was the turning point for the young German. Taken up by Herbert Eimert, a critic at West German Radio (WDR) in Cologne who admired Schoenberg, Stockhausen was invited to Darmstadt, where a series of new music summer courses inspired by Messiaen had started. Pierre Schaeffer, the Italian avantist Luigi Nono and the physicist Werner Meyer-Eppler (whose interest was in chance or aleatory music) were some of the people Stockhausen met that summer. Eimert and Meyer-Eppler would initiate the founding of an electronic studio at WDR that same year. Around that time Stockhausen graduated with distinction.

In 1953 he attended Messiaen's analysis classes at the Paris Conservatoire. The Frenchman's teaching, based on innovation by example and understanding, was an inspiration for Stockhausen. Messiaen, for his part, was convinced that the twenty-five-year-old German was 'an absolute genius'. *Kreuzspiel* (*Crossplay*) of 1951, which isolated points of sound, had certainly been Stockhausen's eleven-minute kick in the face to Romanticism. While in Paris Stockhausen met Pierre Boulez and visited Pierre Schaeffer's studio at Radio France. Soon he was working there on sound analysis and spent just one month coming up with *Study*, a piece which combined electronic sound with concrete music and mixed frequency generator noise with prepared piano. Schaeffer, in search of a wider palette of sound, wasn't impressed and Stockhausen soon found himself back in Germany.

Having long admired the music of Anton Webern, Stockhausen stated in 1953 that his interest was 'in the abolition of very long and very short time values'. He joined Eimert at WDR in Cologne as his assistant and set off on an electronic voyage. He rejected outright the use of instruments and opted to build up new sounds using sine-wave generators, modulators and tape. After months of desperate work involving problems with tape noise, manual synchronization and equipment failure, *Study 1* was unveiled as a fresh distillation of chilling atmosphere. A more obtuse piece, the short *Study 2*, was finished by the summer of 1954 and was reputedly the first electronic score ever published.

Between 1954 and 1956 Stockhausen pursued further studies at Bonn University. He was drawn by Meyer-Eppler's acoustical research into vocoders and sonic measurement. Also stimulated by John Cage's interest in 'chance' music, Stockhausen would soon meet the American and Edgard Varèse, both of whom he greatly admired. Fascinated by the versatility of tape, in 1955 Stockhausen wanted to create an electronic mass for Cologne Cathedral. The idea was rejected but the composer set about writing a section: *The Song Of The Youths In The Fiery Furnace*, later abbreviated to the famous *Song Of The Youths* (*Gesang der Jünglinge*). Using pulse generator, volume meter and feedback filter, Stockhausen spent six months breaking down every element of human speech and matching it to every conceivable sound from sine tone to white noise. The result of this painstaking process was only five minutes of valuable sound; but by May 1956 he had completed a piece lasting thirteen minutes and fourteen seconds. The debut performance of *Song Of The Youths*, projected through five loudspeakers at the broadcasting studio of WDR in Cologne, caused uproar and applause. Electronic music was here to stay and Stockhausen's name would reverberate around the world.

Stockhausen attracted many new musicians and composers to Cologne, including the Hungarian György Ligeti. His next important piece was *Kontakte* (*Contacts*), where tape loops were used to create a kaleidoscope of electronic sounds. Here the acceleration of tape caused pulses to become rhythms, rhythms to become pitches, pitches to become timbres. He famously used a rotary table to splash sound around four different microphones. Photographs of the composer at the time show him lost in the hub of WDR's electronic equipment. And after six months of intense work the premier of this thirty-five-minute piece in Cologne in 1960 proved that Stockhausen was the leader of a new musical revolution.

In Cologne he attracted the interest of many, including the German social philosopher and musicologist Theodor Adorno, the musician David Tudor and a young painter named Mary Bauermeister, who would eventually become his second wife. Meanwhile others raged against Stockhausen's music, the German press describing it as 'a denaturalized montage of noises derived from physics'. But the composer's sheer willingness to experiment and his innovative method of teaching, where new compositions would be worked out in classes, was already being admired throughout the world. In 1963 he founded the Cologne Course for New Music and in 1964 experimented with 'electronically treated sound', in which a traditional orchestra would be split into sections, its various sounds relayed to mixing desks allied to generators and modulators. This concept was to be hugely influential in Ambient music.

After spending much time in the US, Stockhausen visited Japan in early 1966. Influenced by the peace of Kyoto and Japanese culture in general, he made *Telemusik* at the Tokyo NHK studio of Japanese radio. This seventeen-minute amalgam of musical quotations, derived from Vietnam, Hungary, the Amazon, the Sahara and elsewhere and subjected to Stockhausen's electronic vision, would be the occasion of one of his most prophetic statements: 'I wanted to come closer to a music of the whole world, of all cultures and races.' This vision of World Music would implant itself in the collective psyche and resonate through electronic and Ambient music for the rest of the century. On his way back from Japan the composer toured Malaysia, India, Iran, the Lebanon and Turkey.

On a high, Stockhausen arrived in California near the end of 1966 to spend six months lecturing at UCLA. In the firmament he met the leading San Francisco psychedelic groups of the era, Jefferson Airplane and The Grateful Dead. They attended his lectures, he attended psychedelicized concerts at the infamous Fillmore West. Before he left, in the spring of 1967, Stockhausen had married Mary Bauermeister and had expanded his vision of World Music to produce a piece incorporating forty national anthems. Lasting over two hours, *Hymnen* would summarize Stockhausen's impressions of life up to that point in a work which mixed electronic sound and concrete music. Disconnected versions of the German, French and British national anthems caused consternation at the piece's debut at a WDR concert in November 1967. Patriots everywhere were outraged but Stockhausen was just demonstrating the fluidity of new electronic processes. *Hymnen* would go on to become one of his most influential works particularly in the area of experimental rock.

Stimmung (*Tuning In*), a lengthy static work for six voices, was written in 1968 after a trip to Mexico. Its use of erotic poetry dismayed many audiences of the time. Stockhausen called *Kurzwellen* (*Shortwaves*), an improvisation based on Morse code signals, 'a quest for the harmony of the spheres through the guise of technology and electricity'. This idea would be enthusiastically seized upon by the German group Can and their technical boffin, Holger Czukay, in later years. Another development was 'intuitive music', sparked off by the sudden departure of Mary Bauermeister. Going on hunger strike as protest and after four days in isolation, Stockhausen came up with *Aus den sieben Tagen* (*From The Seven Days*) a mystical series of fourteen stanzas full of philosophy and musical instructions. He developed this into a form of 'House Music' at Darmstadt, where people would wander through a scenario filled with musicians improvising and playing from scores.

In 1969 a planned concert with The Beatles never came off but Stockhausen did meet Frank Zappa in New York. At the height of his fame Stockhausen would be the star of the World Fair of 1970 held at Osaka. Inside West Germany's spherical metallic-blue pavilion, dotted with points of light, an instrumental ensemble augmented by electronics would perform over a nine-month period all of the works Stockhausen had written up to then. For five and a half hours each day the composer would balance and control the sound from a large mixing console via fifty-five loudspeakers arranged in seven rings. A total of one million listeners were attracted to this futuristic scenario, reminiscent of 'musical space travel'. A visit to Ceylon would produce two ethno-acoustic pieces, *Ceylon* and *Mantra*. In 1976 *Ceylon* would be released by the British Chrysalis label as a rock album.

With *Mantra* the idea of 'formula music' came into play. This was a technique whereby a simple musical idea could be expanded over time. Miles Davis had done something similar in 1959's *Kind Of Blue* but here Stockhausen was dealing with a piano motif treated by various electronics at a Munich studio. The result was considered to be beautiful and quasi-meditative. More meditative still was *Tierkreis* (*Zodiac*), a series of accessible melodies based on the twelve signs of the zodiac. With versions for percussion, chamber orchestra, clarinet and piano, it was to become Stockhausen's most popular work.

In 1977, having been Professor of Composition at Cologne's Music School for seven years, Stockhausen resigned to devote himself to the creation of an enormous opera cycle, *Licht* (*Light*), for solo voices, solo instruments, solo dancers, choirs, orchestras, ballet, electronic sound and concrete music. This massive concept, encompassing the history of the world and the cosmos and based on the significance of the seven days of the week in various cultures, was Stockhausen's attempt to outdo Wagner by creating the longest 'total-art piece' (*Gesamtkunstwerk*) in the history of music. Each 'day' would have its own opera lasting several hours, and each opera would take three and a half years to execute, with various parts staged around Europe. For technical help Stockhausen turned to his old friend Pierre Boulez at the Institute for the Research and Co-ordination of Electro-Acoustic Music (IRCAM in French) in Paris. The first complete day, *Donnerstag aus Licht* (*Thursday From Light*), was completed by 1981 and premiered in Milan. After more work on the large IRCAM mainframe computer, *Samstag aus Licht* (*Saturday From Light*) was completed in 1984. After switching to a new generation of more compact synthesizers, samplers and effects units, Stockhausen completed *Montag aus Licht* (*Monday From Light*) in 1988. In the early 1990s he worked with his son Simon on *Octophony* for eight groups of loudspeakers, using horizontal, diagonal and vertical movement of electronic sound clusters. The piece was from *Dienstag aus Licht* (*Tuesday From Light*), which was premiered at Leipzig in 1993.

Stockhausen was now ably abetted by the American clarinettist Suzanne

Stephens and the Dutch flautist Kathinka Pasveer, plus members of his family: Simon, his other son the famous trumpeter Markus and his pianist daughter Majella. As he finished *Freitag aus Licht* (*Friday From Light*) in 1995, Stockhausen considered himself to be a 'musician experiencing the mysteries of discovery'. He still had the power to shock as he attempted to stage a helicopter string quartet in a now unified Germany. The concept was objected to in his own country but performed in Holland with the help of the Royal Dutch Airforce as an extract from *Mittwoch aus Licht* (*Wednesday From Light*). With that day completed in 1998 and 1999 spent preparing work on his last operatic day, *Sunday*, again Stockhausen showed that for sheer stamina and dedication to his musical vision, he was in a class of his own. The ideal of having *Light* performed in its entirety at the beginning of the twenty-first century seemed fitting for a composer who gave so much to the twentieth.

Near the end of 1995 the composer was contacted by the BBC and asked his opinion of new Techno music by such Ambient trend-setters of the time as Richie Hawtin, Aphex Twin and Scanner. He was happy to see the young still experimenting and looking for new sounds, as in the telephone sampled work of Scanner. For nearly half a century the guru of Cologne, in long-sleeved Mexican shirts and with flowing blond hair, has exerted a powerful effect on the development of electronic and Ambient music. For Stockhausen the way ahead is clear and unbounded: 'I just don't see any limits in the foreseeable future.'

LISTENING

Stimmung (*Tuning In*) – Singcircle (Hyperion 1986)
Aus den sieben Tagen (*From The Seven Days*) – Ensemble Musique Vivante (Harmonia Mundi 1988)
Mantra – Mikashoff/Bevan (New Albion 1990)
Chöre für Doris (*Choruses For Doris*)/*Chorale* – North German Radio Choir (Stockhausen-Verlag 1 1991)
Electronic Music 1952–1960 (Stockhausen-Verlag 3 1991)
Tierkreis (*Zodiac*)/*Music In The Belly* (Stockhausen-Verlag 24 1992)
Hymnen (*Anthems*)– *Electronic And Concrete Music With Soloists* (Stockhausen-Verlag 10 1995)

The *Stimmung* (*Tuning In*) CD is considered one of the best Stockhausen recordings. The 'Set Sail For The Sun' section of *Aus den sieben Tagen* (*From The Seven Days*) is a successful build-up of extraordinary sounds featuring Aloys Kontarsky's rumbling piano. The *Mantra* disc was recorded in Norway; its packaging and sleeve notes are superb. Since the early 1990s Stockhausen has undertaken to digitally remaster his entire catalogue. The early choral works are collected on *Chore für Doris* (*Choruses For Doris*), a disc which also includes *Kreuzspiel* (*Crossplay*). The *Electronic Music* disc is a tour de force containing the long-lost *Study*, written in France in 1952, the classic *Gesang der Jünglinge* (*Song*

Of The Youths) and Kontakte (*Contacts*) among other works. A 134-page booklet full of photos, scores, extensive notes and much else written by the composer completes an impressive package. *Tierkreis* (*Zodiac*) is a lovely little CD which features the tinkly sound of twelve musical boxes manufactured to Stockhausen's specifications at a Swiss factory. *Hymnen* is a huge four-CD and 200-page booklet affair with two discs devoted to the first version and two devoted to the second with soloists, premiered at WDR in 1967 and 1969 respectively.

MILES DAVIS

The pre-eminent jazz musician of the century, Miles Davis did more than just become a star – he fused musics, broke down racial barriers and demonstrated that the work of Debussy and Messiaen could easily be absorbed into the great black art of improvisation. Up until Davis, real jazz was about speed and frenetic solos. Dizzy Gillespie, John Coltrane, Charlie Parker – the stars of the be-bop post-war urban jazz scene – were all about cascades of notes tumbling out of brass instruments, imitating the speed of modernity. Ornette Coleman took over at the beginning of the 1960s with Free Jazz – a concept veering towards atonality where anything went. Miles Davis, in contrast, stood back, refined the melody down to a sound which was termed 'The Cool'. This new Ambient jazz sound would define jazz for all time.

Miles Davis was born in Illinois in 1926 of affluent parents. His father being a landowning dentist helped when Davis attended the prestigious Juilliard School of Music in 1945 (a New York College which would later tutor such famous Minimalists as Philip Glass and Steve Reich). Many middle-ground jazz musicians have cited Davis's background as the reason for his fame but this is just plain sour grapes. Davis worked harder than most to achieve what he did. When he was very young his family moved to East St Louis. Miles played trumpet in high-school bands and had private tuition which emphasized tone over technique or flashy soloing. As early as eighteen he was playing with the famous band of Charlie Parker and Dizzy Gillespie.

When he arrived in New York to go to the Juilliard, Davis spent more time running around after Charlie Parker than attending his formal studies. Helped by the brilliant pianist Thelonius Monk, he learned his trade playing in the bars and clubs of 52nd Street. In 1947, at the age of twenty-one, he replaced Gillespie in Charlie Parker's band and his career began to take off, although after a year and a half Parker's nosedive into heroin addiction forced the young trumpeter to quit.

In late 1948 Davis met the Canadian arranger Gil Evans, an event which would led to the reshaping of the whole of jazz. Along with baritone saxophonist Gerry Mulligan and others, Davis and Evans cut a series of recordings which in 1949 was released on record as *The Birth Of The Cool*.

Here the idea was to produce 'clouds of sound' which would envelop the listener. The delirious sounds of be-bop had mutated into the Cool sound, where Davis's clipped phrasing, clear spacing and held notes came to the fore. This music was pure Impressionism, linking jazz to Debussy and aimed at achieving a peacefulness that in retrospect could be termed Ambient.

Five years would be spent in his own dark cloud of heroin addiction but by 1954, through sheer force of personality, Davis had kicked the habit. By 1955 he was a star with a big Columbia contract and a quintet which featured the era's finest jazz musicians in the saxophonists Julian 'Cannonball' Adderley and John Coltrane. Again many would criticize Davis's mid-range playing, his tendency to fluff notes and his use of trumpet mute. Many felt he wasn't as good as jazz giants Bix Beiderbecke, Louis Armstrong or Gillespie but Davis was wide open to new ideas. And none was more influential than the recording of *Miles Ahead* in 1957. Here with Gil Evans and an ensemble simply termed 19, Davis pushed orchestral jazz into new dimensions. All the tracks bled into one another and Miles's rounded soft flugelhorn embraced fascinating sounds like his version of the French composer Delibes' nineteenth-century ode to Spain *The Maids Of Cadiz*. In places the orchestration was a bit racy but 'Blues For Pablo', which intersected blues and Spanish idioms, and the allusive 'My Ship' were definitive spare delicacies.

A record titled *Milestones*, released the following year, dangled Miles's ever more elegant trumpet solos over a shifting rhythmic landscape. The idea of modal playing was in the air, George Russell's famous treatise on Greek modes having permeated the mind of John Coltrane in the mid-1950s. Modes, being scales or partial scales, had redefined twentieth-century music via Messiaen and Stockhausen, opening it right out. Sick of years of hearing relentless soloing based on chords crammed up against each other, Miles decided to gamble on a series of modal sketches recorded in April 1959 in New York City. The result was the classic *Kind Of Blue*. With what still is the greatest jazz combo of all time – including Coltrane, Cannonball Adderley and Bill Evans on piano, Davis fashioned forty-five minutes of pristine music which seemed to float, slowly insinuating itself into the listener's consciousness. There was plenty of aural space and the instruments were perfectly poised both in unison and individually. No one soloist attempted to outshine the other. All were in harmony. Both *Flamenco Sketches* and *All Blues* started out like cool summer-night jazz tunes, almost soundtrack music for a film noir of the period, but slowly crossed into the musics of southern Spain and North Africa. 'So What', with its finger-click beat, became Davis's anthem while John Coltrane had never sounded so elegant and restrained.

Back in the studio at the end of 1959 and beginning of 1960, Davis was again working with Gil Evans. And again he was entranced by the music of Spain. Rodrigo's *Concierto de Aranjuez*, written for guitar and orchestra, was in his head and a fruitful recording took place which would become a best-seller. *Sketches Of Spain*, released in 1960, placed Miles's linear trumpet lines in beautifully skeletal orchestrations which emphasized the sinuous character of Hispanic music. There were excerpts from the work of Manuel de Falla, folk melodies and two flamenco song forms done in instrumental style, including the famous Andalusian 'Solea' or song of the lonely. Davis had broken jazz clean out of its confines and demonstrated with incredible aplomb that it was a match for older European music forms.

The album *Quiet Nights* would surface in 1963. It featured some good Iberian-sounding music, notably the famous Brazilian songwriter Antonio Carlos Jobim's 'Corcovado', which inspired the album's title. Miles's raspy, silence-filled trumpet could be heard to supreme effect on the West Coast group track 'Summer Night'. Yet Davis was an ever-changing chameleon never satisfied with one style or commercial setting. Returning to group jazz improvisation, he made some fascinating records like *E.S.P.* in 1965 and *Nefertiti* in 1967 but much of the music was too *active* to evoke the same Ambient effect. Davis would rely more and more on Teo Macero, a top sound engineer and Master's graduate of the Juilliard who had played a key role in the studio since the *Kind Of Blue* period of 1959. Almost ten years later Miles would book into the Columbia label's studio in New York with a new concept. His usual acoustic combo was augmented by electric pianists Herbie Hancock, Joe Zawinul and Chick Corea. A young guitarist named John McLaughlin, who had recently left London, was brought in by chance. Two hours of music was recorded which Teo Macero edited down to two album sides entitled *In A Silent Way*. What began as a simmering low-key pot of rhythmically driven sound became a beautiful sound-painting straight out of the Spanish-flavoured Gil Evans days. 'It's About That Time' finally flung jazz right into the tight beats of 60s rock music. The concept of jazz-rock fusion was invented and Davis did not look back once. Listening to that incredible trumpet sound, carving space in the canyon of shimmering keyboards and guitar, that is *In A Silent Way*, we hear a musician that wasn't afraid to unite Debussy with Stockhausen and most black musical styles in a quest for melodic tranquillity.

LISTENING

Though Miles Davis died in California in 1991, his enormous stature is still lauded right across the musical spectrum. Vast quantities of recordings appear under his name, but if you want the real Cool style at its most accessible *Miles Ahead* (Columbia 1957), *Kind Of Blue* (Columbia 1959), *Sketches of Spain* (Columbia 1960) and *Quiet Nights* (Columbia 1963) are all thoroughly recommended. *Kind Of Blue* is considered the greatest jazz recording of the century, simply because of its perfect elegance and symmetry – short melodies began on one instrument, developed on others, were repeated and then reprised at the end. No self-indulgence was allowed. The album's precise beauty is made more miraculous by the fact that Davis entered the studio with only a few partial scales and one or two chords written down as guidelines for the musicians.

(Though in his 1958 recording of Gershwin's *Porgy And Bess* with Gil Evans, his reading of 'It Ain't Necessarily So' bears more than a passing resemblance to 'So What'.)

Miles Ahead has dated in places but when it's good it's incredible – for example, the little trumpet motif at the end of 'Springsville' which then leads into the languorous, humid and hypnotic 'Maids Of Cadiz'. *Sketches Of Spain* is simply fantastic, Davis's fractured trumpet soloing conjuring up endless vistas of more moonlit Andalusian nights. Neither Davis nor Gil Evans liked *Quiet Nights*, but it is again compact and calm-inducing. *In A Silent Way* limbers up for the big jazz-rock recordings of the 1970s but is more restrained, its textures shifting and blurring; the twenty-four-minute title track summoning all the emotional contemplation from Miles before he dives into the rock maelstrom of the album's closing fifteen minutes.

DAPHNE ORAM

One of the great female innovators in electronic sound, Daphne Oram came to prominence as the key instigator of the BBC Radiophonic Workshop in the late 1950s. As the inventor of a photo-electric music system she realized early that electronics were vital for the development of twentieth-century music. Her continual campaigning for research greatly furthered the cause in the UK, where electronic-music labs on the large-scale, state-funded European and American model simply didn't exist.

Born in 1925 near Salisbury Plain, England, Oram was always interested in sound and experimented with the piano and primitive electronics as a child. A gifted musician, she spurned music college for an engineering job at the BBC when only seventeen. Within a year she was investigating graphic sound-generating systems. Through the late 1940s and early 50s she fought many verbal battles with the conservative corporation about the validity of electronics. When she secretly wired up a radio studio with a batch of recently acquired tape machines it was the drama department which saw the potential of her ideas.

In 1957 various electronic sound effects created by Oram were broadcast and in 1958 she soundtracked a TV play. The same year she became a director of the BBC Radiophonic Workshop but quickly lost interest when she saw no enthusiasm for electronic music in its own right. The turning point came that year when Oram met Karlheinz Stockhausen at a music fair in Brussels. She quickly resigned from her job, using her pension to set up a primitive studio in Kent. By 1962 she received European support to develop Oramics, a highly developed drawn-sound system, as good if not better than optical modes experimented with in Canada and Russia. Oramics consisted of a series of 35mm plastic film strips which travelled over a cluster of photo-electric cells. The application of patterns to the strips caused changes in voltage which could be used to determine musical parameters. The film strips themselves were kept in strict synchronization by an electric motor.

Some have compared the sophistication of this system to the results achieved by the big American synthesizers of the period and given the fact that Oram was working alone at her home in Kent, it was simply down to her genius for electronic music that she went so far with so little. She described Oramics as a 'Digital/analogue compositional technique'. She wrote a piece called *4 Aspects* in 1959 and during the early 1960s lectured extensively on electronic music, concentrating on the importance of the works of Stockhausen and Berio as well as on Oramics.

During the 1960s Oram wrote electronic music for a wide variety of uses, including for the stage, broadcast, film and art environments. She scored the 1961 British film *The Innocents* and in 1965 contributed brilliantly to a Commonwealth cultural exhibition at the Royal Academy whereby her *Pulse Persephone* brought together World Music samples, Oramic sounds, electric guitar and sub-sonic pulse which made the floor rumble. Certainly it was one of the very first examples of environmental Ambient music in the UK. Since then she has scored much for new ballet, toured the world, and written and lectured extensively on Oramics. Having taught for seven years at Christ Church College in Canterbury, the great Daphne Oram spent the end of the 1980s and the beginning of the 90s transferring her pioneering Oramics invention to new digital computer systems.

RAYMOND SCOTT

Only after his death in 1994 at the age of eighty-five did the world realize the importance of the American electronic pioneer Raymond Scott. A musical prodigy and engineer of brilliance, Scott followed Erik Satie's anarchic approach to composition and was influenced by the likes of Friedrich Trautwein and Leon Theremin in the realm of instrument invention. Forever dreaming of an 'artistic collaboration between man and machine' and the idea of 'instantaneous composition', Scott inadvertently prefigured the ideas of twentieth-century Ambience. His trilogy of albums *Soothing Sounds For Baby* (Epic 1963) is an astonishing portent of early-70s German electronica and even the late-80s sound of Chicago Acid House.

Scott was born Harry Warnow in 1908 in New York. His parents were Russian émigrés; his father played violin and owned a music shop. Like Philip Glass, the young Scott grew up in a family fascinated with records. He begun playing the piano at the age of two but later was all set for an engineering career, studying at Brooklyn Polytechnic. But then, on the advice of his brother (a gifted violinist and conductor), Scott, like Glass, attended the Juilliard School of Music. After graduating in 1931 he worked for CBS radio as a staff pianist. He changed his name from Warnow to Scott because it sounded better.

After five years at CBS Scott was married and ambitious for his own band. In 1936 he formed a swing jazz 'Quintette' of six men and Duke Ellington's manager offered them a contract after early radio sessions. Like Satie, Scott named his pieces idiosyncratically: titles like *Celebration On The Planet Mars* and *Dedicatory Piece To The Crew & Passengers Of First Experimental Rocket Express To The Moon* were the norm. His style was a mixture of Debussy and jazz. No scored music was used, Scott directing everything from his piano. He even issued bizarre instructions to his musicians about performance, as Eno would do nearly forty years later when he was making solo rock records. Stravinsky was a fan and within a year of its debut Scott's Quintette was hired by Hollywood.

By 1938 Scott was musical director at CBS, and in 1942 hired their first black and white studio orchestra, which included the two great tenor saxophonists Coleman Hawkins and Ben Webster. In 1943 Warner Brothers purchased a clutch of Scott's tunes for later use in cartoon strips.

Scott worked on Broadway during the mid-1940s and even had his *Suite For Violin And Piano* played at Carnegie Hall. He released albums of exotic jazz in the latter part of the decade and by 1952 had remarried, this time to singer Dorothy Collins, and was pursuing a lucrative career writing advertising jingles and film scores and working in A&R. He even auditioned Bo Diddley and at one stage owned Universal Recording Studios. He used a fortune made in the music business to build electronic instruments by night. Manhattan Music Inc. was the name he gave the laboratory he set up in 1946. Within two years he had spent $100,000 on Karloff, a sound-effects machine. He worked on multi-track tape and by 1952 had seven- and fourteen-track machines installed. Over the next three years he even redesigned the Theremin as the Clavivox, a keyboard that had foot-pedals and allowed greater control over the former's characteristic shivery sound.

In the mid-1950s Scott was living in a four-storey, thirty-two-room house in Long Island stuffed with equipment and a lift. Robert Moog (who was on his way to creating the great Moog synthesizer) designed many circuits and modules for Scott between the mid-1950s and the late 1960s.

An inveterate inventor, Scott created dozens of devices, including the Videola (a soundtrack-recording console) in 1959, the Circle Machine (an early rhythm sequencer) in 1961 and, throughout the 1950s and 60s, his instantaneous composition performance machine, the Electronium. Visitors to his house in 1965 were stunned by an enormous wall of equipment thirty feet long and six feet high: a polyphonic synthesizer-sequencer rigged with telephone switching equipment.

In 1967 Scott married for the third time. His house looked like the inside of a rocket pod, all flashing lights and whirring gadgets. The Electronium was his passion, and produced pulsations which appealed to Berry Gordy, the head of Tamla Motown. After a meeting with Gordy in 1969 Scott and his wife Mitzi were relocated in California and he spent seven years researching electronic equipment for the giant of recorded soul music.

The Electronium was never finished to anyone's satisfaction and a combination of secrecy, seclusion and paranoia meant Scott was overtaken by those, like Moog, intent on providing practical affordable synthesizers for everyday use. Crippled by heart disease during the 1980s, he was by then considered a figure from the distant jazz age who spent too long playing with his gizmos. The posthumous reissue of his electronic music in 1997 saw him ironically dubbed a 'cyberpunk'.

LISTENING

The *Soothing Sounds For Baby* series, released by Epic in 1963, was reissued by Basta in 1997 to much critical acclaim. These lengthy dronal electronic pieces seemed to have more in common with the 1970s and 80s than the era in which Scott made them. *Manhattan Research Inc.* (Basta 2000) is a sumptuously presented two-CD and 144-page book package focusing on Scott's advertising jingles, film music and other futurama from the late 1950s and 60s.

GYÖRGY LIGETI

One of the most extraordinary composers of the twentieth century, György Ligeti came from the Transylvania region of Hungary in the late 1950s to take on modern music and succeeded more than anyone else in creating incredible blocks of sound that rejected all the rules. By concentrating on the vertical characteristics of music rather than traditional linear development, Ligeti showed that that the 'tone-colour' aspect of Schoenberg's Serialism could be extended into unforeseen pastures. So brilliant were his creations that they were used by Stanley Kubrick in the renowned 1968 film *2001: A Space Odyssey* to permeate its atmosphere with a feeling of disquietening stillness.

Born in 1923, Ligeti was from a family that suffered much atrocity and hardship under the Nazis. From 1945 to 1949 he studied at the Franz Liszt Academy in Budapest, where he was impressed by the Ambient reductionism of John Cage and later lectured in music. In 1950, a year he saw as music's chance to begin again from ground zero, he made a concerted effort to create 'a static, motionless music'. Within a year he was constructing pieces from a single note but was frustrated by lack of feedback. In 1956, amid anti-Communist anarchy as the Red Army assailed Budapest, Ligeti accidentally heard Stockhausen's newly completed electronic masterpiece *Gesang der Jünglinge* (*Song Of The Youths*) on the radio. Smitten and inspired, he raced from his war-torn land via Vienna and arrived in Cologne in 1957.

Helped by Stockhausen, Ligeti soon found a post at West German Radio's electronic studio in Cologne, where he conceived *Artikulation* for tape in 1958. The following year he settled in Vienna, and throughout the 1960s was to teach both in Darmstadt and at the Stockholm Music Academy. His keen search to find a music of texture which relied on subtle changes of vertical colour and volume led to two orchestral masterpieces, *Apparitions* (1960) and *Atmospheres* (1961). Here Ligeti laid out his conception of microscopic multi-voicing as wind instruments, horns, trumpets, piano and strings vibrated, appeared and receded but did not travel along any kind of linear plane. The sounds were simply there and then they were gone.

Early in 1964 the American director Stanley Kubrick began working with the science-fiction author Arthur C. Clarke on what was to become the greatest sci-fi film of all time, *2001: A Space Odyssey*. Writing and shooting would last four years. Kubrick felt Ligeti's music was extremely powerful, particularly the way it used volume and timbre to express emotion. He was also impressed by its 'spacey' connotations and knew it would be perfect for his vision. Kubrick used Ligeti's *Requiem* of 1965 to accompany scenes featuring a black alien monolith. Shivering choirs and voices, set against a spartan orchestra, perfectly summed up feelings of deep fear on encountering the unknown. The extreme volume changes of *Atmospheres* accompanied an astronaut's kaleidoscopic trip through a star-gate. Yet it was Kubrick's choice of *Lux Aeterna* (*Eternal Light*) of 1966 that most captured the imagination. Ligeti's nine-minute opus for sixteen-strong choir is stasis perfected as crystalline voices (male and female) blur into one another to form sonic colours of striking beauty. On its own it conveys a unique Ambience but used in conjunction with Kubrick's images of a space capsule silently crossing an authentic lunar landscape *Lux Aeterna* is simply astonishing. Never before nor since has music being used to convey such a sense of limitless emptiness.

During the late 1960s and early 70s Ligeti lectured and composed in West Berlin and California. His dense style became more lucid, as exemplified by his *Melodies For Orchestra* (1971). Interested in Surrealism, The Beatles, clockwork devices, African drumming and absurdist humour, Ligeti used the 1970s to extend himself into areas of avant-garde performance and bizarre opera. A professor at Hamburg Music Academy from 1973, he had some heart trouble in the late 1970s but recovered to return to his assured multi-voiced style in the following decade. In the 1990s he was still living and writing in Hamburg and, full of bravado, had ambitions to incorporate Celtic, Arabic and fractal elements into his art. His theories and use of vertical sound colour have had a huge impact on the evolution of the Ambient music of Brian Eno and many others.

LISTENING

Though Pierre Boulez has recorded some sound Ligeti for Deutsche Grammophon, WERGO have recorded ten discs of his work of which the 1988 recording of *Chamber Concerto*, *Ramifications*, *Lux Aeterna* and *Atmospheres* is highly recommended. Still the best sonic experience of Ligeti's music is the original soundtrack to *2001: A Space Odyssey*, which was remastered by EMI in 1989. Here Kubrick's electronic amplification of *Requiem*, *Atmospheres* and *Lux Aeterna* enhances both their fathomless depth and emotional impact. The disc also includes the serene slow movement from Armenian composer Khachaturian's *Gayaneh* ballet suite (1943), whose spatial Romantic strings Kubrick chose to accompany the fascinating opening shots of the spaceship *Discovery*. In 1996 Rhino reissued the soundtrack in a lavish edition containing extended versions of Ligeti's music.

PIERRE BOULEZ

In the 1950s Pierre Boulez became famous as the *enfant terrible* of twentieth-century French music when he broke with the legacies of Debussy, Stravinsky and Schoenberg to create music that was in essence a violent homage to Anton Webern. Boulez was interested not only in total Serialism (the complete control of all aspects of music) but also in expanding this to electronic and concrete music. In 1951, like his contemporaries Stockhausen and Ligeti, he wanted to start again from a blank page, a year zero where everything could be reinvented. In so doing he embraced electronics and pushed their use way beyond what anyone had done before in his country.

Born in southern France in 1925, Boulez attended the Paris Conservatoire and learned much from Olivier Messiaen in his teens. In his early twenties he worked in music theatre and his first two piano sonatas, written around this time, are marked by a rare intensity of expression. He was an champion of the Ondes Martenot, for which he wrote a *Quartet* and the piece *The Wedding Visage* (both 1946). During the early 1950s he was heavily involved in the Darmstadt new music scene and corresponded much with Stockhausen. In fact he introduced the young German to Schaeffer's Club d'Essai studio in Paris where both composers experimented with early electronica. In 1952 Boulez produced two *Studies* which explored the possibilities of tape and the qualities of individual sounds. Unlike Stockhausen, he hated the idea of John Cage's chance operations even if aleatory (random) threads of sound and silences did creep into his music of the time.

In his search for a totally 'objective' and 'pre-determined music', Boulez saw most pre-Serial music as unimportant. The extreme economy of Anton Webern was his beacon and anybody who didn't want to follow his lead was second-rate. A dedicated teacher in the late 1950s, he also composed at WDR's electronic studio, although he later withdrew a 1958 piece, *Poetry For Power*, for taped electronics and orchestra. In the late 1950s and early 60s Boulez conducted some of Stockhausen's works and in the latter decade he experimented with electric guitar sound and Oriental ideas (inherited from Debussy via Messiaen) but spent much time at odds with French administrators over the direction of electronic music.

His keen interest in mathematics made him want to achieve pure sounds, a 'new musical language' through technology which could lead to 'undreamed of territories'. President Pompidou offered Boulez generous funding for the construction of a huge underground sound lab in 1970. Within seven years IRCAM was up and running. In 1971, during its building, Boulez wrote . . . *explosante fixe . . . (. . . fixed explosion . . .)* for eight instruments and flute. Dedicated to the Surrealist André Breton, the piece used electronic sound projection to change the sound textures of natural instruments. Boulez also used the period of IRCAM's construction to conduct at the BBC in London and for five long years at the New York Philharmonic. From all accounts he was unstintingly radical, not bowing once to any traditionalist repertoire.

When IRCAM opened in Paris 1977 it was heralded as a triumph of French modernism and state intervention in the arts. Its numerous rooms contained state-of-the-art computer technology, an array of flexible studios, recording locations and equipment maintained by teams of assistants and engineers. Its stately 'live' room could be adjusted for any type of music. Boulez then wrote an ambitious sound-filled piece called *Répons* (*Response*) which combined main-frame computer, electronics and chamber orchestra. Though IRCAM attracted the likes of Stockhausen as a solution centre for acoustic and electronic problems which arose with such large-scale works as his opera cycle *Licht*, it didn't take off the way Boulez hoped, a problem made more manifest by the speedy miniaturization and growing cheapness of Japanese music technology. Never-theless this period produced Boulez's most radical collaboration when in 1984 the American rock anarchist Frank Zappa came to IRCAM to record 'The Perfect Stranger', a send-up of early twentieth-century music which Boulez hauled around the orchestral circuit to positive acclaim.

In the 1990s Boulez resigned from the complex administrative duties of IRCAM and resumed his other career as conductor. A painstaking critic of his own and other people's music, a constant revisionist of his own texts, Boulez nevertheless placed the spotlight on the importance of the availability and use of electronic resources in the evolution of modern music.

LISTENING

Most of Boulez's music lies outside the scope of this book. His work is famous for its difficulty and includes pieces like the 1946 *Sonatine For Flute And Piano* which have a beautiful timbral quality. The disc with Sophie Cherrier playing flute (ERATO 1991) also contains the interesting . . . *explosante-fixe . . . (. . . fixed explosion . . .)*, for 'computer-transformed flutes and chamber orchestra'. His third *Piano Sonata* from 1957 (WERGO 1985) contains Ambient elements.

IANNIS XENAKIS

The most famous Greek composer of the twentieth century, Xenakis rose to prominence in the post-war electronic boom. Trained as an architect, he became renowned for his firm grasp of environmental structures and how they related to sound. Many cite his use of statistics and computers as significant when, after the war, he composed electronic music at the Club d'Essai and IRCAM, but it is in his use of nature – light, rain, wind and outdoor locations – that his Ambient credentials can be seen.

Iannis Xenakis was born into affluence in Romania in 1922 and lived there with his Greek family until they moved to Athens when he was ten. Two years later he was studying music but opted for engineering and architecture studies at Athens Polytechnic after he left boarding school. The rise of Nazism brought out a rebellious spirit in him, as in many others, and running street battles during the war led to severe facial injury from a bomb blast. When the British administered Athens after the Second World War he was vigorous in the Greek resistance and ended up in prison and condemned to death as a terrorist. Luckily he escaped in 1947 and on a false passport fled to Paris. The use of huge floodlights in his later open-air pieces is directly related to his war-time experiences.

He quickly found himself a job as an assistant in the Paris offices of the famous architect Le Corbusier. He would hold on to this post until 1960. In 1950, however, he began attending Olivier Messiaen's composition classes at the Paris Conservatoire and in 1952 wrote a paper on 'The Crisis Of Serial Music'. In 1958 he collaborated with Varèse on making music for the Philips pavilion at the Brussels World Fair. He helped design its pointed spires and wrote *Concret PH* for the space where burning charcoal sounds were ordered using the laws of probability.

The rise of computers would help Xenakis master his 'stochastic music' whereby notes and other information would be fed into a programme that would align them in a pre-determined but open way. These *Analogies For Instruments And Tape* (1959) he saw as an answer to Cage's wide-open music based on chance operations. After he left Le Corbusier, Xenakis worked intensively writing concrete music and regularly used the IBM 7090 computer to generate his pieces. In 1965 he became a French citizen. Within a year he had founded the Centre for Automatic and Mathematical Music in Paris and between 1967 and 1972 a similar locus of activity at Indiana University in the US.

During the 1970s Xenakis involved himself in sound and light environments which used pre-recorded taped compositions. *Hibiki-Hana-Ma* for 800 speakers and twelve tapes (1970), *Persepolis* (1971), performed amid ancient Persian ruins, and *Polytope Of Cluny* (1972–4) were three examples of this adventurous spirit. Much small ensemble work was done with Boulez's Intercontemporary Ensemble and in the 1980s and 90s Xenakis wrote more for conventional acoustic instruments, ballet and chorus. An influential twentieth-century hero-figure, he has said that 'architecture is a tragedy'. His real quest has been pursued through all forms of music and their impact on the spiritual plane of man. His fluid use of computers in the late 1950s and 60s certainly opened up their use for future Ambient musicians.

LISTENING

With over 100 compositions to his credit, Xenakis' music has been described as
dense, dazzling, mythological – full of timbral variety and virtuosity. Some of it
he has termed 'symbolic music'. For our purposes two pieces are worth
investigating – *Nomos Alpha* for solo cello, written in 1965 and recorded in
Our Lady of Liban Church in Paris in 1990 (Erato 1992) under the composer's
supervision); and 1978's *Pleïades* (Erato 1992), with its effect of droplets of rain
within a percussion performance that evokes the gamelan of Indonesia.

MORTON FELDMAN

Often seen as the quiet man of American music, Morton Feldman created,
through hushed stillness and subtle, delicate sounds, a body of work which
provided an important bridge between Serialism and Minimalism, Impressionism and Ambience. A close friend of Edgard Varèse, Feldman, born in New
York in 1926, nevertheless drew his main inspiration from the Abstract
Expressionist painters Jackson Pollock and Mark Rothko and the Irish writer
Samuel Beckett.

Though he was well versed in piano, composition and mathematics and
familiar with the musical miniatures of Anton Webern, Feldman sought an
outlet for the more beautiful sounds he heard in his imagination. This outlet was
to be provided in the late 1940s and early 50s when he joined David Tudor and
other avant-garde musicians who gathered around John Cage. His early pieces
experimented with graphic presentation and chance as much as the idea of
innate stasis. *Intermission B* (1953) consisted of two pianists playing monophonic
(one note at a time) lines full of spaces. *Two Pianos* and *Four Pianos* (1957) played
with the notion of lapsed time.

In Feldman's sound world all rhythmic and harmonic content was rejected
for a sense of dissolution. Listening to a piece of Feldman music is akin to taking
an eternal bath – after a while the idea of a beginning or an end just disappears.
Sounds hover in space, slowly displaced by others. When writing for solo
instrument or small collections of instruments, Feldman was intensely interested
in the quality of the sound or timbre. There was a sense of drift but no real sense
of dynamic. This was a music of immersion, its quiet repetition projecting a
sense of unfurling discretion.

After writing the spartan *Rothko Chapel* in 1973 (dedicated to the Russian-
born Jewish painter's posthumously built chapel in Houston displaying his
drained canvases), Feldman said: 'My primary concern is to sustain a flat surface
with a minimum of contrast.' *Rothko Chapel* is written for chorus, percussion
and viola and the bulk of Feldman's work is likewise scored for conventional
instruments, though in strange combinations. His refined sense of sound had

begun in the early 1950s with explorations in tone clusters, something he returned to in the shifting quarter-notes of *Triadic Memories* in 1981. A long-time teacher at the State University of New York, Buffalo, Feldman was a placid individual whose economy of means and sense of tranquillity communicated a rare state of late twentieth-century contentment. He died in 1987, remembered by many.

LISTENING

Almost any Feldman disc will introduce his style of music. His love of soft-pedal piano can be heard on *Pieces For More Than Two Hands* and *Triadic Memories*, two discs on Sub Rosa from 1990 and 1991 recorded in Brussels by Jean-Luc Fafchamps and featuring compositions from the early 1950s to the early 1980s.

MORTON SUBOTNICK

One of the American West Coast's great electronic pioneers, Morton Subotnick was born in Los Angeles in 1933. He studied with Satie acolyte Darius Milhaud at Mills College in Oakland, California. Having seen the rise of the complex RCA synthesizer system in New York, he wanted to make electronics more accessible to actual played music. With this in mind he founded the San Francisco Tape Center in 1960 with Donald Buchla.

Together with Ramon Sender, they developed the 'modular synthesizer' – a machine which comprised manageable units that facilitated easy playability via touch-sensitive pads. What was more exciting about what Subotnick termed 'electric music boxes' was that they were capable of great flexibility. In traditional electronic music complicated tape looping was needed to build up a sequence of sounds, but here repeating sequences could be built up through an array of 'boxes'. Moreover triggered sequences could be used to alter volume and both the quality and direction of sound. This modular approach made the modular synthesizer useful for live performance as well as creative studio experiment.

Subotnick was an integral part of the 1960s, playing at New York's Electric Circus, where light projections, film and other imaging devices were used to bolster his electronic music performances. His plethora of electrical gates, circuits and sequencers were first heard to impressive effect on *Silver Apples Of The Moon* (1967), a half-hour piece which derived its title from the Irish poet W. B. Yeats. *Apples* is famous as the first electronic creation specifically commissioned by a record company and exhibits all the idiosyncrasies of synthetic 1960s music. Blips and burps seem to roll around a giant aural blob, pushed forward by some manic alien hand. Part Two was particularly exciting as looped sequences give a definite Techno sound years before Kraftwerk arrived on the scene.

Subotnick's music was the kind of playful electronica which could be heard on paranoid American corporate or alien-invasion films of the 1960s and early 1970s. *The Wild Bull* (1968) paints a bleaker picture, the heavier and in places scarier sounds used to convey an eerie poem from ancient Sumeria. Subotnick had a studio at New York University at the time and in 1969 became Director of Electronic Music at California Arts Institute. *Silver Apples Of The Moon* was his twenty-first composition; before this he had written for combinations of tape and acoustic instruments. Interestingly during the 1970s he wrote a piece called *Elevator Music*, which, installed in a New York building, 'played itself' when people operated the lifts.

The composer has given successive electronic works colourful titles, like *Four Butterflies* or *After The Butterfly – A Sky Of Cloudless Sulphur*. His 1985 recording for New Albion, *Return (A Triumph Of Reason),* was considered his most approachable work in years. It was a tribute to the return of Halley's comet, written using the then new computerized Yamaha Music System.

LISTENING

Subotnick's *Silver Apples Of The Moon/ The Wild Bull* (Wergo 1994) combines on CD two excellent LPs from the Nonesuch years, digitally remastered and remixed by ex-Tangerine Dream musician Michael Hoenig.

WENDY CARLOS

When her CBS album of classical electronic transcriptions *Switched-On Bach* was a million-seller in 1968, Wendy Carlos became one of the most famous electronic musicians in history. The album thrust the idea of the synthesizer as a musical instrument firmly into the public consciousness and kick-started the use of keyboard synthesizers in all types of popular music. Carlos also became the most famous transsexual composer in the genre, for *Switched-On Bach* was created when she was a man named Walter. Following its success, Walter became Wendy after an operation in 1972, a period which saw her begin to explore various parameters of Ambient music.

Brought up in Rhode Island, where she was born in 1939, Carlos showed huge gifts when she was a child. Already composing for piano at ten, she built a computer when only fourteen. She studied music and physics at Brown University and then advanced to the Columbia-Princeton Electronic Center and worked with the pioneering Vladimir Ussachevsky. There she wrote early tape pieces for acoustic instruments and electronics, displaying a great talent for shaping timbres or quality of sounds. Soon she was working alongside synthe-sizer pioneer Robert Moog on the development of a performance-related instrument.

In 1967–8 she worked with producer Rachel Elkind on a series of electronic transcriptions of the baroque music of Bach. Using a Moog 55, which was made up of several units, she employed a monophonic (capable of producing only one note at a time) keyboard system to painstakingly build tones. These were then stacked on tape to get precise notes, the rich sound giving a new clarity and brilliance to all of Bach's original musical devices. Premiered at the Audio Engineering Society in New York in 1968, Carlos's recordings of Bach's *Air On A G String* with excerpts from the *Brandenburg Concertos* and various *Preludes* and *Fugues* were rapturously received.

When CBS released the music as (to give the album its full title) *Trans-Electronic Music Productions, Inc. Presents: Switched-On Bach* in the same year, worldwide sales quickly topped one million. The famous Bach interpreter Glenn Gould proclaimed it 'the record of the decade'. The American media announced that the synthesizer had arrived as the new piano and many commentators were lured into misinterpretation, for few understood the sheer concentrative force of Carlos's detailed tonal sculpting. The *Well-Tempered Synthesizer*, with its interpretations of Handel, Scarlatti and more Bach, followed in 1969.

A more suitable use of Carlos's gifts was the decision by American director Stanley Kubrick to employ her to write the music for his controversial film about violence and punishment, *A Clockwork Orange*, in 1971. Purcell, Rossini, Beethoven and Carlos's own music were all given electronic treatment which suited the futuristic vision of the film's creator. Soon after came *Sonic Seasonings*, a 1972 double album which featured a season per side – served up as an interweaving of concrete music, electronic sounds and pure Ambience. Having become a woman, Carlos now seemed more comfortable with self-expression than translation.

She returned to the limelight in 1984 with eerie music for Kubrick's nerve-tingler *The Shining*, while her 1984 *Digital Moonscapes* showed how far electronic sound had progressed when she used digital technology to authentically replicate acoustic instruments. The composer has always said that electronic instruments present the greatest possibilities for tuning and timing. Realizing that 1980s digital technology and sampling techniques would make her original 1968 best-seller sound dated in the early 90s, she spent a massive 3,000 hours preparing *Switched-On Bach 2000* in her New York loft.

Here she developed the Moog and tape sounds of old and developed a series of authentic Bach tunings. Everything was played directly into an Apple Macintosh computer with no microphones used at all. The results were magnificent, giving Bach a sheen of electronic Ambience which was wholly advanced, as if classical music had finally caught up with technological progress. At the time of writing Carlos has worked on Ambient and Techno studies of music from *A Clockwork Orange* as well as electronic versions of early church music.

LISTENING

Switched-On Bach 2000 (Telarc 1992) is by far the definitive Carlos album. The use of Dolby Four–Track Surround Sound gives it an incredible depth and the album is a showcase of what such equipment as Kurzweill, Yamaha and Moog synthesizers can do when linked to modern computers, software and digital effects. The CD updates the original album with a nine–minute version of Bach's *Toccata And Fugue In D Minor*. Carlos's own sleeve notes give an minutely detailed history of her electronic journey.

TORU TAKEMITSU

Towards the end of the century Japanese composer Toru Takemitsu reversed the process which Debussy and Ravel had begun nearly a century years earlier. He became prominent in the West as the Japanese inventor of a new type of Oriental classicism. His aerated and often still music, for unusual combinations of instruments and orchestra, was fluidly Western but from a determined Eastern perspective.

Born in Tokyo in 1930 and indoctrinated with strong nationalistic values, Takemitsu grew up resenting Japanese culture. Hearing some French songs played on a record player by Japanese soldiers turned his attention to the West. After the Second World War he became an avid listener to US Army radio and was thrilled by the music of Schoenberg, Berg, Webern, Ravel and Debussy. He then listened to Stockhausen, Cage and Messiaen and took the jump into formal music. Completely self–taught, he moved himself away from a Japanese academic tradition which stressed formality above experimentalism.

Takemitsu pushed for more resources to be poured into new music in Japan. During the 1950s he founded an innovation laboratory for electronic music and worked on several tape experiments which splashed light and colour into the often dense woods of concrete music. He also successfully pushed for a biennial celebration of new music titled Orchestral Space. He equalled Stockhausen at the 1970 Osaka World Fair by fitting out a concert hall with music, lasers and 800 speakers and christening it 'Space Theatre'.

From the start Takemitsu's music was one of both mobility and stasis, ably capturing the Serialism of Schoenberg and Webern but undertowing it with the melodic richness of Messiaen. *Towards The Rainbow, Palma* (1964) is an uncanny meeting between the American orchestral music of, say, Aaron Copland and the delicate quiet of an Oriental sensibility, particularly in the guitar parts. *Music For Trees* (1961) absorbed much from John Cage, as did *Eclipse* (1966), which emphasized the Japanese lute and shakuhachi. Takemitsu broke into the West with *November Steps* (1967), which combined these instruments with orchestra in a very languid style.

From there Takemitsu's floating Ambient imagination produced a slew of works which all sounded as if they were hewn from the same tree, but were equally individual and pleasing to the ear. In 1974 he began the *Waterscape* series, which revolved around rain, water and sea – the concept of endless flow and regeneration being at the heart of Takemitsu's music. Evolving over many years, this cycle produced some minor masterpieces, including *Raintree* of 1981, where mallet instruments and finger cymbals blend exquisitely in a work designed to be performed in near darkness. Another part of the cycle, *Rain Spell* (1982), is a majestic voyage into shimmering silence as flute, clarinet, harp, piano and vibraphone appear and reappear in endless static variations.

Takemitsu's works are not long. Orchestral pieces like *To The Edge Of Dream* (1983) summon up great swells amid the peace and are direct descendants of Debussy. This disquiet in the realm of quiet could be a metaphor for twentieth-century music in general. Many of Takemitsu's works recollect artists like Miró or, in the case of the two-movement orchestral *Visions* (1989), the luminous art of the French Symbolist painter Odilon Redon. His fascination with circulating water, the organic changes of gardens and quiet are thoroughly Eastern, though he has absorbed much from the West.

At the end of the century Takemitsu became Japan's most revered composer. Praised as a synthesist, he composed soundtracks most famously for Japanese director Kurosawa. But his relatively early death, in 1996 from cancer, robbed him of much of the fruits he was beginning to harvest in the West. Takemitsu's aesthetic and themes have been taken up by David Sylvian and ably applied to the field of Ambient rock.

LISTENING

Riverrun and *Waterways* (Virgin Classics 1991), played by the London Sinfonietta under Oliver Knussen, is a great introduction to Takemitsu which includes *Rain Coming* and *Rain Spell* from the *Waterscape* series. *Requiem* and *November Steps* (Denon 1992) is a Japanese recording which features mostly orchestral music and includes the James Joyce-inspired *Far Calls, Coming, Far!* of 1980. The silken tone of Finnish conductor Esa-Pekka Salonen really brings Takemitsu to life on *To The Edge Of Dream*, two different discs released by Sony (1991 and 1993): one a complete cycle, the other an excellent compilation which places the music alongside that of Messiaen and Stravinsky.

KAIJA SAARIAHO

One of a new breed of Finnish composers who did much to break the staid Romantic traditions of the country in the 1980s, Kaija Saariaho was born in Helsinki in 1952. Together with the brilliant conductor Esa-Pekka Salonen, she opened the country's ears to the possibilities of electronic and tape music, possibilities which Boulez and Stockhausen had presented to the world decades before.

A product of the Sibelius Academy in the Finnish capital, she moved to Paris during the 1980s and developed her electronic collage technique at IRCAM. There she met Stockhausen as he worked on *Licht* (*Light*) and was inspired. He would repay her the compliment when he visited Helsinki in 1989 to perform and mix music from his massive opera cycle.

Saariaho's speciality is an arresting mixture of acoustic and electronic sounds, taped actuality recordings and radically transformed instrumental tones, which all combine to communicate a fascinating geological mix. A clear lineage can be traced to Cage but there is a density to her work which is the opposite to the American's Zen-filled sound spaces. After a trip to the US in 1988 she wrote a clutch of pieces, including *Of Crystal* and *By Smoke*, which combined orchestra and string quartet with the best electronic software available at IRCAM. Here singular sounds and instrumental timbres rise up in orchestral swells and then recede, seeming for all their modernity like electronic Impressionism. *Maa*, a ballet in seven scenes, combines pure tape noise and tribal percussion with harp, string quartet, synthesizer and electronics. The introductory section, 'Journey', is extraordinary: thematic archetypes reminiscent of Pink Floyd's *Dark Side Of The Moon* combine with a sense of travelling great distances. The incessant footfalls and continuously altered sonic backdrops (inspired by the composer's Finnish homeland) culminate in a tour de force as the finale of electronic drones and real lapping waves imbue a sense of true serenity.

LISTENING

Saariaho is joined by old friend Esa-Pekka Salonen, conducting the Los Angeles Philharmonic, on an Ondine disc from 1993 featuring *Of Crystal* and *By Smoke*. The Kronos Quartet have their sound remixed at IRCAM and there's even a poem from the late Russian film genius Andrei Tarkovsky. *Maa*, on an Ondine recording from 1992, presents Saariaho's full sound-collage effect.

ELECTRONIC MEDIA

RECORDS

Living in the digital age can obscure the fact that for well over 100 years records dominated the way music was heard. From the day Edison recorded his famous ditty 'Mary Had A Little Lamb' on to a cylinder wrapped in tinfoil in 1877 right up to the late 1980s, electrical vibrations produced by a needle tracing a groove profoundly shaped people's musical experience. Divorced from its sound source and preserved, recorded music could be experienced over and over again, a feature that in time would create the necessary mindset for the arrival of electronic and Ambient music. Moreover records allowed composers such as Darius Milhaud, Paul Hindemith, Percy Grainger and, most importantly, John Cage to explore new avenues in sound. And let's not forget how records gave birth to the Ambient House and Techno music of the 1980 and 1990s.

Surveying the history of records reveals a feverish wish for an ever-improving spectrum of sound evolved by people and enterprises both famous, like Edison, and obscure, like the London Stereoscopic Company or the Gramophone & Typewriter Company of London. Before records history is full of clockwork devices operated by a barrel and pin. Beethoven is reputed to have written something for a clockwork orchestra. Then there was the player piano, which Debussy was fond of. Composers could use it to record performances, which were captured in the form of holes pierced on a paper roll. This could then be used to replay the music using an air-pressure system which activated the instrument's keys. Yet none of it came near true musical fidelity.

Edison's sonic invention was considered a miracle. Within a year of creating the Phonograph in 1877, he had established a company in New York and was sending salesmen all over America armed with blank tinfoil cylinders. In England Lord Tennyson recorded a poem in front of the Royal Institute and by 1879 Edison's 'Speaking Machine' was available on both sides of the Atlantic (in the UK, from the London Stereoscopic Company). Yet it was a novelty of very poor quality. By 1885 Bell & Tainter in Washington had developed a wax cylinder of greater refinement titled a Graphophone. Edison retorted with his Improved Phonograph and in 1888 recorded a young boy playing a piano at his New Jersey laboratory. He even sent equipment replete with large sound-gathering horns over to the Crystal Palace in London to record a Handel festival. By the middle of the 1890s Charles Pathé in Paris had become world-famous for his cylinder recordings.

When all this was happening an inventive German immigrant in Washington DC applied for a patent for his Gramophone. His name was Emile Berliner and he is the father of both records and Compact Discs. Berliner used a flat-disc 'electroforming' technique to create a negative which could then print copies. In 1888 he gave a demonstration at the Franklin Institute in Philadelphia using five-inch hard-rubber discs revolving at seventy revolutions per minute on a hand-cranked machine. He had indeed started a revolution.

While Columbia in America were making money out of cylinders featuring snippets of popular song and opera (sold on a 'return when worn out' basis) Berliner headed for Germany to get manufacturing backing for his Gramophone. By 1891 his machines were available and in 1894 his Washington Gramophone Co. was selling an electric machine playing seven-inch discs. A huge breakthrough came with the invention of shellac in Newark in 1897, which allowed Berliner to make better-quality records. He opened a studio and a record shop in Philadelphia that same year and by 1898 had subsidiary companies in England, France and, in Germany, the famous Deutsche Gram-mophon. More importantly, in Hanover he set up a pressing plant for making innumerable copies from a copper cast. In 1900 ten-inch shellac discs arrived playing at 78rpm but they were still only single-sided, with a playing time of four and a half minutes, and easily breakable.

The early part of the twentieth century was a frenetic period for the recording industry. Berliner had acquired from the His Master's Voice company rights to the legendary painting of a dog listening to a Gramophone. This image would become standard on Gramophone records and the name His Master's Voice (HMV) synonymous with record production in the UK. His company, which became Victor in the US, would famously record Caruso in Milan and, in 1903, Debussy. Up until then records had been seen as novelties, as evinced by the popularity in the US of the nickelodeon, an early form of jukebox. Victor wanted to record classical music, while Columbia went the more popular route. The twelve-inch record arrived in 1903 and in 1904 the double-sided disc.

Though original masters were still recorded crudely with a horn, the popularity of records rocketed five times in the US during the First World War, mainly as a result of the Dixieland jazz boom. In the UK in 1914, HMV released eight single-sided 78s of Beethoven's *Fifth Symphony*, performed in Berlin, the first complete classical recording. They fitted into a box or 'album' which opened out accordion-style to allow access. Hence the word 'album' became associated with serious music and would reverberate down through the century. The same year Decca launched a 'portable' Gramophone.

In 1917 Victor signed Leopold Stokowski and his Philadelphia Orchestra to its Red Label, thus embracing a conductor who was a staunch supporter of new and electronic music. De Forest's pioneering work with the valve led to the appearance of microphone recording and valve amplification in the mid-1920s. The Brunswick Panatrope, made in Iowa in 1925, substituted a loudspeaker for the usual horn, while HMV's Concert Gramophone of 1927 boasted an electromagnetic pick-up. A Tasmanian, Eric Waterworth, tried to float the idea of an automatic record-changer, but the concept didn't take off until 1928 with HMV's Automatic Gramophone. By the end of the twenties HMV had also successfully marketed the idea of a Radiogram (a combined radio and record player designed as a piece of furniture), a product which was still popular in the 1970s.

At the same time the record industry as we know it began to take shape. The Radio Corporation of America (RCA) bought Victor in 1929. In 1931 both Columbia and Gramophone in the UK merged to become Electric and Musical Instruments Ltd, better known as EMI, dragging in all European firms except the fiercely independent Deutsche Grammophon and its sub-label Polydor. But the most important development of the time was RCA Victor's revelatory launch of $33\frac{1}{3}$ rpm records featuring a continuous Beethoven's *Fifth* conducted by Stokowski. Players for the new long-play records cost between $250 and

$1,000. This innovation and a revolutionary stereo system developed by the Bell Telephone Company Laboratories in 1932 which featured Stokowski both failed owing to the collapse of the record industry around this time.

But even though advances in recording fidelity would not pick up until after the Second World War, records were undoubtedly having an affect on musical creation. The French composer and former Satie acolyte Darius Milhaud used records to experiment with vocal and pitch transformations in the 1920s. Between 1929 and 1930 Paul Hindemith and Ernst Toch worked on new acoustical and harmonic ideas utilizing records at the Experimental Radio Centre of the Berlin Music Academy. The eccentric Australian composer Percy Grainger used them as sound sources in the 1930s. During the same period the Hungarian painter, photographer and composer László Moholy-Nagy, along with his colleagues at Germany's Bauhaus school of art and design, attempted radical sound transformations with records. By playing records backwards (fifty or more years before House and Rap DJs) and other means, Moholy-Nagy aimed to alter the way sounds were generated as well as get to the heart of exactly what sound itself was. The closure of the Bauhaus by the Nazis in 1933 put an end to his explorations. It fell to John Cage to put the sound-altering power of turntables and records on the map when, in 1939, his *Imaginary Landscape 1* (using RCA test-frequency recordings) suavely demonstrated that the music had changed the sonic landscape for all time.

While the Columbia Broadcasting System (CBS) had become a giant in America, shellac as a medium for records was ditched in 1943 for a more durable synthetic plastic. Between 1944 and 1946 Decca introduced High-Fidelity, both in terms of the record player's output and the wider dynamic character of the 'full frequency range recording' (ffrr) system. But the watershed came in 1948 with the unveiling of Dr Peter Goldmark's $33\frac{1}{3}$ rpm twelve-inch vinyl 'microgroove' record in Atlantic City at a meeting of Columbia executives. Using a new form of micro-stylus, the records had 200–300 grooves per inch and could hold up to twenty-five minutes of music per side. Until then 78s could only hold five minutes per side. Moreover the new records were nearly unbreakable. They could be played on conventional equipment with an attachment and cost a reasonable $5 apiece. In effect Goldmark consigned all previous record formats to the dustbin. RCA Victor quickly followed in 1949 with the seven-inch microgroove record, which could hold as much as an old 78. Extended Play $33\frac{1}{3}$ rpm seven-inch records, or EPs, were the logical next step.

The accessibility of tape and cheap manufacturing costs brought about a record boom in the 1950s. All forms of music soared in popularity as older buyers replaced 78s and younger teenagers discovered rock and roll. In 1957 in Connecticut, Emory Cork came up with a double-pick-up stereophonic system for playing new records with two separate grooves, one for each channel of the stereo sound. The idea failed. The following year Audio-Fidelity successfully solved the stereo problem by introducing a single groove with forty-five-degree walls to be played by a double-sided stylus. Initially companies like Decca prided themselves on being able to record whole Wagner operas in stereo, packaged in huge boxed sets, but in the 1960s advances in recording fidelity made by groups such as The Beach Boys in the US and The Beatles in the UK turned stereo records into a popular art form.

Having established a standard, the record industry settled down to a period of consolidation. During the early 1970s the idea of quadraphonic, or four-channel, records was mooted. Columbia had SQ, RCA had Quadradisc and, in Japan, the interestingly titled CD-4. High-fidelity groups like Pink Floyd had the concept foisted on them but it didn't take off, even though Ambient and electronic composers had been using multi-speaker systems for years. The seeming balance of two speakers for two ears was enough for average music-lover.

Records in the 1970s became more elaborately packaged, particularly in rock music, where the double or even triple gatefold sleeve was *de rigueur* for a few years. As a form of entertainment the twin turntable of the discotheque, playing twelve-inch 45rpm dance records by the likes of Donna Summer, became an international sensation. Innovations in records themselves became advances in fidelity. Direct Metal Master Cuts were a very popular form of record, and then Denon in Japan pioneered the Digital recording system to radically increase the dynamic range. Telarc in the US and other companies led the market in superior-sounding but more expensive records. By the early 1980s Audiophile Digital standards were the norm for most major classical releases.

In 1982 Compact Cassettes sold more than vinyl records in the US for the first time. In the UK the Compact Disc, or CD, overtook vinyl record sales in 1989. Accounting for only about ten per cent of the market in the 1990s, records were considered outmoded after 100 fruitful years of music reproduction. The oscillations of a moving magnet that created a voltage and hence a sound didn't seem romantic any more in the face of shiny, laser-etched discs. But it was through records that a new music was born in America when the breakbeat was invented in New York in the early 1980s using turntable 'scratch' and 'mix' techniques. The age of Hip-Hop, House and the DJ arrived in the late 1980s and by the 1990s the record was firmly rehabilitated as a medium for radical new music mixed live. And it was through DJs mixing old records that Ambient House was born in the UK. This in itself broadened the experience of listening and allowed a reappraisal both of what actually constituted music and of the substantial sonic legacy of records themselves.

MAGNETIC TAPE

If one could point to the single greatest invention of the twentieth century in electronic music it would have to be magnetic tape. As a flexible carrier of sound, tape opened up whole new vistas, not only in the transmission of music but in its very innovation. As soon as tape technology was up and running in the late 1940s and early 1950s, Cage, Varèse, Schaeffer and Stockhausen eagerly pounced on it to create what had hitherto been only dreamed of. Tape shaped and invigorated the development of electronic and Ambient music in a myriad of ways. Not least in the studio, where the growing sophistication of multi-track recording led in the 1960s and 70s to the creative zenith of the rock era. Also important was the impact of tape technology on Minimalism and, of course, Brian Eno, whose early dronal music came directly from tape loops.

The arrival of plastic tape coated with ferric (iron) particles capable of being magnetized so as to hold sound followed a long and circuitous journey. It all began with Valdemar Poulsen, a Danish engineer who worked for the Copenhagen Telephone Company. He found that he could store electrical information by magnetizing a steel wire. Demonstrated at the Paris Exposition of 1900, his Telegraphone used an electromagnet and piano wire that passed through the device at seven feet per second. The Telegraphone was taken up by a firm in Massachusetts in 1903 with the aim of developing it as a dictation and telephone-answering device. Yet it was cumbersome and of poor sound quality because of its lack of amplification. Unsurprisingly, the enterprise failed. Lee De Forest modified the Telegraphone in 1913 for film experiments he was doing in New York, but the machine would never take off because it was basically a good idea out of context, without suitable technical support.

De Forest was way ahead of everybody in developing a system as early as 1923 for transforming sound into light pulses which, using a photoelectric cell, could be converted back into sound. But in Germany too decisive steps were being taken. Kurt Stille had developed a recording machine which used magnetic steel tape, primarily for use in film. This was bought in 1929 by Louis Blattner for synchronizing film sound at Elstree Studios in the UK but was also marketed as the Blattnerphone. In the same year another German scientist, Fritz Pfluemer, began developing a magnetic coating for plastic tape.

Real changes occurred when the Marconi company bought up the rights to the Blattnerphone in 1931, made refinements and marketed the device as the famous Marconi-Stille Recorder. Several were bought by the BBC and photographs show giant contraptions with huge sprocketed spools arranged vertically. Though erasure was possible, the 'tape' consisted of razor steel travelling at sixty inches per second. Splicing could only be done by welding two pieces of steel together. If the 'tape' spun off it was extremely dangerous and could result in serious injury, such as loss of a limb. Something else had to be found.

Pfluemer's experiments with plastic-coated tape resulted in the invention of the Dictaphone in 1935. This idea was taken up by AEG in Berlin, who developed it as the Magnetophon in the same year. This was the breakthrough that everybody had anticipated – a more compact system using a much more flexible oxide-coated tape which was easily reusable and could hold a number of tracks simultaneously. Improvements were made up to the beginning of the Second World War and it is believed that by the 1940s the Germans had a machine as advanced as anything produced in the UK or US in the 1960s.

There are records of an Ozaphone tape device being produced in the UK around 1937 but nothing more was heard of it. Certainly the Magnecord was the first stereo tape device invented. Primarily for use by engine-testers at General Motors, it was demonstrated in Chicago in 1949 and marketed in New York in 1954 to consumers as the Audiosphere, along with seven-inch tape reels.

Though music, both mono and stereo, was available in limited quantities to consumers in the 1950s, it wasn't until 1958 that real portability arrived with the unveiling of the Cassette Tape recorder by RCA Victor in the US. This was still a reel-to-reel device but now used two four-inch spools of half-inch tape. Playing time was only twenty-three minutes but it was versatile. In Holland, Philips was busy investigating the idea of a miniature tape cassette, and the result was the Compact Cassette, unveiled in 1964 with a tape width of 3.8mm (0.15 inch). This was a revolutionary sound carrier and in itself propelled the growth of the music business to immense proportions. Meanwhile an American physicist named Ray Dolby had long been investigating a way to reduce the immense hiss of ferric tape. In the late 1960s he came up with Dolby A, and in the early 1970s Dolby B, which became a standard. These innovations were instrumental in increasing the fidelity of both produced and recorded music.

Consumer products came and went, like Grundig's DC Cassette from the early 1960s, the infamous Motorola eight-track cartridge and Sony's 1976 Elcaset tape, but then these were nothing more than gimmicks. The Compact Cassette would lodge itself in the marketplace as the best carrier of music. Improvements were made, including high-quality chromium-dioxide and 'metal' tape in the 1970s and 80s, but the basic design would stay the same. The format's biggest boost came in 1979 when the chairman of Sony in Japan, Masura Ibuka, invented a lightweight portable tape player to satisfy the demands of teenagers who were constantly annoying their parents with loud music. Initially called the Stowaway in the UK and the Soundabout in the US, it became the Walkman in 1980. Twelve years later sixty million of them had been sold worldwide. Over the same period annual global sales of cassette players were around 200 million and of cassettes a staggering two and a half billion.

In the 1980s and 90s Dolby C and Dolby S refined the sound of tape, which was facing increased competition from digital sources. One such source was Digital Audio Tape (DAT), a method of storing information on magnetic tape which avoided hiss and sound variance. Originated by Sony and Mitsubishi as a studio medium in the late 1970s, Sony's DAT machines really came into their own in 1987 and by 1990 a Walkman version was an industry standard. Yet DAT's relatively high cost made it the preserve of musicians and professionals, with such companies as Alesis, Fostex and Tascam cleaning up the market for multi-track DAT 'portastudios' by the mid-1990s.

KEYBOARDS, SYNTHESIZERS AND COMPUTERS

What made electronic and Ambient music more ubiquitous in the late twentieth century was the increasing accessibility of equipment which could 'organize' sound. Another word for this idea was to 'synthesize' sound. The search for an instrument which could create, by synthesis, a variety of timbres and put them together like an ensemble was to preoccupy inventors and musicians alike for more than 100 years.

A dip into history shows how much work had to be done. The concept of electromagnetism seems to have dominated the first half of the nineteenth century with Michael Faraday leading the field in the development of electrical transformers by 1831. Soon it was observed that variations in electromagnetic circuits could be used to sustain sound and in Germany as early as the 1850s researchers were already working on the idea of speech synthesis using tuning forks. Attention was focused on communication and during the 1860s the idea of the musical telegraph, one which used keyboards, was in vogue. One of the earliest 'synthesizers' could be said to be Elisha Gray's 1876 instrument, which used steel reeds and electromagnets, but this was designed for Morse code rather than musical reproduction.

A more significant breakthrough was the player piano, first developed in 1850 but refined by the Swiss Matthaus Hipp in 1867. Its ingenious use of a perforated paper roll which acted on the instrument's hammers made it the first digital recording device. The player piano became very popular among composers, particularly Debussy. Once a perfect performance of a piece was executed, it was there on paper for ever. Refinements of this idea led to the German Reproducing Piano of 1904, which was taken up by the Aeolian Company in the US in 1913. Aeolian marketed it as the Duo-Art, which by 1925 had generated sales worth $59 million, its clever use of electric motor and electrical contacts and air pressure for each key making it one of the most accurate digital encoding instruments ever built. Though the depression and the rise of the record effectively killed off the Duo-Art, the survival of piano rolls, notably those played by Percy Grainger and Artur Rubinstein, saw the return of the instrument in recordings by the Nimbus label in the 1990s.

Looking back in time, one can observe dozens of inventions which contributed to the rise of 'synthetic sound'. As early as 1851 the Englishman Henry Gauntlett wished to patent a control device which could be linked to a series of organs and make them all play at the Great Exhibition of that year. It never happened, but the idea was a century ahead of its time. Péchard's electro-acoustic organ of 1868 was the first of its kind and patented in France in that year. In the mid-1880s both Boyle in England and Lorenz in Frankfurt patented instruments which used electromagnetism to create sound. Lorenz is indisputably credited with devising the first 'electric piano', though lacking loudspeakers it was of limited popularity. By the early 1890s in London and Berlin refinements had been made to make the electric piano a future reality. Near the end of the century there existed in Europe isolated inventions which used keyboards to trigger other instruments. But real progress would begin in the twentieth century.

Thaddeus Cahill would begin the century with his unwieldy Telharmonium, which used an array of keyboards and required two players. Lee De Forest, the inventor of the valve and amplifier, actually worked on an electronic keyboard system in 1915 called the Audion Piano. Its use of oscillator frequency interactions would influence electronic instrument design such as that of the Theremin and Ondes Martenot in the 1920s. Significant to the development of 'sound synthesis' was the work of Armand Givelet, a French radio engineer at the Eiffel Tower who applied De Forest's ideas to a series of instruments in the late 1920s. These included a radio-electric piano, an electric organ and, most importantly, a fully programmable music machine which used paper tape to activate electrical circuits and was unveiled at the Paris Exhibition of 1929. Essentially the first synthesizer, this gave more control over the shape and quality of musical notes than any previous device.

A parallel development was 'optical synthesis'. Again this was a product of the genius of De Forest, who had shown as early as 1923 that sound waves could be transformed into light impulses which, when recorded on strips of film and then passed over a photoelectric cell, could generate sound voltages. Of obvious import for the motion-picture sound industry, it also was adapted by various inventors to facilitate sound synthesis. Members of the Bauhaus experimented with 'optical' sound techniques in the 1930s, but it was the German Rudolf Pfenninger who first outlined the real value of synthesizing a range of musical tones from optical sources. He saw that the physical nature of the source, and the use of shading, could greatly affect the musical outcome. In Ottawa Norman McLaren experimented with this idea. So too did Percy Grainger in the dissemination of his 'Free Music' in the mid-1930s. There was also the work of Daphne Oram in the UK. But it was in Russia that the greatest advances were made.

There, in 1932, Yegeny Sholpo invented the Variaphone, a music machine which used imaging in the compositional process. This led to the famous ANS photoelectric optical sound synthesizer constructed by Yevgeny Murzin in the late 1950s. Sited in the Moscow Experimental Studio, this was a terrific advance and capable of great timbral delicacy. A collaboration between Murzin and Edward Artemyev, a graduate of the Moscow Conservatoire, would produce some of the most realistic synthesizer music ever. Some of it, used in the dreamlike films of Andrei Tarkovsky, was incredibly Ambient, particularly the soundtracks of *Solaris* (1972), *Mirror* (1975) and *Stalker* (1979). Only in 1990 was this music available to people in the West (on the Torso Kino CD *Solaris, Mirror, Stalker*) as the Cold War had ruled out any cross-fertilization.

In the West, it was Laurens Hammond who was to make a big impact. At the age of forty Hammond revolutionized the perception of the organ by mass-producing it. His tone-wheeled electric version, powered by his own electric motor, went on sale in 1935. Within three years he had sold 5,000. In 1940 he devised a Solovox, a monophonic (capable of producing only one note at a time) device which could generate chords to go with single-handed piano playing. This chordal idea was applied to the Hammond organ of the 1950s, the fully electronic B3, which was of a more compact design and used a Leslie speaker system to throw out its thick, cheesy sound. Melody and accompaniment were combined in a single instrument which had a three-octave range with ninety-six chord buttons. Other companies, including Allen, Farfisa, Wurlitzer and Lowry, would challenge Hammond in the marketplace but his organ has gone down in history for its sound, enhanced by drawbars and volume pedal. It became a favourite with rock and pop musicians of the 1950s and 60s.

The Hammond organ was bulky, but the growth of miniaturization would lead to smaller and smaller instruments. Farfisa and Vox Continental organs became popular in the 1960s, while Hohner in Germany and Casio in Japan kept refining their organs to achieve greater compactness. Notable for its novelty value, the Stylophone mini-monophonic organ was popularized by Rolf Harris in the early 1970s, and by 1982 the Japanese Casiotone VL-5 and other tiny organs had replaced the need for large machines. One other early keyboard which bridged the gap between the electronic organ and the synthesizer deserves mentioning. The Mellotron, the brainchild of the American Bill Fransen and two Birmingham brothers, was the first 'sampling' instrument. Its name derived from the merger of the words melody and electronic. This keyboard instrument used tapes and magnetic heads to replay instrumental 'samples'. Primarily invented in 1962, it was followed in 1964 by the Mark 2, which was even heavier than a Hammond organ. It had two thirty-five-note keyboards, but each note had three different sounds. Volume, speed and reverberation could be changed and sounds combined. Despite difficulties with the tape mechanisms, this became a very popular instrument, its most famous use being on The Beatles' 'Strawberry Fields Forever'. Refinements were made, the Mellotron reaching its peak in the mid-1970s with the Mark 5, a double-keyboard version weighing 300 pounds and favoured by progressive rock musicians such as Rick Wakeman. Though monophonic, the Mellotron gave a definitive electronic sound, particularly in the 70s music of the German group Tangerine Dream.

The tributaries which lead to the rise of sound synthesis are manifold and complex. Soon after the Second World War studios began to be established around the world to further this aim: the Club d'Essai in Paris (1948), the Columbia-Princeton Electronic Music Center in New York (1951), WDR

Cologne (1951), Japanese Radio, Tokyo (1953), Italian Radio, Milan (1953), Philips in Eindhoven (1956), Siemens in Munich (1957), Polish Radio, Warsaw (1957), the Brussels Studio (1958), Toronto University (1959), the San Francisco Tape Center (1959), the Sonology Institute, Utrecht (1961), the Electro and Psychoacoustic Studio in Ghent (1962) and IRCAM in Paris (1977). All of these studios were used by the illustrious electronic composers of the century. Those at Ghent and Brussels attracted the Belgian electronic composer Henri Pousseur, who stated in 1970 that all old music was dead. The Milan studio was the brainchild of the Italian composers Bruno Maderna and Luciano Berio, whose main interest was the facility of multi-media performance-related electronic pieces. In these sites the equipment was broken up into the substantial components which generated, shaped and amplified sounds and the tape machines which recorded them. They looked like laboratories. By contrast, the 'synthesizer' would compact the equipment and allow composers and musicians much more control over the music they were creating.

Of enormous significance was the invention of the transistor in 1948. Silicon crystals were used during the war in the refinement of radar, but once peace returned Bardeen, Brattain and Shockley would use them in the development of the triode at the Bell Telephone Company Laboratories in New Jersey. Renamed the transistor, the triode was an effective replacement for De Forest's valve and was small, easily managed and almost unbreakable. Its existence led to the development of complex circuits, the lifeblood of any synthesizer. Early versions of the synthesizer were developed by Hugh Le Caine, Harald Bode and Paolo Ketoff. Le Caine's Sackbutt was developed in Ottawa between 1945 and 1948 and was a refinement of earlier instruments; to a touch-sensitive keyboard and a glide strip it added a new pitch-bending facility and voltage control. Bode's Melochord was an American device with two keyboards for controlling studio generators and modulators. Ketoff developed his Fonosynth and Synket (with its three touch-sensitive keyboards) in Rome. All these devices were to fade with the arrival of the Moog.

Robert Moog (rhymes with 'vogue') was to revolutionize the synthesizer. Born in 1934, he studied engineering at Cornell University, where he financed himself by selling self-assembly Theremins in his spare time. During the 1950s Moog had helped the eccentric musician and equipment inventor Raymond Scott to build a series of devices at the latter's home on Long Island. One was a three-octave keyboard version of the Theremin called the Clavivox, which had portamento, vibrato and touch-sensitivity. Moog considered it a proto-synthesizer. More importantly, he supplied parts for Scott's enormous electromechanical sequencer the Electronium, which looked like an old telephone switchboard and could, by the early 1960s, produce rhythms, melodies and timbres. Scott credited Moog with coming up with the word 'sequencer', even though Moog attributes the actual invention of the device to Donald Buchla.

In 1963 Moog met a lecturer, Herb Deutsch, at an electronics conference in New York. Both saw the need to apply the recently invented integrated circuits of transistors to synthesizers. At that time the RCA synthesizer developed by Harry Olson and Herb Belar in the early 1950s was the most advanced model available. Installed in the studio of the Columbia-Princeton Electronic Music Center, it could generate four musical tones simultaneously, various tone colours and other sound characteristics. Everything was communicated through binary (two-digit) code via typewriters attached to the huge synthesizer. Capable of producing one notation every 1/30 second, it was the fastest synthesizer available, but wholly inaccessible to the public.

Beginning life in 1964, the Moog Modular System was the first great analogue synthesizer. This was made up of various boxes controlled by a keyboard. Timbres were built up by the subtraction or filtering of unwanted harmonics from a sound waveform. The quality of these sounds was determined by linking various modules with wire cords. The large 3C version was used by Wendy Carlos to stunning success on 1968's *Switched-On Bach*. Though monophonic, the instrument became extremely popular, so much so that Moog built a portable unit for live performance. Enter the MiniMoog of 1970, one of the all-time classic synthesizers with its pop-up knobs featuring controllers, oscillator bank, mixer and modifier. Its pitch-bend wheels would become an industry standard.

Another popular synthesizer of the era was the EMS VCS3, originally called the Putney – named after the early London base of Peter Zinovieff, the Russian founder of EMS, or Electronic Music Studios. Conceived by Zinovieff and designer David Cockerell, the VCS3 (short for Voltage-controlled Synthesizer No. 3) looked like something out of *Star Trek* with its L-shaped cabinet featuring an array of coloured knobs and a flat console with a sixteen-by-sixteen pin matrix for connecting its internal modules and a funny-looking joystick. Its strange image has fascinated musicians ever since it first went on sale in 1969. Along with its patch bay, oscillators and envelope shaper came a reverb unit. Then Zinovieff and Cockerell added a small keyboard called the DK2. Instantly successful, the VCS3 was used by every 'progressive' rock group of the era, from King Crimson to Yes. In 1971 EMS came up with a suitcase version called the Synthi A (at one time known as the Portabella) – a veritable laptop device, this was used to devastating effect by Pink Floyd on *Dark Side Of The Moon*. The addition of a two-and-a-half-octave touch-sensitive keyboard (which included a digital sequencer) produced the Synthi AKS - a completely portable playable synthesizer. Brian Eno was a famous VCS3 user during the early 1970s and even played the ultra-rare VCS4 large performance model.

By the mid-1970s EMS was concentrating on big synthesizers like the Synthi 100, but it was the VCS3 in all its guises – loved by everyone from The Stones, through Jean-Michel Jarre, to the Ambient and Techno boffins of the 1990s – which was destined to become a classic.

Switches took over from wire connectors in new early-1970s synthesizers from ARP, whose Odyssey and 2600 became popular. New names like Japan's Roland and the US's Oberheim would come on the market but the digital era had arrived to come up alongside the analogue synthesizer. The combination of transistor and circuit in the microprocessor using silicon chips would allow far more information to be stored in synthesizers. In order to understand the implications we must look at the coming of the computer and its impact on music.

By the early 1950s the transistor had made the computer a commercial proposition. Demand was on the increase, though computers were still quite large. One of the earliest applications of computers to music was Lejaren Hiller's *Illiac Suite*, an eighteen-minute string quartet piece generated between 1955 and 1957 by an Illiac computer at Illinois University, where Hiller subsequently taught experimental music. His computer music can be heard on *Computer Music Retrospective* (Wergo 1989). By 1961 the Bell Telephone Company Laboratories had successfully got a computer to synthesize sound. Punched cards, magnetic tape and magnetic discs would all be hold information which was fed into the computer in the form of numbers (hence the term 'digital'). The outcoming information would be transformed using the now famous digital-to-analogue converter. Various models were made of analogue synthesizer components in computer labs. This had significant application to synthesizer design when in 1973 Dr John Chowning, a researcher at Stanford University in California, cracked open the idea of FM, or Frequency Modulated synthesis. His insight made it possible to produce a huge panoply of tones and sounds by altering the frequency of the created sound waves. Computers would be used in the music of Gordon Mumma, who worked with John Cage and who in 1965, at the age of thirty, created the idea of 'cybersonics' or computer-controlled music in Ann Arbour, Michigan; and in the film *2001: A Space Odyssey*, for which HAL's computerized voice was originally conceived in the Bell Telephone Company Laboratories in 1968; and in the quiet, hypnotic music of Mumma's associate David Behrman.

In 1970 Hugh Le Caine developed the first polyphonic (multi-note) synthesizer in Canada. Then Moog brought out the polyphonic Polymoog in 1976. As digital ideas spread, the idea of applying them to analogue instruments came into being. The concept of 'sequencing' (storing an array of notes and playing them back) had been invented by Donald Buchla when he designed his series of analogue electric music boxes for Morton Subotnick at the San Francisco Tape Center in the mid-1960s. But now digital means made on-board sequencing feasible. Oberheim applied it to its Expander series in the mid-1970s. Then in 1978, also from the US, came the Sequential Circuits Prophet 5. This was a synthesizer with five voices – five different synthesizers in one. Gloriously polyphonic, with forty different ways of connecting the sound, the Prophet 5 was fully programmable with control buttons which could be played live. It became a very popular instrument and was a favourite of Tangerine Dream and Terry Riley, to name two.

Within a year there was a new instrument on the block. The Fairlight Computer Music Instrument, or CMI. This was invented in Sydney, Australia and was basically a computer with added keyboard which allowed the composer/musician to create sounds using digital means. It was polyphonic but, more importantly, had a sampler which had eight voices and thus was multi-timbral. The CMI was complemented in the US by the Synclavier, built by New England Digital and a combination of computer and digital/sampling ideas. Unsurprisingly, they were extremely expensive pieces of equipment. The idea of a built-in sequencer or looping was in vogue. The Linn Drum appeared in 1980 and with its programmable sampled acoustic drums would begin the age of the drum machine – an instrument integral to House and Ambient music of the late 1980s and early 90s.

The extensive work carried out in computing and digital synthesis would finally get its commercial launch in the Yamaha DX7. The German PPG Wave had preceded it in the late 1970s but this was bulky and difficult to use. The DX7 was the first of the really important Japanese synthesizers and paved the way for the country's domination of the market at the tail-end of the century. Even though it was reputed to be very difficult to programme, it dominated the market between 1983 and 1987. The DX7 took Chowning's innovation of FM synthesis and put it on a silicon chip inside a highly sensitive keyboard. It had sixteen-voice polyphony, thirty-two memories and four digital channels per note. Full of beautiful pre-set sounds, like those of the old Rhodes piano and various acoustic instruments, the DX7 brought together all the ideas of previous decades into one smooth box. Relatively cheap, it sold in the hundreds of thousands. Through the work of Brian Eno – one of the world's leading experts on the DX7 – and others it became an essential component of Ambient music.

Everything after this was refinement. In the same year as the DX7 came the Musical Instrument Digital Interface, or MIDI. Basically this was a special universal connector that allowed several instruments to be tied together and controlled digitally by a computer. In 1986 the Atari ST computer came with built-in MIDI. In the same year arrived the phenomenal AKAI S900 sampler, a keyboard-less module which had eight-voice polyphony and set the standard for realistic sound sampling in the 1990s. The Japanese continued to dominate the market with the Roland D50, launched in 1987, which had new concepts like stored digital effects and sampled sound waveforms.

Then came the Korg M1 and Wavestation between 1988 and 1990. Korg had been making synthesizers since the 1960s but these were in a class of their own. The M1 was a Rolls-Royce of a machine – multi-timbral, polyphonic, with built-in effects, built-in sequencing and a rainbow of fantastic sounds. It could be a piano, it could be an organ or even a guitar. And it all sounded so natural. The Wavestation came out of the same technology that had produced the Sequential Circuits Prophet 5 in 1978. Korg had acquired the Sequential Circuits company in 1988 and came up with the Wavestation in the 1990s. This specialist synthesizer became famous for its ability to allow a single voice to play an array of sound waves and thus it was synonymous with a generation of 'swirling ambiences'.

As geometric advances in technology continued, the end of the century saw musicians and composers faced with a plethora of digital devices. Digital Audio Tape (DAT) would replace analogue tape in the studio and small eight-track digital recording systems would make extremely high-quality recording available to almost anyone. In the early 1990s Yamaha launched pocket-sized eight-track digital sequencing by means of machines such as the QY-20. Any work done on these in transit could be loaded into a computer or even directly plugged into other instruments using MIDI. By the mid-1990s a musician could do everything inside the brain of the new generation of Apple Macintosh and other home computers, which had powerful internal memories for storing information. A slew of companies offered tapeless recording systems and all sorts of sequencing and editing software was available on floppy computer disc. With the aid of Windows (a multiple-overlap and multiple-access computer operating system), symphonic sound could be orchestrated at the touch of a button and generated from an array of MIDI linked units. Even vintage analogue synthesizers could now be MIDI'd up and controlled from a computer.

Such was the demand for old sounds that as early as 1993 the EMU company built a Vintage Keys module with sixty-eight samples of the Mellotron, Wurlitzer Organ, Prophet 5 and so on. Ambient musicians began to return to the analogue synthesizers of old to both soften and beef up their hypnotic creations. Some spoke of building virtual synthesizers in a computer's memory and playing them in virtual time. In Hertfordshire, England, Martin Newcomb opened a Museum of Synthesizer Technology – a veritable shrine to a century of synthesis. What's interesting about this history is how the piano keyboard has remained an icon of musicality. Through its various mutations through organs, electric keyboards, synthesizer and now, as a veritable computer-control device, the piano keyboard has always acted as an umbilical root to the sources of music. Whatever its future the fact was that the piano keyboard became inextricably linked with synthesizer and computer technology over a century, altering the course of electronic and Ambient music for ever.

COMPACT DISC

The arrival in the early 1980s of Compact Disc Digital Audio, or CD as it quickly became known, opened up a whole new world of sound for the consumer. On a silver disc of just over four and a half inches in diameter could be encoded whole symphonies and concept albums. The sound was high-fidelity and the days of turning over a vinyl album to hear the rest of the music were over. Moreover it was always of the same high quality as there was no contact between the laser player picking up the digitized information and the spinning disc. Also, random accessing and programming of tracks and automatic repeat play were at last in the hands of the consumer. On vinyl records music had to be listened to in sequence or one track picked at a time. A CD could be played in any track order and indeed it could be looked at as a single, an EP, or a complete album. The results of the strides in studio technology could now be heard in all their glory. Sound fidelity, once the preserve of hi-fi buffs willing to pay for expensive turntables, was now within reach of everyone. And above all CDs were virtually indestructible. By the early 1990s one billion were being sold worldwide per year, and by the middle of the decade two and a half billion. Having displaced vinyl as the leading consumer music carrier, CD became the perfect medium for the long aural dreams that comprised end-of-the-century Ambient music.

Developed by the Dutch electronics giant Philips over a period of fifteen years, CD was unveiled at the 1980 Salzburg Festival by the famous conductor Herbert von Karajan, who famously declared: 'All else is gaslight.' Compared to the vinyl record, the technological investment was high. Each disc is made of optical-grade clear polycarbonate with an aluminium reflective coating. This is encoded with over 6,000 million 'pits' of digital information. If a pit were the size of a grain of rice then a CD would have to be as big as any of the world's large football stadiums. But, at about one seventy-fifth of the width of a human hair, they are microscopic and their huge number capable of holding a vast amount of information. The whole is sealed in a clear lacquer for protection.

Philips developed CD jointly with Sony Japan, who by 1982 had readied the requisite laser technology for playing it. The initial market for the medium was seen to be classical music enthusiasts who were fed up with cycles of symphonies and such being spread over boxed sets of vinyl records. In 1983 CD was given its real marketing boost by Polygram (eighty per cent owned by Philips), who launched 300 recordings, mostly classical. Sony and Philips boasted of 'perfect sound for ever' in their marketing. Though players were initially expensive, economies of scale brought prices down so that between 1986 and 1995 worldwide sales increased by 65 million units.

Yet there were latent fears. As early as 1988 various scientific articles began to appear disputing the claim by Sony and Philips that CDs could last for ever. One leading manufacturer, Nimbus, did admit that if air got into a CD when it was being produced the aluminium coating could deteriorate. Certain inks used on the top side of the disc were also causing distortion. Though the mastering process was 100 times cleaner than in a hospital operating theatre, if one spec of dust got into the CD master at the crucial assembly stage then all was lost. Millions of pounds were spent on testing this process and leading manufacturers such as Nimbus, Warner Brothers and Philips had much improved what became known as the Red Book Standard. By 1989 CD had overtaken vinyl as the sound carrier of choice in the marketplace. Three years later Philips declared that CDs could last at least 1,000 years! It was certainly true that, while they could be scratched, they were far more robust than vinyl records and faults were reduced to as little as point one per cent.

The concept of sound waveforms being sampled, converted into numbers and then played back through a machine which could convert these same numbers into analogue sound would tease the music industry for the latter part of the century. Old tape-derived recordings began to be digitally remastered in the late 1980s for fidelity's sake. Then the boxed set arrived in 1990, ushered in by Jimmy Page of Led Zeppelin, who wished to restore his back-catalogue. This led to a rush of similar ventures and the unearthing of hundreds of thousands of old recordings. Instead of killing off old music, as some feared, CD meant even more music. Anything recorded on tape was ripe for remastering and repackaging on to the new format. There was just more music around for everybody. And more music around in digital form for Ambient House musicians, with their need to fill up long, long mixes, to sample.

Initial problems of harsh digital sound were evened out by better and better disc players. In response to DAT and its consumer outcrop Digital Compact Cassette (DCC), Sony launched a Mini-Disc system in late 1992. This was a two-and-a-half-inch disc housed in a case which looked like a small floppy disc. It had seventy-five per cent of the quality of CD as a result of using a system of sound compression to squeeze seventy-five minutes of music on to its tiny surface. Amazingly, it was recordable, erasable and had an anti-skipping device for portability. Hugh Padgham, the producer of Sting and Phil Collins, declared that 'tapeless technology was the future' and endorsed it straight away. The arrival of MP3 in the US in 1999 seemed to bear out this prediction. A tapeless, indeed discless, innovation, this tiny box could, via a computer, download music from the Internet. Yet this futuristic wonder had drawbacks – loss of fidelity due to extreme compression into digital form and a lengthy download time of about five and a half hours for an album.

By the late 1990s CD had lodged itself in human consciousness in a very real way. CD-Rom releases, kick-started by the English rock star Peter Gabriel in 1994, were increasing in popularity. Here music, graphics, text, images and data could all be loaded into a personal computer from the disc. There was CD-I, interactive CD which gave the consumer many more choices about what was heard and how it was heard. Even though the recording industry had been clever enough to encode commercially available CDs with a system to prevent digital copies being made, this did not stop an increasing call for normal CDs to become recordable. In 1996 the first recordable-CD players were made available to the public. Talk of a multi-purpose four-and-a-half-inch disc which could store everything – music, film and computer data – and output it all through a single multi-media device was soon to become reality in the form of Digital Video Disc, or DVD.

BOOK TWO

MINIMALISM, ENO
AND THE NEW SIMPLICITY

DURING THE EARLY 1970s the full impact of Minimalism could be heard around the globe. For in that year two concept albums were released into mainstream consciousness. They topped the charts everywhere and sold in the millions. One helped shape the evolution of rock, one helped start a legendary record company. Today those recordings are still selling. The first was *Dark Side Of The Moon* by the English group Pink Floyd. This concept album was charged by a form of repetition, and in places the chugging of synthesizers bore an uncanny resemblance to the music of the American Minimalist Philip Glass. The second, released only months later in the summer of 1973, was *Tubular Bells*. This was an instrumental suite, conceived and played entirely by one English musician – the twenty-year-old Mike Oldfield. Its interlocking series of notes, repeated throughout the first part of the composition, was originally blueprinted by another American writer of Minimalist music, Steve Reich. The album was so popular it financed the running and prosperity of Virgin Records, a label committed to innovative rock. Minimalist music would go on to influence the mainstream in the late 1970s through the work of David Bowie and in the late 1980s via the sound of Ireland's U2.

But what was Minimalism? And why was it so important? In May 1969 Steve Reich gave a concert of what he described as his 'pulse music' in the Whitney Museum in New York City. He supplied to the audience an essay he had written the previous year titled 'Music As A Gradual Process'. In it could be discerned the bedrock of all Minimalist music. He talked of the 'musical process' as one that determines itself, that 'happens extremely gradually' and that 'facilitates closely detailed listening'. Reich expanded on the theme, noting that the music had a meditative quality, the kind of sounds perceived almost by chance. This allusion to John Cage was made more explicit when he admitted that 'musical processes' had a degree of 'indeterminacy' and that 'once the process is set up and loaded it runs by itself'. Then he drew a line between himself and Cage in that his music and the process behind it were one and the same thing. Therefore the very act of creating a piece of Minimalist music was the music itself! For the listener Reich felt that this music could always sound different, that 'there were still enough mysteries to satisfy all'. He compared listening to Minimalist music to 'watching the minute hand of a watch – you can perceive it moving only after you observe it for a while'. He also compared the experience to listening to the modal folk and ethnic musics popular in the late 1960s and the music of India and electronic music, which used a 'constant key centre' of hypnotic drones and repetition. But the difference here for Reich was that Minimalism wasn't a form 'for improvisation', because the very process determined 'the note details and the form simultaneously'. In the end he aligned Minimalist music with meditation, its ritualistic sense shifting music away from the subjective attention of the listener to an objective appreciation of its very existence.

These ideas were revolutionary, not only for composers looking for a way forward from Schoenberg and Serialism, but also for musicians in other genres and even twentieth-century philosophers. Minimalism's importance was that it offered a new direction, a tangible framework in which twentieth-century music could progress. To understand Minimalism one has to understand how important Schoenberg and his followers had become by the 1950s. The academic world had adopted Serialism as the new ethos and many young musicians and composers simply did not agree. The times were changing and social and political forces were pushing music in another direction. Steve Reich felt that academic music was 'nutty', that the work of 'Schoenberg and Boulez had no rhythm nor melodic organization' and was 'unappealing'. Philip Glass saw it as 'a one-way-ticket – to nowhere. A cul-de- sac'. John Adams shared Glass's despondency in having to study Webern and similar composers; for him it was 'an unhappy time'. Harold Budd spoke of 'getting a heavy-dose of European avant-garde music which I never really cottoned on to'. Jon Hassell and Terry Riley both decided that Serial music 'was a perfect model for twentieth-century problems and the fact that it originated in Vienna at the time of Freud was no mere coincidence'. In fact Riley saw Serial music as truly 'neurotic'. Yet it was one of the ironies of the twentieth century that without something so rigid and formalized as the music of the Second Viennese School, a new form like Minimalism would have had nothing to bounce off.

If traditional Serialism was unappetizing, then the work of John Cage and Stockhausen was more palatable. In fact La Monte Young admired Webern and travelled to Darmstadt to work with Stockhausen in the 1950s. His time there opened up his mind to the idea of the 'single sound'. Back in the US, he said: 'We must let sounds be what they are.' Young was also influenced by John Cage, as were Harold Budd, John Adams and Brian Eno. In a way every person who touched music during the 1960s and 70s was affected by Cage's take on the significance of 'silence'. His writings and ideas crop up again and again as we unfold Minimalism's history. Another influence was the open jazz music performed by John Coltrane and Miles Davis. All the major American Minimalists – Young, Riley, Reich, Glass, Adams – were impressed with post be-bop jazz, particularly the lengthy explorations of John Coltrane. All had first-hand experience of Coltrane and Miles Davis playing live and saw in their extended, often modal, compositions a new way of creating music.

Then, of course, there were the times. According to Jon Hassell: 'The history of drugs in America is inextricably interlaced with early Minimalism. There was a need for a music that one could actually enjoy listening to and that you could float away to.' Finally there was the very social nature of the music. No movement has had so much interaction and cross-pollination from all the main parties. Terry Riley, La Monte Young and Pauline Oliveros all studied together at Berkeley. Jon Hassell performed and recorded with both Young and Riley. Steve Reich performed in Riley's ground-breaking concert performance of *In C* in San Francisco in 1964. He also attended the Juilliard School of Music in New York with Philip Glass. In the late 1960s both Reich and Glass formed an ensemble. Michael Nyman played for a time in Steve Reich's group and also recorded with Brian Eno. John Adams conducted Steve Reich, who was a strong influence on Eno, as had been Philip Glass, whom Eno had seen in concert in 1970. Eno also recorded and produced Harold Budd, John Adams and Jon Hassell. In 1989 Eno produced a new version of *In C* with Terry Riley and Jon Hassell. In the 1990s Philip Glass produced new symphonic versions of albums Eno had recorded with David Bowie in the 1970s. And so on.

But what's most intriguing about Minimalism is the way the very music is a product of individual experience and invention. Each figure, in his very own way, contributed, mosaic-like, to the overall pattern. It's only when we look at each individual in depth that we can grasp the broader picture. A problem with so much work done up to now on Minimalism is that, with exceptions, the area has been rushed over in an attempt to get somewhere else, presumably more interesting. La Monte Young zigzagged his way from Midwestern isolation, through jazz, Stockhausen and Cage, into the Fluxus movement in New York. Then, inspired by Indian music, he formed The Dream Syndicate for what was to become 'a benchmark experiment in drones and tuning'. Terry Riley was inspired by jazz, the psychedelic drug mescaline, Moroccan travels and working in the Paris studio of Pierre Schaeffer and Pierre Henry, to come up with his 'time-lag accumulator', a way of making sheets of sound using two tape machines and keyboards. Steve Reich also worked with tape recorders to invent his 'phase music' and by travelling to Africa and the Middle East arrived at an interlocking music of rich complexity. Philip Glass found his way via Ravi Shankar, the idea of cyclical motion in music enhanced through his travels in North Africa and Asia. John Adams came to Minimalism by working with electronics and synthesizers at the San Francisco Conservatory during the 1970s.

It was down to Brian Eno to synthesize the work of the primary Minimalist composers and bring it into the mainstream. He had seen Philip Glass perform and was impressed by the music's form. He had heard Steve Reich and found fascinating the accidental beauty which came out of Reich's tape-loop experiments. He was intrigued by Riley's use of tape delay and was generally enamoured of La Monte Young, whose music he performed when he was at art college. He fused all this with the philosophy of John Cage and in 1975 invented Ambient music – music that would take on the hues of environment 'just as the colour of the light and the sound of the rain'. He was intrigued with the idea of 'automatic music' and took Reich's aforementioned 'music as a gradual process' to heart. All of Eno's Ambient music was a variation on the theme of the process 'running by itself'. On records and in installations, throughout the 1970s, 80s and 90s Eno allowed several lengths of tape or various pre-recorded discs to run out of synch with each other. The results were unpredictable, but his taste in 'loading' the system always ensured beautiful outcomes. His work highlighted how Minimalism fused strong new ideas with changes in technology to maximum effect.

New Age music is a general fallout from Minimalism and Ambient. Much derided, the movement threw up genuine talent and some fascinating labels like Windham Hill. Though most of the product was essentially facsimile music, its very popularity was denoted by Eno as exemplifying how people's listening habits had changed. It wasn't all 'blurring noises mixed with pretty sounds'. At its worst it could sound like this, as in the prodigious output of Japanese mystic keyboard player Kitaro. The better-quality material, like the music of William Ackerman or Mark Isham, had its roots both in Minimalism and the Cool jazz of John Coltrane and Miles Davis. New Age coincided with a vast increase in disposable income in the West and the change from records to CDs in the consumer market. Dozens of labels proliferated, most offering pleasing instrumental bubble to calm the nerves of anxious young upwardly mobile professional people, or Yuppies as they became known in the 1980s. Some of these labels, like Virgin Venture in the UK, used the niche opened up by New Age to market quality Minimalist music. Hence Michael Nyman scored his biggest successes when his soundtrack music from the films of Peter Greenaway and Jane Campion was released by Virgin Venture.

The aesthetic of Minimalism was nowhere better perceived than in the development of the German label ECM. Founded in 1970 by musician Manfred Eicher, ECM aimed to capture 'the most beautiful sound next to silence'. In the studio gifted musicians were recorded with all the resonance and Ambience possible, adding a texture and tonality that was new to jazz, Eicher's initial interest. The music of wunderkind Keith Jarrett went far beyond simple jazz, his strong melodic fusion of styles subservient to the rich tone of his Bosendorfer piano. Captured on record at Jarrett's unforgettable concert in Cologne in 1975, the audience's applause is made to feel part of the whole listening experience. With its sleek white cover, *The Köln Concert* was Minimalism and Ambience spliced together in a package of sleek sophistication. In retrospect it seems logical that Eicher should be the first to embrace the 'New Simplicity', a term applied to a new wave of spiritual Minimalist music emanating from the former Soviet bloc in the last part of the twentieth century.

On hearing the music of the Estonian composer Arvo Pärt on the radio in the early 1980s, Eicher pronounced that it was the beginning of a new direction for him. He was impressed by the music's 'clarity – the direct path to ear and mind'. He felt that here was 'a music of innermost calm', a 'music of slowly beating wings'. For him this music was still, sensitive to time, with tones that created their own light. Progressing via film music, John Cage, Erik Satie and especially Steve Reich, Pärt had rejected all he was taught. He looked to the music of the medieval church, the use of bells in the Orthodox Church and to silence. He wrote his music of 'time and timelessness' where a single bell marked time and strings scaled an emotional peak and receded into silence; and then promptly fled the country. Later he was to say: 'I am alone with Silence. I have discovered that it is enough when a single note is beautifully played. Silence comforts me.'

The music of Henryk Gorecki was also to capture the public imagination in the 1990s. Having studied Webern and Debussy, Gorecki looked to other sources of inspiration in his native Poland. He found it in nature, Polish prayer and the folk melodies of the fifteenth century. Full of melancholy for the destruction suffered by his country during and after the Second World War, Gorecki used the death of a Holocaust victim to fuel the writing of his *Symphony No. 3*, a luminously deep rendering of Minimalism in which instruments climb a tortuous aural stairway to an angelic vocal.

The English composer John Tavener saw simplicity, silence and repetition as absolute necessities. Through electronics and the music of Messiaen, he sought a unity of sound. He looked to the Orthodox Church and found in its ritualistic, monophonic music an 'intensity' which was also ascribed to early Minimalism. He incorporated all these elements into making what he termed 'lyrical ikons in sound'. His music became so popular that it now stands for a kind of quiet passion. The use of his elegiac *Song For Athene* at the funeral of Diana, Princess of Wales in 1997 confirmed that Minimalism had passed into the everyday lives of ordinary people.

LA MONTE YOUNG

Though the work of La Monte Young stands as a cornerstone of all Minimalist and Ambient music, you would never guess this from the amount of recordings available in his name. Only a handful have ever made it to the marketplace and none has even grazed the charts. Yet his work in the area of pure sound, the sustaining of chords and tones over very long time cycles and his deep developments in the area of tuning spawned American Minimalist music in the 1960s and early 70s. Within Young's work we can observe elements of Debussy, Satie, Webern, Ives, Messiaen and Grainger, but above all John Cage and Stockhausen. By reducing music to the elements of single sounds and multiplying its effect through repetition, Young templated not only Minimalism but also the concept of Ambient rock via his work with the prototype Velvet Underground. Through his lifelong development of the piano work *The Well-Tuned Piano*, Young created, particularly during the 1970s and 80s, the idea of a continuous sound and light environment that would last not only hours but years at a time. This fed directly into the work of Brian Eno and would leave a sustained impression on Ambient club spaces of the late twentieth century.

La Monte Young was born in desolate Bern, Idaho, in 1935. Roughly about the size of the UK and with a population of only a million today, then it was isolation personified. Young is often quoted as remembering his first musical experience as that of wind whistling through the family log cabin by the Bear river. Raised in a Mormon farming community, he started on guitar at four, sang hymns and played the piano. Owing to the effects of the depression, Young's father took temporary employ at an oil plant, where La Monte was impressed with the humming sounds of transformers. In the early 1940s the large family moved to Los Angeles and, though poor, put whatever spare money they had into purchasing La Monte a saxophone. When they moved to another farm in Utah, Young would spend four years developing his technique, taught largely by an uncle steeped in Kansas City jazz. That and the Ambient natural sounds of the forests and lakes would form his early musical mind.

After another move, this time back to LA, Young was living near a trainyard, another potent sound inspiration. At high school he was passionate about be-bop, the sound of the late 1940s spearheaded by Charlie Parker and Dizzy Gillespie. He played in dance bands for money and learned all he could about harmony from his music teacher, Clyde Sorenson, who had been taught by Schoenberg. By the early 1950s Young was addicted to the jazz lifestyle and eventually ran away from home and played the bohemian. Such was the standard of his sax playing that he was taken on by the prestigious LA City College dance band alongside such jazz supremos as Don Cherry. During his three-year stay at the college Young was inspired by Leonard Stein (another Schoenberg disciple) to get into Anton Webern's world of limpid and silence. Young's first major piece, *Five Small Pieces For String Quartet* (1956), was written in homage to Webern.

Young attended LA State College for a year before landing on his feet at UCLA, where he was exposed to much Japanese and Indonesian music; an album of Indian ragas by Ali Akbar Khan was also influential. Having got his Batchelor's degree, Young entered Berkeley to do graduate studies. In the summer of his graduation year, 1958, he wrote *Trio For Strings*, considered to be the benchmark Minimalist piece and an historic moment in the development of music. Instead of polyphonic character and movement, one heard silences and sound that seemed to hover without melodic or rhythmic development. Like Debussy, Young had been deeply affected by Eastern music. His teachers were not amused, but two pupils in his class, Terry Riley and Pauline Oliveros, were impressed.

During the summer of 1959 Young made a pilgrimage to Darmstadt to hear Stockhausen talk of the importance of single sounds and the music of John Cage. There he met David Tudor, the pianist most associated with Cage's music. On his return to Berkeley he became a teaching assistant and staged a series of incendiary avant-garde performances. Audiences were asked to look at each other, witness butterflies hovering around a theatre, look at a fire crackling on stage and, in one of his most famous pieces, *Piano Piece No. 1 For David Tudor* (1960), watch a piano consume a bale of hay and a bucket of water. Another piece from 1960, *X For Henry Flynt*, required the performer to slam his or her arm down on a cluster of piano notes for a long time. Different from the work of Cage and Stockhausen, Young's was a rarification of sound down to its absolute minimum. It's not surprising that Brian Eno was inspired by *X For Henry Flynt* while at art college.

This piece would become a vital ingredient of Young's aesthetic when he moved to Greenwich Village in late 1960. Ostensibly Young had been sent to New York by Berkeley to study electronic music at the New School for Social Research, but the reality was that the famous Californian campus was tired of his antics. Young soon fell in with the Downtown art and music crowd spearheaded by Yoko Ono and George Maciunas, a group of radical artists who would be historically known as Fluxus. Early Young concerts in Yoko Ono's Lower Manhattan loft attracted the artists Robert Rauschenberg and Marcel Duchamp, plus composers John Cage and Morton Feldman, all fascinated by what Young described as the 'Theatre Of The Singular Event'. La Monte Young had arrived.

In 1962 Young wrote two pieces, *The Four Dreams Of China* and *The Second Dream Of The High Tension Line Stepdown Transformer*, where actual pitches of individual notes would be held on instruments, and sometimes frequency generators, for long periods of time. To a casual listener these pieces seemed like simple experiments in linear sound but they would lead to Young's radical invention of 'just intonation', of which more later.

In 1963 Young met and married the calligraphic artist Marian Zazeela, who was also interested in refining form over long periods of time. Her speciality was light art and the pair moved into a large loft space in what is today Tribeca. Here Young practised hard on sopranino saxophone and delved deeper into drones and tunings. In 1963 he also formed what would be one of the most significant groups of all time, The Theatre Of Eternal Music, better known as The Dream Syndicate.

Over from London on a music scholarship, the Welshman John Cale was attracted both to Young and John Cage. By joining The Dream Syndicate, Cale opened the door for The Velvet Underground, which contained in its earliest incarnation Dream Syndicate members Tony Conrad and Angus MacLise. For eighteen months in 1963 and 1964, this group of people would gather in Young's loft every day, seven days a week, and rehearse for hours. Young played intense frenetic saxophone solos over very defined drones held by Marian Zazeela's voice, John Cale's viola and Tony Conrad's violin or bowed guitar. MacLise played Indian tablas. Problems with tuning led to Young just holding vocal notes. Though most of the original master tapes are held in a nuclear bunker in upstate New York, Young has played copies on American radio stations. The pieces *Early Tuesday Morning Blues*, *B Flat Dorian Blues*,

Sunday Morning Blues and *Fire Is Emir* are suffused with an incredibly strong sense of the Orient and reveal Young to be an outstanding sax player. Basically this music has the quality of raga but arrived at by a completely different route – by using just intonation. The result is a series of clouds of sound.

John Cale once told me: 'We achieved something that was culturally pivotal. We encouraged each other to pursue this experimental research into the structural fundamentals of music, both harmonically and intellectually. I wanted to make my mark with the electric viola [restrung with mandolin and guitar strings], so I filed the bridge down and played it with a bass bow. The Dream Syndicate ended up being two amplified voices, a violin and a viola. The strings were the predominant overwhelming force in the music. It still is a benchmark experiment in drones and tuning.'

In 1964 Young conceived his masterpiece, *The Well-Tuned Piano*, described by the *New York Times* as a 'music of spell-binding moods that seeks to produce an immediate deeply-felt sensation'. An astonishing piano tour de force which lasts anything up to five and a half hours, it has been the bedrock of Young's work ever since. In this work, the best example of the power of just intonation, both the soft, silent passages and occasional sprays of notes conjure up a wholly different world. Young's grasp of just intonation has precedents in the use of Eastern modes by Debussy, Satie and Messiaen. He even titled one half-hour section of *The Well-Tuned Piano* 'Hommage à Debussy'. Derived from Pythagoras's work in ancient Greece, just intonation sets out a whole series of notes that go far beyond the Western eight-note octave. Tuning according to the harmonics and overtones contained in every note releases dozens of unheard frequencies which when played produces a shimmering mystical music. Tuning is difficult and has to be limited to a fundamental frequency or else too many notes would have to be catered for. La Monte Young would spend the next seventeen years refining his tunings for his debut recording of *The Well-Tuned Piano*.

Fond of his pet tortoise 49, Young wrote a whole series of pieces in 1964 based on the frequency of its aquarium motor. Ever the anarchist, he gave these drones hilariously long titles, such as: *The blue sawtooth high-tension line stepdown transformer refracting the legend of the dream of the tortoise traversing the 189/98 lost ancestral lake region illuminating quotients for the black tiger tapestries of the drone of the holy numbers*. Most of this would be absorbed into the drone study *The Tortoise, His Dreams And Journeys*, an ever-developing piece.

Marian Zazeela was fast evolving her visual aesthetic alongside Young's. In their Manhattan loft the pair conceived the Dream House, a continuous environment consisting of Young's drones and Zazeela's light creations where precisely coloured calligraphic designs would be used for projections. Their first major collaboration was 1966's *Map of 49's Dream the two systems of eleven sets of galactic intervals Ornamental Lightyear's Tracery*, which lasted for hours. In concert the aim of the concept was to see how periodic soundwaves and synchronized light art affected audiences. In many ways Young and Zazeela were pioneers of the psychedelic light show.

Young conducted many experiments in sine waves in 1967, the most noteworthy being *Drift Studies*. That year he even created some very loud music for films by Andy Warhol. In 1968 Young and his wife unsuccessfully tried to persuade CBS to record them singing at the sea. Most important for Young was his live group The Theatre Of Eternal Music, since John Cale's departure a fluid aggregation in which biofeedback musician David Rosenboom, minimalists Terry Riley and Jon Gibson plus the experimental trumpeter Jon Hassell played as guests. By 1970 it would also include the singer Pandit Pran Nath, a North Indian guru whose precise intonation greatly impressed Young. That year Young and Zazeela became disciples of Nath and his kiranic form of singing, which was in just intonation. This area would become a lifelong study for the composer.

If people at MIT and neurosurgeons were heavily impressed by La Monte Young's studies in tuning, audiences were intrigued by The Theatre Of Eternal Music. Throughout Europe and America, in galleries and spaces during the late 1960s and early 70s, the ensemble created Sound And Light Environments. Both Young and Zazeela were bankrolled by Heiner Friedrich from money earned in oil. Friedrich and his wife were enthusiastic about art, particularly that of Joseph Beuys and Donald Judd. Impressed by Zazeela's unique light art and Young's commitment to sound environments, the Friedrichs created the Dia Art Foundation. Dia Art ran a fifty-seven-day performance of the Dream House in 1975 and following its success invited Young and Zazeela to find a venue which would house performance space, a gallery, a recording studio, an archive, offices and so on.

After finding the old Mercantile Exchange in Harrison Street and then spending years converting it, Young and Zazeela opened the Dream House in 1979. Pandit Pran Nath gave masterclasses while different rooms housed exhibitions and installations of sound and light. The main space was the old trading floor, which featured Young's enormous Bosendorfer Imperial Grand Piano. This instrument had to be previously tuned in Vienna but was now *in situ* permanently and in a constant state of retuning as Young expanded his work on *The Well-Tuned Piano*. Humidity and temperature were constantly monitored. Up to October 1981 the Dia Art Foundation had funded over forty live performances and forty-five recording sessions of the piece before Young was satisfied. The recording in that month of *The Well-Tuned Piano* was Young's greatest achievement. The setting, in the mystical environment of Zazeela's *Magenta Lights*, where magenta and blue light refracted off aluminium mobiles, complemented the music perfectly. Terry Riley stated: 'This is holy work.'

By 1985 La Monte Young was considered by the *Los Angeles Herald Examiner* to be 'the most influential U.S. composer of the last quarter century'. Though Dia Art suffered badly because of the Texas oil crash of that year, Young's influence has since been unassailable. Having moved to a Church Street loft, he has continued to refine his work using synthesizers and computers. His hermetic existence and indifference to the marketplace has helped to magnify his influence. Both he and Zazeela established the MELA Foundation to preserve and extend their archives and during the 1990s Young worked in the area of blues and orchestral score. By being the first to concentrate on extended duration, a minimum of notes or frequencies and the effect on the listener, Young not only changed the art of composition but also the art of performance in all musics.

LISTENING

For years it was almost impossible to hear anything by La Monte Young. There was a Theatre Of Eternal Music recording titled *Dream House* on the French label Shandar from 1973 which featured Jon Hassell on trumpet. There was even a recording with Pandit Pran Nath on *Ragas Of The Morning And Night* (Gramavision). At present four recordings are available. *The Second Dream Of The High Tension Line Stepdown Transformer* (Gramavision 1992) consists of four pitches held on brass instruments derived from childhood memories of overhead cables in the wind. It is a section of his 1962 work *The Four Dreams Of China*. Another work, *Just Stompin'* (Gramavision 1993), is credited to The Forever Bad Blues Band – a misfired attempt to incorporate Young's blues synthesizer playing into the context of a bar-room blues sound. Miraculously the beginning of the twenty-first century saw the release of *Inside The Dream Syndicate Vol. 1 – Day Of Niagara* (1965) on the Table of Elements label; a recording made in Young's New York loft which communicates all the amplified dronal power of the original Theatre Of Eternal Music. The definitive Young album is the five-disc version of the ten-record set *The Well-Tuned Piano* (Gramavision 1994). Originally released in 1987, this is one of the greatest piano works of all time. Recorded using microphones very close to the piano strings, it reaches what Young calls 'the highest levels of spontaneous musical inspiration'. As you listen to clusters of tones, droplets of notes, you can hear the shimmer of Debussy, the rhythm of jazz and blues, the sway of Hindustani classicism, the spatial features of Japanese and Indonesian musics. This work is so special that at each listening it sounds different, peeling back to reveal new layers of meaning and emotion. Here you will find a perfect marriage of his just-intonation tuning and his calligraphic music. Young describes the resultant music as 'tones suspended in the air, as if emanating from the universal source of the eternal sound'.

TERRY RILEY

The incessant pulse of Terry Riley's masterly *In C* of 1964 would push Minimalism out of academia and into the commercial limelight. Riley was the first of the Minimalist and Ambient composers to grasp the importance of commercial records and by exploiting this medium he made himself more famous than his contemporaries. While the release in 1969 of *A Rainbow In Curved Air*, his milestone studio recording of 'spatially separated mirror images', applied pure musical theory to technology, its effect on rock culture (Soft Machine, Curved Air, The Who) was immediate. Moreover Riley's grasp of concert improvisation (derived from the work of John Coltrane and Miles Davis) was hugely popular during the first psychedelic era and that, plus his recorded output, has sifted down to greatly influence modern music both in its use of repetition and style of performance.

Born in the railroad town of Colfax, California, in 1935, Riley could play violin and piano by the age of six. While his father worked on the railways Riley got most of his musical input from the radio and, like La Monte Young, was greatly impressed by be-bop jazz. At high school he extended himself to learn brass instruments and became familiar with Debussy and Stravinsky. Through a combination of fate and timing Riley would be caught up in a series of experiences which would directly shape his music.

After practising piano for two years he entered San Francisco State University in 1955 and abandoned the idea of being a virtuoso pianist. Instead he opted for composition and studied carefully the work of Schoenberg and Thelonius Monk. By 1957 he was married and a father and had to work in an airport and play stride piano at the Gold Street Saloon to boost his finances. He also attended the San Francisco Music Conservatoire. But his big move came when, as a Master's degree student at Berkeley, he met La Monte Young. After hearing *Trio For Strings* Riley felt he had been 'initiated'. Like Young, he was inspired by Stockhausen and Cage but worked towards a new music with the likes of Pauline Oliveros. Working for dance companies, he made several sound collages for tape. When he left Berkeley with an MA in 1961 he invented a piece based on his experiences with the natural psychedelic drug mescaline, using two tape recorders and long tape loops. In 1962 Riley took his family to visit Young in New York and then sailed to Europe to seek inspiration.

Still struck by the work of Coltrane, Miles Davis and Charlie Mingus, he landed in Spain and worked his way across Europe as a pianist, often playing for US Army bases, sometimes supporting variety and circus acts. Struck by Arabic music, he made two extensive trips to Morocco. In Paris he worked with Daevid Allen (the Australian founder of the soon-to-be-famous psychedelic band Soft Machine) and with trumpeter Chet Baker on a soundtrack titled *The Gift* for the Theatre Of Nations. In the studio of Radio France (where Schaeffer and Henry had made such giant strides with *musique concrète*) Riley invented his 'time-lag accumulator' a simple tape-delay system which could repeat the patterns of Baker's trumpet layer upon layer using two tape recorders.

Riley remembers that 'this was a forerunner of *In C* because it was a piece built out of patterns'. Returning to New York in 1964, Riley was impressed by The Theatre Of Eternal Music and Young's experiments with retuning instruments. Yet Riley followed his own path to San Francisco and wrote *In C* – a piece made out of fifty-three different musical cells which the performer had to work through. Repetition of cells was encouraged until boredom set in. The piece started on tape recorders but developed into a pulse piece for ensemble which ignored the traditional falls and swells of classical music or a need for thematic development. In fact everything was in the key of C. Performed in late 1964 at the San Francisco Tape Center with future Minimalists Steve Reich and Jon Hassell in the ensemble, *In C* not only broke ground in 'serious music' but showed how much New Music and psychedelia had in common. The piece came with coloured lights and an up beat. There was joy in repetition. Riley reflects: 'People like Morton Subotnick played. San Franciscan poets like Michael McClure came. There was a very positive response. It was just before the psychedelic era and all these people were looking for new kinds of poetry and music.'

By 1968 *In C* would be on a Columbia record with the original 1964 review from the *San Francisco Chronicle* on the cover. In the spirit of the times this read: 'you have never done anything in your life but listen to this music as if that is all there is or ever will be . . .' Clearly Riley had caused a revolution. Yet in 1965 he moved back to New York and joined The Theatre Of Eternal Music in pursuit of ever more exotic drones. Fatigued by all-day rehearsals, Riley branched out in 1966 and wrote a saxophone piece, *Poppy Nogood And His Phantom Band*. When performing live he would sit cross-legged on a carpet and improvise his sax lines over the dynamic result of two interlocking tape recorders. Today *Poppy Nogood* sounds wholly Indian in its inspiration. Riley recalls: 'By using tape delay I could have a rhythmic structure to play against. The concerts I did in the 1960s used this and tape feedback. Tape was always part of the process and structure of the music. I had a Super Vox Continental electronic organ and the tape recorders with feedback loops in place. Some people from Columbia Masterworks came to see me play at Steinway Hall in New York. After that David Behrman, a well-known producer at Columbia, asked me to record *A Rainbow In Curved Air* – and then things really started happening.'

Even the title of *A Rainbow In Curved Air*, written in 1968 and released on record to universal acclaim in 1969, is apposite, for it plugged right into a music culture rich in social and ideological change. For Riley, it was 'the first music I knew of which used tape delay as a structural element'. Performing on new eight-track tape equipment, he played electric organ, electric harpsichord, dumbec, rocksichord, tambourine and soprano sax. The sound was a glittering array of sequences pushed along by a bubbling electronic pulse. The sheer dexterity and force of attack of Riley's keyboard motifs was astonishing. The sound was electronic, Minimalist but fulsomely optimistic, modern with a strong tinge of classical beauty. Moreover the thematic ideas of old were abandoned for a music of pure sound – a sound so beautiful that time and space seemed to change all around it. Another notable piece to surface from this period was *The Hall Of Mirrors In The Palace Of Versailles*, recorded with John Cale during the *Rainbow* sessions.

As American academics have noted, Riley had introduced 'elements of performer choice, improvisation and chance' into electronic music. But his was a music Technicoloured and amplified by the psychedelic context. Performances of *Rainbow* at the Electric Circus in New York drew many plaudits, most notably from a young Philip Glass, who was dazzled by the sheer energy and volume of Riley's performance. Yet Riley was more interested in Indian music and returned to California to study it. He acknowledges that at the moment of great commercial success he opted for a different path: 'I found that my work was pointing towards the kind of music that was happening in India, North Africa and the Middle East. Even though it had many differences it shared many things, so a study of Indian classical music would be a very valuable thing for me to do – a deep serious study of how the music actually worked.'

Riley's path led him to northern India and the village of Dehra Dun. There in 1970, in the company of La Monte Young, Marian Zazeela and trumpeter Jon Hassell, Riley studied under the kiranic singer Pandit Pran Nath, a guru and 'one of the greatest teachers in India'. Several trips were made, meditational lessons starting before sunrise in the hills, the voice being the main instrument. Lifestyle was as important as practice and the general philosophy of the yogi prevailed. Riley ended up teaching Indian raga at Mills College in Oakland, California until 1980. He specialized in all areas, tabla percussion, vocal dynamics, notation and tuning. The last would influence all his successive music.

Riley's next big piece, *Persian Surgery Dervishes*, was developed over lengthy concert performances in 1971–2. Though the piece is at first seemingly static, the relationship between the repeated organ figures using a cluster of five notes, the repeating organ bass on the tape loop and various processing effects on Riley's own mixer build to an intoxicating sound. At the time one critic wrote: 'opening the Western sensitivity to the fascination of sound figures which are repeated at regular intervals over long periods of time, Terry Riley has created an original music based on the principle of evolutive reiteration – a music which regenerates infinitely in multiple shades.' Another reason for its success was just intonation.

Riley states this clearly: 'All my work from *Persian Surgery Dervishes* on is in "just intonation". All the intervals in this tuning are based on mathematical proportions and these proportions create resonances, which are sounds that are not in the piano instrument when it's tuned in equal temperament. It is used a lot in Eastern music, Indian music, African music, Middle Eastern music and a lot of folk music. They play it naturally. My biggest influence was La Monte Young, even though Californian Harry Partch was the first to use "just intonation" and build his own instruments in the 1930s. He used long tones and when I heard them I realized what its potential was like in Western music. La Monte was the first person to make it clear to me.'

Riley's music had always been described in grandiose terms. A Columbia puff for *Rainbow* had trumpeted that it sounded like 'rock and raga, fugue and fever, basic blues and synthesizer Bach'. The sleeve note to *Persian Surgery Dervishes* talks of a 'music where classical and non-classical elements fuse in the stimulating and lively land of improvisation'. Just intonation went hand in hand with this love of composerly improvisation. By adding resistors to a Yamaha organ, Riley was able to retune it. The output was split in two, one recorded and put into time-delay after the other. The result was *Descending Moonshine Dervishes* (1975), another Riley classic, in which sprinkled high keyboard notes had the quality of Eastern chimes.

After this European phase, as *Descending* was recorded in Berlin and some soundtracks were recorded in France, Riley returned to the US to apply his Yamaha technique to the studio in the form of *Shri Camel*, an album of music first heard on Radio Bremen in 1976. With sixteen tracks at his disposal he turned in four pieces to Columbia records which were far more meditative and influenced by Indian raga than *Rainbow* was over a decade before. Of more import was his acquisition of the recently invented Prophet 5 synthesizer, which had five voicings and was fully polyphonic (capable of playing more than one note at a time). 'I played organs all during the 70s and got my first synthesizer in 1980. I couldn't retune a synth until the Prophet 5. Chester Wood, who was technical engineer, added further oscillators to help this. I loved the Prophet, in fact I ended up with two of them and used them like a double manual organ, linked together.' The resultant *Songs For The Ten Voices Of The Two Prophets* is a famous recording made in 1982 in Munich. Not only does it cleverly pun on the use of the Prophet synthesizer but is at once a vocal and electronic composition. Drawing on the Gospel of Sri Rama Krishna, Riley uses his voice, based on years of training with Pandit Pran Nath, supported by the music of the Prophets. It is here that, in the deepest sense, the spiritual and the technological collide.

Riley involved himself occasionally with both Nath and La Monte Young as part of the Dream House scene which grew out of the Dia Art Foundation in New York. Riley's Eastern drift could be gauged by his work with sitar master Krishna Bhatt. Again the resultant recording, *No Man's Land* (1984), revealed a dazzling synthesizer technique with the Prophet. Riley alludes that this happened by chance. 'This was for a film by Alain Tanner who came to see us play in Geneva. Pieces like *Jaipur Local* are in truth sections from *A Rainbow In Curved Air*.' The main bulk of this work was an epic cycle titled *Songs From The Old Country*, which Riley began in 1978 and which features the composer on acoustic piano and synthesizer, both perfectly in tune with Bhatt's sitar and tablas. The use of modes and precise beat patterns make this phase one of most musically satisfying of Riley's career.

Another avenue which Riley explored around this time was that of the string quartet. At Mills College in the late 1970s he met David Harrington and the Kronos Quartet. They asked him to write for them and, liking the sonorities produced by strings, he produced *Cadenza On The Night Plain*, which the quartet recorded in 1984. This explored the modular writing of *In C*, and adapted ragtime and Vivaldi in Indian style on the outstanding ballad *Mythic Birds Waltz*. Riley made another move towards pure music on *The Harp Of The*

New Albion (1986), a solo piano dedication to La Monte Young using the pitch C sharp and considered an extension of *Cadenza* in his cycle of music on North American mythology. New Albion refers to San Francisco and the harp is considered a sacred North American Indian object which the wind can play at will. This is just-intonation music with a good-time slant.

His reputation now fully established, Riley was continually busy composing, performing and lecturing. He built up a healthy live following in Europe, America and Japan. After he had written ten string quartets for Kronos, *Salome Dances For Peace* appeared in 1989, to critical acclaim. Fascinated with Chinese music, Riley visited Shanghai in early 1989 to see how his *In C* would fair in a new recording. 'We made contact with the film orchestra of Shanghai – the one that did all the Chinese films, a very good and fine orchestra. This was the first time a modern Western piece had been performed in China. When it was performed around the country it became known as *In China*. The recording of same ended up being appropriately mixed by Brian Eno and Jon Hassell in Hollywood.'

Riley had been conjuring up different pieces for different-sounding ensembles – Bulgarian voice choir, saxophone quartet and the brass and percussion group Zeitgeist. In 1991 he wrote a large orchestral piece for the St Louis Symphony. Though he continued to perform with Krishna Bhatt, Zakir Hussain and Pandit Pran Nath, his recorded output became more distilled.

The Padova Concert (1992), where Riley improvises on solo piano themes from *The Harp Of The New Albion* and *Salome Dances For Peace* live in Italy, was like a bejewelled Eastern haze with spiral upon spiral of exquisite piano notes. Two years later Riley's experiments with brass intervals could be heard on *Chanting The Light of Foresight*, in which he used computers and Hindustani scales to communicate the passion of one of Ireland's most famous sagas, The Tain or The Cattle Raid of Cooley, featuring heroism from 500 BC. Maybe Riley was returning to his Irish roots? Other memorable pieces from the 90s were *The Sands*, which commingled Oriental, jazz, folk and East African strains in a dedication to the dead of the Gulf War, and *Cactus Rosary*, an almost static piece.

Whether appearing on television or in person, Riley has always communicated the hearty humour of an Indian mystic. Back in the early 1960s he told Jon Hassell before the realization of *In C* that he considered Serial music, like Freud, to be 'neurotic'. Today his accessible music and pioneering self-contained electronic presentation is seen as a benchmark forerunner of DJ culture. And of course *In C* made Minimalism a going concern. What does Riley think of his own music? 'Well, I like what I'm doing. For me music is about how it feels to the performer. Yet I think of myself as a composer. I definitely like to organize it and of course I need to perform myself in order to do this. Tuning to me is everything. The future will bring instruments which will increase our colour spectrum in music enormously. These will be acoustic and electronic and combinations of the two. This is what fascinates me.'

LISTENING

In C (Columbia/CBS 1968)
A Rainbow In Curved Air (Columbia 1969)
Persian Surgery Dervishes (Sunking 1971)
Shri Camel (Columbia 1980)
Descending Moonshine Dervishes (Kuckuck 1982)
Songs For The Ten Voices Of The Two Prophets (Kuckuck 1982)
No Man's Land (Plainisphare 1984)
Cadenza On The Night Plain (Gramavision 1985)
The Padova Concert (Amiata 1992)
Chanting The Light Of Foresight (New Albion 1994)

More than that of any other of the four original Minimalists, Riley's reputation stands on his recordings. *In C* was first released in 1968 but appeared again on Edsel in 1989 and in the Chinese version on Celestial Harmonies the same year. Both *A Rainbow In Curved Air* and *Shri Camel* were some of the first Columbia Masterworks to be transferred to CD in the mid-1980s and still sound superb. *Shri Camel*, which is divided into four pieces with titles like *Across The Lake Of The Ancient Word* and *Desert Of Ice*, boasts an early use of computerized digital delay. *Rainbow* is an essential late-twentieth-century disc which also features *Poppy Nogood And The Phantom Band*. The 'spatially separated mirror images' of the sleeve note are no idle jest.

Recorded at the same time was *Church of Anthrax* (Columbia 1971) with John Cale. Its release on disc in 1994 did not improve its leaden quality. Only *The Hall of Mirrors In The Palace Of Versailles* is good and that only for Riley's ethereal saxophone style. *Descending Moonshine Dervishes* and *Songs For The Ten Voices Of The Two Prophets* were recorded in Berlin and Munich respectively and reveal Riley's transition from Yamaha electronic organ to Prophet 5 synthesizers. The latter combines voice and Prophets and, as well as being one of Riley's best albums, is an influence on Ambient DJs like the UK's Mixmaster Morris.

No Man's Land involves themes from both *A Rainbow in Curved Air* and *Shri Camel* but placed in a raga context. An outstanding disc in every way, it contains the solo piano piece *Return Of The Dream Collector*, which was reprised on *Cadenza On The Night Plain* with the Kronos Quartet the following year. This could well be one of the most adventurous and interesting string-quartet albums ever recorded. *The Padova Concert* is like a distillation of musical learning, so exquisite is the just-intonation playing of themes from *The Harp Of The New Albion* (1984) and *Salome Dances For Peace* (1988). In 1993 Shanti in Italy reissued *Persian Surgery Dervishes* as a double disc. *Chanting The Light Of Foresight* features the Rova Saxophone Quartet in a series of drones dedicated to Irish legend.

STEVE REICH

One of the most significant American composer-musicians of the late twentieth century, Steve Reich successfully dismantled the cemented bedrock of Western music and rebuilt it in startlingly innovative ways. Drawing on aspects of African, Balinese, Yemenite and Hebrew sound, he continually fashioned new musical models that pushed Western music forward. Having collaborated with Terry Riley on *In C*, Reich moved to tape recorders and invented a phase-shifting technique which not only influenced the work of Brian Eno but also had an effect on black rap music and the Ambient House movement spear-headed by The Orb. In a genuinely absorbed style, Reich synthesizes aspects of eighteenth-century classical music, Debussy, twentieth-century jazz, ethnic and ritualistic music and the happy musical accidents which occur when one uses electronic technology like tape and digital samplers.

Of great significance to Reich's life was the divorce of his parents within a year of his birth in New York in October 1936. His parents were well-to-do Jews whose roots were in Eastern Europe, but the marriage of his strict lawyer father to his singer and lyricist mother June was not made in heaven. His maternal grandfather's occupation as a vaudeville pianist seems to have had a subconscious effect on the baby Reich, and as he grew up the lengthy train journeys between his father's home in New York and his mother's in California would also have a profound significance.

Having taken responsibility for his son, Leonard Reich insisted Steve take a strict classical line. According to Reich: 'There was a keenness for Schubert and Beethoven so I learned a lot of piano. Up to the age of fourteen I'd heard nothing before 1750 or after Wagner.' A move to Larchmont and its high school changed all that. 'It was then I heard be-bop jazz, Stravinsky's *Rite of Spring* and the *Brandenburg Concertos* by Bach. This was a revelation so I decided to be a composer. All the music from Haydn to Wagner I just dismissed. My modern instincts were drawn to the sounds of contemporary music from Debussy, jazz, Africa, Bali to Hebrew chant.' Reich got into jazz drumming and formed a series of groups. Yet his father's expectations made Reich study philosophy at Cornell University between 1953 and 1957.

There he became fascinated by the Austrian philosopher Ludwig Wittgenstein, who had deconstructed language, a fascination that would later lead to Reich's own dismantlings of Western music. A study of music history convinced Reich that twentieth-century composition required more clarity and rhythm. Though accepted at Harvard for more philosophy, he flew in the face of his father and attended the prestigious Juilliard School of Music in New York, where he met both Philip Glass and Meredith Monk. It was here that Reich would strike up a strangely ambivalent relationship with Glass – one of attraction and competition that would run through their parallel careers. Reich has talked about rivalry over a girlfriend but there were other psychological forces at play. While Reich took in the cool sounds of Miles Davis by night, he drank from the lake of Webern and Stockhausen's total Serialism by day. Disenchanted with the Juilliard, he left and married his girlfriend in 1961. Then it was off to California, to Mills College in Oakland, to study with Darius Milhaud and Luciano Berio. Milhaud's interest in melody and Berio's work with electronics would have their impact. Two years were spent on Serial music, but it wasn't to Reich's liking. 'When I went to music school the music that was happening was either like Schoenberg, Boulez or John Cage. Most of it had no melodic organization and I found this very unappealing. I found it very difficult to write Twelve-Tone music. I never transposed a row, I just repeated it. In doing contemporary music that way I stole some harmony in through the back door.' At that time Reich got a bigger buzz from seeing the way John Coltrane generated sheets of sound using modal scales and a steady pulse. Reich graduated from Mills in 1963 with a Master's degree and immersed himself in the flowering art and music scene of San Francisco.

While driving a taxi to make ends meet, he got involved in street theatre and experimental film. Following in the footsteps of Pierre Schaeffer and Pierre Henry, he made tape loops of everyday sounds, ingeniously recording whole segments of his cab journeys. He formed a group with himself as drummer inspired by free jazz. At one 1964 gig Terry Riley famously walked out, but later, after Reich confronted him, Riley asked him to play on *In C*. The pulsing C's on the piano are credited to him. Reich's interest was cohesive innovation, not what he saw as the anarchy of John Cage. 'I respected some of the things he did with voice and folk idioms but much of my early work was done in contradiction to him. I respected his role as a figure but unfortunately I saw many fine composers destroyed by his influence.'

In 1965 Reich embarked on a series of creations which would make him famous. The first, *It's Gonna Rain*, was adapted from a snatch of a black Pentecostal preacher's sermon, captured in San Francisco's Union Square one Sunday afternoon. Reich looped the phrase and doubled it, playing two tape machines against each other. During seventeen minutes of chaotic discord one could hear repeating patterns dropping out of the noise. The time–delay factor inherent in this was to have a powerful impact on Brian Eno while he was at Winchester Art School.

By the time Reich moved back to New York in late 1965 he was intent on developing his concept of 'phase shifting'. A group of black youths had been beaten up and charged with a shop murder. Asked to write something for a benefit, Reich listened to some taped interviews and adopted the phrase 'I had to like, open the bruise up and let some of the bruise blood come out to show them' for his purpose. This was said by a nineteen-year-old who had been forced to prove that he had been beaten up. By looping this phrase and breaking it into fragments, *Come Out* (1966) graphically illustrated race violence and the attendant disbelief by the authorities. Its biggest plus was that here was an invented music as the very words became melody. While working at various part-time jobs – cab driver, social worker, post–office employee – Reich had inadvertently blueprinted rap music decades ahead of time.

Working in his tape studio in Lower Manhattan in 1966, Reich created *Piano Phase* as a live option for one pianist to play against himself. He and people like Jon Gibson played art galleries and were swept along by the Minimalist art movement of the time. By 1967 he had met Philip Glass again and within a year they had formed an ensemble. They even started up a furniture-removal company to make money. Obvious necessity had bonded them together. Reich played with ideas. Typical of the time was *Pendulum Music* (1968), where mikes were swung over amps to create alternating feedback. When they stopped swinging the piece finished. With the help of the Bell Telephone Company Laboratories in 1969 he even developed a 'phase-shifting pulse gate' to mimic his tape experiments live. Most importantly, he published a paper which advocated that the process of his music and its content were identical and that the compositions once set up 'run by themselves'. Again this idea would be critical to Eno's invention of Ambient music.

By the early 1970s the problematic relationship between Reich and Glass had become strained to breaking point. *Four Organs/Phase Patterns* of 1970 was their last recorded collaboration. For a long time Reich had read the book *Studies in African Music* by A. M. Jones because he was fascinated by African drumming. 'I found out from this book that it consisted of basic repeating patterns with the downbeat not coinciding, twelve-metre and a completely different way of putting music together than we were used to. It reminded me of my own work. *Phase Patterns* is drumming on electric organs.' After seeking advice Reich went to the University of Ghana to study African drumming for five weeks in 1970 – the most significant step of his career.

There he studied with the master drummer of the Ewe tribe and played alongside various ensembles. In the Ghanaian *hocket* Reich found an alternating rhythmic pattern which suited his own music. After contracting malaria he came home early and spent the rest of the year writing *Drumming* (1971), his first assured masterpiece. A key work of Minimalism, *Drumming* used no changes in rhythm or key but a build-up and reduction technique where slight changes in pitch and timbre made for a wonderfully bright experience. Hypnotic and shimmering, *Drumming* was a perfect fusion of bongos, marimbas, voices, glockenspiels, whistle and piccolo. Reich had admitted that going to Ghana 'was a giant pat on the back' and confirmed his belief that 'percussion could be richer in sound than electronic instruments'.

Drumming was a touring success. Reich's 1972 *Clapping Music* demonstrated the purist application of his rhythmic ideas which were applied to two pairs of hands. In the fashion of Stockhausen every aspect – size of hands, size of venue, balance of amplification, position of hands – was carefully written down. The drifting process of his electronic experiments was now fully audible in his acoustic settings. Having read and listened to Balinese music for years, and openly influenced by Debussy, Reich wrote the mesmerizing sixteen-minute

Music For Mallet Instruments, Voices And Organ in 1973. Build-up, repeating, lengthening and other devices were used to generate cadence after cadence of shimmering sounds. Critics were enraptured – Steve Reich in their minds had made serious psychedelia. Its most important aspect was the way listening to it seemed to lengthen time. Its release by Deutsche Grammophon in 1973 accompanied by *Drumming* and *Piano Phase* placed Reich on the commercial map.

Reich studied Balinese music at Washington University, Seattle, in 1973 and at Berkeley World Music Center in 1974. He was interested both in the way metal instruments were hit by mallets and the sound of Balinese *kotekan*, or layered rhythms. Debussy was always at the back of his mind. 'Around the turn of the century there was a fork in the road – one way to Wagner, the other to Debussy. After a while I became conscious that what I was doing – repeating the notes in the middle register, changing the bass notes and chords were right out of Debussy's *Prelude To The Afternoon Of A Faun*.

Between 1974 and 1976 Reich then wrote his most famous and influential piece, *Music For 18 Musicians*. With an unforgettable opening which featured breathy bass clarinets this had similarities to some of the material on Pink Floyd's aural masterpiece of the decade, *Dark Side Of The Moon* (the to-ing and fro-ing in the first ten minutes reminded one of the stereo-effect-laden 'On The Run'). As influential on jazz musicians as on Techno DJs, *Music For 18 Musicians* was a perfect fusion – Balinese percussion; classical instruments like piano, cello, violin; Reich's usual xylophones and female voices. The pulsating opening, which rose and fell in a sequence of eleven chords, was breathtaking. Nearly an hour long, the work builds on these chords before returning to the opening. The sounds of Africa and Bali are there, but so is the sound of twelfth-century sacred chanting. According to Reich, the stretching of the chords becomes a pulsing cantus for the whole piece.

The uncanny brilliance of *Music For 18 Musicians* brought Reich mass fame. Concerts were sold out and the classic 1978 ECM album of the piece was a big seller. Though offered thousands of dollars to write scores, Reich was having a different awakening through his personal life. Back in 1963 he had experienced a painful divorce. In 1974 he had met Beryl Korot, a radical and progressive video artist who was also serious about studying the Jewish faith. Reich plunged into the Kabbalah, Torah and Talmud – literature essential to Jewish orthodoxy. His studies brought him into contact with Hebrew singing, or cantillation. Married to Korot in 1976, he went the following year to Israel to record these chants from men steeped in the tradition, some of whom came from Yemen. Studying the results, Reich realized the cellular nature of the music – how small things put together paint the overall picture.

Contractual demands in Holland, Germany and the US meant that he had to come up with three fair-sized works in as many years. *Music For A Large Ensemble* (1978) was scored for thirty players, including winds, brass and strings. Reich used the canonic system of serial repetition to create a wave-like motion. *Octet*

(1979), which is for many more instruments than eight, with players doubling, included woodwinds, pianos and vibraphones. 'After the premier of *Octet*, a guy came up to me backstage, introduced himself as Brian Eno and told me how much he had enjoyed the concert!' Reich continued to expand his instrumental forces with the mellifluous *Variations For Winds, Strings And Keyboards* – a fully repetitive orchestral piece for the San Francisco Symphony.

On a roll, Reich pushed forward and incorporated his Hebrew studies into *Tehillim* in 1981. Based on ancient Hebrew psalms, this work nevertheless included electronic instruments, aspects of the gamelan, folk music and the baroque. Reich's move to the quiet of the Vermont countryside inspired 1983's *The Desert Music*. Lasting nearly an hour, this piece incorporates Reich's ensemble into a large orchestra. A chorus of twenty-seven voices was used to enunciate the apocalyptic poetry of William Carlos Williams, which centred on the moral emptiness of technological progress for its own sake. According to Reich: 'I was concerned with the constant flickering of attention between what the words mean and how they sound.' He wrote a music inspired by vistas he had seen in the real deserts of New Mexico and California. Consisting of five movements, the work had a Romantic lushness under-pinned by pulse and repetition and Reich's favourite ethnic patterns. As well as using synthesizers and electronics it even included a siren à la Varèse that Reich had heard one day in Vermont. It had a Buddhist quality and the whole glistens most tellingly in the delicious instrumental lead-up to the vocal section of the final movement.

When looking at Reich's life it is evident that the music and experience are one. His fierce commitment to creativity is evidenced in the Vermont period of the 1980s, which produced *Vermont Counterpoint* (1982), *New York Counterpoint* (1985), *Sextet* (1985), *Three Movements* (1986), *Six Marimbas* (1986), *Electric Counterpoint* (1987), *Four Sections* (1987) and *Different Trains* (1988). The *Counterpoint* series and *Six Marimbas* saw Reich return to trance elements in his music. *Electric Counterpoint* became a famous piece owing to its masterly performance by jazz guitarist Pat Metheny. Ten guitar parts and two bass parts were pre-recorded, over which Metheny improvised an eleventh guitar part. The gradual changes and trance-like elements reached a climax in the third movement when Metheny tipped into rock territory with some great chordal swipes. The music was so good that The Orb sampled it for live House concerts in the early 1990s.

For Reich his most significant work of that period was *Different Trains*, which eventually won him a Grammy Award in 1990. In 1985 the Kronos Quartet had asked him to write string music. Reich looked back at Bartók but grew frustrated. He started using his favourite sampling keyboards to generate lines based on patterns alternating between speech and string music. Reflecting on his childhood, he decided to evoke the very strong experience of travelling back and forth across the US by train to see his divorced parents. Between 1939 and 1942 he travelled for many hours at a time with his governess while in Germany less fortunate Jewish children were ferried to their deaths in concentration camps on very different trains – hence the title.

Reich was also entranced by the success of Stockhausen's classic *Gesang der Jünglinge* (*Song Of The Youths*) and went out to record his governess and a retired pullman porter. He also sought archive recordings of Holocaust survivors and found authentic train sounds from the 1930s and 40s. Samples of speech were notated, the lot was put on to tape via samplers and computers and given to the Kronos Quartet, who copied the speech melodies on their strings in an overdubbing process which occurred four times. Lasting twenty-seven minutes, *Different Trains* was an astonishing realization of both America and Europe before and after the Second World War. It invented a new documentary music and rightly made Reich famous worldwide. 'It drew a line in the sand and connected all the work I'd been trying to do for years,' the composer said in 1991. 'It was an homage to those people – a memorial to those no longer around and to those living.'

Having started with tape, Reich was now using a combination of Apple Macintosh computers and Casio and Digidesign samplers. He saw synthesizers as a marriage of convenience but saw samplers 'as real sound, the sound of somebody's voice. They have split-second timing and you can contribute to something with them in an instrumental way.' Fired by the success of *Different Trains*, Reich wanted to make a large-scale work based on speech melodies. He and his wife decided to collaborate on a huge piece which took as its basis the Cave of Machpela on the West Bank in Hebron (a site of dual worship for Muslims and Jews). Various bodies, including the Andy Warhol Foundation, provided a total of $1 million for the project. Working from 1989 to 1993, Reich and Beryl Korot interviewed people in Jerusalem, Palestine, Egypt and the US and asked each about the significance of figures like Abraham and Ishmael, from the Bible and the Koran respectively. The answers were edited and provided the basis for the music played by his ensemble. Korot worked hard to get the images arrayed across five eight-foot by ten-foot video screens in a multi-screen process she had templated in the 1970s.

When I saw *The Cave* performed in Amsterdam in 1993 I confessed to being impressed by its rigour and complexity. Ensemble followed speech. Hebrew cantillation was also recorded, as was that of the Muqris, the holy chanters of the Koran. According to Korot: 'We could not fool around with the Koran. In the first act there was no problem in making up musical melodies to the Bible. But the Koranic text has to stand alone. In the second act Steve's music precedes the Islamic text!'

The Cave was definitely Reich's highest-tech endeavour, using the latest visual synchronization and computer techniques. Costing nearly $250,000 per performance in the US, it was not a great commercial success. Artistically it was a triumph. At the end of the first act there was a memorable moment when the cameras panned the interior of the mosque at Hebron, twenty-five miles south of Jerusalem. The resonating sounds of prayer made an A-minor drone which was replayed by the ensemble. The result was an incredible Ambient experience, tantalizing in its exoticism, hypnotic in its effect.

Though the healing effects of *The Cave* were short-lived (a Jewish fanatic would kill twenty-nine Muslims in early 1994), Reich had shown that Minimalism could produce new forms without resorting to the old structures of opera, a pet hate. 'Most opera, whether new or old, is leaden, old-fashioned and boring. There have been some changes in the style of voice plus in the way Kurt Weill presented things, but too many accept the idea of the orchestra in the pit and too many new operas are made for superficial reasons. *The Cave* was about folklore. And to me folklore is technology. We live in an urban folklore which is samplers and drum machines. Even the way *The Cave* used video was very folk. It's folk music for now.'

Reich has always had an ambivalent attitude to the music business, often finding the whole promotional interview process a chore. When I asked him in 1991 about his relationship with Minimalism he told me: 'I learned something from Terry Riley and La Monte Young. Philip Glass and John Adams learned something from me. The rest is journalism.' (Notice the quip against Glass, a remark that could only fuel what had become a legendary rivalry.) Often Reich has maintained that he really doesn't use technology. During the same interview he stated: 'I've been working for twenty years acoustically. In the end I use nothing but mikes!' Having written *Four Sections* in the 1980s, he considered it a goodbye to a very conservative decade. 'I've always had good relationships with ensembles but difficulties with orchestras. Orchestras are elephants!' And that after the London Symphony Orchestra did great justice to his *Four Sections* in 1990.

After *The Cave* Reich seemed to mellow. Returning to New York, he worked with his wife in a studio full of percussion equipment plus his favourite samplers and computers. *City Life*, a complex speech-melody composition based on New York, was released in 1985. One of the sharpest minds of twentieth-century music, Reich is a genuinely invigorating musician whose creations never seem to pale. He has drawn from Debussy and Ravel, Satie and Mahler, the Far East and Stockhausen. He has used technology to create new music and not fallen prey to mere imitation or exoticism for its own sake. Back in 1993, in a lengthy interview, he had this to say to me about modern music: 'I hope there's always a two-way street between popular music and other types of music. If popular music can take something from me. I can take something from them like the sampling keyboard. I'm not interested in electronic music in a laboratory kind of way. Once it hit the streets it signified a number of things – machines do work and are resonant in our culture. I'm happier to be part of an ongoing stream of things rather than being off in a corner. There's a lot of cross-fertilization now but that doesn't mean that everybody has the same background or thinks about the same body of work. House musicians don't rely on notation but on improvisation in playing. In Africa the oral tradition was what was important for passing on rhythmic complexities. Yet the intricacies of harmony did not occur in African music. Now each culture makes up for its own by taking from other cultures which is wonderful.'

LISTENING

Drumming, Six Pianos (Deutsche Grammophon 1974)
Music For 18 Musicians (ECM 1978)
Sextet, Six Marimbas (Elektra-Nonesuch 1986)
Early Works (Elektra-Nonesuch 1987)
Different Trains, Electric Counterpoint (Elektra–Nonesuch 1989)
Four Sections, Music For Mallet Instruments, Voices And Organ (Elektra–Nonesuch 1990)
Variations For Winds, Strings And Keyboards (Deutsche Grammophon 1994)
Steve Reich: Works 1965–1995 (Nonesuch 1996)
Reich: Remixed (Nonesuch 1999)

The Deutsche Grammophon disc *Drumming* was originally the 1974 triple-album boxed set which made Reich a force to be reckoned with in the record business. As well as containing vintage Hamburg recordings the set contains superb self-penned sleeve notes. Included is Reich's famous 1968 manifesto 'Music As A Gradual Process', where some of his most famous quotes are to be found, including his maxim concerning 'closely detailed listening'. Eloquently he expands the idea – 'like pulling back a swing, releasing it and observing it gradually come to rest . . . turning over an hourglass and watching the sand slowly run through to the bottom . . . placing your feet in the sand by the ocean's edge and watching, feeling and listening to the waves as they gradually bury them.' Also he alludes to the important shift of focus away from the personal experience of music and outwards to the impersonal presence of the music itself.

Music For 18 Musicians* is one of those twentieth-century classics that keeps selling. Loved by musicians and DJs from all genres, it is the only place to start. If you only ever have one Reich disc, then the ECM one with its Arabic-styled woven cover should be it. *Six Marimbas* is an intoxicating skein of warbly beats that build up and float down as the instruments interplay and unlock the variations of the eight-tap rhythm. *Early Works* contains *It's Gonna Rain, Come Out, Piano Phase* and *Clapping Music* from the period 1965–72, and is a good way of hearing Reich's inventive phase-shifting procedures.

The pairing of *Different Trains* with *Electric Counterpoint* is great value as it gives two very extreme aspects of Reich's art – the complex and the simple – on one disc. After *Music For 18 Musicians* this is your essential second purchase. Another great recording contains *Four Sections* and *Music For Mallet Instruments, Voices And Organ*. The first piece was Reich's 'hail and farewell to the orchestra'. Encouraged to write it for the London Symphony by conductor Michael Tilson Thomas, he pitted sections of the orchestra against each other in a similar fashion to his earlier phase-shifting experiments on tape. The results bore resemblances to the work of Debussy and Mahler. In this performance by his ensemble *Music For Mallet Instruments, Voices And Organ* is a luminous work as fluttering marimbas, glockenspiels and vibraphone are augmented by repeating cadences of female voice and electronic organ. The original version can be heard on the 1994 DG disc, which is recommended for the inclusion of *Variations For Winds, Strings And Keyboards*, recorded in 1983 in San Francisco and some of the most entrancing music Reich has ever written. *Works* is a summary of the period 1965–95 which contains new versions of classics such as *Music For 18 Musicians*. It also offers the top-notch re-recorded version of *Drumming* from 1987 as well as appraisals from Michael Tilson Thomas and John Adams and an interview with Jonathan Cott. Budget-priced and including archive photographs, this ten-CD set is an essential Reich document. *Reich: Remixed* is a fascinating blend of Reich's music by the likes of Tranquility Bass, DJ Spooky, Coldcut and Howie B in the context of late-twentieth-century Acid, Techno, Hardbeat and Ambient Turntable styles.

BRIAN ENO

One of the pivotal figures of twentieth-century music, Brian Eno introduced a popular voice to a century of musical change. By relocating the essentials of Minimalism in rock music he gave it enormous mainstream exposure. A maverick producer and theoretician, he showed that the ideas of John Cage, La Monte Young and Steve Reich had far-reaching consequences when utilized by non-musicians or those who favoured intuition over scripted music. In every sphere he had success: in composing, producing, collaboration and gallery installations. In the late 1970s he directly influenced record companies to take note of new Minimalist musicians in both the UK and the US. As a record producer he brought Minimalism to bear on rock music, his work with David Bowie in 1977 (*Low*) and U2 in 1987 (*The Joshua Tree*) generating two of the most relevant records of the century. Like Stockhausen, he believed thoroughly in electronic progress but always placed emotion and sheer good taste above the inclination to merely dabble. One of his essential contributions was to highlight the importance of the recording studio as an essential part of the musical experience; a veritable instrument, which in the hands of the right person could work wonders. Between 1975 and 1978 he defined the word Ambient in popular consciousness as a music which was 'as the colour of the light or the sound of the rain', a music defined by his famous maxim 'as ignorable as it is interesting'. Into a popular-music market high on brash excess and short attention spans, Eno brought space and time, time to think, time to reflect. For many people his records and interviews were a doorway into serious music and philosophy. This very book you are now reading would not have developed had it not been for my encounter with Eno's music in my youth.

Indeed beyond that, the whole New Age and Ambient House music genres simply couldn't have existed without his influence.

Eno was born in the small estuary town of Woodbridge in Suffolk in 1948. His father was a postman. Neither of his parents was musical. His grandfather, also a postman, built organs and played the bassoon and other wind instruments – hence Eno's early inclination to disassemble and reassemble tape recorders. Eno was one child in four, born to country working folk in a traditional English community. The unusual name, Eno, has Belgian origins in the area known as East Flanders. Woodbridge itself is an interesting place, its small square featuring a medieval church and an old long-hall tavern, its walls adorned with old photographs, some of Eno's family. Walking along the River Deben one is struck by its essential quietness, the sound of waterbirds and the tinkling of sail cords on the masts of countless boats. A short drive away is Dunwich, where an ancient and important town succumbed to successive landslides and was submerged in the sea, so that only a church, a pub and a few houses survive. The sights and sounds of this quiet English setting would later impact directly on Eno's Ambient music.

Raised a Catholic, Eno was educated by the De la Salle order in nearby Ipswich. He even bears their moniker as part of his lengthy middle name: Peter George St John le Baptiste de la Salle. Eno has spoken to me of the importance of his strict Catholic education, the way it gave him no wishy-washy options. 'When they said no you can't, they meant no you can't.' Hence Eno has always been an option-limiter and prefers working under conditions of constraint rather than freedom. Again his derision of over-complicated synthesizers and studio technique may well derive from his childhood. Eno was taught by the order's nuns and brothers for eleven years from 1953. The special atmosphere conjured by the weekly Latin Mass would leave a lasting impression on the boy.

Another important facet of Eno's growing up was Woodbridge's proximity to two US Air Force bases. Here airmen would be privy to the latest records from the States and during the rock and roll era this brought the 45rpm single right into Eno's home. The American bars and coffee shops all had jukeboxes and Eno's elder sister went out with an American and brought home loads of new 45s, some of which Eno would play over and over again on his parents' auto-change record player. His own response to this new kind of space generated by rock and roll recording would again be fed directly into his Ambient music. 'I lived in rural Suffolk but there were two very large American air bases within five miles of where I lived and the music we heard was urban American pop music. The contrast between that and the environment I lived in was extremely strange to me. I had no context for this music whatsoever, particularly American doo-wop. Subsequent to that I heard Little Richard, Fats Domino, Buddy Holly and Bo Diddley.'

Other musical influences were the easy-listening sounds of Ray Conniff and the hymnal rolls on his parents' player piano. The latter would be reflected in Eno's love of Gospel singing, which he performed in a short-lived teenage vocal combo. Eno's two sisters and younger brother all approached music from a more or less classical perspective. He, on the other hand, did so from the prospect of 'sound' itself. His way into sound was technology. His way into technology was technique and his way into that was the English art-school system of the 1960s. Though his parents encouraged him to get a safe job in a bank, Eno was determined to go to art school.

Ipswich Art School, where Eno did foundation studies from 1964 to 1966, was a hotbed of experimentalism. Pupils and teachers colluded in pulling down the walls of preconception. Eno was particularly affected by the school's head, Roy Ascott, a teacher interested in cybernetics (the study of the interface between machine and biology), who purposefully 'disorientated' his pupils into new ways of thinking. Another teacher, Tom Phillips, influenced Eno's experiments with tape recorders, usually recording one sound over and over to create new textures. Quickly Eno began to see the 'process' of making something to be more interesting than the end result. Like John Adams, he was influenced by John Cage's book *Silence*. He felt that Cage had a deep under-standing of musical possibilities in time and space. At one point in the book Cage discussed Erik Satie's concept of 'furniture music', his hilarious notion to fill up the silences of boring dinner parties with melodious music. Here Cage talks of Satie's music mingling with the 'Ambient sounds'. Eno was also greatly taken by Cage's use of 'chance', specifically the application of the Chinese *I Ching*, or *Book of Changes*, to determine musical outcome. This practice would be mirrored in Eno's use of his own Oblique Strategies oracle cards in his music of the 1970s.

Also at Ipswich, Eno was impressed by the Dada and Surrealist movement of the early twentieth century and its interest in sound generation and automatic writing. The unconscious product of dreams that was a fundamental in Surrealist art would be transferred to his approach to composition – the precept that the work should define itself as much as possible. He saw Allen Ginsberg perform his 'stream of consciousness' poetry but was equally impressed by the structure and intensity of a Buddy Holly performance where the entire band performed through a single Vox amplifier. This balance between precision and indeter-minacy would lend Eno's music an air of both science and art, a quality of spontaneous modernity which made it instantly attractive.

Moving to Winchester Art School in 1966, Eno developed his ideas. He created performances of both paintings and scores, and formed a group, Merchant Taylor's Simultaneous Cabinet, from student friends. Performances involved instructions, locations and ideas similar to those used by John Cage in the 1930s and 40s. He heard the dronal music of The Velvet Underground and enthused about their use of sound and repetition. Eno also admired La Monte Young, both studying and performing his Minimalist music. In 1967 he gave his first public performance, a rendition of Young's *X For Henry Flynt* where he banged on a piano for an hour. The idea was to repeat a note or cluster of notes over and over until something happened. Eno evolved his first great maxim from this experience: 'Repetition is a form of change.' During his stay at Winchester he was also elected student union president. Eno graduated with a Diploma in Fine Art in 1969.

Immediately afterwards he joined the Scratch Orchestra, made up of musicians and non-musicians led by Cornelius Cardew, a Stockhausen pupil and Maoist whose music was both structured and improvised. Also in 1969, Eno teamed up with Gavin Bryars's Portsmouth Sinfonia, an ensemble formed at Portsmouth Polytechnic out of mostly non-musicians. For Eno both these experiments helped him to see how far his ideas would stretch in a new musical setting. In 1971 he saw Philip Glass perform *Music With Changing Parts* at the Royal College of Art in London. The use of repetition and the sheer volume of the electric and acoustic instruments impressed him greatly. Importantly, glam-rock star David Bowie was also in the audience. In that year Eno appeared for the first time on record, in a Deutsche Grammophon recording of Cardew's *The Great Learning*, a seven-paragraph set of instructions mixing music with left-wing polemic.

According to Michael Nyman, Eno had married young at art school and had a young daughter. By now twenty-two, Eno was living in South London and considering a career as an art teacher when one day he took an underground train and met saxophonist Andy Mackay. They had met before at Reading University and Mackay had studied music with both Morton Feldman and John Cage in Italy. Mackay talked about a new group and the VCS3 synthesizer, both of which Eno found interesting. Using his batch of tape recorders from student days, Eno and the group rehearsed. Soon Roxy Music would become the most talked-about group in the UK. With their mix of glam-rock, Hollywood glitz, clever lyrics, decadent sound and the crooning voice of Bryan Ferry, the band met with instant success. They signed to Island Records and their first album, *Roxy Music*, went to number one in 1972. A single, 'Virginia Plain', drenched in Eno's space-age synthesizer treatments of Mackay's saxophone and Phil Manzanera's guitar, was also an instant hit. Eno's stage appearance – full make-up, feather boa and shiny satin – was made all the more shocking by TV coverage. Another album, *For Your Pleasure* (1973), with its trademark glamour-girl cover, featured a similar mix, Eno's synth-twiddling and general ideas lending a strong whiff of Minimalism to the extended instrumental passages. But by the summer of 1973 he was bored with the constant touring and adulation and wanted a change. With no radical alterations in the group's direction coming from the leader, Bryan Ferry, Eno simply departed after a concert.

Eno still sees Roxy Music as crucial to his career. In 1992 he told me: 'As a result of going into a subway station and meeting Andy I joined Roxy Music and as a result of that I have a career in music I wouldn't have had otherwise. If I'd walked ten yards further on the platform or missed that train or been in the next carriage I probably would have been an art teacher now.' Even during the Roxy era, Eno was already experimenting with automatic systems for generating music. When, in the early 1970s, he heard Steve Reich's *It's Gonna Rain*, he was thunderstruck by his simple use of tape-delay montage. In the autumn of 1972 Eno invited the guitarist Robert Fripp to his home to record 'The Heavenly Music Corporation', twenty-one minutes of looped guitar notes using two tape machines rigged to create drones, backwash and an almost infinite repeat-delay effect. Released shortly after he left Roxy Music on the album *No Pussyfooting*, this new approach led to Eno's being hailed for bringing Reich's Minimalist technique into rock for the first time.

Eno was also involved in a solo rock career with Island and two albums were released by 1974. Yet finances were limited and his health suffered. That year he was rushed to hospital with a collapsed lung. Despite these set-backs he completed two collaborations with his heroes John Cale and Nico, formerly of The Velvet Underground, and even performed with them at London's Rainbow Theatre. On the intellectual front Eno had absorbed strong ideas about the dynamics of organizations from Norbert Wiener (the American mathematician and inventor of cybernetics), Stafford Beer (a management guru) and Morse Peckham (an American professor of English). From Peckham he drew the conclusion that art had a biological quality. Beer's thinking led Eno to suspect that any system creates its own dynamics, and gave him the idea for the maxim 'honour thy error as a hidden intention'. In 1986 Eno clarified this: 'The work starts to define you rather than you define it. It starts to tell you what you are doing.' Eno was set to bring everything he knew to bear on the invention of his very special brand of Ambient music.

What was to be one of the most creative years in Eno's life, 1975, began with an accident. In January he was knocked down by a taxi on the way home from a studio session in London. Hospitalized with a suspected skull fracture, he eventually recuperated at home in Maida Vale. One day a singer friend, Judy Nylon, visited him with a gift of eighteenth-century harp music. After she'd gone he put the record on but failed to adjust the volume properly. Too weak to readjust the hi-fi, he lay down and listened to the quiet music mingling with the environment – the sounds of rain outside and the approaching darkness. Early that summer he applied the idea of quiet, environmental music to a series of sounds he'd fed into a synthesizer. Rigging up a delay system using the two Revox tape machines (as on *No Pussyfooting*), he wished to make some background music for himself and Robert Fripp. With the occasional adjustment of timbre through a graphic equalizer he created a soothing, balming music which stayed mostly in the same key and sounded like horns heard through a soft fog. The resultant album, *Discreet Music*, said by Robert Fripp to be made by Eno while they were having tea in his kitchen, became one of the enduring icons of Ambient instrumental music. Favoured both by the public and the artist, it was, in Eno's view, a perfect example of 'automatic music' – a successful realization of Steve Reich's ideas on musical process of more than a decade earlier.

Back on form, Eno spent the summer in Island studios recording *Another Green World*, his third commercial solo album, but this time a mixture of vocal and instrumental concerns. Applying Stafford Beer's ideas. he welcomed the chaos of bringing together a group of widely differing musicians, like violist John Cale, Fripp again and Genesis pop drummer Phil Collins, and putting them in a studio with no score. The instrumentation of treated guitars, piano, fretless bass, percussion, synthesizers and other studio effects was like that of an ensemble, with Eno the conductor of them all as he sat at the twenty-four-track mixing desk. He also used his Oblique Strategies cards, made up of maxims gleaned from years of study, to issue instructions to the players to bring out new ideas from them. The instrumental passages on the record were so inspired that they attracted comparisons with Satie and Debussy. There was a strange other-worldliness to the record, a feeling that the music was coming from somewhere new and disappearing into some other sphere. For Eno it perfectly suited his ideal of creating a sense of new acoustic space that only existed when one heard the recording. Over time *Another Green World* became Eno's most lauded pop album.

The third important release of 1975 was the Fripp and Eno collaboration *Evening Star*. Again this featured the tape-delay system of *No Pussyfooting*, but with a greater synthesizer element. There was the melodic beauty of Fripp's guitar and excerpts from *Discreet Music*, but the album's triumph was 'An Index Of Metals', a highly dense Ambient creation taking up an entire LP side. This piece entranced the listener into a form of contemplation and successfully altered his or her perception of real time through a slowing-down process. By increasing delay lines Eno achieved the same effect as the earlier Minimalist works of La Monte Young and Terry Riley. The beautiful album cover by Eno's artist friend Peter Schmidt would come to symbolize Ambient music.

Yet another signifier of the importance of 1975 to Eno's music was his label Obscure Records, on which *Discreet Music* had been released. Eno had been tantalizing Island with a project to showcase instrumental music for years and in 1975 the label went for it. From late 1975 to 1978 ten records would be released in characteristic black sleeves, each one revealing a different aspect of New Music. Eno's old friend from the Portsmouth Sinfonia, Gavin Bryars, was featured on the first release, *The Sinking Of The Titanic*, and there were subsequent releases of music by John Adams, David Toop, John Cage and Michael Nyman. The quality of this music was that it was unobtrusive and Eno wrote at the time that the concept of mood music or 'muzak, once it sheds its connotations of aural garbage, might enjoy a new and fruitful lease of life'. Michael Nyman and others saw Eno repaying the intellectual stimulus afforded by the likes of Cage and Tom Phillips through the medium of a commercial record. *Irma*, a floating 'opera' by Tom Phillips, was brought to a wide public attention in 1978 through its release on Obscure Records. In fact all of the Obscure artists were exposed to a wider public because of the Eno connection, which always carried the allure of 'interesting', one of Eno's favourite words.

In 1976 Eno moved closer and closer to a music of 'perceptual drift'. That year he released the first of his *Music For Films* albums in a limited quantity of

500. Wrapped in a plain sleeve, it was ostensibly for film directors. Its contents in parts sounded like backing tracks from *Another Green World*, for Eno was always prone to building up a store of unused sounds. One track, 'Slow Water', had the backdrop of a distant plane disappearing into the horizon. This very effect would be later used on Eno's second collaboration with David Bowie, *'Heroes'*. In fact his work with David Bowie from late 1976 to 1977 was a critical career change and would again bring Minimalist ideas to an even wider public as Bowie was the bona-fide rock superstar of the 1970s. Bowie's drug and relationship problems had soared out of control in Los Angeles and his flight to the cooler climes of Europe – he eventually settled in Berlin in the autumn of 1976 – was to have far-reaching consequences for popular music. In search of a new direction, Bowie approached the German groups Kraftwerk and Tangerine Dream for help and in desperation rang Eno in London.

Eno's arrival in Cologne was a gift for Bowie. Working initially in the studio of the legendary German producer Conny Plank, they started to put together their first LP. *Low* was very much a dual affair – Bowie's condensed vocal personality over the first side, Eno's ethereal Ambience spread throughout the second. Sessions were also done in Paris, but the bulk of the record was done at Berlin's Hansa By The Wall studios. Eno played a variety of synthesizers and used a series of electronic effects. His personality is unmistakable in the slow-moving 'Always Crashing In The Same Car' on Side One, the song swimming in a bright, lustrous balm. Another track, 'A New Career In A New Town', begins in the dream world of Eno's diaphanous textures, its repetitive metronomic beat a straight tribute to Minimalism. But it was Side Two that made *Low* famous, its Ambient instrumentals introducing literally millions of young people to the sound of New Music. Eno has said that he literally saved 'Warszawa' and 'Art Decade' from the scrap-heap and mixed and remixed them during Bowie's frequent absences from the studio. The results were astonishing and today *Low* is considered Bowie's greatest work of art. But at the time people were horrified. Bowie's label, RCA, was nervous about even releasing the record. In January 1977 it was issued, but the music press thought it decadent and reeking of Bowie's negative fixation with Germany. It was down to Philip Glass, who recognized kindred spirits in Eno and Bowie (who themselves had cited Glass as an influence on the album, having both seen him perform in London in 1970), to hail it as 'a work of genius'. And to prove how close Eno's instincts were to cultural change, the album automatically hit the top of the charts.

At the time Eno saw music without focus as the way forward. He had spent the previous two years recording and re-recording in London and Cologne when he released *Before And After Science* (1977), the last of his quartet of pop vocal records. Again chance and spontaneity were harnessed together with the help of a motley crew of musicians. Eno spent more and more time on studio processes and a huge quantity of material was generated. The album is famous for the way it begins in an energetic fashion and slowly tapers out, Side Two literally drifting out of earshot. Critically acclaimed, *Before And After Science* included the German musicians Jaki Liebezeit, Holger Czukay and Cluster – all of whom had been influenced by Stockhausen. At the time, and like Bowie, Eno was impressed with German music and hailed *Music From Harmonia* (a 1973 synthesizer-based work featuring the twin talents of Neu! and Cluster) as the best album he'd ever heard. So taken was he with Cluster that in June 1977 he recorded an album with them: *Cluster And Eno*, an electro-acoustic tone poem.

Being in Germany during the summer, Eno went back to Berlin and Bowie, arriving at the Hansa studios with his Oblique Strategies cards and notebooks. Eno on synthesizers, keyboards and treatments worked hand in hand with Bowie on their second album of 1977, *'Heroes'*. At one stage they rang guitarist Robert Fripp to come over and lend them a hand. The result of this specific request was the finest single song of Bowie's career and huge kudos for Eno's background sounds, which proved that Ambience could be loud and potent too. That song was 'Heroes', released in German, English and French as a single. Like *Low*, the album was divided between vocal and instrumental music, its second side (dedicated to German electronic groups Kraftwerk and Neu!) awesome in its conception, with Eno's influence readily audible. 'Sense of Doubt' was a Gothic creation with its Chopin-like funereal piano. 'Moss Garden' was pure inspiration, Eno's fading aircraft sound adapted from *Music For Films* and set against Bowie's plucked Japanese koto. *'Heroes'* was a critical and commercial success and the amount of attention Eno garnered in 1977 meant that by the end of that year he was in a better position than ever to push his own music to its very limits.

Eno would later say that from the mid-1970s he was 'working more and more in a spherative way where I'm very definitely trying to make a place'. His first important release of 1978 was *Music For Films*, which was put out on a new label, EG Records, distributed by Polydor. For this update and expansion of the 1976 limited edition a series of haiku-like instrumental atmospheres were deployed. The musicians were familiar from Eno's solo pop albums but the contents were epiphanous.

In the summer of 1978 Eno moved to New York, settling in Downtown Manhattan's art district. Having for years made Ambient music, that autumn he finally called his instrumental music by that name. *Music For Airports* was a milestone in Eno's career, a distillation of years of thought and experiment, a virtual manifesto of what Minimalist technique, electronics and studio production could produce.

Ambient 1: Music For Airports, to give it its full title, was the gauntlet Eno threw down in his Ambient quest. The cover looked like a blown-up sample of an Ordnance Survey map, its back a series of drawings that could have come from the pen of Stockhausen or Cage. The four tracks had no titles. The first consisted of Robert Wyatt playing some beautiful piano and Eno leaving lots of space for the odd soft electronic effect. The second track was incredible: as if the angels were singing from his childhood, you heard harmonized voices just chanting single notes, but in such a way that as the sound went through Eno's equipment it was subtly electronicized. Track three mixed the elements of the first two and the final mix had all the qualities of a sparsely played church organ and looked back to the horn timbres of *Discreet Music*. *Music For Airports* was as much about silence as sound and is considered today to be a twentieth-century classic. On the inside cover of the album Eno laid out his Ambient manifesto. He divorced his work from mindless canned Muzak and talked about Ambient music containing a 'sense of doubt and uncertainty', its intention being 'to induce calm and a space to think'. The essay ended with his most famous axiom of all, that Ambient music 'must be as ignorable as it is interesting'. Later Eno would talk of how *Music For Airports* was actually made: 'It was mostly physical loops of tape. In the case of piano notes I would wait for the note to completely decay well beyond the threshold of normal audibility and cut the loop there. One of the tape loops was seventy-nine feet long and the other eighty-three feet. I would then synchronize five or six loops and get a repetition which would generate an unpredictable sound or texture which always changes.'

Eno spent the years 1978–83 in the US, but made trips to Europe, Africa and Southeast Asia. Another German collaboration with Cluster (Dieter Moebius and Hans-Joachim Roedelius) came out in 1978. Evocatively titled *After The Heat*, the record had a blue cover that mirrored the cool contents: piano moods, electronic sketches and what would be Eno's final vocal performances for over a decade. The Ambient song 'The Belldog' surfed on a sea of bright, tinkly electronic sounds and understated pulsating synthesizer. *After The Heat* conjured up a new world coming to terms with the encroachment of new technology. Speaking in New York in the late 1970s, Eno felt that culture was moving into a 'post-Science' state, a sort of 'technological primitivism'. Again his gaze was very much on the future.

On settling in New York in 1978, Eno began producing the art-pop group Talking Heads and generally enjoyed the energy of New Wave rock music, which also attracted his old friend Robert Fripp. That year also saw the release of his first work with the American Minimalist Harold Budd, a musician strongly influenced by Minimalist Art. The work, *The Pavilion Of Dreams*, was very much like a sound-painting. In this period Eno professed an interest in returning to painting and saw his Ambient music as sonic mural. Yet he also required something visual.

One day in 1978 he bought a cheap video camera and accidentally left it on the window-ledge of his Manhattan apartment. Over time he discovered that the lopsided images of the New York skyline were pleasing. Nothing much happened but what did – an aircraft coming by or smoke exiting from a funnel – had a slow Ambient quality. He also had to place a TV set on its side to view the results, thus altering his perception of television. These static images, along with the sound of *Music For Airports*, were piped into environments like La Guardia Airport and Grand Central Station in 1980, hectic spaces which Eno felt could be calmed by an Ambient experience. Eno termed the video work *Mistaken*

Memories Of Medieval Manhattan and felt that, like his own Ambient music, the images arose 'from a mixture of nostalgia and hope, and from the desire to make a quiet place for myself. They evoke in me a sense of "what could have been", and hence generate a nostalgia for a different future.'

Eno lectured and spoke at length about his compositional processes. The keyboardist Hans-Joachim Roedelius was awed by his ability to concentrate when he worked with him in Cologne on the Cluster albums. 'He worked twenty-four hours a day, always thinking and doing and organizing and structuring and talking. Always in the middle of the matter.' Eno had devised many strategies for success in the studio, ranging from precise instructions to improvisations. He never saw any time as wasted and generated hundreds of hours of music on tape. He often favoured a technique of 'composting' where taped material unused from one session would be fed into the next. He also loved building sound circuits between an instrument and an amplifier, consisting of loads and loads of effects units. He not only used the synthesizer as a sound source, but fed sounds into it to alter their timbre. He favoured the new polyphonic (or multi-voiced) range of synthesizers that appeared from 1978 onwards but did not see them as a substitute for real creativity. He still made tape loops which would provide repeating sets of oscillating sounds. Using twenty-four-track mixing desks, he spent hours adding or subtracting echo, reverberation and equalization. At one stage he talked about 'composition by subtraction', a notion which would be seized upon by Ambient House musicians such as The Orb in the 1990s.

A great boost to Eno's Ambient experiments was provided by Daniel Lanois, a Canadian musician and engineer who contacted him in 1980. Lanois, together with his brother Bob, had converted a large Victorian house in Grant Avenue, Ontario, into an unusual studio full of nooks and crannies and unusual places to record. Their idea was a large acoustic space where all sounds could be captured. Eno visited and was duly impressed. It was the beginning of a dynamic partnership, where the musical and engineering skills of the quietly spoken Daniel Lanois would be the perfect foil for Eno's ambitious ideas. Their first work together was *The Plateaux Of Mirror* by Harold Budd, an album cited as 'Ambient 2' and with a map-reference cover similar to *Music For Airports*. Budd, who played his characteristic slow piano and keyboards, remembers: 'Eno was willing to accept surprise and take advantage of it. He and Lanois used chorus and delay effects to alter what I was playing and feed it back to me.' Thus Budd was playing to atmospheres which he had inadvertently created. The haloed sound of the music and the occasional use of pitched voices made *The Plateaux Of Mirror* another Ambient tour de force.

In 1980 Eno's record company became Editions EG. It was a time of intense activity. Between lectures and audiovisual installations all over the US, Eno collaborated on lots of records. His 1980 album with Talking Heads, *Remain In Light,* had pushed their sound from spiky to Ambient. During that time he and Talking Heads singer David Byrne had dipped in and out of studios, working on a successful experiment in found voices from various sources. With its roots in the *musique concrète* of Pierre Schaeffer and early Dadaism, *My Life In The Bush Of Ghosts* was a unique blend of ideas. In 1980 Eno also found time to work in San Francisco for six months, collaborating on two more Ambient records: *Ambient 3: Day of Radiance* (with New York zither-player Laraaji) and *Possible Musics* (with trumpeter and La Monte Young protégé Jon Hassell).

The following year Hassell arrived at Grant Avenue to work on a follow-up, *Dream Theory In Malaya*. Lanois remembers Eno's application of large tape loops to create rhythms and the first use of sampling to continuously play back a sound. All these records garnered huge critical praise yet Eno continued to delve. His next solo album, the product of three years' work, was a huge success. *Ambient 4: On Land* (1982) was an acoustic representation of childhood memories. Made in London, New York and Canada, the album also featured Bill Laswell (a future talent in 90s Ambient music.) Each track painted an aural location, many, including 'Dunwich Beach', were representations of real places. Eno cited Fellini's film *Amarcord* (*I Remember*) and Teo Macero's production of Miles Davis as touchstones for the record. It was awesomely powerful material, made from found sounds, electro-acoustic instruments, non-instruments and the active involvement of musicians like Jon Hassell and Laswell. Eno said at the time: 'From *Another Green World* onwards I became interested in exaggerating and inventing rather than replicating spaces. This record represents one culmination of that and in it the landscape has ceased to be a backdrop for something else to happen in front of: instead, everything that happens is part of the landscape. There is no longer a sharp distinction between foreground and background.'

Simple jamming sessions in Grant Avenue between Lanois, Eno and his younger (and classically trained) brother Roger Eno produced *Apollo: Atmospheres And Soundtracks* (1983), an album bathed in beautiful Ambience which conjured up the atmosphere of the American *Apollo* space missions to the moon. Eno was intent on creating acoustic experiences which somehow replicated and resonated with reality. A collaboration with Harold Budd, *The Pearl* (1984), was adrift with a submarine quality, the feeling of creaking galleons at the bottom of a clear ocean teeming with life. The recorded sounds were slowed down by Eno and sent through various delay and harmonizer units. That year also saw Lanois and Eno go to a castle in Ireland and infuse Irish rock group U2 with a large dose of Ambient space. The resultant success of the *Unforgettable Fire* album was a testament to Eno's dogged belief that 'sound' was a musical value in its own right. He would later say: 'Certainly one of the things I tend to offer other musicians is a sense of sound texture. I think that the thing the recording studio has offered to music or electronics in general have offered to music is the possibility of tremendous expansion in the texture of instruments.' The U2 record was also testament to the inspiration of the Eno-Lanois production partnership, a marriage that continued to produce exceptional results in 1985 on the exotic guitar recording *Hybrid* (featuring Michael Brook) and the piano album *Voices* (played by Roger Eno). Roger himself remembers *Voices* as 'the last of the mega Grant Avenue production sounds, using all those great big washes and stuff'.

For his own part, Eno's Ambient music continued to develop. For years his work had been subject to the limitations of vinyl LPs (whose pops and squeaks could ruin the enjoyment of listening to, say, *Music For Airports*). With the advent of CD, Eno saw a medium that would be perfect for his music. In 1985 appeared one of the first works specifically 'designed' for CD, *Thursday After-noon*. Here the music was a series of keyboard clusters which became slowly enveloped by atmospheric tints. According to Eno, a lot of the sounds 'deliberately faded off to the limits of earshot'. What was great about this recording was that the disc could be put on endless repeat play, the music therefore filling the desired location and acting like a piece of acoustic interior design. You didn't just listen to this; you absorbed it at will. In the year when Eno met John Cage and publicly acknowledged his debt to him ('you're the reason why I became a composer!'), *Thursday Afternoon* was a crowning homage to Cage's Ambient doctrine.

Thursday Afternoon had derived from Eno's evolving fascination with video. Commissioned by Sony in Japan, Eno had presented almost static video images of Christine Alicino, filmed in San Francisco. The idea was to convey a slowly changing video representation of the female nude. Again this was vertical format. For Eno it got away from the 'hysteria' of pop video and allowed the consumer freedom to breathe. Another aspect of his internationally in-demand video work was the use of television monitors to create video sculptures and video paintings. The monitor was either surrounded by a shape to create a crystal or was used to diffuse colour on to a flat, opalescent surface. The results were fascinating and were always accompanied by Ambient music in the style of *Thursday Afternoon*. During conferences in Europe at the beginning of 1986, Eno described succinctly where his Ambient work had led him. 'All my work aspires to the condition of painting and what I like about painters is that they stay there, they persist. So I want to make music that has that condition of being almost but not completely static. I want to make it so that it constantly changes but it never really goes anywhere.' Describing the music that went with his new video art, Eno basically summed up his technique of making Ambient music in general: 'The music is made by allowing several cycles [tape loops] to constantly run out of synch. These loops continually fall into new synchronization patterns so that the music never repeats itself. I was really trying to make music I could never predict.'

Eno's work was still strongly allied to Steve Reich's ideas of the 1960s. Reich in 1968 had said of working with equipment: 'Once the process is set up and loaded, it runs by itself.' Eno said in 1986 that his loop system was 'always generating a new music'. Where Eno differed from Reich was in his holistic application, the idea of Ambient as bigger than music. The various *Works Constructed In Sound And Light*, which were seen all over Europe in 1986, spurred his ambition to create a 'quiet club'. The hushed darkness of slowly changing light sculptures accompanied by unpredictable Ambient clusters had all the flavour of an Orthodox or Catholic church and was thoroughly in keeping with Eno's dislike of traditional clubs designed, he felt, 'to speed up what is assumed to be otherwise an average existence'.

Eno's next move was to journey to Dublin and accompany Daniel Lanois in the making of the most successful rock album of the 1980s, U2's *The Joshua Tree*. As Jimmy Page had done in 1970, Eno's wide-screen understanding of texture underpinned an album that had instant appeal in America, where Eno won a Grammy award for his production duties. Importantly, its early 1987 release again put Eno's grasp of Minimalism firmly in the public eye. His aerial synthesizer sounds, generated by a Yamaha DX7, defined songs such as 'With Or Without You' and during the making of the record he had pushed for the inclusion of material that would become future U2 hits.

That year also saw *Music For Airports* used at the São Paulo Biennale in Brazil. Eno's own position had now changed. The U2 album quickly sold fifteen million copies for Island and made Eno's sound a decade-defining one. Other rock artists, like Peter Gabriel and David Sylvian, quickly followed in his path, making what could only be termed Ambient rock. Having been with Editions EG for years, Eno left the company, along with director and future wife Anthea Norman-Taylor. Together they started Opal Ltd. The idea was to further Eno's work and those artists allied to him. Thus he became a 'curator' for people like Harold Budd, Michael Brook, Jon Hassell, Daniel Lanois, his brother Roger and painter Russell Mills. Together they forged a new identity for music and released many records. Eno himself was now happily living back in Suffolk in his own house which included his Wilderness studio. The 1988 compilation *Music For Films 3* showcased all sides of Eno's nexus, including a new Moscow recording of the archetypal electronic instrument, the Theremin, by its inventor's granddaughter Lydia.

This threw up a new avenue of exploration for Eno – Russia. In its glasnost phase the country was opening up to all kinds of ideas and having Eno actually work there was a fascinating thought for thousands of musicians starved for years of outside technical expertise. In 1988 Eno chaired a satellite-TV cultural debate called *Opal-Link Leningrad*. Then he went to Moscow to produce a record by Zvuki Mu, an anarcho-humorist rock group. Of greater import, though, was his collaboration with the classically trained violist John Cale (who had worked with La Monte Young, John Cage and The Velvet Underground), who wished to record an orchestral setting of Dylan Thomas poems in the summer of 1989. The subsequent album, *Words For The Dying* (Land), was also recorded in Moscow but under duress as Eno battled with 'the distraction of a film-crew, a strangely-equipped foreign studio and a large orchestra'. That year also saw Opal release a blissful album of Armenian folk music, *I Will Not Be Sad In This World*, by duduk (flute) player Djivan Gasparayan.

For many years Eno had been fascinated by Ambient spaces. He had found locations such as Rome's Botanical Gardens and the Exploratorium in San Francisco interesting enough places to mount installations in previous years. His 1989 invitation to the Tenkawa Shinto shrine near Kyoto in Japan was an opportunity not to be missed. With the help of Michael Brook, he mounted an Ambient performance inside a crater of a volcano, with music deployed around the site to give it a physical presence. Following in the footsteps of Stockhausen's *Park Music* (1968–71), Eno felt 'it tested the line between performance and installation'. He expanded these ideas at the Winter Garden (aided by Jon Hassell) and in 1990 at the Rainforest Installation at London's Barbican, where the sounds of Colombia and the Cameroons were mixed into Eno's own Ambience in a large tropical setting.

For Eno the 1990s brought consolidation, appreciation, public esteem and a much wider field of activity than ever before. Though he made a pop album in Suffolk with John Cale, he admitted in the autumn of 1990 that *Discreet Music* and *Music For Airports* were his best-selling solo albums of all time. (In a BBC Radio interview Eno declared that *Discreet Music* was 'one of the enduring pieces of Minimal music'.) Having once told me that he felt New Age music was mostly 'blurring noises mixed with pretty sounds', by now he saw it as validation that people were listening to music differently. House music also made him excited. 'I love anything that suddenly cuts the grain, sounding great and full of potential. It belittles the other stuff, which suddenly sounds like Hollywood by comparison.' Eno again joined Daniel Lanois to produce U2, this time in Berlin's Hansa By The Wall studios, the scene of Eno's triumphs with David Bowie in 1977. The resultant album, *Achtung Baby*, got away from the 'glossy LA production style', its discordant post-industrial sound again putting U2 ahead of their rivals.

Eno made three more recordings, two of them released in 1992 by Warner Brothers. Eno preferred not to release *My Squelchy Life*, his first foray into House and Techno styles. Instead appeared *Nerve Net*, a pop album which drew on 'jazz, funk, rap, rock, Ambient and World Music'. Then there was *The Shutov Assembly*, Eno's first proper Ambient album for seven years. Drawn from installation musics, *The Shutov Assembly* aurally conjured up locations, as did *On Land* back in 1982. It was a masterly return to form, Eno's various programmes for the Yamaha DX7 synthesizer imbuing electronic music with a ghostly, spiritual presence. The album, in a typically Enoesque fashion, came along by chance. A Russian painter named Shutov gave Eno a painting. He played Eno's music as he painted. Eno thought he'd put together a tape of unreleased pieces. 'I kept a copy of the tape, and when I started playing it I started to enjoy it and see a thread running through the pieces that I hadn't really seen before. They'd never been put together before, you see.'

Yet music only took up part of his attention. During 1992 he worked hard with friends Peter Gabriel and Laurie Anderson to create a Real World theme park in Barcelona. Other things that drew him were the making of perfumes and working on Hypertext computer links. For his way of 'celebrating a feeling' with U2 he received another Grammy Award and made another album with them in 1993. Through working with U2 he arrived at another famous axiom: 'The process of failure prepares you for the moment of success.' More releases followed: the intensely Minimalist Ambient work *Neroli* ('a continuous permutation of various elements as they fall together in different clusters'), boxed sets of his favourite vocal and instrumental music and the intriguing Philip Glass album *Low Symphony*, where themes from *Low* were expanded by Glass and played by the Brooklyn Philharmonic.

What was always intriguing about Eno was that though he criticized what he saw as the 'classical edifice' he always interfaced with it, at times writing music for string ensemble. Between 1993 and 1995 his 'serious' profile rose. In 1993 he received an Honorary Doctorate from Plymouth University in the field of Technology. The following year he was awarded the prestigious Frankfurt Music Prize for *Discreet Music* and given a lifetime achievement award by the University of California. He became an important patron for War Child, a charity set up to bring long-term aid, education and humanity to war-traumatized children in Bosnia. Through his industry contacts Eno encouraged art and fashion events in 1995 (which included the involvement of Minimalists Steve Reich and Michael Nyman) to raise large amounts of cash for War Child. A rock album, *Help*, produced in one day by Eno, made over £1 million for Bosnian aid. Eno talked and wrote extensively about the diffusion of culture, the decentralization of music, the 'unfinished' nature of art and the paucity of both CD-Rom technology and computers. In 1995 he was also appointed Visiting Professor in Communication Design at the Royal College of Art in London. All this activity was soundtracked by a series of collaborations: with David Bowie, *Outside* (RCA); with Jah Wobble, *Spinner* (All Saints); and with U2 an Ambient and experimental set, *Passengers* (Island). The latter featured opera singer Pavarotti, who invited Eno and U2 to Modena in Italy to perform with him; they accepted and raised hundreds of thousands more dollars for War Child. In fact 1995 was so busy for Eno that he published a 400-page diary of his activities the following year.

Eno's endeavours to find a useful way of computers broke new ground in 1996 with *Generative Music*. For years he wanted to provide the public with Ambient music which couldn't be determined. He saw all his releases, particularly *Music For Airports*, as snapshots of this process. In effect he wanted to provide the process itself. 'I'm interested in a system that you feed material into and *it*, the system, reconfigures the material for you. Working with a company called SSEYO, they have produced something called KOAN. It is basically a machine for doing this.' Basically KOAN interacted with a sound-card in a computer and allowed for the creation of variable sets of musics. *Generative Music* was a software package which provided sound experiences both in Ambient music and in styles ranging from the Renaissance to Schoenberg. For Eno it was 'always different but. like recorded music, free of time-and-space limitations.' Importantly, he saw it as a crucial development of twentieth-century music; a tertiary level; a fine line traced from the performance-based unique concerts of nineteenth-century Romantic music to the modern recordings of the twentieth century and beyond.

Eno again cited Steve Reich as his inspiration. And it is here, among his Minimalist peers, that he fits most easily. His interest has always been in pushing the boundaries, 'looking at new cultural spaces', as he puts it. He's certainly responsible for bringing Ambient and Minimalist music to a broad and multi-faceted audience. And he's a key figure in the appreciation of technology and the recording studio, still his primary tool. Talking about his work in 1997, he stated: 'Music as immersion is really the basis of Ambient music. It moves away from the idea of music as a sort of sonic film unfolding before your ears, and instead suggests a place, a landscape, a soundworld which you inhabit. It emphasizes the textural and dynamic aspects of music over narrative and the directional. It suggests a different role for the listener, and a different set of expectations about how music can be used. It ends up somewhere between Muzak and La Monte Young, somewhere between music and sculpture.'

LISTENING

Another Green World (EG 1975)
Discreet Music (Editions EG 1975)
Evening Star (with Robert Fripp) (EG 1975)
Low (with David Bowie) (RCA 1977)
'Heroes' (with David Bowie) (RCA 1977)
Cluster And Eno (Sky 1977)
Music For Films (Editions EG 1978)
Ambient 1: Music For Airports (Editions EG 1978)
Ambient 2: The Plateaux of Mirror (with Harold Budd) (Editions EG 1980)
Fourth World Volume 1: Possible Musics (with Jon Hassell) (Editions EG 1980)
Ambient 4: On Land (Editions EG 1982)
Apollo: Atmospheres And Soundtracks (with Daniel Lanois and Roger Eno) (Editions EG 1983)
The Pearl (with Harold Budd) (Editions EG 1984)
Thursday Afternoon (EG 1985)
The Shutov Assembly (Opal/Warner Bros 1992)
Brian Eno Instrumental Box 1 (Virgin 1993)
The Essential Fripp And Eno (Virgin EG 1994)
Spinner (with Jah Wobble) (All Saints 1995)
Music For White Cube (Opal 1997)

Like Erik Satie, Eno put himself across as a non-musician, but don't be fooled: his bass, keyboard and synthesizer playing on these records is top-notch. *Another Green World* sets the tone for the future – fourteen Satiesque miniatures rapt with the multi-layering potential of the studio, a perfectly poised mix of electronics and acoustic instruments. The title track, as used by BBC's *Arena* arts programme, became one of the longest-running TV themes. *Discreet Music* is one of Eno's loveliest recordings, effected from the shaky tuning of an old EMS Synthi, a tape-driven Gibson echo unit and the delayed echo of two Revox tape machines. It first came out on Eno's innovative Obscure label, Side Two featuring three variations on the seventeenth-century composer Pachelbel's *Canon in D Major*, whereby fragments of the original piece are fed to an ensemble who play them in such a way as to create a delay and feedback system. *Evening Star* is a development from the tape-loop experiments of *Discreet Music* and contains a fragment of the latter. Fripp (guitarist with rock band King Crimson) is the perfect virtuoso foil for Eno's sculptural studio processes. With a shimmering Peter Schmidt landscape painting on the cover, *Evening Star* is still one of Eno's finest recorded statements.

The Bowie albums *Low* and *'Heroes'* originally appeared on RCA and have to be credited to Eno for their instrumental sides. What major rock or pop star would have taken that much risk in 1977 without Eno on board! Today instrumentals like 'Warszawa' and 'Subterraneans' still sound years ahead of their time. (So impressed was Philip Glass by the pair that he recorded symphonic versions of *Low* and *'Heroes'* in the 1990s.) *Cluster And Eno* gives a good indication of Eno's German orientation, the hypnotic effect of 'He Renomo' benefiting from the input of Stockhausen pupil Holger Czukay. *Music For Films* was the commercial release of earlier work for film directors. Its eighteen brief Ambiences succeed in conjuring up an alien world. *Music For Airports* coincides with Eno's move to a new life in the United States. The piano is played by left-field English musician Robert Wyatt while the angelic voices are those of Christa Fast, Christine Gomez and Inge Zeininger. This is one of Eno's most simple and evocative creations, its silence-filled setting a precursor to CD listening of the 1980s.

Having been used to monophonic synthesizers like the VCS3, its keyboard cousin the EMS AKS and the MiniMoog, Eno embraced the Yamaha CS80 polyphonic synth when he arrived at Daniel Lanois' Grant Avenue studio in 1980. You can hear him use it on *The Plateaux Of Mirror* and his MiniMoog and Prophet work imbues the exotic atmospheres of *Possible Musics*. Jon Hassell, along with Michael Brook, Bill Laswell and others, helped on the impressive *On Land*, which evokes many memories and places from Eno's east Suffolk childhood. *Apollo* is the soundtrack to an Al Reinert film covering the *Apollo* space programme between 1968 and 1972. Shot through with Eno's beloved country idioms, the swimming 'Deep Blue Day' was even used by director Danny Boyle in his genius look at the nature of heroin addiction, *Trainspotting* (1996). *The Pearl* is a beautiful creation on which Eno works flat out with Daniel Lanois to place Budd's piano and keyboards in an oceanic paradise. *Thursday Afternoon* was one of the very first custom-made releases for CD and can be played continuously. It was the soundtrack to a vertical-format video painting which, along with *Mistaken Memories Of Medieval Manhattan* (Eno's New York video work of 1980–1), came out on domestic video in 1987.

The Shutov Assembly is an assemblage of installation musics from all over the world from the period 1984 to 1992. It comes replete with Eno's video-painting ideas. The *Brian Eno Instrumental Box* (1993), as well as containing good released Ambient music, comes with unreleased material from the limited editions *Music For Films* (Director's Edition 1976) and *Music For Films 2* (Director's Edition 1983). It also includes a segment of Eno's extremely Minimalist recording of 1993, *Neroli* (All Saints). *The Essential Fripp And Eno* CD of the same year wonderfully remastered their first 1973 collaboration, *No Pussyfooting*, an album credited with bringing Minimalist tape-delay ideas into the mainstream of rock. It also contains excerpts from *Evening Star* and four unreleased tracks from aborted 1978 Fripp and Eno sessions in New York. Eno made music for a film by Derek Jarman, *Glitterbug*, but refused to release it without the involvement of bassist Jah Wobble. Iranian vocalist Sussan Deihim and famed German drummer Jaki Liebezeit soon joined Wobble. One track, a hypnotic piece of atmosphere and tinkly piano dovetailed on the end, was to appear again as 'Iced World' on 1997's *The Drop* (All Saints), an album generated by applying automatic music principles to computer software and largely devoid of Eno's spiritual presence. Far better Ambient work is to be found on *Music For White Cube*, where Eno took a series of London locations, recorded his voice, and then utilized studio effects to colour, focus and stretch the sounds. Eno's interest in pure Ambience and chance was continued in installation pieces such as *Lightness* (Opal 1997), *I Dormienti* (Opal 1999) and *Kite Stories* (Opal 1999), where about a dozen layers of sound were allowed to overlap at random. The resultant 'quiet' musics were some of the best Ambient experiences ever recorded.

PHILIP GLASS

Much has been written about Philip Glass: about his success, the sheer volume of his written and recorded output, his audacious rebirthing of opera through the avant-garde, his enormous fees and the sheer loudness of his ensemble. As the world's most successful new music composer Glass has had his share of critics among the classical establishment but I've always maintained he approaches his art like a rock and roll musician, as interested in spectacle and great records as any young band.

For me there are two really significant events in Glass's musical career. The first was his teenage years spent working in his father's record store in Baltimore and seeing box loads of Elvis Presley records fly out the door. The excitement generated by popular culture, the sight of Elvis and The Beatles on *The Ed Sullivan Show* was to stay with Glass all of his life. The second was his meeting, when he was twenty-nine, with Ravi Shankar in Paris. Invited to help out on the soundtrack to a psychedelic film, *Chappaqua*, Glass had a collision with Indian music which would change him for ever. Transcribing Shankar's music for Western musicians to play, he had to sit and write directly from Ravi's vocal dictation. When he had finished, the tabla player Alla Rakha shook his head and announced, 'All the notes are equal.' Glass tried to rewrite but it didn't work until he dropped the bar lines. Then he had a vision: 'Instead of distinct groupings of notes, a steady stream of rhythmic pulses stood revealed.' Glass's music and Western music in general would simply never be the same again.

Glass was born to hard-working, first-generation Americanized Jews whose roots were in the USSR. Baltimore, Maryland, was the place and 31 January 1937 the date of his birth. His father repaired radios and sold records in an electrical shop. His mother was a librarian. Glass's first music was classical – Schubert, Beethoven, Haydn – which he heard from his father's collection. But importantly his mother knew Jerry Leiber, a popular songwriter who would go on to become one of the most influential of the 1950s and 60s, with Elvis Presley's 'Hound Dog' just one of a dozen hits. This duophonic musical input would make a lasting impression on Glass. 'When I grew up in the 50s the popular music was Italian crooners – Dean Martin, Perry Como and Frank Sinatra. There were a couple of Irish singers, a couple of Jewish singers. It wasn't really big business. Then in 1948 Les Paul bounced layers of sound using monaural tape recorders. Then in the 50s he and Mary Ford created lush textures with early multi-track equipment. Sam Phillips gave Elvis and Jerry Lee Lewis their deep echoes. Then Phil Spector made multi-layered tracks for the Crystals and Ronettes. What I'm basically saying is that I saw the birth of rock 'n' roll. Popular music became mass media with Elvis Presley. There is no doubt it was then because we were ordering records by the box and selling them by the box because they never got time to get on the shelves. Memories like Ed Sullivan introducing Elvis and then The Beatles stayed in the mind. There was actually a kind of hysteria and what I was seeing was the birth of a new culture – a culture that was very broad and that was something we hadn't seen before.'

Today Glass makes no bones about his precocious intelligence: 'I was considered a local whizz-kid.' He was playing violin at six, flute at eight and attending the Peabody Conservatory. Then it was on to the piano and quickly passing into the University of Chicago to do a tough course in Maths and Philosophy at only fifteen. For Glass these subjects were a passing interest. At night he acquainted himself with the music of Charles Ives and Anton Webern. During the summer break of 1954 he went to Paris to follow in the footsteps of his hero Jean Cocteau and lived the wild life of a student bohemian. At the age of nineteen he graduated and went to New York's prestigious Juilliard School of Music, where he met Steve Reich.

By now Glass was pretty proficient at writing and scoring music. The Juilliard was the second hothouse academic environment he'd experienced as a youth. 'It was a very interesting school, considered the premier American music school of the time. It was really a conservatory, a trade school where you learned a trade. You did nothing at the Juilliard but music. Like Chicago, they put very talented people together to see what would happen. It was very hard to get in, very easy to get out. The teaching programme wasn't very heavy. You had a major teacher who was a musical guru in your speciality (in my case conducting and composition) and then concerts were organized, orchestrations, string quartets – that kind of thing. It was a heady atmosphere with lots of talented people working very hard. There was a dance department and Martha Graham was there. I began to write dance music. I also began to write theatre music.'

Glass had written dozens of pieces in the American neoclassical style of Aaron Copland. He had heard John Coltrane, Yoko Ono and La Monte Young. He had ventured to Colorado to study with Darius Milhaud because of his past connection with Jean Cocteau. He got a Diploma from the Juilliard and by 1962 was in Pittsburgh on another award, as an in-house composer for the local public school. After two years of this he got a Fulbright scholarship to go to Paris and study with Nadia Boulanger, who had taught Copland. In 1965 Glass found himself in a situation where Boulanger ridiculed and bullied him, negating his past work and getting him to start all over with punishing lessons in counter-point and harmony. Beethoven and Mozart were the order of the day. The Serial music which Glass had been constantly rejecting was far from his mind here. When asked to write for a Samuel Beckett theatre piece called *Play* he came up with two static lines of music for saxophones.

'I felt modern music as represented by Boulez was a cul-de-sac. I was very unhappy studying modern music because it seemed to have nowhere to go. I felt it was a one-way-ticket – to nowhere. Boulez really didn't write for the general listening public.' Then along came Ravi Shankar. As he had waitered and worked at airports before he went to the Juilliard, Glass now found himself in need of money. He answered the call of Conrad Rooks, who was looking for an inexpensive young composer to score and transcribe Indian music for a pop film. In a Paris studio Glass met Shankar and the aforementioned insight into reductive music occurred. 'It was a watershed, a new beginning. Nadia had taught me how to go beyond myself. [Ravi] represented a composer who was also a performer. And that's where I got the idea of performing my own music. It was a way to find an audience. From the moment I met Ravi I set my sights on making my way in the world as a composer and as a performer and not through the academic system.'

Indian music had shown Glass that a composition could be made out of cells strung together to make larger forms which are unified by a cyclical process. It's this feeling of cyclical motion which would mark out his later music from that of his contemporaries. Having travelled to Morocco with his future wife, Joanne Akalaitis, Glass set off again another voyage of discovery. 'I decided to look around this new culture which Ravi had acquainted me with. I went again to Morocco and from there it was India through Turkey, Iran, Afghanistan and Pakistan.' Glass and Akalaitis spent months at the base of the Himalayas immersing themselves in Tibetan Buddhism. For him it was a new lease of life. 'I had spent a long time at school, starting at eight and now it was twenty years later! I knew it would be a difficult re-entry into the music world because I was going to come in from a very different point of view altogether.'

Astonishingly, Glass had written eighty pieces before 1966. These he turned away from, vowing instead to start afresh. Back in New York in 1967 he met Steve Reich at a gallery concert of Reich's music. The two spoke and Glass went off to write *Strung Out*, *One Plus One* and *Two Pages*, the latter in honour of Reich. This music was loud, simple, fast and used lines of notes in parallel motion à la Debussy. Moreover the music expanded and then contracted after the manner of Indian raga. By 1968 Reich and Glass had teamed up, fronting the same band. A significant gig was one at the Film Makers' Cinematheque in New York's SoHo, which featured *Strung* Out and *Music In The Form Of A Square*, where the musicians, including Glass, had to play walking around the space because the music was pinned to the wall. The most important aspect of Glass's music then was his fascination with electronics and volume. 'At that time synthesizers were not a practical performance vehicle. Robert Moog's first synth was showing up. Don Buchla's computer was around. I took lessons from a young woman named Suzanne Ciani, who is now famous. But back then was before the era of polyphonic keyboards. We needed ten-finger access and the only thing which offered that were simple electric organs by Farfisa and Yamaha.'

Glass was now settled in Chelsea with Joanne Akalaitis and their two children. He worked as a plumber and moved furniture with Steve Reich. Music flowed out of him – *Music In Fifths*, *Music In Contrary Motion* and *Music In Similar Motion*, all written in 1969, worked with loud wind instruments and keyboards. Through them Glass fleshed out drone and open-form composition.

An extension of the cycle, *Music With Changing Parts* (1970), was Glass's first big hit. Its jazzy keyboards and mixture of voice drones, trumpets and violins were meshed. The distinctive sound came from the insistent pounding of a bass organ. It was funky, it rocked. Yet it was full of long tones – sounds seemed to come from a distance, appear and disappear. It was entrancing, intoxicating stuff. Glass set up his own record company, Chatham Square, to record this work as a double album in 1971. In March of that year he visited London with his ensemble to perform *Music With Changing Parts* at the Royal College of Art. Footage of Glass during this phase shows him hypnotized by his own music, his fingers lost in the groove of the keyboard. Brian Eno and David Bowie were in the audience. They were knocked off their feet by the music, Eno particularly impressed with the sound, which was to him akin to heavy metal without the guitars.

Glass had parted company with Reich a year earlier. He had performed on the latter's *Four Organs* but that was it. The two egos couldn't be contained in one band. Glass cites musical differences – his group being constant, Reich's always changing to the desires of his music. On the age-old rivalry Glass said to me in 1991: 'I had very good relations with Steve. When we worked together he was a terrific character. Now he's gone a little cranky, but that shouldn't be taken too seriously.' Glass now had his own ensemble, put together from old university friends and a series of chance encounters. An important new ally was Kurt Munkacsi, a sound designer who had worked with John Lennon and acquired a mobile studio for Glass to record his first album on. He mixed live, achieving a sheen of sound by blending acoustic and electronic instruments. He also worked with La Monte Young. The minute he teamed up with Glass he custom-built a sound system for him which was in constant evolution. Glass tirelessly played galleries and campuses, occasionally nudging his way into rock venues. Various concerts in Europe and America produced fights and walk-outs. Glass in the early 1970s was really annoying the musical establishment.

Then he had another stab at the record market. His *Music In Twelve Parts* was written between 1971 and 1974 and was nearly six hours long. Parts 1–6 were recorded with Munkacsi and conductor, arranger and keyboardist Michael Riesman between 1974 and 1975. A summation of past techniques and a look forward to the future, *Music In Twelve Parts* evinced archetypes of Glass's style – short motifs, repetition, rising and falling arpeggios, hushed, note-like vocalizations termed solfeggio vocals. In Munkacsi Glass had found a perfect foil and Riesman's arrangements were superb. Between the three of them the sound of amplified winds, keyboards and voices was like a signature tune, for ever associated with Glass. Parts One and Two were released in 1974 – one side slow and hypnotic, the other side ripplingly fast. But Glass had no major record deal and drifted easily into the world of music theatre.

In New York's Downtown scene he had met Robert Wilson, a visionary utilizer of time, space and light. By suggestion and strong imagery Wilson filled stages with a meaning that was more appropriate to image- and noise-filled late-twentieth-century life. A friend of his, Christopher Knowles, was autistic but had an incredible gift for word juxtaposition. The three set about creating the first of Glass's portrait operas, *Einstein On The Beach*. The long haul to create this piece, which lasts four hours and forty minutes, is detailed in Glass's book *Opera On The Beach* and reveals a composer both tenacious and full of self-belief. The opera worked around simple images of a bed, a train, a spaceship. Glass had the Einstein character play the violin as had Einstein in real life. Lucinda Childs choreographed and sang. The work was premiered in Europe, where its hallucinatory power drew a whole new young audience. In November 1976, when it came to the Metropolitan Opera House in New York, it sold out its two performances. There was no intermission, the piece functioning as Ambient backdrop. Scores of hippies attended and Glass became a celebrity, the flag-flyer for a new kind of daring modern opera. Though a critical success, *Einstein On The Beach* lost over $100,000 and Glass had to drive a taxi to make money.

The dazzling music of *Einstein On The Beach* could be compared to the smash-hit rock album *Dark Side Of The Moon*, released in 1973 by Pink Floyd. The flowing, fluid dynamics were similar and the 'Trial/Prison' sequence, where Lucinda Childs repeats in robotic manner the experience of a 'prematurely air-conditioned supermarket' to a series of vocalized numbers before the whole ensemble bursts in at ear-splitting volume, has strong similarities with Pink Floyd's album. Violin and flute passages lent a mystical quality to the whole work.

Glass set about recording *Einstein* for the small Tomato label, which put it out in 1977 on a four-LP set. But the company went bust and it wasn't until 1979, when Glass began his long association with CBS, that the whole work was generally available. That year also saw the completion of his second opera, *Satyagraha* (Sanskrit for 'life-force'), based on Gandhi's experiences in South Africa. For this work, commissioned in Holland, Glass used elements of Purcell's baroque music, and also drew on the lives of Martin Luther King and Tolstoy. Almost classical, *Satyagraha* has some beautiful segments – the lilting strings and Minimalist beauty of its final eight minutes are simply breathtaking.

Glass ended the 1970s with some dance pieces for Lucinda Childs and the painter Sol LeWitt. In 1980 he remarried, this time to a doctor, but it wouldn't last. It would be the start of the most intense decade of his life as commission after commission arrived. His big break came in the form of *Glassworks*, a pop record of short pieces released in 1982 and destined to sell hundreds of thousands of copies. Marketed by CBS like any rock album, this concoction of smooth horns, strings and lovingly coaxed electronics made Glass a star. One of the first digital recordings, it revealed a composer committed to pushing every aspect of his work into the future. It is still Glass's most popular recording. To celebrate, Glass began a new relationship with Candy Jernigan, an album-sleeve designer, one that would nearly last ten years. By 1984 he had bought a nineteenth-century townhouse in Manhattan and had finished his third portrait opera, *Akhnaten*, a tribute to the visionary Egyptian pharaoh who brought monotheism to his country in the fourteenth century BC. Glass had even journeyed to Egypt to research the salient details.

Glass was usually up at six every morning, writing with paper and pencil. Kurt Munkacsi was in a studio in Broadway refining digital recording techniques begun on *Glassworks*. A list of Glass's other 1980s commissions is mind-boggling. *Koyaanisqatsi* (1981 – film soundtrack), *The Photographer* (1982 – play), *CIVIL warS* (1983 – Robert Wilson collaboration), *Glasspieces* (1983 – ballet), *Company* (1983 – *String Quartet No. 2* for Samuel Beckett play), *Juniper Tree* (1984 – opera based on Grimms' fairy tales), *Mishima* (1984 – film soundtrack), *The Olympian* (1984 – theme for Los Angeles Olympics), *Descent Into The Maelstrom* (1985 – theatre piece based on Edgar Allan Poe), *In The Upper Room* (1986 – dance piece), *Songs From Liquid Days* (1986 – album based on lyrics of Paul Simon, Suzanne Vega, David Byrne and Laurie Anderson), *The Making Of The Representative Of Planet 8* (1986 – opera based on a Doris Lessing story), *The Light* (1987 – symphonic movement), *Violin Concerto* (1987), *Pink Noise* (1987 – art installation with Richard Serra), *Mozart Piano Concerto No. 21* (1987 – cadenzas), *Powaqqatsi* (1987 – film soundtrack), *The Fall Of The House Of Usher* (1988 – chamber opera based on Edgar Allan Poe story), *1000 Airplanes On The Roof* (1988 – electronicized drama), *Itaipu/The Canyon* (1988 –

orchestral pieces), *Thin Blue Line* (1988 – film soundtrack), *Dances Nos. 1–5* (1988 – recording), *The Voyage* (Metropolitan Opera commission), *Hydrogen Jukebox* (1989 – drama collaboration with Allen Ginsberg), *Solo Piano* (1989 – recording). There were also meetings in London with Mark Moore of S'Express for House remix projects.

Of the above works, the soundtrack for the 1983 film *Koyaanisqatsi* (Hopi Indian for 'life out of balance') would make Glass's star shine even brighter. Written for experimental film-maker Godfrey Reggio, this mix of sombre vocalize and bubbling electronics perfectly suited Reggio's blend of panoramic nature photography and speeded-up images of modern urban life. The fact that the film was edited to Glass's music was remarkable in itself. The string quartet *Company* revealed Glass's versatility and would be featured on the 1987 debut album by the Kronos Quartet alongside music by Jimi Hendrix. Like Reggio, Paul Schrader edited his 1984 biographical film about the Japanese writer Yukio Mishima to Glass's music. *Liquid Days* (1986) was an awkward meeting of Glass with rock lyricists which may have sounded good on paper but not on disc. The following year's *Violin Concerto* was mellifluous beauty. In 1988 Glass again teamed up with Reggio for *Powaqqatsi* (meaning 'life in transformation'). Though the film was a rather weak portrayal of the effects of capitalism on the third world, Glass's soundtrack was a wonder. In the work he samples instruments such as the dousson'gouni, kora, balafon and tambura, which he knew from having travelled in West Africa, Peru and Brazil.

That year Glass confounded all his critics by receiving $325,000 from the 'Met' to write a new opera (a rarity for a new-music composer) for the 1992 season. It was to commemorate Columbus's discovery of America and would be a talking point for years to come. Meanwhile, after the 1988 US presidential election, Glass was fed up with politics and so decided to collaborate with Allen Ginsberg on *Hydrogen Jukebox*. The beat poet (who died in 1997) furnished poems which covered four decades of American social history, some of it personal and melancholic. Glass's final outing of the 1980s, *Solo Piano*, was a return to simplicity – just Glass at the piano. Over sixty concerts were performed to rapturous applause.

Glass entered the 1990s as the established star of Minimalism. No one else had made this much impact, had so much to show for his endeavour. As he once admitted, he worked 355 days out of every 365, working harder than any Wall Street banker. Up at six every morning to write pages and pages of music, he spent the afternoons in the studio with Kurt Munkacsi and Michael Riesman. On top of this there were rehearsals, ensemble concerts and tours. Glass once admitted to me: 'If we worked bankers' hours we'd get nothing done!'

Having reached a different plateau, he returned to his roots in 1990 by reconnecting with Ravi Shankar for the album *Passages*. Here each presented the other with music to flesh out, in a true collaboration of minds and music. Tragedy struck the following year when, shortly after his marriage to Candy Jernigan, she died of cancer. Glass pushed forward all the same.

Before *The Voyage* was finished he quickly collaborated on *The White Raven* with Robert Wilson. For the latter, based on the exploits of the explorer Vasco da Gama, Glass and Wilson drew on *The Wizard Of Oz* to create a fantastical spectacle in Portuguese! By 1992 *The Voyage* was ready and its $2-million Metropolitan production was another runaway success. Its visual tableaux of spaceship, sailing ship, earth and the stars rooted the story of Columbus in the world of Stanley Kubrick's *2001 – A Space Odyssey*. Following this, Glass turned his attention to writing material based on his greatest hero, Jean Cocteau. *Orphée*, based on the Frenchman's 1949 film, would be a chamber opera. Its 1992 production was much hailed for the perfectionism of its writing. That year also saw Glass transform tracks from David Bowie and Brian Eno's watershed 1977 album *Low* into a series of masterly symphonic sketches in his *'Low' Symphony*. Returning to Cocteau in 1993, he did the curious thing of writing music for his 1946 film *La Belle et la bête* (*Beauty And The Beast*), which was performed in front of the film. He also took time out to play a giant organ in Tennessee and release the results. Film footage exists of this jaunt. Glass seemed to be presenting himself as a Renaissance man capable of fulfilling any fancy, whether it be writing a symphony, as in *Symphony No. 2* (1994), or recasting avant-garde rock for orchestra, as in *'Heroes' Symphony* (1996).

In my encounters with Glass he has always expressed an openness to musical experience. Hence his meetings with Ravi Shankar and his rebirthing of two Eno and Bowie albums that had much to do with him in the first place. Glass had no inhibitions in the late 1980s about working with House musicians in England. Today his work is sampled over and over and he is a guru to creators of loud, repetitive strains of music. No doubt about it, Philip Glass made Minimalism a household word, his *Glassworks* cutting right across the social and economic spectrum to become an instant classic. Many have accused him of diluting serious music, so recognizable is his style, but his intense work methods and incredible output must unnerve the begrudgers.

But it his contribution to electronic music that is most undervalued. It was Glass who popularized the early Farfisa portable organs and brought the polyphonic synthesizers of the 1970s into concert halls. Though most of his material is written on his favourite Baldwin piano, Glass favoured the first generation of digital synths and then the second generation using Midi computer systems, keyboard controllers and samplers. He explained to me: 'We don't hang a mic in front of an orchestra. It's all carefully constructed overdubs. Almost every instrumental section is extended electronically. When you hear an instrument it's that instrument plus a synthesized instrument. When I do an opera I hand a completely synthesized version to the theatre's designer and director, the chorus and orchestras. Hence rehearsals are speeded up because everybody knows the music. In truth my organization gives me a tremendous leverage in the music business. Six to eight people work for me in the studio. The work is only limited by the amount of music I can write and I can write a lot of music. If you have no way of getting the music out of your house it backs up and your productivity slows down. I'm lucky in that my music output is geared to how much I can produce, which is nice.'

LISTENING

Einstein On The Beach (CBS Masterworks 1979)
Glassworks (CBS 1982)
Koyaanisqatsi (Antilles 1983)
Satyagraha (CBS Masterworks 1985)
Powaqqatsi (Elektra/Nonesuch 1988)
Passages (with Ravi Shankar) (Private Music 1990)
'Low' Symphony (Point Music 1993)
Music In Twelve Parts (Nonesuch 1996)
'Heroes' Symphony (Point Music 1997)
Dracula (Nonesuch 1999)

Einstein On The Beach, credited to Philip Glass, Robert Wilson and the Philip Glass Ensemble, is a great place to start. Dazzlingly bright, it features a composer and musicians in the first flush of success. Though Elektra/Nonesuch released a new fuller version (by thirty minutes) in 1993, the original four-CD set is the one to get. All CBS product is now credited to Sony. *Glassworks* is still a beautiful record – the silken sound of cellos, horns, clarinets and violas mixed with piano has an intoxicating balm all of its own. According to Glass: 'That was our first digital recording. We worked very hard at Big Apple recording studios. It was done on twenty-four-tracks but the damn machines were constantly breaking down. It was very expensive and so we had the night hours.' Kurt Munkacsi even ensured that the mix was perfect for the then emerging Walkman market. If you only ever buy one Glass album then this is it.

Koyaanisqatsi is a short CD which packs a punch. It's strangely archaic, with its French horns, trumpets and organ sounds, but when the electronics kick in we hear Glass in all his glory. The other soundtrack for Godfrey Reggio, *Powaqqatsi*, is full of ethnic percussion, which gives it a unique ethnic rock and roll sound. *Satyagraha*, recorded in 1985, used the then new thirty-two-track 3M digital multi-track process whereby Michael Riesman continuously over-dubbed parts rather than using the traditional method of editing together several actual performances. *Passages* is a true merging of West and East as Glass meets Ravi Shankar on equal ground. The idea was given the go-ahead by ex-Tangerine Dreamer Peter Baumann and the work recorded in Madras and New York.

Glass's *'Low' Symphony* confirms his interest in the very avant-garde he helped shape; his repeated listening to Bowie and Eno's album, particularly its Minimalist second side, gave rise to this brooding forty-two-minute symphony. *Music In Twelve Parts* confirms Glass's brave decision to switch from Sony to Nonesuch in 1993. Initially released as a two-parter on Caroline in 1974 and then issued in its full glory on Virgin Venture in 1988, *Music In Twelve Parts* shows how tenacious Glass is as it took three decades to get it right. As he admits: 'By this stage we'd been playing it for years, so it sounds much better.' Nonesuch has a comprehensive reissue programme for Glass, including a *new Einstein On The Beach*, *Koyaanisqatsi* and a 'Works' retrospective. The *'Heroes' Symphony* puts a neo-Romantic sheen on the almost alienated sound of the Bowie and Eno original recorded in Berlin in 1977.

The *Dracula* soundtrack is the first score ever composed for Tod Browning's 1931 horror film starring Bela Lugosi. Its eerie antique feel, provided by the Kronos Quartet, is highlighted by Glass's mesmerizing shifting sprites of sound.

ECM

It all happened in January 1975. A young black pianist sat at a grand piano in Cologne's Opera House and improvised. What came out was a fusion of country, blues, gospel and ragtime bound together by a thorough knowledge of Debussy's Impressionism. The performer's grasp of melody, his ability to couch complexity in simplicity and his sheer virtuosity were astonishing. His name was Keith Jarrett. His photo adorned the resultant double album, which came in a high-quality white sleeve. Inside, the vinyl was thick, pressed direct from the metal masters. Its sound was beautiful, the tone of the Bosendorfer and its resonance perfectly captured. Even the audience applause was incorporated into the overall Ambience. The label was green with three white letters: 'ECM'. That album, *The Köln Concert*, has gone on to sell nearly two million copies. It is responsible for widening public taste, particularly among the young, for new music. With its cool, neutral-looking sleeves and beautiful sounding records, ECM changed the face of jazz in the 1970s and that of contemporary music in the 80s. The sound of ECM became so distinctive that it became known by its slogan 'the most beautiful sound next to silence'. The records' covers, with their framed landscape-format photographs, were mimicked by dozens of 1980s New Age music labels. Fortunately the music was unique, ECM's take on Minimalism being authentic.

ECM, or Editions of Contemporary Music, was founded in Munich in 1970 by the German Manfred Eicher. If ever a label was the vision of one man it is this. Eicher has supervised every single recording. The distilled sound, so peaceful yet so full of wonder, is a product of his endeavours in Oslo, together with his trusted engineer Jan Erik Kongshaug. Eicher attended the Berlin Academy, studied bass and composition, then left to work with the city's Philharmonic as well as doing jazz stints. He even spent time with the *crème de la crème* of classical labels, Deutsche Grammophon. When he arrived at a small mail-order Munich label called JAPO in 1970, Eicher seized his chance. Initially the idea was to record exiled American musicians in Europe but Eicher saw more interest in picking up on the piano ideas of Paul Bley, Chick Corea and the aforementioned Keith Jarrett.

Exploration was the key and soon Eicher began to record unusual ensembles, mixtures of acoustic and electric musics, electronically textured. Though he considered live music important, he preferred to gain a 'live' performance in the studio. Listen to the hue and depth of Chick Corea's 1972 duet with vibraphonist Gary Burton on *Crystal Silence* for confirmation of this fact. While Jarrett made the label famous with such documents as *Solo Concerts* (1973), recorded in Bremen and Lausanne, ECM became associated with outstanding young players like the Norwegian soprano saxophonist Jan Garbarek, the German bassist Eberhard Weber, the American guitarist Ralph Towner and the outstandingly slick American guitar virtuoso Pat Metheny.

Not all of ECM's music is quiet. Works by the Art Ensemble of Chicago, Steve Tibbetts, David Torn and Bill Frisell could be described as fiercely intense. But overall the label has gone for 'new music' whose sound and spatial presence is as important as the instrumentation itself. A look at Jarrett, born in Pennsylvania in 1945, is as good an example as any of ECM's arc. He began piano at three and was an incredibly accomplished writer by his teens. After being kicked out of Berkeley's Music School in 1964, Jarrett moved via Boston to New York, where he began playing with Art Blakey, Charles Lloyd and Charlie Haden. In 1970 he ended up on electric keyboards in Miles Davis's group and toured. The following year he gave up electric music for the acoustic piano and his first solo ECM disc *Facing You*. Within three years he was recording for string orchestra and saxophone on *Luminessence* and then for improvisatory quartet on *Belonging* (both 1974 and both featuring Jan Garbarek). After the summit of *The Köln Concert* he turned to the orchestral suite on the dramatic *Arbour Zena* (1975), back to piano on the twenty-album set *The Sun Bear Concerts* (1977) and then back to ensemble with the lilting *My Song* (1978). In 1980 Jarrett began by recording the sacred music of Armenian mystic Gurdjieff and a fully orchestral composition, *The Celestial Hawk*. There was more piano and organ music in the 80s before a series of eclectic works: *Book Of Ways* (a clavichord album, 1986), *Spirits* (an ethnic-sounding double set, 1986) and two straightforward classical performances on Bach's *The Well-Tempered Klavier* (1988) and *Goldberg Variations* (1989). This period was crowned by Jarrett's receipt of the title of Officer of the Order of Arts and Letters from France's Ministry of Culture.

Jarrett continued to make fairly mainstream jazz recordings for ECM, and his series of interpretations of classic jazz tunes, beginning with *Standards*, with Gary Peacock on drums and Jack DeJohnette on bass, was sustained into the 1990s. Yet it was always the Minimalist and solo work which drew most critical attention. In 1991 Jarrett recorded a resonant piano set at the Vienna State Opera which was as good as any of his piano music of the 1970s. Speaking of its mysterious quietness, the pianist referred to a 'music which finally speaks the language of the flame itself'. ECM also accepted Jarrett's recordings of Shostakovich's *Preludes And Fugues*

(1993), Bach's *Sonatas For Viola And Harpsichord* (1995) and Mozart piano concertos coupled with a symphony (1996). In 1997 Jarrett returned with another piano solo album, *La Scala*, performed in Milan's opera house and including an almost-still evocation of 'Somewhere Over The Rainbow'. Although by 1999 he was suffering from the fatigue syndrome ME, Jarrett was still able to record a wonderful set of love melodies at home in New Jersey. *The Melody Of The Night With You* is lyrical piano Ambience at its most exquisite.

Both Jarrett and the Missouri-born guitarist Pat Metheny provided ECM with economic freedom. Metheny's succulent mix of extended Wes Montgomery-style soft guitar passages, ethnic percussion and voicings, plus the pastel shades of Lyle Mays's piano, was an ECM trademark. Coming to ECM via vibraphonist Gary Burton, Metheny signed a solo deal in 1976. His records are beautifully constructed, full of emotional substance and eloquence. There were many recordings before he left the label in 1984, and a handful – *As Falls Wichita, So Falls Wichita Falls* (1981), *Offramp* (1982), *Travels* (1983) and *Works* (1984) – are exemplars of acoustic and electric restraint with potency. A Minimalism-as-Maximalism aesthetic. As Keith Jarrett once pointed out, ECM music could never be confused with New Age soporifics.

In 1984 Eicher founded ECM New Series for composed music. During the 1970s he had sought out and recorded Steve Reich classics like *Drumming* and *Music for 18 Musicians*. He now embraced such Minimalists as Meredith Monk and the Estonian Arvo Pärt, plus sixteenth-century music by Thomas Tallis and the early-music repertoire of the vocal Hilliard Ensemble. In 1994 the Hilliard Ensemble and the stellar Norwegian saxophonist Jan Garbarek provided an unexpected crossover success with *Officium*. Eicher said of ECM in 1989: 'For me a very important premise is stillness – sensitivity to time, musical time; of letting time have a new relationship to sound. I'm fascinated by the aura of space – by what soundwaves transmit to make a tone sing. I want to capture that tone exactly as I hear it.'

LISTENING

ECM is chock-full of fascinating listens. The guitar works of Norway's Terje Rypdal and Brazil's Egberto Gismonti are some of the cream. The gifted Norwegian tenor and soprano saxophonist Jan Garbarek, whose clear, floating sound is reminiscent of the desolate Scandinavian fiords, has been a mainstay of the label since the early 1970s. He is to be found in group and solo recordings and in tandem with some of Jarrett's most inspired exploratory work. Here are ten ECM albums worth buying:

Crystal Silence (1972). Timbral sound-painting from Gary Burton on vibes and Chick Corea on piano.
Solstice (1974). Guitarist Ralph Towner with Garbarek on saxes and Eberhard Weber on bass turn autumnal shade into sound.

The Köln Concert (1975). Keith Jarrett on piano, footfalls, cries and audience too. Awesomely melancholic.

Folksongs (1981). Bassist Charlie Haden, saxophonist Jan Garbarek and guitarist Egberto Gismonti blend the jazz and folk traditions of America, northern Europe and Latin America to spellbinding effect.

Works (1984). American guitarist Pat Metheny's first summation on ECM. As well as beautiful guitar, includes bells, pipes, organ, voices and Lyle Mays's pianos.

Spirits 1 And 2 (1986). Eastern chant, tape collage, piano Impressionism and more as Jarrett ensconces himself in the studio alone with ethnic percussion and flute instruments.

Making Music (1987). Indian musicians Zakir Hussain and Haraprasad Chaurasia team up with guitarist John McLaughlin and saxophonist Jan Garbarek in this high-quality Ambient exploration.

Private City (1988). Englishman John Surman's baritone saxophone tone is supported by recorders and synthesizers in an artful digital recording.

Vienna Concert (1993). Jarrett returns to solo piano with some magical instrumental meditations.

Officium (1994). This huge crossover success features the Hilliard Ensemble singing medieval Latin texts and Jan Garbarek's horn, recorded for reverberation in a Sussex church.

WINDHAM HILL AND NEW AGE MUSIC

During the mid-1980s a phenomenon known as New Age music percolated through the airwaves. In America it became known as 'hot-tub' music – a form of Minimalism so bland that it was only good for playing as background Muzak in the bath. It was no coincidence that New Age music coincided with the intense increase in the money supply which characterized the 'greedy 80s'. The music was aimed primarily at overheated executives who needed to unwind after a Wall Street-style day at the office. For the most part the music was instrumental, relaxing and soothing the listener with innocuous washes of synthesizer and acoustic guitar. Led Zeppelin it wasn't. Most of it was emotionally shallow, pitching through cover design and title at a quasi-mysticism that was ephemeral at best. The better product picked up a constituency among New Age hippies (who had neglected the workaday lifestyle without ignoring the profit motive) and, after the market swelled, some Minimalism of genuine quality was on offer.

The best place to start is Windham Hill, the *crème de la crème* of American New Age labels of the 1980s. The oft-repeated story is that William Ackerman was a carpenter who played guitar for his friends in Palo Alto, California. He was so impressive that sixty of them gave him five dollars each to record an album, *In*

Search Of The Turtle's Navel, which was distributed by hand in 1975. This instrumental album struck a chord and led to the formation of Windham Hill Records. In terms of album design and quality of pressings, the label was a virtual American edition of ECM in Germany. Even Ackerman's role as fatherly supervisor to recordings mirrored Manfred Eicher's. By 1986 Windham Hill was a $20-million corporation. By 1990 $30 million per annum was going through the books and the company had state-of-the-art recording and video studios in Vermont.

The open homage to ECM may have been a result of Ackerman's having been born a German. Having settled in California at the age of nine, he was adopted by a Stanford professor and began playing acoustic guitar at the age of twelve, inspired by the folk and blues purist John Fahey. He attended Stanford University, played rock guitar, dropped out, became a carpenter in Vermont and returned to acoustic guitar and open-string modal tunings. Here the sounds he was interested in were not far away from the work of Miles Davis and John Coltrane. His early repertoire came from pieces for Stanford theatre productions.

Ackerman's instrumental prowess produced some of the most convincing New Age music of its time. Of his first six records on Windham Hill, *Passage* (1981), *Past Light Visiting* (1983) and *Conferring With The Moon* (1986) were all highly regarded instrumental jewels. His open tunings and use of repetition had a strong Minimalist quality helped by a studio technique which favoured close miking and a clear, ringing production sound. Ackerman differed from serious Minimalism in his preference for melodic decoration over simple additive or reductive process.

Not all of Windham Hill was as good as this. In the label's desire to record atmospheric mood music, a lot of so-called 'soft jazz' was recorded. Combos like Shadowfax and Montreaux recorded easily forgettable sounds and Windham Hill's favoured instrumentalists, pianists George Winston, Bill Quist, Philip Aaberg and Scott Cossu, and guitarist Alex De Grassi (Ackerman's cousin and also a carpenter) dealt in pastel shades rather than satisfying music. Quist did the label no favours in 1979 when he recorded *Piano Solos Of Erik Satie*, an insipid interpretation of some of the finest piano miniatures ever written.

By 1980 Windham Hill very well-pressed vinyl recordings had brought an increase in turnover of 649 per cent. Over the next two years business boomed with George Winston's pallid piano records *Autumn*, *Winter Into Spring* and *December*, which by 1983 had clocked up one and a half million sales on the *Billboard* charts. His soporific records belied this Michigan man's background in wandering blues, stride and rock piano. It was as if all his strong emotions had been left out of the Windham Hill records. And this was exactly what the public wanted at the time – something pleasant but not exacting.

With the coming of CD in the early 1980s, Windham Hill seemed tailor-made for the digital age. And it was at this time that the label signed two of its most important musicians, Michael Hedges and Mark Isham. Hedges was a dazzling acoustic guitar exponent from Oklahoma. When he recorded *Aerial Boundaries* for Windham Hill in 1984 he was likened to Jimi Hendrix. The album's deployment of simultaneous slapping string rhythm and fingerpicking melody, double-handed lead playing, multiple tunings, percussive guitar-body technique and new harmonic ideas earned Hedges a deserved Grammy. In truth Hedges on guitar made every other string-bender on Windham Hill seem like a cocktail musician.

Born in 1953 in Sacramento, Michael Hedges was brought up in rural Oklahoma. By his teens he could play cello, clarinet and flute but listened to rock music, particularly The Beatles. After high school he privately studied piano and eventually went (like Philip Glass) to the Peabody Conservatory in Baltimore. There he studied Morton Feldman, John Cage, Stockhausen and modern composition. 'I made a transcription of Varèse's *Poème electronique*, which impressed me enormously, and listened to ECM records. At night I would play in bars, mainly instrumental versions of Neil Young songs.' When he left he wound up playing an open-air movie house in Palo Alto, California, in 1980. There he was spotted by Will Ackerman and immediately signed to Windham Hill.

Mark Isham was similarly gifted and studied. The son of a violinist and a professor of art and music, this New Yorker was able to cast aside piano and violin in 1964 when he was thirteen for trumpet music. Inspired by Mahler and Miles Davis, he studied hard but after university worked for symphony orchestras in San Francisco. He moonlighted with pop and rock bands such as The Beach Boys before heading into jazz and orchestration with the Irish musician Van Morrison in the late 1970s and early 80s. By the time Windham Hill released *Vapor Drawings* in 1983, Isham's style of soft synthesizers ornamented by trumpet, soprano sax, flugelhorn and piano had become distinctive. An intelligent user of both old analogue synthesizers (Prophet, Arp, Moog) and digital means (for example, the Steiner EVI wind controller) Isham released a second Windham Hill album, *Film Music*, in 1985. This was to define his subsequent career as his themes for the likes of the Diane Keaton-Mel Gibson vehicle *Mrs Soffel* went on to make him one of the most in-demand film composers in the Hollywood of the 1990s.

New Age music spread like wildfire throughout the 1980s. At its height one Tower Record shop employee defined it as 'music for the muesli set with a positive ionizer in the corner who look at their Habitat furniture as they pay off the mortgage on their hi-fi'. As a response to Windham Hill, CODA records was set up in the UK in 1983 with the aim (to quote its founder, Nick Austin) 'to make music for the New Age'. Unfortunately, the instrumental doodlings of rock musicians like Rick Wakeman, Tom Newman and Michael Chapman did not convince and neither did their contrived album covers with the words 'New Age' emblazoned across the top. Eventually CODA diversified into instrumental music television in 1989 with its Landscape Satellite channel.

As CD took over from vinyl the demand for instrumental music increased. Every major label created an offshoot to cater for demand. Polygram had Theta, Virgin had Venture, RCA had Private Music. Some labels were lucky enough to have genuine New Age stars on their books. CBS had the Swiss harpist Andreas Vollenweider, who by 1987 had sold four million albums in the US alone. Bigger still was vapid Japanese synth noodler Kitaro, born in 1953. After years of meditation on Mount Fuji, Kitaro created fourteen celestial albums before being signed to Geffen in 1986 after the worldwide success of his documentary music *Silk Road*. At the time Kitaro could attract audiences of sixteen million in the Far East for one televised concert. There were healthfood-and-meditation labels like Kenwest, Vital Body and New World Cassettes which favoured the sounds of whales and plants to actual music. There was British psychic healer Matthew Manning whose Cloud Nine Music series was designed to improve spiritual well-being. There were earnest electronic labels like Innovative Communications in Germany and Erdenklang in Austria which wished to open minds to future developments in synthesizer and other electronic technology.

And there were plenty of nondescript labels like Ocean Disques, MMC, No Speak and Pangaea, the latter two being offshoots of pop group The Police. No Speak was started by the band's manager Miles Copeland in 1987, and Pangaea was the brainchild of the lead singer and solo pop star Sting in 1988. After a while New Age became a marketing tag, a way of refuelling burned-out careers or just plain making money. The better labels, like Virgin Venture, used this market niche to bring genuine Minimalist talent into the mainstream. Their focus was on neglected electronic pioneers like the Germans Hans-Joachim Roedelius, Klaus Schulze, Holger Czukay and new pieces by composers such as Michael Nyman and Ennio Morricone. Virgin Venture even allowed pop star David Sylvian a chance to record high-quality Minimalist electronica with former Stockhausen pupil Holger Czukay.

Another label which gained respect in the late 1980s was Private Music, founded by Peter Baumann, formerly of Tangerine Dream; it signed the German electronic group in 1985. The Los Angeles label also recorded the sitarist Ravi Shankar, who went on to make an album with Philip Glass for it in 1991. Private Music's roster included artists like guitarist Leo Kottke and violinist Jerry Goodman, but it struck gold with Suzanne Ciani. Having studied with synthesizer guru Don Buchla in the 1960s, Ciani went on to teach Philip Glass synthesizer technique in the 70s. During the 90s she was considered the brightest exponent of New Age keyboard music in the US, achieving substantial sales and Grammy award nominations.

By the end of the century New Age was firmly defined as mystical, meditative accompaniment and a niche market. Genuine composer-musicians who had come to prominence through it grew independent and had their own careers. Those who just used it to cash in sank without a trace. Yet New Age has to be credited with allowing Minimalist music a chance to breathe at a time when the music markets were fiercely competitive and new CD technology was finding its feet.

LISTENING

While the bulk of New Age music is instantly forgettable, there are a few fascinating records. All of Will Ackerman's and Michael Hedges's guitar albums on Windham Hill are worthy of attention. Ackerman's *Past Light Visiting* (1983) and *Conferring At The Moon* (1986) both use subtle electronic and ethnic sounds alongside the guitar. As for Michael Hedges, after making the consummate *Breakfast In The Field* (1981) and *Aerial Boundaries* (1984), he did a New Age vocal album, *Watching My Life Go By*, before recording a concert set, *Live On The Double Planet* (1987), which displayed his rock influences with its homages to Jimi Hendrix, Prince and The Rolling Stones. Tragically, Hedges was killed in a car accident in 1997.

The compilation *Windham Hill – The First Ten Years* (Windham Hill 1990) gives a good indication of what the label was about. Below are listed ten other New Age albums which defined the genre:

Kitaro – *Silk Road 1 And 2* (Kuckuck 1980). Celestial soundtrack for Japanese TV series which made Kitaro a New Age synth star.

Laraaji – *Ambient 3: Day of Radiance* (EG 1980). Cosmic music from New York zither-player, with Brian Eno producing.

Mark Isham – *Film Music* (Windham Hill 1986). Soft piano, trumpet and elegant synth textures defined Isham as the American soundtrack composer of the 1980s and 90s.

Seigen Ono – *Seigen* (Pan East 1986). Dextrous melding of piano and guitar with Ambient backdrops from leading Tokyo studio musician-engineer.

Claire Hamill – *Voices* (Coda 1986). Ground-breaking use of the English singer's voice to generate smooth ensemble instrumental sound.

Andreas Vollenweider – *Down To The Moon* (CBS 1986). The Swiss electronic harpist sold millions with this mixture of country, ethnic and classical styles.

Suzanne Ciani – *Velocity of Love* (Private Music 1986). Keyboardist and synthesist Ciani scored huge FM radio success in the US with her brand of sensual New Age.

Gurdjieff/Thomas de Hartmann – *Journey To Inaccessible Places* (EG 1987). A fine recording by pianist Elan Sicroff of Armenian mystic's musical inspiration. What most New Age should have been but wasn't.

Mind Over Matter – *Colours Of Life* (Innovative Communications 1988). A mélange of taped ethnic sounds and studio electronics make up a record which was like dozens of others in New Age canon. The bordered landscape cover shot and innocuous, placid contents (titles include 'Dreams', 'Peace', 'Spirit Catcher' and 'Spirit of Destiny') by Dutchman Klaus Hoock are indistinguishable from other New Age fare.

Into The Heart Of Love — *WOO* (Cloud Nine 1990) — Pan-ethnic London
New Age music with guitars, clarinets and keyboards made by two brothers
who were part of the New Age traveller community. From here House and
Techno music would absorb mass New Age sensibility.

HAROLD BUDD

One of the great piano stylists of the late twentieth century, Harold Budd wrote
slowly unfurling and haunting compositions that were some of the highlights of
Ambient music in the 1980s and 90s. His technique of atmospheric chords
ornamented by delicate Minimalist motifs was enunciated further by his
collaboration with Brian Eno. Drawing a line from Coltrane through John
Cage, the Minimalist painting of Mark Rothko, the vast deserts of America,
Brian Eno and modern electronics, Budd has fashioned some of the most
beautiful, not to say crucial, recordings in Ambient music.

Born in Victorville, California, a dusty town in the Mojave Desert, in 1936,
Budd had a musical mother from West Virginia who sang Protestant hymns and
played the harmonium. Hank Williams was a favourite on the radio. Budd
started drumming when he was eight and while he was at high school wanted to
drum for John Coltrane and Thelonius Monk, whose music he worshipped.
Today he admits: 'I didn't have the skills or keep up the necessary practice to be
really good.' Something of a late starter, he held down various bit jobs,
including working in an aircraft hangar in LA. Turning twenty, he lit out
for San Francisco but returned without fortune to Los Angeles Community
College, where he met a gifted teacher, H. Endicott Hanson, who grounded
him in music theory. At the age of twenty-one Budd was conscripted and while
in the army met the radical jazz saxophonist Albert Ayler. Soon after that he
attended the University of Southern California, where he met electronic
composer Morton Subotnick.

Budd had become enthralled with music theory, but he was more interested in
American music than European, though he loved Erik Satie. After a heavy dose of
Stockhausen, Webern and Boulez he started to grow weary of what he strangely
described as 'the tyranny of the European tradition'. Budd became captivated by
Charles Ives and John Cage. After attending a lecture by Cage in 1961 he felt that he
wasn't alone. 'That really blew me away. Here was the ticket to a new music. After
that I became interested in painters, particularly Mark Rothko and Ellesworth
Kelly, who went strictly for surface, for brilliant blasts of colour. My early music was
based on chance and the theatre pieces I did and were very open-ended and
improvisatory like Cage.' In 1970 Budd wrote his famous *Candy Apple Revision*, a
piece whose entire content was its title and the chord D flat major. In his own words
Budd had 'minimalized himself out of a career'. From then until 1976 he lectured in
music at the California Institute for the Arts.

By 1977 Budd had written an elaborate score for celesta, harp, marimba, vibraphone and pianos. It had taken him six years and had aroused the curiosity of Brian Eno, who in England had started the experimental label Obscure Records. The two spoke and Budd went to London to record an album of gorgeous impressionistic hue called *The Pavilion Of Dreams*. This 1978 opus included Michael Nyman, Gavin Bryars and saxophonist Marion Brown. It was a wondrous creation and established Budd as one of finest exponents of Ambient minimalism of the period. Eno was keen to document Budd's composerly ability and Budd was equally keen to see how the producer worked in the studio. Within two years the two had reunited for the collaboration *The Plateaux Of Mirror*, where Budd witnessed first-hand how Eno used the studio as another instrument. 'We did good pieces quickly, just piano and ambience. What I was playing was going through a configuration of processing machines and I was hearing that as I played, so that the treatments influenced what I played. This was a brand-new world of making solo music that was hardly solo.'

Back in America, Budd worked productively between 1981 and 1983 to produce two recordings – *Serpent In Quicksilver* and *Abandoned Cities*. The first explored various keyboards and synthesizers intertwined with pedal-steel guitar. The second involved two lengthy atmospheric pieces for an installation at the Fisher Art Gallery in Los Angeles. Intense and majestic in design, these electronic tone-poems displayed Budd's acumen in the studio. Soon after he was back with Eno, this time with Daniel Lanois in the Lanois brothers' studio in a big, rambling house in Ontario. For weeks in 1984 they recorded *The Pearl*, an album of ultramarine quiet which would make its mark with the public. 'This was much more cohesive and focused than *Plateaux*. By then we had all become mature in that musical language.'

Unlike the traditional classical pianist, Budd did not see himself as a performer. 'I think of myself as a composer who occasionally plays the piano.' His path into music – rural desert upbringing, love of the country and lack of interest in the urban rush – had given him a uniquely relaxed approach. Therefore he didn't raise an eyebrow when lots of harmonizer and reverb were applied to the acoustic and electric pianos he used on *The Pearl*.

In 1985 Budd was in the apartment of Michael Hoenig, a keyboardist who had played with Tangerine Dream. There he discovered the Synclavier keyboard and wrote a lengthy piece with Japanese drum rolls titled *Gypsy Violin*. At the same time he heard some cassettes by the Scottish group The Cocteau Twins and in 1986 returned to London to record two records, *Lovely Thunder* and *The Moon And The Melodies*. The first featured ideas he had fleshed out on Synclavier and Fairlight Computer Music Instrument in LA, while the second was a strange collaboration with the operatic vocals and treated guitars of The Cocteau Twins.

In 1988 Budd concluded his UK work with a final collaborative album with Eno, *The White Arcades*. In 1990 he returned permanently to California, where he travelled the desert and wrote about Indian legend. He focused this in an album of instrumentals and poetry, *By The Dawn's Early Light*, which was recorded in Daniel Lanois's French colonial mansion in New Orleans. For this ensemble piece of guitar, viola, harp and keyboards Budd remembers 'covering the Steinway piano with horseblankets to get a muffled, muted sound'. The idea was to get 'chords flowing freely in space'.

Budd continued to live a Buddhist existence, indifferent to material gain. Even the destruction of his piano by a Californian tremor in 1994 did not faze him. Instead of writing for keyboards he wrote poetry and collaborated with musicians like Andy Partridge and Hector Zazou.

Budd maintains that at one point he clocked up 200,000 miles travelling around the world 'concertizing', as he puts it. His reputation established, he maintained strong links with the art world. In fact he always considered himself 'an artist who likes working with ideas'. In a hot, dusty Arizona town called Mesa he produced the stunning keyboard solo album *Luxa* in 1996. Its superlative contents were a homage to his favourite twentieth-century artists. On its release Budd praised the Minimalist tradition, particularly the work of Terry Riley, Philip Glass, La Monte Young and rock group Pink Floyd. He stated simply: 'I feel a kinship.'

LISTENING

Many of Budd's recordings have become classics of the genre. *The Pavilion Of Dreams* (Obscure 1978) is Ambient ensemble design at its best. Both *Serpent In Quicksilver* and *Abandandoned Cities* (released as a single disc, Land 1989) convey Budd's drained but poignant desert visions. *The Pearl* (EG 1984) catches the Eno-Lanois production team at a time when they were limbering up for U2. Nobody has conveyed the sense of an ocean world like Budd before or since. *Music For Three Pianos* (All Saints 1992) is a miniature masterpiece, while as a career summation and a deployment of Budd music *Luxa* (All Saints 1996) is hard to beat.

JON HASSELL

One of the most significant catalysts of the twentieth century, the American trumpeter Jon Hassell acted as a nexus for a confluence of different musics which integrated aspects of Miles Davis, Stockhausen, La Monte Young, Terry Riley, Pandit Pran Nath, Brian Eno and latter-day Hip-Hop, Trance and Trip-Hop styles. On the release of his significant *Possible Musics: Fourth World Vol. 1*, Hassell stated: 'I propose a kind of classical music of the future which is as structurally well defined as, for example, a symphony. I want an integration of the best qualities in Western music and the freedom that exists in all great non-Western classical music.'

His integration of Third World sounds with First World equipment created a hybrid he dubbed 'Fourth World Music', an instrumental form which initiated the World Music explosion in Western music of the 1980s.

Hassell was born in Memphis, Tennessee, the birthplace of rock and roll, in 1937. Therefore he is the same age as the other major minimalists Glass, Reich, Riley and Young. His father worked for the Internal Revenue Service but played a cornet. Inspired by the dance bands and trumpeting of Harry James, Stan Kenton and Maynard Ferguson, Hassell took up the instrument. He often frequented black bars and had many black friends despite the racial segregation of the times. Yet his academic inclinations directed him towards New York and after high school he enrolled in the Eastman School of Music in Rochester. During his second year, while playing hotel lounges and rooftops, he acquired a scholarship and studied composition and orchestration. Hassell remembers Eastman as a conservative school but by the time he got his Master's degree he was into the wave of European Serial music which had spread after Webern and was being spearheaded by Stockhausen.

Impressed by Stockhausen's *Gesang der Jünglinge* (*Song Of The Youths*) and what he described as the German's 'thoroughgoing out and out musical dedication', Hassell enrolled for two and a half years in the Course for New Music in Cologne. Here he was exposed to all manner of new musics. He heard for the first time the work of Luciano Berio and Pierre Boulez, and Stockhausen himself performed a Minimalist piece by La Monte Young. On a personal level Hassell shared classes and rooms with Irmin Schmidt and Holger Czukay, who would go on to form the most important German rock band of the 1960s and 70s, Can. He took his first LSD trip with Schmidt and was greatly taken by the almost surrealistic character of Czukay.

In 1967 Hassell returned to America. He met Terry Riley at the Center for Creative and Performing Arts at Buffalo University, New York State. Riley had formed an ensemble to perform *In C* and so Hassell took up the trumpet again. Interest from David Behrman at Columbia meant Hassell ended up on the first Minimalist recording of *In C* in 1968. Hassell told me: 'Terry was very influential during his semesters there. A chance remark of his when we were hanging out together made me sit up and think. He described all Serial music as "neurotic" and since psychoanalysis and Freud were happening in Vienna at the same time it seemed to make sense. We talked about a music that one could float away to and that was actually enjoyable to listen to. And because of the times it made sense. The history of drugs in America is inextricably linked with early Minimalism.'

Hassell pursued a PhD in musicology at Buffalo while creating such pieces as *Solid State* (1969), a tuned sound mass which became a hit on the US art circuit. He involved himself with La Monte Young in New York and performed live and on record in the latter's Dream House concept. Back in Buffalo in the early 1970s, he again met Terry Riley, who presented him with a tape of the North Indian singer Pandit Pran Nath, a specialist in the ancient kiranic style of singing.

Later, at the Documenta festival in Rome, Hassell, in tow with La Monte Young, shared a bill with Nath. Influenced by Miles Davis's *Bitches Brew* and *On The Corner*, Hassell was using wah-wah pedal with trumpet and putting it through electronic effects. Nath heard this and started improvising a vocal. Hassell saw it as 'a lens back through five centuries pure music a drawing of a line that is pure raga'. The upshot of this was that Hassell accompanied Young, his wife Marian Zazeela and Pran Nath on a pilgrimage to Dehra Dun, in northern India. Meditating in mountain temples before dawn and coming down to improvise music was the stuff of mystery and imagination. Pran Nath would be beckoned to the US by Young and Riley, while Hassell incorporated more Indian raga into his style. By 1977 he wanted to begin a recording career with a sound that was 'so vertically integrated that you were not able to pick out a single element as being from a particular country or musical genre'.

After a couple of records Hassell hit his stride in 1980 with *Possible Musics: Fourth World Vol. 1*, the album which introduced his breathy, digitally altered trumpet lines to the world. Backed by Brian Eno's subtle synthesizer sounds, the record had a totally individual feel. Hassell played and recorded with the pop band Talking Heads and in 1981 made another influential recording, *Dream Theory In Malaya*, which integrated various ethnic sounds with the water-splash rhythms of Malayan aborigines. His influence was duly recognized by Peter Gabriel, who requested his presence at the first World Of Music, Art And Dance (WOMAD) festival at Bath, England, in 1982. His performance with the Master Drummers of Burundi and the Royal Court Gamelan of Indonesia made World Music a visible force in the UK for the first time.

In Europe Hassell became a celebrity of the new primitivism and was fêted by French and Italian cultural ministers. In 1983 he returned to Canada to record his favourite album, *Aka-Darbari-Java (Magic Realism)*, a meld of Indian Darbari raga motifs over Senegalese drumming, Aka pygmy voices from the central African rainforest, Gamelan percussion from Java and the five-octave vocal range of 1950s singer Yma Sumac, orchestrated by Les Baxter. It was called 'unearthly', 'a unique blend of magic and science'. Hassell says he felt 'like a painter blending all these things into a place that was both familiar and very strange'.

From there Hassell became a constant on the world art and music circuit. He collaborated successfully with David Sylvian, the former singer of the UK group Japan, and recorded more records with the U2 production team of Brian Eno and Daniel Lanois. In 1989 he shaped the theme music to the Martin Scorsese film *The Last Temptation Of Christ* and reunited with Terry Riley for a performance of *In C* in China with the Shanghai Film Orchestra. In 1990 so impressed was he with the Africanness of black American Hip-Hop and rap culture that he made a record around it, *City: Works Of Fiction*, which 'ends with quiet African drums and his familiar trumpet chords'. In the 1990s Hassell was hailed as a visionary by such diverse Techno and Ambient musicians as The Orb, 808 State, Tricky and Howie B.

LISTENING

Possible Musics: Fourth World Vol. 1 (EG 1980) is a silky-smooth listen abetted by Eno's sound textures. *Dream Theory in Malaya* (EG 1981) is more primitive but with fascinating sleeve notes. *Aka-Darbari-Java (Magic Realism)* (EG 1983)is essential late-twentieth-century music which conjures up the aural impressions of the fiction of Gabriel García Márquez. *Power Spot* (ECM 1986) is another fine album, as is *Flash Of The Spirit* (Intuition 1988). Hassell's contributions to David Sylvian's *Brilliant Trees* and *Words With The Shaman* (Virgin 1984–5) are excellent and his involvement in Peter Gabriel's *Passion* (Realworld 1989) noteworthy. His 1994 album *Dressing For Pleasure* (Warner Brothers) further investigates American black music culture while drawing on the fountain of inspiration of Miles Davis.

Hassell even collaborated with the atmospheric American guitarist Ry Cooder for an album couched in the Ambience Indian flute and tambura titled *Fascinoma* (Water Lily 1999). He then entered the twenty-first century by making breathy trumpet contributions to the Ambient soundtrack of the Wim Wenders-Bono film *The Million Dollar Hotel* (Island).

MICHAEL NYMAN

Throughout the 1960s and 70s Michael Nyman was the UK's chief advocate for Minimalism. In fact it was he who invented the term to describe the wave of new music coming from the minds of Terry Riley, Philip Glass and others. During the 1980s and 90s he was the country's most successful Minimalist composer, clocking up album sales in the hundreds of thousands and eventually in the millions. His 1993 soundtrack for the Jane Campion film *The Piano* made him a *cause célèbre* all over the world and sold in excess of two million copies. Nyman's importance doesn't derive just from his commercial success, but also from his writings, his embracing of the studio and his own realization that the music of the past can be a rich source for the music of the present.

Born in London in 1944 of Jewish parentage, Nyman always looks at his musical upbringing as conventional. 'My parents were not remotely musical. I got a whole grounding in musical history from a very dedicated music teacher in Northeast London. I listened to everything from Monteverdi to Stravinsky. I learned the symphonic repertoire and went to the opera a lot. It was an amazing experience and I had it from the age of ten when I started playing piano.'

He attended the Royal Academy of Music in London from 1961 to 1964 and there studied the normal musical elements: history, composition, keyboards. During that time he wrote four pieces of music after the lugubrious style of Shostakovich, which all got a public airing. In 1963–4 he actively involved himself in the atonal and Serial music of Peter Maxwell Davies and Harrison

Birtwistle. Seen as revolutionary young turks at the time, they impressed Nyman with their nerve. 'I admired them but I couldn't sit down and express what I wanted to express in this post-Webern medium.' Instead he opted for musicological research.

Nyman went to King's College, London for further studies. There he met Thurston Dart, a keen early-music specialist, who encouraged his interest in the great seventeenth-century English composer Henry Purcell. In the words of Nyman: 'He presided over my (still unfinished) PhD thesis on sixteenth- and seventeenth-century repetitive and systems music!' These were works more akin to the electronic experiments of Steve Reich and Terry Riley, but Nyman had no problems applying them to the canons and rounds of Purcell's day. In 1965 he even went to Bucharest to research into Romanian folk song. On finishing this study in 1967 Nyman still felt unsure as a composer. He worked on reclaiming authentic versions of baroque music for a year and even edited for the German music publisher Universal Edition until 1972.

His most important role, though, was as a music critic for various British publications: the *Spectator*, *New Statesman*, *Music And Musicians*, and the *Daily Telegraph*, where he openly espoused new music. He began in 1968 by supporting the more radical ideas of Boulez and Stockhausen but by the end of the decade had shifted his perspective to the work of John Cage, Terry Riley and Englishmen like Cornelius Cardew and Gavin Bryars. He coined the word Minimalism to describe this new, American-influenced sound, and became its greatest English champion. More than that, he played with the makers of the music – with Cardew's Scratch Orchestra and with the Portsmouth Sinfonia, where he met Brian Eno, and most importantly joined Steve Reich's Musicians for the year of 1972. Also during that time he experimented with a VCS3 Putney synthesizer, developed in London by the scientist Peter Zinovieff's company Electronic Music Studios, or EMS.

Nyman collected his writings in the ground-breaking book *Experimental Music: Cage And Beyond*, which was published in 1974 and was enthusiastically received in the US. From that time he made his living as a music lecturer, being a prominent figure in the art departments of colleges such as Maidstone and Goldsmiths as well as the famous Slade School of Art. Again he met Eno and Cornelius Cardew. In 1976 two significant things occurred to revitalize Nyman's own music. First, he was asked by his old friend Harrison Birtwistle to organize eighteenth-century gondolier songs for a production at London's National Theatre. He formed a band that would play loud versions featuring medieval instruments mixed with brass, keyboards and electric guitars. This would eventually become The Michael Nyman Band.

Secondly, Brian Eno recorded Nyman's debut album, *Decay Music*. Nyman's own reminiscences are important here. 'That was the first time in my life I'd ever been in a recording studio. I'd known Eno through the Portsmouth Sinfonia and myself and my contemporaries like Gavin Bryars, Cardew and Tom Phillips had collectively fed into Eno's education as an art student.

Suddenly he came up with this label Obscure Records. He recorded pieces by John Cage and John Adams and I helped him out in the second phase. It was a new opportunity. Eno was quite a glamorous figure with a lot of power, the power to put records out and the power to be able to record in a good twenty-four-track studio – a first for me.' *Decay Music* was recorded in Island's studios with Eno producing. Considered now to be a fairly mechanical example of Nyman's 'systems' music for piano and bells, it nevertheless kick-started his recording career.

The album had started its life as a rejected soundtrack for a Peter Greenaway film. Greenaway was a reclusive Englishman who organized surreal tableaux into highly objective films. He had met Nyman during the 1960s and by the early 70s they were collaborating on a children's film – Nyman banging out a soundtrack on his synthesizer. The film was never made. But, from 1978 onwards, Green-away's experimental non-narrative works, like *A Walk Thru H*, *The Falls* and *Vertical Features Remake*, all carried Nyman's music. Then, in the early 1980s, Greenaway visited Nyman's West London home to discuss music for a new film. The story, set in late-seventeenth-century England, concerned a man who was commissioned to make twelve different drawings of a country house. Nyman was to score each drawing to fix it in the viewer's mind. There was no script and the music would be used, in Nyman's words, 'to lubricate the plot'.

The result was *The Draughtsman's Contract*, the work which established both Nyman and Greenaway at the cutting edge of English film and music in 1982. Nyman's score of burping horns and humorous harpsichord snatches was perfectly suited to an ironic look at be-wigged high jinks in post-Restoration England. Henry Purcell was the inspiration for Nyman, who adapted his ground basses for a more modern Minimalist music with sure aplomb. Excerpts like the hypnotic 'Garden Is Becoming A Robe Room' were a fresh window into the past, as was the film's arch look at aristocratic exploitation of an honest artisan.

Production of *The Draughtsman's Contract* album was done by David Cun-ningham, an electronic musician who Nyman had met through the pop group The Flying Lizards. Cunningham would handle most of Nyman's recordings from this point. Over the next nine years the Nyman-Greenaway soundtracks would become legendary. There was the quirky *A Zed And Two Noughts* (1985), the Mozart-inspired *Drowning By Numbers* (1988), the choral Gothic of *The Cook, The Thief, His Wife And Her Lover* (1989) and the vocal and instrumental lushness of *Prospero's Books* (1991), which marked the end of their relationship. Greenaway has said that Nyman's music 'shows its skeleton admirably, delights in repetition, has an ironic sense of its own existence and is nicely self-reflexive'. Nyman found the separation of music from film in his partnership with Greenaway (music always preceding shooting) an unpredict-able and exciting way to work.

All the soundtracks have beautiful static moments, where deftly manoeuvred strings, horns, reeds and brass float in unison through aural space. The Shakespearian origins of *Prospero's Books* provided Nyman with much material, and the album provides a valuable insight into Nyman's advanced techniques. Yet Nyman objected to the discrepancy between the film music and the soundtrack released on record. His objection led to a break with Greenaway: 'It was the longest process ever. Nearly a year. I'd given Peter a bunch of music which he liked. That was fifty per cent of it. The rest of the music was composed especially – a series of songs and a miniaturized opera. Peter had grown quite attached to the initial music. There was the actual soundtrack and the idealized soundtrack recorded for the album. In the end I felt the discrepancy was too great between what he used in the film and what I achieved on the album.' In Nyman's mind the Decca album was superior and a fruitful partnership had been muddied.

Outside his work with Greenaway, the 1980s was the decade where Nyman established himself as a left-field composer of merit. In 1982 he wrote *I'll Stake My Cremona For A Jew's Trump* for electronically modified violin and viola. This became a film directed by Sara Jolly. Another film connection was his arrangement of 'Spread A Little Happiness' for pop star Sting in the movie *Brimstone And Treacle*. Two years later Nyman wrote the music for a video opera, *The Kiss And Other Movements*, an energetic take on ensemble pieces which, according to Nyman, 'used repetition to emphasize change'. It became an EG album in 1985.

Around this time Nyman collaborated on many dance pieces, notably with Rosemary Butcher, Lucinda Childs and Ashley Page. In 1986 came his most ambitious project, a full touring opera based on a book written by the neurologist Oliver Sacks. The book concerned a man suffering from distorted vision – literally *The Man Who Mistook His Wife For A Hat*. Nyman wove his insistently repetitive patterns around tunes by Schumann and was taken to task by the classical establishment for picking at musical history in this piece lasting over seventy minutes. Ignoring the criticism, he went high-tech to record the opera with David Cunningham in 1988 for CBS Masterworks. Then he teamed up with dancer Shobana Jeyasingh in a televised combination of string-quartet music and Indian classical rhythm. The Cannes film festival heard Nyman's music in 1989 when he scored the Patrice Laconte film *Monsieur Hire*, based on a detective novel by Georges Simenon. The composer's pen had also fulfilled many commissions for ensembles around the world and his own Michael Nyman Band (like the groups of Glass and Reich) was constantly touring.

At that time Nyman emphasized the constant stream of commissions and work: 'I have to appear in a straight festival one day, a rock festival the next, a dance thing the day after and a film-music convention the day after that.' His attitude to the classical establishment was ambiguous – he disliked its suspicion of repetitive music but as a composer desired its patronage.

The times were changing as musical styles began to blend and overlap. In 1991 Nyman was signed to Decca Records (original home of The Rolling Stones) but allowed to maintain his association with Virgin. His first two records were show-stoppers, recorded in the most up-to-date digital fashion in

London's Abbey Road Studios, made famous by The Beatles. *Prospero's Books* for Peter Greenaway I've already mentioned. *Songbook*, with Ute Lemper, was a cycle of songs for the Berlin chanteuse dubbed the new Dietrich. Her Brechtian style was reminiscent of 1930s cabaret and very theatrical. Nyman chose texts credited to the German poet Paul Celan, Shakespeare, Mozart and Rimbaud. A stream of string quartets and concertos would also be released but Nyman's biggest challenge was yet to come.

The New Zealand director Jane Campion had come to prominence with *An Angel At My Table*, a powerful film about a writer institutionalized by her own family. Her next film, *Piano Lesson*, again looked at exploitation and disability. Nyman's own reflections are interesting here: 'Its main character, Ada, played by Holly Hunter, has been dumb from the age of six. She uses the piano as a means of expression. It acts as a possession from the old world into the new and becomes a means of exchanging sexual favours with Harvey Keitel. Ada was this untutored, eccentric, strong-willed character who composed anything she wanted. Holly Hunter, who's a fairly good pianist, performed my music on shot. With Peter Greenaway I just threw my music at him; with this I had to write the music around the character. The music had to be suitable for the medium, be derived from late-1860s Romantic and Scottish folk song and be mobile and emotional enough to support the content of the film's plot.'

The film, now titled *The Piano*, was a runaway success on release in 1992. Nyman's addictive but simple piano themes were indeed a memorable ingredient. Moreover Nyman was inspired by Holly Hunter's Oscar-winning performance. He recalls: 'She took the work under her wing and made it very intense and very personalized. It was fluid and lyrical and much less mechanistic than if I'd done it. For *The Piano* album [1993], an actress showed me how to perform my own music.'

By this stage Nyman was composing in South-west France, where he had a house fitted out with a studio. He had used electronic keyboards in the past and here he had a computer and keyboard set-up. Though he liked technology his favoured means were the acoustic piano and paper. *The Piano* album and film seemed to define Nyman. He made several more recordings of the music and toured it to ecstatic audiences. At the time he was getting offers that before were unthinkable. He commented: 'Before, it was occasional concerts – National Theatre foyer; bandstands on beaches; outside art galleries rather than inside art galleries – pretty scrappy. Now people, particularly in the film industry, know I exist.' In 1997 Nyman appeared alongside popular musicians like Lou Reed, Laurie Anderson, Ryuichi Sakamoto (all inspired by Minimalism) and the author Salman Rushdie in a gala new-music event in London's Festival Hall. After a mesmerizing performance of the reiterative folk theme from *The Piano* Nyman received a standing ovation. Having persisted in championing Minimalism in the UK, he had finally triumphed.

LISTENING

The Draughtsman's Contract (Charisma 1982)
Drowning By Numbers (Virgin Venture 1988)
The Cook, The Thief, His Wife And Her Lover (Virgin (Venture 1989)
The Nyman-Greenaway Soundtracks (Virgin Venture 1989)
Prospero's Books (Decca 1991)
The Piano (Virgin Venture 1993)
Michael Nyman Live (Virgin Venture 1994)

From the very first time Nyman went into a studio he fell in love with the layering process of multi-track recording. When he began working with Peter Greenaway, the violinist Alexander Balanescu, saxophonist John Harle and producer David Cunningham would all play key roles. *The Draughtsman's Contract* is still Nyman's most spritely and immediate recording, alternating between humorous reworkings of baroque music and sonorous arrangements. *Drowning By Numbers*, influenced by Mozart's *Sinfonia Concertante*, is beautifully reflective and elegiac. *The Cook, The Thief, His Wife And Her Lover* is part strident, part melancholy, and accurate in its aural representation of a lurid Jacobean passion-killing starring Helen Mirren. More importantly, it features the first Nyman choral writing for film. *The Nyman-Greenaway Soundtracks* is a boxed set.

Vocal writing would be fully expressed in Nyman's splendid final collaboration with Greenaway, *Prospero's Books*, in 1991. At the time Nyman reflected on recording soundtracks: 'When doing a soundtrack there is usually one recording and three mixes – a rough mix to work/edit to, a final playback mix for the film and another mix for the album.' Nyman and engineer Mike Dutton did extensive work on *Prospero's Books* in Abbey Road Studios. The album involved digital recording and computerized mixing techniques. Lots of electronic effects were also used to alter and improve the sound. The results are sumptuous, running the full gamut of Nyman's abilities.

At the time Nyman told me of his perceptions of recording music, among the clearest insights ever into the process: 'Classical recording is vertical and incomplete. Complete texture is derived from short takes which are in the end edited together. My way is horizontal but incomplete. The texture is in the tracks I lay down but the picture is not complete until the mix.' The multimillion-selling album *The Piano* was recorded in Munich with members of The Michael Nyman Band and the Munich Philharmonic. Nyman's own piano pieces are a career best. *Michael Nyman Live* is a summation; recorded in Spain, it features *The Piano* and music recorded with Moroccan musicians.

JOHN ADAMS

After nearly twenty-five years of creativity the American Minimalist composer John Adams made a statement in early 1997 which in essence is the watchword for this entire book: 'There's a vast synthesis happening now. All genres are beginning to collapse.' His belief that several styles could inhabit the same musical experience meant that his creations were cross-pollinations which skitted across the entire century of music and beyond. Adams used Minimalism to forge a more expansive expression, one that embraced both popular and classical music, and one that became increasingly successful with the public. He revealed that Minimalism was versatile enough to embrace contemporary news story (*Nixon In China*, 1987), top-quality commercial recordings (*The Chairman Dances*, 1986) and pure electronic music (*Hoodoo Zephyr*, 1993). In many ways he is the twentieth century's last great Minimalist creator.

John Adams was born in 1947 in Massachusetts to a pair of musicians. His sax-playing father met his mother, a popular singer, in a New Hampshire dance hall by a lake one summer in the 1940s. Adams's childhood was full of movement around New England, from Boston to East Concord via Woodstock. In his family no lines were drawn between the classical music of Haydn and Mozart and the jazz styles of Duke Ellington and George Gershwin. Adams started on the clarinet at eight and was composing at the remarkably young age of eleven. He joined his father's marching band and was considered so gifted that by his early teens he was conducting his own music in the community orchestra.

A local hero, Adams easily gained a scholarship to study at Harvard University in Boston after leaving high school in the mid-1960s. He immediately connected with several orchestras, including the Boston Symphony and, following in the footsteps of his hero Leopold Stokowski, began to make a name for himself as a conductor. Like John Cale before him, he was invited by Leonard Bernstein to Tanglewood Conservatory. Also like Cale (who would go on to fame in the proto-Minimalist rock band The Velvet Underground), Adams was impressed by the possibilities inherent in rock music and admired the intense psychedelia of Cream, The Doors and Jimi Hendrix, who all sprang to fame in 1967. He dallied with the hippie mood of the times and by 1969 was investigating Donald Buchla's synthesizer, which the Harvard music department had installed that year.

Like most young men of his era, Adams got a draft notice to fight in the Vietnam war. He avoided this by staying on at Harvard for another two years to do a Master's degree. Most of his time at college had been spent studying fairly difficult Serial music and though he admired Schoenberg, Webern and Berg, he did not feel his own musical instincts were completely in that direction. By 1971, inspired by the writings of John Cage and William Burroughs, he was thinking of new avenues. John Cage revealed to him that 'silence' was as important an instrument in music as sound. Burroughs's cut-up method and pliability with words showed that technique need not be a barrier to humour or popularity. In the summer of 1971 Adams headed west, to San Francisco and a new life in music.

His first year there was inconspicuous, spent in manual labour on the docks. In 1972 he was taken up by the San Francisco Conservatory, where he taught and cajoled students into New Music. He conducted their Ensemble and in 1973 came up with the 'dream polyphony' of *American Standard*. Here Adams used reeds and strings to evoke an extreme melancholy. Long-held notes and isolated tones gave it the elegiac flavour of American nostalgia. Divided into three parts, 'John Philip Sousa', 'Christian Zeal And Activity' and 'Sentimentals', it had a middle section which contained found material related to evangelism while the third section quotes directly from Duke Ellington. Adams allowed a Cageian openness in the work's preparation. This highly original piece, inspired by Cornelius Cardew in the UK, was one of the first recordings which Brian Eno chose (with the help of English composer Gavin Bryars) for his Obscure Records label in 1975. Because of this Adams instantly became aligned with Ambient music and was seen as being among the cream of new American composers.

That year he made *Lo-Fi*, derived from old speakers, car radios, 78rpm records and broken turntables. He also began building his own synthesizers and through trial and error achieved a fairly effective range of integrated circuits and filters. Adams was to spend three years in this study, refining the systems he was building. In electronics he had found a fresh approach to music, one that did not accord with the rigidity of his Serial musical education. Themes of tonality and pulsation were also being echoed in the music of the first generation of Minimalists as Steve Reich and Philip Glass performed in San Francisco with their respective ensembles. Adams loved Reich's *Drumming* and even conducted his luminous *Music For Mallet Instruments, Voices And Organ* in 1977. In response Adams came up with *Phrygian Gates* and *Shaker Loops*.

These pieces of music, dating from 1977–8, exemplify Adams enriched sonic vocabulary. *Phyrygian Gates*, for rhythmical piano, refers in its title to both old Greek musical modes and voltage controls, or 'gates'. *Shaker Loops*, an oscillating work for seven strings, owed its title to the seminal tape loops of Steve Reich and a childhood memory of an old religious Shaker colony in New Hampshire. At nearly thirty minutes apiece, these creations established Adams as a purveyor of an unpredictable branch of Minimalism where rigid systems were passed over for a greater emotional content. One minute an Adams composition could be as still as anything by Brian Eno, the next it could burst through with all the force of a Mahlerian flourish. Nineteen seventy-eight also saw Adams given the post of new music adviser to the San Francisco Symphony Orchestra, of which he would become composer in residence in the 1980s.

Adams opened the decade with the exceptional *Common Tones In Simple Time*, a floating, glistening, vibrating hue of strings, pianos, oboes, flutes and finger cymbals which recalled Japanese and other Eastern musics. In contrast,

Adams's large pieces of this period seem to recall a Romantic spirit. *Harmonium* (1981) required a cast of nearly 300 players and singers. More relevant was the controversial *Grand Pianola Music* (1982), which divided critics and audiences. In just over thirty minutes Adams conjoins the shimmering quality of American Minimalism with an almost cartoon array of big-band climaxes, Hollywood sirens, marching-band drums and Wagnerian excess. Its winds, brass, and hefty percussion are augmented by two pianos, which open the two movements of the piece in pure Reichian mode, one played slightly behind the other. As other instrumentation delicately entered, no one could expect the sheer boom of sound that would follow. This sounded more like a Busby Berkeley soundtrack of the 1930s or that of a 40s Broadway spectacular, its evolving piano bombast not unlike that of Liberace. Adams was roundly criticized for vulgarizing American music. Yet taken on their own, the Minimalist passages were masterly.

During a return visit to New Hampshire Adams met theatre director Peter Sellars and writer Alice Goodman. They had a novel idea to set to music the former US president Richard Nixon's ground-breaking visit to Mao Tse-Tung in 1972. The opera *Nixon In China* would take Adams nearly four years to write. The excerpt titled *The Chairman Dances* – intended to convey the dancing scene of Nixon and Mao and their wives in the great banqueting hall in Beijing – is full of both humour and nostalgia for a bygone Hollywood era. The piece became the title sequence for an impressive album released in 1986, a record which contained a box of Adams jewels including the incredibly quiet, slowly moving, mysterious and almost ethereal *Tromba Lontana* (*Distant Trumpet*).

Nixon In China was premiered in 1987 at the Houston Grand Opera. It travelled America and made Adams a star. Here were the distinctive triads of classic Minimalism used to highlight an historic situation which was contemporary and ironic. Both Nixon and Mao were now consigned to memory but back in 1972 were at the height of their media lives. The opera had the realistic feel of television newscast but was an ironic send-up of the bloated self-confidence of Nixon, Kissinger, Mao and his calculating wife Jiang Ching. It was eventually broadcast on US television to millions of viewers. The Elektra-Nonesuch recording of *Nixon In China* won a 1989 Grammy Award for Best Contemporary Composition. Adams was now seen as the voice of New Minimalism.

Like Aaron Copland and Charles Ives before him, Adams was forging a distinctly American music full of popular idioms. *Fearful Symmetries* (1988) was a rumbustious kinetic creation which used brass, pianos, horns, synthesizers and samplers and filled the listener with the train rhythms of American travel and Adams's trademark big-band blast-offs. Contrary to that were two requiems for death, both finished in 1989. *The Wound Dresser* was written at the time Adams's father was succumbing to a fatal illness. This piece for voice, violin and trumpet was based on a Walt Whitman poem from the American Civil War. Equally plaintive was the instrumental *Eros Piano*, dedicated to one of the great originators of Ambient music, Morton Feldman.

Adams showed in 1991 that he was adept at intense emotionalism when he used classical choral writing and Eastern and Greek dramatic settings for his next opera, *The Death Of Klinghoffer*. Again this had a contemporary theme, the Arab-Israeli conflict played out against a single event: the 1985 Palestinian hijacking of the cruise ship the *Achille Lauro* and the subsequent murder of a Jewish passenger, Leon Klinghoffer. Most observers were wont to ask if John Adams was a Minimalist any more. His *Chamber Symphony* (1992) and *Violin Concerto* (1993) were so fulsome and complex in their lyricism that they seemed to be drawn from the grand classical tradition rather than any strain of Minimalism. Then Adams released an entire album of electronic music, brimming with all the Minimalist ammunition in his creative armoury.

Hoodoo Zephyr (1993) features eight tracks of pulsing, shimmering Minimalist music. It uses various modern synthesizers, keyboards, sampling boxes, effects units and an Apple Macintosh computer running sequencing software, all of which gives the recording its repetitive Minimalist character. Adams said at the time: 'I have always been interested in electronic instruments and one thing that keeps me composing is the possibility of discovering new sound worlds. Since the 1960s synthesizers have become more sophisticated, more malleable, and combining them with acoustic instruments is like a new form of alchemy.' Adams admitted to loving the smoothness of transitions. *Hoodoo Zephyr* also functions as a sonic tapestry full of Americana from Ry Cooder-styled desert guitar paintings to hypnotic soundtrack.

Adams would apply his new-found love of technology to his next important creation, *El Dorado*, which appeared in 1996. Here he blended sounds from his synthesizers and samplers with the timbres of an orchestra. Like Glass, he accentuated the acoustic instruments with a sampled, electronic equivalent in a process called 'doubling'. The accentuation suited the haunting music, particularly the serene passages in the first and second movements. *El Dorado* was Adams's take on the discovery of the New World. In line with the Christopher Columbus celebrations of 1991 (when it was written), Adams wished to sonically capture the rape of the earth in the first movement, 'The Dream Of Gold', which he described as 'a series of upward moving vectors'. 'Solitudes', the second movement, conveys the tranquillity of the rainforest, plopping sounds accentuated later by rising strings which hark back to the insistence of *Shaker Loops*.

At the end of the twentieth century, Adams redefined Minimalism. Like Ives (who connects with Adams's background through his famous *Concord Sonata* of 1920), he has embraced American popular culture and made historical connections to a music which ends up being neither new nor old. Mindful of innovators like Edgard Varèse and John Cage, Adams has absorbed Serialism, psychedelic rock, the core Minimalism of Glass, Riley and Reich, jazz, Broadway musical and pure electronic music to create a synthesis entirely his own. In 1996 he premiered *I Was Looking At The Ceiling And Then I Saw The Sky*, a cycle of twenty-five 'songs' based on the writings of the black poet June

Jordan. This creation honoured black music history. Another symbol of Adams's open vision of music was the 1997 release of his conducted version of the film music of Toru Takemitsu, a celebration of another modern composer who looked to popular art form for inspiration.

LISTENING

Ensemble Pieces (Obscure 1975)
The Chairman Dances (Elektra/Nonesuch 1986)
Fearful Symmetries (Elektra/Nonesuch 1989)
American Elegies (Elektra/Nonesuch 1991)
Hoodoo Zephyr (Elektra/Nonesuch 1993)
Grand Pianola Music (Elektra/Nonesuch 1994)
El Dorado (Elektra/Nonesuch 1996)
Shaker Loops (Nonesuch 1996)
The John Adams Earbox (Nonesuch 1999)

The English conductor Simon Rattle once said that he had no interest in Minimalism until he heard the music of John Adams. And it is certainly worth hearing. The Obscure disc, from 1975, did much to establish Adams in European consciousness as it was produced and released by Brian Eno. Adams shares space with Gavin Bryars and Christopher Hobbs but his *American Standard* is a singular Ambient work which is made all the more memorable by the interpolation of a radio argument between a cynical broadcaster and a religious zealot. The next album, *The Chairman Dances*, was a classic disc in 1986 and still is. Released on CD only a year after its record pressing, it is played by the San Francisco Symphony under Adams's friend Edo De Waart. The disc contains another version of 'Christian Zeal And Activity' from the Obscure disc but also the archetypal Minimalist creations *Tromba Lontana* and *Common Tones In Simple Time*. The futuristic *Short Ride In A Fast Machine* (at only four minutes) became Adams's most played piece. The title track (also known as *Foxtrot For Orchestra*) is a variation on a theme from his hit opera *Nixon In China*. With its image of Chinese villagers welcoming a dignitary, *The Chairman Dances* is one of the best albums ever released by a Minimalist musician.

Those who like their Minimalism with a lot of verve will love the Orchestra of St Luke's under Adams on *Fearful Symmetries*, a piece which is packaged with the doleful *The Wound Dresser*, a tribute to the dead and wounded of the American Civil War. *American Elegies* is a wonderful disc of Adams, orchestra, Dawn Upshaw's voice and Paul Crossley's piano. It includes the 1989 piece *Eros Piano* and various pieces by Morton Feldman (the dedicatee of *Eros Piano*) and one of Adams's great heroes Charles Ives. *Hoodoo Zephyr* is an essential Adams electronic album, created entirely in his writing studio in Berkeley. The music is enriching and sublime and reveals just how good new computer music and sampling technology is in the hands of a master craftsman. *Grand Pianola Music* is one of Adams's most derided pieces, but also contains some of his most mellifluous instrumentations. *El Dorado* is a deft melding of orchestration with spooky electronic tones. The disc also contains Adams's arrangements of *Cradle Song* and *The Black Gondola*, two elegies, the first to Ferruccio Busoni's mother, the other to Wagner by Franz Liszt, the latter revealing Adams's love of Romanticism. Both were recorded in London. *Shaker Loops* is a recording of the 1993 orchestral version of the 1977 septet. It still holds together all of Adams's stylistic flair: furtive but insistent string playing, tonal pools of still sound, rising and subsiding oscillations and a sense of sadness. Adams is happy to comment in the sleeve note that *Shaker Loops* was quoted in the soundtrack to *Barfly*, an LA-set film starring Mickey Rourke and Faye Dunaway based on the alcoholic skid-row life of writer Charles Bukowski.

The John Adams Earbox is a century's-end career summation containing twenty-four works on ten CDs and a fabulous 180-page booklet. It includes three new recordings of the orchestral works *Harmonium*, *Lollapalooza* and *Slonimsky's Earbox*.

ARVO PÄRT

In 1984 Manfred Eicher of ECM was convinced that he had to begin a new branch to his already successful ECM label, for composers. His New Series, as he described it, was as a result of hearing the spiritually resonant music of Arvo Pärt on the radio. Eicher's reaction to the music is worth quoting. 'What moved me in his music was clarity – the direct path to ear and mind, a drama of quiet passion. The music was cathartic, a music of slowly beating wings. A drawing-inward of all feeling, as if the music were burying itself in a crypt of its own making: pitiless and solitary. A music of innermost calm demanding concentration from the musicians as well as from the listeners. These compositions didn't make the vulnerable soul turn inward; they created a dialectic of action and stillness.'

Pärt's music is simple – organs, bells and voices but sounded with maximum effect and timbre. Silence is an appropriate portion of his compositional style, as is his use of Gregorian chant and simple triadic scales. Many who heard his almost religious ECM debut, *Tabula Rasa*, in 1984, were struck by the use of a single church bell and the audacious placing of the voices, which piled one on top of another until the volume reached breaking point. If Pärt seemed to, shaman-like, stumble out of the Orthodox Church of his Estonian past it was all down to the music of Steve Reich, which he heard in the 1970s and which confirmed his own rejection of Serialism. Pärt's arrival in the West in the 1980s (sonically speaking) was heralded as part of the 'new simplicity' – a take on Minimalism which had its roots in the very different cultural experiences of those who for years were shrouded from view by the Iron Curtain.

Pärt, like the American Minimalists, was born in the 1930s, 1935 to be exact. He grew up in Estonian isolation but had been taking piano lessons since the age of eight. Starved of musical stimulus, he plumped for marching-band music in the Russian forces during his National Service years. By 1958 he had enrolled in the Music Conservatory in Tallinn and simultaneously got a job as a technician at Estonian Radio. He experimented with musical styles, drawing first on Russian composers and then Schoenberg. In fact the minute he aired Serial technique, the authorities were down on him. Not for the first time was he considered a musical subversive.

During the 1960s Pärt was influenced by the dense writing of Ligeti and even the 'indeterminacy' of John Cage. Yet some of his writing was accessible enough to win prizes in Moscow in 1962. He graduated in 1963 but stayed on at Estonian Radio. His symphonic work continued to be heavy-going but in 1968 his *Credo* looked to both Jesus Christ and choral peace for resolution. It was outwardly banned by the Russian government and Pärt left the radio station to write for Soviet films, a task he relished as it involved neither deep thought nor much emotional commitment. This he was keeping for his own music, which was going to undergo a radical change.

During the 1970s Pärt punched out more than fifty film scores but all this time he was refining his personal vision. He studied and studied: Franco-Flemish choral music, Gregorian chant, polyphonic (multi-voiced) singing from thirteenth-century Notre-Dame and Renaissance music. The results could first be heard in the uplifting *Third Symphony* (1971). More study and reflection led Pärt to the sounds of the Orthodox Church, with its bells, incense-laden ritual and mellifluous echoed chanting. In 1976 he published the Satie-like *Für Alina* (*For Alina*), its quiet triadic style finding no favour with the Composers' Union. Tired of Soviet restrictions, he fled to Vienna with his wife and two children, gained Austrian citizenship and settled in what was then West Berlin in late 1981.

Pärt had brought with him new compositions of extraordinary simplicity and grandeur. He had heard Satie, he had heard Reich. He noticed something important about John Cage's avowal of the importance of 'silence'. He made equations with ages-old abbeys and their fondness for bells. In searching for a music of 'time and timelessness' he came up with *Cantus In Memory Of Benjamin Britten* (a melody which dates from the time of the English composer's death in December 1976). In this short but devastating piece the emotional swelling of the famous *Adagio* from Mahler's *Symphony No. 5* can be heard in tandem with slowly building voices and the tolling of a single bell. Another work, *Fratres* (*Brothers*), isolated violin drones and decorative Minimalist piano notes. Silence and simple triads filled *Tabula Rasa*, for piano and violins, composed, like *Fratres*, in 1977. All these pieces were released by Manfred Eicher in 1984 to worldwide acclaim.

Living almost like a hermit in Berlin, Pärt prefers silence to hustle and bustle. 'Here I am alone with silence. I have discovered that it is enough when a single note is beautifully played. This one note, or a silent beat, or a moment of silence, comfort me. I work with very few elements – with one voice, with two voices. I build with the most primitive materials – with the triad, with one specific tonality. The three notes of a triad are like bells.' He was unrepentant about taking five years to come up with new material. In 1987, having been moved by the death the previous year of Andrei Tarkovsky – the Russian film-maker who made a virtue out of his religious faith and slowly changing, almost static, tableaux – Pärt sanctioned the release of *Arbos* (Latin for 'tree') with its extreme but wholly convincing series of organ, string and voice works aimed on high.

Pärt's penchant for the Orthodox Mass and the suffering of Jesus Christ on the way to the Cross was revealed on three recordings for ECM from the late 1980s and early 1990s: *Passio*, *Miserere* and *Te Deum*. *Passio* is an eighty-minute rendition of St John's suffering. Strings, voices, organ and the echoes of a cavernous church are combined to bring back the music of a bygone age, an age when faith alone was enough philosophy to live by, the celebration of that faith and its musical affirmation, the very life force itself. Yet Pärt's music sounds incredibly modern, his adaptation of Minimalism for a spiritual music is precise, never overblown or bombastic. His work is shorn of all the conceit and sheer luxury of Romantic music and in its strange way rejects any of the mechanical sleight of hand of the poorer examples of Minimalism. Pärt's creations are a 'new simplicity' but in their profound content they have a spiritual resonance eagerly appreciated in the last years of the twentieth century and at the beginning of the new millennium.

LISTENING

Arvo Pärt's music is essential listening to anyone reading this book. *Tabula Rasa* (ECM 1984) is simply astonishing, the *Cantus In Memory Of Benjamin Britten* riveting, the descending power of the Stuttgart Orchestra recalling Mahler and Wagner at their most potent. Keith Jarrett (piano) and Gidon Kremer (violin) hit it off wonderfully on *Fratres*. Jarrett, in particular, has rarely played such spartan but effective notes. *Arbos* (ECM 1987) begins Pärt's successful recording partnership with the Hilliard Ensemble and contains a variety of pieces. *Pari Intervallo* ('with equal intervals'), written in 1976, is a beguiling meditation for organ which seems to slow down time. *Stabat Mater*, which dates from 1985, is a gorgeously hypnotic unflowering of voices and strings. Silence and choral celebration are intertwined on *Te Deum* (ECM 1993), sung by the Estonian Philharmonic Chamber Choir and recorded in a Finnish church. As an introduction to Pärt's choral works, *Beatus* (*Blessed*) (Virgin 1997) includes four new works plus performances by the Estonian Chamber Choir and is supervised by the composer himself.

In 1999 ECM made available new recordings of *Für Alina* (*For Alina*) and *Spiegel im Spiegel* (*Mirror Within A Mirror*) – spare works for piano and strings

which achieved the composer's intended effect of 'calm, exalted, listening to
one's inner self'.

HENRYK GORECKI

As a fount of the 'new simplicity' there is no better example than the Pole
Henryk Gorecki. In 1992 his *Symphony No. 3*, or *Symphony Of Sorrowful Songs*,
was released in the West to unprecedented acclaim. Not alone did this arcing,
almost religious work top all the classical music charts but it even got to number
one in the rock and popular music charts in the UK. With over a million sales to
date, Gorecki's *Symphony No. 3* has become a symbol of post-Holocaust, post-
Communist spiritual fortitude and carries a resounding empathy with human
suffering everywhere. Rooted in fifteenth-century Polish prayer and folk song,
the slow ascent to the vocal and down again has all the resonances of
Minimalism – but a Minimalism of emotion rather than form.

One could liken Gorecki's vocal music to the early choral works of Stockhausen. Both men come from backgrounds of adversity, both have suffered
because of oppressive regimes. Both went on to transcend their backgrounds
and gain fame and fortune in the modern music market. The potency of
Gorecki's music comes in no small way from Poland itself – a land invaded by
the Nazis at the start of the Second World War and then annexed by Soviet
Russia in its aftermath. Born in the coal-mining region of Silesia in 1933,
Gorecki first opted for teaching before gaining admittance to the Conservatory
in Katowice, the region's capital. This was in 1955, when Gorecki was
fascinated by Anton Webern and Serialism. In the wake of Stalin, Gorecki,
like others, threw himself into the avant-garde, and both *Symphony No. 1* (1959)
and *Scontri* (*Collisions*)(1960) explored extreme sound spectrums in orchestral
music.

Scontri made a spectacular impact at the 1960 Warsaw Music Festival but
outraged Communist officialdom. This furore coincided with the graduation of
the recently married Gorecki and his departure to Paris for further study. After
returning to Poland, Gorecki had to resign himself to the country's growing
conservative climate but was determined to live there and went back to
Katowice to raise a family. In 1963 he wrote *Three Pieces In Olden Style*, a
slow Ambient creation for strings with harmonic elements close to Debussy and
the modality of sixteenth-century Polish folk music. In the late sixties came *Old
Polish Music*, an orchestral work built out of Gorecki's love of medieval and
Renaissance music.

Gorecki taught and wrote, continuously refining his style. His *Symphony No.
2*, dedicated to the famous astronomer Copernicus, arrived in 1972, full of
prayers and the plainsong style of fourteenth-century choral music. Gorecki
found spiritual sustenance in both the rural hinterland of Katowice, with its

Tatra Mountains, woodlands, valleys, farmers and craftsmen, and the Catholic Church. His *Amen* of 1973 is an extraordinary Minimalist composition, with its repetition of a single word and the slow build-up of potency until the harmonies form a wall of echoing sound. In this grand expression of spiritual thankfulness Gorecki had already laid the foundations for his future triumph.

This work of greatness was to precede a period of acute illness and withdrawal. To ease the pressure of academic work he took up a job as rector at his old school in Katowice in 1975. Though he is said to have embroidered elements of Beethoven and Chopin into its fabric, *Symphony No. 3* (1976) has its roots in church and folk music, not to mention the terrible legacy of the Holocaust. Katowice is situated close to the site of the notorious Nazi death camp Auschwitz and it was in another camp, at nearby Zakopane, that Gorecki found something extraordinary. There, on a wall in one of the cells, was a simple inscription from an eighteen-year-old girl, dated 1944: 'No mother, do not weep, most chaste Queen of Heaven.' This would form the centrepiece of a remarkable creation, located between Monastic church song from the fifteenth century and regional folk melody. Using the centuries-old technique of the canon, where theme is passed from one instrument to another, Gorecki fashioned three movements that were sonically symmetrical and packed a huge emotional wallop. On paper it was strings and one soprano voice, but in acoustic space it was Minimalism of rare emotional ferocity.

In 1977 Gorecki deservedly took up his place as Professor of Music at Katowice Conservatory. He continued to write for a variety of instruments but in 1979 he resigned his post in protest at the harsh economic and social conditions prevailing in Poland at the time. In 1980 along came Lech Walesa and the Solidarity movement – a time when Gorecki was eulogized in America for the Minimalism of his *Harpsichord Concerto* and honoured by having his *Beatus* performed for the then recently elected Pope John Paul II, the first Polish pope in nearly half a century. Gorecki continued to fashion serenely beautiful music, and his *O Domina Nostra* (*To Our Lady*), written in 1982 for voice and organ, is another example of his devotional Minimalism coloured by his love of folk song.

Illness returned in the mid-1980s but Gorecki again displayed a fierce will to live by composing another piece of aural serenity in *Totus Tuus* (*Wholly Thine*), specially written for a High Mass in Warsaw celebrated by Pope John Paul in 1987. Gorecki was getting interest from the Kronos Quartet in the US and several Polish recordings of *Symphony No. 3* were circulating in the West. He went to the UK in 1989 to prepare for the classic recording of the work in 1991. The following year he visited the US and his celebrity quickly spread.

Working in his own way he continued to base himself in Katowice with his wife and two children. Revenues from the Nonesuch recording of *Symphony No. 3* allowed him to buy a house in his beloved Tatra Mountains, the better air and setting intended to ease his delicate health. His instrumental writing could be harsh, as in his string quartet work, but there is no doubt that his quieter, more spiritual output like the *Miserere* of 1994 cemented the idea of a new kind of Minimalism worldwide.

LISTENING

There are now many recordings of music by Gorecki on the market. The essential million-selling *Symphony No. 3*, or *Symphony Of Sorrowful Songs* (Nonesuch), features the American soprano Dawn Upshaw in a performance of a lifetime. Recorded in London in 1991 by the London Sinfonietta under conductor David Zinman, the disc not only represents a zenith of the 'new simplicity' but one of the best orchestral recordings of all time. The panoramic sound was achieved by rock engineer Bob Ludwig. *O Domina Nostra* (*To Our Lady*) (ECM 1992), for organ and voice, was produced by Manfred Eicher and again achieves the perfect balance between Minimalism and folk spirituality. It is dedicated fittingly to the symbol of Polish independence, the Black Virgin of Jasna Gora. *Ikos* (EMI Classics 1994) places Gorecki fittingly in the company of John Tavener and Arvo Pärt. The album's two spiritual prayers are crystalline evocations of Gorecki's art, *Totus Tuus* climbing from near-silence to grand expression with the minimum of means – the Choir of King's College, Cambridge and the resonant acoustics of the church.

Ambient Trance producer William Orbit released electronic versions of Gorecki's 1963 work *Pieces In Olden Style* on his long-awaited modern classical *opus Pieces In Modern Style* (WEA, 2000).

JOHN TAVENER

During the 1990s John Tavener sprang to fame as the UK's most popular composer of the 'new simplicity'. His spartan vocal and instrumental compositions evolved from a deep Christianity, the hallowed ground of the Greek and Russian Orthodox Church and its rituals. His use of repetition, major chords and monophonic voices made his textures seem simply translucent. The runaway popular success in 1992–3 of creations such as *The Protecting Veil* and *The Last Sleep Of The Virgin* was due to the fact that, like the work of Arvo Pärt and Henryk Gorecki, Tavener's music simply spoke to the world in a quiet but crystalline fashion. Like the Minimalism of the 1960s and 70s, his work seemed egoless, unfettered by pretension or complexity. Hence the use of his 1993 *Song For Athene* at the funeral mass in London in 1997 of Diana, Princess of Wales.

Tavener was born in London in 1944, a year before the end of the Second World War. He was brought up a Presbyterian, his father playing organ in their local Hampstead church. He went to nearby Highgate School and had decided to become a composer after hearing the late sacred music of the century's most famous pagan, Igor Stravinsky. Tavener quickly gained admittance to the Royal Academy of Music in the early 1960s. There he met David Lumsdaine and Lennox Berkeley, two composers who introduced their young protégé to electronics and modern French music, particularly Messiaen. Like the latter, Tavener began to play church organ, and he was still at the Academy when he began to give recitals in St John's Church, Kensington. On graduation in 1965 he won a prize in Monaco for his version of the biblical story of Cain and Abel, a piece combining text and music which drew on medieval and Catholic sources.

Though Tavener has often decried the popularity of Serialism during his education, the severe simplicity advocated by Webern and the sound of early Stockhausen have flowed unchecked through his music. Indeed his early use of tape owes much to Stockhausen. Tavener was to have almost instantaneous success in 1968 when two works were premiered, *In Alium* (*Ever Changing*) and *The Whale*. Both used voice, orchestra and tape, the latter being more lavish in its use of electric keyboards and sound. Tavener was ingenious in his use of silence to heighten the effect of his work. *The Whale* recalled the biblical story of Jonah being swallowed by a whale and spat out again. It had instant appeal among the hippie generation and attracted The Beatles. Alongside his *Celtic Requiem* (1969), which displayed an interest in both Celtic mysticism and children's singing, *The Whale* was featured on an album released on The Beatles' Apple label in 1970. Tavener was at once a popular success and was also fêted by the academic world, having become Professor of Music at Trinity College, London, a year earlier.

But Tavener was looking for a deeper spirituality. He wanted to leave works like *Three Surrealist Songs*, a 1968 piece for voice, piano, bongos and tape, behind him. He lost himself in the writings of St John of the Cross and drew guidance from the Irish prior of a Carmelite Monastery in southern England. When the prior died in 1972, Tavener wrote a tribute, *Little Requiem For Father Malachy Lynch*. In this one can hear the use of voices, followed by stingingly Minimalist instrumentation – a humming effect known as unison. His tributes to saints and Catholicism were overshadowed by a shift to the iconography and teachings of the Orthodox Church, notably its Russian and Greek variants. In 1974 he married a Greek lady, Victoria. His 1976 dedication to the Russian orthodoxy, *Canticle Of The Mother Of God*, was followed in 1977 by complete conversion. From then on Tavener's music became more progressively stripped of ornamentation, more steeped in the austerity of ritual. Even his titles had an archaic ring about them – for example, *The Immurement Of Antigone*, from the late 1970s, which concerns the walling up of the Greek mythical heroine after the story by Sophocles.

Tavener could never be accused of resting on his laurels. A glance at his output reveals that he written more than forty works by 1980. Yet those for which he is best known were yet to come. There was *Funeral Ikos* (1981), a simple sung alleluia which rises and then falls to rest, '*ikos*' being the Greek word for sounds. Then came *The Lamb* in 1982, a simple melodic interpretation of a part of the mystic poet William Blake's *Songs Of Innocence And Experience*. In *Ikon Of Light* (1984) Tavener set out his stall for all to see. Over forty minutes one heard intense repetitions followed by echoing silences, single Greek words sung in canons or rounds, Byzantine chant, descending and ascending scales, drones and an epiphanous or light-filled sound. Its central theme was a mystic prayer by the Orthodox poet St Simeon Stylites, which talked of the 'uncreated light of God' which, in the liturgy, can only be seen by those filled by 'divine grace'. Through careful Minimalist means, Tavener wanted to create other-worldly music which reached back as well as upwards for its inspiration.

This impressive work was followed in 1985 *by Two Hymns To The Mother Of God*, clear but bright choral pieces, dedicated to the composer's late mother. His love of William Blake was again celebrated in an effulgent choral setting, *The Tyger* (1987), which in itself quotes the mode of *The Lamb*. Tavener's most famous piece, *The Protecting Veil*, was also written in 1987. Penned for the cellist Steven Isserlis, this work again drew its inspiration from Orthodox religion – this time a tenth-century vision of the Virgin Mary in Constantinople seen by Greeks during a Saracen attack. Tavener described this effusive piece for cello and strings as 'an attempt to make a lyrical ikon in sound'. Its constant cello sound, swinging from swallow song to Slavic exquisiteness, was so captivating that on its release in 1992 the Virgin album hit the top of the classical charts and sold in the hundreds of thousands. The piece, though often mawkish in its use of strings, made Tavener internationally famous.

Tavener's elegiac music was popular because it was sincere. There was simply no contrivance. Tavener chose to close the 1980s with *Eonia*, a short musical tribute to a painter friend based on a haiku sung in Slavonic and English. In producing this, Tavener would be helped by Mother Thekla, the Orthodox Abbess of a Yorkshire monastery, who also functioned as a spiritual guide. During the 1990s Tavener would spend lengthy creative sojourns on the Greek island of Ennoia, his writing alternating between huge choral works and shorter meditations. In 1991 came his Ambient masterpiece *The Last Sleep Of The Virgin*, a work for handbells and delicate strings where performers were instructed to play still and quiet. Even listeners at home were instructed to turn down the volume.

In 1993 came another melancholic creation, *Song For Athene*, which Tavener dedicated to his friend the actress and poet Athene Hariades, who had been tragically killed in a road accident. Again a sense of calm was created by the use of drones. An example of Tavener's use of sound space and exotic sources is *Innocence* (1995), which is reminiscent of Ligeti's work in its use of vertical blocks of massed voice and draws on Islamic chant. Like many of his creations, this was written for the dimensions of Westminster Abbey. Therefore in 1997 it seemed fitting that *Song For Athene* should be performed in the Abbey at the close of the funeral service of Diana, Princess of Wales. Like the Princess's simple compassion, Tavener's elegiac Minimalism always seemed to strike a chord with a wide public.

LISTENING

There are a lot of Tavener discs on the market. Those new to the composer should hear compilation albums like *Ikon Of Light* (Collins 1994) or *Innocence* (Sony 1995), which include most of the music discussed above. Tavener is usually paired with Gorecki and Pärt on selections of choral music – for example, *Ikos* (EMI 1994) and *20th Century Choral Music* (EMI 1996). The best-selling *The Protecting Veil*, played by cellist Steven Isserlis and the London Symphony Orchestra, is on Virgin Classics (1992); but *The Last Sleep Of The Virgin* (Virgin Classics 1994) is a superior creation and possibly the definitive recording.

OTHER MINIMALISTS

Lou Harrison was born in Portland, Oregon in 1917. He allied himself to the West Coast music scene and was one of the first to investigate Asian pitch systems and instruments. He was taught by Schoenberg and worked with John Cage in the 1930s. Cage excited Harrison's interest in the Javanese gamelan and in 1961 he studied in Korea and Japan. Such pieces as *The Perilous Chapel* (1948) are renowned for the delicacy of their organization and the use of drones. He incorporated elements like tuned water bowls, finger cymbals and exotic scales in his search for a 'transethnic planetary music'. Hear the excellent disc *The Perilous Chapel* (New Albion 1994) for a wide selection of Harrison's lovely Minimalism.

Alan Hovhaness is included here for his long-standing incorporation of Eastern music into Western tradition. Like Debussy, Stockhausen, Cage and the major American Minimalists, Hovhaness strongly believed that the modal musics of the Orient brought a calming, meditative quality to the brash sonorities of traditional orchestral music. Born in Massachusetts in 1911, Hovhaness was the son of Scottish and Armenian parents. He studied astronomy and sacred Armenian composition. During further studies at a New England conservatory he avidly read the cultural histories of Armenia, China and Japan. Long walks in the New Hampshire hills honed a contemplative spirit. His early compositions were championed by the conductor Leopold Stokowski. During the late 1950s he studied Carnatic raga in Madras in India, and in 1962 he went to Japan to study the timeless court style of the Gagaku. He became famous in the early 1970s for his use of electronic whale song in his orchestral piece *And God Created Great Whales*.

The author of hundreds of pieces, Hovhaness composed in a style characterized by lustrous settings whose use of ethno–modal scales and Oriental instrumentation lent his work a dreamlike air. Sadly, he died mid-2000. A good introduction is the compilation *Hovhaness Collection* (Delos 1997).

One of the most enduring Ambient/Minimalist recordings ever made is by the English composer Gavin Bryars. His *The Sinking Of The Titanic* was the debut album on Brian Eno's Obscure label in 1975 and over the years its reputation blossomed to such a degree that it was reissued, in a fuller version by Philip Glass, in 1994. Bryars, born in Yorkshire in 1943, studied composition and became a bassist accompanying a host of variety performers, from fire-eaters to magicians. He also allied himself to the burgeoning British jazz scene until 1966. Subsequently he went to America and worked with John Cage. He returned to Portsmouth Polytechnic and founded the Portsmouth Sinfonia, which was made up of inspired amateurs, among them Brian Eno. Moved by a report that a wireless operator had heard and seen the house band of the *Titanic* play until the ship sank on 14 April 1912, Bryars wrote a piece in 1969 based on the poetic idea that the music continued to play underwater and would one day be heard again when the wreck was salvaged. He even had the piece performed by John Adams in San Francisco, but it was the 1975 Obscure recording that made its name. The funereal slowness of the string music is accentuated by spoken fragments from survivors and the sound of a music box. The music draws from the hymn 'Autumn' (reportedly the final music heard on the *Titanic*) and various folk and ragtime sources also heard by other survivors. As an Ambient wash combining memory, repetition and chance elements, *The Sinking Of The Titanic* is a twentieth-century classic. Its original 'b' side was another Bryars masterpiece: the plaintive voice of a London tramp, tape-looped and offset against a series of incremental melodies played by an ensemble including Michael Nyman. This work, *Jesus' Blood Never Failed Me Yet*, was again a classic use of repetition, filled to the brim with emotion. In 1993 Philip Glass commissioned a new version for his Point Music label – an expansion which now featured full orchestra and choirs. Realizing its importance, Virgin Venture eventually reissued the original Obscure album on remastered CD in 1998. Bryars has also recorded for ECM New Series.

Wim Mertens is another latter-day composer who has made valuable contributions to Minimalism. Born in Belgium in 1953, Mertens studied at the universities of Leuven and Ghent, majoring in Musicology. In 1980 he published a ground-breaking study of *American Minimal Music*, which in 1983 was circulated in Japan, America and the British Isles and reissued in the 1980s and 90s. As well as being a thoroughly musicological survey of early Minimalism it also delved into the historical and philosophical implications of the music in terms of French 'sexual philosophy' and the dialectical thinking of the German social philosopher and musicologist Theodor Adorno. Mertens produced various concerts by Glass, Reich and Terry Riley for Belgian radio and travelled widely, popularizing the form. In 1981 he formed his own group, Soft Verdict, who recorded avidly for the Belgian label (Les Disques du) Crépuscule. He has shown an interest in the sounds generated by microprocessors, in Gregorian chant and in the ensemble sound of both Philip Glass and Michael Nyman. Championed by Nyman, he went on to score the Peter Greenaway film *The*

Belly Of An Architect (1987). Also during the 1980s, Mertens worked with the Stockhausen pupil K. Goeyvaerts and signed to the New Age Windham Hill label. His recent work has been directed towards voice and piano.

American vocal gymnast and multi-media and performance artist Meredith Monk is aligned to the development of Minimalism in that much of her stylizations grew out of the form. She has devoted an enormous amount of time to the sheer sound of the voice and located this in pared-down repetitive musical settings. Her theatre and opera creations recall those of Philip Glass and Robert Wilson. Monk was born in Lima, Peru in 1943. She grew up in New York with a family heritage of Hebrew chant and opera singing. She was a prodigy, reading music and playing piano at three. As a teenager she combined studies in music with those of dance, film and the theatre. By 1965 her voice had a three-octave range and could command extensive wordless improvisations. She was part of the Downtown New York avant-garde scene and presented many 'happenings'. Her early 1970s work involves tape, acoustic instruments and massed voices. The ECM label released her chamber setting *Dolmen Music* (1981) and the stripped-down electronica of her *Turtle Dreams* (1983), both of which gained classic status. She has won many international prizes for both her music and her video and film presentations. Though the range of Monk's voice can sometimes jar, she has written some fine music deeply indebted to John Cage, as can be heard on the Cage-Monk disc *The Tale And Other Compositions* (Koch 1993).

Roger Eno defined a style of Minimalism in the 1980s and 90s which drew on French Impressionism and English pastoralism for its inspiration. A consummate musician and composer, he made valuable contributions to the Brian Eno album *Apollo: Atmospheres And Soundtracks* (1983) and to the soundtracks of the movies *Dune* (David Lynch, 1984) and *9 $\frac{1}{2}$ Weeks* (Adrian Lyne, 1985). Born in Woodbridge, Suffolk in 1960, Roger Eno was encouraged to compose by a tuba-playing schoolteacher. At Colchester Institute he studied the euphonium, music history, harmony and performance. His interest in piano was purely timbral, long, rising tones being an abiding passion. He taught himself guitar and in 1979 went to busk in London, after which he worked as a music therapist to young sick children. His brother Brian rang him from New York in 1983 to ask for his help on the recording of *Apollo: Atmospheres And Soundtracks* in Canada. Playing piano and DX7 synthesizer, Roger Eno co-composed four tunes including 'Deep Blue Day' (heard in the 1996 film *Trainspotting*) and the intensely evocative 'Always Returning'. Revisiting Canada, the younger Eno made his first solo album there with Daniel Lanois – *Voices* (1985), a sound-painting inspired by Debussy, Fauré, Ravel and, most of all, Erik Satie. Its ghostly harmonized washes would define Roger's twin interest in electronics and formal music. Another record, *Between Tides* (1988), revealed a more English side, its woodwind, string and brass additions mindful of both Delius and Elgar. Later works expressed an interest in song and instrumentals and the use of orchestral samples. *Lost In Translation* (1994) features Latin texts inspired by Eno's Flemish background while *Swimming* (1996) reveals his love of folk song and its modalities, fired by reverence for English composers such as Vaughan Williams and George Butterworth. Eno considers himself a pianist at heart and as recently as 1997 has produced *The Music Of Neglected English Composers* for Resurgence. In 1998 he released a melancholic English-sounding chamber album titled *The Flatlands*. Early recordings are on Editions EG and his 1990s work is on All Saints, a label which also features him in collaboration with the ensemble Channel Light Vessel and the respected reed instrumentalist Kate St John.

Acclaimed by John Cage for her psycho-acoustic work, the American electronic musician Pauline Oliveros made a decisive contribution to Minimalism in the form of her 1980s forays into 'Deep Listening'. Whether it be in the caves of Lanzarote in the Canary Islands or in subterranean spaces in North America, Oliveros has combined acoustic instruments with delay and echo units to produce some of the most compelling dronal music ever heard. Born in 1932 in Houston, Texas, she quickly aligned herself with the West Coast tradition, studying during the 1950s for six years alongside Terry Riley and Morton Subotnick. In the 60s her multi-media tape-based work brought her into contact with dancer Merce Cunningham and musician David Tudor, two spearheads of the avant-garde. She was a vital asset at the San Francisco Tape Center for experimental music and became its director in 1966 when it transferred to Mills College, Oakland. There she worked on the Buchla synthesizer and then in performance with Terry Riley, whose tape-delay system influenced her later sound investigations. She applied Riley's delay techniques to the accordion, her favourite instrument, whose system of keyboard, buttons and bellows provided an awesome range of notes for subsequent processing. This was allied to her adoption of La Monte Young's just-intonation tuning for the instrument and the formation in the 1980s of The Deep Listening Band, a trio combining trombone, didgeridoo, accordion and an electronic relay system full of delay lines and effects units.

A move to New York in the late 1980s led to the Pauline Oliveros Foundation for new music. The composers' work of this decade can be sampled on the New Albion disc *Deep Listening* (1989), while the Ambient boxed set *Driftworks* (Big Cat 1997) fully convinces one that Steve Reich's 'detailed listening' could be extended to other areas of sound.

Jon Gibson was born in Los Angeles in 1940. Working with saxophones, the visual arts and composition, he performed with Steve Reich, Terry Riley, Philip Glass and La Monte Young from the 1960s onwards. His work ranges from simple Satiesque melodic pieces to sound-textural improvisations as exemplified by *Extensions 2* (1992) for sax, drones and natural sounds. His *In Good Company* (Point Music 1992) is a showcase of Minimalist work performed by Gibson. The disc includes material (some unheard) by Adams, Reich, Riley, Glass and Terry Jennings. The latter was born in California and introduced La Monte Young to the ideas of John Cage. Jennings studied with Young and was a member of the

Fluxus group. It is he who is credited with composing, during the 1950s, the first pieces using the Minimalist elements of reduction, repetition, steady pulse and expansion of time.

David Toop became a mainstay of UK Ambient music in the 1990s through his Virgin recordings, his writings and his performances. He came to prominence in 1975 when Brian Eno recorded the album *New And Rediscovered Musical Instruments* for his Obscure label. It featured the sound sculpture of Max Eastley on one side and the voice, flute and prepared instruments of Toop on the other. Toop, like Eno, developed through the English art-school scene, attending Hornsey College of Art in the 1960s. Starting on guitar, Toop displayed an interest in John Cage and Terry Riley but was also attracted to Ornette Coleman and Free Jazz. The early 1970s saw a blending of ideas, and Toop's performances involved tape, ethnic music and electronics. He teamed up with instrument inventor Max Eastley but after the Eno recording went to Venezuela to record the curing ceremonies of the Yanomani Indians. His return to the UK saw him involved with the pop group The Flying Lizards in 1979 and then the reggae of Prince Far I. By the 1980s he was immersed in black Hip-Hop music, writing and a growing fondness for synthesizers and computer technology. Toop describes his exotic, often opaque Ambient music as 'a mixture of live and sampled, the outdoor and indoor, hi- and low-tech. Of interesting contrasts.' In 1994 came the second Eastley and Toop album, *Buried Dreams* (Beyond). The following year saw the publication of a highly personalized look at Ambient music in the book *Ocean Of Sound*. Since then Toop has collaborated with the Virgin label on a series of Ambient compilations and released the albums *Screen Ceremonies* (1995), *Pink Noir* (1996) and *Spirit World* (1997).

BOOK THREE

AMBIENCE IN THE ROCK ERA

THE ROCK ERA of the late 1950s to the 1990s was one of unprecedented sonic change. It was a revolution in popular music facilitated by transformations in both economics and technology. An upswing in the post-war economies of the West meant that by the 1960s young people had a degree of financial power. Through the exercise of this new freedom the records of The Beatles began to sell in huge quantities. Moreover technological advances in sound recording meant that rock music became a locus of innovation and experiment. In the studio multi-track recording afforded The Beatles the luxury of making state-of-the-art rock like 1967's *Sgt. Pepper's Lonely Hearts Club Band*, which birthed the era of the concept album. The collision between expanding studio facilities and new guitar, keyboard and synthesizer equipment meant that rock releases such as a Jimi Hendrix or Byrds album had enormous social impact. As the industry grew, rock became more sophisticated and absorbed more influences from sources ranging from classical to World Music. Its evolution has fascinated generations of listeners, the perennial phrase 'rock is dead' usually undone by another startling release from a U2 or lesser-known band. What's most interesting here is how rock opened listeners' minds to new perceptions in sound; how through its necessary innovation it served as a perfect vehicle for new Ambient and electronic ideas.

Our story begins with those people whose lives and work shaped the very history of the genre. Innovators like Americans Les Paul and Leo Fender. whose classic electric-guitar designs of the late 1940s would define the sound of rock for decades. Both the Fender Stratocaster and Gibson Les Paul had huge potentialities for sound manipulation, advantages that were exploited to the limit by rock musicians during the 1960s and 70s. Les Paul was also an early advocate of overdubbing and, like Stockhausen, used record discs for his early experiments in the 1940s. By the early 1950s he was multi-tracking vocals on tape and making hit records. In the UK producer Joe Meek was the first to use the studio itself as an instrument in recorded sound. Beginning in the 1950s, Meek's maverick approach to taped music led to the first transatlantic number-one hit for an English rock group – 'Telstar' by The Tornadoes.

Which brings us to The Beatles. Their contribution was a quantum leap in terms of sound and quality on almost everything that had come before them. By the late 1960s each of their albums had become an event, a benchmark example of what could be done inside a studio with the best technology and a group of musicians at the very apex of their creativity. *Revolver* (1966) was an incredible achievement – its mixture of tape effects, Indian raga, pocket symphony and sustained songcraft has frequently earned it the epithet 'greatest album of all time'. *Sgt. Pepper's Lonely Hearts Club Band* (1967) inaugurated a new era of rock sophistication, its runaway sales defining a new youth–culture demographic. In the US others worked as hard as The Beatles to push rock forward. Bob Dylan brought the quality of a great novelist and poet to songwriting and allied it to a considered approach to record production. His mid-1960s work with the black producer Tom Wilson kick-started 'folk-rock' while later Dylan albums saw him pursue a more distilled Ambience in sound. The Beach Boys had a surrealistic quality to their music as envisioned by their chief songwriter and sound–shaper Brian Wilson. In a constant rivalry to keep up with The Beatles, Wilson spent the best part of 1966 crafting 'Good Vibrations' – a mini cornucopia of electronic and acoustic sounds.

If Wilson used the singular droning sound of the Theremin to enhance 'Good Vibrations', then Jimi Hendrix used everything he could lay his hands on to paint his colours in sound. Hendrix played the electric guitar like nobody before him or since. His *Are You Experienced* (1967) has never been bettered as a guitarist's album in terms of vision and sheer sound experiment. Hendrix used the Fender Stratocaster like an electronic gizmo, constantly manipulating ideas in feedback, sustain, sound-swirl, octave displacement and much more to create the boldest tapestry of guitar sound in history. Even in the studio his use of effects such as backwards-tape editing matched that of The Beatles. By 1968's *Electric Ladyland* his recording processes was akin to sound-painting.

Paul Simon and Art Garfunkel are more often remembered for their beautiful folk-rock ballads than their technical savvy. Yet, like Hendrix, they were excited by new developments in musical technology. With their perfect harmonies, multi-tracked voices and endless overdubbing, courtesy of new eight-track recording equipment, their 1966 single 'Scarborough Fair' was a sonic miracle. By spending months and months in the studio and investigating the new possibilities of sixteen-track tape Simon & Garfunkel came up with *Bridge Over Troubled Water* in 1969, in the process heralding the era of High-Fidelity rock.

Besides great leaps in technical know-how, other influences shaped the rock era. Ravi Shankar single-handedly introduced Indian music to the West. Constant touring and recording made him talk of the rock fraternity by the mid-1960s. Both The Byrds and The Beatles were directly influenced by him to expand their sense of melody and harmony. Shankar's appearance at the Monterey Pop Festival in 1967 was momentous. As noted earlier, Ravi Shankar influenced Philip Glass, in the same way that the Minimalist La Monte Young influenced The Velvet Underground. The latter experimented with drones and repetition in a new form of subversive rock documented by MGM in late 1960s recordings such as *The Velvet Underground And Nico*. Their New York base made for a more graphic, street-wise art which, in the hands of leaders John Cale and Lou Reed, resulted in an extreme form of electric music.

Like The Velvet Underground, The Rolling Stones are often seen as rock rebels though in truth their interest in exotic sound design made them as progressive in outlook as The Beatles. During the late 1960s Brian Jones was using the Mellotron as well as a variety of ethnic instruments, including the sitar. In 1968 Jones made a location recording of Moroccan music which was then subjected to a phasing process by one of Jimi Hendrix's engineers. At the same time Mick Jagger was toying with the very Moog synthesizer which would eventually define Tangerine Dream's sound. The Stones' work in the studio with producer Jimmy Miller would come into its own in the 1970s, their own Rolling Stones Mobile studio capturing some of the great rock albums of the decade. The early 1970s was also the era of the soul-baring singer songwriter. Van Morrison had laid out his vision of spiritual ecstasy on 1968's *Astral Weeks*. His stream-of-consciousness style, coupled with lush Ambient settings, resulted in marvellously energetic works like *Moondance*. His huge canon of work provides some of the most stirringly profound emotional expression in rock. Marvin Gaye took soul music to new levels with his song cycle *What's Going On* (1971), an album so compelling that it induced Stevie Wonder to work with synthesizers. And then there was David Bowie, an artist whose space-age visions were born as man landed on the moon and whose *Space Oddity* (1969) was an electro-acoustic miracle. Bowie is as strongly associated with rock of the 1970s as The Beatles are with the 1960s. As he moved through the decade his love of change and radical innovation would peak in Berlin in 1977, when the master of the surreal compressed pop song met the diligent Brian Eno and they literally suspended time in sound. *Low* not only unfolded new vistas in synthesizer and Ambient music but also predicted the insistent beat of Techno years before it happened.

The story continues with tendencies in rock which saw electronic and Ambient styles become more acceptable in mainstream consciousness. Psychedelia was a dominant force in 1960s rock – the creation of music influenced by hallucinogenics such as LSD, mescaline and marijuana altered not only the way music was recorded but how it was listened to. In the UK, as Ian MacDonald has succinctly pointed out, psychedelia was all wrapped up in pastoral moods: 'the nostalgic innocent vision of the child'. Most UK psychedelia concentrated on wigged-out guitar solos and strange arrangements on seven-inch singles. With exceptions, such as the albums of Pink Floyd and The Pretty Things, psychedelia was seen as an interesting novelty. In contrast, American psychedelia was a frontier voyage, the album and the live concert the natural place to dive into a world of improvisation and on-the-spot inspiration. It blossomed on the West Coast, in the Californian sunshine of Los Angeles and San Francisco. LA's mixture of glamour and showbiz lent the city's psychedelic outpourings a certain whiff of decadence. The Byrds, whose masterly 'Eight Miles High' (1966) was a great blend of Indian raga and Rickenbacker guitar noise, were as interested in the trappings of success as they were in the workings of the Moog synthesizer. The Doors and Love were decadence on high, both creating visions of dread of a strange acidic potency. In the studio Arthur Lee's ear for classical sound made Love's *Forever Changes* a finely etched masterpiece while Ray Manzarek's substantial keyboard ability pushed The Doors way beyond their blues roots. When Neil Young came to LA and joined Buffalo Springfield he found the perfect vehicle for his high-flown visions. Within both acoustic and electric contexts, Young was willing and able to push rock way beyond perceived boundaries. When he began making sound collages on *Buffalo Springfield Again* (1967) he showed that, for him, studio production was as important as content. The sheen of LA psychedelia was not replicated in San Francisco. Here the form was organic, communal and born out of a social and political imperative. The early music of Jefferson Airplane and The Grateful Dead was recorded intuitively, the feeling conveyed in sound more important than tweaky perfectionism. Yet the emotional, let-fly nature of San Francisco psychedelia did not exclude an interest in technology or experimental composition. The Grateful Dead embraced eight- and sixteen-track facilities, blended live and studio music and were as interested in noise and feedback as much as melodically beautiful ensemble playing. Two albums from 1969, The Dead's *Live/Dead* and Quicksilver Messenger Service's *Happy Trails*, epitomize true San Francisco psychedelia, where fluid instrumental music and Ambience conjoin in epic flights of electric fantasy.

The natural tendencies of many musicians in the British Isles during the 1960s and 70s was to go in the direction of Folk Ambience. Traditional English, Irish and Scottish musics lent themselves to dronal and ornamental exploration. With electric instrumentation and new production techniques, British folk–rock blossomed. Donovan became an early star of the genre, assisted by producer Mickie Most. His interest in Eastern music and the presence of guitarist Jimmy Page made *Sunshine Superman* (1966) a wonderful listening experience. Also from Scotland was The Incredible String Band, a duo whose colourful compositions were grounded in medieval melody and Arabic and Eastern instrumentation. Their affinity with modal scales and timbral diversity made *The Hangman's Beautiful Daughter* (1968) a truly ground-breaking album of original folk music. Fellow Scot Bert Jansch had made a name for himself in acoustic guitar circles with his open-tuned compositional style. His group Pentangle really pushed the idea of amplified acoustic music as being on a par with the best rock improvisation. Of course the crown for greatest-ever UK folk–rock band has to go to Fairport Convention. In 1969 three albums were released under their name which changed the UK scene for ever. With the captivating vocals of Sandy Denny and the encyclopedic musical knowledge of guitarist Richard Thompson, the band flew higher than most. Other significant contributions were made by Nick Drake and John Martyn, two musicians who prided themselves on their studio craft and their ability to make a great song become a vehicle for Ambient exploration. This all came to a head with the Irish group

Clannad, who used the Prophet 5 synthesizer to conjure up a silky web of voices on the track 'Theme From Harry's Game' (1983).

Which neatly brings us back to the 1970s, the decade when rock evolved and built upon the pioneering work of the 1960s. For Clannad were influenced by 10cc, specifically the vocal ambience of the Manchester band's UK and US mega-hit 'I'm Not In Love' in 1975. Written by Eric Stewart and Graham Gouldman, this memorably romantic song was electronic rock at its most delicious. Using a sixteen-track recorder in their own Strawberry Studios, 10cc painstakingly recorded single-note vocal harmonies which were then put on tape loops and blended through the mixing desk. Combined with Fender Rhodes piano and MiniMoog synth, this produced a sound that was a perfect meeting of emotion and technical brilliance.

Like 10cc, Pink Floyd will always be identified with the 1970s. From the beginning they were seen as the last word in big experimental rock, and even their late-60s music with Syd Barrett was full of electronic sound effects. Yet it wasn't until the 1970s that the world at large would see how far Pink Floyd could travel. *Dark Side Of The Moon* (1973) became the most famous deployment of the EMS VCS3 synthesizer in history while *Wish You Were Here* (1975) still stands as a colossal achievement in Ambient rock – an album where ringing guitar, absolute silence, keyboards, synthesizers and studio magic all combine in one great glorious burst of sound. Compared to Pink Floyd, the work of so-called 'progressive rockers' Keith Emerson, King Crimson and Yes seems crude in retrospect, but it did have flashes of brilliance and fully embraced new musical hardware. Far better were the folk-inspired creations of Led Zeppelin and Mike Oldfield. Zeppelin's Jimmy Page was a master of studio technique, and his open-plan production 'Stairway To Heaven' was another highlight of early 70s rock. Mike Oldfield was proclaimed a rock saviour when his multi-instrumental studio-enhanced take on Minimalism, *Tubular Bells* (1973), sold millions.

Another source of great electronic and Ambient music was German rock, or 'krautrock' as it became known in the UK. The young musicians who sprang from cities such as Berlin, Cologne, Düsseldorf, Hamburg and Munich during the early 1970s had no interest in aping Anglo-American rock. Their German identity necessitated a reinvention and this was facilitated by radical approaches to recording and an emphasis on long instrumental tracks. Can, with their background in Stockhausen and jazz, were masters of 'instant composition' whereby long, improvised tracks were laid down in their self-built studios for later 'editing' by their technical boffin Holger Czukay. In fact Czukay continued to work with tape and in the 1980s made successful solo albums as well as great Ambient collaborations with David Sylvian. The Hamburg-based communal formation Faust made an excellent collage album, *The Faust Tapes* (1973), while metronomic drumming and strange electronic sounds were the province of Düsseldorf's NEU!. Tangerine Dream emerged from Berlin as a trio of synthesizer experts whose thorough knowledge of the potential of electronic rock produced magnificent sound tapestries like *Rubycon* (1975) and *Stratosfear*

(1976). Their purposeful exploration of electronic rhythm would result in the invention of computer sequencing software. The spiritually enriched music of Munich's Popol Vuh graced many a Werner Herzog soundtrack while Hans-Joachim Roedelius's keyboard genius (inside and outside Cluster) was so thoroughly Ambient that Brian Eno proclaimed his music some of the best the 1970s had to offer. Many 70s German musicians would directly influence Techno music of the 1990s. Ash Ra Tempel's guitarist Manuel Gottsching would become famous due to the 1994 remix of his hypnotic tour de force *E2–E4*. MiniMoog maestro Klaus Schulze became a firm collaborator in the 1990s with the Frankfurt Ambient star Pete Namlook. Yet the most influential German group of the 1970s was undoubtedly Kraftwerk, a Düsseldorf quartet whose slick modernistic creations defined an entire electronic sound world. A union of self-designed synthesizers and drum machines with a perfectionist approach to recording resulted in such conceptual triumphs as *Trans-Europe Express* (1977) and *The Man Machine* (1978) – recordings that influenced David Bowie, US Hip-Hop and the entire history of Techno.

Rock was so eclectic that it was fed and nourished by developments in synthesizer music. From the late 1960s to the early 1970s the likes of The Byrds, Mick Jagger and Van Morrison all availed themselves of the skills of Beaver & Krause, two California-based Moog synth specialists. As the Moog was notoriously difficult to tune, Beaver & Krause were happy to contribute their know-how, even recording some good experimental albums along the way. In New York the duo Tonto's Expanding Headband customized a series of Moogs and made such compelling electronica that they were hired by Stevie Wonder to help make a series of classic rocking-soul recordings like *Innervisions* (1973). Some rock musicians preferred to become synthesizer stars in their own right. Tim Blake transferred from the UK to France to become a touring sound-and-light sensation, an act made more impressive by his futuristic glam-rock image and virtuosity on keyboard and synth. Destined to outsell every other 'synthesist' was France's Jean Michel-Jarre, a serious avant-garde musician who was inspired by Pierre Schaeffer and Stockhausen to delve into the world of analogue synthesizers. The kinetic power of *Oxygene* (1977) was as convincing an argument as any that electronics could make very human music. Jarre enthusiastically embraced everything from computer music to huge urban laser-light displays, his high-profile endorsement of electronic music leading to a staggering sixty million album sales worldwide.

If emotion was what was needed from keyboards and synths then Greek star Vangelis provided it in spades during the 1980s. One of the great exponents of the Yamaha CS-80 polyphonic synthesizer, Vangelis became a star when he won an Oscar for the film theme to *Chariots Of Fire* (1981). His moving Ambient score for the film *Blade Runner* (1982) is a twentieth-century highlight.

During the late 1970s a new rock force appeared which is best described as the Indie Wave. Independent, and mostly British, labels provided an outlet for music driven by the availability of cheaper and more compact electronic equipment.

Cabaret Voltaire, from Sheffield, were inspired by Stockhausen and Eno to make sound collages with tape machines and small synthesizers. Their interest in sensory overload due to new information technology led them to Chicago House and beyond into the pure datastream of Techno. In Manchester, Joy Division's debut album, *Unknown Pleasures* (1979), not only spawned the legendary Factory Records label but also invented a form of isolationist rock where desolate synth and tape sounds were as important as the familiar drum, guitar and vocal timbres of old. As the group developed, their music became more Ambiently ravishing, and the death of their singer Ian Curtis and a name-change to New Order did not halt the process. Their 1983 release 'Blue Monday', with its accelerated bass and drum patterns, was one of the most celebrated twelve-inch dance records of all time. Factory was also home to Vini Reilly, who recorded under the name The Durutti Column. His singular classical–cum–Ambient approach to rock guitar produced a whole series of beautiful-sounding albums. In London the 4AD label attracted a series of fascinating musicians. When Colin Newman left the ironic new-wave band Wire, he found a comfortable stable at 4AD for which he recorded a number of Ambient–cum–experimental rock LPs in the early 1980s. The defining sound of 4AD came from the Scottish trio The Cocteau Twins, whose combination of treated guitars, keyboards, studio processing and the operatic voice of Elizabeth Fraser resulted in a sparkling, sheen-like music. Their emphasis was on total sound space, and albums like *Treasure* (1984) and *Blue Bell Knoll* (1988) were so individual that not even Fraser's indecipherable vocalise detracted from their accomplishment. Other 'indie' groups opted for the route of an opaque insular sound universe.

Americans Sonic Youth produced a blizzard of guitar noise and sound distortion on the exemplary *Daydream Nation* (1988) while Anglo-Irish group My Bloody Valentine blazed white-hot on the sound-morphing *Loveless* (1991). Indie rock minimalism and mantric guitar drones were taken to their farthest limits by Sonic Boom and Jason Pierce in Spacemen 3. *The Perfect Prescription* (1987) celebrated John Cage, The Velvet Underground and psychedelia. By the late 1990s Pierce was creating hypnotic rock in Spiritualized while Sonic Boom delved into pure electronic music with Spectrum and EAR.

Our survey of Ambience in the rock era concludes with those musicians whose contribution to the latter part of the twentieth century marks them out as true individualists. The Italian Ennio Morricone embraced the drama of rock recording to create some of the most memorable theme music of all time. Once heard, such soundtrack work as *The Good, The Bad And The Ugly* (1966) was not easily forgotten. Philadelphian rock star Todd Rundgren was one of the first to show that if a musician was able enough, new technology could allow him or her to do anything in the studio. His *Something/Anything* (1972) seemed to sum up the entire history of rock sound on one incredibly eclectic album. After Jimi Hendrix, Yorkshireman John McLaughlin was one of the few guitarists able to face down the instrument with a new musical vocabulary. His mixture of Indian music and jazz, along with his interest in guitar-synthesizers, computers and new fusions, enriched rock for decades. The self-taught English guitarist Robert Fripp went way beyond the bounds of 'progressive rock' when he made some of the earliest Ambient records with Brian Eno. His constant interest in new sounds and a considered approach to the instrument made him a sought-after collaborator, his guitar Ambience on David Bowie's *'Heroes'* (1977) a pinnacle of under-statement. Like Fripp, Peter Gabriel emerged from UK 'progressive rock'. Even in Genesis his interest in studio innovation led to the dry, compressed drum sound which would dominate the 1980s. His slow, meticulously detailed approach to recording absorbed all available analogue and digital technology to produce *So* (1986) – an Ambient rock masterwork. Though a contemporary of Gabriel, guitarist Bill Nelson opted for capturing moods in short compositions which also used keyboards and synthetic percussion. His instrumental works, particularly those of the 1980s, had a Satiesque brilliance.

American Laurie Anderson brought the sound of voice synthesis into millions of homes with her 1982 hit 'O Superman'. Influenced by Philip Glass, Anderson became rock's best-known performance artist and one of the world's most inventive users of digital sampling technology. Influenced by Debussy, The Beatles and Steve Reich, the Japanese musician Ryuichi Sakamoto made a valuable bridge between East and West in the 1980s. With his talents in film music, arranging and electronic sound, his work was a rock or pop equivalent to that of the Japanese composer Toru Takemitsu. Sakamoto worked extensively with the English pop star David Sylvian, whose debut solo album *Brilliant Trees* (1984) brought the experimental approaches of the likes of Minimalist Jon Hassell into full public view. Sylvian's interest in Ambient music and instru-mental sound reached a rich outflowing with German Holger Czukay during the late 1980s. Around the same time the Canadian Michael Brook celebrated the success of his Infinite Guitar, a self-built instrument capable of infinite sustain. Brook attracted the interest of both Brian Eno and the Irish group U2 for his atmospheric tone-coloured music. The latter's chiming rock sound was full of Ambience courtesy of Brian Eno's production and The Edge's echoing, harmonically rich guitar style. U2 were fearless in the studio, and recordings such as *The Joshua Tree* (1987) and *Achtung Baby* (1991) were brilliant realizations of what could be achieved with synthesizers in rock. Some of their atmosphere they owed to the Canadian Daniel Lanois, who helped midwife the above two albums. Lanois produced Peter Gabriel and believed that studio recording should emphasize the environment as much as the music. After working with U2 he salvaged Bob Dylan's career not once but twice, first in 1989 and then in 1997 with the superlative *Time Out Of Mind*. By the last decade of the century it seemed that everything possible in electronic rock had been achieved. Then along came Enya with a new sound. Her speciality lay in creating myriad multi-tracks of her voice and blending its hushed choral properties with finely drawn synthesizer and keyboard lines. An album like *Shepherd Moons* (1991) was state-of-the-art electronic music which sacrificed not a jot of emotion. Enya's worldwide multimillion album sales made her the first true Ambient star.

INNOVATORS

LEO FENDER

In the rock era the single most important invention was undoubtedly the electric guitar. It transformed acoustic music into amplified sound capable of a wide degree of alteration and effect. The psychedelic era was all mostly guitar-led, the awesome achievements of Jimi Hendrix and Jeff Beck (who both endorsed the Fender guitar) ushering in the progressive rock era of the 1970s and the guitar Ambience of both Led Zeppelin and Pink Floyd. Fender's guitars continued to be a classic instrument of change for rock groups of the 1980s and 90s.

Leo Fender was born in California in 1909 and by the 1940s was manu-facturing guitar amplifiers for a growing market. Friends and clients complained of constant distortion problems arising from amplifying an acoustic guitar. He designed a new pick-up. History states that a number of people, including Les Paul, arrived at the solution of the solid-bodied guitar at around the same time, but it was Fender's prototype which became the electric guitar of the twentieth century. With its multiple pick-ups and unmistakably clear sound the Fender Broadcaster was invented in 1947 to go into mass production a year later. By 1950 the guitar was so popular it name was changed to the more expansive-sounding Telecaster.

In 1953 Fender put all his knowledge into the design of the Stratocaster, an amazingly versatile instrument which would become the ultimate guitar as deployed by Jimi Hendrix – with its simple volume and tone controls and its tremolo arm to increase sound effects off the fretboard. Fender worked on other instruments, including Precision Basses and Jazz guitars in the 1950s, but the Strat was his work of genius. Having founded the small Fender Electrical Instrument Company in 1946, he was prompted by illness to sell it to CBS in 1965 for a staggering $13 million, a year before Jeff Beck and Jimi Hendrix showed the world the true potential of the Telecaster and Stratocaster. Over time Fender regained his health and continued to innovate through research, design and consultancy. He died in California in 1991, having revolutionized electronic guitar sound for ever.

LES PAUL

Although Les Paul is best known for his precision-built electric guitar, manufactured by Gibson in 1952, he was also a tremendous pioneer in the area of recording. During the 1940s he plunged into the world of tape manipulation, speeding up recordings to get strange effects. Moreover he originated the concept of overdubbing instruments and multi-tracking the voice in popular music during the late 1940s.

Les Paul was born in Wisconsin in 1915 and as a child was a music fanatic, playing a number of instruments. By the age of twelve he was playing guitar and recording with self-built apparatus. He was a local DJ and played guitar with country ensembles. By 1936 he was in New York, where he came under the influence of Django Reinhardt and hence saw a future in amplified jazz guitar. In 1940 he began to recognize the potential of a solid-bodied (as opposed to semi-acoustic) electric instrument. Though Gibson was wary of putting money behind Paul's idea, the success of Fender guitars in the late 1940s made the company think again. As a result, the Gibson Les Paul electric guitars of the 50s became a classic instrument.

The Les Paul was small but very strong. It had a number of pick-ups and acute tone, which made it very good for both rock and jazz. Its high quality of sustain made it a perfect foil for Jimmy Page when he made the guitar his very own during the heady days of Led Zeppelin between 1969 and 1975. Paul himself continued to play music after his great invention, and was known for his tasteful guitar work, recording with Nat King Cole in the late 1940s. Then living in Los Angeles, he married the singer Mary Ford in 1949 and in 1950 had a huge American hit with the country ballad 'Tennessee Waltz' (a version of which appeared in Antonioni's 1970 film *Zabriskie Point*).

During the early 1950s Paul and Ford had a string of million-selling US hits on Capitol, all full of multi-tracked voice and other sounds achieved through Paul's own home-made eight-track equipment. Paul's sound being two decades ahead of its time, it was, ironically, doomed by the coming of no-nonsense rock 'n' roll in the late 1950s. In fact a parallel can be drawn between, on the one hand, his sophistication and the simplicity of early rock, and, on the other, the complexity of late-1970s English 'progressive' music and the coming of punk rock. Though divorce in the 1960s and health problems in the 1970s set him back, Paul continued to work on new electronic components for his guitar. By the 1990s he was hailed as a genius, a favourite guest at music fests, often playing alongside Jeff Beck.

JOE MEEK

Joe Meek is certainly the most innovative producer to come out of England before The Beatles entered the Abbey Road studios. He was the first to use the recording studio as an instrument, pre-dating Brian Eno's ideas by fifteen years. He was the first to see that recording was in itself an electronic process to transform sound, not just to document it. He was also the first maverick technician, pushing primitive technology beyond its limits and leading the way for equipment manufacturers to follow musicians' dreams and desires.

Meek was born in Gloucestershire in 1929. Before he reached his teens he was dabbling in radio and television construction. After being called to serve in the RAF, where he applied his talents to radar, he left to pursue sound experiments with tape machines and work as a radio and TV repair man in Gloucester. In 1950, long before Steve Reich and Brian Eno experimented with tape, Meek was already making important concrete-sound studies and collages using two primitive tape machines.

After moving to London in 1954 he joined IBC studios, first as a junior then as senior engineer. There he began to experiment with microphone placement, live-studio mixing and sound distortion from the recording environment and the use of echo and compression on the resultant sounds themselves. A mixture of hostility and paranoia led to his resignation in 1957. He continued to work with jazzmen Acker Bilk and Chris Barber at Lansdowne Studios but soon tired and left to found his own Triumph record company at the beginning of the 1960s. He even recorded a legendary LP, *I Hear A New World*, full of outer- and inner-space connotations, but, incredibly, the company foundered on its own success. Demand for Triumph's hit singles simply outstripped its limited ability to supply.

Still undaunted in his quest for independent prestige, Meek set up a production company called RGM Sound on the Holloway Road in North London. A live-music room and a recording room stuffed with primitive equipment was all he required. Here Meek put down backing instrumentals, then compressed and limited them to extremes before sending them out again to be played along to by the lead vocalist or instrumentalist. The parallel with Eno's later experiments with Harold Budd in the 1980s is uncanny. A forest of cables and tape, Meek's studio also employed the John Cage approach of preparing pianos with drawing pins and using unusual sound sources like industrial and garden springs for reverberation. As Daniel Lanois did later with U2, Meek would also place microphones all over the premises and use natural reverberation in bathrooms and in attics to enhance sound.

In 1962 Meek scored his biggest hit record with the brilliant novelty 'space' single 'Telstar' by The Tornadoes. It was a number-one hit in the UK and the US and the first recording by a British beat combo to scale the top of the American charts. This futuristic instrumental is still selling today. By now everybody wanted to know Meek. Crooners like Tom Jones admired him, while guitarists like Jimmy Page and Ritchie Blackmore (to become giants of 70s hard rock) were more than happy to record sessions with him.

As he upgraded his studio in 1963 with new American limiting and reverb equipment, The Beatles arrived on the scene and Meek's sound was swamped by the new Beat music. A combination of declining business, manic depression, conflict over his homosexuality and sheer exhaustion led to his untimely death in 1967 from self-inflicted gunshot wounds. Today an entire range of audio equipment is dedicated to Meek – equipment designed to apply that other-worldly sound to work which may owe its very existence to Meek's passionate vision.

LISTENING

'I Hear A New World' surfaced on an RPM CD in 1992 and by 1995/1996 equipment builder Ted Fletcher had updated Meek's optical control system and other circuitry to build a series of compressors and enhancers which gave new recordings the classic Meek sound of old.

THE BEATLES

The lasting impression left by The Beatles is one of overwhelming innovation resulting from unprecedented popularity. It is easy to forget that Lennon and McCartney had been working together for ten years before the landmark release of *Sgt. Pepper's Lonely Hearts Club Band* in June 1967. Having spent nearly 2,000 hours performing, the group had paid more than their dues by the Summer of Love. Moreover they always wanted to make it on their own terms, their leader, John Lennon, desiring more than the trappings of material success. So by 1966 The Beatles were headily exploring the work of Cage and Stockhausen. *Sgt. Pepper* is a homage to these twentieth-century iconoclasts, its rich, tape-manipulated sound also owing something to Pierre Schaeffer. The fact that it is the best-selling album ever in the UK attests to the absorption of electronic-music ideas into mainstream rock and pop.

All four Beatles were born in Liverpool in the early 1940s and all were proudly working-class. Paul McCartney (whose father was a professional pianist) had serious trumpet lessons as a child. John Lennon had his own group, The Quarrymen, which McCartney joined in 1957. Lennon immediately knew that the younger McCartney had a perfect understanding of harmony and pitch. George Harrison, for his part, was addicted to the guitar from the age of thirteen. Ringo Starr's bass kicks and tom-tom fills were a perfect counterpoint to the chiming guitars and vocal lushness of The Beatles' sound, one inspired by American soul, blues, country and, of course, rock 'n' roll.

It is said that The Beatles had played some 800 amphetamine-fuelled gigs in Hamburg and Liverpool before their fateful meeting with George Martin at EMI in 1962. Even so, they'd been turned down by four major labels and their sound was still rough. Martin was a visionary producer who would become the 'fifth Beatle'. Born in 1926, he had studied piano as a child, going on to pursue the gamut of classical-music studies at London's Guildhall. A formidable orchestrator, oboist and pianist, he then worked for the BBC before joining EMI. Made head producer at the EMI subsidiary label Parlophone when only twenty-eight, he was destined to meet The Beatles, and over the next eight years he would be their in-house sonic maestro – able to turn any idea, no matter how far-out, into gorgeously realized music.

By 1963 Beatlemania had taken hold of Britain, driven by such songs as the repetitively delicious 'She Loves You'. Their first album had been recorded on two-track tape machines, virtually live, in ten hours! Their second LP, also recorded in 1963, saw the introduction of four-track equipment at Martin's insistence. Vocals could be easily doubled and separated from the other instrumental colours, which were expanded to include Spanish guitar, African percussion and bongo drums. Even though the group were singing infectious pop singles like 'I Want To Hold Your Hand', their studio techniques were already evolving.

In 1964 they hit America but, bar the hysteria, their most important encounter was with Bob Dylan in a Manhattan hotel room, where they smoked marijuana for the first time. Their hectic schedule left them little time to digest the experience, but their sound began to subtly alter – now incorporating twelve-string guitars and guitar feedback. Inspired by Dylan, they also began writing all their own material as exemplified on that year's *A Hard Day's Night*. More importantly, they began to stretch out recording sessions, spending time between February and June 1965 putting down *Help!*. This time the four-track Abbey Road equipment was used to layer instruments, Harrison for his part using volume-pedal and more intricate chordal devices to enrich his guitar sound. Two songs on *Help!* stood out. Lennon's 'You've Got To Hide Your Love Away' was an acoustic folk charmer which included maracas, tambourine and ornate flutes. McCartney's 'Yesterday' was pure inspiration, a classical melody and harmony creation improved by Martin's string-quartet arrangement. It was a turning-point, and from then on The Beatles' music would embrace complexity as a matter of course.

The group were still touring in Europe and the US, but after the Shea Stadium concert in late summer of 1965 they had their second important drug experience. They met David Crosby and Roger McGuinn of The Byrds at a house in Los Angeles, where, aided by LSD, Lennon and Harrison were struck by the Indian cadences produced by Crosby's twelve-string guitar. The Indian sitarist Ravi Shankar was mentioned and The Byrds were only months away from creating the epic raga-rock of 'Eight Miles High'. Back in London that autumn, The Beatles laid down a track directly inspired by this meeting, 'Norwegian Wood', full of Harrison's double-tracked sitar.

This would be the stand-out song on *Rubber Soul* (1965), the first great Beatles album. Recorded in a matter of a month, the album was the first Beatles record which was noticeably drug-influenced. Introspective, moody and at times bitter, it was famous for its warped group photo and pop-art title. It was full of great sounds – sitar, bouzouki, harmonium, Byrdsy twelve-string Rickenbacker guitars, bright ethnic percussion and filtered vocals. The antique sound of the acoustic guitars on 'Norwegian Wood' was full of drones, Lennon's lyric about a one-night stand very 1960s. The album is famous for

Martin's half-speed piano fill on 'In My Life', a classical touch which in retrospect sounds contrived. In my opinion the greatest song on *Rubber Soul* was 'Nowhere Man', which burst forth with all the gusto of newly discovered psychedelia. Lennon's cheesy vocal luxuriates in an opiated haze of production and Harrison's Fender Stratocaster solo fuzzes with all the right hallucinatory sparkle. No wonder it was used again on the soundtrack to the psychedelic cartoon fantasy *Yellow Submarine* (1968).

Yet this was only a promise, for the greatest album in The Beatles' canon was yet to come. Fully confident that the sounds and visions of mind-expanding drugs led to a deeper musical fountain, the group experimented liberally with tape recorders in their own home studios. The aim was to catch these feelings and observations in music, and with *Revolver* The Beatles rose to the occasion like no other group before them. At times saturated in drugs, the mood of *Revolver* nevertheless captured everything the group was about – jollity, great rock music, peaking innovation, masterful songwriting and new studio techniques. The album's vibe opened up millions to the potential of psychedelic music, the exotic finales of some songs promising a whole universe of sonic dreams. The recording sessions at Abbey Road, which took place in the spring and summer of 1966, began with the most portentous psychedelic song ever written. 'Tomorrow Never Knows' was Lennon's interpretation of LSD guru Timothy Leary's mantra 'Turn off your mind, relax and float downstream'. Over Starr's repetitive, effects-laden tom-toms, Lennon recited this mantra to a kaleidoscope of electronically treated sounds. Five tape loops were spun into a mix full of Mellotron flute, treated sitar, backwards guitar and organ drones. Every signal was vari-speeded, compressed or echoed. Lennon's voice was altered by putting it through an artificial double-tracked tape process, and in the course of this procedure the term 'flanging' was born. His voice was rarefied even further by directing it through a rotating Leslie speaker cabinet.

If listening to 'Tomorrow Never Knows' was like taking a trip, hearing Lennon's acid-drenched 'I'm Only Sleeping' left one in no doubt as to where its author was coming from. Again the sound of this aural delight evoked the drugged state of its writer. The trebly tone of the acoustic guitars was a perfect foil to Lennon's languid tone, in what was possibly the world's first 'chill-out' pop song. Harrison's backwards guitars seemed to have an intended hypnotic quality, and the conclusion of the song all the flavour of an electronic raga. Brilliantly this led into Harrison's own authentically Indian-sounding 'Love You To', whose tabla and sitar improvisation in the finale was gloriously uplifting. The devotional ending of Harrison's 'I Want To Tell You' was equally optimistic, while 'Good Day Sunshine' had a raga-like edge to its mirrored vocal climax. *Revolver* was an album of superb timbral variety – French horn, strings, clavichord and so on, its series of flawless sound constructions nowhere better heard than on McCartney's classically perfect creation 'For No One'.

Amazingly, Lennon, ever the adventurer, wasn't satisfied. Working in

Weybridge, near London, on his Mellotron, he wanted to make an even better sound collage than 'Tomorrow Never Knows'. At Abbey Road over eight days in the winter of 1966, he pushed the group into recording an open-ended modal creation titled 'Strawberry Fields Forever'. Featuring backwards cymbals, cascading Indian harp, riveting Harrison guitar solos, timpani, bongos, trumpets and cellos, this was the lushest music The Beatles had recorded up to then. The song was also recorded using two four-track machines, the final take being a splice of a rock version and an orchestral version. From its weird Mellotron opening to its fake drum forward reprise where a voice could be heard saying, 'I'm very stoned', 'Strawberry Fields Forever' inaugurated 1967 like no other song on earth.

Just before its release McCartney spent five hours at Abbey Road recording his psychedelic improvisation 'Carnival Of Light', a work of fourteen minutes full of the results of tape-editing experiments in his London home. Never released, it nevertheless shows that both Lennon and McCartney were coming under the influence of experimental composers, particularly Cage and Stockhausen. Recorded in the first four months of 1967, *Sgt. Pepper's Lonely Hearts Club Band* would bring all these interests into accessible focus. In essence the album was less psychedelic than its predecessor; its sounds were totally upfront, leaving little to the imagination. Achieved by wiring two four-track tape machines together, the deep stereophonic sound of *Sgt. Pepper* was the best audio rock result of its times. The album's majestic red cover was a veritable gallery of the famous and inspired, including Aldous Huxley, Edgar Allan Poe, Stockhausen, Dylan and Oscar Wilde. In truth, *Sgt. Pepper* was psychedelia for the masses, a pop-sensitive pot-pourri of mixed-up studio effects which caught the public imagination like no album before it or since.

Sgt. Pepper is soaked with all the echo, vari-speed tape, compression and artificial double-tracking gimmicks of The Beatles' 1966 sessions, but a lot of the songs don't sound that good on close listening. 'Fixing A Hole' begins with a lovely harpsichord and has McCartney dreaming away, but the rough guitar and ordinary rock instrumentation let it down in the end. Some of the squealier guitar tones on the album (courtesy of McCartney) were inspired by Jimi Hendrix. There are, though, three outstanding cuts on *Sgt. Pepper*. 'A Day In The Life', which began the sessions and finished the album, was masterly. A mixture of two different songs by Lennon and McCartney, the track was characterized by its stoned vocals and Cageian string instructions, which had forty players from the Royal and London Philharmonics sliding up the scale until the piece ends with the climax of twelve pianos ringing on one Ambient chord for nearly a minute. More Ambient was Lennon's incredible 'Lucy In The Sky With Diamonds' a gossamer-like evocation of childlike psychedelia. Like Jefferson Airplane in *White Rabbit*, Lennon quoted *Alice In Wonderland* to McCartney's echoed and vari-speeded Lowry organ. But if the drift of psychedelia was what you wanted, its luxuriant Ambience was best summed up by Harrison's 'Within You Without You' – the product of nearly a year's study with Ravi Shankar. The song's Hinduistic lyric was framed by beautiful strings and a variety of other Indian lutes, harp and tamburas. Its main feature was a wobbling tabla and sitar. This and its purity of tone led one to believe it had a Northern Indian quality. Yet the use of strings (playing Indian scales) had its roots in the Southern Carnatic tradition. Whatever was in Harrison's mind, he brought in Asian musicians to play the parts, creating the most timeless piece of dronal psychedelia ever recorded.

Having left live performance behind (the last tour ending in California in the summer of 1966), The Beatles continued to be preoccupied with studio experiments. Inspired by author Ken Kesey and his cross-country bus journey with his Merry Pranksters, McCartney dreamed up *Magical Mystery Tour*, a filmed psychedelic odyssey. Some of the music taped in the autumn of 1967 was inspiring. Lennon's 'I Am The Walrus' was gushingly hallucinogenic and used Stockhausen-like random radio samples. An instrumental take, 'Flying', included Lennon getting Indian flute sounds from a Mellotron. Harrison used more backwards editing and other tape effects on the dreamlike 'Blue Jay Way', a song which seemed to fall out of his interest in transcendental meditation. In fact in early 1968 Harrison was in Bombay recording Indian music for a film. Out of this came the raga 'The Inner Light', another beautiful Indian composition, released as a single. Soon after that Lennon recorded the mantra-full 'Across The Universe', a veritable acoustic dream song, and then the whole group journeyed to India to meditate with their guru the Maharishi Mahesh Yogi.

That year, 1968, saw The Beatles embrace many other musics through their Apple label, including those of the spiritual Minimalist John Tavener and Ravi Shankar himself. In India they wrote and wrote and came back to London to record *The Beatles*, better known as 'The White Album', in the summer and autumn. Thirty songs made up this double album, of which Lennon's eight-minute twenty-second 'Revolution 9' was the most important. Here Lennon effectively paid his respects to Stockhausen, whose *Hymnen* of 1966–7 embraced forty national anthems. Tape loops, record snippets, radio edits, Mellotron, backwards tape, echo delay, bits of *Sgt. Pepper* and lots of voice samples and dialogue built up a picture of repetitive chaos. A voice repeatedly intoning the words 'number nine' gave the track its Minimalist edge. It's worth noting that Lennon had just met Yoko Ono, who'd worked with the American Minimalist composer La Monte Young in New York. Lennon, Ono and Harrison spent days preparing the tapes, the result only coming together over a further two days of mixing in the summer of 1968. This time was the peak of The Beatles' interest in Stockhausen's electronic composition, Cage's chance music and Schaeffer's concrete music. Stockhausen himself commented in 1980 that at that time: 'Lennon often used to phone me. He was particularly fond of my *Hymnen* and *Song Of The Youths* and got many things from them.' The stylistic similarity between the 1956 work *Song Of The Youths* (*Gesang der Jünglinge*) and *Revolution 9* was uncanny.

Another song on 'The White Album', Harrison's haunting ballad 'Long Long Long', was noteworthy for its Ambient production. Yet tensions were running high and time was running out for The Beatles. Ringo had briefly given up on the group during the 1968 sessions. Harrison would walk out during the filming of their next 'live studio' project, provisionally called *Get Back* but to become *Let It Be* in 1970. Then marital and financial arguments clouded the first part of 1969. Nevertheless Harrison's new-found interest in synthetic sound would shape their last masterpiece, *Abbey Road*. He had purchased a Moog synthesizer on the advice of the electronic duo Beaver & Krause at the end of 1968 and it was used on the new album. (Krause also helped Harrison record an album of Moog doodles, *Electronic Sounds*, which saw the light of day on the Zapple label in the spring of 1969.)

Recorded on new eight-track equipment, *Abbey Road* was destined to be The Beatles' best-sounding record. Moreover a lot of the songs repeated melodic lines, parts of the album forming fantastic song and sound suites which still have wondrous effect. The record opened with Lennon's call to Timothy Leary, 'Come Together', with its fine electric piano and tape-manipulated drum sound. Lennon's awesome 'I Want You' was constructed in an endless series of takes and overdubs, its character Minimalist in its repetition, ambitious in its changes of metre, coolly elegant in its jazzy instrumental break and overtly experimental in its Moog 'white noise' finale, which simply cut off. The Moog was again heard on 'Because', a tune which magically begins with George Martin repeating the melodic motif of 'I Want You' on electric harpsichord, and continues into a sound world of massed vocal harmony and quirky synth timbres reminiscent of Wendy Carlos. Its understated opening was then mirrored by McCartney's soft piano entry on 'You Never Give Me Your Money', which ends with his guitars repeating Lennon's lead guitar on 'I Want You'. This merged with wind chimes and looped cricket noises to open up the Mayan trance of 'Sun King'. Later in the record 'Golden Slumbers' also opened with McCartney's understated piano before leading into 'Carry That Weight', which featured backing from a thirty-strong orchestra. This reprised in brass the melody of 'You Never Give Me Your Money' and concluded again with the descending line of 'I Want You'.

As an example of cyclical ideas in pop and rock *Abbey Road* was a masterpiece. Released in the autumn of 1969, it was a fitting swansong to nearly a decade of innovation. (The Beatles were never happy with the Phil Spector post-produced *Let It Be*, which appeared in the summer of 1970.) In terms of production the group had greatly expanded the studio's technical possibilities. Many followed their lead. In terms of sound The Beatles had opened millions of listeners' ears to the world of electronic composition. Harrison's interest in Indian classical music had brought ethnic music into homes the world over. Through the medium of rock and pop The Beatles achieved a position so rarefied that innovation was their only true outlet. Their courage in the studio irrevocably changed the course of twentieth-century music.

LISTENING

All The Beatles' recordings mentioned above are essential listening. All bear the Apple and Parlophone logos and are credited to EMI in the UK. In the US Capitol issued The Beatles' records and veered from British custom by including singles on albums. Thus *Magical Mystery Tour* (1967) came out as an album in America but as a double EP in the UK. With its lovely Ambient piano fade on the title track, *Magical Mystery Tour* included 'Strawberry Fields Forever', 'I Am The Walrus', 'Flying', 'Blue Jay Way' and 'Baby, You're A Rich Man', among other nuggets, thus making it the most psychedelic album The Beatles ever released. Issued in the UK in 1976, it is an essential purchase, as is *Revolver* (1966), my favourite. After Lennon's death, George Martin and the remaining Beatles compiled a series of out-take albums, *The Beatles Anthology 1–3* (1995–6). Credited to Apple Corps Ltd, the series was a great glimpse into the working methods of the group, throwing up many unissued takes and tracks. The second and third albums of *The Beatles Anthology*, which detail sessions from *Help!* to *Abbey Road*, are especially interesting.

BOB DYLAN

When Bob Dylan began putting his own stamp on American folk music in the early 1960s he blueprinted the future of rock. His was the gift of storytelling allied to sound fidelity. What Dylan did best was to crystallize his outstanding vision in excellent records. When he 'went electric' in 1965 he harnessed an earnest conscience to the new power of rock music. With his able black producer Tom Wilson, Dylan would bequeath a licence to express to hundreds of American musicians, including The Mamas & The Papas, The Byrds, Tim Buckley and Simon & Garfunkel. Jimi Hendrix consistently honoured his debt to Dylan throughout his brief but highly influential career. The Velvet Underground were stimulated by Dylan's presence as well as being produced by his studio wizard Tom Wilson. Dylan's impact on the British Isles was enormous, inspiring the work of many, including The Incredible String Band, Fairport Convention and Clannad. Over time it became clear that Dylan was a genius at capturing mood in the studio; so adept was he that he attracted the attention of the Canadian 'sonic sorcerer' Daniel Lanois, who produced some excellent atmospheric recordings for Dylan in the 1980s and 90s.

At the beginning of his career the Minnesota kid had a very 'hit and run' attitude to recording. In 1961 Dylan's first Columbia album was dispatched in two days at the label's New York studios. He and Tom Wilson got through some of his finest songs, such as 'Chimes Of Freedom' and 'My Back Pages', in one intense session for *Another Side Of Bob Dylan* in 1964. It was on the following year's *Bringing It All Back Home* that Wilson began to reveal to Dylan the secrets of tape overdubbing in an album which mixed rock and folk instrumentation, and one which took longer to record. Wilson achieved his best recording on 'Like A Rolling Stone', where Dylan played piano, guitar and harmonica to Al Kooper's organ and Mike Bloomfield's guitar. As Wilson had accepted an offer from Verve, staff producer Bob Johnston produced the rest of what became known as *Highway 61 Revisited* (1965). Did his country roots affect Dylan's trajectory? From listening to this famous album, it's not obvious, but subsequently Dylan did record a lot of material in Nashville.

LSD was more of an influence. Certainly the undulating flow of 'Desolation Row' had the quality of druggy reverie. This beautiful piece clocked in at eleven and a half minutes and was reputedly the product of six weeks' consideration. Yet amid all the furore over Dylan going electric 'Desolation Row' was acoustic Ambience of a very special quality. He had mastered a technique of distorting time by putting a harmonica break at a judicious point in the song's flow and then, instead of ending it there, going back to yet more verses to build up the tension all over again. Dylan would repeat this device on his 1966 album *Blonde On Blonde* (the first double album of self-penned rock songs) when he devoted a whole side to the curling love song 'Sad Eyed Lady Of The Lowlands' – a number which took him a full seven hours of Nashville Studio time to record.

After his 'motorbike accident' in July 1966 Dylan returned to basics with the two-day Bob Johnston-produced *John Wesley Harding* (1968), a recording which stimulated Jimi Hendrix into recording its tracks 'All Along The Watchtower' and 'The Drifter's Escape'. Put down in Nashville with seasoned session musicians, it was a strange record to fire rock's premier guitarist.

A trip to Mexico in early 1973 to film Sam Peckinpah's *Pat Garrett And Billy The Kid* produced Dylan's finest instrumental flourish. The twin challenge of acting and doing the soundtrack took Dylan out of his usual environment. His instrumentals were later multi-tracked in California with added cellos, flute, harmonium and fiddle. Roger McGuinn of The Byrds also appeared. The result was a lovely lilting acoustic soundtrack album which included the angelic 'Knocking On Heaven's Door'.

Dylan's ability to capture the mood never left him. *Blood On The Tracks* (1974) was in places utterly poignant. *Desire* (1976) had a wonderfully thick overdubbed sound deriving from sixteen-track. Though the album was both written and recorded in New York, Scarlet Rivera's gypsy violin and an assortment of mandolin, trumpet, harmony vocals and multiple guitars gave *Desire* the exotic air of having been recorded South of the Border. *Infidels* (1983) drew on the reggae talents of Sly and Robbie. Dylan produced his share of poor records, but the powerful *Oh Mercy* (1989) and *Time Out Of Mind* (1997), recorded in New Orleans and Miami respectively, benefited from the magical production of Daniel Lanois. Says the French Canadian, who has also produced U2: 'It's all about putting care into the organization of the music. Bob's a very good guitar player and a good piano player. He can support himself so well when he plays in the studio.'

LISTENING

Dylan has always been a Columbia recording artist. All the records noted are worth hearing. For those looking for the twittering insects and swampy guitars of the Deep South, Daniel Lanois' production on *Oh Mercy* is superb. Equally atmospheric is his work on *Time Out Of Mind*, which includes the mind-stretchingly Ambient sixteen and a half minutes of 'Highlands'.

THE BEACH BOYS

With their barbershop close harmonies, blond image and string of early-1960s hits about sea, surf and girls, The Beach Boys epitomized the Californian fantasy of white America. It seemed fitting that on his debut album of 1966 Jimi Hendrix should say, 'May you never hear surf-music again', so alien was The Beach Boys' sweet music to his exalted vision of psychedelia. In truth, the group's image was a manufactured one based on the insular genius of Brian Wilson, their songwriter. Wilson had started ingesting LSD as early as mid-1965. When this produced mini-symphonies on *Pet Sounds* (1966) and the incredible song 'Good Vibrations' – an inspired piece of linear production where organ, Fender bass, bongos, piccolo, cellos and the swooshing sound of the Thereminvox were poured on to tape and mixed through echo-chamber then topped off with repeating vocals – Wilson duly earned his place as one of the great sound-shapers of the century, influencing The Beatles and the whole production of rock and pop from then on.

Although Wilson's growing paranoia, insecurity and drug use made him a virtual recluse until rehabilitation in the 1990s, this sad history has not affected his standing. Today he is still considered 'a shy genius', whose unreleased unfinished 1967 mega-opus *Smile* (of which 'Good Vibrations' formed a part) is spoken about in the same hushed tones as *Sgt. Pepper*. In fact the baroque sound of a treated organ, first heard on *Pet Sounds* and then during the *Smile* sessions, resurfaced on The Beatles' 'Lucy In The Sky With Diamonds'. Certainly Paul McCartney was a visitor to Wilson's Los Angeles studio during that time. And it was the recording innovations of first Phil Spector, and then The Beatles in the pop and rock field, that spurred Wilson on to even greater heights.

Wilson was born in 1942, in the Hawthorne district of Los Angeles, to a petit-bourgeois family. He studied music at school but was introverted, awkward and dominated by his ogre father, Murry Wilson. Even so, by his late teens he had formed a close-harmony group with his brothers, a cousin and a neighbour. The Beach Boys' mix of rock 'n' roll, surf guitar and harmony heaven got them signed to the Capitol label in 1962, for which they recorded 'Surfin' USA' the following year. Wilson admired Phil Spector's 'wall-of-sound' vertical recording techniques, which massed instruments and voices on top of one another. Away from Capitol's in-house producers, he spent more time at Western Studios twiddling knobs. Endless hot-house recording sessions and tours drained Wilson, and after breaking down on a flight at the end of 1964 he withdrew from the world, unwilling to play his own music live. An LSD trip in the summer of 1965 laid out his whole life in front of him and he claimed to have seen visions of God. When The Beatles' *Rubber Soul* came out in December 1965, Wilson wanted to make 'feeling music'.

With the other Beach Boys on tour in Japan and unwilling to go along with Wilson's mental trip, the twenty-two-year-old employed advertising tunesmith Tony Asher to co-write the songs for *Pet Sounds*. What they came up with has been described as one of the great pop albums of all time. The minimal involvement of the rest of the group in *Pet Sounds* has led many to see it as a Brian Wilson solo recording. Wilson achieved 'an airy spaciousness' on the album, an ethereal compression where strange percussion, sleigh bells, water bottles, harpsichord and a myriad of other sounds were used. A melancholic alienation runs through 'God Only Knows' and 'I Just Wasn't Made For These Times', the latter including Wilson's first use of the Theremin. On the instrumental 'Let's Go Away For Awhile' Wilson multi-layered twelve violins, piano, four saxophones, oboe, vibes, basses and guitar to come up with a fabulously dreamy piece of high-quality muzak. Even today it's hard to believe the whole thing was recorded in mono.

Paul McCartney was justified when he said that Wilson's songs like the breathtaking harpsichord-punctuated 'Caroline No' was his favourite music of all time. Recorded at the beginning of 1966, *Pet Sounds* was not surfing music and did better in the UK than in the US. From February to September of that year Wilson laboured at various LA studios on 'Good Vibrations' in fits and starts. The resultant three-and-a-half-minute single, released in October 1966, changed the course of rock and popular music. Wilson's layering process on *Pet Sounds* gave way to an almost classical arrangement of sounds and melody which evolved through the listening experience. This was sound-painting of the highest order, owing much to the inspired use of the trembly Theremin and marvellously echoed vocal harmonies.

As 'Good Vibrations' topped the charts and sold in the millions all over the world, Wilson desired to extend the use of the studio as instrument. Harnessing the songwriting talents of the classically trained Mississippi musician Van Dyke Parks, he wanted to create 'the next step in the evolution of record production'. Wilson had his own 'crew' of session musicians and invited guests such as the veteran jazz guitarist Barney Kessell to help out. For the ambitious 'Elements Suite' he even made Ambient tape loops of rain, wind and sea for authenticity. Tirelessly recording and re-recording, arriving in studios like Goldstar at all times of the morning and taking copious amounts of speed and marijuana made

Wilson unhinged. Several deadlines for a new LP, titled *Smile*, came and went, but when a demented and paranoid Wilson threatened to burn the master tapes, all was lost. The album was cancelled in May 1967, and after *Sgt. Pepper* came out a few weeks later Wilson withdrew into himself. What can be heard today displays Wilson as a pop Mozart with an uncanny feel for soft, delicate, Ambient arranging. 'Wind Chimes', 'Wonderful' and 'Cool Cool Water' are delicate watercolours in sound. But the cream is the masterly song 'Surf's Up', a mystical paean to childhood and God, picked out on piano, which begins in a minor chord with subtle trumpets, bass and bells and ends as a lullaby. Ironically, it's as far from the original surf music as Wilson could get.

LISTENING

Capitol's remastered and extensively annotated *Pet Sounds* (1990) is a great release. In 1998 the label also issued a three-disc boxed set of the entire *Pet Sounds* recording sessions. Having abandoned *Smile*, Capitol released the compromised *Smiley Smile* album in September 1967 and this surfaced again, on disc, in 1990. Though The Beach Boys' versions of tracks from *Smile* aren't a patch on Brian's originals, this disc contains various sessions and takes of 'Good Vibrations' which open up Wilson's creative process in the studio. Original takes of *Smile* have always been available on bootleg discs replete with the original cover, the best being an Australian double pack on Vigo (1993). *Surf's Up* retained its brilliance when it was finally released by The Beach Boys in 1971.

JIMI HENDRIX

The pre-eminent guitarist of the twentieth century achieved his lofty position by treating the guitar not as an instrument with strings but as an electronic magic box. Fuelled by an infinite musical imagination, Jimi Hendrix used every electrical device he could lay his hands on to amplify the Technicolor sounds he heard in his imagination. The trilling guitar sound of this musical visionary of bottomless resources became the psychedelic soundtrack of the 1960s. His death at only twenty-seven, when his ambitions were pushing his work towards a grand fusion of classical music, jazz and rock, robbed the world of a true innovator.

Much has been written about the life of Hendrix, one so full of event that it often threatened to overshadow the very music that he lived for. Yet, amid the endless stories of his Swinging 60s lifestyle, lies a body of work that awed such talents as Miles Davis and Brian Eno and was respected by each and every successive generation of musicians, including those from House and Techno persuasions. Why was Hendrix so important? The answer lies in the music itself.

Hendrix was born in Seattle in 1942. He was an African American but with a mixture of Irish and Cherokee Indian in his blood. His upbringing was unstable, though he spent some valued time on an Indian reservation with his grand-mother. His first encounter with music was Gospel but at thirteen he acquired a cheap guitar. Over the years he taught himself how to play, mimicking rock and blues standards he heard on the radio. He played in school bands but in 1961 joined the parachute division of the US Air Force. Stationed in Kentucky, he slept with his guitar, which he wanted to make sound like the wind. There he met another musician, bassist Billy Cox. He played the blues, learning much from the Chicago veteran Muddy Waters. So desperate was Hendrix to play that after he was discharged from the Air Force he ended up as a sideman to the black stars of the day such as Little Richard and B.B. King. In 1964 he went to New York and played with the Isley Brothers. That year he also bought his first Fender Stratocaster, the instrument he would make famous. Being a left-hander, Hendrix held the guitar upside down, with the electronic controls nearest him. Hence his hand would naturally touch the volume and tone knobs, the pick-up switch and most famously the tremolo arm, which was used to give a variety of effects, from quickly trembling notes to controlled feedback. Of course, this expertise came with practice.

By 1966, having honed an outrageous stage act which included playing the guitar in every conceivable position, even with his teeth, Hendrix became the toast of New York. Spotted by a girlfriend of Rolling Stone Keith Richards, he was brought to London, where he became an instant star. That winter he met a young Royal Naval acoustics expert named Roger Mayer who had been interested in avant-garde electronics since the early 1960s. He gave Hendrix a self-built Octavia unit which boosted the guitar's octaves, giving a harmonic mirroring effect. This was used to singular effect on Hendrix's breakthrough single of 1967, 'Purple Haze'. Mayer provided a variety of similar distorting, touch-sensitive guitar devices, which Hendrix used right up until his death in 1970.

Though he was immediately lionized by the cream of London's rockocracy, including The Beatles, Hendrix's own interest lay in the studio. During the winter of 1966 he tried various venues but it wasn't until early the following year, at Olympic Studios, that he met Eddie Kramer, an engineer who was open and willing to transform Hendrix's ambitions into realistic sound. Kramer's approach was to get as much as possible out of four-track tape recorders. Two tracks were used for Mitch Mitchell's jazzy multi-roll drumming with its big bass kick, one track for Hendrix's rhythm guitar and another for the bass. These would then be mixed down to two tracks, leaving two open for Hendrix's vocal and lead guitar overdubs. The sound thus generated was big and crystal-clear.

Hendrix and his manager, Chas Chandler, also took the then unorthodox route of paying for the recording sessions themselves, allowing more time in the studio to perfect the music. They worked intensively on Hendrix's first album, *Are You Experienced* (Track 1967). 'May This Be Love' (also known as 'Waterfall') had a rhythm and sensibility derived from American Indian culture. Its crystalline guitar sound was multi-imaged by means of backwards guitar and stereo panning from one channel to another. Hendrix seized on tape manipulation as a way forward in sound – a backing track would be reversed and a lead guitar solo inserted so that when the track was played in the normal direction the guitar would have a much more impactful entry, with rapid decay. Nowhere was this better heard than on the incredible psychedelic title track 'Are You Experienced', which set a peerless standard for what could be achieved with the electric guitar. With its ratchety entrance and swirling, fibrillating solos, this was awesomely advanced music, drenched in an electronic sound never before captured on disc.

Hendrix was a master of instrumental sound. *Are You Experienced* proved that he wasn't just writing songs with musical accompaniment but also creating word- and sound-paintings. The Ambience of his tone was everything, nowhere more successful than on the near-seven-minute aural extravaganza 'Third Stone From The Sun'. The song seemed to have been cut from a modal-jazz improvisation with a dollop of effects thrown in. Hendrix adapted Roger Mayer's various harmonic, fuzz and boosting devices on the succulent guitar solos here; vocals were spoken words where even Hendrix berated The Beach Boys. Controlled feedback, deft mixing and Kramer and Hendrix's panning on the console made this a stand-out performance.

During the summer of 1967 Hendrix worked on 'The Burning Of The Midnight Lamp' in London and New York. This was rock soul saturated in even more adventurous Hendrix sounds. Here he used an electric harpsichord, the early Mellotron sampling instrument and the guitar accessory that he was best known for, a Vox wah-wah pedal. The latter gave the guitar a wave-like fluttering sound and would be modified by Roger Mayer for Hendrix's next album, the lilting *Axis – Bold As Love* (Track 1967). During the thirty takes of 'Burning' Hendrix would meet engineer Gary Kellgren, a friend of Tom Wilson (the legendary black producer of Dylan, Simon & Garfunkel and The Velvet Underground). Kellgren would be important in shaping Hendrix's later American recording scene.

Back in London, Hendrix spent much time at Olympic Studios with Eddie Kramer, pushing for more extraordinary music. Recorded in the summer and autumn of 1967, *Axis – Bold As Love* was inspired by Hopi Indian symbology and full of colour and number associations. The Technicolor sound of this record was achieved by the use of phasing, a new procedure invented by Olympic second engineer George Chkiantz whereby an instrument's frequency seemed to whirl out of the speakers. The Beatles had tried something similar with Eddie Kramer using double-tracking in the early summer of 1967, but the real thing in stereo was achieved by Chkiantz and Kramer at Olympic. The whole idea was that two signals were superimposed on one another, one at a slightly different speed and frequency.

If phasing was heard to devastating effect on the outro of the title track of

Axis, its subtle use was detected on Hendrix's vocal on 'Little Wing', one of his finest achievements. A beautiful short lullaby, this immaculate composition featured glockenspiel, Hendrix's mellifluous guitar fed through a small revolving Leslie speaker, and the use of a Pultec filter. The Leslie speaker gave the guitar a shifting Doppler effect while the Pultec made Hendrix sound as if he was singing from a great height. Another ballad, the wonderfully picturesque 'Castles Made Of Sand', had one of Hendrix's most heartfelt backwards guitar solos ever. The album made extensive use of Octavia, fuzz and wah-wah pedal. Again Hendrix had ventured to the very frontiers of studio sound.

Hendrix's greatest work, *Electric Ladyland*, would hit the top of the American charts in the autumn of 1968. A double-LP celebration of his black roots, this was the most potent electric blues ever recorded. Full of soul and Gospel touches, *Electric Ladyland* contained its share of studio live playing but also a tremendous amount of Ambient electronica. Recorded between early spring and late summer 1968, it benefited from being put down in a new studio, the Record Plant, opened by Hendrix's old friend Gary Kellgren with Tom Wilson's help. The studio boasted one of the first twelve-track tape machines in the industry. Eddie Kramer was brought over from London to engineer and Hendrix was its first prestigious client. The album opened with the ninety-second sound collage 'And The Gods Made Love', a science-fiction Ambience of backwards voice and cymbals, echoed drums, tape loops and delay, all mixed manually by Hendrix and Kramer. The album included 'Midnight Lamp' and lots of wah-wah pedal on other tracks.

Each side of the double album summoned up a different mood – its first the blues, its last incendiary protest. But the best track was '1983 (A Merman I Should Turn To Be)'/'Moon Turn The Tides Gently Gently Away' – a near-fifteen-minute subaqueous Ambient odyssey. Hendrix played all the instruments himself except the flute, which was contributed by Traffic's Chris Wood. Sounds were speeded up and slowed down, the effect of crying seagulls was coaxed from feedbacking headphones and tape-altered African bells adorned the mix. Kramer and Hendrix decided that the panning, fading and sound effects would be mixed as a performance with no edits. Throughout the flow and eddies of '1983' Hendrix displayed a magician's understanding of volume, tone, colour and timbre, and in the process put down guitar solos of such majesty that everyone knew on hearing them that this was the work of a maestro. Some have even remarked on the classical structure of the piece, its harmony chordings recalling the sonata form of old.

A further example of this kind of sound-painting was done at TTG studios in Los Angeles the very month that *Electric Ladyland* came out. Equipped with a sixteen-track tape machine, Hendrix used lots of backwards guitar and a lead guitar with the warbly tone of a new Uni-Vibe effects unit. This instrumental also featured altered drums and was called 'New Rising Sun', the phantasmagoric intro to Hendrix's fourth, unfinished album. Having played Woodstock in 1969, Hendrix spent much time in America with black groups such as The Band of Gypsys. He had his own studio in New York, Electric Lady, and continued to record. With former Air Force buddy Billy Cox on bass and Mitch Mitchell still on drums, the rippling hypnotic instrumental 'Pali Gap', recorded in the summer of 1970, had a mythological feel, its ethnic guitar sound deriving from the use of the Uni-Vibe unit. Another example of this cleaner sound could be heard on the burring intro to 'Hey Baby', recorded during the same period.

So near the end of his life, Hendrix was refining his musicality. It's no secret that he sought to widen his vision at the same time as many around him wished him to continue performing the hits in the old flashy manner. Hendrix was interested in working with Miles Davis and an orchestral recording arranged by Gil Evans was definitely in the pipeline. His vibrato-full guitar style seemed to connect directly to people of both his own and successive generations. A musician capable of playing lead, harmony, rhythm and singing at the same time, he had a gift that seemed to stretch the bounds of human capacity.

Live, Hendrix plugged his Fender into a personalized array of effects pedals and boxes, a system which included his wah-wah, fuzz and Uni-Vibe units as well as the octave-jumping Octavia gizmo. With an instrument tuned in complex flat and sharp keys, his palette of sounds seemed limitless. On top of this, Hendrix had a consummate understanding of feedback – the noise created by a looping signal going from loudspeaker to electric guitar through a loud amplifier. Hendrix knew exactly how to control this noise, standing in the right place, tapping different parts of his Fender (including the springs at the back) to achieve startling effects. His greatest live epitaph was 'The Star Spangled Banner' at Woodstock in 1969, an interpretation that saw Hendrix pass into the realms of myth. Brian Eno once commented to me: 'He was heroic, really. At Woodstock he had enough suss to continually make the corrections necessary to work around a completely out of tune guitar. He was amazing really, a real Paganini. He was absolutely one of the few people one could call a genius.'

LISTENING

In 1992 Castle Communications issued a disc titled *If 60s Were 90s* attributed to Beautiful People. This was an exciting House mix of Hendrix material by two Surrey musicians, Luke Baldry and Du Kane, facilitated by imaginative use of an Akai S1000 sampler and unprecedented access to the tape vaults. In 1993 Polydor reissued the core Hendrix catalogue in tastefully remastered CD editions with deluxe booklets. In 1995 they released a disc called *Voodoo Soup*, which attempted to approximate Hendrix's final album. Compiled by producer Alan Douglas, it contained 'New Rising Sun' and 'Pali Gap', its back cover featuring a rare shot of Hendrix performing in front of a black audience in Harlem, New York, in 1969.

By 1996 Paul Allen, of the giant Microsoft corporation, had closed years of litigation by getting the Hendrix catalogue returned to Hendrix's remaining family in Seattle. A deal was done with MCA/Universal for the release in 1997 of an entirely new catalogue, this time digitally remastered by Eddie Kramer. *Are You Experienced, Axis – Bold As Love* and *Electric Ladyland* are all essential twentieth-century recordings. 'Pali Gap' and 'Hey Baby (New Rising Sun)', originally released on *Rainbow Bridge* (Reprise 1971), can be heard on *First Rays Of The New Rising Sun* (MCA 1997) and *South Saturn Delta* (MCA 1997) respectively.

RAVI SHANKAR

If both psychedelia and Minimalism had the effect of suspending time in the listener's head, it is no surprise to find that both were fuelled by the West's discovery of traditional Indian music. Ravi Shankar, in particular, became the great guru of that tradition, his influence leaving an indelible mark on the music of The Beatles, The Byrds and Philip Glass. In fact the entire 1960s fascination with Indian music can be traced to Shankar, whose appearances at Monterey Pop in 1967 and Woodstock in 1969 cemented his reputation. His meeting with Philip Glass in Paris in the mid-1960s led the young American composer to reject rigid bar lines for undulating rhythm, thus forming the basis for a new kind of writing known as Minimalism. Most importantly, Shankar's continual recording and performances exposed listeners to a form of music which was open-ended, modal and improvisatory. Without Shankar the idea of Ambient sound would have taken longer to evolve.

To appreciate the contribution of Ravi Shankar, it is interesting to understand a little about the music itself. Shankar is the chief exponent of Northern Indian or Hindustani music. (His namesake the violinist L. Shankar is the most visible face of Southern Indian or Carnatic music, a music made famous by his 1970s recordings with John McLaughlin in the group Shakti.) The Northern Indian tradition goes back 2,000 years and its chief instruments are the stringed sitar and double tabla drums. Accompanying instruments, such as the stringed sarod, dronal tambura and bamboo flute, are also used. The huge musical form known as the 'raga' came to a fixed resolution as late as 1800. The raga was born out of seventy-two scales which use the microtones between tones to generate greater variety. There are many inflections and ornamentations of the notes, and the knowledge of these has been passed down through an oral tradition over many centuries.

A similar structure exists in most of Ravi Shankar's sitar recordings. Firstly there is the *alap*, or opening scale, which is simply played forward and then reversed to set the mood. Next comes the rhythmical exposition known as the *jod*. Then there is the best-known element, the *gat*. In this we hear the kernel of the piece, its song, so to speak. Here also there is improvisation, the tablas speeding up to push the sitarist to greater heights of virtuosity. The tabla playing itself is incredibly intricate, with hundreds of beat cycles to choose from. The sitar is a complex musical tool with moveable convex frets and underlying sympathetic strings. It takes about twenty years of study to become a true virtuoso on either instrument.

Ravi Shankar was born in 1920 in the holy city of Varanasi, famous for its silk. When only ten he went to Paris to work with his brother Uday's Hindu dance and music troupe. He danced and played both the sarod and sitar. On tour with the master sarod player Allauddin Khan, Shankar impressed him with his musical gifts. When Shankar was eighteen he journeyed to the Northern Indian town of Maihar to study with Khan and his son Ali Akbar. Shankar spent sixteen hours a day practising the sitar, on a musical and spiritual voyage that would last eight years.

He began performing in the late 1940s and by 1949 was a musical director at All-India Radio. During the six years he worked there he wrote much music, including film scores, most famously for Satyajit Ray's *Pather Panchali* (1955). When Ali Akbar Khan recorded with violinist Yehudi Menuhin in that year, Shankar was inspired to go on a tour of Europe and America. He gave recitals and expositions of Indian music all over the world in the decade preceding his meeting with George Harrison. He founded his own Kinnara music school in Bombay in 1962 and recorded with both Yehudi Menuhin and the Ambient flautist Paul Horn. Shankar was also accessible to the jazz world and influenced the American Minimalist La Monte Young.

Having spent so much time in France when he was a boy, Shankar was fully open to the modernity of be-bop jazz, abstract art, new-wave cinema and everything else that the 1960s had to throw at him. He even worked with Philip Glass in Paris on a film soundtrack in 1965. Yet, having been taught by a master court musician, he embodied much Indian tradition. Shankar's increasingly popular recordings were having a huge effect on rock music. The Byrds' David Crosby was so obsessed with Shankar that he pushed his own group and The Beatles towards raga-rock in the autumn of 1965. Both The Beatles' 'Norwegian Wood' and The Byrds' 'Eight Miles High' came out of an intense, trippy discussion the two groups had about Shankar in Los Angeles before their recording. Moreover the melismatic highs and sitar and tabla delights of *Revolver*, released in 1966, were a direct product of Harrison's increasing fascination with Indian music. That summer, during the recording of the album, Shankar and his tabla player, Alla Rakha, met Harrison in his country house. An emotional and a spiritual bond was made that saw Harrison journey to Bombay that autumn and spend six weeks in intense study with Shankar. This friendship would make Ravi Shankar's name world-famous.

Having established a Californian arm of his music school in 1967, Shankar was guest of honour at that year's Monterey International Pop Festival, where he played for two and a half hours and was later remembered, alongside Jimi Hendrix, as the highlight of the show. His star in the ascendant, Shankar was a 1960s touring sensation with best-selling records in the US and Europe. He was not at all interested in drugs himself, but his growing constituency was largely drawn from drug-taking hippies immersed in a vague Indian mysticism. He even played Woodstock in 1969. After organizing and playing the Concert For Bangladesh (New York 1971) with George Harrison, Shankar toured the US in 1974 with the ex-Beatle, who had facilitated his rise to fame and helped disseminate his music through releases on Apple and Dark Horse.

During the tour Shankar suffered a heart attack. Removing himself from the rock scene, he wrote concertos for sitar and interested himself in ballet during the 1970s. In the early 1980s he joined the Californian Institute of Music. His second great film success came with Richard Attenborough's *Gandhi* (1982). Now living in California, Ravi Shankar is a constant on the concert platform and lecture circuit. Not only did he educate the West in the sound of Northern Indian music, he also incorporated many elements of its more florid Carnatic counterpart in his performances and recordings. His influence on rock and subsequent Ambient styles is immeasurable. With George Harrison's help, Shankar published his autobiography, *Raga Mala*, in 1998, an exotically presented boxed item which came with joss-sticks and two CDs of new and archive recordings.

LISTENING

There are dozens of Ravi Shankar albums on the market, many little more than live recordings. A great one to start with is *The Sound Of The Sitar*, which came out in 1966 and was remastered in Cambridge, England, in 1993 for the Beat Goes On label. In fact BGO had released an entire series of vintage Shankar albums on disc, including, in 1994, *India's Master Musician* from 1959. There are various recordings in the 'Raga Moods' series, all of which are interesting. The classic *In Concert* recording from 1972, featuring Shankar with Ali Akbar Khan and Alla Rakha, is now available again in a two-CD set on The Beatles' Apple label. Remastered in 1996, it is one of the best examples of sitar, sarod, tabla and tambura interplay ever recorded. There's a sublime 1970s disc on Deutsche Grammophon titled *East Greets East* (featuring Shankar and Rakha with Japanese classical musicians) and a great recording with Philip Glass, *Passages* (Private Music 1990). Partly recorded in Madras, this was the setting for work on *Chants Of India* (Angel 1997), produced by George Harrison. Their long friendship also saw Harrison fund and oversee that year's retrospective four-disc Shankar set *In Celebration* (Angel).

In 1998 EMI won the rights to the entire World Pacific/Angel catalogue and began releasing new editions of Shankar's vast output. Recommended discs are *Improvisations* (1962), *Live at Monterey* (1967) and *West Meets East*, a superlative compilation of recordings made in the late 1960s and 70s with the great violinist Yehudi Menuhin.

THE VELVET UNDERGROUND, NICO AND JOHN CALE

The Velvet Underground represented the confluence of pure Minimalism, glamour and European Decadence in rock. Their emergence in the New York of the late 1960s coincided with the moment street culture became high art, most visibly embodied in the success of their patron Andy Warhol. Their extremely radical music, which used intense repetitions and distorted volumes, became a touchstone for musicians such as Can, Joy Division, Brian Eno, Sonic Youth and Spacemen 3, to name some. Yet the Velvets could make some of the quietest music in the history of the genre, often for the voice of the mysterious German chanteuse Nico. Their primary importance derives from the evolution of Minimalism into a rock context – masterminded by the gifted composer John Cale and streamlined by the talent of the classically trained songwriter Lou Reed. With the media sheen provided by Warhol, the group were to become icons of subversion, their albums such as *The Velvet Underground & Nico* (1967) and *White Light/White Heat* (1968) regarded as some of the most fantastic creations of the twentieth century.

The kernel of The Velvet Underground was the strange, often fierce creative relationship between its principals, Cale and Reed. Cale was impressed by the intelligence of the writing which Reed brought to rock. Reed was awed by Cale's unpredictable spirit and his so-called playing of 'unauthorized music' on amplified viola. John Cale was Welsh, born in 1942 in Garnant to a coalminer father. Hymns and both composition and performance ran in his blood. He began piano at three, viola at five and gave his first BBC performance at eight. At the beginning of the 1960s he entered Goldsmiths College in London to pursue formal music studies, including a projected thesis on the relationship between Webern's Serialism and secret codes. Instead he became obsessed with the work of John Cage and La Monte Young. After three years he was expelled but gained a Bernstein scholarship to study with the Greek composer Iannis Xenakis at Tanglewood in Massachusetts. There he alienated his mentors by physically attacking his instruments in performance. His hero became the Surrealist artist Marcel Duchamp.

In the autumn of 1963 Cale and Cage performed a piece by Erik Satie. The repetition of the French composer's 180-note piano piece *Vexations* the required 840 times took more than eighteen hours and made New York headlines. It was then that Cale would forge one of the most important musical relationships in history, that with La Monte Young in The Theatre Of Eternal Music, better known as The Dream Syndicate. The basis of this group, which included Young, his wife Marian Zazeela, the violinist Tony Conrad and percussionist Angus MacLise, was the extreme concentration on drones – the use of repetition and extension to achieve a trance-like Ambience. Formed in 1962, the group grew out of Young's jazz and raga leanings but with the arrival of John Cale in 1963 became more purely scientific. According to Cale: 'We were working with the cross-over point of physics in sound and what the basic nature of a fundamental was – the results were all these resonating tones.'

Young played high-pitched saxophones and was persuaded by Cale, at times, to hold vocal notes as he and Conrad droned away on strings. The results, like *B flat Dorian Blues* (1963), sounded as if they derived from an Indian Ashram but the 1964 recording of *Fire Is Emir* introduced electronic sounds. Cale believed the whole Dream Syndicate experience to be pivotal: 'I felt I could make my mark with the viola. I filed the bridge down and played it with a bass bow. It was collaborative improvisation, an experiment with harmonics and fundamentals, with strings being the overwhelming force in the music. It was, and still is, the benchmark experiment in drones and the famous "just intonation" system of tuning.' Though it attracted the interest of Terry Riley, the importance of The Dream Syndicate to Cale was Young's military discipline, the coming together every day to practise and repeat music over and over until it was wholly absorbed and understood. This would formulate the early working routines of The Velvet Underground. Both Cale and Conrad left The Dream Syndicate for pastures new in 1965.

Lou Reed came from a totally different scenario. Born in New York to a tax accountant in 1942, the young Jewish boy had classical piano lessons, read poetry and was a good athlete. He moved to Freeport, Long Island, when he was twelve but was so disturbed as a teenager that he was subjected to electro-shock therapy at seventeen. Then he went to New York University but didn't last a year. In 1960 he signed up at the leafy Syracuse University in upstate New York, where he studied literature and philosophy but also took classes in music theory and composition. Always interested in rock 'n' roll records, Reed played a lot of music, often with Sterling Morrison, whom he met on campus in 1961. Reed was also into writing, inspired by his mentor the poet Delmore Schwartz. Heavily into drugs, Reed barely graduated in 1964. From there he went to work at Pickwick Records in Long Island as a hack songwriter.

Early in 1965 he wrote a song which involved a completely open-tuned dronal guitar, a track which he, Cale and Conrad recorded as The Primitives. The group died a death but soon Reed and Cale were living together on Manhattan's Lower East Side and making music. They were joined by Reed's old friend Sterling Morrison on guitar. Morrison, born the same year as Reed, had studied classical trumpet until thirteen, when he discovered black blues and rock and Django Reinhardt. Academically disposed to English literature, he nevertheless went for what Cale and Reed were doing. Cale's old friend from The Dream Syndicate, Angus MacLise, provided support on tablas. Early demos saw Reed play harmonica à la Bob Dylan and the recording of songs with slow, raga-like exposition. Cale recorded everything on reel-to-reel tape. Tony Conrad gave the group their name after an erotic book he found in the street. MacLise, not interested in playing live, was replaced by Maureen 'Moe' Tucker, an acquaintance of Reed and Morrison from their college days. Tucker, born in 1946 and from Long Island, worked in computers but was obsessed with African drumming. Her approach was a steady-pulse beat using bass drums and toms. The Velvet Underground was born in December 1965.

Playing a residency in Greenwich Village, they were spotted by Andy Warhol, who was then moving into films and rock music. He was attracted by their unstinting music, with its lyrical basis in the Decadence of nineteenth-century French writers such as Baudelaire, Lautréamont and Mirbeau. Attired all in black with shades to match, The Velvets played noise-drenched music that celebrated death, sadomasochism and drugs. It fitted in perfectly with Warhol's desire to shock. At the very beginning of 1966 Warhol was providing equipment, rehearsal space at his studio, The Factory, and organizing concerts. He changed the band by insisting on the presence of a statuesque German singer, Nico, who would front the group.

Nico (Christa Päffgen) was one of the great stars of the 1960s. Born in 1938 in Cologne of German and Slavic parents, Nico was multi-lingual, had learned piano and harmonium as a child, had appeared in Fellini's *La Dolce Vita*, studied method acting with Marilyn Monroe and was an international cover model for such magazines as *Harpers* and *Vogue*. Moreover she had recorded with Jimmy Page and Bob Dylan in London in 1965, hung out with The Rolling Stones, appeared on TV and was considered one of the most beautiful women of the decade. Tall, blonde and with a unique contralto voice which was instantly recognizable, Nico was 'Pop Girl of 1966'. Her presence with The Velvet Underground just added to their allure.

For about a year and a half Warhol incorporated the new-look Velvet Underground into a multi-media show called The Exploding Plastic Inevitable, which was basically The Factory on tour. Films, lights and strobes were projected on to the group as dancers and other members of Warhol's travelling theatre 'freaked out' around them. The media were awed at the 'discordant music, throbbing cadences and pulsating tempo'. In Chicago one paper alluded to Baudelaire by describing The Exploding Plastic Inevitable's performance as a 'total environment with the flowers of evil in full bloom'. In San Francisco The Velvets' sound was seen as 'shatteringly contemporary electronic music'. Warhol's next objective was to get them on record and he approached both Columbia and MGM. Columbia put up some money for a day's work in an old Manhattan studio with Andy Warhol, but Tom Wilson, the producer of Dylan and Simon & Garfunkel, felt he could do better work on four tracks – 'I'm Waiting For The Man', 'Heroin', 'Venus In Furs' and 'Sunday Morning'. The bulk of this was done in Los Angeles. Basically The Velvets' first album was recorded in two days in the spring of 1966.

The Velvet Underground & Nico (Verve), subtitled 'Produced by Andy Warhol', wouldn't be released until the summer of 1967 and was far too innovative even for the Summer of Love. The record was shot through with total contrasts between ballads and sound constructions that teetered on the brink of white noise. Nico sang soft, emotional songs written for her by Reed, such as 'I'll Be Your Mirror' and 'Femme Fatale', yet her finest moment was the riveting 'All

Tomorrow's Parties', which sounded as if it came from the Middle Ages. Here both Reed and Cale incorporated much of their Minimalist knowledge into the construction. Piano keys just kept repeating chords while Reed tuned his guitar strings to the same note and played a Byrds-like raga lead. Tucker hit her drums in perfect time. This metronomic element was best heard on 'I'm Waiting For The Man', a fast rocker whose persistent beat and wall of rough guitar chords were the very essence of Minimalism. The detuned instruments and Cale's severe viola drones were brilliantly realized on the sadomasochistic shocker 'Venus In Furs'. What Cale had done with The Dream Syndicate could be best heard on 'The Black Angel's Death Song' while his 'concrete music' subversiveness and The Velvets' entire noise aesthetic exploded on 'European Son'. In short, *The Velvet Underground & Nico* was one of the most inspired debuts in rock history.

Performing live, The Velvets increased the noise element, their feedbacking guitars topped by Nico's wailing, shivering voice. Nico starred in Warhol's film *Chelsea Girls* and went to the Cannes Festival in 1967. Increasingly interested in furthering her solo career, she recorded her first solo album, *Chelsea Girl*, with Tom Wilson in New York that year. It was full of material penned by The Velvets, the haunting 'It Was A Pleasure Then' basically a Velvet Underground excursion into painted sound. Nico's sometimes harsh voice was softened by added flutes and strings which she didn't want; in her own words: 'I was heartbroken.'

Nico continued to record – both *Marble Index* (Elektra 1969) and *Desertshore* (Reprise 1971) were midwifed by John Cale and featured Nico singing and playing harmonium. Her dramatic, almost Gothic style was inspired by Jim Morrison, whom she loved until his death. In a life dogged by drug problems, Nico's last great moment was an atmospheric recording of 'My Funny Valentine' in 1985, but her peripatetic lifestyle took its toll when she suffered a heart attack and brain trauma in Ibiza in 1988.

Back in Velvet-land, sans Nico The Velvet Underground were becoming a top-line rock band. Songs from the spring and summer of 1967, like 'Guess I'm Falling In Love', were full of chugging, changing tempos. In the autumn of 1967 they were back in the studio with Tom Wilson for the recording of *White Light/White Heat* (Verve 1968). Lou Reed was getting into guitar effects gizmos of the kind made by Vox, who were endorsing the group. The album was a salvo of distorted noise, even though Reed played piano and Cale organ. The Minimalist repetition was still there but, as on the title track, the sound was saturated with volume. In contrast, 'The Gift' was sheer sonic theatre as Cale recited the story of a guy mailing himself to his intended with churning, feedbacking guitar as background. Reed relieved the tension on the relatively light 'Here She Comes Now' but let it all out on the brain-searing 'Heard Her Call My Name', where his screaming Gretsch guitar meets Tucker's belting hammer-drum drone. Much has been made of the concluding seventeen-minute improvisation 'Sister Ray'. Though it was brave at the time, history makes it sound like a mish-mash. Certainly its effect pales in comparison with 'I Heard Her Call My Name'.

John Cale was thrown out of the group in the autumn of 1968 and the classic Velvet Underground was no more. Reed took control and developed his confessional songwriting approach on the introspective, Hollywood-recorded *Velvet Underground* (MGM 1969) and *Loaded* (Cotillion 1970), laid down in New York. *Loaded* was recorded in a soft-rock style with some stand-out tracks but with nothing of the innovative spirit of the first two albums. Reed went on to become a rock star while Tucker had children and worked in a supermarket. John Cale became one of the most prolific producers, arrangers and creators of the subsequent decades. Between 1968 and 1972 he worked for Elektra, CBS and Warner Bros. His first important album was *Church Of Anthrax* (CBS 1971) with Terry Riley. Cale played harpsichord, among other things, but Riley walked out of the New York sessions, leaving only the composition *The Hall Of Mirrors In The Palace Of Versailles* bearing his customary stamp of tape-delayed organ and saxophone. *The Academy In Peril* (Reprise 1972) was recorded at Virgin's Manor studios in Oxfordshire with the Royal Philharmonic and contained some lovely quiet instrumentals. Cale then fused atmosphere with pop lyricism on the resonant *Paris 1919* (Reprise 1973). He returned to rock recording with Eno and others for the Island label, his crowning Ambient achievement being the evocative sound-film 'The Jeweller' of 1975.

Relocated in New York, Cale recorded the harrowingly introspective *Music For A New Society* (Island 1982) and began working on ballets and string quartets as the decade wore on. Warhol's death in 1987 prompted a reunion of The Velvet Underground's two most potent creators, Reed and Cale, on *Songs For Drella* (Sire 1990), 'a work for guitar, viola and Midi System', according to Cale. This resulted in a short Velvet Underground reunion in Paris which sprouted into a full-scale European tour in 1993. Significantly, at that time Cale considered Arvo Pärt, Percy Grainger and Miles Davis to be some of the greatest musicians ever.

LISTENING

In 1995 Polydor gathered together all known Velvet Underground tracks for the indispensable five-CD boxed set *Peel Slowly And See*. One of the finest collections ever, it included all the original albums, out-takes, live material and a lavishly illustrated booklet written by *Rolling Stone* writer David Fricke. (The only minus point was his hazy knowledge of Nico, which had her born in Budapest!) If you buy only one Velvets album *The Velvet Underground & Nico* has to be it. All Nico and Cale albums cited above are worth hearing. In addition Cale's dedication to the Welsh poet Dylan Thomas, *Words For The Dying* (Land 1989) is interesting for its arabesque orchestral interludes and floating synthesizer lines. Unsurprisingly, it was produced in Moscow and in Suffolk by Brian Eno. Obviously inspired, Cale went on to record a series of Satie-like piano miniatures for the film-maker (and old Nico cohort) Philippe Garrel titled *23 Solo Pieces for La Naissance de l'Amour* (Crépuscule 1993).

SIMON & GARFUNKEL

In search of 'records full of breathing', Simon & Garfunkel pushed studio technology to its limits to achieve some of the finest production jobs of the 1960s. Influenced by The Beatles, the modal sound of English folk and the sweet harmonies of The Everly Brothers, Simon & Garfunkel continually expanded the horizons of the recording procedure until the beginning of 1970 saw them release an album, *Bridge Over Troubled Water*, whose sixteen-track cinemascopic sound defined a new era of sonic fidelity.

Like those of The Beatles, Simon & Garfunkel's songs were full of instrumental niceties, subtle drop-ins and strange sounds. With Simon's deft use of acoustic guitar and Garfunkel's irresistibly sweet falsetto, a Simon & Garfunkel song was like taking an exotic shower, so full was it of aural surprise. Ably assisted by 'third member' their engineer Roy Halee, they could spend months on a song. Art Garfunkel talked of going through hundreds of takes to get the vocals of the Gospel masterpiece 'Bridge Over Troubled Water' right. And Paul Simon spoke about the 'closely worked-out harmony, doubled right-on using four voices' – basically having the technical ability to re-record a line precisely as it was sung before using two voices.

Simon & Garfunkel's closeness was typical of two New York middle-class Jewish boys born in the early 1940s and growing up in the same neighbourhood. From an early age they sang together and fiddled around with tape recorders in Garfunkel's basement. They worked on gruelling diction exercises and in the late 1950s had an early chart success with the chuggy rock 'n' roll number 'Hey Schoolgirl'. While attending different universities in New York, Simon studying English, Garfunkel majoring in architecture, they both worked at the Brill Building song factory.

Simon felt the folk circuit in Britain offered a better avenue and in 1964 dropped out to do a poverty-stricken trek around the country. Over two periods in 1964 and 1965 he would write some of his first great works, like 'Kathy's Song' and 'Scarborough Fair', influenced by the new English folk-guitar style of Bert Jansch and Davy Graham. Here expanded open chordings more akin to jazz and Indian music lent Simon's guitar an exotic flair.

During this time the producer Tom Wilson was excited enough by some Simon & Garfunkel demos to offer them a shot at recording. The October 1964 album *Wednesday Morning 3 A.M.* had a strong folk feel and one great song, 'Sound Of Silence'. The duo spent part of 1965 in London and, so the story goes, Wilson got some Bob Dylan sidemen and rocked up 'Sound Of Silence'. It went to number one in November of that year. The single was quickly followed by the *Sounds Of Silence* album, recorded on four-track tape at various Columbia studios in New York, LA and Nashville. The 1966 album sparkled with material conceived during Simon's English sojourn, his version of the instrumental guitar piece 'Anji' especially impressive.

Three to four months were spent on *Parsley, Sage, Rosemary And Thyme* (1966) with a new producer, Bob Johnston. Roy Halee and the duo persuaded him to use new eight-track recording, and according to Simon they were the ones who pushed Columbia into using the technique. The album produced another bona-fide sound classic, 'Scarborough Fair', a version of an Irish folk song which saw Simon & Garfunkel's voices meld in pure tones.

Equally impressive was their own year-long production job on *Bookends* (1968), which produced a side-long suite of quiet introspection, including 'Bookends Theme', 'Overs' and 'Old Friends'. Garfunkel's vocal on 'America', a quintessential view of their roots, remains a standard. As the album neared completion, the soundtrack to *The Graduate* was released to universal acclaim in February 1968. Produced by Miles Davis's producer Teo Macero, it contained strong instrumental flavours, including a fine harp and flute interlude on 'Scarborough Fair'. Drones and congas personified the stand-out signature tune 'Mrs Robinson'. That LP and *Bookends*, released in April, saw Simon & Garfunkel garner two number-one albums and Grammy awards within a matter of months.

Having punched in loads of vocal overdubs on *Bookends*, Simon wanted to go further in search of the 'total record'. He got Roy Halee to hook up two eight-track machines at Columbia to record a mini-epic in sound. This new sixteen-track process could be distinctly heard on 'The Boxer', a brilliant sound-novel, introduced softly by acoustic guitar but building up over five minutes into a string-soaked epic with a huge, repeating outro. On the way, bass harmonica, trumpet, pedal-steel guitar and echo effects were all employed. Released as a single in 1969, it was only a promise of what was to come.

Bridge Over Troubled Water (1970) was conceived in the turmoil of the previous year. Simon had argued with Garfunkel about the finale of 'The Boxer' while Art's growing closeness with Mike Nichols landed him parts in the films *Catch 22* (1970) and *Carnal Knowledge* (1971). His absence from the studio resulted in Simon planning a lot of tracks with Halee which evoked his love of early rock 'n' roll, ethnic music and folk. Garfunkel is very present on 'So Long, Frank Lloyd Wright', a tribute to the American architect, and of course the title track. 'Bridge Over Troubled Water' was a Gospel inspired by the massed Phil Spector sound. Because of its high-falsetto vocal it was given to Garfunkel by Simon on the former's return from filming. Recorded in LA and New York, the song was nailed down in the winter of 1969. It took four whole days to get Larry Knechtel's piano part right and two whole days for Art to perfect the tri-part vocal, the last verse of which is considered his finest-ever performance. Two basses, vibraphone and drums transmitted via an echo-chamber on to reverberating tape were all added and then flushed down by a huge Los Angeles string ensemble. Even after the writing and arranging were complete, the number took two weeks of non-stop work to record. This was high-fidelity rock of such grandeur that it made Simon & Garfunkel superstars. As the album rode for ten weeks at number one on the US album charts Simon & Garfunkel split up at the zenith of their collective powers.

LISTENING

In 1972 Columbia released the remarkable *Simon & Garfunkel's Greatest Hits*. A million-seller, it contained four unreleased live tracks – 'For Emily', 'Kathy's Song', '59th Street Bridge Song' and 'Homeward Bound' – which all display the Simon & Garfunkel sound at its very best. Better still was that all the tracks dovetailed into one another. Released on CD in the late 1980s, this a fantastic place to start. The individual albums, *Sounds Of Silence*, *The Graduate*, *Bookends* and *Bridge Over Troubled Water*, all contain their requisite of sonic gold. A triple-disc set, *Old Friends* (Columbia Legacy 1997), contains fifteen unreleased tracks and charts the duo's history.

THE ROLLING STONES

Though the Rolling Stones are often perceived as the world's most famous exponents of no-frills rock 'n' roll, some aspects of their story are very relevant to the progress of Ambient and electronic music. During the late 1960s Mick Jagger, Keith Richards and Brian Jones all did things that had a huge effect on musical history, familiarizing the public in the process with exotic instrumentation and the Moog synthesizer and thus opening the way for the arrival of Trance music and Rave culture.

Jagger, Richards and Jones had been born in England in the early 1940s. By 1966 they were riding a high of popularity and were one of the most successful draws on the concert circuit. By that time a string of recordings had revealed that Brian Jones was a multi-instrumentalist of exceptional talent. The baroque 'Lady Jane' featured his dulcimer, he played sitar on the urgent 'Paint It Black', the ethnically flavoured 'Under My Thumb' had him on marimba and the yearning 'Ruby Tuesday' included a marvellous flute performance by Jones. By the summer of 1967 he was in charge of the brass and Mellotron sections of the psychedelic droney 'We Love You'. (Around the same period he even contributed oboe to The Beatles' 'Baby, You're A Rich Man'.)

During the extended recording of *Their Satanic Majesties Request* (Decca 1967), The Stones' hazy reply to The Beatles' *Sgt. Pepper's Lonely Hearts Club Band*, Jones appeared on Mellotron, flute, sitar and bongos. His instrumental talents also extended to harpsichord, piano and guitar. From 1965 to 1967 Jones had taken frequent trips to Morocco. In 1968, through a complex web of contacts that included the writer and musician Paul Bowles and the painter and writer Brion Gysin, he was able to take recording equipment to Morocco to record indigenous music. In the spring of 1968 he recorded the music of the black Gnawa musicians of Marrakesh but the results were poor. A better recording (using two Uher reel-to-reel tape machines) was achieved in the Rif Mountains that autumn with the Master Musicians of Jajouka. This village featured a musical tradition which stretched back 4,000 years to a pre-Islamic Sufi era. The music was driven by *tebel* drums and high-pitched *ghaita* flutes; bamboo flute was also played. The emphasis was on reaching a trance-like state through repetition and rhythm.

Such a bold step was marred by Jones's death at twenty-seven. In London the tapes were remixed by George Chkiantz at Olympic Studios, who phased the drum sound as he had done on the music of Jimi Hendrix. Only pressure by Brion Gysin and the Master Musicians of Jajouka themselves saw the release of *Brian Jones Presents The Pipes Of Pan At Jajouka* (Rolling Stones) in 1971. Yet the recording was a seminal one. Praised by William Burroughs and Philip Glass, to name two, it opened up whole new vistas for a generation of rock lovers, paving the way for the coming of World Music and later Trance. As a tribute The Stones later returned to Tangier to record 'Continental Drift' with the Jajouka musicians for their CBS album *Steel Wheels* (1989).

There are elements of tape manipulation on *Their Satanic Majesties Request*, but without a knowledge of Stockhausen, Cage or other pioneering composers, the 1967 Stones found themselves in a muddle, unable to come up with an album as consistently original as *Sgt. Pepper*. When they met an American producer with a bias towards rocking black music, they reverted to form. Jimmy Miller was instrumental in defining The Stones' crisply recorded sound. He began working with them in 1968 and stayed on board for seven years and seven albums. He guided them from four-track recording into the era of sixteen-track. He encouraged Richards' famous cassette demos plus open tuning and the use of wah-wah pedal on his guitars. From the sitar and tambura-laden highs (courtesy of Brian Jones) of 'Street Fighting Man' (1968) to the Jamaican sessions which produced the US number-one ballad 'Angie' (1973), Miller was there. He also oversaw a period in which the group's Rolling Stones Mobile recording studio became a prominent feature of European on-location rock recording. Its most famous use was on Led Zeppelin's untitled fourth album, recorded at a run-down mansion in Berkshire called Headley Grange in early 1971. There the Stones Mobile helped track the landmark sessions for the acoustic-rock classic 'Stairway To Heaven'.

Finally Mick Jagger's interest in the Moog synthesizer had a startling out-come. In 1967 he purchased a Moog Modular synthesizer at a very exorbitant price. Ostensibly it was to be used for a Kenneth Anger film, *Invocation Of My Demon Brother* (1968), a Californian homoerotic art-movie short. Jagger's single-note stabs on the instrument showed a lack of patience and an underestimation of the complexity of the instrument. The synthesizer ended up as a prop on the set of *Performance*, a violent and druggy period piece shot in 1968 and featuring Jagger as a faded rock idol. Interested, the American Moog expert Paul Beaver coaxed more laudatory sounds from the instrument for the film's eventual 1970 soundtrack. Unable to see a use for the Moog, Jagger sold it to the Hansa By The Wall recording studio in Berlin. It languished there until 1973, when Christoph Franke bought it for $15,000. Franke had practised on that very Moog for years, and even though it took hours to tune, with its spaghetti junction of patching and drifting oscillations, he found it the perfect instrument for an entirely new sound. That sound was sequencing and Franke was then a member of Tangerine Dream. Hence Jagger and one of the most important group's in electronic music history are linked by that Moog synthesizer.

LISTENING

The 1960s recordings of The Stones are on Decca/ABKO. The major 1970s recordings are now on Virgin. *Brian Jones Presents The Pipes Of Pan At Jajouka* was reissued by Philip Glass on his Point Music label in a new CD edition in 1995.

MARVIN GAYE AND VAN MORRISON

There are many artists who could be lauded for their contributions to the Ambience of the voice but no two have had such a profound affect on the twentieth century as Marvin Gaye and Van Morrison. Gaye literally transformed the entire recording process for black soul singers, showing with his early-1970s masterpiece *What's Going On* that a sweet voice could deliver substantial depth worthy of a consistent thematic album. Van Morrison, for his part, used the vocal setting as a vehicle for 'inducing states of meditation and ecstasy'. His spiritual quest in sound led to some of the most memorable Ambient vocal music ever committed to tape.

Amazingly, Marvin Gaye was a very shy musician who grew up a musical prodigy. Born in Washington in 1939, Gaye first performed publicly by playing the organ in his father's church. His musical gift saw him in the high-school orchestra before various vocal groups attracted his interest in his late teens. On a trip to Detroit with one group he was spotted by Tamla Motown boss Berry Gordy and signed to the label as a drummer. By the early 1960s he was singing, his lush velvet voice making evergreen classics of songs like 'How Sweet It Is To Be Loved By You' (1964) and 'I Heard It Through The Grapevine' (1968). As with The Beatles and their hit singles, the huge success of the latter (a transatlantic number one) allowed Gaye to get away from the restrictions of the three-minute single.

Despite Gaye's reputation, Motown was very nervous about him ruining his winning formula. Detroit studio sessions for his 'concept album' dragged through the summer of 1970, with more work done in the spring of 1971. Inspired by his brother's Vietnam War experiences, Gaye urged his songwriting team to come up with a continuous suite of songs full of social observations. Poverty, the loss of faith, despair, ecology and the need for love were the overwhelming themes. Most importantly, the potent lyrics were couched in very accessible upbeat arrangements which seemed to swim along in their own atmosphere. The list of musicians was vast, including vibes, percussion, celesta, harp, nine violins, four violas, three cellos, two trumpets, two flutes, trombone, a range of saxophones, bongos and conga, along with the usual guitars, basses, piano and drums. David Van DePitte's skilful orchestration and Gaye's subtle production touch allowed the arrangements to breath with an incredible clarity.

Though Berry Gordy was bewildered by the results, *What's Going On* (1971) went on to become one of Motown's biggest-selling albums of all time, spawning million-selling singles. Like *Sgt. Pepper*, it opened up whole new sound worlds, this time for black soul music – Gaye's manipulation of tape inspiring Stevie Wonder to dive headlong into analogue synthesizers. In effect *What's Going On* started where Jimi Hendrix's *Electric Ladyland* had left off. Gaye used his new-found vocal confidence at the mike to record an album of aural erotica, *Let's Get It On* (1973), but the real icing was the fabulous *I Want You* from 1976, a celebration of his love for teenager Janis Hunter. The album was recorded, like its predecessor, in California, but this time production was by Diana Ross's brother and another Motown musician, Leon Ware. A year was spent with lengthy vocal overdubs, Gaye covering all the ranges with a multi-harmony technique. Instrumentally *I Want You* featured a group but with the emphasis on ethnic percussion, wonky off-key bass parts and wah-wahing guitars. 'After The Dance' even had an instrumental version with what sounded like a pitch-bent synthesizer lead from outer space. Melodic parts emerged, disappeared and reappeared several times. Sections of the album sounded as if they were mere fragments of a larger performance, its overall feel echoed by the cover art, which showed a cool black house party. *I Want You* was an intoxicating example of vocal/instrumental Ambience from an artist at the very peak of his genius.

One could say the same about Van Morrison's *Astral Weeks*, but that 1968 opus was only the beginning of a remarkable career. Morrison himself saw all his previous rhythm and blues recordings as false starts. Born in 1945 in East Belfast to working-class Protestants, Morrison had an atypical upbringing in that his shipbuilder father loved American jazz, blues and Gospel records while his mother liked jazz dancing and singing. He grew up listening to Leadbelly and Debussy. His locale was surrounded by all kinds of churches, including Baptist and Jehovah's Witness fraternities. Morrison's later visions of hills, rivers, foghorns, listening to the radio and suchlike can all be traced to what was for him a time of inner peace.

At secondary school he took up the guitar and involved himself in simple skiffle music. When he was thirteen he taught himself saxophone and joined a showband looking for a Beat life on the road. He played in Germany before returning to Belfast and forming Them in 1964. A successful beat group in the Rolling Stones mould, Them toured, eventually reaching the US West Coast and touching base with The Doors and Love. Even before he returned to America in 1967, Morrison had sketched out elements of *Astral Weeks*, an outpouring of emotions relating to his love for Californian beauty Janet Planet. He had a hit with 'Brown Eyed Girl' in 1967 but was not happy until he moved to New England and began going in a jazz direction, working in the context of flute and upright bass. After a deal with Warner Bros., producer Lewis Merenstein added vibraphone and percussion plus the formidable talents of musicians who had played with Miles Davis and Charlie Mingus. Recorded in two evening sessions at Century Sound in New York in the autumn of 1968, *Astral Weeks* was a revelation. Acoustic bassist Richard Davis talked of 'the Ambience of the day going into the evening' on recordings which were often one-take improvisations. Again the mood was one of something lifted from a greater whole, subtle vibraphone, classical guitar and wind-blown flute framing the effervescent lyrics with a golden glow. Certainly 'Beside You' and 'Slim Slow Slider' held an awesome emotional power, Morrison ululating his feelings as sound-visions pulling the listener into a vortex of overflowing expression. The unique results quickly established themselves as a classic of the rock canon.

Morrison quickly grasped that free-expression rock lyrics coloured by the timbres of jazz and blues was an original approach. Horn sections, woodwinds, acoustic piano and guitar gave him more room to emote at the microphone. At the New York studio where he recorded *Moondance* (1970) he spent months getting the balance right, the perfect Ambience of 'Crazy Love' one of the album's many highlights. After a move to California and a number of years of commercial music-making Morrison returned to expansiveness on *St Dominic's Preview* (1973), recorded in San Francisco. Its closing ten-minute, twelve-string acoustic-guitar meditation 'Almost Independence Day' even featured Bernie Krause on a Moog Modular synthesizer. Flute, recorder and acoustic guitar were much in the foreground of *Veedon Fleece* (1974), a mood-suite which celebrated a visit to Ireland and was recorded in his own sixteen-track studio.

An interest in the English mystic-poet William Blake and other 'New Age' philosophies brought Morrison back to Europe in the late 1970s. He was now working with New Age horn player Mark Isham, and *Common One* (1980) closed with the fifteen-minute Ambient excursion 'When Heart Is Open'. Living in London and expanding the spiritual element of his music even further, Morrison embraced Scientology and recorded *Inarticulate Speech Of The Heart* (1983), which was full of Isham's ethereal synth work. Tracks like 'Connswater' and 'Rave On John Donne' were singularly atmospheric. Now, in all his recordings, he matched his love of blues and soul music with transcendental themes. He thoroughly believed in the healing power of music and in 1986 even lectured on the subject. The instrumentals 'Spanish Steps' and 'Celtic

Excavation' from 1987's *Poetic Champions Compose* derive from this period. After working with the traditional Irish group The Chieftains in 1988, Morrison seemed to find renewed energy in his homeland. 'Coney Island' from 1989's *Avalon Sunset* was a rich sound-poem which married images of coastal weekend touring with a lush string setting. Morrison is alone in making simple reminiscences of childhood in Northern Ireland have a profound sonic presence. On *Hymns To The Silence* (1991) the effect was magnificent. 'Pagan Streams', with its sonorous piano and upright bass, brimmed with exaltation for 'the silence'. 'On Hyndford Street' returned to his birthplace with the Ambient sound of a synthesizer voiced in hymnal mode, Morrison narrating memories of sounds drifting across the Beechie River, days of ice-cream, picking apples, boyhood meetings, Radio Luxembourg, Debussy, jazz, Jack Kerouac and 'being lit up inside'.

LISTENING

Motown remastered Marvin Gaye's catalogue for CD in 1993–4. Van Morrison's catalogue has had many changes. *Astral Weeks*, released on CD in the 1980s, is an essential purchase yet much unreleased music from the 1968 sessions remains in the Warner Bros. vaults. In the UK, recordings from *Tupelo Honey* (1971) onwards were reissued on remastered CDs by Polydor in 1998, a company Morrison had signed to in 1989.

DAVID BOWIE

Dazzled by an array of popular images ranging from androgynous 1960s hippie to space-age rock god, from glam superstar to cocaine-numbed 'thin white duke', David Bowie's critics have often overlooked the substantial effect of his music on both musicians and listeners. The ambitious futuristic single 'Space Oddity' of 1969 ushered in an era of sophisticated pop-single production exemplified by the work of the Manchester group 10cc. Comfortable with new synthesizer technology, Bowie influenced and was influenced by Kraftwerk. Willing to open his music to both Tangerine Dream and Kraftwerk in Berlin in 1976, he settled on the synth drones and tape treatments of Brian Eno to create two of the most influential albums in rock, the 1977 duet of *Low* and *'Heroes'*. Influenced by the Minimalism of Philip Glass, these recordings would themselves be reinterpreted by Glass in the 1990s, a decade which saw Bowie once more work with Eno and explore Trip-Hop and Ambient Jungle styles of black British stars such as Tricky and Goldie.

   Born David Jones in Brixton, London in 1947, David Bowie grew up in the south-eastern suburb of Bromley. At school he showed an interest in the recorder, choral singing, the ukulele and the piano. He took up the acoustic guitar at ten and, impressively for a left-hander, played it right-handed. A year later he attended Bromley Technical College, where he studied art and design. Inspired by the free jazz of Charlie Parker, he took lessons on a plastic saxophone in the early 1960s. During that decade he involved himself with Buddhism and a series of Beat groups such as David Jones And The Lower Third. As well as an interest in Bob Dylan he was fascinated by the cabaret croonery of Anthony Newley and the theatrical mime of America's Living Theatre group.

Bowie was very much part of the hippie times, and his Beckenham Arts Lab of 1969 combined recitations, folk guitars, mime and festivals. Bowie's breakthrough album, *Space Oddity* (Philips), was an acoustic-electric package which included the moving 'Letter To Hermione', an open declaration of love to a ballerina girlfriend. The title track was a huge chart hit in the winter of 1969. Produced by Gus Dudgeon at Trident studios, this five-minute wonder was a sonic delight which began with Bowie strumming a faded-up twelve-string guitar and ended in the swimming sound of stereo-panned, tape-distorted cello. The introduction also featured Bowie playing a Stylophone (a simple electrode signal-generating device which used a pen to make contacts) while the finale had him on kalimba (a type of African thumb piano), whose sharp pitches gave the song its weird outer-space feel. Aided by electric guitar harmonics, Rick Wakeman's airy Mellotron, backwards taped piano and guitar sounds, Paul Buckmaster's placing of cello and woodwind, Terry Cox's splashy drums, handclaps and Bowie's sophisticated approach to both melody and chordal development, the song was undoubtedly a classic rock production.

Though the public would be more interested in his chameleon-like shifting persona, Bowie was always interested in the technical details. On *The Man Who Sold The World* (RCA 1971) he availed himself of the sound of a Moog Modular synthesizer while the lavish song cycle of *Hunky Dory* (RCA 1971) also featured the keyboard strengths of Rick Wakeman. In 1972 Bowie sat in the producer's chair for former Velvet Underground singer Lou Reed's *Transformer* (RCA). He and guitarist Mick Ronson were responsible for the filmic reed and string arrangements on 'Walk On The Wild Side', a hit single memorable for its supple double-bass sound. By 1975, when Bowie was living out a cocaine and amphetamine-fuelled rock-star existence in Los Angeles, he was still awed by the cyclical style of Philip Glass, whom he had witnessed at close quarters mesmerize an audience in London in the spring of 1971 with *Music With Changing Parts*. The Minimalist influence can be heard on the chugging-train intro of 'Station To Station' and the taut repetitions of 'Golden Years', both recorded in California in 1975. Though the album *Station To Station* (RCA 1976) endeared Bowie to black audiences in America its Minimalist undertones should not be ignored.

Filming of the time-warping futuristic Nicolas Roeg film *The Man Who Fell To Earth* followed, during which Bowie considered writing a synthesizer score. On the subsequent 'Station To Station' tour he played tapes of Kraftwerk and offered them the support slot but they remained reclusive in their Kling Klang studio in Düsseldorf. Via Switzerland Bowie eventually settled in West Berlin in the autumn of 1976, immersing himself in the music of Kraftwerk, NEU! and Cluster. Living in a damp flat in a modest quarter, Bowie was still taking drugs and drinking heavily. Admiring what he termed 'the timeless music' of Tangerine Dream, he met Edgar Froese for coffee-house summits which petered out owing to Froese's touring commitments. In another part of Germany Brian Eno was successfully recording with Cluster. Both Eno and Bowie would meet in Conny Plank's Cologne studio for the beginning of an historic partnership.

Bowie and Eno shared 'glam-rock' roots, both had arty backgrounds and both liked Philip Glass. Ostensibly, *Low* (RCA 1977) was produced by old Bowie cohort Tony Visconti, who was American and a multi-instrumentalist. Sessions were divided between a château near Paris and the Hansa studio, near the Berlin Wall, during the final quarter of 1976. With some musicians from *Station To Station* and various others, including Iggy Pop, the result was electronic rock of a unique vitality. Synthesizers and strange dry drum sounds dominated. In album form, Side One was seven short 'songs'. 'Speed Of Life', an instrumental, opened the proceedings, Bowie going for broke with a descending ARP synthesizer riff. 'Breaking Glass' was memorable for its cut-off drums and Eno's fanning MiniMoog surges. The compressed, speeded-up 'What In The World' contained some of Eno's craziest synth-box machinations. 'Sound And Vision' was almost instrumental, with crooning vocal backing by Eno and Bowie and a synthetic drum hiss that would take its place over a decade later as the trademark of Techno music. 'Always Crashing In The Same Car' was the record's first masterstroke, a burbling wash of Eno treatments suffused around Bowie at his most elegiac. Though uncredited, the diaphanous opening of 'A New Career In A New Town' would have been unthinkable without Eno, its metronomic smothered bass-drum accompaniment a pure antecedent to all House music.

Side Two was four instrumentals which brought Eno and other aspects of Minimalism to a mass audience. The first half of the side featured the extensive use of the Chamberlain, an early 1960s version of the tape-based Mellotron sampling keyboard. 'Warszawa' was funereal, an epic soundscape of piano, MiniMoog bass rhythm and synth-derived organ and flute melodies. Finely textured by Eno, it arced to an upper register caught some minutes in by Bowie's instrumental vocalise, a twist which Eno much admired. 'Art Decade' had the whiff of Berlin pre-war decadence and was reshaped by Eno during one of Bowie's frequent studio absences. Again it was noticeably slow and melancholic, synthetic percussion pushing along sad melodies on piano and accompanying treatments with strings and shifting electronic sounds punctuating the atmosphere. Both 'Weeping Wall' and 'Subterraneans' were built from soundtrack ideas Bowie had for *The Man Who Fell To Earth*. 'Weeping Wall' was a stuttering, rhythmic creation with interesting struck percussion, quavering vocalise and the radio-signal sound of an ARP synthesizer. Again the sluggish character of 'Subterraneans', with its ARP tones, would not have been predictable in the Bowie canon without Eno's intervention.

The release of *Low* at the beginning of 1977 saw Bowie enter the élite of the avant-garde. In a country where Stockhausen had literally invented electronic music, the thirty-year-old Bowie had embraced it with aplomb. The critics hated the record but it went to the upper reaches of the UK album charts. *'Heroes'* (RCA 1977) could be seen as an extension album to *Low*, the pair forming one unit. Yet on close inspection there were differences. Recording began in the summer of 1977 at Hansa with Bowie on a health-conscious exercise kick. Hence the songs on *'Heroes'* are more defined in their attack, having less of the indefinability of much of the contents of *Low*. Eno became a fully fledged band member, credited with synthesizers, keyboards and guitar treatments. The division between song and instrumental was more defined. Eno used his own Oblique Strategies chance cards to come up with quick results and Bowie favoured minimal overdub and retakes.

The first great moment on *'Heroes'* was the title track. Here Robert Fripp's oblique guitar was surrounded by a myriad of Eno sounds, with Bowie giving the best reedy croon of his career. Impressed by Kraftwerk's just-released *Trans-Europe Express*, Bowie dedicated the busy 'V-2 Schneider' to them, even adding Kraftwerk-like synthetic vocals. 'Sense Of Doubt' was a death-like dirge for piano which included windy synth washes, wobbling, glassy keyboard notes and what sounded like Bowie inhaling hard in the background. This was relieved by the Eastern promise of 'Moss Garden', where Bowie played Japanese koto over widescreen Eno treatments and various sound effects. The tranquil atmosphere of Bowie's Buddhist interest could be felt in the gongs, birds and the distant sound of an overhead plane. This Ambience was continued into the watery eddies of 'Neuköln', which concluded in the long, screaming tones of Bowie's alto saxophone. During a period when drug withdrawal and marriage break-up threatened his very sanity, Bowie had been rescued and replenished by Eno's Ambient and electronic music.

LISTENING

Tired of poor RCA reissues, Bowie had his entire back-catalogue remastered via Rykodisc in the US and released on new CDs in 1991. EMI handled the catalogue in Europe. *Low* came with two lost tracks, the sublime lullaby 'Some Are' and the sharding electronics of 'All Saints'. *'Heroes'* included 'Abdulmajid' (dedicated to Bowie's Somalian second wife), a brilliant slice of ethno-Ambience. Eno appeared on all three. *'Heroes'* had been mixed at Mountain Studios in Switzerland and there Bowie and Eno reconvened in 1995 to make *Outside* (an album as detective novel) based on similar chance procedures. The proof that *Low* and *'Heroes'* were 'landmark recordings' came when Philip Glass used some of their contents to write a series of symphonic movements in his unmistakable Minimal style. Both *Low Symphony* (1993) and *'Heroes' Symphony* (1997) were released on Glass's own Point Music label.

PSYCHEDELIA

The word 'psychedelic' is derived from the Greek and means 'expanding the mind'. It was coined in the early 1950s when the writer Aldous Huxley was discussing the nature of mescaline and LSD with a doctor friend of his. A tide of psychedelic drugs like mescaline, psilocybin and, most famously, LSD 25 (better known as acid) enhanced the production and the perception of rock music during the 1960s. Influentially, The Beatles embraced the power of hallucinogenics to expand the texture, form and sound of their music. In the studio these drugs allowed producers and musicians to push rock way beyond perceived limitations. English writer Chris Cutler has commented: 'The music was now based on repetition, invention and extemporization. It was experimental, progressive and based around electric instruments and volume.' The repetitive element was borrowed from the East, thus allowing a greater appreciation of drones and modal scales. Hence the ubiquitous presence of Indian instruments such as the dronal tambura and modal sitar in psychedelia of the late 1960s. The connection with Minimalism, Ambience and the greater use of Electronics is obvious.

Psychedelia was also more than music. It was a new awareness, a spiritual transcendence of the everyday, a lifestyle, a religion, a political movement. Its roots were not in the 1960s but in the nineteenth century, specifically the world of the Decadents, their literature and the Symbolist art movement which grew up around them. The drugs of choice were then opium and hashish, which inspired the reveries of such French writers as Baudelaire, Rimbaud and Gautier. These authors were matched visually by the radiant work of Gustave Moreau, whose dream paintings were uniquely psychedelic. In Britain the Christian visions of William Blake spurred on the Pre-Raphaelites, a group of young idealistic anti-materialist artists who lived the bohemian lifestyle, wore their hair long and painted luminous exalted portraits of damsels and knights. Led by Dante Gabriel Rossetti, the Pre-Raphaelites directly influenced the visual style of English psychedelia in the 1960s.

Lewis Carroll, the author of *Alice In Wonderland*, was a friend of Rossetti. He too influenced the development of psychedelia, as did countless other nineteenth-century writers, including Thomas De Quincey, Samuel Coleridge and Edgar Allan Poe. In the twentieth century it was the turn of Aldous Huxley, Allen Ginsberg and William Burroughs to evoke the disorientated feel of LSD through their literature. After the synthesis of LSD 25 by Albert Hofmann in Switzerland in 1938 it would take until the early 1960s for the drug to become truly influential. When experienced by author Ken Kesey and academic Timothy Leary, LSD became a social and spiritual touchstone for a generation.

The psychedelic effect on rock music differed widely between the US and the UK. Carlos Santana once told me: 'Everybody in San Francisco in the 1960s was experimenting with peyote, LSD, mescaline and marijuana. The music was known for its merging of Ravi Shankar, Jimi Hendrix and Duke Ellington. The hippies were responsible for the elastication of musical taste. Miles Davis learned a lot from the San Francisco scene, as can be heard on 1970's *Bitches Brew*.' As writer Harry Shapiro has pointed out, the word 'hippie' has its origins in African language, where it meant 'someone who has opened his or her eyes'. And no group opened more people's eyes and minds than Jefferson Airplane. One of the greatest of San Franciscan bands. the Airplane crystallized the whole psychedelic scene with their sparkling 1966 album *Surrealistic Pillow* (RCA). With two lead guitarists in Paul Kantner and Jorma Kaukonen and two lead singers in Grace Slick and Marty Balin, they were the business. The album had an electric feel, an organic quality born out of communal musicianship and laced with sun-refracted ballads and fulsome ecstatic rock. If 'Embryonic Journey' was acoustic guitar bliss, then the *Alice In Wonderland*-influenced 'White Rabbit' was nirvana as it interwove Ravel, Indian raga and rock in an historic tribute to hallucinogenic drugs.

The work of other San Francisco groups, like The Grateful Dead and Quicksilver Messenger Service, is considered later; as is that of their Los Angeles peers, like The Byrds, Love and The Doors. Pushed forward by the Beat movement of the 1950s, American psychedelia can be broken down into three categories. There was the pop psychedelia of, say, The Beach Boys and Buffalo Springfield. There was the acid jams of San Franciscan bands like Country Joe And The Fish. With much of this music, particularly the latter's, albums were all-important. Then there was the music inspired by the 'English Invasion' groups like The Beatles and Yardbirds. Taking the three-minute single as their cue bands such as The Seeds, The Chocolate Watch Band, The Nazz and The Electric Prunes all made wigged-out psychedelic songs. Texan jug-band blues outfit The 13th Floor Elevators devoted the entirety of their 1966 International Artists debut album, *The Psychedelic Sounds Of The 13th Floor Elevators*, to singing the spiritual praises of LSD. The best of this sub-genre was collected by guitarist Lenny Kaye on the classic 1972 Elektra compilation *Nuggets*.

Psychedelia in the UK was very different, with greater emphasis on the seven-inch single as a vehicle for expression. Stylistically it differed in four ways. First, rhythm and blues played a greater part, with distorted guitars and loopy organs giving the desired psychedelic effect. Secondly, Britain's connection with Asia since the days of Empire meant abundant use of sitars, tamburas, bongo drums and other instruments associated with Indian classical music. Thirdly, studio effects were exploited as a psychedelic sensitizer, with phasing, backwards tapes and other synthetic effects being added to music to make it sound strange and trippy. In fact drum, guitar and vocal phasing was much overused in UK psychedelia of the late 1960s. Finally, there was an antiquated aspect of the music which drew on things like Victorian musical boxes, carnival sounds and music–hall nostalgia. In all it was a strange hybrid.

In many ways The Beatles covered all the above aspects and more. It was under their influence that every major UK group of the 1960s made their psychedelic contribution in one form or another. The Yardbirds' 1966 'Happenings Ten Years Time Ago' (Columbia) was R&B at 100mph as guitarists Jeff Beck and Jimmy Page had the guitar dual of their lives. Cream, The Who, The Hollies, The Moody Blues and many others made psychedelic albums but it was the lesser-known groups who made the best contributions. Dantalian's Chariot (with future Police guitarist Andy Summers) cut an album for CBS in 1967 full of sitar tracks and clever if over-heated psychedelia. At the time only the brilliant song 'Madman Running Through The Fields' saw the light of day. Tomorrow (with future Yes guitarist Steve Howe) recorded the studio–effects masterpiece 'My White Bicycle' for Parlophone in 1967. There were equally brilliant contributions from Simon Dupree, Fleur De Lys, Nirvana and Kaleidoscope between 1966 and 1968.

If Pink Floyd and The Jimi Hendrix Experience seemed to vie with The Beatles for the moniker of 'greatest sixties albums band' there were many other groups who made fantastic psychedelic albums. Possibly the finest were The Pretty Things, an R&B group from Kent who changed personnel in 1967 to record the first psychedelic rock opera, *S. F. Sorrow* (Columbia 1968). Full of images of war, the album charted a young man's life from birth to death, with Dick Taylor's guitar and Norman Smith's ambitious production pushing the music along at a cracking pace. Unsurprisingly, the album was recorded in Abbey Road at the same time as The Beatles and Pink Floyd were recording *Sgt. Pepper* and *The Piper At The Gates Of Dawn*. Having learned much during the making of *S. F. Sorrow*, The Pretty Things then produced *Parachute* (Harvest 1970), which featured a spatial, almost Ambient, production sheen. From the sound of falling rain to the unnerving dissolving pitch of its final forty seconds, *Parachute* was nothing less than astonishing.

Though often associated with the multicoloured sitar-laden 1967 singles 'Paper Sun' and 'Hole In My Shoe' Traffic were from the off committed to album-making. Hailing from the Birmingham area, they were a democratic unit where the ideas of Steve Winwood, Dave Mason, Chris Wood and Jim Capaldi all held sway. Six months were spent in a cottage in Berkshire jamming a mixture of sitar, flute, sax, guitars, Hammond organ and percussion. Spending five times the normal budget, the group worked with Jimi Hendrix's engineer Eddie Kramer at Olympic Studios in London to make *Mr Fantasy* (Island 1967). This debut album was memorable for its dizzying array of clockwork sounds, Indian music, ballad, jazz improvisation and superlative guitar-rock songs. Without a doubt the group were sonically influenced by their friend Jimi Hendrix.

Traffic's guitarist and sitarist Dave Mason also produced Family's *Music In A Doll's House* (Reprise 1968). A quintessential UK psychedelic album, it featured strings, brass, reeds, guitars, sitar and much else. It sounded as antiquated as its cover looked, with the strangled vocal of Roger Chapman adding much colour. Most obvious was its use of phasing – not surprising as it was recorded with the technique's inventors, George Chkiantz and Eddie Kramer. Even though it was done at Olympic on four-track, the album had a huge range – medieval music, guitar rock, wistful acoustic ballads, rhythm and blues, choral music, keyboard instrumentals, violin-led progressive rock, sitar music and even the British national anthem, which closed the album in chaotic fashion.

Certainly there was a feeling of light-heartedness and whimsy in UK psychedelia that was only discernible in the garage-band equivalent in America. Uniquely, Syd Barrett was capable of straddling the Atlantic divide for he injected the early Pink Floyd singles with the necessary humour and was capable of lengthy Grateful Dead-style extemporization in his 'Interstellar Overdrive'. (Soft Machine followed the Floyd's free-wheeling groove but were more jazz-oriented.) Even after the 1960s, psychedelia had a place in British hearts. In 1980 the Cambridge quartet The Soft Boys recorded a modern pop psychedelic masterpiece in *Underwater Moonlight*. Their leader, Robyn Hitchcock, went on to make a series of psychedelic-influenced solo albums. Another pop group, XTC, formed The Dukes Of Stratosphear, whose Virgin creations *25 O'Clock* and *Psonic Psunspot* of the late 1980s summed up what was best in UK psychedelia. Even in the 1990s such sitar-drone acoustic recordings as *Magic Carpet* (Mushroom 1972) by London collective led by Alisha were still finding new audiences.

LISTENING

Jefferson Airplane were honoured by a sumptuous three-CD boxed set in 1992 titled *Jefferson Airplane Loves You* (BMG/RCA). The US edition *of Surrealistic Pillow* got a first-time UK CD issue in 1998. One often-overlooked San Francisco group was It's A Beautiful Day, led by violinist David La Flamme. Their mellifluous, mantra-like music could be heard on the albums *It's A Beautiful Day* (1968) and *Marrying Maiden* 1969), reissued as a single Columbia disc in 1998. The original Nuggets album has had many reissues, the most extravagant being the 1998 Rykodisc boxed-set with ninety-one extra tracks! Of the more eccentric American garage-band-type psychedelia the most interesting came from The 13th Floor Elevators and The Electric Prunes. Albums such as The Elevators' *The Psychedelic Sounds Of The 13th Floor Elevators* (1967*)* and *Easter Everywhere* (1968) and The Prunes' 1967–8 *I Had Too Much To Dream Lastnight, Underground* and *Mass In F Minor* (yes, a psychedelic mass!) (all 1967) are worth tracking down on any format and label. Singular praise must given to Californian Captain Beefheart (Don Van Vliet) for his 1967 recording 'Electricity', one of the earliest composed psychedelic songs and one that featured a Theremin! Beefheart's strange, multi-phased, improvisatory acid music can be best assimilated by hearing *Strictly Personal* (Liberty 1968).

In the UK there has always been a proliferation of psychedelic records. The Moody Blues' *In Search Of The Lost Chord*, reissued on Deram CD in 1986, even had a tribute to Timothy Leary. Dantalian's Chariot's only album was finally issued on disc by Wooden Hall in 1996. Tomorrow's self-titled 1967 album came out on See For Miles in 1991. Kaleidoscope had much of their late-60s music compiled into *Dive Into Yesterday* (Fontana 1997). The Pretty Things' *S. F. Sorrow* and *Parachute* were reissued by Edsel in the late 1980s, with new editions coming out on labels like Snapper Music in the late 90s. Some of Traffic's best music was lovingly anthologized in the 1991 Island set *Smiling Phases*. Their psychedelic debut, *Mr Fantasy*, was remastered for CD issue in 1999. Family's *Music In A Doll's House* appeared on a new See For Miles CD in 1998. Two great latter-day psychedelic CDs are The Dukes Of Stratosphear's *Chips From The Chocolate Fireball* (Virgin 1987) and The Soft Boys' *Underwater Moonlight* (Rykodisc 1992).

THE BYRDS

When The Byrds recorded the chiming 'Mr Tambourine Man' in Los Angeles in January of 1965 they set forth on a journey which would change the history of rock sound. In their Chicago-born leader Roger McGuinn they had a musician who was unafraid to exploit electronics and absorb them into a musical vision which embraced folk-rock, raga-rock, jet-rock and eventually space-rock. In fact The Byrds made Columbia's '360-Sound' logo a reality with their dizzying Rickenbacker guitar effects and stereophonic phasing. One of the first mainstream rock musicians to endorse the Moog synthesizer, Roger McGuinn purchased one from Beaver & Krause directly after the Monterey International Pop Festival of 1967. But it's the legacy of their 1960s recordings, culminating in the symphonic psychedelia of *The Notorious Byrd Brothers* in 1968, that so radically altered the landscape of rock.

The Byrds' original instrumental prowess came from the fact that they had their roots in folk and bluegrass outfits like The New Christy Minstrels and Lex Baxter's Balladeers. Initially Jim 'Roger' McGuinn, singer-writer Gene Clark and melodious vocalist and twelve-string rhythm guitarist David Crosby were the acoustic threesome The Jet Set. With the addition of mandolin-playing Chris Hillman and boyishly beautiful drummer Michael Clarke a quintet was born who set out to emulate The Beatles. Early material was recorded at World Pacific studios, and one number, 'The Airport Song', trademarked the ethereal and stylish instrumental style of the group. After a recommendation to Columbia by master trumpeter Miles Davis, The Jet Set were signed and changed their name to The Byrds.

Everything about them was inspired by The Beatles' 1964 film *A Hard Day's Night* – including their haircuts and the fact that Roger McGuinn bought his twelve-string Rickenbacker guitar and Clarke his Ludwig drum kit after seeing The Beatles playing the instruments on screen. An admiration for Bob Dylan made them choose, with producer Terry Melcher, the song 'Mr Tambourine Man' as their debut. Cut in January 1965 with session musicians, the version featured the glorious tri-part double-tracked harmonies of McGuinn, Clark and Crosby plus the ringing sound of McGuinn's Rickenbacker strummed in the 'plagal cadences' of Gregorian chant. This incredibly sweet melodious sound became a transatlantic number-one smash and The Byrds were airborne.

The group quickly entered the pop fray with the debut album *Mr Tambourine Man*, but it was their second disc of 1965, *Turn Turn Turn*, which really cut the mustard. The title track had its roots in choral litany and drew on the classical structures of Bach. Gene Clark's mellifluous ballads were endorsed by The Beatles, especially 'Set You Free This Time'. His 'If You're Gone' involved the use of harmonies as drone. Having experimented with LSD, The Byrds were already trying out new instrumental structures.

It must be remembered that the group were very much a 'pop rock' phenomenon who were pressured to innovate within the format of the single. Over time they were recognized as an albums band. After taking LSD with The Beatles and smoking copious amounts of marijuana in both the US and the UK, The Byrds were now turning their attention to the modal musical landscapes of John Coltrane's meditative classic *A Love Supreme* (1964) and the sitar improvisations of Ravi Shankar. Recorded in two different studios in two bursts at the end of 1965 and the beginning of 1966, 'Eight Miles High'/'Why' was an extraordinary achievement. McGuinn soaked up the sound of Coltrane on his Rickenbacker for the mesmeric drug song 'Eight Miles High', which seemed to float on the interlocking flashing guitars of McGuinn and Crosby. 'Why' saw McGuinn put his guitar through a walkie-talkie speaker to get an hallucinogenic trance-like effect. In fact backwards tape and much other studio trickery was used by McGuinn and Co. to make this single combination one of psychedelia's greatest achievements on its release in the spring of 1966.

Ironically, people thought the sitar was all over the 'raga-rock' of those songs and others on the album *Fifth Dimension*, released in the summer of 1966. But throughout both Crosby and McGuinn achieved bending, distorted guitar sounds on their own electric instruments and on '2-4-2' they actually recorded the sound of a Lear Jet as a form of tribute to their early days of gazing at planes at LA's Airport Boulevard, under runway twenty-five. By 1967 The Byrds were in full flight under producer Gary Usher. *Younger Than Yesterday*, released that spring, was an embarrassment of riches and saw David Crosby's plangent style of composition for guitar and voice reach full glory on the exquisite ballad 'Everybody's Been Burned'. Roger McGuinn emulated Karlheinz Stockhausen on 'CTA-102', an electronic rollercoaster ride which utilized oscillator, dissonant piano and microphone distortion, while backwards-taped guitars featured heavily on both 'Thoughts And Words' and 'Mind Gardens'.

After the band lost Gene Clark (apparently from fear of flying) in 1966, the recording of their masterpiece *The Notorious Byrd Brothers* in the latter half of 1967 also saw the departure of David Crosby and Michael Clarke owing to in-fighting. The album is a continuous play cycle where songs bleed into one another, spectacular sound effects and sonic fidelity its hallmark. Chris Hillman's 'Natural Harmony' was drenched in Moog synthesizer, 'Draft Morning' a wondrously smooth ride on Hillman's bass and jingle-jangle guitars plus vocal harmonies which protested against Vietnam and all wars through use of electronically modified sound effects. In fact the album had an orchestral quality, magnified by the use of harp, celesta and cello on the plaintive childhood reverie ballad 'Goin' Back', written by the Brill Building song-factory duo Carole King and Gerry Goffin. Another Goffin-King creation, 'Wasn't Born To Follow', with its flowing guitar phasing, became associated with the 1969 hippie film *Easy Rider*.

In fact the latter song featured country-guitar specialist Clarence White, who would go on to grace The Byrds with his Stringbender, an electronic mod-ification which allowed an electric Fender to have the quality of a pedal-steel guitar. The raga-like 'Change Is Now' from *Notorious* is full of White's sharp attack. A harpsichord appears on 'Old John Robertson' and guitars are made to sound like other things on both 'Change Is Now' and 'Dolphin's Smile'. The album reached its zenith on the synthesizer and guitar sound-effects soup 'Space Odyssey', where The Byrds seem to wave goodbye as they sonically journey to outer space. In essence The Byrds were the first electronic pop group who didn't just use technology to sound better but made electric sounds the very nature of their exploration.

LISTENING

The Byrds' extensive Columbia discography has always been in print. After *The Notorious Byrd Brothers* they met Gram Parsons and discovered country-rock until the whole thing fizzled out in 1971. One album, *Untitled* (1970), sparked a return to form, with 'Chestnut Mare' quoting Bach on its wonderful acoustic middle section and 'Well Come Back Home' featuring Buddhist chant. Its inner sleeve portrayed founding member Roger McGuinn at home in front of his trusty Moog synth, which he used extensively on the ecological 'Hungry Planet'.

The Byrds were one of the first to get the boxed-set, remastered treatment. The four-CD *The Byrds* (CBS 1990) is still considered a classic. In 1996 Columbia began reissuing the original albums in deluxe disc versions with bonus tracks. *Fifth Dimension* contained earlier versions of 'Eight Miles High'/ 'Why'. *Younger Than Yesterday* included the hypnotic acoustic Crosby song 'It Happens Each Day'. The best, as ever, was *The Notorious Byrd Brothers*, which included 'Moog Raga', McGuinn playing Indian music on his Moog and 'Triad', the Crosby ballad which supposedly broke up the original band. Included at the end of the instrumental 'Universal Mind Decoder' is a 'secret' track featuring an intense band argument during the recording of 'Natural Harmony' which illuminates Crosby's departure.

Early 2000 saw the release of *12 Dimensions: The Columbia Recordings 1965–1972*, a four-CD box containing latter-day Byrds albums, including *Untitled* (which came with a bonus disc of unreleased tracks, *Unissued*) and a 'lost' live album, *At The Fillmore 1969*.

LOVE AND THE DOORS

Two Californian groups, whose wonderfully packaged Los Angeles psychedelic rock sound was first captured by the fledgling Elektra label in 1966, epitomized some of the coolest-sounding Ambient rock of the late 1960s. The timelessness of some of their best music comes down to an understanding of sound organization and the curious blend of influences from bossa nova to Bach that percolated through it. Scored for acoustic guitars and cushioned in a wonderful string and brass arrangement, Love's *Forever Changes* (1967) is now considered one of the finest achievements of the psychedelic era. Equally fabulous are the literary ballads of The Doors, whose classically trained keyboardist Ray Manzarek brought a rigorous discipline to the music, nowhere better observed than in 'Riders On The Storm' (1971).

The very first Love song I ever heard was Bryan Maclean's 'Softly To Me', with its rising strummed guitar intro and mantric repetitive candy-coloured rhythm which was lightly tinged with the sound of Latin America. It was sweet, light, lovely but totally original. That was the essence of Love – the intersecting of two originals in Arthur Lee and Bryan Maclean. The first was black and from Memphis and born in 1945 but moved to Los Angeles when he was five. Always hell-bent on rock 'n' roll, he ended up producing an early session for Jimi Hendrix in 1964. By 1965 he had seen The Byrds and met a roadie of theirs, Bryan Maclean, who was from an affluent white background and was interested in orchestral American music like that of George Gershwin. Lee had been playing with the excellent black guitarist Johnny Echols, who favoured a small double-necked Gibson guitar and even a customized double-necked instrument with twelve strings on top and six on the bottom. His speedy hammer-on left-handed style and use of distortion would define the strange sound of Love's occasional guitar breaks.

Initially Lee's smooth vocal style was suited to Burt Bacharach and you can hear it on the first album, *Love*, recorded at Sunset Sound in January 1966. The mercurially talented Lee could also play piano, rhythm guitar, harmonica and even drums when needs must. Included in the rush of R&B-inspired rock songs were such balladic gems as Lee's poignant 'A Message To Pretty' and Maclean's aforementioned 'Softly To Me'. In the autumn of 1966 Love recorded *Da Capo* at RCA Victor studios, an album spruced up with gorgeous jazz and Latin-American flavours, including the sounds of flute and harpsichord. Live, they had an awesome electric reputation but on parts of *Da Capo* they were making miniature acoustic masterpieces. Maclean's 'Orange Skies', sung by Lee, was so subtly arranged that one writer described it as 'psychedelic Muzak'. In fact one acoustic pocket symphony, *The Castle*, was used subsequently as television theme music.

Having lived communally and been open to a mixture of smack and LSD, it's incredible that Love ever recorded *Forever Changes* at all. With trusty old Bruce Botnick at the controls, Arthur Lee and Bryan Maclean began recording the disc at Sunset Sound with session musicians in the summer of 1967. Even Neil Young was considering as producer but only got as far as arranging 'The Daily Planet'. This galvanized the rest of the group into action over a series of short sessions in late summer and early autumn of 1967. One of the last songs to be recorded was the fulsome opener 'Alone Again Or', written by Maclean and sung by both him and Arthur Lee with a fantastic meshing of Hispanic acoustic guitar flourish and the famous Mexicana horns. David Angel added a seven-man string and five-man horn section to arrangements Maclean and Lee had made after the album was completed. The ballads 'Andmoreagain' and 'Old Man' were dappled with pure Californian sunshine while the orchestral dynamic of 'Good Humour Man' (a song from 1965 originally titled 'Hummingbirds') and 'You Set The Scene' make the album still sound contemporary. The precise placing of instruments and voices made *Forever Changes* the equivalent of psychedelic Vermeer.

So much has been written about The Doors that most of it obfuscates the music itself. Jim Morrison was born in Florida in 1943 and came from a naval family. Highly educated, he attended several Florida colleges before ending up in 1964 at UCLA's film school, where he met Chicago-born Ray Manzarek. The latter had a classical education, an economics degree and played a lot of piano. Also studying at the film school, Manzarek eventually got a Master's degree. The two met again on Venice Beach in 1965 and decided to form The Doors. The rest is history, as they say, with Morrison ending up in Père Lachaise cemetery, having taken French Symbolist poet Arthur Rimbaud's ideal of the 'systematic derangement of the senses' to the farthest human extreme.

The Doors were signed to Elektra in the summer of 1966 after Love's Arthur Lee persuaded the label's founder, Jac Holzman, to check out the demonic Doors at the infamous Whiskey A Go Go. Once the svengali had witnessed the shamanic ritual of 'The End' with John Densmore and guitarist Robby Krieger (both from LA) extending out Indo-classical improvisations in sound, the group's fortune was made. Their debut album, *The Doors*, recorded at Sunset Sound, was released in January 1967 to much acclaim. 'The Crystal Ship' had a haunting poetic quality urged on by Manzarek's 'Bach-like organ solo' and 'Light My Fire' used repetition between Krieger's wispy guitar and Manzarek's cloudy organ to convey a Grand Guignol effect. The eleven-and-a-half-minute 'The End' topped off the whole theatrical event.

More soundtrack, more thoughtful was *Strange Days*, recorded in the summer of 1967 with Paul Rothchild again in attendance. There was a liquid, semi-hallucinogenic quality to this record, as evidenced by Krieger's use of wavering bottle-neck guitar sound. It included the first Doors song, penned in 1965, 'Moonlight Drive', and the extraordinary 'I Can't See Your Face In My Mind', where Manzarek played marimba and described its glistening haze 'as a languid, oriental Bolero'. This languid Latino feel continued on 1968's *Waiting For The Sun*, especially on 'Summer's Almost Gone'. Flamenco guitar featured on 'Spanish Caravan' and 'Yes, The River Knows' succumbed to the cool sound of West Coast jazz.

Because bass figures were played by Manzarek with his left hand The Doors' sound was always in the high register. (Manzarek famously played a Vox Continental organ with plastic keys with the addition of a Fender Rhodes piano bass. Halfway through *Waiting For The Sun* he switched to a Gibson combo organ which included a wide variety of sound-altering devices. Its flat top could still accommodate his Fender Rhodes piano bass.) Densmore's drumming thus veered towards percussion rather than mere rhythm. It's not surprising that the group recorded Albinoni's *Adagio in G Minor* in 1968 and went for more orchestration. On their last album, *L.A. Woman*, recorded in 1970, they effectively caught the 'mysterious ambiance', to quote Densmore, of their surroundings in the incredible 'Riders On The Storm', where rain and thunder, whispered vocal and that tremulous electric piano sound combined to make an instrumental performance of rare Ambient potency.

LISTENING

Love's best music can be found on all manner of compilation discs. The best are *Comes In Colours*, a 1992 Raven item compiled by Love expert John Tobler, and the essential *Love Story* (Rhino 1995), a two-disc set which includes the entire *Forever Changes* album, digitally remastered. Michael Stuart's Ambient drumming on the latter disc is one of the many highlights of Arthur Lee's inspired production technique on one of rock's evergreen classics.

The Doors are amply served on disc, though the moments I've highlighted are to be gleaned from the individual recordings. Elektra's soundtrack to Oliver Stone's 1991 film *The Doors* is a good place to start. In 1978 a Jim Morrison album, *An American Prayer*, was put together to convey Morrison's cinematic and poetic vision. Elements of this, like 'The Hitchhiker', make for a warped kind of noirish soundtrack. It was reissued on CD in 1995 with bonus tracks. The rarities-packed four-CD *Doors Box Set* (Elektra 1997) is for fans only.

THE WEST COAST POP ART EXPERIMENTAL BAND

The weird and wonderful LA group The West Coast Pop Art Experimental Band appeared on the scene in 1966 amid a blaze of publicity. Live, they were considered to work with 'incredible crescendoes of sound . . . sustained walls of sound that seemed to have a physical presence in the room'. On Sunset Strip, at the time, they were regarded in some quarters as one of 'the weirdest most original man-made sensations' in experimental rock. Over three albums they pushed their sound so far out that by *A Child's Guide To Good And Evil* (1968) they were following John Cage's dictum and working with total silence!

The Pop Arts, or Artex as they became known, was the brainchild of Bob Markley, who opted out of his oil-rich Oklahoman family to work as a musician in LA. In 1964 he met Shaun and Danny Harris, bass- and guitar-playing brothers whose parents were both classical musicians. They started out as The Snowmen and had a hit record but by 1966 they were The West Coast Pop Art Experimental Band. Their blond surfing good looks drew lots of attention as they played up and down the Strip, but their first album, *Part 1*, recorded in 1966, contained music of real originality. After opening with mingling psychedelic guitars, it then chartered areas such as Lo–Fi and the baroque as well as the usual chiming Byrds and Beatlesy harmonies of the time.

Breaking Through – Vol. 2 (1967) was better recorded. It combined a Monkees craziness with biting social and political satire, the latter most overt on 'Suppose They Give A War And Nobody Comes'. Trance and raga moods were all there on the lengthy Ambience of 'Smell Of Incense', with its cascading strings and guitars. Their third album, *A Child's Guide To Good And Evil* (1968), was their most bizarre and benefited from exploration of multi-track recording. Amid the spoof-horror sounds, tape manipulations, ironic jests ('Eighteen Is Over The Hill'), and genuine political jibes ('Until The Poorest People Have Money To Spend', on welfare equality, and 'A Child Of A Few Hours Is Burning To Death', on the Vietnam war) there was a real sense of musical adventure. At times the album was sleepily Minimalist and in the tour-de-force 'Anniversary Of World War 3' – the empty crackling grooves of the vinyl itself was the music. Overlooked and almost forgotten, today The West Coast Pop Art Experimental Band are considered everything their name implied.

LISTENING

The original trio of 1960s Reprise albums are now highly collectable gems of their era. Sundazed began a comprehensive reissue programme of their music on CD in the autumn of 1997, drawing the critical response 'brilliant'.

NEIL YOUNG, BUFFALO SPRINGFIELD AND CROSBY, STILLS & NASH

The 1960s and 70s have left no better artefacts in recorded sound than the work of those musicians who seemed to orbit around the maverick vision and quivering voice of Neil Young. By the time that Crosby, Stills, Nash & Young were recording in 1969 the general view was that they were privileged Californian hippie musicians coasting on the back of successful band careers. Yet the actual reasons for the huge success of *Crosby, Stills & Nash* (1969), Young's subsequent solo recordings and the respect still awarded to the early Buffalo Springfield albums is the fact that they pushed recorded music into a new level of definition and complexity.

With their four-part harmonies and intertwining triple guitar sound which mixed folk music with electronalia, Buffalo Springfield made music of such dynamism that in the late 1990s it was sampled by Hip-Hop musicians. Springfield was the product of a 1966 meeting between Neil Young and Stephen Stills, famously in a Los Angeles traffic jam when Stills spotted Young's black hearse! Young was born in Ontario in 1945 and suffered from polio in the 1950s. After moving around Canada with a series of bands like The Squires and The Mynah Birds, Young and the classically trained bassist Bruce Palmer headed for California in 1966. Stephen Stills was born in 1945 in Dallas, went to military academy in Florida and spent time in Costa Rica and New Orleans in the early 1960s. In New York in 1964 he met the clear tenor singer Richie Furay. This quartet crossed paths in the famous traffic jam of 1966 and immediately formed Buffalo Springfield with the addition of Dewey Martin, another Canadian, on drums, their name taken from a Toledo, Ohio, steam-roller company.

The chemistry gelled as they played the famous LA music club the Whiskey A Go Go and they were quickly signed to Atlantic Records. 'For What It's Worth', penned by Stills when high on peyote, was recorded at Columbia's eight-track facility at the close of 1966 and is famous for its close-miked thumping bass–drum sound and Young's ringing harmonic guitar notes. That year also saw them recording at Gold Star, a four-track facility Young favoured because of its associations with 'pop' sound pioneers Phil Spector and The Beach Boys' Brian Wilson.

If their debut album, *Buffalo Springfield* (1966), caught the euphoric rush of their talent, it also saw Young's growing disillusionment with psychedelia, as evinced on 'Flying On The Ground Is Wrong', an anti-LSD song. Young, with his childhood polio and now chronic epilepsy mingled with diabetes, was closed physically to the overt excesses of 60s rock. Almost solipsistic, Young sought out the help of the Michigan-born arranger Jack Nitzsche to flesh out his ever-more complex ideas. Young's interest was in 'airy drums, drums more like a sound effect'. As he worked alone with Nitzsche he was even asked to produce Love's *Forever Changes*, and got as far as arranging 'The Daily Planet' before turning back to his own work in the summer of 1967. The result was the incredible sound collage 'Expecting To Fly', orchestrated by Nitzsche and overdubbed by Young and Bruce Botnick over three weeks. It used double-tracked acoustic and electric pianos, rising tonal orchestral introduction and stereophonic panning.

If that was over three and a half minutes of sonic bliss, then at nearly twice the length 'Broken Arrow' was an overt tribute to The Beatles' *Sgt. Pepper*, replete with Beatles screams at the beginning. Recorded in three different movements with fairground sounds and jazz instrumentals thrown in for good measure, the miniature epic seemed to put Young's own paranoia over fame plumb in the middle of historical Americana, with his favoured American Indian as a central motif. One hundred hours of studio time went into that one.

And these were only two cuts from *Buffalo Springfield Again* (1967), the quintessential Springfield album, recorded in three studios that year. Other highlights were Stills's flat-picked acoustic guitar showcase 'Bluebird' and 'Everydays', the latter inspired by Miles Davis, played in 3/4 time and featuring Young sustaining a low, fuzz-toned guitar note throughout. The album was topped off by the elegiac and slow Richie Furay song 'Sad Memory', again made sonically interesting by Young's use of deep reverb echo.

Fierce competition drove the group apart and their posthumous album *Last Time Around* (1968) was disowned by Young, though it contained some strong material, including a clutch of fabulous countryesque ballads by Furay. One critic referred to it as the sound of 'soft summer rain'. Young signed to Reprise in late 1968 and continued his experiments with Jack Nitzsche and producer David Briggs. Elsewhere in Los Angeles, Stephen Stills had teamed up with former Byrd David Crosby and Graham Nash of the UK group The Hollies. Together they made 'air mixes' with their 'locked-in harmonies'. With the cream of Laurel Canyon musicians in attendance the trio made an album of thick acoustic guitar tones, backwards guitar effects, electric organ and the purest of pure harmonic blends. The twelve-string sound and floating flavour of 'Guinnevere' was just one of the many delights of *Crosby, Stills & Nash* (1969).

Soon Neil Young joined them and *Déjà vu* (1970) was recorded over 800 hours in Wally Heider's San Francisco studio in late 1969. A disjointed affair, it nevertheless benefited from a fantastic production sound, acoustic instruments being placed in clear sound hierarchies. Again with Jack Nitzsche's help, Young came up with the complex organ-driven 'Country Girl' while his 'Helpless', a reminiscence of Ontario, was recorded in the early hours at almost slow-motion speed. Back in Los Angeles, Young would then team up with Crazy Horse to make music like the trance-inducing 'Down By The River' (1968), which Young sometimes extrapolated out in concert to half an hour.

Young's career from here on in would be split between electric guitar duelling with Crazy Horse and other bands, complex studio designs and straight-ahead acoustic music. *After The Goldrush* (1970) seemed to mix these styles as Jack Nitzsche helped out – the album's acoustic title track and the spacious 'Don't Let It Bring You Down' were in contrast to the incendiary 'Southern Man'. Yet, as in his brilliant guitar solo there, Young never dropped into the clichéd riffing style of many of his rock contemporaries. Always his cue was the making of original sound experiences.

Back problems and related health blips did not stop Young recording *Harvest*

(1972) in London, Nashville and on his Californian ranch during the latter part of 1971. The album again mixed guitar rock with acoustic gems and Nitzschean orchestration. Topping both album and singles charts in 1972, this made Young a superstar. Since then Young has never stopped recording, changing styles and generally confounding his admirers. His best album ever, the bitter *On The Beach* (1974), took years to gain CD release. On *Zuma* (1975) Young recorded his greatest piece of Ambiosonics, the slow, torturous but endlessly fascinating electric-guitar meditation on the plight of the ancient Aztecs, 'Cortez The Killer'.

Another fascinating track from the same period was 'Like A Hurricane' (not released until 1977), which again saw Young extend guitar melody into the upper reaches of noise and feedback without losing the listener's interest. After a period of confusion when at one point he was sued by his record company for making 'uncommercial music', Young returned to his old form on *Freedom* (1989). In 1991 he released *Arc-Weld*, a two-and-a-half-hour journey into the sonic outreaches of Neil Young live with Crazy Horse, including half an hour of instrumental free-form noise inspired by Sonic Youth. In 1992 the ever-mercurial Young changed tack again with the belated sequel to *Harvest* in *Harvest Moon*, with Jack Nitzsche in tow. A natural outflowing of four decades of sound exploration was Young's 1996 collaboration with the American film-maker Jim Jarmusch. Recorded on a mobile studio in San Francisco, Young played pump organ, detuned piano, acoustic guitar and distorted, effect-laden electric guitar for the soundtrack to *Dead Man*, an hour-long Ambient master-work.

LISTENING

There have been many Buffalo Springfield compilations on Atlantic and all the original records are available on disc. *Buffalo Springfield Again* (Atco 1967) is essential. Both *Crosby, Stills & Nash* (1969) and *Déjà Vu* (1970) got the Ocean View digitally remastered treatment in 1995 and are available on Atlantic. Neil Young's catalogue is vast, though incomplete on CD. *Decade* (Reprise 1977) was a brilliant personal triple-album overview handpicked by Young himself. As well as containing 'Expecting To Fly' and 'Broken Arrow' from the Springfield days it also weighed in with 'Cortez The Killer' and 'Like A Hurricane' on one record side. Its repackaging on to double CD in 1996 was a welcome reminder of Young's huge contribution to rock. Other mentioned recordings are on Reprise except *Dead Man*, which came out on Vapor Records in 1996. Since 1988 Young has been working on an almost mythical series of boxed sets intended to showcase a wealth of unreleased material. Young appears on David Crosby's *If I Could Only Remember My Name* (Atlantic 1971) alongside what sounds like the entire Airplane-Dead San Francisco music fraternity in a commendable sound experiment.

SPIRIT

The sublime music of the LA band Spirit stood the test of time to be reappraised in the 1990s as 'classic'. They even blueprinted the chord sequence for the most successful acoustic rock song of all time, Led Zeppelin's 'Stairway To Heaven'. I wrote in 1992 about Spirit that 'there was something timeless about hearing this mixture of jazz, pop and rock'. Spirit mixed subtlety with taste, classical with jazz, vocal with instrumental. Their take on psychedelia was not a heady rush but thoughtful arranging, suites of songs edited together to make sound-films, and impeccable musicianship extending melodic arrangements to outer territories. To listen to a Spirit album was to take a journey into a music of unexpected twists and sound flourishes. With their fourth album, *The Twelve Dreams Of Dr Sardonicus*, they seized on studio and synthesizer technology to produce some of the most futuristic music of the period.

Randy California had met Jimi Hendrix in 1966 when trying out Fender Strats at a guitar shop in New York. California joined Hendrix's group for six months before the Seattle man's supernova transfer to London. California, still in his early teens, moved back to the West Coast and at a 1967 LA 'love-in' formed Spirit's Rebellious with his stepfather Ed Cassidy, Mark Andes and Jay Ferguson. Cassidy was a veteran jazz drummer with an interest in Latin and avant-garde music, Andes a blues-loving bassist and Ferguson a classically trained all-round musician with a talent for writing. With the addition of keyboardist John Locke the band were signed in 1967 and immediately set about getting 'a pure and crystalline sound' in the studio.

Living in a big yellow house in Topanga Canyon, the group committed themselves totally to music. Lou Adler, who'd signed them to his Ode label, went for a light touch and *Spirit* (1968) is the airiest of psychedelic records of the time. Each track was different and a jazzy undertow sprinkled itself throughout. Even the use of sitar was tasteful and restrained. On 'Taurus' (the only California composition), flute, strings and harpsichord cushioned a wonderful descending acoustic chord sequence. On a subsequent European tour the group met Jimmy Page and Robert Plant, who appreciated this arrangement no end. Three years later it would resurface as the intro to the legendary 'Stairway To Heaven'.

Influenced by The Beatles' *Sgt. Pepper* and much of the experimentation in West Coast music of the times, Spirit pushed in two directions – rock-single success and more complex albums. The second 1968 album, *The Family That Plays Together*, featured on Side One a suite of songs mostly credited to ace arranger Jay Ferguson. Here the classical flavour of 'Taurus' was spread through a series of imagistic filmic compositions. Elsewhere the group successfully placed one song inside another ('Dream Within A Dream') and became interested in background music. In fact a lot of instrumental music was recorded – Ferguson's considerable keyboard skills intertwining with Locke's piano, Cassidy's subtle drumming and California's linear electric-guitar playing, which seemed to hum on one note for ever.

Unsurprisingly, the group were asked to score a film, Jacques Demy's *The Model Shop*, in which they appeared. Having already tried their hand at Ambient music, they wrote more for the film, some of it quite jazzy, some of it exquisitely beautiful. Pieces like 'Ice' and 'Clear' seemed to stand time still, so considered was their unfolding. The best of it was to surface on the subsequent album, *Clear* (1969). But Spirit wanted to produce a rock masterpiece and to this end recruited Neil Young producer David Briggs to work on their next project

In 1970 five months were spent in Sound City Studios experimenting with Moog synthesizer, reverse tape sounds, close-miked acoustic guitars and pipe organ. Briggs brought the suitable width of screen to a group who always painted their music as soundtrack. Both 'Space Child' and 'Love Has Found A Way' utilized the Moog synth in an imaginative way while the continual use of song-merging made for an eventful listening experience. For example, the appearance of the short, mantra-like acoustic jewel 'Why Can't I Be Free' is still an arresting experience to this day. *The Twelve Dreams Of Dr Sardonicus* was unveiled in the winter of 1970 to an indifferent public. Despite two tours and much publicity, Spirit disbanded in 1971. Over time people began to appreciate the advanced electronic feel of *Sardonicus*. By the late 1970s it had sold over half a million copies and today is considered a rock classic.

LISTENING

In 1991 Epic/Legacy released the two-disc set *Time Circle*, which admirably charts the band's career. Including instrumental out-takes from 1968 like 'Fog' and unreleased soundtrack material from the film *The Model Shop*, it's a good entry point. More impressive is the selection of Epic/Legacy remastered discs released in 1996. All came with unreleased tracks and generous sleeve notes. *The Family That Plays Together* (1968) is particularly impressive. The sequence which begins with 'It Shall Be' and continues through 'Poor Richard'/'Silky Sam'/ 'Drunkard'/'Darling If' has the quality of classical music. It also contains a generous amount of instrumental music penned at the time. *Clear* (1969) continues the trend, its poetic 'Give A Life, Take A Life' so perfectly realized that it could have come from Brian Wilson or Lennon and McCartney at their peak. *The Twelve Dreams Of Dr Sardonicus* (1970) was so well produced it still holds the power to startle.

TIM BUCKLEY

This American singer-songwriter travelled from folk to the very outer reaches of experimentation with the constant ambition to capture the 'mood'. From the late 1960s to the early 1970s Buckley used mostly acoustic instruments and a five-and-a-half-octave voice to create some of the most compelling experiences in 'song' ever put to tape. Such recordings as *Happy Sad* (1968) and *Blue Afternoon* (1969) conjure up such extreme moods of presence it's as if the sound of the music itself is the lived experience. Even though he flirted with rock, jazz and avant-garde it's his cool style of minimal improvisation that best sums up his genius.

Buckley was born in Washington DC in 1947. He arrived in California when he was ten and later began playing folk and country guitar in various Los Angeles clubs. Through a connection with freak rocker Frank Zappa, he was signed to Elektra and recorded an album at the tender age of nineteen. By 1967 he was playing in New York and even attracting the attention of The Beatles with his lithe twelve-string guitar style and a voice which could move from baritone through tenor and upwards. His melancholic style was best heard on the baroque folk-rock masterpiece *Goodbye And Hello*, recorded that summer in LA with musical stalwarts Lee Underwood on guitar and C. C. Collins on congas. 'Hallucinations' was pure dreamy, effect-laden Ambient psychedelia. 'Once I Was' presaged the dense acoustic sound of Neil Young while 'Morning Glory' was a chamber icon of rare angelic intensity.

Happy Sad (1968) veered away from the instrumental lushness of its predecessor, but kept to the nucleus of Buckley, Underwood and Collins with added vibraphone and marimba by David Friedman and Johnny Miller's acoustic bass. 'Strange Feeling' seemed to float on its gossamer, jazz-tinged groove, the overall vibe of the record being one of brooding melancholy. 'Love From Room 109 At The Islander On Pacific Coast Highway' opened with the sounds of crashing waves and through its lengthy arrangement emerged the sound of desolation. With its moody cover shot of Buckley, *Happy Sad* was aural reality blues of a unique frankness. It is still my favourite Buckley album of all time.

Buckley's next recording, *Blue Afternoon* (1969), which appeared on his manager's Straight label, was a more playful selection with shorter songs. It still had the ensemble feel and the brooding, introspective melody but it was delivered with a certain buoyancy. One track, 'Cafe', was stillness itself, a slow-motion fog of languidly plucked guitar and aching vocal. *Lorca* (1970) began the avant-garde experiments with voice and electronically coloured instrumentation which would reach their zenith on the difficult *Starsailor* (1971). Yet the best piece on *Lorca* was the deliberately meditative, raga-like 'Driftin''. Unable to settle down to one style, Buckley dallied with rock, easy listening and soul until in 1975 he accidentally overdosed after a concert in Dallas, Texas.

LISTENING

All the Elektra albums were reissued on CD in the late 1980s. *Goodbye And Hello* and *Happy Sad* are particularly recommended. *Blue Afternoon* came out on

Rhino CD in 1989. Two excellent live documents catch Buckley at the height of his powers in his early twenties. *Dream Letter – Live In London 1968* (Demon 1990) covers the early Elektra period. As a single-disc introduction, *Live At The Troubadour 1969* (Edsel 1994) is a fantastic opener, containing excellent material from *Happy Sad*, *Blue Afternoon* and the career pinnacle, the majestic 'Driftin'' from his final Elektra album, *Lorca* (1970). One of the finest versions of a Buckley song, 'Song To The Siren', was recorded by The Cocteau Twins and appears on the compilation *This Mortal Coil – It'll End In Tears* (4AD 1983).

THE GRATEFUL DEAD

Of all the experimental rock groups to emerge from San Francisco during the psychedelic 1960s, the one to stand the test of time and connect directly with the Techno and Rave culture of the 80s and 90s was The Grateful Dead. Much misunderstood, especially during the late-70s punk–rock explosion, The Grateful Dead did more than any other collective to bring the ideas of Cage and Stockhausen to a new generation. Moreover their studio experiments went far beyond the pop format of The Beatles in that they pushed the very sonic experience to the limits. They seized on every kind of equipment possible and in the best electronic tradition, remodelled it to create even newer sounds. Whether on record or live, The Grateful Dead created a spatial dimension where electronic and Ambient music sounded right, and years before the very notion became mainstream parlance in the 1990s.

It is no accident that any history of the San Franciscan music scene of the 1960s only ever gives you glimpses of The Dead. So woven into the very fabric of American psychedelia were they that they are the backdrop for everything else happening around them. Their Beat-generation connections, their association with LSD and author Ken Kesey, their Haight-Ashbury home, their lengthy improvisatory interstellar sets led by Jerry Garcia's liquid Gibson guitar solos, their drug busts and very lifestyle have all passed into legend. The fact that The Dead entered the 1970s more than $200,000 in debt to Warner Bros. didn't bother them one jot. What was important was the music; as Jerry Garcia put it, 'the search for the form that follows chaos!'.

The form was born out of a mixture of blues, rock 'n' roll, Gospel, jug-band folk, soul, Miles Davis-John Coltrane jazz and the electronic mindscapes of Stockhausen. The pure musicianship of Jerry Garcia, born in 1942, met the composerly Phil Lesh, born two years earlier, in San Francisco in 1958 and a bond was made for life. Garcia played folk guitar from the age of fifteen and after nine months in the US Army dropped out in 1959. Lesh graduated, could play violin and studied classical trumpet and composition at Mills College in Oakland with the Italian composer Luciano Berio. Yet the modal explorations of Coltrane fired his imagination.

After the army Garcia enrolled in San Mateo College, played coffee-houses and worked in a music shop. He soon met poet Robert Hunter (whose windowpane lyrics would surface on later Dead albums), young rhythm guitarist Bob Weir, bluesy organist Ron 'Pigpen' McKernan and percussionist Bill Kreutzmann. Interest was in acoustic music and Garcia went through a series of combinations under crazy names such as The Harte Valley Drifters (with Hunter) and then Mother McCree's Uptown Jug Champions. By 1965 the group were an electric band called The Warlocks with Phil Lesh on electric bass. They became the band for a range of 'Acid Tests' conducted at Stanford University. In 1966 Garcia changed their name to The Grateful Dead and until October of that year, when LSD became illegal, they were the number-one group of inner-space exploration. They became synonymous with the Acid Tests of Ken Kesey and His Merry Pranksters and made a connection with Neal Cassady, who drove the Pranksters' psychedelicized bus and was the real hero of Jack Kerouac's Beat novel *On The Road*. As Jerry Garcia noted: 'We could experiment freely.'

The open chemical experimentation of the Acid Tests, where light-shows, music and drugs were mixed freely, were the whole template for the US psychedelic experience. Here the essence of psychedelia was a communal alternative, the reaching of another level of consciousness which together could form a viable alternative to the strictures of American government and authority. And The Dead were its soundtrack. Here their extended proto-Ambient jams, which evoked Arabic calligraphy as much as the influence of Minimalism and pure electronic music, were born.

By the summer of 1966 The Dead were fully ensconced in a rambling Victorian mansion at 710 Ashbury Street. They played for free, anywhere they could, even setting up their equipment on flat-back trucks and jamming away for whoever would listen. Eventually they drew the crowds, up to 20,000 at a time. Their equipment was fine-tuned by Augustus Owsley Stanley III, one of the most famous acid chemists in America. In 1967 Warner Bros. signed the band and put them in a four-track studio to make an album of rock and blues in a matter of days. Except for the affecting version of Tim Rose's 'Morning Dew' and the accelerated instrumental of 'Viola Lee Blues', the band mostly disowned the album, simply titled *The Grateful Dead*. Come late 1967 the Asia-oriented drummer Mickey Hart and the pianist Tom Constanten had joined the group. Constanten had also studied with Berio at Mills College, knew Phil Lesh and had an energetic interest in experimental music. Aptly, after graduation, he went to Europe to study with Boulez and Stockhausen. Now seven, the group would make one of the most daring moves in rock history.

For their next album, *Anthem Of The Sun* (1968), they wanted something which caught the magic moments of their live sets where instrumentally they would fly off into the sonic ether. They also wanted more quality. With Warner Bros. producer Dave Hassinger they had visited eight-track studios in LA and New York in late 1967 to record takes but only got as far as parts for three tracks before demands by Lesh and Weir to record the sound of 'heavy and thin air' drove Hassinger from the production seat. Assisted by engineer Dan Healy, who had helped convert a studio to eight-track in North Beach, San Francisco, The Dead aimed to combine live tracks from a tour of the Pacific North-West with studio material.

This was painstakingly done through the first half of 1968, when the group literally played the studio as an instrument. Huge technical problems were presented by the use of different tape machines and different four-track mixers at different gigs. All these had to be hand-synched by Dan Healy to the studio multi-tracks. Constanten came in and converted a piano, using gyroscopes, coins and suchlike, to a 'prepared' instrument à la Cage. Bob Weir aimed at getting Stockhausen's 'coloured silence' out of the tapes. Such unlikely sounds as those of backwards piano and tympani were also incorporated. After months of jump-cuts, drop-ins and cross-fades the group ended up with two continuous eight-track edits. Then Lesh, Healy and Garcia manually mixed them for two distinct performances on album. So complex was the whole process (aided by the use of laughing gas and other drugs) that Garcia likened it to 'a collage – an approach that was more like electronic or concrete music'.

For *Aoxomoxoa* (1969) The Dead used new Ampex sixteen-track recording for a more enhanced sound. They alternated between lysergic delicacies like 'Rosemary' and 'Mountains Of The Moon' to experiments in phasing and filtering exemplified by the seriously weird 'What's Become Of The Baby'. Again Constanten's classically flavoured harpsichord and keyboards enhanced the sound no end. For their most famous album, *Live/Dead* (1969), the group took a number of stellar performances from the spring of 1969 at Fillmore West and the Avalon Ballroom and edited them into one continuous sequence of music. 'Dark Star' was masterly – over twenty-three minutes Garcia's spiky guitar eddies traced a composition that had much to do with raga and Ambience and which at times burst into intense psychedelic climaxes. So descriptive was 'Dark Star' of an LSD trip that the Italian director Michelangelo Antonioni used an edit of the piece, plus some beautiful warbly Garcia guitar instrumentals, for his rapturous 1970 hippie film *Zabriskie Point*.

The further adventures of The Grateful Dead are the stuff of social history and legend. In 1970 the group survived huge debts and embezzlement, not to mention the loss of Hart and Constanten, to record two acoustically mellow albums, *Workingman's Dead* and *American Beauty*. Their European tour of 1972 yielded a terrific album which in its later stages ably showcased how brilliant an Ambient music group The Grateful Dead could be – Garcia's cellular, additive, flashing guitar solos propelled by Lesh's deep, thick bass runs and the deftest of percussion ensembles. Even the death of Pigpen in 1973 did not stop them becoming one of the most successful live bands of all time, by 1974 sporting a 'wall-of-sound', twenty-five-ton, 641-speaker stack. In 1978 they even performed at the pyramids of Giza during a total eclipse of the sun. Their reputation for live musical improvisation just drew more and more crowds. From 1984 onwards they earned more from live concerts than any other rock group on the planet save The Rolling Stones. After they had an MTV hit with 'Touch Of Grey' in 1987 they became even more successful. But after selling millions of records and playing to millions of people, Captain Trips himself, Jerry Garcia, died suddenly of a heart attack in the summer of 1995. It was noted, at the time, that Eric Clapton considered him to be 'the greatest guitarist in popular music'.

The Grateful Dead truly embodied the spirit of America. It's no coincidence that from the very start the American flag, with its stars and stripes, was an important ingredient in the band's imagery. Their anti-establishment stance was religiously sincere – it spoke eloquently in a music that mixed everything but served itself. (In 1983 the group even established the Rex Foundation, which gave handsome donations to experimental composers.) The essence of The Dead is in the instrumental Ambience of such albums as *Live/Dead* and *Europe '72*. In 1988 Sonic Youth (then flying the flag of noise-rock) stated that The Dead were the only group they really wanted to play with. The Dead encouraged bootlegging and saw music as 'something to be given away to those who couldn't afford to pay for it'. As revolutionary psychedelians their experience was a late-twentieth-century mirroring of the entire Acid House and Techno-Rave culture and the music of such groupings as Spiritualized. In truth The Grateful Dead are a fundamental of how music evolved in the rock era.

LISTENING

The Grateful Dead were one of the first groups to benefit from CD technology. The remastering of *Live/Dead* in 1989 at last allowed the listener to hear the seamless flow of 'Dark Star', 'St. Stephen', 'The Eleven' and 'Turn On Your Love Light', which before had been broken down to three album sides. This 1969 Warner Bros. album is definitely the first port of call for the uninitiated. From the hallucinatory acid flashes of the incredible 'Dark Star' to the intense 11/4 time shifts of 'The Eleven' and onwards into the deep blues of 'Death Don't Have No Mercy' and feedback electronica of 'Feedback', this is The Dead *in excelsis*.

Other ports of call are the densely layered psychedelia of *Anthem Of The Sun* (Warner Bros. 1968) and the baroque-flavoured *Aoxomoxoa* (Warner Bros. 1969). Unforgettable are the Hunter lines 'lady finger dipped in moonlight, writing "what for" across the morning sky' from the latter's opening cut, 'St. Stephen'. *Workingman's Dead* and *American Beauty* (both Warner Bros. 1970) are acoustic jewels. Jerry Garcia himself combined electronica with country ballads on his first solo album, *Garcia* (Warner Bros. 1972), and Phil Lesh explored bio-electronics on the album *Seastones* (Round 1975). *Seastones* became something of a curio as it featured Ned Lagin playing a Buchla-innovated digital-poly-phonic synth and a digital computer, both firsts. Lesh played an electronic Alembic bass and even Garcia appeared with treated guitar. Lagin, a graduate of MIT, described it as 'cybernetic biomusic'. Rykodisc put *Seastones* on CD in the

ustav Mahler in 1907, the year he became
lusical Director of the Metropolitan Opera,
ew York.

Erik Satie in a portrait taken in 1918, the
year of his 'static sound décor' *Socrates*.

Claude Debussy, a
true visionary of
universal Ambient
music, contemplates
the dawn of the
twentieth century.

Influenced and influencer: Brian Eno with Ambient guru John Cage, London, 1985.

Leon Theremin, demonstrating his ingenious hands–free 'ether wave' electronic instrument, London, 1927.

Karlheinz Stockhausen playing his famous Kandy drum during a performance of *Ceylon*, France, 1973.

he coolly elegant Miles Davis in 1956, a year before he began making orchestral jazz
cordings with arranger Gil Evans.

obert Moog in 1998, proudly displaying
e most significant 'compact performance
thesizer' ever invented, his 1970 Mini Moog.

A smiling Terry Riley on the cover of his
1969 hit album of electronica *A Rainbow In
Curved Air*.

Eno playing the classic VCS3 synthesizer during an open-air concert with Roxy Music, London, summer 1972.

Steve Reich in 1987, the year his early 'phase-shifting' music was reissued by Nonesuch.

Philip Glass in 1989, at the time the highest-paid Minimalist in America, following his daily routine of writing music with pencil and paper.

Keith Jarrett. While on ECM the pianist was responsible for breaking down barriers between jazz, classical and popular music.

Californian Harold Budd, possibly the world's finest Ambient keyboard composer, pictured in the late 1980s.

Jon Hassell in the early 1980s, as his 'Fourth World' music concept was reaching fruition.

Michael Nyman in 1985, the composer-musician who coined the word 'Minimalism'.

John Adams, the cross-pollinating Minimalist, in 1989 after the worldwide success of his opera *Nixon In China*.

Arvo Pärt, Estonian beacon of 'the new simplicity'.

Britain's John Tavener, whose unfettered musical style was inspired by Orthodox religious ritual.

Max Eastley and David Toop rejoin forces in 1994, nearly twenty-five years after their ground-breaking debut album *New And Rediscovered Musical Instruments*.

The Beatles, summer 1968, just before the release of *The White Album*, in Paul McCartney's Japanese outhouse, St John's Wood, London.

Jimi Hendrix in California, summer 1969, a few months before his legendary Woodstock performance.

Ravi Shankar, India's most famous sitarist, had a profound impact on Western musicians from The Beatles to Philip Glass to Ambient House and Techno.

Lou Reed, John Cale and Nico in quintessential Velvet Underground reunion mode, Paris, January 1972.

Space-rock pioneers The Byrds in 1965, a photograph used later on the rarities album *Never Before*.

David Bowie, the consummate European in 1977, sporting the bomber- jacket style of *'Heroes'*.

he Grateful Dead at the height of their powers in February 1970, just after the release of *ve/Dead* and just before the premiere of Antonioni's psychedelic film *Zabriskie Point*, which tured their unforgettable 'Dark Star'.

Led Zeppelin's Robert Plant and Jimmy Page, bringing 'light and shade' to hard rock during the early 1970s.

vid Gilmour of Pink Floyd, live in the 70s. His chiming guitar solos would fine Ambient sound for decades.

English multi-instrumentalist
Mike Oldfield at the piano.
In 1973 his *Tubular Bells* was
considered 'the future of music'.

Can, live in 1974, the most electrifying German rock
group of all time. From left: Holger Czukay, Jaki
Liebezeit, Michael Karoli and Irmin Schmidt.

Tangerine Dream touring *Phaedra* in Europe 1974–5: Peter Baumann, Edgar Froese and
Christoph Franke at the controls.

...aftwerk in their Kling Klang Studio in Düsseldorf: the vintage line-up of Bartos, Schneider, ...r and Hütter which recorded *Trans-Europe Express* in 1976.

...n-Michel Jarre, 1986, accompanied by dry ice ...d a luminous circular keyboard for his ...endez-Vous' spectaculars.

Elizabeth Fraser, the ethereal voice of her generation, with The Cocteau Twins, London, 1993.

The audacious and dazzling film composer Ennio Morricone, conducting a score in a 1987 promo shot.

Laurie Anderson, the world's best-known performance artist, playing her trademark electric violin during the 1980s.

David Sylvian (left) goes all Ambient with Holger Czukay in 1988.

no, Daniel Lanois, Bono and The Edge at Slane Castle, Ireland, during the making of U2's *ne Unforgettable Fire* in 1984.

The uniquely brilliant Donna Summer, who turned Disco to Techno in the late 1970s.

iya, high priestess of Ambient, finds peace the Irish countryside in the late 1980s.

Frankie Knuckles, New York-born but the undisputed innovator of Chicago House.

Derrick May, the intellectual figurehead of Detroit Techno.

The Stone Roses in 198 reinventing rock for the Acid House generation. From left: Ian Brown, John Squire, Mani Mounfield and Reni Wren.

he Orb reach number one in the UK. Alex
terson and Thrash Weston in 1992, the
ar of *U.F. Orb*.

Frankfurt's Ambient Techno supremo Pete
Namlook in his studio surrounded by
analogue synthesizers, circa 1994.

ll Laswell in 1989, tireless champion of studio Ambience and multi-cultural 'collision' musics.

A young William Orbit in the late 1980s, before he plunged into Progressive House, Trance and producing Madonna.

Goldie, whose 'time-stretching' orchestral take on Drum and Bass made him an Ambient star in 1995.

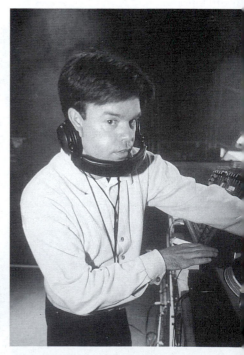

Lee 'Scratch' Perry. His Jamaican Dub innovations of the 1970s are still reverberating throughout music.

Paul Oakenfold, the world's number-one Trance DJ of the 1990s, at the decks as usual.

early 1990s as well as Ambient field recordings by Mickey Hart, who had studied Indian percussion with Ravi Shankar's tabla player, Alla Rakha.

There are so many Dead discs on the market only the really knowledgeable know what to choose. Those looking for the more experimental electronic side should listen to *Infrared Roses* (Grateful Dead 1991) and *Grayfolded* (1995). The first is a collection of 'free music' from various concerts, those passages where the group plunges totally into free improvisation. The latter is an awesome two–disc remix of almost every version of 'Dark Star' The Dead have ever played by Canadian 'plunderphonics' expert John Oswald. In contrast, anyone who wants the best distinct example of Garcia's crystal–sweet guitar lines should hear the *Zabriskie Point Soundtrack* (Rhino 1997) for its 'Dark Star' excerpt and 'Love Scene' solo guitar adagio. But the essence of The Dead is live. Nobody can fault the free–flowing genius of the instrumental stream which follows 'Truckin'' at the Lyceum in London on *Europe '72* (Warner Bros.). A 1968 show from the Shrine Auditorium came out in 1992 as *Two From The Vault* and again benchmarked The Dead as an incredible live psychedelic experience. One disc highlighted the *Live/Dead* material (the segue from 'The Eleven' to 'Death Don't Have No Mercy' is simply wondrous) and the other took in material from *Anthem Of The Sun* while also including 'Morning Dew' from the first album. After that a series of live sound–board recordings titled 'Dick's Picks' were released by Grateful Dead Records, *Vol. 4* (1996) and *Vol. 8* (1998) both highlighting the band at its peak in 1970.

In 1999 came what many considered the impossible – a Grateful Dead boxed set. Compiled from the best sources by Dead scholars and friends of the band, *So Many Roads (1965–1995)* (Arista) was, incredibly, a five–CD package of unreleased live and studio material; a veritable treasure-trove for anyone interested in the group or the history of rock music. The 1971 track 'Beautiful Jam' is as close as anything to Dead perfection – open, transcendental and Ambiently beautiful.

COUNTRY JOE AND THE FISH

One of the wildest psychedelic groups of the American 1960s, Country Joe And The Fish were part political agenda, part acid rock. In their best music they fused an almost classical sense to their hallucinogenic sound, which many consider to be to the closest thing to aural LSD ever put to tape. They certainly understood that raga–style instrumentals, which washed the ears with sound, conveyed and enhanced the feeling of mind expansion.

The linchpins of the group were writer–singer Joe McDonald and guitarist Barry Melton. It has been noted that their bond grew out of similar back-grounds, most importantly that both had leftist fathers who had been persecuted by the FBI. McDonald was born in California in the 1940s and studied trombone and played in orchestras. He then took up guitar and while still a teenager spent four years in the US Navy in Japan. A return to college led him to Berkeley and a meeting with Melton. They recorded the first protest-full 'Rag Baby' EP in 1965 and after calling themselves the Instant Action Jug Band became the electric Country Joe And The Fish in honour of China's Mao Tse-Tung!

Now with additional organist, drummer and bass player, Country Joe And The Fish cut a second 'Rag Baby' EP early in 1966. This was definitive Berkeley Bay Area psychedelia of the times. 'Section 43' was an undulating instrumental derived from Norwegian composer Edvard Grieg while 'Bass Strings' was a dreamlike paean to all hallucinogenics. At the time the band liked to perform them high on the natural psychotropic mescaline. They were the central compositions of their debut album for Vanguard, *Electric Music For The Mind And Body* (1967), a recording notable for its effective use of electric organ and variable electric-guitar sounds courtesy of Barry Melton and David Cohen.

Having recorded their debut in Berkeley, The Fish and their producer, Sam Charteris, went to New York to record *I-Feel-Like-I'm-Fixin'-To-Die*, also released in 1967. Again the group flawlessly mixed political sentiment with appealingly decorative composing. 'Pat's Song' included tasteful use of bells; the translucent 'Magoo' involved the sound of a thunderstorm; 'Janis', McDonald's tribute to his lover Janis Joplin, featured harpsichord. The finale was even more breathtaking – Barry Melton and David Cohen playing raga-like electric guitars to Chicken Hirsh's military drumming on 'Eastern Jam'. Then the instrumental outro continued into 'Colors For Susan', where simple chords were strummed to decay and then repeated, embellished here and there by percussion and bells.

By 1968 The Fish were using expletives in their songs and generally getting up the noses of the establishment. On *Together* their anarchic nature produced a confusing album which only recalled past glories in its closing moments. In 1969 they were heroes of Woodstock but their fourth album, *Here We Are Again*, sounded distracted. With only McDonald and Melton left of the original group a final effort, *C.J. Fish* (1970), bid farewell to one of the great American groups of the 1960s in a return to form with country tinges.

LISTENING

All the original Vanguard albums were put to disc in 1992. Even the 'Rag Baby' EPs surfaced on a Sequel disc around the same time. These first recordings, made between 1965 and the late 1960s, are considered some of the purest psychedelic music ever to come out of the Bay Area. The first two albums, *Electric Music For The Mind And Body* and *I-Feel-Like-I'm-Fixin'-To-Die* (both 1967) are quintessential recordings, essential listening for anybody interested in the history of sound or psychedelic rock. The finale of *Electric Music*, 'Grace', sounds as though it was recorded in the desert at night, as water and other sound effects drip through the production.

H. P. LOVECRAFT

A perfect example of a 1960s group who captured the pure essence of psychedelia and made music which was wholly American in its inspiration. By drawing on the literate Gothic tradition of Edgar Allan Poe and fusing it with a ritualistic synaesthetic music, they produced in *H. P. Lovecraft 2* (1968) one of the great classics of the genre. Moreover this vertiginous, effect-laden sound ably communicated the lysergic experience in more than just personal terms. The very sonic experience of *H. P. Lovecraft 2* was a trip in itself and an able pointer to what Ambience in the rock era could achieve.

H. P. Lovecraft were the brainchild of George Edwards and Dave Michaels, two Chicago musicians who had strong experience of the mid-1960s beat-rock scene. Edwards had even played with the Texan guitarist Steve Miller. They put together a five-piece group based on intense vocal harmonies, a mixture of keyboards and rhythm guitars and textured percussion. Their name was derived from the reclusive Rhode Island writer of fantastic horror fiction, Howard Phillips Lovecraft (1890–1937), whose 1931 novella *At The Mountains Of Madness* is still considered a Gothic masterpiece.

H. P. Lovecraft's first album was recorded in Chicago in 1967 and drew immediately on their namesake's writing by including a long, dreamy song, 'The White Ship', based on a Lovecraft short story. Moreover the use of harpsichord, clarinet, recorder, tympani and other orchestral instruments showed that the group were as interested in texture as in sound. A move to the West Coast in the spring of 1968 prompted the loss of former Shadows Of Knight guitarist Jerry McGeorge.

In California, H. P. Lovecraft fully immersed themselves in the psychedelic subculture, performing and recording while tripping on LSD. Live, San Francisco became their favourite stomping ground and they were apt to play Billy Wheeler's 'High Flying Bird', which had become a staple of Bay Area bands like Jefferson Airplane. But on record they were a different proposition. *H. P. Lovecraft 2* saw them find an aural space which married the dramatic terror of Gothic fiction with some of the cleverest psychedelia ever put to disc. The album ranges from gossamer sound effects ('Electrallentando'), through hippie reverie ('Mobius Trip') and psychological disturbance ('Nothing's Boy') to climax at the shore of the fantastical soundtrack 'At The Mountains Of Madness' – as great a homage, in form as well as content, as you will hear to any writer living or dead.

LISTENING

For years the music of H. P. Lovecraft was a legend which could only be bought on the original Philips Records label for exorbitant prices. In 1988 Edsel released in the UK a handsome double-album package, *At The Mountains Of*

Madness, which featured their first two records in the original psychedelic sleeve of their debut with bonus tracks. In mid-2000 they arrived on a Collectors' Choice CD. Listeners must be warned of the variety of the material contained therein. The first album mixes folk styles with Ambient nuggets like 'The White Ship' and 'That's How Much I Love You Baby'. The great *H. P. Lovecraft 2* (1968) lures you into a song and then scene-shifts in such a cinematic way that the intended sense of disorientation actually occurs.

QUICKSILVER MESSENGER SERVICE

If any group could attest to capturing the intense American psychedelic sound at its most distilled, it has to be Quicksilver Messenger Service. They were a bunch of urban cowboys who lived the hippie dream and played themselves into oblivion but not before leaving two fascinating documents of the era, full of electric instrumentals drenched in the modal jazz of Miles Davis and shifting time signatures of Dave Brubeck. Their story reads likes a picaresque novel of seduction, drug busts, near escapes and fantastic music. Yet in *Happy Trails* (1969) they devised a whole album side of twin-guitar improvisation which still stands up today. The very nature of Gary Duncan and John Cipollina's traded instrumentals on Bo Diddley's vamping 'Who Do You Love' are at once psychedelic and Ambient.

Formed in North Beach, San Francisco in 1965, Quicksilver Messenger Service were Gary Duncan (guitar, vocals), Dino Valenti (guitar, vocals), John Cipollina (guitar), David Freiberg (bass, vocals) and Greg Elmore (drums). The name was astrological in source: all five shared birth signs and some shared birthdays. Valenti was soon imprisoned for possessing marijuana. The others soldiered on in much poverty, playing live and living in various shacks and even a farm in Marin County. Incidents with teenage girls and band squabbles did not stop the band honing their sound in live performance, making a impressive debuts at Fillmore West and the Avalon Ballroom in 1966.

With producer Nick Gravenites Quicksilver attempted to capture their alchemical live sound on record. Most important was Cipollina's acidy and piercingly clear Gibson guitar, which used a lot of trembling on the whammy bar. After two uproarious attempts, *Quicksilver Messenger Service* arrived in the summer of 1968 and revealed a wonderful fluidity, particularly on the jazz-inflected 'Gold And Silver'.

Following a US tour, the group and their very young families compiled a 'live' treasure-trove at Golden State Recorders titled *Happy Trails* – its moniker inspired by the George Hunter album-cover painting of a psychedelicized horseman waving his girl goodbye in the old West. A classic of aesthetics and content, the choked clean guitar style of Duncan was ably matched by Cipollina's shivery approach. Freiberg's plopping propulsive bass and Elmore's finely deployed, almost-jazz drumming rounded off one of the most impressive forays into San Franciscan psychedelia ever captured on tape.

Sadly too much gun-play, drugs, ego battles and the return of Dino Valenti at the end of the 1960s caused havoc. Slowly Quicksilver lost its key members, first Duncan in 1969, then Cipollina in 1970. The early 1970s saw a slimmed-down group recording with Valenti in Hawaii but the days of *Happy Trails* were over. In retrospect Quicksilver Messenger Service acted out the existential acid experiences of LSD as an organic unit. Once shorn of the camaraderie that came with youthful poverty, the heightened live experience of the times and the intense competition of their guitarists, the band couldn't possible relive history.

LISTENING

Capitol in the US and BGO in the UK have seen fit to reissue the original LPs on disc. *Quicksilver Messenger Service* (1968) is embroidered with fine playing, from the liquid intimacy of 'Pride Of Man' to the tour-de-force time-changes of 'Gold And Silver' (inspired by Dave Brubeck's evergreen early-60s jazz classic 'Take Five')and concluding with the psychedelic suite 'The Fool'. *Happy Trails* (1969) still sounds fantastic on LP – a testament to its production and the band's musicality on stage. A nerve-tingling experience, the wonderfully smooth entrance of Gary Duncan's guitar solo on 'When You Love' is still breathtaking today. Other tracks, like 'Maiden Of The Cancer Moon' and 'Calvary', evince pure sound exploration and are in essence the LSD experience as sonic adventure.

THE STEVE MILLER BAND

One of the most innovative groups of the 1960s and the only one to come out of the San Francisco psychedelic scene to fully explore the potential of multi-track recording was The Steve Miller Band, whose ambitious singer-guitarist leader ably survived to make high-fidelity rock over three decades. Though an interest in blues, soul and outright rock 'n' roll has been a major focus of his career, Miller has always embraced technology to enhance the Ambience of his sound. His 1968 albums *Children Of The Future* and *Sailor* are both considered sonic milestones, while his embrace of polyphonic synthesis on *1976's Fly Like An Eagle* makes for one of the most memorable top-flight sounds of the rock era.

Miller was born in Wisconsin in 1943 but raised in Texas. He was a middle-class kid, his father a doctor and violinist who loved tape recorders. His mother was a singer. Early on he was introduced to the innovations of Les Paul and by the age of five was playing guitar. As a child he also met the innovative jazz bassist Charlie Mingus. At a private school in Dallas he formed his first group with another singer–guitarist, Boz Scaggs, when he was only twelve. Miller's life from then on was a series of bands and gigs – white soul at Wisconsin University, gigging with blues heroes like T–Bone Walker at night, then on to Chicago and gigs with bluesmen like Muddy Waters and Buddy Guy.

Here was a prodigy who loved to play but who also liked sound. Ending up as a studio engineer in Tucson, Miller felt San Francisco offered the best opportunity for advancement. In late 1966 he arrived at Haight-Ashbury and put together a group at Berkeley University which included Scaggs. In no time at all they were playing the ballrooms and by the spring of 1967 Miller was extemporizing modal ragas on his guitar live! The quality of his musicians, like bassist Lonnie Turner and drummer Tim Davis, was so high that they were signed to Capitol Records in 1968 for a huge advance. At once Miller went to London to hire the services of Beatles engineer Glyn Johns.

The first album, *Children Of The Future* (1968), was in terms of production, the best-sounding debut from any San Francisco band extant. Its first side comprised a suite of songs linked by extensive use of studio-enhanced effects. In parts it sounded like the Farfisa organ-led music of Pink Floyd, in others like film soundtrack. Its second side opened with Scaggs's harpsichord ballad 'Baby's Calling Me Home' and concluded with more typical rock and blues material. Everything was segued, the finale 'Key To The Highway' an Ambient treatment of the Big Bill Broonzy blues more faithful than Eric Clapton could ever be.

Not missing a beat, Miller immediately brought Johns to California to record the astonishing *Sailor*, also in 1968, still considered the most advanced rock album of the 1960s after *Sgt. Pepper*. Opening with an Ambient collage of foghorn, keyboard and lush guitars, the soundscape pirouetted into 'Dear Mary', with its rain, choir-like Miller vocal, treated drums and Beatlesy 'Penny Lane'-styled horns. This was fantastic stuff indeed. Though most of the rest was slick American rock, the quality of such tunes as the trance-inducing 'Quicksilver Girl', with its use of repetitive textures, had never been heard before then.

Though many have pointed to Miller's disaffection with the San Francisco scene, documents exist of him jamming with a supergroup made up of Country Joe And The Fish and members of The Grateful Dead and Jefferson Airplane at Fillmore West in 1969. Boz Scaggs's departure from the group after 1968 led to a period of unease and it wasn't until Miller retired to Nashville in 1970 that he regained the finely textured sound of old. In terms of electronica his next high point was the fabulous 1976 album *Fly Like An Eagle*, which consolidated his star status.

LISTENING

As one of the most commercially successful American rock acts of the 1970s and 80s, Steve Miller's catalogue has consequently never been out of Capitol/EMI print. *Children Of The Future* and *Sailor* are two 1968 albums of incredibly advanced music which make most of the other San Franciscan groups of the time sound like amateurs. *Sailor*, in particular, is an essential purchase whose Ambient sound is still a healthy shock to the system. Miller's penchant for lush acoustic ballads and impeccable recording can be further sampled on *Number 5, Best Of The Steve Miller Band 1968–1973* and *Fly Like An Eagle*. The latter's 1976 appearance again showcased Miller's interest in lush Ambient rock, its opening numbers, 'Fly Like An Eagle' and 'Space Odyssey', amply decorated with Miller's imaginative use of Roland synthesizer.

SANTANA

The Latin polyrhythms and stinging guitar tones of Santana have brought the group and its Gibson-specialist frontman lasting fame in the rock pantheon. For ever associated with Central and South America, the group actually emerged from the psychedelic San Francisco of the 1960s, a fact often hidden by the hot silkiness of some of their best instrumental music. Though infectiously poly-rhythmical at the time, Santana's direction led to a cool sound with its roots in Miles Davis and endless feedback sustains afforded by post-Hendrix use of guitar technology.

Initially Santana were a collective of musicians from vastly differing back-grounds – white urban Gregg Rolie (vocals, keyboards) and Michael Shrieve (drums), black urban David Brown (bass) and street conga-player and Latin-music freak Michael Carabello teamed with the Nicaraguan percussionist Jose 'Chepito' Areas and Mexican guitarist Carlos Santana. This was the group who made a devastating appearance at Woodstock in August 1969 and whose debut album that autumn flew up the US charts in one long, sinuous groove.

Carlos Santana himself was born in Mexican poverty to a mariachi musician father in the late 1940s. He studied violin, then switched to guitar and as a teenager played the brothels and saloons of Tijuana. Affected by imported black American blues (especially that of B.B. King), he went to San Francisco in 1966. There he discovered Miles Davis, John Coltrane, LSD and the blues guitar of Mike Bloomfield. With pressure from music svengali Bill Graham, The Santana Blues Band was formed in 1967, with studied musician Mike Shrieve and timbales expert Chepito Areas arriving in 1969 in time to support Jimi Hendrix at Woodstock. The debut album, *Santana*, rode on a wind of Latin and African rhythms; its outstand-ing cut, 'Evil Ways', was the most entrancing groove ever heard at the time.

The group favoured long, intense studio sessions, sometimes up to twelve hours at a time, from which a segment would be honed to perfection live. For their second set, *Abraxas* (1970), they got a $1-million advance for an album which on its release topped the US charts. Here they adapted the Peter Green blues 'Black Magic Woman' to a sultry, shimmering production with added salsa, blues, Latin and flamenco elements in an elaborate jigsaw.

Intense tours, full of stories of drug excess and groupies, dogged the band's progress. Second guitarist Neal Schon was added late in 1970 but Carlos Santana was deeply dissatisfied with *Santana 3* (1971). That summer the band performed an incredible version of Miles Davis's 'In A Silent Way' to close Fillmore West. It was also the end of the original Santana. With Carabello and Brown out of the band, a more painterly approach was taken on *Caravanserai* (1972), whose two LP sides opened with exotic sound canvases.

Subsequently Carlos Santana became undisputed leader, his spiritual leanings helping to perfect the guitar sound he had stormed the world with from 1966 to 1972. His openly trilly sound and use of lengthy feedback sustains was a compliment to Jimi Hendrix. His composition style a virtue of Miles Davis's modality. His instrumentality a product of blues intersecting with Latin-American virtuosity. In 1973 he displayed his devotion to Eastern guru Sri Chinmoy by recording an album with the English guitarist John McLaughlin dedicated to John Coltrane. In 1987 Santana's 'Blues For Salvador' project was considered heartfelt and musically impeccable while he repaid his debt to the blues by playing with blues elder statesman John Lee Hooker in the 1980s and 90s.

LISTENING

The vast Santana catalogue on Columbia/Sony may be a bit intimidating for the first-time buyer. In 1995 Sony Legacy put out an excellent three-CD boxed set, *Spirits Dancing In The Flesh*, which included live music from Woodstock and Santana's awe-inspiring version of the open-groove Miles Davis composition 'In A Silent Way' from 1971. In 1998 Columbia began reissuing all the original albums on remastered CDs with expanded booklets and extra live tracks. *Abraxas* (1970) is a good first port of call but the best Ambient experience is derived from *Caravanserai* (1970), where the guitarist excels himself on 'Waves Within' and the Neal Schon guitar duel 'Song Of The Wind'. Other members Shrieve and Areas display outstanding taste on the sound designs 'Eternal Caravan Of Reincarnation' and 'Future Primitive'. Santana's own collaboration with John McLaughlin, *Love Devotion Surrender* (CBS 1973), may have produced much electric guitar sizzle but the quiet contemplation of Coltrane's 'Naima', played on acoustic guitars, is peerless.

Santana's comeback album, *Supernatural* (Arista 1999), sold over seven million copies and earned an unprecedented nine Grammy awards in the US.

FOLK AMBIENCE

The cross-over to rock music which Bob Dylan had so effectively executed during the mid-1960s had an enormous impact on the folk scene in Ireland,

Scotland and England. Irish and Scottish folk, with its inherent ornamental character, and the dronal quality of English folk music were seized upon and revamped in terms of electric instruments and new studio production techniques. If Anglo-Irish formations like Sweeney's Men and Steeleye Span were formative electric-folk ensembles, it was the music of Donovan, The Incredible String Band, Fairport Convention, John Martyn and Clannad that really assimilated the new electronic and Ambient possibilities of the late twentieth century.

Though often dismissed as ersatz Dylan, Scottish musician Donovan, born in 1946, made quite a contribution in the form of his studio albums. With the help of producer Mickie Most and contributions from Jimmy Page and John Paul Jones (later of Led Zeppelin) his studio work of the mid to late 1960s was atmospherically sophisticated. Its delicate Romantic quality was apparent when Donovan broke upon the UK scene in 1965 with such gracious music as the sound documentary of 'Sunny Goodge Street' or the vibrato vocal-filled 'Turquoise'. *Sunshine Superman* (Epic 1966) was a huge stride forward. Recorded in London and Los Angeles, this album featured string arrangements, Indian sitar and drones plus the guitar of Jimmy Page. With its tributes to folk-guitar ace Bert Jansch, American psychedelians Jefferson Airplane and Arthurian legend it was perfectly in tune with its times. Travels to Greece and Mexico were reflected on Donovan's 1967 album *Mellow Yellow* (Epic). Flutes, glockenspiel, electric harpsichord, strings and various acoustic guitar styles mixed with jazz elements on another rich collection. *A Gift From A Flower To A Garden* (Pye 1967) was a two-album boxed set of baroque folk laced with organ, vibraphone, harpsichord, flute and percussion produced by Donovan himself in London. Its acoustic 'For Little Ones' disc featured sampled sea and bird sounds. Eclectic and whimsical in turn, *Hurdy Gurdy Man* (Epic 1968) showed a return to the strictures of traditional Gaelic music but refracted through a consciousness familiar with Moroccan climes. The title track was virtually Led Zeppelin with Donovan as lead singer! By 1969 Donovan was rocking out with guitarist Jeff Beck, leaving his gentle gossamer suffused creations to posterity.

With their melismatic vocal techniques, use of medieval scales and exotic instrumentation, The Incredible String Band opened people's ears to a carnival of acoustic sounds. Formed in the early 1960s in Edinburgh with a nucleus of Dylan fan Mike Heron and Celtic troubadour Robin Williamson, they gravitated to Glasgow, where they opened a club featuring chimes, gongs and stringed instruments picked up in junk shops. Admired by fellow Scots Bert Jansch and John Martyn, they also spent a lot of time in Ireland, where they first aired the hypnotic 'October Song' from their self-titled 1966 debut on Elektra. Handled by Bostonian Joe Boyd, they then travelled widely, Williamson bringing back various strange instruments from Morocco for the London sessions of *The 5000 Spirits Or The Layers Of The Onion* (1967). Bowed gimbri, flute, sitar, tambura, mandolin, acoustic guitars and Danny Thompson's bass supported a series of short compositions that were at once strange, mysterious and affectionate. Presented in an earthy psychedelic cover, its fifty minutes of music seemed to last much longer as the sounds eddied into North African and Asian harbours. If that was great, the next album, *The Hangman's Beautiful Daughter*, was truly astonishing. Fully competent in playing every instrument they could get their hands on, Heron and Williamson stretched song structures up to thirteen minutes. Modal, even microtonal scales were on offer as Williamson acquitted himself on fifteen instruments, including water harp, chahanai and pan pipes. The album's second side was a tour de force, fully embracing the depth of spirit of Indian classical music. Admired by George Harrison, this was as authentic as Western musicians could get without bowing to parody. Loved by Led Zeppelin, the band widened their troupe, lived as a commune in Wales, embraced Scientology and multi-media and played Wood-stock. By 1970 they were on the Island label and, excepting the raga-like qualities of songs like 'Maya' and 'Dreams Of No Return', their successive releases edged them further towards a bland folk-rock and away from the wonderful acoustic stillness of their best work.

Bert Jansch was another Scot who made waves. Influenced by Mississippi blues and the modal picking of Davy Graham, his open-tuned baroque guitar style became famous in London during the mid-1960s. When he teamed up with guitarist John Renbourn their sound influenced the careers of both Jimmy Page and Neil Young. Pentangle came into being in 1967 when they were joined by singer Jacqui McShee and the jazzy rhythm section of Danny Thompson and Terry Cox. With albums on Transatlantic and later Reprise, the group created a popular hybrid of folk, blues and jazz with extended bass and twin-guitar improvisation. Bassist Danny Thompson had already played with many Indian classical musicians, so the feel of many of their amplified acoustic albums is raga without necessarily playing particular scales or Indian structures. *Sweet Child* (1968) was a paired live and studio set, *Basket Of Light* (1969) included the famous BBC theme 'Light Flight', *Cruel Sister* (1970) featured one track lasting an entire vinyl side, while *Reflection* (1970) was their best-sounding studio album.

Folk-rock was a difficult hybrid to muster. Many failed to see it was more than just amplifying acoustic instruments and putting a back-beat to it. The finest English folk-rock group of their era were undoubtedly Fairport Con-vention. Though led by bassist Ashley 'Tyger' Hutchings, the group has always been identified with guitarist Richard Thompson and their incredible singer Sandy Denny. Thompson grew up in the leafy areas of north London and started playing guitar at ten with his eye on classical music and Django Reinhardt. In 1967 Fairport Convention was formed, with Ian Matthews, Simon Nicol, Judy Dyble and Martin Lamble joining Thompson and Hutch-ings. Produced by Joe Boyd in the same Chelsea studio, Sound Techniques, as The Incredible String Band recorded at, *Fairport Convention* (1968) was a folk-rock experiment which included Dylan and Joni Mitchell songs. Sandy Denny then took over from Dyble as vocalist for a trio of quite brilliant albums released by Island records in 1969. The first, *What We Did On Our Holidays*, interwove Denny's beautiful creamy vocal with a richly sewn tapestry of electric and acoustic instrumentation. Sitar, strummed zither and the twin guitars of Nicol and Thompson were all in evidence but the most notable quality was the spatial Ambience of such pieces as 'The Lord Is In This Place' and the definitive version of Irish ballad 'She Moves Through The Fair'. Bob Dylan still featured in their songbook but Fairport Convention were fast becoming a stellar group of unique quality. *Unhalfbricking* featured the mesmerizing folk-rock of 'Autopsy' and the lengthy improvisation of 'A Sailor's Life'. By their third Island album, *Liege And Lief* (1969), Denny was in full flight as she rocked out with Dave Swarbrick and Dave Mattacks, who had come in to replace the departing Ian Matthews and Martin Lamble, who died in a road accident. On an album which was more pronouncedly rock in one way and more traditionalist in another, Denny's more intimate contributions were peerless in the genre. After this Mattacks and Hutchings formed Steeleye Span with an Irish duo and folk-rock was truly established. Reflecting back in 1989, Richard Thompson thought the band had been young and still finding its voice when it came asunder in 1970. The music he considered to be Celtic was 'a blend of drones and melodies in English, Irish, Scottish, Italian, French and North African which originally came from India'.

Joe Boyd managed most of these artists through his Witchseason Productions. One of his most mercurial talents was Nick Drake, a well-bred and much-travelled young musician with a sound grasp of classical piano and the uses of horns and reeds. Born in Burma in 1948, Drake was brought up in luxury in the English Midlands. His mother sang and while at public school he embraced Dylan, Bert Jansch and the emerging London scene of rhythm and blues music. Before attending Cambridge University in 1967 he spent months in France and Morocco writing. Entranced by Tim Buckley and Van Morrison, he began performing his exuberantly sad songs. Again Joe Boyd stepped in and put him in the Sound Techniques studio with engineer John Wood in 1968 to record *Five Leaves Left* on eight-track. Richard and Danny Thompson helped out on guitar and bass and Drake made ample use of conga, flute, cello and strings. The recording process took over a year, Drake painstakingly building up the songs with several arrangers. Released on Island in 1969, the album boasted a strident plucked guitar style, mature lyrics beyond Drake's twenty years and wonderfully extended Ambient songs like 'River Man', 'Three Hours' and 'Cello Song'. Living in Hampstead, Drake then spent months working on the lighter *Bryter Layter* in 1970. Featuring most of Fairport Convention, John Cale and sundry instrumentalists, it had some great sonic delights, like the expansive, wave-like 'Hazey Jane I'. Soon after the album's release in 1971, Drake retired to his parents' house in the Warwickshire countryside and became depressed. A spell at a Spanish villa did nothing to arrest his emotional decline. Yet he dredged up enough strength to record *Pink Moon* (1972) on sixteen-track in Chelsea completely solo. Again the guitar and vocal sound was mesmerizing. His drug-related death at the age of twenty-six was a real tragedy.

A great friend of Drake, and yet another folk musician associated with Joe Boyd, was John Martyn. Like Drake, he was born in 1948, but to two opera singers in Glasgow. His childhood was spent in a houseboat on the English canals with his mother. An early interest in the acoustic guitar led Martyn to leave school early and play in pubs and clubs. Influenced by the Incredible String Band and a personal tutor from an early age, he was keen to combine modern technology with the lilts and airs of traditional Gaelic folk music. In 1968 he was spotted, signed to Island and from the off was putting his acoustic guitar through effects boxes and using phasing and other tape manipulations. A spell in America introduced him to jazz and he first started using the Echoplex guitar unit in Woodstock. Back in the UK, he played with Danny Thompson (who had come from working with John McLaughlin) and the sonority of his Echoplexed guitar built up a ricocheting, bouncing sound and led to a crescendo of overtones. By adding that and a fuzz tone to his acoustic guitar Martyn achieved a sound similar in effect to that of La Monte Young on piano or Terry Riley on electronic keyboards. *Bless The Weather* (1971) was a fine showcase of Martyn's talents – dextrous interweaving acoustic playing, silken jazz-folk vocals and the six-and-a-half-minute Echoplex and piano Ambience of 'Glistening Glyndebourne'. *Solid Air* (1973), often considered his master-piece, was a tribute to Nick Drake and again showed the sonic improvement of Sound Techniques' sixteen-track facilities. Danny and Richard Thompson were again on board and organs, keyboards, vibes and reeds pushed the music towards Easy Listening. Yet Martyn's sense of dynamic, how he framed a song and emphasized the instrumental qualities made songs like 'Man In The Station' addictive creations. Used sparingly on *Solid Air*, the Echoplex would take centre stage on *Inside Out* (1973), the track 'Outside In' a virtual homage to the off-beat technique. The album also featured a full blend of Moroccan, Indian and Gaelic styles. Touring with Danny Thompson and drummer John Stevens produced the atmospheric home-produced album *Live At Leeds* (1975). Mar-tyn's final 1970s album was *One World* (1977), produced by then Island boss Chris Blackwell on twenty-four-track equipment. Admiring Jamaica's dub-reggae king Lee Perry, Martyn was developing a more African-inflected style. Various musicians, including Danny Thompson and keyboardist Stevie Win-wood, helped out on what was one of his most ambitious achievements in sound. 'One World' itself was like listening to slow-motion music underwater but pride of place went to the eight-and-a-half-minute Ambience of 'Small Hours'. Here Martyn's slowly echoing electric guitar was backed by a heartbeat rhythm, percussion instruments made to sound like sea gulls and dripping water; the tone expanded halfway through by MiniMoog synth solo.

Folk Ambience reached its full electronic potential with the Irish group Clannad. The name was derived from the Irish 'clann a Dore', meaning 'family from the town of Dore', Gweedore in Donegal. During the early 1970s their interest was in The Beatles and The Beach Boys, music they played for relaxation after the constant reels and jigs of their father's pub. The nucleus was Maire (harp, vocals), Pol (flute, guitars) and Ciaran (bass, keyboards) Brennan, with help from two uncles as a rhythm section. They won a festival, got more equipment and became a famous gigging group, particularly in Scandinavia. They negotiated their own contracts and signed with Philips in 1973. *Clannad 2* (1974) featured Moog synthesizer with upright bass, flute and African percussion. By 1980 they were working in Cologne with the German producer Conny Plank and with their younger sister, Enya. *Fuaim* (1982) featured Enya and a Prophet 5 synth. According to Ciaran Brennan: 'I studied classical music, was into Schoenberg and interested in drones with the Prophet 5. I wanted to add colour and space to the music.' The fact that Clannad used Irish as their first language didn't deter anybody from appreciating the sonic beauty of their output. In 1982 they signed with RCA and went into Dublin's Windmill Lane studios with 10cc engineer Richard Dodd. Inspired by 10cc's beautiful pop masterpiece 'I'm Not In Love', Clannad used the Prophet 5 to sample their own voices, which were then keyed into the mixing desk. The misty harmonies of their break-through 'Theme From Harry's Game', from the album *Magical Ring* (1983), were produced by the group sitting at the desk and fading them up in massed harmony as required. Awards and acclaim quickly followed, 1985's *Macalla* featuring David Sylvian's producer Steve Nye and Bono from U2. Pol's departure to work at Real World studios in 1989 didn't prevent *Anam* from going gold in the US in 1990. By 1993 they were even more famous, owing to writing the hit theme from the film *The Last Of The Mohicans*. Clannad's dreamy mood music was the product of working in their own Dublin mountains studio with sixteen-track, a computer, a couple of keyboards and a number of samplers. Ciaran loved to wire three Yamaha DX7 synths together in a room and experiment with delays and reverbs. Though they had spent years collecting traditional songs and working on their melodies, Clannad's step into electronic folk was a natural evolution – but one which did not mask the pure tone of Maire Brennan's voice nor the earthiness of their acoustic arrangements.

LISTENING

EMI released Donovan's *The Trip*, a collection of music from his 1960s albums, in 1991. *A Gift From A Flower To A Garden* was reissued on a single disc by BGO in 1993. In 1994 came *Four Donovan Originals*, EMI's remastered reissued box of each individual US album from 1966 to 1969 in original miniature sleeves. The Incredible String Band had two archive BBC sessions reissued by Strange Fruit in 1997, the *On Air* set featuring the flowing raga interpretation 'Dreams Of No Return' from 1970. Both *The 5000 Spirits or The Layers Of The Onion* and *The Hangman's Beautiful Daughter* are essential Incredible String Band albums, reissued on Elektra CD in 1992. Even sessions from *The 5000 Spirits* recorded in Chelsea in 1967 surfaced on Pig's Whisker in 1997.

Those interested in Pentangle should look to *Live At The BBC* (BOJ 1995) and the expansive *Sweet Child* (Castle 1996). Fairport Convention were at their peak on the three 1969 albums, *What We Did On Our Holidays*, *Unhalfbricking* and *Liege And Lief*, which were all reissued on Island Masters CDs in 1990.

All of Nick Drake's albums were also issued in 1990 on CD. During the summer of 2000 Island reissued Drake's three key albums in remastered deluxe versions. John Martyn's *Bless The Weather* and *Inside Out* were issued on the same imprint but in 1992 Island released the fabulous twin set of *Solid Air* and *One World* in one box. *Live At Leeds* was reissued on disc in 1992 by Awareness.

Clannad have a long and honourable discography, though most of it emphasizes the RCA years. *Magical Ring* (1983) is a worthy starting point, as is *Pastpresent* (a good 1989 compilation), as both contain the definitive 'Theme From Harry's Game'. Later discs, like *Banba* (1993), *Lore* (1996) and *Landmarks* (1998), are full to the brim with that special Clannad Ambience. *Lore* came with a bonus CD, *Themes And Dreams*, featuring their hit film and television themes.

ROCK EVOLVES

PINK FLOYD

When Pink Floyd began making psychedelic rock in 1966 they embarked on a musical journey so significant that it would alter the entire history of late-twentieth-century sound. From the start their founder, Syd Barrett, had a complete understanding of psychedelia, allowing the Floyd to be one of the few UK bands to create expansive hallucinogenic music akin to that of such San Franciscan groups as The Grateful Dead and Jefferson Airplane. Moreover they thoroughly embraced technology and looked on instruments as sound sources which could be utilized to paint a landscape. Their art and architecture backgrounds dictated a considered approach to recording and presentation, their immaculately crafted masterpieces *Dark Side Of The Moon* (1973) and *Wish You Were Here* (1975) finding an equivalence only in the 1960s work of The Beatles. Their perfectionist attitude to sound in the studio and on stage was seen as part of 'progressive rock' during the early 1970s but they far outgrew the pretensions of their peers. Their aim was simply to improve the quality of everything – composition, melody, structure, concept and spectacle. Between 1966 and 1975 they did just that and in the process made some of the most beautiful instrumental rock ever imagined. *Wish You Were Here* still stands as the defining moment of Ambience in rock, a work of such resonance that it was an automatic sampling choice for The Orb when they began their sonic odyssey in 1989.

The Pink Floyd story is one of an enigma which has endured for decades. Though well over 100 million albums have been sold and countless books and articles written, the general public knows next to nothing about how their music was generated. Moreover their brilliant Hipgnosis-designed album sleeves communicated little about the band line-up or what instruments they played. The twenty-fifth anniversary of the release of *Dark Side Of The Moon* allowed, for the first time, a detailed look at the making of a thirty-million-selling recording which, according to Philip Glass, was one of the best examples of Minimalism in rock. This element of reductionism, which made Pink Floyd's best music sound both symphonic and accessible at the same time, seemed to permeate all aspects of the band's life. Even though the group had exploded into acrimony by 1985, the legacy of their music still holds a deep mystery – one which deserves to be unravelled.

All the members of Pink Floyd were post-war children who flowered in the expanded consciousness of the 1960s. Roger 'Syd' Barrett, Roger Waters and David Gilmour had all grown up in Cambridge. Richard Wright was born in London while Nick Mason was from Birmingham but grew up in London's leafy Hampstead. All were distinctly English and middle-class. All had good educations and looked to the arts as a natural career. Barrett grew up with a father obsessed by classical music. He was playing piano as a child and then took to the ukulele and banjo. Soon enough he was playing guitar, mimicking rock 'n' roll tunes he heard on the radio. After meeting David Gilmour he went electric. Both Barrett and Gilmour attended Cambridge College of Art in 1962. In between their respective art and language courses they experimented with guitars, echo effects and marijuana. Gilmour had been given a guitar when he was thirteen and assiduously studied American folk styles.

That year Roger Waters (who had had a brief naval career) went to London to study architecture. He blew his first year's grant on a guitar and indulged his love of American jazz and blues. By 1963 he had met both Wright and Mason and formed the group Sigma 6. Richard Wright had gone to a private school, as had Mason. Wright, Mason and Waters were studying architecture at Regent Street Polytechnic. By 1964 Barrett (who'd been at the same Cambridge school as Waters) had gone to London to study at the prestigious Camberwell School of Art. At the same time Gilmour was making a name for himself with a Cambridge band, Jokers Wild. In the summer of 1965 Barrett and Gilmour went on a busking holiday to St Tropez. Back in London, Barrett, Waters, Mason and Wright intermingled. They formed a group called Spectrum 5. Barrett took pure LSD with another Cambridge friend, Storm Thorgerson (who went on to create the Floyd's lavish record sleeves), and the stage was set. Wright became interested in Stockhausen and left architecture to study piano at the London College of Music. With an open mind to guitar feedback and other sound distortions, Barrett (with the help of Wright) envisioned a new music away from the staple rhythm and blues of most British bands. In the winter of 1965 The Pink Floyd Sound was born. By 1966 Pink Floyd were in business.

Barrett was a huge sponge. He absorbed everything from children's rhymes to French Symbolist poetry, with a nod to mysticism and other esoterica along the way. He was inspired by the modal music of John Coltrane, the baroque of

Handel, the West Coast sound of Love and copious amounts of LSD to create 'Interstellar Overdrive', a lengthy free-form electronic experiment which featured his electric guitar going through a Binson Echorec effects box. The Binson was an Italian metal recording device with controls which affected the volume, tone and length of a signal plus other controls to create echo, repeats and reverbs. It even had a mixer, was quite small and featured only six dials. Until their use of VCS3 Synthi in 1972, the Binson Echorec would define a major part of Pink Floyd's sound.

By the end of 1966 Pink Floyd were defining a new concert concept in terms of 'happenings' and 'raves', which were held in purpose-built venues such as the UFO club in London. Their music was billed as 'coloured sound' and featured liquid-light displays and projected films. One film-making acquaintance of Barrett, Peter Whitehead, wanted to film the emerging psychedelic London scene. He made a deal with the Floyd that he would pay for studio time if they allowed him to film the sessions. This he did in January 1967, when he made an extraordinary document of them recording 'Interstellar Overdrive' at Sound Techniques in Chelsea. Eventually released as part of the film *Tonite Let's All Make Love In London* in 1968, the Floyd footage showed Barrett playing his electric guitar flat with metal objects and coaxing strange sounds from the Binson echo box. Moreover Rick Wright was putting his Farfisa Duo electric organ through another Binson Echorec to get that distinctive shimmering keyboard sound. Even Mason's tom-tom playing and cymbal work looked as if it was designed to entrance.

This session had been produced by American Joe Boyd and resulted in other material, including the incredible psychedelic pop single 'Arnold Layne', notable for Wright's glimmering Echoreced organ. Literally chased by record companies, Pink Floyd were signed by EMI as an 'albums band' and 'Arnold Layne' was released to huge popularity. While Waters (now on bass) was in the background, he did provide limits within which Barrett could fly. Ensconced in Abbey Road studios during the spring and summer of 1967, they recorded their first album under the eye of former Beatles' engineer Norman Smith. In a strange twist of fate, The Beatles were recording *Sgt. Pepper's Lonely Hearts Club Band* in the building at the same time and a meeting occurred as a result of McCartney's Stockhausen-assisted vision of a new electronic music. Nothing happened at this meeting. We are left to speculate whether it was a class division (Liverpool working class meets Cambridge privilege) or temperamental differences.

By the summer of 1967 Pink Floyd were using a quadraphonic surround-sound system, the Azimuth Co-Ordinator, live. Another single, the soaring guitar-and-organ extravaganza 'See Emily Play', was released, a piece sprinkled with speeded-up piano and a dreamy Ambient production sound. Live, Pink Floyd were also using found sounds, like wind and rain randomly taped. Their quick absorption of the ideas of John Cage and The Beatles could be heard all over their debut EMI album, *The Piper At The Gates Of Dawn*, released at the end of the summer of 1967. If lyrically Syd Barrett drew much from his LSD experiences, astronomy, the *I Ching* and his love of fairy-tales and children's rhymes, he was predominantly affected by English nostalgia and rural heritage. The last two tracks of *Piper* crystallized this very English perspective – the lilting acoustic 'Scarecrow' and the vaudevillian 'Bike', which concluded with a door opening on a Victorian clockwork-toy shop and the sound of quacking ducks! Though recorded on standard four-track, the album was full of tape manipulation, random edits, double-tracked vocals, Echoreced guitar, reverb and Wright's glittering Farfisa organ.

Pink Floyd were now the darlings of the psychedelic scene. They were welcomed in Europe and America but Barrett's increasing use of LSD and erratic stage presence (no strings on his guitar, staring blankly into the audience) made life impossible for the rest of the band. In the autumn of 1967 Barrett cut a strange hybrid of acoustic rock, brass band and electronica at a London studio titled 'Jugband Blues'. Soon after, sessions commenced on the Floyd's second album, *A Saucerful Of Secrets*, to which he contributed little. That Christmas David Gilmour came in to help out on guitar and vocals. By the spring of 1968 Barrett was out of Pink Floyd, his condition declared 'incurable' by the noted psychiatrist R. D. Laing. The group would spend the rest of its working life coming to terms with this loss.

Recorded in patches, *A Saucerful Of Secrets*, released in the summer of 1968, saw Pink Floyd in true experimental mode. Along with 'Jugband Blues', Barrett had contributed to 'Set The Controls For The Heart Of The Sun' and 'Remember A Day'. The former was a hypnotic Waters creation with Chinese roots played out to throbbing bass, shivering vibraphone, treated organ, Mason's distinctive soft-malleted drums, sampled seagull sounds and much stereo panning. The latter was a dreamy Wright piano piece with an effects-warped backing. Outside these the stand-out creation was the twelve-minute title track, which at the time was compared to the work of Stockhausen. *A Saucerful Of Secrets* was a creation which began with Chinese gong rumbles, wind chimes and that typically foresty Farfisa organ sound. It went on to showcase Mason's circular drumming technique, random piano clusters, backwards-taped guitar sounds and noise tape loops. Waters and Mason had written the piece like a Cageian diagram. It concluded in a stately fashion, all grandiose organ and syllabic harmonies. Gilmour, for his part, was eschewing blues guitar riffs for a more Barrett-like attack on the instrument – utilizing any object to attack the strings as the instrument lay horizontal.

On tour Pink Floyd continued to develop their 'Azimuth Co-Ordinated' quadraphonic sound system. Much of their show contained Ambient sounds such as bells, footsteps, clocks and voices. Waters was now playing a Fender Precision bass and Gilmour had a couple of Fender electric guitars and a lap steel guitar for playing slide passages. Wright had his electric organs and Mason played the drums. This may sound basic but Pink Floyd had an uncanny knack of extracting the maximum out of limited resources. Commissioned to write for film, the group recorded *More* in the early part of 1969 without seeing Barbet Schroeder's hippie Formentera-located flick it was destined for. Released that summer, *More* was full of great music. The opening Waters track, 'Cirrus Minor', was pure Ambient bliss. The sound of woodland wildlife opened a song which drifted into acoustic guitar and concluded with Wright's oscillating organ sound floating out into space. The sound was mind-expanded, but precise. The result was a mental trip one could do without drugs. The rest of *More* was a mixture of good acoustic ballads, bad rock songs, ethnic drum, whistle and Spanish guitar tunes plus typical Floydian electronica.

Though Norman Smith was credited as producer, *Ummagumma* (1969) was really the Floyd producing themselves. A double album of live and studio recorded material, it featured the first great surrealistic sleeve of receding band portraits by old friend Storm Thorgerson's company Hipgnosis. Like its silly Cambridge erotic slang title, the studio album was terrible. Each member went into Abbey Road and tried to create a solo suite. Only two pieces were up to standard. Gilmour's 'The Narrow Way (Pt One)' was a take on Jefferson Airplane's acoustic guitar melody 'Embryonic Journey' (1966) bookended by tape-effected electric guitar. Waters's 'Grantchester Meadows' was the best – a perfect recreation of a lazy summer's day by the River Cam of his childhood, replete with acoustic picking, the sounds of birds, bees and swans. It concluded with the humorous recording of someone coming down the stairs and swatting a bee in a room. Much better was the live album, which was all good, especially the scintillating Waters exploration 'Careful With That Axe, Eugene'. Recorded as a 'b' side at the end of 1968, the piece had taken on a life of its own. A throbbing hypnotic Ambience of bass and organ backdropped by angelic voice, its ethereal quality hid the ferocious dynamite blast of sound which erupted a little over three minutes in. After this veritable sonic apocalypse the piece trailed into the quiet of subtle cymbals, organ tones and softly stroked guitar. The piece was to influence the work of one of the great film-makers of the twentieth century, Michelangelo Antonioni.

Having seen the psychedelic Floyd in London in 1966 during the making of his award-winning *Blow-Up* (1967), Antonioni wanted the group to soundtrack his new American counter-culture film *Zabriskie Point* (1970). With a $7-million MGM budget Antonioni could afford to invite the Floyd to Rome for a fortnight at the end of 1969. Enjoying the best French cuisine, they worked every night into the next morning for a month, recording over an hour's worth of music. Here the group were really able to develop their ideas. From Nick Mason's heartbeat drumming at the beginning, all the way through to the incredible end sequence where a plush desert mansion blows up, to a spellbinding version of 'Careful With That Axe, Eugene' (then renamed 'Come In No. 51, Your Time Is Up'), the music which Pink Floyd were now making was full of great ideas. Unfortunately, fifty minutes of material was left unused, some of it only surfacing in 1997 when issued by Rhino. One instrumental, 'Love Scene 4', was a serenely attractive piano piece by Rick Wright which floated on a love for both French Impressionism and jazz. Some of Wright's lyrical piano creations were said to pre-date the trance keyboard part of 'Us And Them' from 1973's *Dark Side Of The Moon*.

Back in the UK in 1970, the group had serious financial problems to deal with. In a way this was the year they stepped back from innovating to consolidate their situation. In a fashion they looked back to their past, various members helping the temporarily recovered Syd Barrett to record two albums, *The Madcap Laughs* and *Barrett*, for EMI Harvest. More pressingly, they had to create a hit album, and this they did with the very English *Atom Heart Mother*, which featured images of cows and stoned songs about Cambridge. The centrepiece of the album was the twenty-three-and-a-half-minute title track, which featured brass, choir and solo cello. The group were helped out on this by an eccentric electronic composer friend, Ron Geesin, who scored and arranged the piece around the rock instrumentation. This piece was certainly too English in its preoccupations and sounded too much like bad Prog-Rock. Its only saving grace was Gilmour's milky lap steel guitar playing and a 'funky' Rick Wright Hammond organ solo halfway in. The rest of the album's tracks were still foggy with a druggy post-60s hangover. Wright's jaunty 'Summer '68' was good enough, while Gilmour's 'Fat Old Sun' featured real church bells and some tasteful guitar work. The record hit its nadir on the sound-effects romp 'Alan's Psychedelic Breakfast'. Probably because of its transparency and obvious 'pop' accessibility, it was Pink Floyd's first UK number-one album. Interestingly, it was recorded on Abbey Road's fairly slick eight-track equipment and was part engineered by Alan Parsons, a young technician who'd worked with The Beatles. Parsons would play a crucial role in Pink Floyd's future fortunes.

With a big commercial success behind them Pink Floyd entered Abbey Road in early 1971 to begin recording on a high. In the grand experimental tradition they wanted to make a recording with the probable title *Music For Household Objects*, but the planned series of melodies derived from the timbres of glasses and cutlery did not transpire. Various musical fragments were produced on normal instruments, the music honed over seven weeks of recording which saw the group use other studios such as Morgan, AIR and Command during the summer and autumn of 1971. AIR studios had a new sixteen-track facility and Command was used to create a quadraphonic mix. Pink Floyd were determined to create a form of Hi-Fidelity rock and with *Meddle* (1971), their sixth original album, they succeeded admirably.

Housed in a mysterious untitled green sleeve which looked like a textured image from the heavens (but in reality was a submerged ear), the album opened with 'One Of These Days', which began with the sound of wind and a ricocheting bass sound. The bass was basically two basses, one played by Gilmour, the other played by Waters through the ever-present Binson Echorec unit. The rest of 'One Of These Days' consisted of Mason's backwards-recorded cymbals, another Gilmour bass put through a high vibrato amplification setting, a searing lap steel guitar tuned to an open E chord, organ and drums. This was only a taster for the magnificent 'Echoes', a veritable cerebral voyage in sound. 'Echoes' was the first time that Pink Floyd truly conveyed the profundity of their vision on disc. Millions would lie back and close their eyes and just travel to this heavenly music. The piece began with Richard Wright's grand-piano 'ping', an effect accidentally found by putting the natural piano sound through a rotating Leslie speaker. When Wright played the piano it had a 'watery' effect akin to an electronic harp. A series of backwards-taped drums and cymbals accompanied Gilmour's creamy guitar, which led to the first series of dreamy subaqueous verses (sung by Wright and Gilmour). After a fine instrumental passage the phenomenal sound of Echoreced bass with drums, rhythmic organ and scorching electric guitar kicked in at the seventh minute. Halfway through the entire creation this dissolved into a ghoulishy dark phase of screaming gulls, rumbling sounds and spooky effects created by high-fretted guitars and by moving metal objects on bass and guitar strings. Ten minutes from the end this was superseded by sustained organ chords, then the 'pinging' piano, a ratcheting bass, the play of cymbals, the increasing volume of loud guitar and finally the upward chromatic slide of Gilmour's electric guitar, leading to the comparative quiet of the last two verses, which referred to the sunlight as the 'quiet ambassadors of morning'. The listener was left in no doubt that this was an aural voyage similar in sensibility to a good LSD trip. My favourite Pink Floyd music of all time occurs in the last three minutes, where the loud drums give way to a rising vocal wind effect faded into sun-dappled soft guitar, piano and soft bass with spatial percussion. This gorgeous instrumental was resolved with a windy sound loop similar to the album's beginning and the pinging of the treated piano.

When given the opportunity to play this brilliant new music in a Roman amphitheatre and have it filmed, Pink Floyd jumped at the chance. The French director Adrian Maben did a wonderful job on *Pink Floyd Live At Pompeii* (1972), filmed in Italy, Paris and Abbey Road at the end of 1971 and the beginning of 1972. The result was an eye-opening glimpse into the Floyd's working method. Now available on video, it shows that the Floyd's live instrumentation was nothing elaborate – Gilmour played his Fender Strat through a number of effects units, Waters played Fender bass, Mason had a double drum kit and Wright still banged away on his Farfisa Duo organ. In fact Wright had the lion's share of sound equipment, using the Binson Echorec and augmenting the sound with a Hammond organ and grand piano. The WEM amplification was standard but large for its time. The group's Chinese gong was also present. Also striking were the characteristic flat black and gold Sennheiser microphones. The studio footage showcased the group in Abbey Road writing stuff for *The Dark Side Of The Moon*, later to become simply *Dark Side Of The Moon* – their high-concept best-seller.

Most people think of the album as having been recorded in one simple stretch of six months but in fact *Dark Side Of The Moon* was achieved over a staggeringly short studio time of thirty-eight days, two sessions in the summer and autumn of

1972, and another at the outset of 1973. More beguiling is the fact that the group were up to their necks in work – tours of Britain, Japan and North America; another film soundtrack for Barbet Schroeder (*The Valley*, which featured tribal chants); and a French ballet tour. At the close of 1971 Roger Waters begun tinkering around with a musical suite about things which irritate in the everyday life of a travelling group. Hassles about money, travel, time and the loss of one's bearings were all worked into a loose concept titled *Eclipse* in a North London rehearsal studio at the very beginning of 1972. Rick Wright, for his part, came up with lots of keyboard instrumentals while Roger Waters worked hard on the lyrics. As with The Beatles' *Sgt. Pepper*, this led to the subsequent deployment of found tape sounds, electronic sequences, repeating motifs and a willingness to explore areas defined by such composers as Stockhausen and Cage. In truth, thirty-six years after Cage had made his famous speech about the future of music encompassing 'all sounds of the imagination and time', Pink Floyd would embrace all of that to make *Dark Side Of The Moon* a classic album.

The recording sessions at Abbey Road were divided into three blocks in the early summer and late autumn of 1972, and January 1973, between tours of the US and Europe. Engineer Alan Parsons recorded the basic band structures on sixteen-track with no noise reduction. Almost all effects were generated by tape machines. A second sixteen-track tape process was used to give more space for the complex overdubbing the album required. Because of tape hiss problems, Dolby noise reduction was used here. Other recording aspects were direct injection of instruments into the console without amplification, simple reverb and a customized EMI tone box. The real glamour of *Dark Side Of The Moon* lay in its use of electronic and tape sounds. The electronics derived from the usual Binson Echorec and, most importantly, two Synthi A synthesizers coupled with a three-octave Synthi keyboard. (These were portable synthesizers made by EMS which both Waters and Gilmour found invaluable for producing a variety of original electronic effects.) Gilmour used another EMS guitar gizmo and a phasing pedal. Mixed with an excellent palette of Wright's piano and organ tones plus silken female singers and Dick Parry's breathy sax, the results mingled the strange with the familiar in a way that guaranteed a timeless quality.

Dark Side Of The Moon quickly graduated into a thematic album about communication, death, belief, violence and insanity. Roger Waters laced the record with taped interviews, most notably from two Irishmen – the reflective Abbey Road employee Jerry Driscoll and the guitarist Henry McCullough. There was the recurring heartbeat drum sequence which opened and closed the record. There was Clare Torry's extraordinarily effusive scat performance on 'The Great Gig In The Sky', but above all there was a feeling of interlocking perfection which saw ideas and melodic fragments surface and submerge only to reappear in a different guise later in the record. One of the last things recorded was the opener, 'Speak To Me', with its heartbeat drum, ticking clocks, voices, cash-register noise, ominous synthesizer whirrs, Torry's spine-tingling scream and then the wonderfully arcing and treble-full steel sound of Gilmour's guitar as it led into 'Breathe'.

One of the most important tracks on *Dark Side Of The Moon* was 'On The Run', which featured a rolling synthesizer sequence generated from the Synthi A. This took ages to generate. Philip Glass has remarked how much this borrowed from Minimalism, its robotic character pre-dating the famous Techno beat. 'On The Run' was incredibly impressive for its time, with its darting sound effects of planes, trains and a climaxing explosion. With the addition of running steps, heavy breathing and oscillator noise, the effect of humanity being literally annihilated by speeded-up transport has never been more graphically realized in sound. Equally, 'The Great Gig In The Sky', with Torry's wordless 'outburst' and Wright's elegiac piano, was one of the greatest of rock instrumentals. 'Money', with its seven-note bass riff, was memorable for Wright's humid Wurlitzer Electric piano playing and Gilmour's effects-laden guitar solos. 'Us And Them' came from some unused Ambient piano material Rick Wright had written for Antonioni in 1969. The use of Wright's wavering Farfisa organ, a waltz-like slow tempo and much echo-delay made this song sound like aural hypnosis. 'Any Colour You Like' was another awesome electronicized instrumental full of shimmering Synthi keyboard and a Gilmour guitar solo put through a Uni-Vibe chorus box in honour of Jimi Hendrix. Here lengthy electronic tones generated by the Synthi could be heard in the background.

Dark Side Of The Moon was more than just a record – it was a defining cultural moment. Ever since *Atom Heart Mother* Hipgnosis had designed album covers for Pink Floyd which left out their name and the album title. This air of mystery generated by the seemingly anonymous covers increased interest in the group and its music. For *Dark Side Of The Moon* Storm Thorgerson went all out and ended up with a ray of light refracting through a prism on a black sleeve. The emblem for the record was the Great Pyramids and the millions who bought it felt they were getting a profound rock experience. Quickly it became an American number-one album and Pink Floyd became famous, even attracting the interest of Andy Warhol. During their tours of 1973 they used a giant mirror-ball and searchlights, but by the summer of 1974 they were using a forty-foot circular screen to project films to complement *Dark Side Of The Moon* during its performance. Completed with lasers and inflatables, the post-*Dark Side* live arena and stadium shows would define the colossal sound and light extravaganzas of subsequent years.

Though the Floyd had reached an advanced state of the art in sound on record and with their customized quadraphonic live system, they were still not satisfied. The winter of 1973 saw them try to resuscitate the *Music For Household Objects* project from 1971 with little success. By the spring of 1974 they were rehearsing new material for more concerts. Out of these sessions came a four-note ringing guitar arpeggio by Gilmour in G minor. This note struck Waters as being so mournful it became the basis for 'Shine On You Crazy Diamond', a song about human withdrawal from society, a veritable homage to Syd Barrett. This would be the main focus of their next album, *Wish You Were Here*, a recording which was done under conditions of complete physical and emotional exhaustion (and around two North American touring jaunts) during the first seven months of 1975.

Wish You Were Here was by far Pink Floyd's greatest achievement and still stands up as the most encapsulating of 1970s records. It is a perfect realization of Ambient rock; its twenty-six-minute, nine-part 'Shine On' suite saw Gilmour, Wright, Waters and Mason achieve a purity of sound that other 70s acts could only dream of. Moreover it worked on several levels. As a statement it summed up Pink Floyd's life-story as a group, from the loss of their founder Syd Barrett (who turned up during the mixing phase) to the corporate wheelings and dealings of a band who commanded a $1-million Columbia advance in 1974. Its sound was full of sheen, Rick Wright's keyboard vamping at times alluding to the glitz of disco. If the group had their origins in a 60s haze of hallucination, *Wish You Were Here* was more in keeping with its cocaine-fuelled times. Even its white cover had an air of 70s chic, coming with a postcard of an exotically located diver. Again Storm Thorgerson's cover art was a stroke of genius. With its front image of a Hollywood back-lot handshake as one executive burns, its back shot of a faceless and bodyless businessman in the desert and its inner sleeve showing a drifting scarf and a splashless diver, the sleeve art was one continuous observation. Each photo even had an allusion to its elemental representation – burning, falling sand and spouting water. The whole was housed in black cellophane with only a sticker on the front of interlocking robotic hands against a representation of the four elements, earth, air, fire and water.

Wish You Were Here's opening and closing track, 'Shine On You Crazy Diamond', took six weeks to get right. Work at Abbey Road was difficult, getting the correct drum sound and fitting the parts together, but the results were justifiably magnificent. Rick Wright, in particular, shone with the mix of MiniMoog synth, electric organ and Fender Rhodes electric piano he applied to the enterprise. And David Gilmour's guitar was at its most lyrical and varied. The opening of 'Shine On' featured an almost inaudible dripping sequence from a Synthi A, followed by a rising electronic organ chord held for two and a half minutes in G minor, overlaid by the MiniMoog switched to a horn setting augmented by Gilmour's heavenly piercing liquid guitar. After about four minutes (delicate tinkling chimes in the background), Gilmour's famous open-stringed four-note G-minor chord was heard for the first time, its overtones defining a physical space all around it. It was eight and a half minutes before Waters's melancholic lyric was heard. This quickly faded out and just after the eleventh minute the windy sax of old Cambridge friend Dick Parry arrives as if from heaven, backed by Gilmour's slowly strummed electric chord. In contrast the subsequent track, 'Welcome To The Machine', was centred around a myriad of electronic effects – vari-speeded tape, automatic double-tracking and repeat echo. Beginning with the sound of opening and clamping shut mechanical doors, its defining quality was the relentless throb of the VCS3 Synthi with its boom echo-repeat used in conjunction with a high-frequency Moog synth. The title track featured the sound of Gilmour's guitar without the bass frequencies, car-radio interference, Gilmour's finest-ever acoustic guitar intro and Waters' best-ever lyric, sung by Rick Wright. The album climaxed with the rest of 'Shine On You Crazy Diamond'; the sound of wind followed by the MiniMoog, much lap steel guitar, and in its final six minutes Gilmour picking harmonic notes off his electric guitar to Wright's wonderfully reverberating jazz-tinged Fender Rhodes piano. The album ended as it began with Wright's horn-like synthesizer enveloped in the receding electronic washes of the VCS3 Synthi. Recorded on twenty-four-track equipment, it was the very best amalgam of acoustic, electric and electronic instruments. It was also the last time the four members of Pink Floyd would work together as a cohesive unit.

Wish You Were Here was a number-one album on both sides of the Atlantic on its release in the autumn of 1975. The group did a subsequent quadraphonic mix and built the Britannia Row studio in a North London chapel. There they recorded *Animals* (1977), much of it based on material they had rejected during the *Wish You Were Here* sessions. Dominated by Waters's jaundiced view of society (and a nod towards George Orwell's novel *Animal Farm*), *Animals* was less ambitious than its predecessors, with much of the emphasis placed on Waters's biting lyrics. The album was well received and made famous by its cover shot of a pig floating between the smokestacks of Battersea power station. (This cover would later be adapted by The Orb.)

Waters became disillusioned by subsequent tours and wrote *The Wall* (1979), a double album of personal antagonism, recorded over a year in France, Los Angeles and New York with the Canadian producer Bob Ezrin. Despite its American number-one position, it was pure conceit, and only memorable for Gilmour's guitar composition 'Comfortably Numb'. In fact Rick Wright was fired during the sessions. Subsequent ego battles, poor recordings, financial problems and such were to make the tabloid headlines but are of little interest here. Waters officially resigned in 1985 but two years later Gilmour again toured Pink Floyd as a trio with backing musicians. Musically, both Waters's solo effort, *Amused To Death* (1992) and *The Division Bell* (1994) by Gilmour, Wright and Mason (as Pink Floyd), have interesting moments, but they lack the completeness of both *Dark Side Of The Moon* and *Wish You Were Here*, where the group reached the apogee of their art.

LISTENING

The bulk of Pink Floyd recordings are on EMI Harvest in the UK and Columbia in the US. *Dark Side Of The Moon* was the first CD release by EMI in 1984. The original engineer, Alan Parsons, supervised the remastering of the album in 1992, though personally I prefer the less trebly original CD. The first set of digital remasters appeared in a boxed set titled *Shine On* in 1992.

Subsequently they achieved individual remastered CD release in 1994–5. *Wish You Were Here* is by far the best Pink Floyd album on CD, its quiet passages fully illuminated by the medium. For those in search of great Ambiences in sound, both that album and *Meddle* are essential. For those interested in psychedelia, *The Piper At The Gates Of Dawn* is one of the great 1967 albums.

The best visual document is *Pink Floyd Live At Pompeii* (Polygram Video), with all the *Dark Side Of The Moon* studio footage intact. EMI reissued the fascinating soundtrack to *More* in 1996 with an expanded booklet of stills from Barbet Schroeder's film. Rhino's 1997 reissue of the *Zabriskie Point* soundtrack contains valuable rare Pink Floyd out-takes from the sessions for Antonioni in Rome in 1969. If you are interested in latter-day Floyd check out *David Gilmour* (Harvest 1978), Rick Wright's *Wet Dream* (Harvest 1978), Roger Waters's *Amused To Death* (Sony 1992) and Pink Floyd's *The Division Bell* (EMI 1994). As David Gilmour has pointed out, this album showed himself, Wright and Mason back playing at full strength; Dick Parry was on saxophone, there were soulful backing vocalists and the theme of broken communication was topped off by another Storm Thorgerson sleeve. Luscious, creamy and often mellifluous, *The Division Bell* was a creditable post-Waters comeback.

KEITH EMERSON, KING CRIMSON, YES

What's fascinating in hindsight is that one of the most criticized movements in 1970s music, 'progressive rock', was at the time known as 'flash-rock', 'space-rock' or, more accurately, 'techno-rock'. The latter title derived not only from the form's fixation with new synthesizer and keyboard technology but also with its love of complex musical structures, changing time signatures and strange classical ambitions. In terms of sound, 'progressive rock' was a compressed medium, its busy alternating textures more at home with nineteenth-century Romanticism than the New Minimalism coming from America. In a way 'progressive' was really 'regressive' rock, happily harking back to older forms and ancient times (myths, legends, medieval history) to convey an aura of mystery. Hence musicians such as Pink Floyd and Mike Oldfield have little in common with the worst conceits of 'progressive rock', which included playing double- or triple-necked guitars and making triple-gatefold overblown concept albums. A very English phenomenon, the form reached its most absurd on the David Greenslade keyboard album *The Pentateuch Of The Cosmogony* (EMI 1979), meaning 'the book of the universe', which came out as a boxed double album with a lavish forty-seven-page fantasy book.

Ignoring the tripe, 'progressive rock' did produce some great music and created some important ripples in the history of Ambient and Electronic music. Keith Emerson, King Crimson and Yes all distinguished themselves in the field and though they all released too many bad records some of what they did has lasting value. Keith Emerson was a Yorkshireman, born in 1944, who had ambitions as a classical pianist. A move to London in the 1960s saw him playing rhythm and blues on the round-toned Hammond organ. Soon he was backing soul singer P.P. Arnold with a group which became The Nice. Emerson was an incredible showman who emulated Jimi Hendrix with his on-stage antics. His Hammond was brutalized nightly, stabbed with daggers, whipped and set fire to. Leonard Bernstein was furious at their use of his 'America' and had The Nice's single version rescinded in the US. Five Mercury albums were released between 1967 and 1970, all drawing heavily from such classical composers as Bach, Tchaikovsky and Sibelius. Impressed by the sound of the Moog synthesizer on Wendy Carlos's *Switched-On Bach*, Emerson paid a small fortune for a row of Moog modules in 1970.

This infatuation with the Moog led to the formation of Emerson, Lake & Palmer, whose eponymous album for Island in 1970 featured the Moog sound. One song, 'Lucky Man', was a big hit in America and so impressed was Robert Moog that Emerson became one of his most valued customers. Moog met Emerson in 1971 and Moog's factory took special care of his system, even customizing performance trigger-boxes so Emerson could reset it without effort on stage. Emerson's group, now known as ELP, became a stadium-rock sensation in the US, performing below proscenium arches and eventually touring with orchestras. The approach was technical excellence in the studio, leading to constant overdubbing of tracks. Live it was spectacle, with Emerson performing in front of a huge Moog tower. The 1973 opus *Brain Salad Surgery* (Manti Core) even included a version of Aaron Copland's *Fanfare For The Common Man*. By then Emerson's Moog had been customized to include two huge sequencers, lines of programmers and a TV set with a waveform pattern blinking across it. On stage Emerson placed his four-cabinet Moog stack behind his Hammond organ and surrounded himself with every other type of keyboard, piano and synth he could lay his hands on. He also used the Moog's large ribbon controller to launch fireworks! If this all sounds silly, Emerson's giant Moog is still going today, having been modified by the original technicians. At seventeen square feet and an astonishing 550 pounds it has to be one of the most famous vintage synthesizers in operation.

King Crimson were a different proposition entirely. According to founder member Robert Fripp, the band was 'a social/political/economic experiment with a life of its own. In essence a form of anarchy with no leaders, interchangeable roles and no one really in charge.' Fripp's ideal was to capture a vibrancy and this occurred when a group of musicians, mostly from Bournemouth, started rehearsing in the basement of a London café. The music was full of flutes and acoustic guitars while Pete Sinfield's lyrics veered from fairy-tale to dark portents. Greg Lake was an excellent bassist and singer. Mike Giles was a powerful drummer and Fripp's electric guitar could switch from velvet subtlety one moment to awesome virtuosity the next. Flautist Ian McDonald also played keyboards, including the Mellotron, perhaps the most defining characteristic of

Crimson's sound. Their Mellotron Mk2 had two thirty-five-note keyboards with each note able to play one of three audio tapes which could last up to nine seconds. These tapes were filled with musical 'samples', usually organ, strings or harpsichord, which made it a very versatile tool that could even blend timbres. King Crimson used it to devastating effect on their Island debut album of 1969.

In The Court Of The Crimson King is one of the defining rock moments of the twentieth century. It is said to have augured 'progressive rock' and certainly its screaming-head cover art and song titles, which broke down into subparts, went a long way to support that view. Yet its contents were unique, drawing from a variety of sources, including jazz, flower-power ballad and orchestral music, particularly Fripp's interest in Dvořák and Stravinsky. The album had a precision in the arrangements and the lengthy movements of the title track and 'Epitaph' were cunningly achieved. Recorded in just eight days, on its release it established Crimson as 'one of the world's best performing rock groups'. Even before the album was out their reputation saw them support The Rolling Stones at a free concert attended by 650,000 in London's Hyde Park during the summer of 1969. Fripp viewed King Crimson as very much 'in the moment', for the first incarnation split up on tour in the US at the close of the 1960s. Greg Lake left in 1970 to form Emerson, Lake & Palmer. Pete Sinfield continued to experiment with a VCS3 Synthi until he too departed the fold in 1971. Crimson went through at least nine line-up changes in the 1970s (a classic formation from 1973 to 1974 included Yes drummer Bill Bruford and two Mellotrons) but did not regain its momentum until 1981 with *Discipline* (EG), an album which included a gorgeous instrumental dedication to Paul Bowles's novel *The Sheltering Sky*.

Yes seemed to dominate the 1970s albums market, particularly with those eye-catching fantasy sleeves of mountain lakes, ocean floors and frozen ancient terrains courtesy of Royal College of Art graduate Roger Dean. In their day they crystallized the best and worst of what 'progressive rock' had to offer. Most importantly, *Close To The Edge* (1972) still conveys a unique sound world. Yes were a product of the 1960s, formed in 1968 in London by Lancashire singer Jon Anderson and public-school-educated bassist Chris Squire. With teenage jazz drummer Bill Bruford in tow Yes featured a Hammond organ and a music heavily influenced by West Coast American rock and pop soul group The Fifth Dimension. Theirs was a sweet, aerated sound topped off by Anderson's distinctively high alto vocal. Made for Atlantic, early records like the orchestral *Time And A Word* (1970) lacked real confidence, but the arrival of psychedelic guitarist Steve Howe and producer Eddie Offord changed all that in 1971. Offord was keenly interested in what Keith Emerson had done with the Moog synth and had one set up in Advision studios, where he worked with Yes. Londoner Howe had distinguished himself in Tomorrow, even learning the Indian sitar. *The Yes Album* (1971) was a huge leap in quality, with Howe contributing a brilliant effects-laden guitar solo to 'Starship Trooper'.

After an American tour Yes lost their organ player and recruited Rick

Wakeman, who played not only the Hammond organ but also the Mellotron, MiniMoog synthesizer, Fender Rhodes electric piano, harpsichord, pipe organ and anything else with keys. Born in 1949 in London, Wakeman was innately musical, attending the Royal College of Music at sixteen. Attracted to lucrative session work, he quit college to go professional, playing the Mellotron on David Bowie's eerie 'Space Oddity' single in 1969. With the definitive line-up of Anderson, Bruford, Wakeman, Squire and Howe, Yes cut their first Roger Dean-illustrated album, *Fragile* (1971), which showcased Squire as an excellent propulsive and technically visionary bass player, especially on 'The Fish'.

Three months in the making, *Close To The Edge* (Atlantic 1972) was another decade-defining sixteen-track marvel full of wonderful tape effects and synthesizer noises. Both Squire's bass and Howe's guitars seemed to be put through every gizmo then available. Howe even played a Coral electric sitar on the album, an electric instrument which had thirteen resonating strings to go with the additional six. The title track took up an entire album side and began with the incremental volume of tape-looped natural wild birdsong backed by a metallic hurdy-gurdy sound. Then began an unforgettable elastic bass and electric guitar twin solo and a series of jaw-dropping time changes and instrumental flourishes as the piece zigzagged its way across an incredible soundscape. After eight and a half minutes the piece became Ambient – all keyboards and guitars being made to mimic the sound of watery terrain, complete with dripping-water effect. Wakeman's reverberated piano here was at its minimal best. Ostensibly the end of the subsection 'I Get Up I Get Down', this special aural space was completely ruined by a gratuitous Gothic church-organ solo by Wakeman.

It was here that 'progressive rock' lost its way, for in 1973 Wakeman recorded a whole suite of keyboard musics dedicated to the deceased wives of the Tudor King Henry VIII. Not content with using two Mellotron 400s, four Mini-Moogs and everything else, Wakeman saw himself as some caped, blond-haired crusader of Arthurian legend. The outcome was the egotistical *Myths And Legends Of King Arthur* (A&M 1975), whose London premier on ice featured a ninety-piece orchestra and choir, a rock band and skating clashing knights. This came after extensive touring with Yes had produced the triple-live *Yessongs* (1973) and the bloated double-album single-composition nightmare of *Tales From Topographic Oceans* (1973), only remembered for Dean's impressive sleeve painting of fish swimming in a nocturnal underwater dream world of stars and Mayan pyramids. Curiously, the more pompous the music got, the more successful it was, both Wakeman and Yes racking up UK number ones and high US chart placings in 1974.

LISTENING

Emerson, Lake & Palmer's self-titled first album and *Brain Salad Surgery*, released in 1970 and 1973 respectively, were reissued on disc by Essential in 1996. Both King Crimson and Yes were given the CD boxed-set treatment in 1991, with

Frame By Frame (Virgin) and *The Yes Years* (Atco). Back in 1988 Robert Fripp and engineer Tony Arnold remastered the entire Crimson catalogue. The new CD version of *In The Court Of The Crimson King* was released in the US in 1989, in the UK in 1991 and again in a de-luxe gatefold-sleeve format by Virgin in 1999. Later tracks, like the acoustic-guitar 'Peace A Theme' (1970) and the Mellotron flute-led 'Trio' (1974), are some of the loveliest Crimson instrumentals put to disc. Yes made a comeback of sorts in 1974, approaching Vangelis to join them before settling on classical Swiss keyboardist Patrick Moraz. 'Soon', from the album *Relayer*, had an expansive overflowing richness. But *Close To The Edge* (Atlantic) is the definitive Yes album, remastered by Joe Gastwirt in 1996, its simple green cover-art making it stand out from the rest of the Yes oeuvre. Other 'progressive' groups of note were Soft Machine, Caravan, Van Der Graaf Generator and Wishbone Ash. Soft Machine featured drummer-vocalist Robert Wyatt and were part of free-form psychedelia before recording a debut album with Tom Wilson in 1968. Caravan made high-quality jazz pop and combined flute and electric organ to impressive effect on their first two Decca albums, *If I Could Do It All Over Again* (1970) and *In The Land Of Grey And Pink* (1971). Van Der Graaf Generator hailed from Manchester and specialized in a sheets-of-sound vocal and instrumental style with no lead guitars. 'House With No Door' from their third album, *H to He, Who Am The Only One* (Charisma 1970), still stands up. Finally Wishbone Ash specialized in a multiple-guitar velvet rock sound so smooth that *Argus* (MCA 1972) sounds today as if it came from some mist-shrouded castle in the sky.

LED ZEPPELIN

At the time of their meteoric rise to fame during the early 1970s, Led Zeppelin were seen as another English blues rock band or at best a 'heavy-metal' group. Distance and the emergence of their music on one of the first CD boxed sets, *Led Zeppelin* (Atlantic 1990), saw them undergo a huge re-evaluation. The CD medium afforded a deeper impression of a music that was full of 'light and shade'. Guitar shaman Jimmy Page emerged as a formidable producer, his work in the studio, especially with Jimi Hendrix engineer Eddie Kramer, standing up as some of the greatest Ambient rock ever committed to tape. Zeppelin's true ability was in drawing from a wide palette of blues, modal folk music, Eastern music and electronica and painting it on to tape in glorious cinemascopic sound.

Born in Greater London in 1944, Jimmy Page began serious guitar playing at fourteen, inspired by early rock 'n' roll records. Soon he was practising blues and folk styles. He joined various ensembles before ill-health saw him enter Croydon Art College. Afterwards he became a session guitarist, his Fender Stratocaster and customized Gibson Les Paul appearing on some very famous records. Two of his greatest achievements were his electric playing on the intensely psychedelic 'Happenings Ten Years Time Ago' by The Yardbirds in 1966 and on Donovan's 1968 opus 'Hurdy Gurdy Man'. During the mid-1960s he was house producer for The Rolling Stones' manager Andrew Oldham and even recorded with the German singer and actress Nico. His fearsome guitar duets with Jeff Beck of The Yardbirds were caught on film for posterity by Michelangelo Antonioni in his award-winning 1967 film *Blow-Up*.

By that stage Page was playing a Fender Telecaster. Soon he became chief guitarist in The Yardbirds, their 1967 album *Little Games* (EMI 1967) showcasing his absorbing interest in the 'folk baroque' style of acoustic guitarists such as Davy Graham. 'White Summer' was basically a version of the old Irish tune 'She Moved Through The Fair' with a raga bent. Page had shown an interest in the Indian sitar but found it impossible to play. Studying the work of Rodrigo, he transferred modal tunings to electric and acoustic guitars. This feature alone would give Led Zeppelin's music a distinctive edge.

Led Zeppelin came out of 1967 sessions with Kent-born John Paul Jones. Keyboards, arranging, strings, woodwinds and bass were Jones's specialities. Led Zeppelin became a band in 1968 when the two met a pair of musicians from the British Midlands, drummer John Bonham and vocalist Robert Plant. Bonham would become the most sampled drummer in history and Plant's incredible vocal range, from cooing intimacy to full-flight falsetto, would define a whole new style of rock phrasing. All shared a love of the blues and a belief in the power of music to transform. Their first album was recorded in Olympic Studios, London in thirty hours during the autumn of 1968. Its release in the first month of 1969 invented a new form of 'heavy rock' music, establishing Page (with his lightning-fast leads and stop-start-stop chordal riffs) as the next evolutionary step in electric-guitar music after Hendrix.

If live Page impressed audiences with a violin bow across his Telecaster, then in the studio 'Black Mountainside' evinced an absorption of Indian tabla music and the open-tuned modal folk music of Scottish guitarist Bert Jansch. *Led Zeppelin 2* was recorded on the run in 1969, Page using two engineers associated with Jimi Hendrix, George Chkiantz in London and in New York the legendary Eddie Kramer. The latter's expertise influenced 'Whole Lotta Love', a song full of backwards Echoplexed guitar. On stage Page would get the same effect using a Thereminvox and thus became the second most famous user of the Russian invention after The Beach Boys. By now Page had made the Gibson Les Paul his electric guitar of choice.

The summer of 1970 saw Led Zeppelin go to Wales to write material in a country cottage. This folk-accented material was then recorded on the Rolling Stones Mobile at a deserted mansion in Hampshire called Headley Grange. Other studios were also used, including Electric Lady in New York with Eddie Kramer. *Led Zeppelin 3* boasted the strange, Eastern-tinged 'Friends', which included a Moog synthesizer and John Paul Jones conducting Indian string players. Another highlight was the open-G tuning of the nirvanic acoustic-guitar ballad 'That's The Way'. As a producer Jimmy Page was nearing his goal of creating a total Ambience in studio sound.

During the beginning of 1971 Headley Grange and the Rolling Stones Mobile were again the background for extraordinary recording sessions for Zeppelin's fourth, 'untitled' album (later dubbed *Led Zeppelin IV*). This time Page pushed equipment and location to its limits in order to get an other-worldly atmosphere. The mixture of hard-rocking blues and folk strains continued but with a greater emphasis on space and atmosphere. 'The Battle Of Evermore' was a beautiful acoustic guitar and mandolin instrumental powered by a duet between Plant and the dulcet tonsils of Fairport Con-vention's Sandy Denny. 'Going To California' was another open-G-tuned Page diamond while the construction of 'Stairway To Heaven' recalled the cyclical nature of US Minimalism. From its rustic opening of woodwinds and acoustic guitars to its eight-second fading chorus, 'Stairway' was destined to become the most famous song in rock. Finalized at Island studios, it contained what is for many the best Fender Telecaster lead-guitar solo ever recorded. Its famous descending chord sequences required Jimmy Page to use a specially built double-necked eighteen-string Gibson ES electric guitar on stage.

'Stairway To Heaven' was symphonic rock of rare grandeur yet it had super-clear definition. Early in 1972 Page and Plant extended this idea to recording with the Bombay Symphony Orchestra. Then that spring the entire group retired to Mick Jagger's country mansion, Stargroves, to again record on the Rolling Stones Mobile. Later mixing was done at Electric Lady in New York with Eddie Kramer at the controls, for what was titled in 1973 *Houses Of The Holy*. This album featured the apex of Page's orchestrated rock visions. 'The Rain Song' was without doubt Led Zeppelin's greatest achievement. It used a variation of Page's favoured open-G tuning and merged acoustic and electric guitars in seven and a half minutes of finely honed overdubbing. Moreover John Paul Jones's Mellotron and piano parts were masterfully interwoven. Jones, a dab hand at the Hammond organ, was also a VCS3 synthesizer buff. Its warbling sound was heard throughout the atmospheric tone-painting 'No Quarter', along with some discreet Jones piano touches.

A trip to Morocco would inspire 'Kashmir', recorded in 1974 at Headley Grange and recognized as the peak of Led Zeppelin's interest in Indian, Turkish and Moroccan music. Using an upward and downward sliding note formation in another one of his open guitar tunings (this time a form of D), Page created something suitably exotic, its sensuous Oriental feel matched by Jones's Mellotron and carefully scored orchestral accompaniment. Post-Zeppelin Page and Plant would revisit this terrain for *No Quarter* (Fontana 1994), a reunion album which featured a live 'Kashmir' with an eleven-man Egyptian ensemble. The project had begun with the duo writing around African drum loops sourced in Paris. The resultant 'Wonderful One' featured an open-chorded guitar tuning similar to that used on 'The Rain Song'. Another trip to Morocco saw them record with the Gnawa trance musicians of Marrakesh. They even returned to Snowdonia to rekindle the folk sound of *Led Zeppelin 3*, this time with added bodhran and hurdy-gurdy accompaniment.

LISTENING

By the late 1990s Led Zeppelin were Atlantic's most successful recording act ever, with the second most lucrative back-catalogue in the world. Jimmy Page had remastered the entire back-catalogue in 1990, appearing on two impressive boxed sets in 1990 and 1993. The individual remastered discs came on the market in 1994. The appearance of *No Quarter* in early 1995 featured not only old Zeppelin material with a twenty-nine-piece English string orchestra but also four new songs couched in African and Arabic instrumentation. Outside Led Zeppelin, Jimmy Page has used his extensive home-studio facilities to record music for film, notably for Kenneth Anger's early-70s film *Lucifer Rising* and Michael Winner's early-80s *Death Wish* series.

MIKE OLDFIELD

When Mike Oldfield's multimillion-selling debut album *Tubular Bells* was released on the fledgling Virgin label in May 1973 most critics could not understand its nature. They saw it as a breakthrough for 'classical rock', a work akin to that of Debussy, full of logic and flawless musicianship. The fact that Oldfield was only nineteen when it was conceived, and played all the instruments himself, made it seem a daunting feat. The work was seen as a 'concept album' and comparisons were made with other 'progressive' music made by Pink Floyd, Emerson Lake & Palmer and The Electric Prunes. When Oldfield performed the two-part opus lasting nearly fifty minutes at a London concert hall in 1973 he incorporated brass, woodwind, organ and a choir. Even his old friend David Bedford recorded an orchestral version with the Royal Philharmonic in 1975. No wonder it was seen as a classical work.

By the mid-1970s rock historian Tony Palmer was declaring Oldfield the future of music, its veritable saviour no less. *Tubular Bells* went on to sell sixteen million copies globally and establish one of the most visionary rock labels of all time in Virgin. But a listen to the recording makes it abundantly clear why it was so successful. Not yet familiar with American Minimalism, critics did not have the tools with which to analyse the music. Simply put, *Tubular Bells* was the first commercially successful use of Minimalism in rock. Its beautiful opening (used as the theme for the 1973 film *The Exorcist*) is a wonderful example of Minimalist composition. A cycle of nine notes is played on piano, then repeated with the last note dropped. This nine-eight phrase is then played on a glockenspiel. Accompanying this trance-like sound is the sound of an E drone played on a Farfisa organ. This phrase is returned to again and again throughout the course of 'Part One', resolving itself at the end of twenty-four minutes in a lovely antique guitar coda. What's interesting is that it is in a modal key of C, played on the white notes of a piano. Hence it is an heir to Terry Riley's *In C* of 1964, one of the first Minimalist compositions. Moreover its shifting accent on the downbeat is mindful of the work of Steve Reich. Oldfield and Reich shared a love of African drumming and its hypnotic beat structure.

Oldfield was born in Reading, England, in 1953. A shy introvert, he escaped through music. At an early age he explored both classical and folk styles, spending all his time outside of school practising various instruments, especially the guitar. He made an album with his folk-singing sister Sally in 1968 and joined a rock band fronted by Kevin Ayers. When he left that in 1971 Oldfield set about a creating a composition by rebuilding a Bang & Olufsen tape machine to make four tracks. He made the rounds of record companies to no avail. At the time Richard Branson was establishing a mail-order record business and a recording studio. By the end of 1971 Branson had said no to Oldfield's tapes.

A crucial figure in the Oldfield story is Tom Newman, a musician, producer and engineer who helped shape Branson's Manor studios in Oxfordshire. Highly influenced by The Beatles' *Sgt. Pepper*, Newman and his group July had cut a psychedelic album in 1967 using such Beatles standards as phasing, backwards recording, vari-speed tape, echo and distortion. Newman even sought advice from The Beatles' producer, George Martin, on installing eight-track equipment in the country-house setting of the Manor. By 1972 it was a live-in facility boosted to sixteen-track recording with Dolby stereo, very good for its time.

Oldfield impressed Newman with his tapes and literally moved into the Manor. Branson gave the go-ahead and *Tubular Bells* was recorded over a month, the major first half recorded in a single week. Oldfield overdubbed all the guitars, basses, piano, organ, percussion and tubular bells himself. Thousands of tape overdubs were done with around twenty different instruments while Newman and engineer Simon Heyworth rigged up new equalization gizmos to boost frequencies. Tape loops were also used and lots of echo incorporated from various sources such as a steel platter and a rewired speaker-amp system. Branson attempted to sell the results to others early in 1973 but with no interest risked releasing the work himself. He called the label Virgin and by the summer of 1973 *Tubular Bells* was a number-one album.

Highlights from the recording were the sound of double-speeded instruments, the wave-like boost in volume which heralded the first entry of the ringing tubular bell sound four minutes in, the effortless melodic invention of Oldfield himself on various guitars, the serial role-play of instruments in the finale (introduced by comedian Vivian Stanshall) and its glorious stereophonic sound. The often-forgotten 'Part Two' featured some lovely Hammond organ and Spanish guitar Ambience sixteen and a half minutes in. Certainly Oldfield was a musician who could paint a mood with sound.

Early success at twenty did not hinder his musical ambition, though *Hergest*

Ridge (1974) was a disappointment by comparison. By 1975 Oldfield had returned to form with *Ommadawn*, an elaborate album of instrumental timbres featuring Celtic harp and bodhran, Greek bouzouki, synthesizers, Northumbrian pipes and African drumming. As with *Tubular Bells*, *Ommadawn* featured Sally Oldfield on backing vocals but expanded the contributors to timpani, brass, strings and the sound of uileann pipes courtesy of The Chieftains' Paddy Moloney. Even Oldfield's brother Terry played the pan pipes. The African drummers of Jabula came into their own on the drifting finale of the nineteen-minute 'Part One'. They would be heard again on Oldfield's 1978 double-album *Incantations*. By 1984 Oldfield was making great folk-rock songs with Maggie Reilly such as 'To France' and that year he also scored Roland Joffe's award-winning film *The Killing Fields*. Yet his first success would not go away and in 1992 Warner Bros. encouraged him to record *Tubular Bells 2* using modern digital techniques. Even The Orb acknowledged Oldfield's importance by remixing part of this. While living in Ibiza, Oldfield was inspired by rave culture to record the beat-oriented *Tubular Bells 3* (WEA 1998).

LISTENING

During the faddish 1970s the original *Tubular Bells* was even remixed for quadraphonic listening. The analogue CD issue from the late 1980s still sounds great but a superlative boost in quality was achieved by Simon Heyworth and Tom Newman for Virgin's twenty-fifth anniversary gold edition of 1998 (which includes rare photos in a de-luxe booklet). *Ommadawn* is another great disc while an excellent overview of Oldfield's Virgin years can be found in the *Elements* CD boxed set of 1993.

THE GERMAN SCENE

One of the great mythologies of rock literature is how German rock and electronic music from the early 1970s came to be known as 'krautrock'. In 1993, in an article about the rebirth of the German band Faust, former jazz journal *The Wire* stated that it was 'the London music press, with characteristically snide xenophobia, which dubbed it "Krautrock"'. Over a year later the same magazine ran a leader article about 'krautrock' as if it was a *de facto* term, with large excerpts from a highly personalized account of 'The Great Cosmic Music, 1968 Onwards' by the eccentric English indie musician Julian Cope.

In response I wrote a letter to the magazine which described the word 'krautrock' as an 'Anglophile term derived from a post-war hangover'. In reply *The Wire* contended rather speciously that such groups as Cluster and Can had adopted the term. In fact this was never the case (though Faust did name a track 'Krautrock' when they recorded their fourth album in England in

1973). Moreover most writers accuse the eminent British musicologist Ian MacDonald of inventing the label during the early 1970s when he wrote about German music in the *New Musical Express*. In fact during December of 1972 MacDonald published three articles consecutively titled 'Germany Calling', two of them double broadsheet pages. In not one line did he mention the term 'krautrock'!

Instead MacDonald gave a jaw-droppingly accurate description of German rock of the late 60s and early 70s. For openers he stated that in the UK there was a total ignorance of continental rock. Secondly, there was a strong revolutionary spirit among Germany's youth since 1968. They disliked rich Anglo-American groups playing in their country and a lot of students demanded free entry. The concept of 'the revolutionary head' was paramount, a concept which 'challenged every accepted English and American standpoint'. The roots of new German rock were thus traced to a rejection of all previous forms, an acceptance of open improvisation, with 'no leaders'. Hence guitar heroes and singer-stars were out, group instrumental expression was in. MacDonald dubbed the resultant music 'tonally free sound improvisation'.

In this setting it was no wonder that electronics took over, 'the other-worldly capacities of the synthesizers' as MacDonald described them. He feared the dematerialization of humans as machines became more and more important to the Germans, Kraftwerk of course following the 'Man Machine' concept to its furthest extreme as they famously celebrated the coming of 'The Robots' and a 'Computer World' in their music. In great detail MacDonald went on to elucidate the various labels and the importance of the group studio where anything could happen. Fascinatingly, he pointed out that managers had to play in the band according to German law at the time and, more interestingly, the Arbeitsamt (Labour Exchange) did not allow any musician to be unemployed. If he or she was kicked out of a group, its officials quickly found another group to take them on.

Importantly, MacDonald noted that a lot of new German music was ignored in Germany until it found critical favour in the UK. As he sifted through band histories he laced his detailed observations with much humour. Records which Julian Cope would later ludicrously drool over in his *Krautrocksampler* (1995) were stylishly dispatched to oblivion. Of the early jams of Munich commune Amon Düül MacDonald said: 'The most valuable sociological inference to be made from these execrable records is that the early years of German rock coincided with a colossal boom in the sale of bongoes!' Most surprisingly, he did not go the standard route and had things to say about unknowns such as Mythos, Limbus 4, Embryo and the 'quite mortifying' Floh De Cologne. He found Kraftwerk lacking in any emotion and saw a future for a type of new German Romanticism based on a meeting of Wagner and the Moog synthesizer.

If MacDonald found Kraftwerk 'heartless' he considered NEU! to be 'tender', but reserved great praise for Can, the most powerful example of

German rock, some of their music 'as hypnotically engrossing as Bob Dylan's "Sad Eyed Lady Of The Lowlands"'. Cluster, Tangerine Dream, Klaus Schulze, Amon Düül and such were all given their due but he was genuinely impressed by Faust, who with their 'self-designed equipment made truly avant-garde music'. MacDonald presciently saw the mixture of revolutionary ideas and inadequate techniques as a genuinely strong basis for innovation. Nowhere did he ever mention the word 'krautrock' and I have to conclude that subsequent articles and arguments deriving the epithet from this source are pure myth.

CAN

The most potent expression of German experimental rock undoubtedly came from Can, a group of highly experienced composer-musicians formed in Cologne after the Paris youth riots of the summer of 1968. Can's approach to limitation and 'instant composition' soon became legendary, all facilitated by recording their own music in their own time at self-built studios in a castle and a cinema. With the basis of an ethnically derived rhythm section, tape collages and electronic keyboards were all absorbed into a mix which openly acknowledged the influence of Stockhausen, Cage, Pierre Schaeffer and American Minimal music. Normal rock and blues references were relegated to the background while New Music ideas were brought to the fore. Can believed in finding a new language through constant experimentation and improvisation, and thus album tracks often took up entire sides of LPs. Continuously testing the parameters of sound, they were one of the loudest groups in the history of rock but were capable of beautiful and elegiac compositions. A direct influence on the likes of Joy Division and New Order, Cabaret Voltaire, The KLF and The Orb, Can became a touchstone for what was most creative in modern music.

Founder Irmin Schmidt, born in 1937, had a strong background in classical music – piano and French horn – and had attended many music schools, including the Essen Academy, from which he graduated with a superlative distinction. He conducted the Vienna Philharmonic but on hearing the new sounds of Messiaen, Feldman and Cage opted to study ethnic music. During the 1960s he worked with Stockhausen and Cage at Darmstadt, where he met Holger Czukay and Jon Hassell. Having worked in art journalism and written music for various media, Schmidt journeyed to New York in 1966 and met the Minimalists Young, Reich and Riley. This meeting convinced him to form a new kind of group.

Back in Germany, Schmidt contacted flautist David Johnson and Holger Czukay. Born in 1938, Czukay was Polish with a background in choral music. After the war he had famously blown up a Russian ammunitions dump just to hear the sound of the explosion. He had worked in an electrical shop, studied bass at the Berlin Academy and worked with Stockhausen, who inspired his interests in tone building and sound analysis. In 1966 in Switzerland he met Michael Karoli, a Bavarian guitar player. Karoli, born in 1948, was a multi-instrumentalist from the age of four; by the early 1960s he could play anything on electric guitar from Mozart to Arabic music. He had a particular love of gypsy music and played the violin. To complete the line-up Schmidt rang free-jazz drummer Jaki Liebezeit, born in Dresden in 1938. Liebezeit could play piano and trumpet but turned professional drummer in Cologne after leaving high school. During the early 1960s he played cool jazz with Chet Baker and others in Barcelona before returning to Germany in 1966 and the free-jazz movement. Tired of formless music, he joined Can after impressing Schmidt with the depth and variety of his orbital drum technique.

Experiments began in a Cologne flat but were soon moved to Schloss Nörvenich, a castle in the suburbs, where the group, first known as Inner Space, played a music which incorporated the taped sounds of Gregorian chant and the Paris riots of 1968. Czukay played bass but was technically responsible for tape manipulations and mix-downs. With only a few microphones and two two-track tape machines the group were forced to produce their music live. Irmin Schmidt played organ and keyboards. The arrival of an American sculptor and musician, Malcolm Mooney, precipitated the exit of David Johnson and a change of name to Can.

The process of playing live for long periods of time, allowing Czukay to edit the results, produced the debut album, *Monster Movie* (1969), credited to The Can. Issued first on a small Munich label, it was quickly taken up internationally by United Artists. Undoubtedly an impressive first album, this was the most dynamic and powerful rock music ever to come out of Germany. Can played with an intensity as if it was their last breath. The meshing of instruments was fabulous to hear – Czukay and Liebezeit laid down a heavy, thick rhythm section while Karoli literally insinuated his spidery sustaining Fender guitar in between that and Schmidt's Ambient organ sounds. The music reached a peak of innovation on the side-long 'You Doo Right', a droning repetitive rock tribute to Minimalism. With the majesty of the hypnotic 'Mary Mary, So Contrary', nobody, but nobody sounded as good as Can.

After the recording of some more sessions vocalist Mooney suffered a nervous breakdown and was replaced in the summer of 1970 by Damo Suzuki, a Japanese busker the band spied during a trip to Munich. On *Soundtracks* (Liberty 1970) Mooney was heard on some fine ballads but the almost opiated performance of Suzuki on the groove-laden fourteen-and-a-half-minute 'Mother Sky' was a revelation. Working far into the night, Can created some of the most distinctly potent music of the era with *Tago Mago* (Liberty 1971). They were capable of wonderful shimmering music which entranced the listener ('Paperhouse') and Schmidt was performing some remarkable feats of electronic wizardry like the detonating explosions derived from a modified Farfisa organ and Alpha 77 synth on the brilliant 'Oh Yeah'. Again 'Hallelujah' was a side-long locked groove which merged the constancy of machine music with ancient ethnic beats. Hildegard Schmidt, Irmin's wife and Can's manager, insisted on the group including a second disc of free-form instrumental music with the album.

So popular were Can in 1971 that they even had a number-one hit single in Germany, 'Spoon', taken from their next album, *Ege Bamyasi* (UA 1972), which was recorded in their new studio, a converted cinema about twenty miles from Cologne. The album's short pieces, specifically 'One More Night' and 'Sing Swan Song', revealed Can as masters of trance-inducing dexterity. The record also featured one of the first uses of drum-machine patterns, adapted from Schmidt's Farfisa organ. Reviews, particularly in the UK, recognized Can as the finest experimental rock band of their era. After time off the group returned with arguably their best record in *Future Days* (UA 1973), an album which found them expressing environmental sounds through their instruments and using tape loops of Indian birdsong. The title track alone sounded as if it were recorded in a mist, the production slowly uncovering another of Can's erotic grooves.

Can's idea of 'instant composition', playing in unison 'like an orchestra', was only possible because of the wealth of musical ability of the participants. Irmin Schmidt said: 'We always rejected the term improvisation.' The departure of Damo Suzuki allowed Karoli to play more violin and sing. The new Can sound was even more atmospheric as evinced on the descending semi-tones of the soundtrack piece 'Gomorrha' (1973), a mood and sound which would resurface on their next mighty album. Again *Soon Over Babaluma* (UA 1974) was a classic, with a whole side devoted to the explosive 'Quantum Physics/Chain Reaction', which concluded in the arena of volume-manipulated, tape-edited Ambience.

And this is really the end of Can's great period. A switch to Virgin and to sixteen-track recording resulted in *Landed* (1975), with only the Ambience and collage of 'Unfinished' coming close to their previous experiments. Subsequently they worked with David Gilmour of Pink Floyd and musicians from Malaysia, Jamaica and Ghana. Fully exploring their interest in folk and ethnic music, Can played out the 1970s with a series of diminishingly interesting albums. The release of *Cannibalism* (UA 1978), a first-rate compilation of their music up to 1974, highlighted the lack of genuine discovery in their late-70s work and coincided with the break-up of the group. Having shown that the ideas of Stockhausen, Cage and the Minimalists could be adapted to rock to produce new and startling results, Can became a legendary influence on subsequent generations of exploratory musicians.

LISTENING

In 1980 Hildegard Schmidt reissued the original Can albums on Spoon, and these vinyl pressings are the very best place to hear Can albums like *Monster Movie* (1969), *Future Days* (1973) or *Soon Over Babaluma* (1974). In 1989 Mute in London reissued the first six Can albums, up to 1974, on CD, but *Tago Mago* in particular is better on record. In 1991 the same company reissued the Virgin Can catalogue on disc, including the excellent out-takes compilation from 1976 *Unlimited Edition* (which includes 'Gomorrha'). Between 1986 and 1988 the original Can with Malcolm Mooney reunited at the old studio for a new product, *Rite Time* (Phonogram 1989), filled with the new beat sensibility of House music. A logical extension was the Can remix album *Sacrilege* (Mute 1997), which saw musicians as diverse as Brian Eno, Sonic Youth, The Orb and A Guy Called Gerald take original Can songs and put them through their own personal electronic processes.

To celebrate Can's enduring legacy, Spoon and Mute collaborated to release *Can Box* (1999), a huge extravaganza comprising a double CD, 480-page book and video archive material.

FAUST

Much loved by the British rock intelligentsia, Faust were one of the most extreme rock groups ever to come out of Germany. Unfortunately, the bulk of their music was and still is unlistenable. More a socio-political experiment in hippie and free-music aesthetics, Faust had the dubious honour of being nominated the best 'krautrock' band of all time – an unattractive epithet which they nevertheless acknowledged on their fourth Virgin album, released in 1974. Their popularity in the UK stems from their adoption of the noise + melody + accident = cool music aesthetic of The Velvet Underground. As far as I'm concerned their true importance lies in their use of tape-collage and chance, a sort of rock-soup meeting of Cage and Stockhausen and the fact that they sold 100,000 copies of these tape experiments in 1973 to an unsuspecting audience.

The background to Faust makes pretty funny reading. Two underground Hamburg bands meet a middle-class revolutionary magazine editor named Uwe Nettelbeck in the late 1960s. He has persuaded Polydor records that the sound of youthful unrest would sell. With two drummers, the Frenchman Jean-Hervé Peron on bass and guitar and various others on keyboards and tapes, the groups merge into Faust and are given money by Polydor. They get a house in the country and settle down to a diet of pure LSD 25 and electronic experiment. Polydor, thinking that more money will improve the sound quality, provide them with the means to convert an old school house in Wumme (between Bremen and Hamburg) into a state-of-the-art studio. Sound engineer Kurt Graupner customizes synthesizers and sound effects into black boxes which can be triggered at will. Tape is the chief tool, and Gunther Wusthoff its main manipulator. The group live in the studio, growing their own marijuana and recording in bed!

Faust (Polydor) 1971, marketed in clear vinyl with a clear-perspex sleeve, was the first result of Faust's collage-improv rock. It began with excerpts from The

Beatles and The Stones and went downhill all the way to the end. *So Far* (Polydor 1972) improved on the raggedness of sound, but sounded like the dope-rock it was. Faust's real strength lay in their studio experiments and their ability to collage these into a meaningful whole. Attracting the attention of American violinist Tony Conrad (who had played with the pre-Velvet Underground Dream Syndicate), they then recorded an experiment in repetitive music titled *Outside The Dream Syndicate* (Caroline 1973). Alienated from Polydor, they were picked up by the fledgling Virgin label, who marketed *The Faust Tapes* (1973) for all of 49p. The album sold in six figures and brought German rock to a mass British audience. The album would be Faust's best stab at capturing the open experiment of their studio excursions. Not just a jumble of studio out-takes, instead *The Faust Tapes* seemed to lay out in a series of twenty-six edits the grand electro-acoustic sweep of their vision.

Plagued by German revolutionary factions, the group opted to tour the UK in a disastrous on-stage experiment in pure noise. A final Virgin album, *Faust 4* (1973), was recorded in England at the Manor but the game was up. A fifth album was attempted in luxurious surroundings in Munich but the group folded, heavily in debt. Various sporadic albums of unreleased material appeared on the London-based avant-garde Recommended label during the 1980s. Since 1990 Jean-Hervé Peron has led a slimmed-down Faust on various American and British concerts, all of which have featured radical takes on 'performance'. In 1994 they played in Death Valley in California and in London for some gigs in 1996 they brought amplified power tools, an arc-welder and hay-threshing machinery on stage.

LISTENING

The Faust Tapes (Re CD 1993) is well worth the effort for its ability to amble along Ambiently in the background. Snippets of French, English and German dialogue often intrude, occasionally an excerpt from a tune comes into view, but it's the whole that really counts. Capable of many plays, it always sounds strangely different each time. *Faust 4* (Virgin CD 1992) arcs from the noise-mantra 'Krautrock' to the relative quietness of 'Run'. Approach 1990s albums of new material on Table Of Elements with extreme caution. In 1998 an album with the wacky title *Faust Wakes Nosferatu* appeared on Think Progressive discs.

NEU!

One of the most overrated bands in the history of rock, NEU! impressed English and German critical consciousness with their stripped-down metronomic beats, no-nonsense album covers and a sense of primalism in the early 1970s. With the release of their third album, *NEU! '75*, the group reached their peak as machine-like drumming, chilly synth textures, abrasive industrial rock and pieces of pure tape-manipulated Ambience combined to blueprint a uniquely introspective and German sound. Often credited as being a template for English punk rock, NEU!'s music never wholly convinced. What did, though, was the talent of guitarist and keyboardist Michael Rother, whose work with Harmonia (Brian Eno's favourite group of the 1970s) and subsequent solo recordings revealed a true maestro of electronic and Ambient sound.

NEU! (meaning 'NEW!') emerged from the industrial heartland of Düsseldorf. Michael Rother and Klaus Dinger had, in fact, been closely involved with Kraftwerk and the music they had been recording with engineer-producer Conny Plank in the Star studio in Hamburg. Leaving Kraftwerk in the summer of 1971, Rother and Dinger went back to Hamburg to record an album with Conny Plank which was released on the experimental Brain label. Simply titled *NEU!*, it went on to sell 35,000 copies, wrapped in a plain white sleeve on which a sharply underlined 'NEU!' was scrawled in red. It opened with a fiercely stripped-down mechanistic beat and rhythm guitar with the odd treated synthesizer surfacing and disappearing back into the mix. The track 'Hallogallo' defined the NEU! sound. Elsewhere there were the timbres of cymbals distorted by tape recorders, the sound of a boating journey augmented by eerie electronic tones ('In Luck'), the disconcertingly noisy entry of a pneumatic drill, some grinding slow rock and finally, on 'Dear Honey', the whole is deconstructed between pained slow-motion vocal and pure tone before returning to the Ambience of boats on water.

Unwisely the group then rush-recorded *NEU! 2*, an album so appalling in its results that Rother left the group. In fact the recording seemed to be dominated by Dinger's monotonous drumming, its entire second side mostly taken up with speeded-up and slowed-down versions of a single track, 'Newsnow'. Disaffected, Rother joined Cluster in an old farmhouse near Hanover and began recording. According to Hans-Joachim Roedelius of Cluster, at one time it was NEU! and Cluster all in one room but it didn't work out and Dinger exited to form La Düsseldorf with his brother. Anyway Rother and Cluster formed Harmonia and recorded two albums for Brain, of which the second, *Deluxe* (1975), is the best – a recording which seemed to take the autobahn fantasies of Kraftwerk and make them more intricate.

Impressed with this new atmospheric sound which combined electronics and rock instrumentation to make self-contained instrumental soundscapes, Brian Eno performed with Harmonia in 1974 and joined them in their home studio in 1976 for an Ambient album, *Harmonia 76*, left unreleased until 1997. Meanwhile Rother joined Dinger's musicians for a new NEU! album, *NEU! '75*, recorded wisely with Conny Plank. With two extra drummers, Dinger now concentrated on guitar, piano and organ, with Rother taking his usual keyboards and guitar synthesizer role. The spatial quality of the music, particularly on 'Isi' and 'Fare Thee Well', was quite impressive and the album showed the group had not run out of potential. Again the record appeared in a simple sleeve, this time all black with the underlined 'NEU!' scrawled in white.

Subsequently Dinger made records with La Düsseldorf and Rother engaged himself with more exotic Ambient tableaux with the drummer from Can, Jaki Liebezeit. *Flaming Hearts* (Sky 1977) was again recorded with Conny Plank and was prettier than most NEU! music, lacking Dinger's obvious austerity. *Starvalley* (1978) and *Catmusic* (1979) followed a similar vein and Rother continued to record into the 1990s. Unfortunately, during that decade dubious items put out as *NEU! 4* (1996) and *NEU! Live* (1996) came from Dinger's dusty tape pile and should never have seen the light of day.

LISTENING

Though the early NEU! catalogue was officially released on United Artists in the 1970s it only appeared in the mid-1990s on bootleg Germanofon CDs. Harmonia's *Deluxe* (1975) is worth searching for on import CD. The group's 1976 album *Tracks And Traces* (Sony 1997) features 'Lüneburg Heath', a location near which Faust had their Wumme studio. Michael Rother's *Flaming Hearts* appeared on Random Records in a laudable 1993 CD edition which included Ambient remixes of the title track. Avoid all latter-day product on Captain Trip CDs, especially *NEU! 4*, taken from aborted 1986 NEU! sessions.

TANGERINE DREAM

In the rock era they were the ultimate synthesizer group, who produced an other-worldly music which drew vast crowds to cathedrals and amphitheatres. Like Stockhausen, they believed in a total electronic music and harnessed embryonic analogue synthesizers to create vast instrumental sound tapestries. During the 1970s many rock musicians used the evolving synthesizer to support both acoustic and electric instruments but Tangerine Dream stood almost alone in placing all their faith in electronica. As time passed they became the virtuosos of the sequenced rhythm, their own research leading directly to sampling technology and sequencing software. By the 1990s Tangerine Dream were fêted as the forerunners of Techno music, their beauteous warm landscapes championed by Mixmaster Morris and Future Sound of London to name some.

Before Tangerine Dream recorded their benchmark synthesizer album *Phaedra* for Virgin in 1973, they had spent six years developing their unique sound. Founder Edgar Froese was born in Lithuania in 1944 and studied classical music while young. In his teens he went to West Berlin to study painting and sculpture. By his twenties he was playing bluesy guitar and even visited arch-Surrealist Salvador Dalí in his Catalonian home on several occasions. There Froese was struck by Dalí's 'melting images' and felt the painterly technique could be applied to music. At that time Berlin was buzzing with the new musical theories of Cage, Stockhausen and Xenakis, who all often lectured there. On hearing Jimi Hendrix and particularly The Beatles' *Sgt. Pepper*, Froese formed Tangerine Dream in 1967.

Froese was soon drawn to Berlin's Zodiak Free Arts Lab, established by Hans-Joachim Roedelius and cellist Conrad Schnitzler in 1968. In this experimental club strewn with tone generators and amplifiers, early Tangerine Dream shows mimicked the Pink Floyd sound of 'Interstellar Overdrive'. By 1969 Froese was playing with Schnitzler and a young drummer, Klaus Schulze. The three recorded *Electronic Meditation* (Ear) on a two-track tape machine in a factory. Though it owed an obvious debt to Pink Floyd's *A Saucerful Of Secrets*, it was much more risqué. Schulze has called it 'the primary electronic album', a recording where unusual sound sources like an office calculator jostled with the sounds of Farfisa organ and strings, all modulated by reverbs and delays. By 1970 Schulze had embarked on a solo career and the following year Froese recruited Berliner Christoph Franke, one of the ablest musicians in Germany. Franke, born in 1952, came from a family of musicians and was building his own studio by the age of fifteen. By the time he met Froese in a Berlin studio, the nineteen-year-old Franke had studied trumpet, violin, piano and composition and was considered the best young drummer in the country.

Franke impressed Froese with his collection of Stockhausen and Ligeti recordings. The result was the meditational electronic feast of *Alpha Centauri* (Ear 1971), a record made on eight-track with Hammond and Farfisa organs, flutes and the EMS VCS3 Synthi, a new dimension in the Tangerine Dream sound. The group had made their first 'space-rock' album.

Soon after Peter Baumann joined the group. Baumann had studied at the American School in Berlin, played organ, liked Surrealist art and had an acutely structuralist approach to composition. For many the trio of Froese, Franke and Baumann became the classic Tangerine Dream line-up. Working in an eight-track studio in Cologne, they produced *Zeit* (meaning 'time') (Ear 1972), a wafting double-album Ambient-classical creation using two VCS3 Synthis, four cellos and a large Moog Modular synthesizer courtesy of Florian Fricke. Recorded in the same studio, *Atem* (meaning 'breath') (Ear 1973) had a dense ritualistic air heightened by the first use of an out-of-tune Mellotron.

At this stage Tangerine Dream were like a group of lab technicians hunched over their growing armoury of keyboards and synth modules. Baumann took a sabbatical in India and Nepal while Froese and Franke made a 'sound research' album called *Green Desert* in Berlin. Unreleased until 1986, this boasted one of the first drum sequencers, a PRX rhythm controller from Italy and a MiniMoog synth. Its advanced, accessible sound was lapped up by Virgin, who immediately signed the group. Franke had for years been experimenting with a Moog Modular synth which The Rolling Stones had sold to Hansa studios in Berlin. He found it difficult to rig up but was fascinated by the endless rhythms or sequences it could generate. The sound reminded him of the repetitive metres of Indian classical music and with it he knew he could build a music of 'dreams and meditations'. With $15,000 of the Virgin advance Franke bought the synth from Hansa, his first 'big Moog'. History in the making.

The driving bass notes of the Moog were the key feature of *Phaedra*, Tangerine Dream's debut Virgin album, recorded at the Manor studios over six weeks at the end of 1973. Having produced Mike Oldfield's *Tubular Bells*, Virgin was committed to instrumental music and not disappointed with *Phaedra*, which went Gold in seven countries and stayed on the UK charts for fifteen weeks after its release in early 1974. The mythological washes and aquatic eddies of burbling VCS3, foresty double-keyboarded Mellotron Mark 5 and the finale of Romantic flute drones were all achieved in painstaking fashion. The aim was to achieve a human, emotive music using only electronic means. This aim achieved, Franke purchased another big Moog from the English pop group The Moody Blues. The Moogs had red light displays and with the blinking lights of their VCS3s and PRX console, the three-man Tangerine Dream made an impressive sight live.

At the time Peter Baumann asserted that Tangerine Dream were always moving closer to the 'colour of sound'. For *Rubycon* (1975), again recorded at Virgin's Oxfordshire studio, the group added a Modified Elka organ and an Arp synth to their battery of Mellotron, Moogs and VCS3s. Spliced into two seventeen-minute tracks, *Rubycon* openly paid homage to Stockhausen (opening of 'Part 1') and Ligeti (opening of 'Part 2'). Other highlights were the characteristic Moog sequences, backwards-taped piano sounds and the elegiac slow finale. Though a touring sensation, Tangerine Dream had extreme problems transporting their equipment, particularly Franke's double Moog set-up, which was damaged on a subsequent Australian tour and gave him a nasty electric shock when plugged in. After that Tangerine Dream worked on developing a safe transportation system for electronic instruments. The live album *Ricochet* (1975) boasted extensive sixteen-track overdubbing from cathedral concerts in Europe that year.

The year 1976 began with Tangerine Dream recording a soundtrack for William Friedkin, the director of the classic horror film *The Exorcist* (1973). In a small Berlin studio with an eight-track Ampex recorder, thirteen short compositions, full of throbbing suspense, were created for *Sorcerer*. Unusually the film was shot around the resultant music. In late summer of 1976 the group tried out Audio Studios in Berlin for their next studio album, *Stratosfear*. A favourite among fans, the record mixed electronic instruments with acoustic sources like harpsichord, guitars and harmonica. Though an orchestral studio, Audio proved a jinxed location, the recording process costing a small fortune owing to faulty multi-tracks, exploding Dolby units and a mixing desk which spontaneously combusted. Baumann also had many problems with a new Projeckt Elecktronik computer sequencer which had taken a year to build in Berlin. Despite the problems, *Stratosfear* (1976) was Tangerine Dream's most accessible album up to then.

American tours followed in 1977, the group adding new equipment such as an Oberheim eight-voiced polyphonic synthesizer and first digital synth from Wolfgang Palm, the PPG Wave, which Tangerine Dream were investing in. With their synth racks on wheeled metal boxes and help from Projeckt Elecktronik, their sold-out America jaunts were successful enough to record on four-track. The resultant *Encore* (1977) cut stylistically across ten years of Dream music, from Froese's Gibson guitar solos to pure Ambient sound-paintings. The last date of the tour in Colorado that autumn saw the surprise exit of Peter Baumann, who wished to pursue a solo career in electronic music. After a period of instability which included the recording at Hansa of the futuristic *Force Majeure* (1979), containing the Techno excursion 'Thru Metamorphic Rocks', Tangerine Dream stabilized once again with new member Johannes Schmoelling.

A young sound engineer with an interest in piano and organ music, Schmoelling was also keen to develop electronic collages. When he met Froese he was mixing sounds for Philip Glass's opera collaborator Robert Wilson at a Berlin theatre. Schmoelling was an excellent technician and pianist and injected 'more structured elements and composed melodies' into the music. Franke taught him how to use the MiniMoog and their first studio album, *Tangram* (1980), revealed an extensive use of new polyphonic synthesizers, including the Roland Jupiter 8, which Chris Franke helped design. Moreover Franke's cinema space in Berlin had become a $1.5-million complex full of twenty-four-track recording equipment. Approached by talented director Michael Mann to score the suspenseful heist thriller *Thief* (1981), the group produced a soundtrack that made them famous in America, particularly for the organic quality of the electronic music on display. The album also boasted one of the early uses of Bell Laboratories' GDS computer synthesizer.

The Fairlight Computer Music Instrument, drum loops, long tape loops and extensive use of voice synthesizer, or vocoder, characterized Tangerine Dream's 1981 album *Exit*, a cutting-edge electronic release whose lyrical melodicism was years ahead of the work of any of their rivals. The evolution of digital sampling and sequencing technology from PPG Wave and the Japanese Roland company allowed greater progress in the Tangerine Dream sound. Another Michael Mann film, *Risky Business*, benefited from the Roland MC-8 sequencer, which could store thousands of musical notes. Programmable sequencers also facilitated a more Minimalist sound in the vein of Philip Glass and Steve Reich, and pulsations were heard to their fullest effect on the soundtrack to Mann's Gothic sci-fi thriller *The Keep* (1983). Sampled drum sounds, electronic sitar and tabla sounds were just some of the lush textures which made up the eloquent *Hyperborea*, also released in 1983.

As the years progressed Tangerine Dream consolidated their lead as researchers and innovators in electronic music. Froese built up an extensive sound library while Franke would leave to work with Steinberg on the CUBASE Audio computer sequencing software, one of the most popular computer-music tools ever invented. Johannes Schmoelling had left in 1984 and developed his own studio in Berlin. His replacement was a young Austrian classical musician, Paul Haslinger, whose computer-software expertise helped shape the three-month creative process of *Underwater Sunlight* (Jive 1986), an album which included the formidable Ambient masterpiece 'Song Of The Whale'. The pressure of touring and soundtrack work proved too much for Chris Franke, who left in 1988 to work in Los Angeles with Steinberg. His 1991 Virgin recording *Pacific Coast Highway* revealed his sonorous instrumental abilities outside the group. The 1990s saw Edgar Froese work with his son Jerome, a computer and synthesizer enthusiast and, for five years, with former Austrian model, classical keyboardist and saxophonist Linda Spa. *Goblin's Club* (Castle 1996), using Korg and Roland keyboards plus an exotic list of sampled acoustic sources, was a convincing return to form. Two latter-day film soundtracks, *Oasis* (1997) and *Great Wall Of China* (2000), both released on TDI and both credited to Edgar and Jerome Froese, show Tangerine Dream to be the masters of flawless chugging electro-Ambience. By now the group had studios in Vienna and Berlin and one of the most formidable equipment stores in the world, so it was no idle boast when Froese told me in 1994: 'Tangerine Dream's music is a diary of the history of musical instruments in the 1970s, 1980s and 1990s.'

LISTENING

In 1994 appeared *Tangents*, a five-disc reappraisal of the Virgin years, 1973–83, which was extensively remixed and remastered by Edgar Froese himself. The period 1994–5 saw the release of the individual remastered Virgin discs, of which *Phaedra* (1974), *Rubycon* (1975) and *Stratosfear* (1976) come highly recommended. In 1996 another five-disc box (again remixed by Froese) covering Tangerine Dream history before and after their Virgin decade was released by Castle Communications. Individual remastered albums also appeared, including the fascinating *Alpha Centauri* (1971) and *Zeit* (1972) and the impressive *Poland* (1984) and *Underwater Sunlight* (1986).

Peter Baumann's contribution to electronic music should not be underestimated. In 1976 he contacted E-Mu systems in America to develop a combined computer and analogue synthesizer. His first two solo albums for Virgin, *Romance '76* (1976) and *Trans-Harmonic Nights* (1978), were full of edgy sequenced lines which pre-dated UK electro-bop and House music by years. During the 1980s he set up the New Age label Private Music in the US, eventually signing Tangerine Dream in 1988. Unfortunately, this gifted musician left the music business in the 1990s, his solo gifts duly celebrated on the Virgin compilation *Phase By Phase* (1996).

Surprisingly, Edgar Froese also had a solo contract with Virgin during their successful Virgin period. The amorphous, bubbling quality of *Aqua* (1974) was enhanced by the three-dimensional 'Artificial Head' recording system developed in Germany. *Epsilon In Malaysian Pale* (1975), recorded after a trip to

Southeast Asia, was a veritable homage to the Mellotron. The well-structured *Stuntman* (1979), recorded at Hansa studios in Berlin, saw Froese use the Roland Guitar synth and various sound waveforms produced by new PPG equipment. His last Virgin solo, *Pinnacles* (1983), was an even more streamlined use of digital sampling and Korg and Roland polyphonics, influenced in mood by a trip to the Australian outback. In 1995 Virgin released a collection of remastered and remixed material from Froese's solo tape banks titled *Beyond The Storm*.

POPOL VUH

No one ever forgets the opening scene of Werner Herzog's spellbinding movie *Aguirre, Wrath Of God* (1972). An angelic choir is heard as we travel through the clouds of the High Andes. Slowly the mist clears to reveal a giant mountainside from which tiny figures descend. There is the sound of a strange keyboard instrument, in this case a Mellotron, and the sight of heavily armoured conquistadors blindly thrashing their way through jungle highlands in search of El Dorado. The music is shrouded in an air of mystery, its makers Popol Vuh probably the most mysterious group to emerge from German rock of the 1970s. Over dozens of albums Popol Vuh drew on Oriental and Indian philosophies to create mantras in sound, using both acoustic and electronic instruments. Their almost mystical sound became a key ingredient in the films of German director Herzog. The music eventually transcended all fashion so that by the 1990s it was able to absorb Trance and Techno styles without losing its unique identity.

Popol Vuh has always been driven by musician and composer Florian Fricke, born near the German–Swiss border in 1944. He studied classical piano in Freiburg and composition at Munich Conservatory. While still a teenager he transferred to film school, where he met Herzog and bonded a fruitful friendship. He even played jazz-rock with the future founder of ECM, Manfred Eicher. During the late 1960s he followed the hippie trail to Nepal, taking in Africa and India before studying Tibetan choral music in the Himalayas. He returned to Munich and in 1969 bought one of the first big Moog synthesizers in Germany. With this he founded Popol Vuh, a group whose name derived from the sacred book of the Mayas. Their debut album, *Affenstunde* ('time of the monkeys'), was released on Liberty in 1971 to great acclaim. Recording natural elemental sounds, Popol Vuh combined these with electronic Moog drones to great effect. At the time the synthesizer's inventor, Robert Moog, commented: 'This is beautiful music.'

Another meditation on the sixty-one-keyed Moog followed, its spooky sound driven by conga drums and climaxing in a celestial coda for percussion, electric piano and splashing water. Titled *In Pharaoh's Garden*, it was released by Pilz in early 1972, the year that Fricke contributed Moog synth solos to Tangerine Dream's fourth album, *Zeit*, and wrote the music for *Aguirre, Wrath*

Of God, starring Klaus Kinski. Consisting of theme and exposition, along classical lines, this work had such an other-worldly quality that it has featured on Popol Vuh compilations ever since.

In 1973 Fricke turned his back on electronics and formed a new Popol Vuh featuring piano, harpsichord, oboe, tambura and violin. Djong Yun, from Korea, sang and the resultant album, *Hosianna Mantra*, was one long devotional hymn. Fricke explored a more rock-oriented music over the next few years with the addition of Daniel Fichelscher (of German rock band Amon Düül II) on electric Fender and percussion. This phase came to a climax on the 1975 album *The Holy Song Of Solomon*, which contained some of the creamiest rock ever recorded.

Always changing, Fricke recorded the solo album *Yoga* in 1976, just two tracks of uplifting sitar-led music recorded with Indian musicians at his studio in Munich. Again in 1977 Fricke arrived at a unique music for Herzog's film *Heart Of Glass*, a dreamlike series of instrumentals which complemented Herzog's controversial use of hypnosis on the cast. More important was his music for the Herzog version of *Nosferatu* (1978), which again starred Kinski and contained Fricke's finest creations since *Aguirre*. Released on Brain as *Brothers Of Darkness – Sons Of Light* in the same year, it was a powerhouse of Ambient guitar, piano and sitar mantra. The title track alone lasted seventeen minutes. The becalming 'Oh Hear, Thou Who Darest' used the still Ambience of decaying piano notes and in retrospect was a precursor to Eno's sound-alike *Thursday Afternoon* of 1985. More wanderings in the Himalayas, studies in Indian tantra and so on led Fricke to consolidate various line-ups of Popol Vuh for the recording *Night Of The Spirit – Tantric Songs* (1979), which featured Amazonian chants, acoustic guitar passages, chanted mantras, percussion instrumentals and Ambient piano pieces. At this point Fricke began holding workshops in creative singing and breathing therapy. Eventually he would become an authority, lecturing on the subject internationally.

In 1982 Herzog requested more Popol Vuh music, this time for his ambitious *Fitzcarraldo*, again starring Kinski, here in the role of a crazed Irishman who dreams of building an opera house in the Amazon jungle. During filming Herzog attempted to defy nature by dragging a paddle-steamer across a mountain. Dotted with the early 78rpm recordings of classic operatic performances, the soundtrack was best remembered for Popol Vuh's raw, ritualistic percussion and unnervingly primal chanting. A more commercial recording, *Agape-Agape*, appeared on the Norwegian Uniton label in 1983 and seemed to sum up all of Popol Vuh's stylistic changes to date. It concluded with the still Ambience of the piano track 'Why Do I Still Sleep'. Even better was 1987's *Spirit Of Peace*, an album which explored spatial piano notes and lengthy, trance-inducing guitar mantras. Part of it was then used on Herzog's 1987 film *Cobra Verde*, the soundtrack of which also featured Fricke coaxing beautiful textures from his Synclavier keyboard.

Having influenced the 80s group The Cocteau Twins, Popol Vuh's music became during the late 1990s a reference point for electronic musicians interested in 'isolationist' tendencies. Musicians like Dortmund's Thomas Köner and Norway's Biosphere could relate the static and the spiritually uplifting in Fricke's music to their own explorations of slowly unfolding time and motion. Often touching on the careers of such legendary German groups as Tangerine Dream and Amon Düül II (whose Renate Knaup joined as vocalist in the late 1970s), Popol Vuh have always existed in their own space, making a music that has reference points and influences way beyond the rock spectrum.

LISTENING

During the early 1990s Spalax Music in Paris began reissuing the extensive Popol Vuh catalogue on CD. Up to then it was well-nigh impossible to hear some of the finest Ambient-electronic music ever recorded as it was spread over a dozen European labels. *Affenstunde* (1991) and *In Pharaoh's Garden* (1994) are certainly worth hearing because of the innovative use of Moog, while *The Holy Song Of Solomon* (1992) contains some fine rock instrumentals. The bulk of the Herzog material is brilliant, particularly the soundtracks to *Aguirre, Wrath Of God* (1996) and *Nosferatu* (1993) (which came in two versions). Be warned: the *Fitzcarraldo* soundtrack of 1996 is littered with classic opera performances on 78 by Enrico Caruso.

For a general Herzog-Fricke disc choose *Best Of Popol Vuh–Werner Herzog* (Milan 1993). In 1994 Fricke teamed up with Popol Vuh founder member Frank Fiedler to record a more Techno-influenced album, *City Raga* (Milan), sampling the voice of a young singer travelling in the Yucatan. The follow-up, *Shepherd's Symphony* (Mystic 1997), refined these Trance-Dance elements even further. Mystic released a commendable sampler, *Not High In Heaven*, in 1998, featuring new mixes and out-takes from the period 1970–85.

ROEDELIUS, CLUSTER, HARMONIA

Hans-Joachim Roedelius is a key ingredient in the genesis of German electronica from the late 1960s until the end of the twentieth century. He forms a vital link between the pioneering electronic work of Tangerine Dream, Klaus Schulze and Ash Ra Tempel; the music of his own group Cluster and that of Brian Eno; and his influence goes right through the fashionable soothing Ambience of the 1980s and on into the chilly Techno soundscapes of the following decade. Initially a pioneer of German electronic experimentation, he slowly shifted to acoustic piano and electric keyboards, his style of repeating melodic motifs and cascading arpeggios producing some of the most distinctive and beautiful Ambient music ever recorded. It is no exaggeration to proclaim him the finest keyboardist to emerge from German rock.

Roedelius was born in Berlin in 1934 to a church-going mother and a dentist. His boyhood, like Stockhausen's, was marred by the horror of war and after a failed attempt to escape the Nazi regime he was imprisoned in East Germany for desertion. He was later released to a compulsory physiotherapy course and remained in the East until 1961, when threats to his family subsided. He then crossed to West Berlin and became a masseur. Through all this he maintained an interest in the piano and an appreciation of the Impressionistic music of Satie, Ravel and Debussy. At night he played with theatrical, jazz and mixed-media groups. He travelled to Paris and, colourfully, opened a restaurant in Corsica.

Sympathetic to student unrest, he returned to Berlin in 1968 and started the Zodiak Free Arts Lab with a friend, Conrad Schnitzler (a founder member of Tangerine Dream). It became a locus of experimentation to which the Dream, Klaus Schulze and Ash Ra Tempel all owing the beginning of their careers. Roedelius himself used the space as a forum for experiments such as 'electronically treated sounds, handmade flutes, alarm clock and voice used in conjunction with amplification and tape delays'. The Zodiak closed in May 1969 and Roedelius and friends went off to North Africa on a musical quest. Within a short time he was back in Berlin and formed Kluster with Schnitzler and another musician, Dieter Moebius. They played long pieces of electro-acoustic music. 'Just keyboards, musical cycles, tone generators, voltage things used in conjunction with odd sources like metal plates linked to contact mikes. Moebius played an electronically treated battery with microphones wired through amplifiers and echo machine!' Roedelius also confessed to playing organ and cello. The others also played the more conventional violin, cello and guitar.

Roedelius always stated that he had no formal training and worked his way towards his consummate style through a combination of emotion, instinct and concentration. Kluster played the hippie music circuit in Germany, even supporting Jimi Hendrix at one open-air festival. After two years Schnitzler left and Kluster became the legendary duo Cluster of Moebius and Roedelius. Even more legendary was Conny Plank, a Cologne engineer who offered to produce Cluster's albums in Hamburg and later in his own studio in Cologne. He even played synthesizers and was virtually a third member of Cluster. Early recordings like *Cluster 2* (Brain 1972) sounded like a host of machines left running overnight! Eventually Cluster set up their own studio in a stone room in Forst in north-west Germany.

In 1973 Cluster were joined by Michael Rother of the Düsseldorf group NEU! and made *Music From Harmonia* (Brain 1974), an album of oscillating rhythms and 'cosmic music'. Harmonia was a form of supergroup that very quickly attracted the attention of Brian Eno, who thought the album one of the greatest ever. In 1974 he performed on stage with Harmonia in Hamburg and in 1976 went to Forst to record an album of superior electronic Ambience before continuing his German odyssey with David Bowie in Berlin. Of course that resulted in *Low* and *'Heroes'*, two 1977 albums which in essence brought the work of Cluster and other German experimentalists to a mass audience.

Harmonia released one last album, *Deluxe* (1975), a critically acclaimed set, before Cluster became a duo again. In 1976 they released the burblingly accessible *Sowiesoso* ('anyway') on Sky. For many the peak of this fruitful period came when Eno again collaborated with Cluster and Conny Plank on the Sky albums *Cluster And Eno* (1977) and *After The Heat* (1978), two fine examples of digestible electronica which brought Roedelius and Moebius to a world audience.

Contemplating a solo career, Roedelius moved to Vienna in 1978 and released his first solo album, *Through The Desert*, which was two years in the making with Conny Plank. His next album, *Jardin Au Fou* (1979), produced by ex-Tangerine Dream synthesist Peter Baumann, marked Roedelius's transition from electronics to more serene acoustic tableaux. In 1980, with a grant from the Alban Berg Endowment fund, he purchased a Bosendorfer grand piano. His method was to overdub himself on tape, adding subtle saxophone or guitar tracks. For the most part the waterfall piano style, cushioned by an instinctive use of acoustic space and hypnotic tempos, would produce brilliant results time and time again. The albums *Gift Of The Moment* (1984), *Like The Whispering Of Winds* (1986) and *Momenti Felici* (1987) are masterpieces of 'texture and mood'.

Having worked alone for many years, Roedelius ended the 1980s by teaming up with other musicians and writing *Fortress Of Love* (1989) for Virgin, an album full of different moods and poetic recitations. The 1990s saw his Blumau studio in Austria attract lots of musicians. Now working with Korg synthesizer and sampling keyboard as well as a lot of reverberation and delay, Roedelius began composing for the German theatre. In 1993 he started to work with a guitar, sax and keyboard trio which became known as Aquarello and in 1995 reunited with Moebius for a live Cluster album, *One Hour*. By the end of the 1990s Roedelius was a hero to many, his quietly insistent music hailed by DJs such as the UK's Mixmaster Morris and Japan's Ken Ishii and endorsed by rock stars such as David Bowie.

LISTENING

Roedelius is an archetype of Ambient and electronic music, so almost all of his discography is worth hearing. So sublime and often luminous is his work that, once heard, many claim that it is essential to hear more. Most records have been reissued on CD. Early Cluster albums are often little more than treated electronic tones but *Sowiesoso* (Sky 1976) is fantastic upbeat stuff. The two Eno collaborations, *Cluster And Eno* (Sky 1977) and *After The Heat* (Sky 1978), are very stylish exercises in electronic exploration. Can's Holger Czukay appears on the first. Roedelius's work with Harmonia appeared on bootleg disc in the 1990s but in 1997 Sony S3 reissued 'the legendary lost Eno album' *Harmonia 76*, whose sound is often that of single vibrations being dropped into liquid space.

Those interested in acoustic and chamber music need look no further than the pastoral bliss of *Gift Of The Moment* (EG 1984), the Ambient piano minimalism of *Like The Whispering Of Winds* (Cicada 1986) or the dancing keyboard patters of *Momenti Felici* (Virgin Venture 1987). Brian Eno sponsored some of the tonal pieces on the Japanese collection, *Pink, Blue And Amber* (Prudence 1996). For a fresh overview of everything Roedelius has to offer, try *Aquarello* (All Saints 1998).

MANUEL GÖTTSCHING AND ASH RA TEMPEL

One of the most mellifluously gifted guitarists to come out of the German rock scene of the early 1970s was Manuel Göttsching. His fusion of guitar improvisation with electronic treatments made his first group, Ash Ra Tempel, one of the most exciting German bands of their era. By the mid-1970s he was a solo inventor, allying his Fender and Gibson guitar streams with effects to the modern recording studio. He became adept at combining the instrument with soft synthesizer washes and hypnotic grooves. His output reached a crucial peak on the 1984 release 'E2–E4', so successful a marriage that it became a benchmark Ambient House and Trance recording for the 1990s.

Ash Ra Tempel were formed in 1970 by Göttsching and Klaus Schulze in Berlin. Their first album, *Ash Ra Tempel* (Ear) was recorded by Conny Plank at the Star Studio in Hamburg in 1971 and released that year. It was basically electronically treated rock, one track per side of LP. The second track, 'Dream Machine', was full of cavernous atmospheric sounds. The group's second 1971 album, *Oscillations* (Ear), added more instrumentation and players but lost Schulze to a solo career. It played around with rock but culminated in the region of cosmic music, 'Search'/'Love', featuring electronically treated vibraphone and an electronic Ambient haze.

A journey to Berne in Switzerland saw them jam with the American acid guru Timothy Leary on the highly self-indulgent *Seven Up* (Cosmic 1972). From the early days with Conny Plank most of the recordings were produced or supervised by Dieter Dierks, who had a studio in Cologne. By 1973 Ash Ra Tempel were down to a duo of Göttsching and Rosi Müller, who made the hippie-folk *Starring Rosi* (Cosmic), replete with Mellotron, harp, vibes, synths and conga drums. Sweetly affecting it was, serious innovation it was not.

For this Göttsching had to go solo, spending two months in the summer of 1974 in his own studio in Berlin with guitar, effects and a four-track Teac tape machine. Mixed by Dierks, the resultant *Inventions For Electric Guitar* (Cosmic) is now considered a benchmark recording. Over three compositions Göttsching harnessed bubbling rhythm tracks, plaintive electronic sonorities and wonderfully colourful tone poems from his guitar. Often it was impossible to discern what he was playing, so consummate was the skill involved. *Inventions* was to become a name-checked Ambient classic.

Now signed to Virgin as Ashra, Göttsching was to begin by effortlessly combining his sweetly toned guitar style with mellow synthesizer and keyboard sounds. *New Age Of Earth* (1977) danced along on a rush of brightly textured sounds, lapping on the shores of Fleetwood Mac blues one moment, taking off into the cosmic ether the next. Here texture was everything, Göttsching going out of his way to create an interplanetary sound of the future. *Blackouts* (1978) was less convincing but his guitar glowed as usual. *Correlations* (1979) and *Bell Alliance* (1980) had their moments but Göttsching was increasingly at odds with the technology, some of the drum-machine tracks sounding positively awkward. Sensing his music needed more concentration, he took time off and during the last month of 1981 recorded the astonishing *E2–E4* (INTEAM 1984), a wonderfully dancey rhythm track with enough space for liquid sounds, funky bass keyboard grooves, hesitant nervy keyboard motifs and the silken guitar notes of old. At nearly an hour long it occupied a space all of its own, thus becoming one of the most-sampled records of the House explosion of the 1980s and 1990s – a veritable soundtrack for the E generation.

KRAFTWERK

Considered the most influential group to come from Germany during the 1970s, Kraftwerk went out of their way to fashion a pure electronic aesthetic which encompassed all aspects of modernity. Each album became a complete concept in its own right, from motorways to trains, from radios to computers. Each new phase was marked by a startling new image, a process which saw the Düsseldorf group move in the direction of cybernetics, as actual robots took their places on-stage. They played the pop game to the hilt, building up a huge reputation for themselves as each recording widened their audience. They had a direct effect on the music of David Bowie and with Afrika Bambaataa's 1982 club smash 'Planet Rock' (which sampled the rhythmic sections of *Trans-Europe Express* and *Computer World*) they became hip with young black Americans. It was their adoption by Detroit Techno musicians that made Kraftwerk gurus of the new Ecstasy generation, their sleek, machine-like creations at one with the new culture of cyberspace.

Ralf Hütter and Florian Schneider-Esleben, to all intents and purposes, embodied Kraftwerk. The word loosely denotes 'power station' and has a strong gender connotation of 'men at work'. Hütter was born in Krefeld in 1946, the son of a doctor. He studied piano while young and then took up the electric organ at Düsseldorf Conservatory. Schneider-Esleben, the son of a prominent architect, was born near the Swiss-German border in 1947. The family moved to Düsseldorf when he was a toddler and over time he developed an interest in concrete music, particularly the work of Pierre Henry. He also attended Düsseldorf Conservatory, studying the flute. Later he would drop the 'Esleben' from his surname, becoming simply Schneider. Both were '*hoch bourgeoisie*', gentlemen of the refined and affluent German classes. They formed a close friendship at the Conservatory and began making music.

Schneider had a strong interest in electronic equipment – the potentialities of loudspeakers, echo machines and sound synthesis. Hütter was keenly interested in composition and rated The Beach Boys very highly. Both admired Stockhausen and the Futurists. In 1968 they formed Organisation, a loose industrial rock group. They played with Can and recorded *Tone Float* (RCA 1970) but considered the results undisciplined. Their focus became an evocation of the North Rhine industrial heartland of the New Germany. Hence Hütter and Schneider renamed themselves Kraftwerk and worked with Conny Plank, the engineer most likely to produce positive and contemporary results.

From 1970 to 1971 two albums were made for Philips, their new label. In the heart of Düsseldorf they had found 180 square feet of studio space, which they christened Kling Klang Studio. There they began amassing equipment – tape machines, self-invented drum machines, oscillators and such, Hammond organ and of course Schneider's beloved flutes. *Kraftwerk* (1970) was pure sound manipulation, a product of their LSD experience of the late 1960s, a nerveracking ride through machine sounds which ended with a veritable recreation of aerial bombing. 'Coming Down From Heaven' was a reminder that these young Germans had inherited a painful cultural memory of the war. *Kraftwerk 2* (1971) was a huge jump in sound quality, its opening track, 'Klingklang', bringing in the soft percussive sequences overlaid by flute which would become a Kraftwerk trademark. During this period they had temporarily worked with Michael Rother and Klaus Dinger, who would form NEU!. Surprisingly, even Hütter had left for six months, confused over his musical direction. The commercial success of *Kraftwerk 2* gave the duo confidence to go on.

Ralf And Florian (Philips 1973) is my favourite Kraftwerk album and their finest Ambient statement. Having honed their skills in live performance and improved their self-made synthesizers and drum machines, the group recorded this album at Kling Klang and in Cologne and Munich with Conny Plank. No longer was it a case of exploring the avant-garde loves of their youth but playing real music. The album was full of Schneider's treated flute sounds, their presence adding a real dimension of German Romanticism, mindful of Mahler. More incredible were the glacial and insistent sequences, so advanced that they would still sound contemporary a quarter of a century later. 'Tone Mountain' was as if the electronics were jumping out of the grooves. In effect this was dance music and to highlight the fact they even recorded a track titled 'Dance Music'; again the interlocking electronic rhythm, graced ever so slightly with bright percussion and angelic voices, was wonderfully fresh and accomplished. There were plenty of interesting sounds on this album – Hütter's excellent touch on the piano, the synthesized sound of waves and the altered sound of Hawaiian guitar on 'Pineapple Symphony'.

By 1974 Hütter had invested in a MiniMoog synthesizer. Inspired by their constant Volkswagen trips on the new autobahns, Kraftwerk decided to base an entire album around a car journey. Again they chose Conny Plank to oversee the recording, this time in his new studio near Cologne. Using electronicized voices and the hypnotic sequences so well conceived on *Ralf And Florian*, Kraftwerk produced a twenty-two-minute track titled 'Autobahn', which began with the sound of a car starting up. The resulting album, *Autobahn* (Philips 1974), charted all over the world. That year also saw the addition of two new members, Wolfgang Flur (a Frankfurt design student who drummed) and Karl Bartos (another conservatory student from Düsseldorf with orchestral ambitions). Kraftwerk thus became four and toured America as such in 1975.

Their next project, *Radio-Activity* (Capitol 1976), would turn their early Romanticism to a kind of wistfulness, a sense of something lost in the future. Its equivalent would be Brian Eno's feeling of the 'nostalgia for the future' he experienced when he began filming the water towers of Manhattan during the late 1970s. Kling Klang was now a laboratory, Kraftwerk's image that of white-coated scientists. Schneider had come up with better drum machines and was fond of short-wave radio sounds. It all came together on *Radio-Activity*, a powerful statement of high-definition electronics. 'Radioland' involved metronomic and slow percussion overlaid by an entire panoply of squirmy, squishy, electronic noises panned in wonderful stereo effects. This literal celebration of the early joys of radio included a synthesized voice singing the words 'electronic mu-sic'. The album, with an old picture of a radio as the entire cover, shifted considerable quantities in France, where the title track sold one million copies as a single.

Used to spending much time travelling by train all over Europe, Kraftwerk then fashioned an album on the concept of the European rail network. *Trans-Europe Express* (Capitol 1977) is a radiantly concise statement, the album cover again harking back to the past, the four members of Kraftwerk dressed in 1930s suits with very short hair. Another inside-cover shot pictured them sitting at an outdoor luncheon table which could have come from a traditional Bavarian postcard. The only sign that these four gentlemen were musicians came from Schneider's trademark minim badge on his left lapel. The album was a masterwork of wonderfully gilded sequences that recurred with Minimalist simplicity. Their tone on all keyboards and synthesizers had reached a new peak of fidelity and sheen. The show-piece title track mimicked the movement, sound and sights of a train journey with a humorous reference to 'Iggy Pop and David Bowie'. The finale, 'Franz Schubert', is one long, hypnotic multi-sequence with again a wistful synthesizer undertow. It leads to the climax of the vocoded 'Endless Endless', which brought one back to the album's opening sequence.

While *Trans-Europe Express* was mixed in Los Angeles, *The Man Machine* (Capitol 1978) was entirely recorded in Düsseldorf. The album is often considered the pinnacle of Kraftwerk and highly influential on British electro music and subsequent Techno offshoots. *The Man Machine* realized Kraftwerk's fullest ambition of the futuristic meeting of man and machine as in cybernetics.

Yet tracks like 'The Robots' sound completely mechanized. Another track, 'The Model', became a number-one hit in 1981 owing to its pop commercial appeal but the real guts of *The Man Machine* lay in 'Neon Lights', again a piece filled with a wistful longing for a future that seemed to be past. There was a textural beauty to the synthesized flute passages, a jewel-like luminessence to the keyboard sequences which repeated themselves in Minimalist style for over ten minutes. In terms of concept the cover was another classic: four red-shirted men in stiff formation standing on a staircase and facing east, their faces super-pale, their lips covered in rouge. The cover was credited to the Russian Constructivist artist El Lissitzky and it was obvious that Kraftwerk saw themselves as workers for a new electronic future. In the studio they had built workstations which could be taken out on tour. Dummies were even designed to look like the group which could humorously take the place of the musicians on stage. There was a wicked irony at play here which wasn't lost on their burgeoning audiences. In response Kraftwerk, now wealthy enough to spend time in summer houses and follow intellectual pursuits, did not even bother to tour the album.

In effect the great period of Kraftwerk was over. The rest was consolidation. *Computer World* (EMI 1981) was again a short album at just over thirty minutes. (By having fewer tracks on vinyl, Kraftwerk could get better sounds out of fatter grooves. Hence the high sound quality of their later records.) An excellent paean to the computer, the album spawned a technologically impressive world tour where the Kling Klang studio was taken on the road and audiences were treated to state-of-the-art video screens and customized hand-held synthesizers. Florian Schneider even played a completely synthesized flute. In the US they encountered the new dance culture which centred around DJs looping their very own records. By 1982 Afrika Bambaataa would make Kraftwerk a real influence on black music culture.

Yet offers from even Michael Jackson were allowed to dissolve as Kraftwerk spent years digitizing Kling Klang. Hütter became obsessed with cycling and the album *Technopop* was recorded on analogue equipment ready for release in 1983. But Hütter shelved this and continued to upgrade, purchasing a Synclavier computer sampling synthesizer from New England Digital at enormous personal expense. Kraftwerk had always wanted to be ahead in terms of technology. During the early 1970s they had used electronic drum pads, by the mid-1970s they were using sixteen-step sequencing and by the early 1980s were perfectly synchronizing multi-track tape equipment to synthesizers. For them digital technology had to be embraced. The first fruits was the multi-lingual, danceable *Electric Café*, (EMI 1986), Kraftwerk's first CD release.

Yet all wasn't well. Hütter, who drove himself to the limits, hardly ever sleeping, collapsed in England in 1986 with a suspected heart condition. Five years would then be spent remixing old Kraftwerk tunes digitally for the new Techno generation. Karl Bartos remembers two years literally spent programming a new Yamaha DX7 synthesizer! Since Kling Klang was hermetically sealed (Hütter and Schneider refused to have telephones, faxes or secretaries) both Flur and Bartos felt completely isolated. In 1990 they left the group and Kraftwerk was again a duo. For *The Mix* (EMI 1991) familiar Kraftwerk tunes were Housed up, given a Techno sheen to fairly impressive effect, but the results only showed that Kraftwerk's sound was now commonplace and not advanced.

Kraftwerk then toured with two studio engineers and got the likes of studio whiz William Orbit to remix some old music. In 1992 they supported U2 in Manchester in a protest against nuclear waste disposal. As the century came to a close Kraftwerk became more conspicuous musically but physically seemed to disappear into the fabric of their closely guarded studio. In 1997 they made a surprise appearance at Luton for that year's Tribal Gathering rave. The following year they played Sonar '98 in Barcelona – an array of men in black behind their electronic consoles, chiming their greatest hits for an appreciative electronic generation. After they toured Japan and the US rumours were rife that this was their last-ever concert appearance. In terms of impact, Hütter and Schneider had followed Stockhausen's famous dictum that man should control machines. By allying a classical education and a progressive attitude to electronics with perfect (and often ironic) pop concepts, Kraftwerk used the medium of LP records to achieve a tremendous cultural impact. Though often seen as over-simplistic and too mechanized in their approach, they nevertheless humanized electronic music for a mass audience.

LISTENING

For many years Kraftwerk's CD releases were in disarray. In 1994 I was forced to purchase my CD copy of *Trans-Europe Express* in New York because it was not available in the UK. *Ralf And Florian* (Crown 1995) is their supreme Ambient release, a wonderfully warm and spiritual music which pre-dates their so-called 'mechanized' phase. *Radio-Activity* (EMI 1987) and *Trans-Europe Express* (EMI 1987) have much to recommend them, but the value of *The Man Machine* (Fame 1988) is overstated (though 'Neon Lights' is exemplary Kraftwerk music). *The Mix* (EMI 1991) is pure fun, a Techno-ized snapshot of their entire career.

KLAUS SCHULZE

One of the great electronic musicians, Germany's Klaus Schulze became a synth star during the 1970s, a decade in which he went out of his way to break down prejudice towards the medium. His view was simple: 'With Pierre Schaeffer, Stockhausen and Boulez you had people building notes from scratch. They really worked hard to create a framework for us. When I began using synthesizers I too learned how to build notes. All the stuff had to be done by hand.' Influenced by Pink Floyd, Schulze entered the 1970s by venturing into the then uncharted realm of synthesizer music. By 1977 he was famous, his uncannily intoxicating *Mirage* still one of the finest electronic albums of the twentieth century. He declared his music to be 'a dream without the isolation of sleep'; his interest in science fiction, particularly the writings of Frank Herbert and William Gibson, infusing his work with self-contained atmosphere. By the mid-1990s Schulze was a favourite among Techno musicians and recorded a series of albums with the Frankfurt Ambient guru Pete Namlook.

Schulze was born in Berlin in 1947 and as early as five began playing the guitar. Within two years he was receiving classical guitar tuition but by fifteen he had tired of playing Bach pieces. He switched to drums but also attended the University of Berlin, where he discovered Stockhausen and Ligeti while honing his music writing skills. From 1967 he played and recorded with a number of German groups, including Tangerine Dream and Ash Ra Tempel, with whom he recorded debut albums. Though he was impressed with producer Conny Plank and guitarist Manuel Göttsching he saw little future in drums. Once he heard Pink Floyd's second album, *A Saucerful Of Secrets*, he decided that keyboards were the way forward.

Inspired by the likes of Wendy Carlos, La Monte Young, Terry Riley and Ravi Shankar, Schulze made home experiments with a Teisco electric organ and tape devices. Aided by strings, these spidery droning organ meditations were first aired on 1972's *Irrlicht* ('eerie light'), a recording which made Schulze a musician to watch. Associated with various German labels such as Ear, Cosmic Music and Brain, Schulze continued to expand his interest in synthesizers, adding the UK's classic EMS VCS3 Synthi A and the accessible American ARP range. These synthesizers became increasingly popular because they looked good, were relatively small, produced unique sounds and didn't require a bird's nest of wires to hook them up. Along with much echo and a Farfisa Duo organ (like Pink Floyd's), Schulze produced the pleasing *Picture Music* in 1973 – just two long tracks where the ARP synth was used to generate the percussion.

The period 1974–5 marked a turning-point for Schulze. He acquired two MiniMoog synthesizers for live soloing, worked with the Japanese synthesist Kitaro and experimented with a new German surround-sound technique called the 'artificial head' recording system. He also signed with Virgin for two ground-breaking albums, *Blackdance* and *Timewind*, distinguished by their Daliesque Urs Amann gatefold-sleeve paintings. *Blackdance* (1974) was unusual, mixing classical ideas with new technology. Recorded in Delta Acoustics in Berlin, the album featured piano, twelve-string guitar, bass voice, the usual Farfisa organ and various timbres derived from a Farfisa Synthorchestra. The general mood was forlorn melancholy, 'Some Velvet Phasing' being an example of Romantic adagio played through electronics. In contrast, *Timewind* (1975), reputedly recorded in Schulze's Berlin home studio in two single sessions, was spectacular. Aided by a custom-built Synthanorma sequencer, Schulze repeated keyboard patterns pulsed forward to the cricket-like dripping tones of the Synthi A. Wind effects and other synth tones created an auralscape which fitted the surreal overtones of the sleeve art. The entire first side was called 'Bayreuth Return' and the album was dedicated to Richard Wagner. Schulze called it 'real floating music that carried the listener away'. So different was Schulze's music that *Timewind* won 1975's prestigious Grand Prix award for best new 'classical' album, an honour that a long-haired Schulze accepted in Paris in the company of Pierre Boulez. To top it all, Schulze performed alongside his heroes Steve Reich and Philip Glass at a Berlin music festival.

With the success of *Timewind*, Schulze could now afford to buy from the US a huge Moog Series 3 synthesizer made up of six different cabinets, and this gave him even greater control over the electronic sounds he generated. He dubbed it the 'Big Moog'. He also added an eight-track recorder and a brass and strings synth to his arsenal. Live, Schulze sat in front of the Moog like an altar, surrounded by a phalanx of keyboards and synthesizers, his trusty VCS3, ARP and MiniMoogs never far from his fingertips. Complete with a mixing desk, his set-up was a virtual studio on stage.

This synth-maestro image was celebrated on *Moondawn* (1976), whose mind-wrenching sleeve photos were better than its contents of synth washes allied to a real drummer's beat. Far more creative was *Body Love* (1976), made in Frankfurt for an erotic movie but containing some well-structured electronica plus the great piano-led Ambience of 'Blanche'. This kind of still atmosphere would be celebrated on his next recording, *Mirage*, which turned out a masterpiece. Schulze admired the sheen of Pink Floyd's 1975 opus *Wish You Were Here* (whose MiniMoog sound he described as 'a human and beautiful thing') and wished to achieve the same level of instrumental cohesion. Envisioned as 'an electronic winter landscape', *Mirage* comprised two side-long album tracks subtitled by science-fiction references such as 'Destinationvoid'. Moreover Schulze's own sleeve note hinted that the music was a celebration of creativity in the midst 'of our dying planet life'. 'Velvet Voyage' aurally summoned up visions of a journey to a cold polar landscape outside our experience. 'Crystal Lake' began with Minimalist bell sounds (cue Steve Reich and Mike Oldfield) and continued with chiming metronomic rhythms to bass keyboard changes, and until halfway through its thirty-minute length the whole thing was awash in atmosphere. Schulze's own sound sources were now so complex that few, if any, could source many of the sounds on *Mirage*. He was now using the Big Moog, at least five smaller Moog synths, original computer sequencers, a customized phaser unit, various reverbs and tape echoes, and all his old equipment plus three Crumar keyboards. Yet little on *Mirage* sounded as if it was earth-made. Its other-worldly quality made it an instant classic when it was released by Island in the spring of 1977. To celebrate, Schulze performed the whole album at the London Planetarium, the scene of the public unveiling of Pink Floyd's *Dark Side Of The Moon* four years earlier.

Incredibly, Schulze was able to follow up *Mirage* with another tour de force in *X* (Brain 1978), the title indicating that it was the tenth solo album he had issued. A lavish double-album package full of writing, photos, music score and

Stockhausen-like diagrams, *X* was a return to electronic classicism. Featuring cello, violin, chamber orchestra, a real drummer, a Mellotron and a multi-voiced Korg synthesizer alongside his usual kit, Schulze created six musical portraits. Wagner's eccentric patron King Ludwig II of Bavaria was honoured, as were Nietzsche, the Austrian poet Georg Trakl and the sci-fi writer Frank Herbert. The music ranged from choral synth backdrops fronted by dancing percussive keyboards to finely accented flute-like electronic miniatures. There was driving rock-styled synth and drum music contrasted by brooding Ambient slow stuff full of atmosphere. Event-filled soundscapes gave way to bare mindscapes of dream music. Schulze had proved that analogue synthesizers and real instruments could mix to make music with the same integrity as classical music.

Around this time Schulze moved from West Berlin to a remote village near Hanover to live and work in a large glass-walled studio space in a forest near a river. He acquired the Yamaha CS-80 synthesizer, a crucial instrument which was polyphonic (with eight different voices) and touch-sensitive. Moreover, tired of spending hours building up sounds on his old Moog and ARP equipment, he decided to embrace new computerized equipment and form his own label, Innovative Communications. The impressive *Trancefer* (1981) was the first result. In 1983 he acquired the famous Fairlight Computer Music Instrument and in 1984 released one of the most influential German albums of all time, Manuel Göttsching's *E2–E4*, on his own INTEAM label.

Schulze absorbed most new advances in technology as they came his way. Now using twenty-four-track digital recording, he made the rhythmic *EN = TRANCE* (Brain), which included the mesmerizing 'FM Delight', the number-one electronic radio track in Europe and the US in 1988. Inspired by Russian electronicist Edvard Artemyev, Schulze played behind the then Berlin Wall before recording *Miditerranean Pads* (Brain 1989), a velvet fusion of percussion pads and finely tuned keyboard-triggered samples.

During the 1990s Schulze's ambition was to merge the experience gained through years of working with vintage synthesizers to newer more malleable computer systems. His interest in exotic sound samples was borne out on *Beyond Recall* (Venture 1992). Schulze also returned to his classical roots, penning an opera in 1994 and releasing *Goes Classic*, a series of electronic reshapings of music by Beethoven and others. He documented his own career with special ten-disc sets, like *Historic Edition* (1995), and continued to write for film. His 200-square-metre Moldau studio became a place of pilgrimage as it boasted almost every electronic instrument, effect and keyboard ever invented. Pride of place went to his old Moog synthesizers and so attached was he to Robert Moog's invention that he made more than half a dozen Ambient recordings dedicated to the instrument (and its American inventor) with Pete Namlook between 1993 and 1998.

LISTENING

Klaus Schulze's classic recordings for Brain were reissued by Metronome during the 1990s. In the UK Magnum Music issued various items, including *Mirage* (1991). On CD, Schulze's 'electronic landscape' is a wonderful experience, conveyed through icy synth textures and a panoramic sound production. Consummate is the best description for *X* (Brain 1994), a double disc which ably mixes rock, classical and synth tones. Both *EN = TRANCE* (Magnum 1991) and *Beyond Recall* (Venture 1991) track Schulze's interest in digital and sampling recording methods. His 'Dark Side Of The Moog' project, with Pete Namlook, began in his Moldau studio in 1993 but then moved to Frankfurt to include Bill Laswell on a series of discs which explored various Ambient stylings. Their titles punned on Pink Floyd's work – the fourth disc, released in 1996, was cleverly titled *Three Pipers At The Gates Of Dawn* after the Floyd's first album.

HOLGER CZUKAY

Once I described Holger Czukay as 'a thorough-going eccentric with one foot in the avant-garde and the other in the outer fringes of modern pop sensibility'. On leaving Can in 1977 he unexpectedly became their most successful member with the commercial success of the multi-edit album *Movies* (EMI 1979). Czukay's irreverent attitude to the studio; his use of short-wave radio snippets, dictaphone and extreme tape-splicing made him one of the first 'sampling musicians' in rock.

Czukay was born just before the Second World War in Danzig, where his earliest musical interest was in church music. After the war his family moved to West Germany and he turned to organ music and conducting. His work in an electrical shop sparked a fascination with electronics. In 1957 he saw Stock-hausen perform in Duisburg and became a convert. While he was studying double bass at the Berlin Academy in the 1960s, he followed the composer around Germany, seeing him as a strong individualist 'who made uncopiable music'. Czukay wrote orchestral scores and played popular guitar. He went to Switzerland in 1966, ostensibly to conduct, but ended up teaching. There he met Michael Karoli, who turned him on to The Beatles. Soon after, Can were born.

Czukay loved the idea of limited overdub possibilities in Can, the sheer risk of coming from a place of minimal options – a notion which would be influential on Brian Eno. He recorded a unique album in 1968 called *Canaxis 5* (Music Factory) with another Stockhausen pupil, Rolf Dammers. It was an experiment in exotic sound collecting – electrically altered sounds mixed with Vietnamese, Tibetan, African and Indian music. Czukay continued in an experimental vein after leaving Can in 1977. He worked with Conny Plank in Cologne and contributed to late-1970s albums by Cluster and Eno. The result of 1,000 edits, *Movies* (EMI 1979) was a solid commercial success which attracted many to Czukay and Can. David Sylvian, of the UK group Japan, was converted on hearing this record.

A second solo album, *On The Way To The Peak Of Normal* (EMI 1981), proved that Czukay was a master of studio Ambience. He continued to work with various members of Can as well as musicians as diverse as The Eurythmics, The Edge (of U2) and Jah Wobble. His best work came with David Sylvian, with whom he began working in 1984. Czukay would distort found voices on an old IBM dictaphone and drop them into Sylvian's sonorous mixes. Their two duo albums, *Plight & Premonition* (Virgin 1988) and *Flux + Mutability* (Virgin 1989), were benchmarks of Ambient music as pulses and tones formed by tape loops provided the canvas for a wonderful collage of sounds. Czukay always championed analogue over digital recording, and in his private studio in Cologne worked with vintage analogue equipment. A lover of many forms of music, he has often cited James Brown and Lee Perry as major influences.

LISTENING

In 1987 Czukay made one of his greatest records, *Rome Remains Rome* (Virgin), which sampled an Easter blessing by Pope John Paul II. During the 1990s many of his best recordings, like *Canaxis 5* and *On The Way To The Peak Of Normal*, were reissued on CD via Mute. All his work with David Sylvian is essential, especially the late-80s Virgin recordings *Plight & Premonition* and *Flux + Mutability*.

In 1999 came *Good Morning Story* (Tone Casualties), one of Czukay's best albums as it featured the lithe drumming of Jaki Liebezeit among a host of guest spots. Sampled short-wave radio snippets, humour and sound collaging abound.

SYNTHESIZER MUSIC

BEAVER & KRAUSE

Paul Beaver and Bernie Krause were two outstandingly innovative musicians who came together in the 1960s with an eye to popularizing the Moog synthesizer and then in 1971 concocted the classic album *Gandharva* – a true amalgam of blues, rock, gospel, Ambient and electronic sound. At the time they equated the extremely varied contents of the album to Hindu mythology and the very concept as a 'score to a non-existent film'. Like Tonto's Expanding Headband, *Gandharva* had caught a vogue for aural mind-expansion, but in retrospect it was a luminously successful voyage into electro-acoustic synthesis.

Krause was born in Detroit, had a stint with The Weavers folk group in the early 1960s, then produced for Motown before moving to Jac Holzman's Elektra label and working in California. Beaver was a jazz musician who discovered the wonders of oscillation, filter and modulation devices. He did one of the first electronic scores for a film, *The Magnetic Monster* of 1953. When the Moog synth appeared he became an advocate and after he met Krause they each bought one for the then huge sum of $15,000. After the rock explosion of 1967 the likes of The Byrds, The Beach Boys, Neil Young and Simon & Garfunkel all wanted Beaver & Krause's ingenious skills on the Moog. Moreover Hollywood beckoned and the duo's sounds would adorn such films as *The Graduate* (1967), *Catch 22* (1970) and the strange, hallucinogenic Mick Jagger vehicle *Performance* (1970).

Utilizing, à la Steve Reich, the everyday sounds of San Francisco, animal sounds, acoustic instruments from tablas to flutes and the sounds of Hammond organ and Moog synthesizer, Beaver & Krause came up with *In A Wild Sanctuary* (1970), their first recording of 'environmental impressionism celebrating life'. Better by far was their second Warner Bros. outing, *Gandharva*. The pair had persuaded Jac Holzman to let them record in San Francisco's Grace Cathedral, using the then new Quadraphonic Process and Ray Dolby's 'S' noise-reduction system. The space was 150 feet long and ninety feet high with a seven-second echo delay. A film crew was dispatched to record the event for posterity. Beaver & Krause assorted an interesting conclave of musicians, including jazz reedsmen Gerry Mulligan and Bud Shank. The results were mellifluously magnificent, fully exploiting the Ambience of the cathedral itself.

Early in 1975 Beaver died suddenly of a seizure. Krause continued to innovate. Having invented the first guitar synthesizer as far back as 1967, he went on to investigate the world of bio-acoustics and fuel the New Age scene of the 1980s with dozens of recordings of natural phenomena. During the 1990s he was lecturing in California, advocating ecology and 'audio-expressionism'.

LISTENING

The sleeve notes to Beaver & Krause's debut album, *In A Wild Sanctuary* (1970), are dedicated to, among others, Friends of the Earth, *The Whole Earth Katalog* and nineteenth-century poet Ellen Glasgow, who gave them the title. *Gandharva* (1971) is an adroit amalgam of sounds. Its early stages feature the blues guitar of Mike Bloomfield along with bristling shards of Moog synthesizer. 'Walkin'' is the sound of hymnal gospel graced by Satie-like piano. The final four pieces are thoroughly spiritual, the Moog sounds wonderfully augmented by Beaver's Hammond and pipe organ. The horn and flute sounds seem to drift upwards, while the finale, 'Bright Shadows', involves a wonderful double harp interspersed with fragments of reed and woodwind which trail-off into silence. Reissued on CD in 1993, *Gandharva* can be found paired with *In A Wild Sanctuary* on a Warner Bros. US edition.

TONTO'S EXPANDING HEADBAND

The appearance of Tonto's Expanding Headband in 1971 was as much a shock to psychedelic enthusiasts as it was to mainstream rock fans. Here were two long-haired hippies standing next to their space-age-looking Moog synthesizer on the back of a gatefolded album drenched in garish reds and blues. The cover painting of *Zero Time*, their debut album, was titled *Apollo On Mars*. The album folded out to reveal another lurid psychedelic painting, *Seed Dream*. Lyrics to a mystical reverie titled 'Riversong' were also enclosed.

Then when one heard the record it was totally electronic, in fact a mini-electronic symphony. That 'Riversong' was a totally synthesized vocal mantra was an astonishing discovery. Moreover Malcolm Cecil and Robert Margouleff were two high-level musicians with an encyclopedic knowledge of engineering and sound-design. They worked at Jimi Hendrix's Electric Lady studios in New York and had specifically studied the Moog synthesizer and its scope for polyphony or simply playing more than one note at a time.

In 1971 they came up with 'Tonto', short for 'The New Timbral Orchestra', which rigged up a number of Moog Series 3 synthesizers together with three keyboards in customized wooden cabinets. The resultant music was warm and lifelike and showed the world that sound synthesis was not a dehumanizing experience. In fact *Zero Time* is an exceptional example of electronic Ambience in the rock era. Margouleff and Cecil went on to become in-demand sound-shapers; their polyphonic synthesizer gracing the work of many pop records, most notably the early 1970s work of Stevie Wonder. They were awarded a Grammy for their contribution to Wonder's 1973 opus *Innervisions*. After that they moved to Malibu in California and continued to sound-design. By the 1990s they were working on solar-energy recording and computer sound-morphing via the Internet.

LISTENING

The original Atlantic album is still highly collectable. It was reissued on CD by Prestige in 1996 as *Tonto Rides Again*, such classic tracks as 'Jetsex' and 'Cybernaut' enhanced by the addition of seven newly discovered pieces recorded between 1972 and 1974 in California.

TIM BLAKE

One of the leading lights in synthesizer music of the 1970s, Tim Blake became famous in France and has often been considered a French musician. Nevertheless he was born and raised in the UK, where he benefited from a classical trumpet education. Having gigged with a number of bands in the 1960s as a virtuoso harmonica player, Blake turned his attention to the embryonic synthesizer technology and headed for France in 1971.

Soon he teamed up with Daevid Allen's infamous hippie troupe Gong and helped them shape what became known as the *Radio Gnome Trilogy* between 1973 and 1974. After touring and recording two more live Gong albums, Blake left to follow a path towards New Age enlightenment. Many consider his merging of New Age philosophy with a growing understanding of the timbral beauty of synthesizers to be a key factor in triggering the New Age music phenomenon. Certainly his next phase would reap spectacular success. Not only was *Crystal Machine* (1977) a staggering deployment of synthesizers over a series of short but incisive melodic compositions, but the accompanying laser and light show by Patrice Warrener was a smash hit throughout the UK, France and Japan. Blake's shiny jump-suit, gaudy make-up and long, flowing hair complemented a stage full of electronic equipment and mind-warping special effects.

Blake was exceptionally proficient on EMS Synthi, MiniMoog and Elka Strings and used a strong arsenal of effects. At the time he was endorsed by the English progressive musician Peter Gabriel but took a left turn on his next project, *New Jerusalem* (1978), where he inadvisedly sang his way through a series of New Age poems, even quoting his namesake, the great English mystic poet William Blake.

After that he was recruited by the English space-rock band Hawkwind for two albums in 1980 and then retired for a decade to a Breton mill to develop his compositional technique. In 1991 he returned to live performance, touring the world, including the US, with a new vocal and synthesizer concept called *Magick*. Blake's achievements may seem minor in comparison to, say, Tangerine Dream but his excellent *Crystal Machine* was many rock fans' first introduction to synthesizer music.

LISTENING

During the 1990s Mantra Records in France reissued Tim Blake's first two albums on disc. *Crystal Machine*, taken from concerts in 1976 and 1977, is still the definitive Blake album — its phantasmagoric sleeve of the alien Ziggy-styled synth guru festooned with technology in the eye of a wave, a brilliant New Music icon. If you can take Blake's fairly thin vocals the music of *New Jerusalem* (1978) is still very captivating. In 2000 Voiceprint UK reissued both *Crystal Machine* and *Magick*.

JEAN-MICHEL JARRE

One of the twentieth century's most successful creators of synthesizer music, the Frenchman Jean-Michel Jarre had racked up worldwide sales of thirty-five million albums within ten years of recording his first international hit, *Oxygene* (Polydor 1977). His highly defined rhythmic music, which relied on a strong sense of structural discipline within which memorable keyboard and synth lines were articulated, remained a successful art form right through the 1990s. Aided in no small way by his gargantuan stage shows, which used major cities like Houston and London as backdrops to his kinetic laser and light shows, Jarre's album sales were over sixty million as the century came to a close.

With Jarre it's easy to get lost in a maze of statistics and forget his real contribution to electronic and Ambient music. Initially he was inspired by the use of everyday sounds by his compatriot Pierre Schaeffer in his *musique concrète* and openly embraced analogue synthesizers such as the Moog and the EMS VCS3 as used by Brian Eno and Pink Floyd in the early 1970s. It was the combination of such instruments with equipment custom-built by engineer Michael Geiss and with devices such as the Fairlight Computer Music Instrument which made Jarre's electronic soup sound so state-of-the-art. With the advent of the sampler he drew on Stockhausen's concept of 'universal music' in 1984 to make *Zoolook*, an album created out of the voices and tongues of the whole world.

Born in 1948 in Lyon, Jarre was from a family with an impeccable electronic-music pedigree. His grandfather was the inventor of the first French mixing board, his father an avowed follower of environmental music. Jarre started on piano at five and attended the Paris Conservatoire in his teens, studying harmony and composition. Bored with Serialism, during the 1960s he joined Pierre Schaeffer's Research Group For Concrete Music and explored the 'analogue sampling' used in this music. By the late 1960s he wished to turn away from acoustic sounds and left the Group to follow Stockhausen's lead in 'pure electronic music'. Jarre wrote pieces like *The Cage And Eros Machine* (released in France in 1971) and over the next few years supplied electronic scores for ballet and the cinema. Yet he did not find an international outlet until the creation of *Oxygene* in 1976.

Jarre had worked for years with equipment specialists and musician-engineer Michael Geiss, and *Oxygene* proved a milestone in synthesizer music. As well as customized technology it featured famous analogue synthesizers like the ARP and VCS3, plus Farfisa organ and even a Mellotron. The album's very simplicity, warmth and accessibility made it a chart success in many countries and thus broke down barriers between the public and electronic music. Synthesizers were now seen as fun, an integral part of modernity. Jarre's high-profile relationship with the English actress Charlotte Rampling also helped his growing reputation as the world's most successful French musician.

Equinoxe (1978) followed the pattern of *Oxygene*, a single electronic theme punctuated by many variations. It was a hit in thirty-five countries, its success crowned by the record-breaking debut concert at the Place de la Concorde in Paris, attended by one million people. Jarre dubbed the extravaganza 'a musical fête'. The more rhythmic *Magnetic Fields* (1981) preceded huge concerts in

China with traditional Chinese musicians heard by a staggering half a billion people. The resultant live album again sold in huge quantities.

Then Jarre did an about-face. Like Eno, he decided to make an environmental album. He made only one copy of *Music For Supermarkets* (1983). This single artefact was then played on the radio before its auction at a Parisian hotel for $10,000. The proceeds went to the support of struggling artists. Another change came with *Zoolook* (1984), an album of vocal effects derived from language samples from all over the world coaxed into melodic tracks. By 1986 he was back to spectaculars, lighting up the panoramic skyscraper-filled Houston skyline with an incredible laser-filled light show in honour of the birth of Texas and NASA. Dubbed 'Rendez-Vous', the concerts were memorable for Jarre's use of a huge circular keyboard which lit up as he played it.

By this stage Jarre was incorporating a wide variety of sources in his live and recorded music. As well as the ethnic sounds of Japan and Africa he also involved opera singers and choral groups in his live shows. He used the vocoder on his 1988 album *Revolutions* and staged another spectacular at London's Docklands Arena. Again he changed tack by releasing *Waiting For Cousteau* in 1990, an album in honour of the great French diver Jacques Cousteau; its lengthy title track was one slow Ambient tribute to the aquamarine world. Within a few years Jarre was back playing stadiums, dazzling all comers with his array of giant searchlights, his circular illuminated keyboard and his laser harp. The latter was a series of light lasers which pointed vertically from the stage, allowing Jarre to pass his hands through them and create music.

Always wishing to better previous performances, Jarre continued to tour what could only be described as a 'sound and light experience'. He was made a UNESCO goodwill ambassador in 1995 and in 1997 his Disques Dreyfus record label signed a new deal with Sony. Living in a suburb of western Paris with Rampling and three children, Jarre reflected on his years of success. He maintained a commitment to analogue recording and favoured old synthesizers over new digital ones for their hands-on approach. Michael Geiss's contributions were still preferred over the latest gadgets. Jarre's aim was always spontaneity in creativity and realism in sound. And just to prove it he returned to his roots by making a sequel to *Oxygene* titled *Oxygene 7–13*, his first 1997 release for Sony.

Jarre celebrated the dawn of the twenty-first century with a lavish spectacle at the pyramids of Giza and a spanking-new album, *Metamorphoses*, which featured Laurie Anderson, Natacha Atlas and the Irish violinist Sharon Corr in a form of planetarium electronic which cross-pollinated his trademark synth sounds with House, Techno and Middle Eastern influences.

LISTENING

Many find Jarre's take on electronic sound extremely commercial and often rockist in nature. Yet his first two Polydor albums (now on Sony CD), *Oxygene* and *Equinoxe*, are worth investigating. *Oxygene* (reissued in 1999) had an enormous influence on Techno Trance music of the late 1990s. *Zoolook* (1984) is an extremely good indicator of early sampling techniques and the use of the Fairlight Computer Music Instrument. It also features the voice of Laurie Anderson. Other albums, such as *Waiting For Cousteau* (1990), *Chronologie* (1993) and *Oxygene 7–13* (1997), all have their moments.

Metamorphoses (Epic 2000) showed Jarre, at fifty, to be completely in touch with modern pan-global music.

VANGELIS

'I function as a channel through which music emerges from the chaos of noise,' Vangelis once said. Yet so textured and rhapsodic has been the music produced by this keyboard genius that one often wonders if the noises in his head originate from the Elysian Fields of ancient mythology. Certainly he's one of the great popularizers of the synthesizer, the first to win an Oscar for his completely synthesized score of the 1981 film *Chariots Of Fire*. At the core of Vangelis's success is his humanization of electronic means, his unwillingness to get caught up in artificial avenues of creation and determination to rely instead on pure instinct. His body of work over the years attests to his own belief in emotion over machine. His soundtrack to the Ridley Scott film *Blade Runner* (1982) still stands as one of the twentieth century's greatest achievements in sound.

Vangelis Papathanassiou was born in southern Greece, a post-war child prodigy who was playing piano at four and performing his own compositions at six. After a military coup and the arrival of dictatorship in Greece in 1967, Vangelis fled the country for Paris the following year. He soon became a member of the Greek expatriate band Aphrodite's Child with singer Demis Roussos and was renowned as a keyboard and synth virtuoso. A reclusive character, he soon tired of psychedelic rock and began to concentrate on keyboard-based symphonic music. He began a fertile relationship with the director Frédéric Rossif in 1970, writing for a number of art and wildlife films. Such soundtracks as *Animal Apocalypse* and *The Savage Feast* blueprinted Vangelis's style of sonorous glistening keyboards couched in wonderfully clear acoustic arrangements.

In 1974 he visited London, ostensibly to audition as new keyboardist for progressive band Yes. He opted instead to stay and build his own studio. On the top floor of an old film studio near Marble Arch, Vangelis laid out a personal space of nearly 1,500 square feet with a sixteen-track recording facility, grand and electric pianos, organs and synthesizers. He also filled the space with eccentric mobiles, statues and figurines. He christened it Nemo Studios and soon got a contract with RCA. His first UK album, *Heaven And Hell*, came out in 1976 and he also developed a strong working relationship with Yes vocalist Jon Anderson.

Nemo Studios became a hive of activity, the workaholic Vangelis recording and producing every single day, all day. The studio could handle choirs and a huge assortment of percussion instruments, including tubular bells. In 1977 Vangelis went polyphonic and embraced the new Prophet 5 and Yamaha CS-80 synthesizers. One of the first musicians in the UK to own a CS-80, he loved it for its touch-sensitivity and it ended up being his trademark instrument. Over this period he expanded to twenty-four-track recording and acquired drum machines and sequencers. Daily Vangelis would fill up reels and reels of multi-track tape. Some would be edited, but many were not, as he preferred a spontaneous approach. Such albums as *Spiral* (RCA 1977) and *China* (Polydor 1979) were the result of this direct electronic expression.

In 1981 Vangelis improvised direct to the film *Chariots Of Fire* without any synchronization. So evocative of the tale of great British runners was his music that Vangelis won an Oscar and became a famous film composer. The following year he created his most important music when he scored Ridley Scott's ground-breaking futuristic vision of life gone wrong, *Blade Runner*. Eerily evocative of a very plausible future, Scott's vision was perfectly complemented by Vangelis's unearthly score, which deployed grand pianos, keyboards and synthesizer to memorable effect. That year also saw him score Costa-Gavras's intense political thriller *Missing*. From that year on Vangelis was in such demand that he devoted the greatest part of his time and energy to film, theatre and ballet commissions.

In 1987 Vangelis left the UK to travel and write in the US and Europe, using a mobile synthesizer set-up. While in Rome to work on a film score, he began writing themes in his hotel suite which he later used to depict Paris and made into an album called *The City* (East West 1990), acclaimed for its filmic quality. Famously shy of all publicity and wary of the music business, Vangelis has nevertheless used his position of exotic keyboard maestro to dazzling commercial advantage. As a lover of pure sound and pure expression he despises the complexity of much modern digital equipment, preferring the 'spontaneous playability' of vintage synths and keyboards. A disliker of demos, overdubs and editing, Vangelis in recent years has taken to designing his own equipment so it will have a 'real-time response', aiding his quest for pure, automatic music.

LISTENING

No one need go any further than Vangelis's brilliant music to Ridley Scott's film *Blade Runner* (1982). The textures which Vangelis coaxes from Fender Rhodes piano, Yamaha CS-80 synthesizer and Steinway acoustic piano are fabulous. So luminous are his touches on the keys, and so spatial the production sound, that again and again the effect is one of ensemble music or the lustre of organic instruments. It's often his placing of individual sounds, his incorporation of the voice of Mary Hopkin or Dick Morrisey's shimmering saxophone on 'Love Theme', that does the trick. For Vangelis, electronic and organic sounds are both legitimate sources of material with which to beautify a work. Inexplicably, the soundtrack was never properly released until East West did so in 1994. Other recommended recordings are the tranquil *Soil Festivities* (Polydor 1984) and the atmospheric electro-acoustic *The City* (East West 1990), which features Ambient Parisian recordings with the film director Roman Polanski.

THE INDIE WAVE

CABARET VOLTAIRE

One of the most radical groups to come out of UK punk-rock, Cabaret Voltaire took sound itself as an inspiration and, casting themselves in the role of media terrorists, created a catalogue of wonderful artefacts. Inspired by Pierre Schaeffer, Stockhausen, Can, Brian Eno and the literary 'cut-up' techniques of the American writer William Burroughs, Cabaret Voltaire went from being an electronic-industrial band to being a vital force in the electro-dance scene of the early 1980s. As UK pioneers in the use of breakbeats and Hip-Hop styles they naturally graduated to Chicago House in the late 1980s and by the 1990s were easily assimilating Techno and Ambient music.

During the early 1970s in Sheffield a group of youngsters were influenced by the original Dadaist club set up by Hugo Ball in Zurich in 1917. It was called The Cabaret Voltaire and so the name was adopted. Keen on manipulating sound, Chris Watson, Stephen Mallinder and Richard H. Kirk took to rehearsing weekly with an oscillator, some cheap guitars, clarinets and a VCS3 synthesizer and Revox tape machine loaned by the music department of Sheffield University. Working mostly in the realm of Schaeffer-like aural collages, the trio wrote to Eno during the mid-1970s for inspiration. Using film, handouts and Dadaist tricks to gain attention, they performed alongside Joy Division in 1976 and were signed by Rough Trade in London, the label agreeing that they could retain an insular independence in their home city. Renting an old factory space near Sheffield University which was to become their legendary Western Works studio, they installed a four-track Revox tape recorder.

From the beginning sound and texture were what guided Cabaret Voltaire. Though their 1979 'Nag Nag Nag' single made them punk heroes, the contents of the record, its drum-machine pulse and treated vocals, actually had an electronic bias. Their debut album, *Mix-Up* (1979), went further into the arena of tape loops and found sounds. At a happening in Belgium that year they performed with the Beat writers William Burroughs and Brion Gysin, regarding them as kindred spirits. In 1980 they released *Three Mantras*, excellent dronal music of an uncertain ethnic and electronic origin lasting over forty minutes. Resolutely uncompromising, Cabaret Voltaire were only willing to play the music-business game their way – staying in Sheffield and sending their 'finished product' to London.

Their métier quickly extended to videos and soundtracks. Their record covers were like art-school collages while their continual left-field interest in taboo areas only strengthened their appeal. Cabaret Voltaire's third Rough Trade album, *Red Mecca* (1981), sold in huge quantities, establishing them in the US and Japan. Its 'wash of colour' sleeve and sombre, almost primeval music meant   Cabaret Voltaire were perceived as resolutely independent sound manipulators. Unwilling to tour or be drawn into more traditional music making, Chris Watson left soon afterwards to pursue 'sound research' at Tyne-Tees Television and eventually at the Royal Society for the Protection of Birds.

Kirk and Mallinder continued to expand Cabaret Voltaire's music. In 1982 they supported the Polish solidarity movement and performed in Japan. Using a myriad of late-twentieth-century visual imagery, they played in front of an array of TV monitors all synched to their continuous pulse. Kirk specialized in the raw material for their film and video work and played guitars, wind instruments and synthesizers. Mallinder concentrated on voice, bass, drum and percussive effects. Though still seeing their 'art' as a kind of reportage, they easily embraced 'disco' sounds in 1983 when they signed to Virgin. With Mallinder now extending himself to keyboards and trumpet and with Kirk on Japanese shakuhachi the resultant album, *Crackdown*, was a surprisingly commercial beat-laden affair. Yet it contained a bonus album of instrumental music, some of it the most beautiful Ambient work of their career.

Through their own company, Double Vision, Cabaret Voltaire extended their work to include other artists like Derek Jarman, David Bowie and Andy Warhol. Their music became more exploratory of rhythm, the *Micro-Phonies* album of 1984 a veritable homage to James Brown. Their final Virgin album, *The Covenant, The Sword And The Arm Of The Lord* (1985), was assembled after touring America and contains endless snippets from US TV documentaries on religion and firearms. After moving to The Beatles' old label, Parlophone, in 1987, they went to Chicago to meet House innovator Marshall Jefferson. Their return to favour in 1990 saw them work with Manchester's A Guy Called Gerald and top remixer Paul Oakenfold. Having been British pioneers of the breakbeat, Cabaret Voltaire were able to move with ease into Techno and Ambient electronica. Their new music on *Body And Soul* (1991) had the sophistication and smoothness derived from computer sampling techniques, yet it contained first-rate atmospheric instrumentals. In 1993, at the time of release of *International Language* (reputedly two albums mixed into one) and Richard Kirk's extremely painterly *Virtual State*, Kirk himself acknowledged the continuing importance of twentieth-century composers: 'Stockhausen is more of an influence than ever. Both he and John Cage in terms of attitude to sound, Ambience and "found" recordings.'

LISTENING

The full discography of Cabaret Voltaire is vast and doesn't concern us here. In 1990 Mute Records in London reissued the core Rough Trade catalogue on CD. *The Living Legends* pulls together all their significant singles from the late 1970s and early 80s. In 1988 Crépuscule in Belgium released *Eight Crépuscule Tracks*, a marvellous disc of trio recordings from the early 1980s revealing their experimental-Ambient and proto-House roots. The Virgin discs are still available. Made after Western Works relocated to more comfortable surroundings in central Sheffield, latter-day albums like *Body And Soul* (Crépuscule 1991), *Plasticity* (Plastex 1992), *International Language* (Plastex 1993) and *The Conversation* (Apollo 1994) all display an uncanny knack of making technology work to create a deeply satisfying trance music.

NEW ORDER AND JOY DIVISION

After the rage of punk in Britain, rock literally reinvented itself in the late 1970s and early 80s. Replacing the pomp of 'progressive rock' was a leaner, more realistic music which happily embraced electronic technology. Important was the arrival of more compact polyphonic synthesizers, sequencers, drum machines and cheaper monophonic synths, especially from the Japanese Roland company. Groups like The Human League, Depeche Mode and Soft Cell all came to the fore, making good rock and pop using quirky synth and sequencer sounds. Vince Clarke of Depeche Mode would go on to make a strong career as the techno-boffin in Erasure but of all these artists the most significant was Joy Division, later New Order.

Joy Division were the product of the bleaker parts of Manchester in the depressed late 1970s. Their music echoed the emotional and psychological pain of living in a post-industrial wasteland. In Ian Curtis they had an Existential poet on a par with the visionary French Symbolist Arthur Rimbaud. Curtis's emotional creativity was caught on two extraordinary albums, *Unknown Pleasures* (1979) and *Closer* (1980), by producer Martin Hannett. Joy Division were a primary influence on the genesis of U2. After Ian Curtis committed suicide in 1980 the rest of the group carried on as New Order. Instead of ploughing their old furrow they opted for a new kind of music aided by American sequencers and drum machines.

Their first big breakthrough came in 1983 in the form of 'Blue Monday', which defined the era of twelve-inch dance singles and changed the course of popular music. With its fat, irresistible drum thump, 'Blue Monday' was the biggest selling twelve-incher of all time and without doubt the beginning of modern House music. Through ownership of Manchester's Hacienda club, New Order became sponsors of the Rave generation and via a series of great records continued to experiment at the crossroads of emotion and technology.

When the four principals of Joy Division met in Manchester in 1977 they were all just entering their twenties. Bernard Sumner, a graphic artist, and Peter Hook, a council worker, had both started to teach themselves guitar the previous year. They were joined by the brilliant drummer Steven Morris, whose Germanic style was heavily influenced by Can. Ian Curtis, the lyricist and melodist, was a huge fan of The Velvet Underground and David Bowie's Berlin period. It's no secret that the group's first name Warsaw was derived from Bowie's Eno-assisted *Low* of 1977. Their earliest music had 'punk' written all over it but quickly their style gelled – Curtis's declamatory lyrics, Hook's razor-sharp sliding bass style, Sumner's Minimalist chordal guitar chops and Morris's piston-like mechanized drum beats. Various demos were done for RCA and WEA but it was television producer Tony Wilson who offered them the opportunity to record in 1978. By the following spring everything was ready.

The location for the recording of *Unknown Pleasures* was 10cc's famous Strawberry Studios in the Manchester suburb of Stockport. Here one of the finest groups of the 1970s had built a fine twenty-four-track studio. As Joy Division's producer, Martin Hannett was interested not only in capturing the group's visceral intensity but also in colouring it with tape effects, synth noises, found sounds and synth drones. Emphasis was placed on getting a crystal-clear drum sound, with different drums recorded independently. Microphones were set up in separate rooms and Ambiences created using digital delay and reverb. Hannett was brilliant at conjuring up a landscape of late-night desolation as the doors of far-off lifts opened, analogue synthesizers oscillated splintered tones, radio frequencies hummed, glass smashed and car horns honked. The album recalled the atmosphere of Kraftwerk's *Radio-Activity* (1976) and even the drum patterns of 'She's Lost Control' seemed to replicate automotive patterns on Kraftwerk's 1978 opus *The Man Machine*. Housed in a dark sleeve and illustrated with only the spidery form of radio waves from a dying star, *Unknown Pleasures* was a bona-fide classic and defined the style of Wilson's Factory Records.

In the autumn of 1979 Joy Division recorded 'Atmosphere', another realization of chilled beauty, with its perfect layering of organ, drums, chiming percussion and emotional vocal. The single would prefigure the recording of *Closer* (1980), put down exactly one year after *Unknown Pleasures*. This time Pink Floyd's Britannia Row facility in London was chosen. Sessions were lengthy, band and producer often sleeping in the studio to absorb its atmosphere. According to Steven Morris, recording was done in a recreation room because Hannett liked the ambience. Side One of *Closer* was very live, with the odd cheesy synth on display. Side Two was extraordinary and possibly the reason for the continuing myth around the band. Funereal, baroque, Ambient, eerie and eloquently beautiful, the four tracks which made up this long adieu were some of the most elegiac creations in rock. Hannett spent long nights routing stuff through his mixing desk, adding tweaks here and there, pummelling and shaping performance into electronicized composition. Everything was discreet, the sound of analogue synthesizers no more than a tint in the expanse. Curtis sang of isolation and desperation on 'The Eternal' as machines whirred all around him, broad synthesizer chords framing the harmony. Ravaged by epilepsy and barbiturates, Curtis would hang himself only weeks after the completion of *Closer*, the album serving as a testament to tortured genius.

Joy Division became New Order with the addition of Gillian Gilbert at the end of 1980. Born in the early 1960s, Gilbert, an art student, came in as guitar and synth player to allow the musically talented Bernard Sumner to do more things. Early work with Hannett sounded like Joy Division but Gilbert's presence brought a fresh direction. She played a polyphonic Arp Quadra synth and Sumner started building sequencers from manuals. A 1981 album, *Movement*, marked the end of New Order's relationship with Hannett but their growing fascination with programming synthesizers such as the Prophet 5 led to a growing independence. Their music started to chug along on the energy of machines, overlaid by soulful vocals from Sumner and Hook's complementary bass-as-lead-guitar style.

With a combination of an eight-voice Emulator digital keyboard sampler, an error in the programming of an Oberheim DMX bass drum-machine sound and some electronic drums, New Order came up with 'Blue Monday' in 1983. This lengthy piece of repetitive dance heaven was truly futuristic for its time. The group even tried to mix in an Apple Mac-synthesized voice when they were recording at Britannia Row but technical difficulties resulted in the use of Sumner's voice instead. It didn't make any difference to the fortunes of the million-selling single or the future perception of New Order as dance rockers. The album recorded at the same time, *Power, Corruption And Lies*, saw the group fully enveloped in new technology. In addition to the 'Blue Monday' equipment, two months of production saw New Order avail themselves of Moog and Prophet synthesizer sounds that humanized the relentless flow of beats. With Sumner's now ecstatic songs dominating the proceedings, New Order were a near-perfect meeting of heart and mind.

Their next album, *Low Life* (1985), was an exuberant celebration of the new hybrid, Gilbert playing bass and synth over lovingly programmed sequencers. Some tracks were improvised in the studio in one take as the more sequencer-based pieces took up much Britannia Row studio time. The album featured sampled frogs and a wonderful Ambient synthesizer and guitar instrumental (written by Sumner) titled 'Elegia'. For *Brotherhood* (1986) the group opted to split the album between real drum sounds and programmed drums. Featuring extensive use of acoustic guitar, it made musical nods to Pink Floyd, Lou Reed and even old Joy Division music. In terms of equipment, the group were in the land of the early large, floppy-disc-driven systems from Emulator and Voyetra. They were also using various Roland drum programmers, including the now famous TR 808 drum machine, a staple of the later Acid House scene.

New Order were becoming fully competent with interface computers and were learning sequencing software designed by Steinberg. *Brotherhood* was partly recorded at the Windmill Lane studios in Dublin, and for *Technique* (1989) New Order spent four months divided between Ibiza, Spain and Peter Gabriel's Real World studios. With their favourite engineer, Michael Johnson, in tow, New Order filled all acoustic space on forty-eight tracks of recording equipment. Three Apple Mac computers were used and the group augmented this set-up with their own sixteen-track facility. Steven Morris's drums were even sampled and the result was state-of-the-art Techno rock of the times.

LISTENING

After *Technique* New Order's members pursued various solo projects, including *Electronic* (1991), Sumner's impressive electro-acoustic collaboration with Smiths guitarist Johnny Marr. After a period of uncertainty New Order signed with London Records and released the cheerful *Republic* (1993). All the albums mentioned above were original Factory Records releases and were graced by admirable sleeves designed by Peter Saville. Early Joy Division music and the first two albums by New Order chart substantial advances in Ambient and electronic music as it developed in the UK. The austere beauty of Joy Division was celebrated in a comprehensive four-CD set called *Body And Soul* (London 1997).

THE DURUTTI COLUMN

In the squall of noise that was British indie rock circa 1979, one album stood out like a beacon. *The Return Of The Durutti Column* was the product of a frail Mancunian guitarist named Vini Reilly. In eschewing most of rock's pyro-technics in favour of classically inspired guitar-arpeggiated instrumentals, the record shocked the established music press. Pastel shades, chamber music, new psychedelia it was; indie rock it was not. Yet Factory Records, Reilly's label, was founded with him in mind. And over the years this unassuming genius, plagued by ill-health, would make a series of fascinating recordings which explored not only instrumental music but also new formats such as CD, DAT and CD-Rom.

As a post-war child Reilly grew up listening to a lot of Fats Waller and Art Tatum records. His father also loved opera and Benjamin Britten and encouraged in the young Reilly a love of classical music. The boy studied piano, had a number of day tutors and then was taught by a professor of music. At ten he got his first guitar and tried to play it. Then he met a German lady who specialized in medieval music and played the spinet. She coached him in the fundamentals of composition and performance. Over the next twelve years she would be his mentor, exposing him to the music of Bach, the Czech composer Martinů and the paintings of the Frenchman Yves Klein.

By his early twenties Reilly was playing folk and jazz, but switched to punk in 1977 when he joined a group called The Nosebleeds. A friend, Tony Wilson, who worked for Granada TV, wanted to do something in the music business and had informed Reilly he wanted him to join 'a bunch of Didsbury hippies' called The Durutti Column. The nucleus of this group would go on to form Simply Red in 1986. The Durutti Column recorded the first Factory sampler EP in late 1978 and then split up. Reilly was now alone and entered various Manchester studios in the spring and summer of 1979 to make history with the maverick producer Martin Hannett. With occasional support from a drummer and bass player, Reilly's album *The Return Of The Durutti Column* came out a masterpiece.

The sound was ethereal, delicate, isolated, profound and elegiac all at the same time. Beginning in the psychedelic haze of 'Sketch For Summer', it reached a climax on the awesome 'Conduct', the Echoplexed electric guitar ringing out loud and clear against a thunderous rhythm section. The album was released in January 1980 and, according to Reilly: 'At the time it was a surprise. The music press called the record Ambient and compared it to the work of Robert Fripp. It was recorded in a couple of hours with no overdubbing. The response put me on the road with Joy Division. For me the whole experience was a form of therapy.'

Reilly saw 'the production of a very tranquil music in 1979 as an anarchic gesture'. The name 'The Durutti Column' had been derived from an idealistic hero of the Spanish Civil War and the Situationist Internationale of Strasbourg in the late 1960s. The Situationists had published a sandpaper-sleeved book called *Return Of The Durutti Column* with the aim of destroying other books on store shelves. The first Durutti album, likewise wrapped, did so much damage in record shops it was deleted and released in a normal sleeve late in the summer of 1980. In effect Reilly was bringing anarcho-punk ideals to Ambient music.

Reilly suffered from anorexia nervosa, for which doctors would keep him on tranquillizers until 1995. But this debilitating condition did not affect his output and he was so prolific that he had to release material on two other European labels, Crépuscule and Factory Benelux. I've described some of his early work as like tears rolling off records, so expressive were his repeated and delayed harmonic guitar lines. His next Factory album, *L.C.* (from the Italian radical political slogan '*lotta continua*', 'the struggle continues'), filled the mind with images of autumn breezes, soft rain, misty mornings and all the colours of spring. Reilly recorded the album, released in 1981, spontaneously in five hours with percussionist Bruce Mitchell after receiving a gift of a four-track Teac tape machine from Yorkshire guitarist Bill Nelson.

During a conversation in the 1990s Reilly confessed to me: 'Although people perceive me as a guitarist, I write all my music on piano. When I get to the piano the music arrives fully formed.' Hence it's not surprising to see him expanding his instrumental palette early on, adding cor anglais and trumpet for his 1982 album *Another Setting*. After recording in Portugal, Reilly spent 1984 working on *Without Mercy* – a musical setting of Keats's poem 'La Belle Dame Sans Merci' – which featured an additional chamber ensemble. A tour of Japan (where The Durutti Column were extremely popular) resulted in 1985's *Domo Arigato*, the first-ever CD-only release by a rock artist. In 1987 The Durutti Column ventured to the US, where a version of Jefferson Airplane's 'White Rabbit' was recorded in Los Angeles. That year also saw the release of the first commercial DAT album, *The Guitar And Other Machines*, which featured more complex production and three backing vocalists. Late in 1987 Reilly began working in Bath with the producer Stephen Street on the debut solo album by the former Smiths vocalist and lyricist Morrissey. The resultant *Viva Hate* (EMI 1988) was a number-one smash, bathed in Reilly's lovely guitars, arrangements and orchestrations.

Influenced by House music, Reilly was intrigued by the ability of a keyboard to trigger vocal samples. During the summer of 1988 he assembled the voices of Otis Redding, Annie Lennox, Tracy Chapman and the Australian opera singer Joan Sutherland. 'I actually used her voice and long sustained notes to play tunes. It was a wild dream of mine to have the greatest opera singer of this century on my record.' The resultant album, *Vini Reilly* (1989), was a powerful mix of electro and acoustic ballads, flamenco guitar and electronic hues.

By the early 1990s Reilly was openly flirting with House music but this paled in comparison with the 1991 release of *Lips That Would Kiss*, a collection of released and unreleased work from the 1980s on various European labels. In 1994 a new album, *Sex And Death*, was the first to get a simultaneous CD-Rom and Internet site release. On this excellent return to form Reilly used a Fender Rhodes master keyboard to trigger a classic selection of old analogue synthesizers, including the VCS3 and Moog. The album was inspired by hearing a thunderstorm outside his French windows at five o'clock one morning and recording it as background sound. Though the album featured a variety of lively electric and acoustic guitar music, Reilly attests to its Ambient origins.

LISTENING

In 1996 and 1998 Factory Once reissued eight original Durutti Column albums, digitally remastered with bonus tracks. Almost all of Vini Reilly's output is worth hearing, though his first two albums, *The Return Of The Durutti Column* (1980) and *L.C.* (1981), are masterpieces. The newly restored *Another Setting* (1982) and *Without Mercy* (1984) offer further rewarding glimpses of his impressionistic chamber-music style. As an alternative view of rock both *Vini Reilly* (1989) and *Sex And Death* (1994) are high-class art. Such compilations as *Durutti Column – The First Four Albums* (1988) and *Lips That Would Kiss (From Prayers To Broken Stone)* (1991) are definitely worth seeking out.

COLIN NEWMAN

As a member of the strange, often Dadaistic London punk group Wire, Colin Newman created some wonderful recordings of which the quirky 'pop' singles 'Outdoor Miner' (1978) and 'Map Reference' (1979) achieved a sheen of sound without compromising the group's individuality. The latter song came from the EMI Harvest album *154*, on which Wire worked with producer Mike Thorne in a way that integrated electronic keyboards and studio effects into the mix.

This approach was extended on Newman's first solo album, *A–Z* (Beggars Banquet 1980). Strewn among the claustrophobic, often angry band music were two impressive Ambient works. 'Image' used short guitar strums, synthesizer drones and tape-manipulated sounds. 'Seconds To Last' involved an extended instrumental coda with a Japanese-flavoured keyboard sound. Seizing on the possibilities of the Ambient sound, Newman extended the idea on the wonderfully titled *Provisionally Entitled The Singing Fish* (4AD 1981). With help from Wire's former drummer Robert Gotobed on only one track, Newman played, recorded and produced the whole album at Scorpio Sound in London.

Provisionally Entitled The Singing Fish comprised twelve 'Fish' creations, each one a haiku-like exploration of a certain timbre. Hence 'Fish 2' has a Chinese lute sound, 'Fish 4' is an enchanting atmospheric coloration of discreetly treated sounds, 'Fish 10' a simple piano repetition. Newman's next album, *Not To* (4AD 1982), returned to the compressed band sound, this time employing tabla, vibraphone and 'assorted instrumentation'. The title track, 'Not To', conjured up its own unique sound universe where Ambient drone was the order of the day.

In the late 1980s Newman re-formed Wire, this time exploring the use of computer sequencers. His association with former Minimal Compact singer and instrumentalist Malka Spigel led to more solo recordings and the formation of the Swim label in 1993. Even though Newman railed against 'designer wall-paper', his interest in digital synthesis, Midi sequencing and twelve-bit sampling saw him embrace the Ambient Techno music of the time. Through releases by the seminal US Techno musician Mark Gage and the *Immersion* project (Newman and Spigel as a duo), those initial Ambient adventures of the 1980s helped Newman touch base with ease in the 90s.

LISTENING

The 4AD recordings are particularly recommended on disc. The high, trebly, tweaky sounds throughout *Provisionally Entitled The Singing Fish* (1981) are uniquely redolent of what marine life might sound like. During the mid-1990s Newman spoke of downloading Swim sound excerpts on the Internet.

THE COCTEAU TWINS

The darlings of the British 'indie' music scene of the 1980s, The Cocteau Twins were in many ways the most original group to come out of 'punk'. Significantly, they married a maximalist approach to minimal technology, extracting enormous leverage from the imaginative use of drum machine, treated guitars and keyboards and the incredible coloratura voice of their lead vocalist and lyricist Elizabeth Fraser. Singing in tongues, in a vocalise of her own making, Fraser could coo a lullaby one minute and whoop it up into the high registers of opera the next, an ability which made her the finest rock vocalist of her era. With track titles such as 'Great Spangled Fritillary' or 'Ella Megalast Burls Forever' allied to a swirling whirlpool of music, The Cocteau Twins soon came to signify the ineffable in sound, existing quite resolutely in a world of their own making. So steadfast was their own creative vision that even a meeting with Brian Eno after he had worked with U2 did not convince them they should change their highly individual ways.

Liz Fraser, Robin Guthrie and Will Heggie were all born in the early part of the 1960s in Scotland and attended school in Grangemouth, an industrial town near Edinburgh. Guthrie and Heggie saw music as a way out of working-class poverty. After leaving school they worked as part-time DJs, Guthrie also holding down a job as a control engineer on an oil refinery. Guthrie played guitars, Heggie bass. They had a little studio and one night in 1980 in a nightclub met the sixteen-year-old Fraser and asked her to come for an audition. The minute she opened her mouth, The Cocteau Twins were born. The three moved to Falkirk and gigged. Two demo tapes were brought to London in the winter of 1981 – one for DJ John Peel, the other for the record label 4AD, which immediately signed the trio on the recommendation of the Australian poet and rocker Nick Cave.

Their first album, *Garlands* (1982), was hermetic, Romantically pretentious and heavy on drum machine. It became a favourite among fanciers of the Gothic, particularly as it sampled excerpts from the German group Popol Vuh's 1978 soundtrack for the ghoulish horror film *Nosferatu*. Everything changed for The Cocteau Twins in 1983. After a fifty-two-date European tour Will Heggie left and as a duet Guthrie and Fraser produced *Head Over Heels*, which marked the beginning of the classic 4AD period and had complementary organically abstract cover art designed by Vaughan Oliver. So taken was the legendary rock writer Barney Hoskyns with the new music that he described the effect as 'carrying this girl away in a swirling, swooshing mist of sound'.

Near the end of 1983 they met keyboardist and all-round London musician Simon Raymonde, and immediately went to work on a track for a 4AD in-house album project by various musicians collectively called This Mortal Coil. For this album, *It'll End In Tears*, they made a version of Tim Buckley's 'Song To The Siren' so affecting that when released as a single it charted not just once but twice. Now a threesome again, the group cut their teeth on another song for the project, an epic version of Roy Harper's folk–hippie standard 'Another Day', as well as an entire album as The Cocteau Twins, *Treasure* (1984). The latter stretched Fraser's voice to the limit and tough bass and drum machine chugged along as the sounds of distorted guitars exploded out of the mix and trailed into sonic blackness. Yet at times the record became an object lesson in how to make hypnotic instrumentals. Though loathed by its makers, *Treasure* has since become an archetypal Cocteau Twins record.

Established, the group set up their own studio and sound lab in West London and then toured Japan, Scandinavia and the Far East. The two-LP set *Tiny Dynamine/Echoes In A Shallow Bay* (1985) further consolidated their original dreamlike sound. In 1986 *Victorialand* saw the duo of Guthrie and Fraser seek meditational solace in their native land on an album where acoustic guitar, strings, saxophone and Indian tablas were the only backing. That same year the three Cocteaus collaborated with the American Minimalist Harold Budd on the strange *The Moon And The Melodies*. Guthrie would go on to work on Budd's lustrous 1988 album *The White Arcades* (Land).

Also in 1988 came their most forthright and ecstatic album of the decade, *Blue Bell Knoll*. Better production and a more cohesive structure graced an almost perfect work. Subsequently, in their new, equipment-strewn September Sound studio overlooking the Thames, The Cocteau Twins divulged to me their working practices. Guthrie took guitars and channelled their sounds through a myriad of reverb and chorus effects. Raymonde played a variety of instruments as well as bass guitar. Sounds were sampled and put through more compression, equalization and delays. Synthesizers were hardly ever used but sound was deconstructed and reconstructed, the studio being the vital ingredient. A Japanese Tokai Stratocaster copy had been the guitar of choice on *Blue Bell Knoll*. Analogue multi-tracking was still preferred. Usually music was finished before Liz Fraser arrived in the booth to sing her meticulously prepared 'wordese'. Years of critics gushing verbiage seemed to miss the point that these three musicians worked very hard to achieve their heavenly sound. In 1990 the group celebrated birth and marriage as well as artistic success with the joyous 4AD album *Heaven Or Las Vegas*.

LISTENING

Many of the albums mentioned above are worth hearing, especially the This Mortal Coil album *It'll End In Tears* (1984) on which The Cocteaus can be heard on seven tracks. *Blue Bell Knoll* (1988) and *Heaven Or Las Vegas* (1990) certainly define the late 4AD period. A change of label to Fontana saw them refine their sound further on the soothing *Four-Calendar Café* (1993). The strained personal relationship between Guthrie and Fraser would eventually tear The Cocteau Twins apart, but not before they left a richly elegant album, *Milk And Kisses*, and an extraordinary EP, 'Twinlights' (both 1995). The latter sees the trio for the last time in their September Sound studio, aided by a string quartet. With Fraser now singing intelligibly audible words, her performance on 'Half-Gifts' recalls Leonard Cohen at his most emotionally quiescent. Simon Raymonde's charming first solo album, *Blame Someone Else* (Bella 1997), involves contributions from Fraser and Guthrie but on separate tracks.

SONIC YOUTH

Emerging from the dissonant reverberations of Glenn Branca and the jarring chords of Rys Chatham (two classically knowing experimentalists), Sonic Youth rose like a blazing phoenix in an incendiary clang of guitar feedback and overtones. Their 80s music wrought beauty from formalized chaos, their grandest statement, *Daydream Nation* (1988), stretching the massed guitars until the sparkling notes collided in beauteous psychedelic combustion. Dubbed 'the electric cyberpunk breakthrough' in rock, Sonic Youth drew directly on the music of Can, Roxy Music, Neil Young, The Grateful Dead, Cabaret Voltaire, Lou Reed and Jimi Hendrix. Their environment was Downtown New York, the locale which galvanized the original Minimalism. Their radical approach to tunings, inspired by the late-70s massed-guitar pieces of the Pennsylvanian composer Branca, was linked to a consciousness of the new electronic science fiction which predicted an inevitable merging of man and machine. Parts of Sonic Youth's music were like vapour trails from some sound machine built by the Tyrell Corporation in Ridley Scott's 1982 film *Blade Runner*. In truth they were the only group to elicit real Ambient beauty from the chaos of grunge rock.

The principals – Thurston Moore, Lee Renaldo and Kim Gordon – were not from New York at all, though they all met in Manhattan and lived in one another's apartments. Moore was born in Florida but grew up in Connecticut. Renaldo was from Long Island and Gordon a native of Los Angeles. All were about thirty when *Daydream Nation* exploded into the rock consciousness in 1988. Moore had a strong affinity with art and cited a 1970s New York performance of Brion Gysin's 'spirit music' as an inspiration. Gysin, an original Beat artist, invented the cut-up technique so beloved of William Burroughs and David Bowie and pioneered the idea of the 'dream machine', a light modulator used in conjunction with trance music.

Between 1977 and 1979 New York succumbed to the No-Wave movement, a sort of post-punk 'avant-punk' rock. Glenn Branca was part of it but after toying with a number of groups he decided to write guitar symphonies based on a series of instruments tuned at different intervals to create fields of chords. Accordingly, in 1979, as art-rock became fashionable in New York, Branca changed tack. Working on the harmonic series, he wanted to create chord cloud clusters, just as La Monte Young had done in his Minimalism. Mallet-struck flat guitars were used and open tunings adopted. Both Thurston Moore and Lee Renaldo performed with Branca's Guitar Army for two years. As Branca wanted to go in 'a symphonic direction', Lee and Thurston adopted these tunings and structures to rock. Hence Sonic Youth was born in 1981.

The key to their sound was this tuning approach, with its basis in La Monte Young and Indian music. According to Lee Renaldo: 'We used modal tunings, open tunings (ones we made up), octave pairs, two or three strings tuned to the same note, same-gauge strings in different places or even half-step tuning like a pair of D strings and then a pair of D sharps.' Sonic Youth's recorded output was a series of uncompromisingly anarchic EPs, twelve-inch singles and indie albums. A 1984 Rough Trade twelve-inch, 'Halloween', included explosions, glass breaking and a needle scratching a record. Another song from that source, 'Flower', featured Kim Gordon disconcertingly baying to dreamlike erotic rapture. These would be included on the CD version of the album *Bad Moon Rising* (Blast First 1985), which consolidated Sonic Youth's position in experimental rock and included samples from Jimi Hendrix and from Lou Reed's 1975 electronic statement *Metal Machine Music*. This period also saw the arrival of Michigan-born Steve Shelley on drums.

Recorded between 1986 and early 1988 under the name Ciccone Youth, *The Whitey Album* (Blast First) was Sonic Youth's grand send-up of pop, with lots of sounds thrown in for good measure. Instrumentally it sounded like a tinny industrial version of Can and though it featured strange covers of Robert Palmer's 'Addicted To Love' and Madonna's 'Into The Groove', other tracks drew on early Kraftwerk and NEU! for inspiration. They even called a track 'Two Cool Rock Chicks Listening To NEU', which was Kim Gordon and a friend talking as they listened to 'Negativland' from NEU!'s 1971 debut album.

Recorded in the summer of 1988, *Daydream Nation* (Blast First) would make Sonic Youth famous. The double-album or single CD summed up all the great aspirations of their music. This was anarchic 'big' music for all disaffected urbanites. Lyrically it sucked in much from the great post-modern sprawl that was late-twentieth-century American life but its real greatness was in the instrumentalities. Now that Sonic Youth carried over thirty guitars with them you could hear all the ringing overtones in this music. The three-and-a-half-minute coda to 'Sprawl' was like sharding glass reconstituting itself into magnificent sound. Feedback guitars never sounded so nirvanic. The flame-driven sound of 'Providence' was equally enthralling – intense burning coupled with distant piano, the interruption of a distorted answerphone and the background pigment of descend-scale slide electric guitars. The promise of all guitar rock since Hendrix was the pyrotechnics of sound, the attainment, through volume and intense distortion, of a peak of emotion that would literally burn in sound. With 'Providence' and indeed the whole of *Daydream Nation*, Sonic Youth came close to perfecting that ideal.

LISTENING

Sonic Youth were signed to Geffen after *Daydream Nation,* leaving their indie cloisters for the big distribution world of a major label. *Dirty* (1992) had its moments and was midwifed by Butch Vig, who had produced Nirvana, the grunge-rock group who went on to benefit most from the work of Sonic Youth. This and *Experimental Jet Set, Trash & No Star* (1994) were great rock albums, but the blissful unorthodoxies pulled off on *Daydream Nation* (Blast First 1988) have no equal. It's truly their greatest album.

DEAD CAN DANCE

What was possible in rock after the cleansing effect of punk was nowhere better exemplified than by Dead Can Dance, a group born out of Melbourne 'new wave' and transferred to the British Isles to reap a rich harvest of influences as diverse as Gregorian chant, Renaissance music, and Spanish and Celtic folk music. These were mixed with the group's own love of ethnic rhythm and the incantatory wordless vocalise of Lisa Gerrard. By 1993 Dead Can Dance were selling huge quantities of records and defining the very words 'world beat'. In reality their music reached back to an older melismatic tradition whose use of vocal and percussive drones defined a new Ambience for the 1990s.

Many people witnessing the famous 1993 Santa Monica concert will remember Dead Can Dance as an ensemble fronted by a Pre-Raphaelite singer in long, luminous robes and wreathed red hair. While Lisa Gerrard played her Chinese dulcimer and opened her throat, a knightly bearded Brendan Perry provided ample forte vocal and guitar accompaniment. The rest was all percussion. Perry and Gerrard owed their exotic intermingling of influences to their being Anglo-Irish and transplanted to the Antipodes – he to New Zealand, she to the Irish, Greek and Turkish district of Melbourne. Perry was exposed to a lot of Irish folk music and Broadway soundtracks, but remembers his very first album purchase to be the intense psychedelia of Pink Floyd's *The Piper At The Gates Of Dawn.* Gerrard, for her part, picked up piano–accordion and began to mimic the ethnic singing of her environs. The purchase of a 2,500-year-old Chinese *yang t'chin* hammer dulcimer when she was seventeen changed her life.

The pair met as late teenagers in 1979 in Melbourne and developed through the same 'new wave' music scene as the poetic Nick Cave. Dead Can Dance were formed in 1981 and quickly moved to London to find a recording home with 4AD, whose Ivo Watts-Russell was struck by their 'dedication and motivation'. Having begun as a four-piece rock sort of band, they were down to Lisa and Brendan for their dronal contributions to 4AD's concept album of etherea *It'll End In Tears.* After they had recorded three earnest LPs the big break came in 1988 with *The Serpent's Egg*, which burst into view with the hypnotically baroque 'The Host Of Seraphim', Gerrard's voice so richly expressed that it bathed you in the colours of ancient hymns and folk song.

By this stage Gerrard was living in Barcelona and Perry in a converted church in County Cavan in Ireland, where he built a studio. They extended themselves to film music and acting and seemed to journey further back in search of what they sought as a transcendental music. *Aion* was released in 1990 and sounds like it comes from the Middle Ages or the early Renaissance. The apex of the record was 'Song Of The Sybil', so evocative of sixteenth-century Spain that one could almost smell the incense coming out of the speakers.

Work continued on theatre and festival projects and worldwide acclaim followed the use of 'The Host Of Seraphim' in Ron Fricke's ethnographic documentary *Baraka*. By 1993 they were throwing African and Middle Eastern rhythms into an instrumental and sampled mix which freely used eighteenth-century Irish folk melodies. The resultant *Into The Labyrinth* easily sold half a million copies on release. By this time based in the Snowy Mountains in Australia, Gerrard regularly jetted to the Quivvy church in Cavan, where some of the most singularly innovate Ambient rock was recorded for posterity. World tours, huge album sales and the use of their music in such places as television's *Miami Vice* and Michael Mann's 1995 film *Heat* assured Dead Can Dance their place in history.

LISTENING

There are over a dozen discs credited to Dead Can Dance and their music has appeared on many compilations – for example, *It'll End In Tears* (4AD 1984). Once signed to 4AD in 1983 they began recording solemn, almost Gothic rock, drawing on sources such as New Guinea death ritual and nineteenth-century Symbolism – for the latter see *Spleen And Ideal* (1985). After studying classical music theory their first great record was 1988's *The Serpent's Egg*. Then came *Aion* (1990) with its mix of fourteenth-century Italian dance music, sixteenth-century Catalan folk, Slavonic and Greek music, drums, pipes, among other styles. For the uninitiated the brilliant compilation *A Passage In Time* (1991) and consummate live recording and video *Toward The Within* (1994), taken from the Santa Monica concert of the previous year, are definitely the places to start. Some of their most accessible music can be also heard on *Spiritchaser* (1996), its high point being a trance-like remake of The Beatles' 'Within You Without You'.

SPACEMEN 3, SONIC BOOM, SPIRITUALIZED

Undoubtedly the true heirs of The Velvet Underground sound, Spacemen 3 made music that is best described as 'dream rock'. Their lengthy excursions into guitar mantras, droning feedback and hypnotic sound was, according to their founder, Sonic Boom, 'inspired by one chord Minimalism, John Cage and The Velvet Underground'. Their orientation was also psychedelic – in the words of an early demo album: 'Taking drugs to make music to take drugs to.' The drugs in question were hallucinogens like LSD and marijuana, and even though their best Ambient track was titled 'Ecstasy Symphony', they did not endorse the use of electronics to generate dance beats. Their music had the resonance of rarefied spiritual highs and when the group split up in 1990, its leading lights went on to make some of the most inspired electronic rock of the 1990s.

Sonic Boom (Pete Kember) was only seventeen when he founded Spacemen 3 at Rugby College of Art, England. His co-conspirator was Jason Pierce and the year was 1982. Their early interest was in noise, feedback and fuzz-tone, drawing much from American rock history. They even founded a venue for psychedelic experimental music called The Reverberation in Rugby in 1985. Their first album, *Sound Of Confusion* (Glass 1986), evoked this period but then Kember and Pierce felt that quiet ballads could convey more. In short, 'the more Minimal the music the more maximal the effect'. The new songs, like 'Feel So Good', shared the same space as Lou Reed's more acoustic work in The Velvet Underground circa 1969.

Working in a small sixteen-track studio in Rugby, with a modest effects rack, the duo came up with their finest work, 'Ecstasy Symphony', in 1987. Here was a veritable sea of electronic sound, of no recognizable origin, which bathed the listener in a gleaming hush. One could mentally reach inside the sound and focus on veritable objects, like jewels in a gleaming stream. Kember got the idea from John Cage's music for 'prepared piano' and translated it to electronics. One keyboard note was recorded over and over, each time with a different effect, including chorus, flange, echo, reverb and phasing.

Kember was obsessed with single-note repetitions. He used a Vox Starstream guitar, played in open-tuned fashion. It was a late-60s guitar with built-in tuner, bass and treble boosters plus effects like wah-wah and fuzz-tone. This was used on the album version of 'Ecstasy Symphony', which segued into a heavenly version of 'Transparent Radiation' (an obscure track by 1960s Texan psyche-delians The Red Crayola) which featured strings. The album in question was called *The Perfect Prescription* (Glass 1987), a wonderfully narcotic-sounding document of introspection and spiritual wonder. Kember confessed to having a 'non-strict Catholic background'.

Spacemen 3 were also interested in sampling, but not to create House tracks; instead they generated samples from feedback – that realized from keyboard and synth effects. These resulted in drone music like the 1987 'Ecstasy In Slow Motion', inspired by La Monte Young. Their next album, *Playing With Fire* (Fire 1988), mixed the electric repetition of The Velvets with atmospheric songs of a cavernous, numinous brilliance. Its blipping echoing sound was the product of a Vox keyboard and stuttering tremolo effects. Unfortunately, as fame approached, tension pushed the principals apart and on *Recurring* (Fire 1990) Kember and Pierce had one LP side apiece.

Pierce, whose work on *Recurring* leaned towards a use of horns in a soul and blues way reminiscent of The Rolling Stones, opted for a more conventional indie-rock career. Playing Telecaster guitar alongside Doors-like Vox Continental organ, he went for a big sound with Spiritualized. Their first album, *Lazer Guided Melodies*, (1992) was a huge acoustic-electric soup with a commercial edge. Their 1995 album *Pure Phase* featured the Balanescu String Quartet, horns, woodwinds and reeds, along with the usual guitars and drones. Mostly good indie pop, only its title track looked back to the undiluted electronica of old. Spiritualized reached their apogee in 1997 with *Ladies And Gentlemen We Are Floating In Space*, an album sold in pharmaceutical packaging whose swelled instrumentalities made the sound of orchestral rock. The electronic edge was still there and at times – like on the emotion-baring 'Broken Heart' – Ambience was pursued, but on the whole this was an album where the song and not the sound reigned.

Kember opted for a more interesting trajectory. His first solo outing, *Spectrum* (Silvertone 1990), included the extraordinary 'If I Should Die' – tape-manipulated Minimalism, backwards guitar, treated drones and lots of distant electronic tones. Now calling his group Spectrum, Kember spent twenty months recording the highly ambitious *Soul Kiss (Glide Divine)* (Silvertone 1992). This work was full of electronically generated sound effects (wind and water sounds created by feedback) and the looping keyboard of 'Drunk Suite' conveyed dizziness before the album concluded on the droney tremolos of 'Phase Me Out (Gently)'.

Delving deeper into sound, Kember formed Experimental Audio Research, or EAR, an affiliation of sonic adventurers including 'glide guitarist' Kevin Shields and percussionist Eddie Prevost. *Mesmerised* (Sympathy 1993) carried on where Spacemen 3 left off, but pushed the territory entirely into instrumental hallucinations. Having always wanted to emulate Jimi Hendrix's way of translating the feelings of drugs into music', Kember became increasingly more studio-oriented, forming his own label (Space Age) and releasing more and more music. By the late 1990s there was little difference between his Spectrum work and that with EAR, save for the former having a vocal element. A growing interest in classic analogue synthesizers such as the Theremin, EMS Synthi and OSCar led to such phantasmagoric electronica as Spectrum's *Forever Alien* (Space Age 1997) and his working with Delia Derbyshire (famous for 'realizing' the swooping/bubbling 'Dr Who' theme in 1963). The creative mind of Kember links many kinds of electric Ambience – from Joe Meek to Hendrix, from John Cage to the Velvets and through such New York synth groups as the 1960s' Silver Apples and 70s' Suicide (both duos who favoured the throbbing of the machine.)

LISTENING

Spacemen 3's majestic 'Transparent Radiation' EP has been released often on disc – see *The Singles* (Tang 1995). A chunk of it appears on the sublime *The Perfect Prescription* (Fire 1989). Their final disc, *Recurring* (Fire 1990), contains five bonus tracks and is recommended. In 1994 a worthwhile collection of live and studio drone experiments from 1987–8 was released by Sympathy as *Dreamweapon – An Evening Of Contemporary Sitar Music*.

By the turn of the century Sonic Boom had begun reissuing on Third Stone a comprehensive set of remastered Spacemen 3 albums with much bonus material. Recommended are *Playing With Fire* (1999), *Taking Drugs To Make Music To Take Drugs To* (a band favourite) and *Forged Prescription* (a lavish expansion of *The Perfect Prescription*. All Spiritualized albums are on Dedicated.

INDIVIDUALISTS

ENNIO MORRICONE

The most famous composer to adapt the techniques of rock to soundtrack recording, Morricone evolved a music of atmosphere, mood and feeling by juxtaposing dramatic elements on tape. With his background in Italian popular songs he was adept at arranging material in the studio for recorded release. Thus when it came to soundtracks he vitalized his scores by the use of strong contrasts and lots of acoustic space. His rhythms were simple, highlighted by a harmonica, Jew's harp or guitar melody and bathed in an Italian pastoral Romanticism of lush strings and operatic harmonies. His flair for blending electronically treated sound with ethnic instruments was unmatched. He believed that his scores should not 'limit the film in time and space' and thus his distinctive music has often become the star of films such as *Once Upon A Time In The West* (1968) and *The Mission* (1986).

Though Morricone is most commonly identified with Sergio Leone's 1960s 'Spaghetti Westerns' starring Clint Eastwood, the composer was an all-rounder. Born in Rome in 1928 to a bandleader and trumpeter father, he loved the radio as a child and would transcribe the popular songs he heard on it. He learned jazz trumpet but then enrolled at the Conservatory of St Cecilia to study classical trumpet and composition. Influenced by Hollywood soundtracks and Verdi's opera music, Morricone began writing scores which included found sounds from everyday life. Precocious and fast-moving, he turned a standard classical education into something quite different when he joined Rome's bustling Cinecittà studios in the 1950s. Here he did stints in orchestras, tried his hand at arranging and odd-jobbed it as a pop-song writer before launching himself into composing film scores in the early 1960s. His time coincided with the post-war rise of Italian cinema, which was exemplified by the international success of Fellini's *La Dolce Vita* (1959).

On the request of his old friend the film director Sergio Leone, Morricone set about writing a score for a new type of Western. Shot in Spain and starring Clint Eastwood, *A Fistful Of Dollars* (1964) began the Spaghetti Western craze that would be trademarked by Morricone's music. 'I simply wanted to express my feelings about the wide open spaces and solitude one finds in them,' Morricone later said. To achieve this he adopted a compressed recording technique more akin to rock, with strong features highlighted to provide contrast. Leone shot the films to the music, thus lending the results an operatic edge, particularly in the gunfight scenes. Morricone was skilful at incorporating everyday sounds, as in the memorable 'ticking watch' music of the finale of *For A Few Dollars More* (1965). This use of symbolic sounds reached its zenith on *The Good, The Bad And The Ugly* (1966), whose outrageous theme featured block percussion, American Indian flute, whistling, vocoder, Shadows-styled twangy guitar, shouted backing vocals, chiming bells, Spanish trumpets, maracas and distorted vocals.

So talented was Morricone in his thirties that he was able to broaden the Ambience of his sound and still retain his own distinctiveness. The 1960s saw him score films by other directors beside Leone, such as Bertolucci and Polanski. His score for Leone's masterly epic *Once Upon A Time In The West* (1968), starring Charles Bronson, Claudia Cardinale and Henry Fonda, was characterized by female operatic soprano and honeyed strings. Its title music was an excellent example of sound-painting, the extremely plaintive harmonica opening up a vista for melancholic horns, a fiercely distorted guitar, suspenseful string section and an emotionally charged operatic background music. This theme ended with the peal of a bell and the harmonica dissolving into silence – usually the cue for a gut-wrenching gunfight. But in fact Morricone and Leone began the film with the Ambient sounds of a desert way-station, in one of the most audaciously dazzling opening sequences in cinematic history.

By the latter part of the century Morricone had written over 350 soundtracks for film and television, to become the most popular soundtrack composer in history. In 1983 his use of Andean pipes and strong emotional Ambience added much to Leone's sprawling Robert De Niro-led epic movie *Once Upon A Time In America*. Three years later he received an Oscar for his memorable theme to Roland Joffe's film *The Mission*, which mixed oboe and Indian pipe melody with choral and string music, the plangent instrumentalities arranged and recorded with a wonderful feel for texture. Morricone revealed his avant-garde music in the difficult *Chamber Music* album (Virgin Venture 1988), writing for strings punctuated only by a quiet piano fugue, but returned to his familiar landscape of breezy tunes, lucid melodies and moving meditations for Zeffirelli's *Hamlet* (1991). The recipient of many awards, both in Italy and outside, Morricone scored Adrian Lyne's controversial remake of *Lolita* in 1998. He created fantastic moments in film sound by simply understanding the importance of sonic space and, not surprisingly, he has been sampled by House musicians, most famously The Orb.

LISTENING

The world is littered with recordings of Morricone's work. A great place to start is *Film Music 1966–1987* (Virgin 1988), a two-CD set which nicely collects some of his choicest cuts, including the twangy Ambient theme from the 1969 film *The Sicilian Clan*, starring Alain Delon. A single-disc version, *Film Music By Ennio Morricone* (EMI/Virgin), came out in 1993. A very worthwhile investment is the two-CD *Singles Collection Vol. 2* (DRG 1997), featuring music for a range of European films made between 1969 and 1981 and starring the likes of Marcello Mastroianni, Catherine Deneuve and Natassja Kinski. There's an ice-cream-parlour Ambience to much of this music and though Morricone's syrupy production can border on schmaltz, the sudden intrusion of an emotive trumpet or lone oboe always saves the day.

TODD RUNDGREN

Seen by many as the Prince of the 70s, Todd Rundgren was an American whizz-kid who could write, sing, play, arrange, produce and engineer his own material to a high standard. He stretched the limitations of the vinyl record and, more importantly, pioneered the early use of drum-machine rhythms and vocoder. And then there was the synthesizer, which in his hands was made to create uncharacteristic atmospheres and sounds.

Rundgren was born in Philadelphia in 1948 and grew up addicted to all forms of music – classical, orchestral jazz, black soul and simple rock. In his teens he formed a number of bands, including the important psychedelic group The Nazz. Here his penchant for catchy and harmonized lyrics was offset by his dazzling electric-guitar technique. The band's second Screen Gems set, *Nazz Nazz* (1969), contained the lengthy suite-like creation 'A Beautiful Song', a sign of what was to come. So much in demand were Rundgren's production and engineering skills that he was signed by Bob Dylan's manager, Albert Grossman, to his New York-based Bearsville label.

Between solo albums and other duties, Rundgren couldn't stop working. He hit his peak early, his third Bearsville outing, *Something/Anything* (1972), becoming a rock classic in the process. Recorded in various studios in LA and New York (including Hendrix's old haunt the Record Plant) this double album cut across all genres – ballad, rock, soul, electronic music, ensemble playing, tape music. Providing something for everyone, it was an exuberant and technically brilliant offering. 'Hello It's Me' had been a big radio hit for The Nazz but on *Something/Anything* it became a masterpiece of production and blended harmonies. Everywhere stereophonic sounds poured out of the mix – the hurdy-gurdy of 'Carousel Broke Down', the pad drums and sequencer of 'Breathless' and the hi-fi test tones of 'Intro'. Throughout the album Rundgren used a VCS3 synth with DK3 keyboard extensively, but with such skill that it merged with the other instruments, nearly all of which he played himself.

Rundgren broke most records with the follow-up, *A Wizard A True Star* (1973), nineteen tracks lasting nearly an hour, but his ingestion of mescaline led here to an erratic work which never has matched up to its predecessor. *Todd* (1974) was much better and included 'Spark Of Life', a wonderful synth and guitar tune which sounded as if Jimi Hendrix had met Tonto's Expanding Headband on Mars for a six-minute jam. After this Rundgren headed into the land of space-rock with his synthesizer group Utopia, which would include Roger Powell, a former employee of ARP who had pioneered the use of the portable ARP 2600 synthesizer in the early 1970s.

Utopia were much denigrated as a 'prog rock' group who spouted mysticism and performed amid much spectacle. As if to highlight the excess, the Zen Buddhist-laced 'cosmic' solo concept *Initiation* (1975) was, remarkably, a single album over an hour long, and that nearly a decade before CD. Rundgren never forgot his debt to The Beatles, Hendrix and The Beach Boys and dedicated his next solo album, *Faithful* (1976), to them. A new line-up of Utopia, but still featuring keyboardist Roger Powell, recorded *RA* (1977), an Egyptology-led concept album which made the band stars of the 'techno-rock' era. Away from the limelight, Rundgren continued to produce (most successfully, the theatrical 1978 Meatloaf album *Bat Out Of Hell*) and innovate new ideas in video, recorded vocals, sampling and Ambient music during the 1980s. In 1993 he again scored a first with the Interactive CD *No World Order* (Philips). By the late 1990s Rundgren had shortened his name to TR-I and was releasing albums exclusively on the Internet.

LISTENING

Something/Anything was reissued by Castle Communications on double CD in 1989 and still possesses an incredible power, particularly on the textured vocal performances such as 'Torch Song'. Like Prince, Rundgren often suffered from over-production, yet a track like 'Spark Of Life' from *Todd* (1974) played an important role in the long-term task of achieving acceptance for electronic rock. In 1999 Castle Communications celebrated Rundgren's contribution to twentieth-century music with the release of the lovingly compiled and presented two-CD collection *Go Ahead Ignore Me – The Best Of Todd Rundgren*. This was followed by the reissue of his solo Bearsville catalogue and Utopia recordings in digitally remastered versions.

JOHN MCLAUGHLIN

One of the few guitarists to seize on the possibilities opened up by Jimi Hendrix and push them into new directions, notably jazz-rock and acoustic fusion music mixing Indian and flamenco scales, John McLaughlin has successively explored both Ambient and electronic areas while being popularly known as the fastest and one of the loudest electric guitarists in the world. This reputation stemmed from his days with the Mahavishnu Orchestra in America, but his work with Miles Davis and the Indian group Shakti, his investigation of guitar synthesizers and then his exploration of flamenco with Paco De Lucia resulted in some of the most satisfying instrumental music of the century. McLaughlin himself would emphasize that the meditative aspect of his music, which has always informed his best work, has flowed directly from his spiritual quest.

McLaughlin was born in Yorkshire in 1942 and prompted by his mother, who was an amateur violinist, he began studying classical violin and guitar from the age of seven. His three brothers were into blues guitar, particularly the music of Leadbelly and Robert Johnson. McLaughlin acquired one of their guitars at eleven and started working on blues scales. At thirteen he became interested in flamenco guitar and then the crisply picked jazz recordings of Tal Farlow and Barney Kessell. Abandoning school, McLaughlin went to work in a musical instrument shop and practised incessantly. He sat in with local groups and when he heard Miles Davis's *Milestones* album in 1958 decided to turn professional. He gigged in Manchester and arrived in London in the late 1950s as Miles Davis was laying down his ground-breaking modal jazz in New York with John Coltrane.

McLaughlin wanted a mixture of jazz and blues guitar, and also liked amplification. He played around the London clubs but eventually became a studio guitarist, performing on Rolling Stones sessions, teaching Jimmy Page a thing or two and befriending The Beatles' producer, George Martin. Disillusioned with odd-jobbing, in the late 1960s he formed his own group and recorded the extraordinary album *Extrapolation* (1969), where acoustic and electric guitar was used in a non-blues way within a jazz format. The tracks had a 'modal' quality reminiscent of Miles Davis, an open-endedness, a restive centre. The concluding 'Peace Piece' had the flavour of Indian raga, while the whole conveyed the sense of a musician on a spiritual journey. The East was very much a part of McLaughlin's spiritual interests.

When he got a call from New York to join drummer Tony Williams in a band he went for it. He arrived early in 1969 and the very first day met Miles Davis and his milieu. The minute he played his guitar Davis booked him in to record the ground-breaking album *In A Silent Way* with a bunch of electric keyboard players. McLaughlin went on to appear on several Davis albums which defined the very idiom of jazz-rock, his open and fluid guitar style lending *Bitches Brew* and *Jack Johnson* (both 1970) the quality of urgent musical fragments plucked from the ether. During that time McLaughlin even played with Hendrix at the latter's Electric Lady studios.

Practising yoga every day, McLaughlin soon became a devotee of the Eastern mystic Sri Chinmoy, who dubbed him Mahavishnu. This led to the recording of the extraordinary *My Goal's Beyond* (Douglas 1971), an album made up of eight acoustic guitar pieces and two lengthy meditative improvisations based around violin, tablas, veena (an Indian stringed drone instrument), horns, bass and acoustic guitar. This beautiful sound would soon be adapted to electric music, McLaughlin playing double-necked Gibson guitar with lightning flashes of notes which did not resort to the blues scale but mixed Indian and jazz musics at the ear-deafening volume of Hendrix's rock. The twelve-string guitar was for arpeggios, the six-string for his dazzling solos. In 1973 McLaughlin recorded with Carlos Santana, a meeting which produced some very distinctive tributes to John Coltrane.

In that year McLaughlin met a series of inventors from Emulator in Santa Cruz. They discussed the design of a guitar-synthesizer made up of six mini-modules. McLaughlin later called it 'elephantine' and a 'nightmare' but didn't give up on the idea. He had also been working with a group of Indian musicians, particularly the classical violin player L. Shankar. A live recording from 1975 was released as *Shakti* (CBS 1976), the name of the group. Here McLaughlin used a specially adapted Gibson acoustic guitar with seven 'sympathetic' strings across the sound-hole. These were used for dronal qualities during performance and recording. Shakti released two more CBS albums, *A Handful Of Beauty* and *Natural Elements*, both in 1977. The music had a deep spiritual quality, guided by McLaughlin's serious studies of Indian classical music in California and Connecticut.

Next, McLaughlin and Paco De Lucia teamed up for an exploration of what could done with the acoustic guitar trio, first with Larry Coryell and then Al Di Meola. McLaughlin considered the resulting album, *Friday Night In San Francisco* (CBS 1981), to be one possessing 'magic' properties. The same year also saw the release of *Belo Horizonte* (WEA), a delicate merging of acoustic guitar and light classically flavoured jazz which used the synth and electric keyboard skills of his partner the pianist Katia Labèque. By 1982 McLaughlin was working with NED in Vermont on the development of the Synclavier 2 guitar synthesizer, contributing to the design of the computer software which linked the guitar and the synthesizer.

McLaughlin produced velvet-smooth, reed-like sounds for his 1984 album *Mahavishnu* (WEA). His aim was to achieve the dynamic range of acoustic guitar on an electric instrument. In 1988 he admitted to me: 'I've played all the guitar synths, including the Photon, the Stepp DG1 and the Shadow GMT6, with varying results. You can replace the sound but never the physical effort of playing an instrument.' As if in response, the previous year had seen the release of the elegant ECM album *Making Music*, an all-acoustic meeting in Oslo with tabla player Zakir Hussain, flautist Haraprasad Chaurasia and Norwegian saxophonist Jan Garbarek. The impressive result was produced by ECM's founder and boss Manfred Eicher.

Living in Monaco, McLaughlin worked on a fusion of computer music and acoustic instrumentation. Deriving inspiration from Debussy and Ravel as well as Iberian composers like Manuel de Falla, he wrote *Mediterranean Concerto* (1990), a breezy take on the age-old meeting of flamenco and classical music. It was performed worldwide before he formed an improvisatory acoustic trio with L. Shankar and the Indian tabla player Trilok Gurtu. A multi-national project, bringing in almost every high-profile musician McLaughlin had ever recorded, was released by Verve in 1996 under the title *The Promise*. This CD had its fair share of Ambient-flavoured and sun-baked atmospheric instrumentals. In the same year McLaughlin recorded *Paco De Lucia, Al Di Meola And John McLaughlin* (Verve), returning to a form of acoustic music which resonated with the peace of his own spiritual journey – an undertaking which had taken in the ideas of the Sufis, Zen Buddhism, Lao-Tsu, Padre Pio, Thomas Merton and Carlos Castañeda.

LISTENING

The bulk of John McLaughlin's work has surfaced on CD since the late 1980s. *Extrapolation* appeared on Polydor in 1990. The essential *My Goal's Beyond* was released by Rykodisc in a stellar version in 1992. The collaboration with Carlos Santana, *Love Devotion Surrender* (Sony 1992), contains the gorgeous acoustic pieces 'Naima' and 'Meditation'. The Shakti records appeared on Sony CDs in the early 1990s and are worth hearing for 'Lotus Feet' (from *Shakti*) and 'Isis', 'India' and 'Two Sisters' (from *A Handful Of Beauty*). Columbia released *Friday Night In San Francisco* in 1990. *Live At The Royal Festival Hall* (Mercury 1990) features the Trilok Gurtu trio. During the 1990s Columbia reissued the groundbreaking Mahavishnu Orchestra recordings, including the illuminating previously unreleased third album from 1973, under the title *The Lost Trident Sessions* (1999).

ROBERT FRIPP

Though for ever associated with the 'progressive' sound of King Crimson, English guitarist Robert Fripp always stood out as an individual, preferring tea and a good book to the excesses of early-70s rock. Forging a unique style on the electric guitar, Fripp borrowed from jazz, flamenco and classical music. The left-handed Fripp's adoption of the right-handed guitar led to an emphasis on extended fretting, particularly in various modal scales. His considered approach led him to always play the instrument seated. From the early 1970s he found fresh pastures in Brian Eno's tape-delay systems and made Ambient records with him. After leaving King Crimson in 1974, Fripp absorbed the practical philosophy of the Armenian mystic Gurdjieff. By 1977 he was recording again, this time with Peter Gabriel and David Bowie. His work with Bowie and Eno in Berlin on *'Heroes'* he considered some of his best. During the 1980s he again worked with King Crimson, now with guitar synthesizers. He also recorded with Andy Summers and David Sylvian. He continued his work with Sylvian into the 90s, a period during which he also collaborated with Ambient Techno musicians such as The Orb, The Grid and The Future Sound Of London. His own Ambient work had evolved into 'Soundscapes', a series of environmental performances recorded around the world, featuring washes of guitar put through a customized effects rack.

Robert Fripp was born in Dorset in 1946 and showed a keen interest in English literature while young. Receiving an acoustic guitar as a Christmas present in 1957, he went on to study music theory at a local college. In his teens he was playing Bournemouth hotels and listening to rock 'n' roll and Django Reinhardt. He also took professional lessons in jazz and flamenco guitar. Pressure from his parents made him study economics and his future would have been in real estate if he hadn't dropped out of college at the age of twenty. An interest in Stravinsky and Bartók, along with hearing The Beatles' *Sgt. Pepper* in 1967, convinced him his destiny lay in rock music.

Fripp's success with King Crimson is outlined earlier in this book. He once described Crimson to me as 'being in a group which is coming from a place where safety isn't one of the key elements'. Yet by 1974 numerous line-up changes and the slog of touring had taken their toll, leading Fripp to announce that he was leaving the music business 'for ever and ever'. Yet his fluid Les Paul guitar style was always in demand. Invited to dinner at Brian Eno's London home in 1970, he witnessed the effect of two Revox tape machines linked together. Plugging in his guitar, Fripp was bemused by the echoes, delays and fluctuating volumes this system produced. Even tape loops could be generated into a sound mass. He dubbed the outcome Frippertronics. Released in 1972, *No Pussyfooting* (Island) was a take on Minimalist Ambience, arrived at purely by chance by Fripp and Eno. The duo toured the music and in 1973 Fripp contributed a brilliant noise-rock guitar solo to Eno's glam masterpiece 'Baby's On Fire'. He was again present during the making of *Discreet Music* in Eno's home studio. The same system produced their second Ambient album, the masterly *Evening Star* (EG 1975). Fripp found Eno's studio treatments of his guitar fascinating and continued to contribute to his colleague's solo projects throughout the 1970s.

Yet Fripp's private search led him to the teachings of Gurdjieff through his English disciple John Bennett, whom the mystic had met in Turkey in the early 1920s. Gurdjieff had spent years in the East absorbing esoteric knowledge and beliefs and believed in the attainment of a higher awareness based on relaxation, complex movements, concentrated labour and new symbolic ideas, particularly in music. He was fascinated with the effect of musical vibrations on the body and theorized about music endlessly at his Institute for the Harmonious Development of Man near Paris. In 1949 Gurdjieff died in a Paris hospital after a car crash, but it wasn't until the early 1970s that Bennett continued his work. Founding the Society for Continuous Education, Bennett set up two centres at country estates, Sherborne House in Dorset and Claymount Court in Virginia. Robert Fripp spent nearly a year at Sherborne House in 1975–6, a period of intense self-realization which resulted in his editing Bennett's entrancing taped lectures.

In 1977 Fripp journeyed to Toronto to record with Peter Gabriel on his lavish studio-treated debut album for Charisma. That year also saw Fripp move to New York's Bowery district, where he got involved in the New Wave music scene. One night he got a call from Eno, who was in Berlin. David Bowie came to the phone seeking inspiration. Fripp said he'd do his best and within days was laying down some of the most exciting music of his career. The slow-tempoed electric guitar of 'Heroes' sharded through Eno's tape treatments for the Bowie song and was a pinnacle of understatement.

Back in New York, Fripp continued to work as sideman and producer to the likes of Peter Gabriel, Blondie and Talking Heads. In 1979 came his first solo album, *Exposure* (EG), a strange amalgam of dinner conversation, Frippertronic Ambience, furious rock, ballad, white soul, John Bennett's voice, Eno's synthesizer and a gorgeous song by Peter Gabriel. Amid a flurry of activity Fripp undertook a Frippertronics tour of unusual venues such as record shops, cinemas and factories across North America and Europe. Using effects pedals, the two tape machines and a guitar, Fripp was a veritable one-man electronic band. Inspired, he formed a new group, Discipline, with former Yes and King Crimson drummer Bill Bruford and Americans Tony Levin (bass) and Adrian Belew (guitar). After a brief European tour Fripp sensed the spirit of old in the group and readopted the name King Crimson. The debut album, *Discipline*, (EG) was recorded in three weeks in Island Studios, London. Its stand-out track, 'The Sheltering Sky', featured clipped African percussion, ground-swelling bass, jangly guitar and Fripp's mirage-like guitar – a distinctive sound courtesy of his new-found love of the Roland GR300 guitar synthesizer.

Fripp liked the rehearsed group, fresh into the studio off the road. It recalled the original 1969 King Crimson. But subsequent albums would be written in the studio, much to Fripp's chagrin. He diverted some of his energy into work with ex-Police guitarist Andy Summers, a musician whom he had met in Bournemouth during his teens. Two albums were recorded in Dorset, of which *I Advance Masked* (A&M 1982) contained some heavenly Ambient music, its atmosphere enhanced by Moog and Roland synthesizers. Exhausted again by the music industry, Fripp found himself once more at the Bennett institute, this time in the US as president of the Claymount Court Society. Associated with this appointment was Fripp's production of an extraordinary 1985 recording of piano music credited to Gurdjieff and his Russian musical associate Thomas De Hartmann. *Journey To Inaccessible Places* (EG 1987) featured a series of modal Eastern musics translated to piano. The held-pedal nuances and slow, enraptured melodies recalled Satie, though the content was doused in a mystical vapour. Revitalized, Fripp began giving guitar seminars in Virginia using a new tuning, a variation on C major no less! Playing an Ovation acoustic guitar with a built-in pick-up, Fripp began to develop his philosophically based guitar-tuition system known as Guitar Craft. Students not only learned new techniques but lived the music as well. Fripp found constant challenges for his charges, like the album *Robert Fripp And The League Of Crafty Guitarists* (EG 1986), recorded in the US at a few days' notice by eighteen guitarists on a twenty-four-track mobile studio.

At this time Fripp became involved with the enigmatic English musician David Sylvian. He contributed to the film soundtrack of *Steel Cathedrals*, recorded in Tokyo and London in 1985, but it was on Sylvian's ambitious second solo album, *Gone To Earth* (Virgin 1986), recorded in England, that Fripp's presence was really felt. Intensity and quietude were there in abundance, the title track even containing voice excerpts from Bennett. Fripp was impressed with Sylvian's 'studio sculpting' approach to making records. In the studio Fripp was now using a Tokai Les Paul guitar with customized electronics to trigger synthesizers. He toured Japan with Sylvian in 1992 and later recorded *The First Day* (Virgin 1993) in the US. Again an intense listening experience, this album produced the bona-fide Ambient classic 'Bringing Down The Light'. A live recording from a subsequent world tour, *Damage*, was released by Virgin in 1994 to almost universal acclaim.

Fripp had long ago kissed goodbye to analogue tape machines and was instead using a personalized rack-mounted system of effects, delays, processors and harmonizer alongside his guitar and Roland guitar synthesizer, all activated by foot pedals and switches. Ambient work produced on this system became known as Soundscapes. Fripp's approach to music-making was always practical, yet over and over he has stressed the importance of 'being in the flow of music, to be in the moment where music comes directly into people's lives'. A firm hater of industry-driven music – he once told me that he felt 'the bulk of 70s "progressive rock"' was 'frankly loathsome!' – Fripp respected anything with real spirit. For this reason he admired the pioneers of Ambient House and in 1994 collaborated with The Orb, The Grid and The Future Sound Of London.

LISTENING

In 1989 Robert Fripp remastered most of his complex back-catalogue with the assistance of the Dorset-based engineer Tony Arnold. The King Crimson material benefited, as did *Exposure*, his eclectic debut solo recording. Fripp's collaborations with Eno still sound superb and were brought together on *The Essential Fripp And Eno* (Venture 1994), a highlight being the resonating harmonic guitar of 'Evening Star'. That year also saw the first releases from Fripp's own Discipline Global Mobile record company set up in Wiltshire, where Fripp was now living. From 1994 to 1997 half a dozen Soundscapes live solo albums credited to Fripp were released, including the double Ambient *Gates Of Paradise*. The label was also a fount of King Crimson material old and new.

The beginning of the twenty-first century saw the release of a brand-new King Crimson album, *The Construkction of Light*, featuring a new four-piece band that included Fripp and the old stalwart Adrian Belew. It was as good as anything in the Crimson-Fripp canon, offering powerful instrumentals, wondrous guitar playing and lots of Ambience.

PETER GABRIEL

One of the most interesting musicians to come out of the much-derided arena of UK 'progressive rock' of the 1970s, Peter Gabriel combined a self-absorbed artistry with an astonishing grasp of new technology. His theatrical flair, first exhibited with Genesis, came into sharp focus when he worked with new video technology in the 1980s and then with computer imaging in the 1990s. His enduring empathy with human rights and his overall philosophical outlook have been absorbed into some of the best Ambient rock of the late twentieth century.

Gabriel was born in London in 1950 and brought up in Surrey. He began his musical life as a drummer and was also interested in the film world. His time at Charterhouse public school, where Genesis came into being, was always a sticking point with a UK rock press obsessed with class. Despite this, Genesis, in which Gabriel was the vocalist, flourished, though in retrospect the band seems grandiose in its artistic pretensions, which mixed theatre with leaden music. Gabriel left in 1975 and later recorded a solo album, *Peter Gabriel* (Charisma 1977), in Toronto. With the help of the guitarist Robert Fripp and an orchestra, Gabriel managed to produce a fascinating insight into personal and global crisis. There was something special about the sound of the album – 'Solsbury Hill' used an addictively repetitive synth motif while 'Humdrum' had a wonderful spatial quality, replete with electronicized vibraphone, percussion, synthesizer and orchestration. A second album, also called, like the third and fourth, *Peter Gabriel*, appeared in 1978 on Charisma.

In 1977 Gabriel acquired an electronic rhythm box and recorded the anti-apartheid anthem 'Biko', which appeared on his third album (Charisma 1980), a work influenced by African rhythm, the music of Can and Eno, and the Fairlight Computer Music Instrument – one of the early sampling tools. This was used to more extensive effect on the fourth album (Charisma 1982), where a World Music flavour seemed more in evidence. This release also saw Gabriel become the finest exponent of the new MTV video age with his direction of the thrilling promotional video for his song 'Shock The Monkey'.

With the help of the Canadian engineer-musician Daniel Lanois, Gabriel came up with the impressive instrumental soundtrack for Alan Parker's film *Birdy* (Charisma 1985). Lanois felt that the location in lush English countryside near Bath helped with the production of atmospheric work, as he had recently done with Eno in Canada. Gabriel, a self-confessed 'tortoise of the music business', put a year's effort into *So* (Charisma 1986). (This was a year that saw Gabriel briefly locked in a room by Lanois until he had come up with some music and the duo's adoption of the hard-hat and lunch-pail image of site workers in order to get them into production mode.)

With contributions from singer Kate Bush, bassist Tony Levin, drummer Stewart Copeland and Lanois himself on acoustic and electric guitars, the result was the finest Ambient rock of its generation. There was a deepness to the sound, an acoustical space which showed an immaculate intelligence at work. Lanois admitted that 'a small toolbox' was used, with most of the sounds created by acoustic piano, Yamaha CS-80 keyboard, an old Prophet 5 synth and the Fairlight Computer Music Instrument Series 2. On the consummately Ambient 'Don't Give Up', Gabriel and Lanois coaxed a bass performance from Tony Levin which is so determinedly beautiful that it has no equal in the rock canon. As an object lesson in how to meld new digital and old analogue recording techniques the album positioned Gabriel at the very forefront of high-fidelity production.

Since 1982 Gabriel had been involved in World Of Music And Dance, or WOMAD, a platform for the cross-pollination of World Music. This seemed to overlap with his growing involvement with human-rights organizations such as Amnesty International. With the financial success of *So* and help from MIT and US computer companies in California's Silicon Valley, Gabriel built a state-of-the-art recording studio. Real World was born in an eighteenth-century mill house in the village of Box, near Bristol. The complex would record musicians from far-flung locations, house the WOMAD offices and be the HQ for Gabriel's new Real World record label.

In 1988 Martin Scorsese invited Gabriel to write the music for his controversial film *The Last Temptation Of Christ*, which portrayed Christ as a human figure full of doubt and weaknesses. The resultant twenty-one-track album, *Passion* (Real World 1989), was again an object lesson in how to make a brilliant soundtrack. Gabriel drew on the music of Morocco and Egypt, mixed in elements of electronic keyboards, synthesizers such as the Prophet 5 and his recent research work on the Fairlight Computer Music Instrument Series 3; then added elements from Turkey, Ivory Coast, India, Bahrain, New Guinea, Senegal and Russia. The performances of the huge cast of musicians, enhanced by the use of multi-track drones, were breathtaking.

Gabriel has often sought unusual experience as a source for his intensely felt music. Flotation tanks and bio-feedback were just two avenues of exploration in the late 1980s. In the following decade Gabriel continued to spend hundreds of hours recording video footage for stirring genre-leading product. His 1992 album *US* (Real World) again featured Daniel Lanois and Tony Levin as well as a cast of players which included Indian violinist Shankar, Brian Eno, noted mixer William Orbit, regular Gabriel drummer Manu Katche and Irish chanteuse Sinead O'Connor. In 1994 he spent £500,000 on the most advanced CD-Rom of its day, *Xplora 1*. Pushing further into new media, his 1997 CD-Rom *Eve* combined visuals, screens, music and animation in a non-stop interactive experience lasting more than sixty hours.

LISTENING

All of Gabriel's latter-day product is available on Virgin discs, as is his back-catalogue. For a quick overview, listen to the 1990 Virgin compilation *Digging In The Dirt*. His 1977 debut, *Peter Gabriel*, still sounds impressive. (Note that his first four albums, of 1977, 1978, 1980 and 1982, are all called *Peter Gabriel*.) *So* is a mandatory purchase – a revelation of what rock could sound like at the very apex of the genre in 1986. For its breadth of vision and sheer diversity of instrumentalities *Passion* (Real World 1988) is my favourite album. A companion disc, *Sources* (Real World 1989), reveals the ethnic roots at the core of the Scorsese project. *US* (Real World, 1992) has lots to commend it in terms of great atmospheric sound and its clever use of House and Techno drum loops.

Ovo (Real World 2000), though the soundtrack to a theatrical event, is full of beautifully produced Ambiences and fascinating multi-ethnic sounds. It also includes a superb guest spot from the Scottish chanteuse Elizabeth Fraser.

BILL NELSON

Spanning three decades of glam-rock, new wave, electro-bop, Ambient music, and working with figures such as the ex-Japan vocalist David Sylvian and the American Minimalist pianist Harold Budd, the English guitarist Bill Nelson made a huge contribution to electronic and instrumental rock, putting out over fifty albums. His music exhibits an eclectic range of influences, from American outer-space fantasies of the 1950s to the art and thinking of the French artist, writer and film director Jean Cocteau. Nelson's Ambient music of the 1980s, when he was a practising Rosicrucian, is some of the finest in the canon. A champion of the short form à la Erik Satie, Nelson has always seen his work as creating moods and painting pictures for a higher purpose than mere entertainment. At the height of his powers, after the release of his incredible *Chance Encounters In The Garden Of Lights* (1988), Nelson told me: 'My music is painterly, an extension of my art studies and intended to be visual. It is also therapeutic. In truth, it has a great healing power and it allows for the subconscious to come forward without the hindrance of the day-to-day orthodoxy.'

Nelson was born in Yorkshire in the late 1940s to a father who was a saxophonist and bandleader and a mother who was a tap-dancer. At school he began playing acoustic and electric guitar, influenced by the Beat music of the early 1960s. As psychedelia dawned with Syd Barrett's Pink Floyd, Nelson was at Wakefield Art College by night and in various 'way-out' acid-rock bands by night. After finishing his studies he joined a religious group, The Gentle Revolution, and persuaded a local record shop to finance his impressive folk-rock debut album, *Northern Dream* (1971). The album won support from the BBC DJ John Peel and EMI in London. Soon Nelson had formed Be-Bop Deluxe, one of the finest flash-rock bands of the 1970s.

Influenced by the glam of David Bowie and Roxy Music but drawing on Nelson's own fantastic futuristic visions plus his gorgeous Gibson guitar solos, Be-Bop Deluxe made a string of impressive albums for EMI Harvest which culminated in the 'ecstatic Jimi Hendrix homage' *Sunburst Finish* and the futuristic bravura of *Modern Music*, both released in 1976. The electro elements of Nelson's vision were then adopted by Gary Numan's Tubeway Army and David Sylvian's Japan, among others. Between 1977 and 1978 he was one of the first to fully explore the concept of 'guitar synthesis', using a Hagstrom Patch 2000 guitar to trigger a Mini-Moog synthesizer. Then Nelson formed Red Noise and made the album *Sound On Sound* (Phonogram) in 1979, a blueprint of home-studio tape manipulation, treated guitar and electronic percussion.

As well as releasing poppier vocal albums, Nelson began making instrumental records, often included as free bonus albums with his mainstream releases. For the Yorkshire Actors' Company he recorded the soundtrack for *The Cabinet of Dr Caligari* (Cocteau 1981), which he put together at his home studio, Echo Observatory, using a four-track tape machine, a MiniMoog, various instruments and the aleatory (or chance) principles of John Cage. *Sounding The Ritual Echo* (Phonogram 1981) seemed designed to enhance a mood of wakeful dreaming and was recorded on 'broken and faulty tape machines and speakers'. (In a gesture of good faith, Nelson gave the guitarist Vini Reilly of The Durutti Column the Teac tape machine on which he had recorded this material for Reilly to use on his 1981 album *L.C.*) During this period Nelson even concocted an electro-acoustic soundtrack to Cocteau's film *La Belle et la bête* (*Beauty And The Beast*), given away free with his impressive 1982 album *The Love That Whirls* (Phonogram). Later Nelson would admit that his growing fondness of sonic brevity was down to a Japanese sojourn of the time with composer Ryuichi Sakamoto and his experience of sushi.

In between doing film and television work and producing (his own records and others), Nelson continued to explore the arcane in sound. It all came to a head on his first boxed set on his own Cocteau label, a 1984 affair called *Trial By Intimacy* in which eighty-three tracks were spread over four discs lovingly titled *The Summer Of God's Piano*, *Pavilion Of The Heart And Soul*, *Chamber Of Dreams* and *Catalogue Of Obsessions*. Though he contributed tasteful acoustic guitar to David Sylvian's exploratory *Gone To Earth* of 1986, Nelson himself investigated further and further the achievement of sonic atmosphere through tape and instrumental manipulation. Echo Observatory was a veritable sound laboratory, of which his 1987 *Map Of Dreams* soundtrack was a typical product.

Of the twenty-five albums Nelson admits to making in the 1980s, the finest in my view is the incomparable *Chance Encounters In The Garden Of Lights* (Cocteau 1988). Over forty-nine instrumental vignettes (sixty-three on the US Enigma version) Nelson conjured up a uniquely mysterious sound. He wrote at the time: 'This music marks a consolidation of several years of musical and philosophical practice. Almost every piece was conceived during moments of intense stillness or "magical vacuity". For this I acknowledge the influence of the late Austin Osman Spare and his technique of "automatic drawing".' He went on to outline the ritual and meditational aspects of the electronica contained therein.

In many ways Nelson had reached a zenith in his personal quest. In 1989 he released on the Cocteau label another four-disc boxed set titled *Demonstrations Of Affection*. This was made up of a series of rock love letters to his second wife, Jan. Though a slew of albums followed, a proposed Be-Bop Deluxe reunion was aborted owing to managerial difficulties and Cocteau was no more. Nelson quickly established a new studio, Rose-Croix, in the loft of a Yorkshire farmhouse and kept working. He had a small film soundtrack studio, lots of guitars, effects boxes, a sixteen-track mixing desk and a few synthesizers, notably analogue MiniMoog and digital Yamaha DX7. He often used an E-Bow gadget on his guitars to achieve an infinite sustaining tone. In 1991 he collaborated with both the re-formed Japan (named Rain Tree Crow) and Harold Budd, the latter in New Orleans.

Since signing with David Sylvian's Opium management company in the early 1990s, Nelson has continued to produce records both instrumental and vocal. He has worked with Roger Eno, lived in Japan and still pursues the concept of 'automatic music'. Though he has dedicated albums like *After The Satellite Sings* (Resurgence 1996) to Americana and Beat literature, his greatest inspiration has always been a form of Western spiritualism associated with Rosicrucianism and the Golden Dawn movement. Though Nelson contends that his spiritual philosophy is very personal, it has produced Ambient electronica of great communicative power and originality. By the late 1990s he was talking of making a film, *Evocations Of My Radiant Childhood*, its title taken from his mesmerizing *Chance Encounters In The Garden Of Lights*.

LISTENING

In 1998 DGM, a label associated with Robert Fripp and King Crimson, released *What Now, What Next*, a double-CD compilation of Nelson's most innovative music from the Cocteau years. All of the instrumental albums are worth investigating, from theatre projects such as *Dr Caligari* right through to the immense instrumental soundscapes of *Chance Encounters In The Garden Of Lights*. If they can still be found, *Duplex* (Cocteau 1989) and *Simplex* (Cocteau 1990) are well worth investing in.

LAURIE ANDERSON

The most high-profile 'performance artist' of the late twentieth century has always been associated with rock music. Brought up a classical violinist, Laurie

Anderson became convinced, after moving to New York, that theatrical originality and punchy albums were more advantageous to her career. Her voice-synthesized masterpiece 'O Superman' (1982) broke new ground and went on to sell nearly one million copies. Subsequently she worked with Peter Gabriel and Brian Eno on albums which emphasized her quirky story-telling electronica. Her genius for theatrical presentation, catalysed by the operatic successes of Philip Glass, saw Anderson present mixtures of narrative, song, images, film and music with the latest in technology. Famous for her neon-bowed digital violin, she blended, in presentations such as *Empty Places* (1990), the rock dynamics of Jimi Hendrix with an unusual melancholy.

Laurie Anderson was born in an affluent Chicago suburb in 1947, one of a family of eight. So musical was her family that they even wrote their own compositions, and she began serious violin lessons at the age of five. At school she loved art but kept up intensive violin studies until she was sixteen, when she showed a distaste for the post-Serialist approach of American conservatory teaching. During the early 1970s she arrived in New York to study art history but soon steeped herself in almost every aspect of fine art. Her interest in sculpture and film-making led her to Philip Glass. She remembered sitting in on his rehearsals for up to six hours at a stretch listening to 'perfect thinking music which went up and down and which had a very concentrated atmosphere'. Inspired by the Downtown milieu which included Glass and Steve Reich, Anderson struck out on her own with a collage of music and visuals. Her first famous piece was called *Performance Art* (1973) and consisted of Anderson perched atop a block of ice in the street playing the violin. She wore ice-skates and the piece was over when the ice melted.

As the art scene of New York's SoHo district grew, so did Anderson's reputation. She performed in galleries until the desire for better acoustics took her to other venues. After witnessing the critical success of Glass's *Einstein On The Beach* in 1976, she became more determined to raise the level of her art. During the early 1980s she readily absorbed new digital technology and was one of the first to use New England Digital's Synclavier computer synthesizer. In 1982 came her big breakthrough, the single 'O Superman', with its dulcet vocal cadences synthetically enhanced by digital vocoder. A UK number two, the song was followed by the Warner Bros. album *Big Science*, which saw Anderson cross into the mainstream.

Still thinking of Glass's opera works, Anderson used her Warner Bros. advances to fund *United States I–IV* (1983), an ambitious sixteen-hour presentation which toured the world. Words, film and images, plus acoustic and electronic sounds, dazzled audiences. Anderson played a special violin, customized by New England digital, which, when touched by her glowing white bow, produced both voice and music samples. Her 'talking violin' became more impactful when played by Anderson dressed in black with only her neon-enhanced lips visible. *United States I–IV* was a satire on corporate America, an alternative US history from Red Indian to rock 'n' roll.

In 1984 Anderson moved towards rock with the album *Mr Heartbreak*, a recording assisted by Peter Gabriel, Bill Laswell and King Crimson guitarist Adrian Belew. Anderson would keep in contact with Gabriel, visiting his Real World studio and touching base on the latest in studio technology. Co-production on her 1986 album *Home Of The Brave* went to the famous David Bowie collaborator Nile Rodgers and its subsequent concert movie (of the US and Japanese tour) featured a rock band and the cult author William Burroughs. By 1989 Anderson was mixing the ethereal with an ever-widening range of instrumental colours, including flamenco, African, Gospel and folk music, on the album *Strange Angels*. Instrumentally she had a fantastic grasp of technology, her Eventide Harmonizers working like a 'ventriloquist's box', allowing her to sound like man or a girlie chorus at the touch of a switch. She was fond of Akai samplers and loved the multi-timbral Korg M1 and Roland D70 synthesizers. By this stage she had moved to a Zeta digital violin which allowed her to play sub-octaves with a full bass sound.

Anderson shot a lot of film, took a lot of slides and used the new computer animation to generate images of bluebirds for the 'Strange Angels' tour, which took on a life of its own as 'Empty Places' in 1990. Anderson used five background screens, a KX remote keyboard, various drum pads, her violin and foot pedals to access her different harmonized vocals. Each venue was treated to vocals in the local language, including Czech, Slovak, Greek, Hungarian and many others. Yet for all the technical brilliance the concerts presented simple clear visuals – images of snow falling through an open window to soft electric guitar music, Anderson in trademark spiky hair, violin by her side.

At the time she expanded her twenty-four-track studio in New York to include a film and video facility, darkroom and rehearsal space. In 1994 came a new album, *Bright Red*, a floating amalgam of blues, folk and Gospel styles textured by Brian Eno's electronic treatments. The spiky mop now gone, Anderson was singing in a natural angelic soprano. The album also included contributions from the former leader of The Velvet Underground, Lou Reed, with whom Anderson had begun a relationship. She had also written a 300-page diary, *Stories From The Nerve Bible*, which she subsequently channelled into performances. In 1995 she collaborated with Eno on the London-based installation *Self-Storage* (a series of rooms full of interesting art and music 'exhibits') and interested herself in CD-Rom and Internet technology. Her curatorship of the Meltdown Festival of 1997, held at London's South Bank arts complex, culminated in a gala performance of leading lights from all corners of the New Music spectrum, including Anderson herself, Ryuichi Sakamoto, Michael Nyman, Philip Glass and Lou Reed.

LISTENING

All the albums mentioned above are on Warner Bros. in the US and WEA in the UK. Anderson provided music for Wim Wenders's film *Wings Of Desire*

(1987) after a chance meeting at a Paris airport. The collaboration was continued on *Faraway So Close* (1993). Her *United States I–IV* came out on Warner Bros. in 1991 as a four-CD set. One of her best recordings is on the extensive tribute to John Cage *A Chance Operation* (Koch 1993), where Anderson, in a cadential voice, reads 'Cunningham Stories' (a text written by Cage in 1968) to a suitably Ambient electronic backing.

RYUICHI SAKAMOTO

One of the world's most gifted organizers of sound, Ryuichi Sakamoto achieved a reclamation of Japanese music after decades of post-war erosion. In a country that so often looked outward for inspiration, Sakamoto used a phenomenal understanding of music to achieve some of the most accomplished recordings of his generation. His was an ability to absorb the best of what the West had to offer and fuse it with traditional Oriental instrumentation and structures. His innate good taste helped him make great soundtracks, for one of which, the impressive *The Last Emperor* (Virgin), he was rewarded with an Oscar in 1987.

Sakamoto was born in 1952, the son of a literary editor and fashion designer. He began composition work at the Tokyo University of Fine Arts at the age of ten. As the 1960s progressed Sakamoto became interested in different musics, such as that of The Beatles and John Cage. He begun writing poetry and worked in radical theatre. After finishing high school he returned to Tokyo University to take his degree in composition, drawing much inspiration from French Impressionism and Minimalism. During the 1970s his interest turned to Stockhausen and he gained a Master's degree in electronic and ethnic music. After this he became a famous arranger and pianist, often working as a session musician. He also became a male fashion model.

When he heard The Beatles' *Rubber Soul* (1965), Sakamoto was impressed by the mixing and arrangements, 'the instrumental timbres that had loads of atmosphere, that were even Ambient in sound'. He thought Steve Reich 'one of the great inventors of tape manipulation' and Brian Eno's work to be 'abstract and Romantic'. To Sakamoto, Debussy was the master of 'sound colour', while Kraftwerk's *Trans-Europe Express* (1977) was 'Minimalism with hypnotic rhythm, a richness of overall sound that blueprinted Technopop'. It was the latter that Sakamoto explored with the new-wave glam group the Yellow Magic Orchestra (YMO) in 1978. Seven albums were recorded between then and 1983, during which time Sakamoto became a big star in Japan.

But frustration would leave him to desert the YMO for greener pastures in acting, writing and developing a solo career in music. He had already met the talented studio maverick Seigen Ono and the charismatic lead singer of the English group Japan, David Sylvian. (It was Sakamoto's wife Akiko Yano who helped Sylvian with the synthesized vocal lines on Japan's best-selling LP *Tin Drum*, released in 1981.) They started making records together, Sakamoto impressed by Sylvian's acoustic vision, Sylvian simply awed by Sakamoto's musical acumen. In 1983 came the soundtrack album for the hit 1982 film *Merry Christmas, Mr Lawrence*, a recording which included Sylvian singing the main theme in a vocal version titled 'Forbidden Colours'. Sakamoto not only wrote, arranged and performed the entire electro-acoustic score but also acted in the movie, sharing the bill with David Bowie.

What was impressive about the musical collaboration was the fruitfulness of the meeting of East and West – Sakamoto's discreet Japanese touches on synthesizers did not sound out of place with the Western orchestral accompaniment. He continued to work on his Ambient music with Sylvian, their cooperation culminating in Sakamoto's acoustic-electronic arrangements on *Secrets Of The Beehive* (Virgin 1987). Yet it was the soundtrack to Bertolucci's 1987 film *The Last Emperor* that would bring him global recognition. Here he drew on Chinese folk music, Mahler's Romanticism and the strident Minimalism of John Adams to fashion an array of memorable tunes. Using a simple four-note melody, Sakamoto developed it through a palette of different settings, some orchestral, some drawing on traditional Chinese lute, zither and violin styles. 'Variation 1' was probably the finest piece of the film as synth atmospheres backdropped a beautifully expressive Chinese lute solo.

In concert Sakamoto played a Yamaha grand piano (with MIDI interface to trigger sampled sounds and synthesizers). In the studio he preferred to use an old Prophet 5 synthesizer, an Apple Macintosh computer for creating note sequences and the Fairlight Computer Music Instrument for sampling. He had made pop music albums since the late 1970s, but his most elaborate effort was *Beauty* (Virgin 1990), recorded in America and Tokyo in a variety of languages with an international cast of musicians such as the Senegalese star Youssou N'Dour, Beach Boys composer Brian Wilson, Indian violinist Shankar and English vocalist Robert Wyatt. Japanese choral music could be heard alongside the music of Africa and Arabia. Sakamoto's influence throughout was a series of Japanese haikus and Zen poems found in a New York bookshop. In 1990 Sakamoto also worked with the Royal Philharmonic Orchestra on the emotionally charged soundtrack for Bertolucci's screen version of Paul Bowles's renowned novel *The Sheltering Sky*. Sakamoto spent six months agonizing over the score in London before going to live in New York's Greenwich Village.

This period saw Sakamoto working more and more with computers and samplers. He spoke to David Sylvian about a possible collaboration with Toru Takemitsu, Japan's great post-war composer. The looping, sampled beat of New York Hip-Hop informed the excellent pop album *Heartbeat* (Virgin 1992), another exercise in exquisite taste as DJs, the guitar of Jimi Hendrix and David Sylvian all appeared in the seamless sonic daze of Sakamoto's vision. Sakamoto worked relentlessly at home with his computers and keyboards, in studios for his soundtrack work, often conducting the orchestras himself. He has worked with other directors, such as Pedro Almodovar, and his music opened the 1992 Olympics. A believer in total digital sound recording, he nevertheless has an impressive collection of old analogue synthesizers such as Moog and Arp.

The Yellow Magic Orchestra re-formed in 1993 and in 1998 Sakamoto achieved a breakthrough with the deeply moving *Discord*, an orchestral piece written out of sorrow for world economic, political and social upheavals. Strong, aerated string themes were coloured by distant piano and samples from DJ Spooky, and the final movement 'Salvation' included Cageian voices, flute and harp.

LISTENING

Sakamoto has never had any problem making memorable instrumental music full of the Ambience of his Oriental roots. All his work with David Sylvian is recommended, particularly the 1985 soundtrack *Steel Cathedrals* (Virgin). His soundtracks are superb, particularly those for Oshima's *Merry Christmas, Mr Lawrence* (Virgin 1983), and Bertolucci's *The Last Emperor* (1987) and *The Sheltering Sky* (1990), both on Virgin discs. His pop albums often drift into Ambient interludes (as in *Heartbeat* of 1992) but *Smoochy* (Milan 1996) is laden with lovely piano and collaged instrumentals. *1996* (Milan 1996) is a chamber setting of some of his best-known music. In its two fantastic string movements, *Discord* (Sony 1998) perfectly mirrors Sakamoto's complete synthesis of East and West.

SEIGEN ONO

In the 1980s a new breed of roving electronic musicians combined engineering and production skills as a matter of taste in the search for beautiful and exotic sounds. Among them was Seigen Ono, who in the latter part of the decade recorded in studios in Japan, France, America and Brazil. Initially Ono was seen simply as a leading light of Japanese New Age music but the sheer quality and diversity of his output plus his acknowledgement of the importance of Brian Eno and Stockhausen put him in a league of his own.

Seigen Ono was born in Kakogawa in western Japan in the late 1950s. By his own admission, New York was nearer in spirit than Tokyo. He listened to the work of Brian Eno all the way through high school. At twenty he played various styles of rock, African music and jazz with friends. On hearing David Bowie's *Low* in 1977 and the effect Eno's studio techniques had on the pop icon, Ono was convinced that his career lay in the studio. In Tokyo he knocked on many doors before landing a job in the prestigious Onkio Haus complex with its six studios and film synchronization facilities. Working from the ground up, Ono became a respected engineer-producer, and in 1982 famously engineered Ryuichi Sakamoto's soundtrack to the film *Merry Christmas, Mr Lawrence*.

After becoming a freelance he showed equipment no respect and continually sought the 'quality of sound in the music'. Putting his own ideas to tape, he eventually assembled musicians to record *Seigen* (1983), a whirling orchestral debut full of clipped acoustic guitars, water-drop piano notes and electronica. Soon he was working with the likes of Robert Fripp and David Sylvian. Ono's aim was a synthesis of electronic sound, sampling and more conventional console mixing, tape loops and quality instrumental performance. Following Eno's lead, he saw that modern music allowed the roles of engineer, producer and musician to merge.

Since releasing *Seigen* he has worked all over the world, in demand as a collaborator on a myriad of projects from John Lurie's Ambient jazz project *The Lounge Lizards* in the US to composing music for the French fashion house Comme des Garçons. He has spent much time in Brazil and has worked with leading American avantists the saxophonist John Zorn and guitarists Arto Lindsay and Bill Frisell.

LISTENING

Seigen Ono's recordings are some of the best Oriental Ambient and electronic music available. His 1983 debut album *Seigen*, issued in the West by Pan East in 1986, overflows with inspired sounds, its maker ecstatic at the very thought of recording. *Steel Cathedrals* (1985), his collaboration with David Sylvian, is a classic of the Ambient genre. Ono's two albums for Comme des Garçons (both Virgin Venture 1989) illustrate his wonderful versatility. *Nekonotopia Nekonomania* (*Made To Measure*) (1991) sees him on twelve-string guitar and synthesizers, combining Latin music with tonal ambiences.

DAVID SYLVIAN

Of all the pop and rock musicians to emerge in Britain during the early 1980s no one embraced the philosophy of Ambience and silence as thoroughly as David Sylvian. With its forceful emphasis on image, his group Japan became one of the finest acts to emerge from the New Romantic scene – a cluster of musicians whose talents were on a par with their sophisticated Eastern-tinged stage presence. Even then Sylvian was absorbing the influences of both Toru Takemitsu and Karlheinz Stockhausen. Though an excellent tenor, he wished to broaden the instrumental aspect of his recorded music. Ryuichi Sakamoto, Robert Fripp, Jon Hassell, Holger Czukay and Bill Nelson would all play their part in the recording of a stream of brilliant albums, some of which became the most ambitious and satisfying Ambient music of the last decade and a half of the twentieth century.

Sylvian was born in Beckenham, London in 1958. Like David Bowie, whose glam influences had an indirect effect on Japan, he moved around South London with his working-class parents. At secondary school painting and music were escape routes for the desperately shy and introverted Sylvian. He played guitar and eventually formed Japan with bassist Mick Karn, keyboardist Richard Barbieri and drummer Steve Jansen (Sylvian's brother). By 1976 they had good management and their combination of a confident image and a music which mixed Sylvian's svelte vocals with an exotic sound of supple bass, atmospheric keyboards and feather-light drumming made Japan pop stars. By 1980 they were making good records but it was *Tin Drum* (Virgin 1981) which defined their unique style. Helped by the classically trained Ryuichi Sakamoto, Sylvian had studied traditional Japanese music and applied its emphasis on space to the album's slower pieces. He also credited Stockhausen with inspiring 'the abstract synthesizer melody lines' on the song 'Ghosts'.

Differences between himself and Mick Karn led to the demise of Japan at the end of 1982. At the invitation of Sakamoto, Sylvian contributed a vocal to the film soundtrack *Merry Christmas, Mr Lawrence*. Retreating to Tokyo, Sylvian recorded the theme 'Forbidden Colours' in 1983 and was able to observe Sakamoto at work on the film score. This was a fundamental experience for the Englishman as he saw that in Onkio Haus studios Sakamato was inspired to create 'a sense of place, a landscape in the mind of the listener'.

Back in London, Sylvian began writing on a four-track Teac tape machine with a combination of guitar, percussion and Prophet 5 synthesizer. He imagined roles for other players and in the winter of 1983–4 set about 'creating an unspecified aural landscape'. He even journeyed to Berlin to get what he wanted. In Steve Nye he found an engineer-producer he could trust. Supported by two former members of Japan, Jansen and Barbieri, Sylvian extended his sonic palette to take in the pitch-shifted trumpet sound of Jon Hassell, various horns and reeds, upright bass and the unique contributions of Holger Czukay. The ex-Can musician was adept at splicing short-wave radio samples into the mix and also used an old 1950s IBM dictaphone to create hissy sound loops. Ryuichi Sakamoto also played synthesizers and piano and the resultant album, *Brilliant Trees* (1984), was a tour de force. Sylvian openly acknowledged Brian Eno's influence on the structure of the album and his adoption of the studio as a musical instrument during the recording. In the studio Sylvian worked with each musician individually, a one-to-one process he would later describe as 'emotional layering'.

Fired by the possibilities of instrumental electro-acoustic Ambient music, Sylvian returned to Japan near the end of 1984 to record some African-inflected material with Seigen Ono and Sakamoto. Asked for some music by the Japanese film-maker Yamaguchi, he spent further eight days recording nearly eighteen and a half minutes of pulse and Ambient atmospherics. A Japanese guitarist even banged a tuning-fork on a flat guitar to get unusual sounds. Back in London in 1985, Sylvian brought in Robert Fripp and a flugelhorn player. *Steel Cathedrals* was defined by a slap-drum rhythm, Sakamoto's stark piano 'noises' and

Czukay's 'treatment' of sounds on the three-inch tape-loop facility of his dictaphone. It remains an astonishing example of the creation of pure atmosphere.

Sylvian continued recording in London, now with Czukay and Jon Hassell. Czukay brought in an entire bag of sampled voice cassettes to put into the mix. The most impressive product of these 1985 sessions was 'Awakening', a piece of trance music full of ethnic percussion and Jon Hassell's familiar 'Fourth World' trumpet. Both the Japanese Ambiences of 1984 and the newer pieces would form the entirety of *Alchemy − An Index Of Possibilities*, a cassette-only release. Sylvian was keen to create a 'kind of fascination' in his instrumental sounds. Privately he was expanding his mental horizons, absorbing the teachings of Buddhism, Christianity, the Jewish Kabbalah and Rosicrucianism. He felt his music should show 'an appreciation of nature and a love for life and its value'. Unsurprisingly, he collaborated with two avowedly philosophical musicians, Bill Nelson and Robert Fripp, on his next album.

Gone To Earth (1986), recorded in Oxfordshire and Sylvian's favoured Town House studio in London, was a huge twin-album concept. One LP mixed rock and ballad and was full of bright sonorities. The other was a rich instrumental creation, elemental and Christian in tone. Throughout, Nelson's ecstatic guitar bursts were contrasted by Fripp's sharding broadsides. Fripp's other contribution was influencing Sylvian to use excerpts of the voices of the German artist Joseph Beuys and J. G. Bennett, a disciple of the mystic Gurdjieff. The recording approach on *Gone To Earth* was painstaking in that Sylvian often began with a rhythm machine on tape, then a drum sound, then the chord shapes, followed by guitar parts and vocals. These demo ideas were then brought to the studio, where his brother, Steve Jansen, would lay the drum foundation.

So open was Sylvian to new challenges that 1986 also saw him abandon vocal music completely for an extraordinary collaboration with Czukay. One night after a meal with Czukay and the writer Karl Lippergaus in Cologne, Sylvian was shown around Can's famous Innerspace studio, converted from a cinema. 'We created a sound environment by setting up guitar loops, tape loops and drones from pre-recorded radio signals,' he recalled. Czukay's expertise in sound fields led to an eighteen-and-a-half-minute creation which featured telephone signals, flute, string whirls, pan pipes, guitar treatments, synth noises, random edits, the sound of a train, lots of hiss, piano and garbled radio transmission in Italian, Greek and Arabic. Titled 'Plight', it was extensively re-edited by Czukay in 1987. A second night in the studio led to 'Premonition', defined by its sailing treatments and bubbling short-wave radio transmissions. Piano sprinkles and welling and ebbing keyboard treatments were punctuated by distant radio voices, Morse code, wind sounds and a constant electronic tone over sixteen and a half minutes. On its release in 1988 the album *Plight & Premonition* was greeted with astonishment. With its multi-processing, excessive tape distortions, found sounds and organic, other-worldly eeriness, it was one of the richest Ambient music recordings ever released.

As a singer and vocalist Sylvian had felt the need to write an album of short songs based on orchestral arrangements and acoustic instruments. Influenced by his Japanese girlfriend the visual designer Yuka Fujii (who had introduced him to the folk Ambience of Nick Drake and John Martyn during the writing of *Brilliant Trees*), Sylvian was now avidly listening to the ECM catalogue. Two and a half months were spent in studios in France, London, Holland and Bath recording *Secrets Of The Beehive* (1987). Ryuichi Sakamoto was again in attendance on keyboards, organ, woodwind and string arrangements. Amid the crafted horn, string, double bass and acoustic guitar was an extraordinarily atmospheric creation full of taped voices and tape loops titled 'Maria'.

In 1988 Sylvian spent a fortnight on holiday in Cologne with Czukay. Again they retired to the Can studio, with drummer Jaki Liebezeit helping out. This time the aural environment of arcing guitar treatments, radio and dictaphone signals was driven by Liebezeit's trance drumming. Called 'Flux', the near-seventeen-minute piece they created was completed when Michael Karoli on guitar and Markus Stockhausen on flugelhorn overdubbed their parts. So Sylvian met most of Can and created another Ambient jewel. He even told me that its companion piece, the transcendent 'Mutability', was recorded in one day with a couple of keyboard and guitar overdubs. Jaki Liebezeit played African flute in a twenty-one-minute cycle of uplifting sonorities which was convincingly heaven bound. *Flux + Mutability* (1989) was, without doubt, another Ambient classic.

On a creative roll, Sylvian then experimented with different tonalities and tunings in the programming of synthesizers for the single 'Pop Song'. By the autumn of 1989 he was enthusiastic enough to re-form Japan and record a new album based on studio improvisation. Over two months were spent at locations in the South of France and Venice, laying down material with Jansen, Barbieri and Karn. More work was done in studios in London, Bath, Dublin and Paris but by the spring of 1990 finance was low and Sylvian was under pressure to christen the project *Japan*, when he preferred *Rain Tree Crow*. Refusing to bend, he financed the mixing himself and again the group dissolved. *Rain Tree Crow* (1991) was made during a period of depression for Sylvian yet it was a success because it was a true group effort which featured two Prophet 5 synthesizers with more up-to-date electronic instruments from EMU and Roland. The mix of real sounds, computer sequencing, Karn's flexi-bass and the extensive use of sampled drums made it a satisfying sonic surprise. It also featured extensive instrumental sound paintings.

Another 1990 collaboration was with Sylvian's long-time artist friend Russell Mills on *Ember Glance*, a Tokyo installation based around the concept of memory. In this work Sylvian felt he was moving towards a more fulfilled inner spirituality and with Mills (a frequent visual collaborator with Brian Eno) he had found the perfect resonator. With its hanging veils, light-boxes and golden cloud, the presentation was quite effective, stimulating composer

Takemitsu to say: 'Enclosed within are both the stillness of eternity and the fury of instant conflagration.' Released as a book-and-CD package in 1991, *Ember Glance* saw Sylvian collaborate with musician Frank Perry on another Ambient excursion. Bells, gong and synth drones made up the disc, which included a voice sample of poet Seamus Heaney. A meeting with Ingrid Chavez (a singer and actress associated with the soul star Prince) changed Sylvian's life completely. They married in 1992, he left London to settle permanently in the US, primarily Minneapolis, Prince's hometown.

Nineteen ninety-two also saw another collaboration between Sylvian and Robert Fripp. Invited to tour Japan, the duo wrote material for this purpose. After another tour in Italy it was obvious that Sylvian was exorcizing a lot of personal pain through a raucous music. Working at studios in New Orleans, Woodstock and New York with Peter Gabriel's engineer David Bottrill, the duo came up with *The First Day* (1993), whose highlight was the optimistic Ambience of 'Bringing Down The Light', a composition not far in spirit from Fripp's mid-1970s work with Eno. In 1993–4 Sylvian and Fripp toured Japan, Europe and the US with support from the guitarist Michael Brook. A live album, *Damage* (1994), produced some exceptional ballads. By now a family man, Sylvian spent many years building his own studio at his American home, basing it around a twenty-four-track Amek desk. When I talked to him in 1995 he confessed to 'having a variety of synthesizers which are used in conjunction with a number of outboard effects. My work involves fine-tuning treatments to enhance the sounds I programme myself into the synth modules. I also sound-sculpt on a Macintosh computer – literally create soundscapes using samples from a diversity of sources.'

By 1998 Sylvian was living in San Francisco and had readied for release a new album, *Dead Bees On A Cake*, a recording shot through with a Hindu spirituality and Indian tabla. Ranging from Trip-Hop to a personal mix of folk blues, chamber and Ambience, the album benefited from the glow of the Fender Rhodes electric piano. Now a dab hand at sampling, Sylvian absorbed the sounds of The Mahavishnu Orchestra, John Cage and John Lee Hooker without ever losing a jot of his style.

Sylvian has always been a Virgin recording artist. He and Ingrid Chavez appeared on Ryuichi Sakamoto's *Heartbeat* (Virgin 1992). Two interesting outside collaborations were with Hector Zazou on *Sahara Blue* (Crammed 1992) and Italians Alesini and Andreoni on *Marco Polo* (Maso 1995), where he was featured alongside Harold Budd and Roger Eno.

LISTENING

Of the albums considered above, *Brilliant Trees* (1984), *Alchemy – An Index of Possibilities* (1985), *Gone To Earth* (1986), *Plight & Premonition* (1988) and *Flux + Mutability* (1989) are essential Ambient purchases. Also recommended is *Weatherbox* (1989), a beautiful five-disc artefact, designed by Russell Mills, which featured the first CD version of *Alchemy*. In 1999 Virgin reissued 1990's *Ember Glance* as part of the Ambient CD *Approaching Silence*.

MICHAEL BROOK

A good example of the new kind of Ambient rock which emerged in the 1980s and 1990s is the music of the Canadian guitarist Michael Brook. By marrying studies in non-Western music to emergent technology, Brook carved himself a niche as an in-demand producer, engineer and instrument builder to a wide cross-section of the musical fraternity. His invention of the 'Infinite Guitar' brought a chiming new sustained guitar sound that was readily heard on U2's 1987 multimillion-selling album *The Joshua Tree*. During the 1990s he pushed the production of World Music into unforeseen areas through his painterly approach to performers such as the fêted Pakistani singer Nusrat Fateh Ali Khan, whose album *Night Sky* won Brook a Grammy award in 1996. Brook's constant dealing in timbre, texture and drones has had a lasting impact on film music. Though he is seen as a rock musician, his real roots go back through Jon Hassell to the benchmark Minimalism of La Monte Young.

Brook was born in the early 1950s in Toronto. His first important musical memories were from the 1960s, when he heard the 'distorted sounds of amplified electric instruments' on imported albums by Cream, Jimi Hendrix and The Beatles. He played in Toronto bar-rock bands before attending Ontario's York University, ostensibly as an art student with an interest in photography. Soon, though, he was studying African music, American Indian music and working in the campus electronic studio. At the time, under the influence of the instrument builder Hugh Le Caine, there was a very positive attitude to electronic music at Canadian universities. Brook formed a group at York which 'primarily mixed ethnic music and electronics'. While working as a teaching assistant as part of his studies he met the renowned American trumpeter and Minimalist Jon Hassell.

After college Brook worked as a video technician in an art gallery and met Hassell again in 1974. This time Hassell introduced the young musician to the teachings of La Monte Young and the Hindustani classical singer Pandit Pran Nath. Through Hassell, Brook would also meet Brian Eno and Daniel Lanois, who were working hard on Ambient recordings in the Lanois brothers' Grant Avenue studio in Ontario. Brook worked on Hassell's debut album, *Vernal Equinox*, in 1977 and then toured with him. Eventually Brook became house engineer at Grant Avenue, a situation that was 'determined to be open-minded in that the "studio" was instruments, recording equipment and effects boxes all together'. There he helped record Martha & The Muffins, a pop band whose success in the late 1970s and early 80s saw him join them on the road as guitarist.

At that time Brook's technical and musical skills surfaced on a series of Grant

Avenue Ambient discs by Eno and Jon Hassell. In 1985 his first solo album, *Hybrid* (with help from Eno and Lanois), was a soothing mix of African percussion, nature recordings and drones wrapped up in a thick coverlet of swampy sound. The latter was provided by Brook's first finished version of his Infinite Guitar, basically a Fender Stratocaster copy with additional electronics to enable it to provide unlimited sustain as long as a finger was touching a string. Brook traced the guitar back to his 'love of Indian notation and drones'. He wanted to play longer phrases and, inspired by the kind of controlled feedback wizardry exploited by Jimi Hendrix during the 1960s, he wanted to make such guitar sounds readily available. With its sitar-like scalloped neck and the addition of fuzz boxes and echo-volume pedals, Brook's invention was a formidable instrument which would be seized upon by U2's The Edge for the recording of *The Joshua Tree* in 1986.

That year saw Brook collaborate with The Edge on the soundtrack recording *Captive*, which introduced singer Sinead O'Connor to the world. Again Brook's penchant for mixing electronics with instrumental sound yielded a particularly impressive form of ethnic Ambience. By the late 1980s he was a key figure in Eno's Opal stable of artists, performing live with the likes of Minimalist pianists Harold Budd, Hans-Joachim Roedelius and Terry Riley in exotic venues such as the caves of Lanzarote and Rome's Botanical Gardens. In addition he provided strong technical support to Eno's installation sites in various parts of the world and even performed an open-air Ambient concert with him at a Shinto shrine in Tenkawa, Japan, during the summer of 1989.

After two acclaimed 1990 ethnic productions (for Youssou N'Dour and Nusrat Fateh Ali Khan) Brook worked long and hard at using technology to make a more direct and focused instrumental sound – a veritable electric form of ethnic music. On *Cobalt Blue* (1992) what was achieved was a multi-layered landscape of percussion deftly filled by some of the most beautiful guitar sounds ever played. With its shimmering Eastern textures, repetitive phrases and the deceptive use of synthesizers to generate 'acoustic sounds', *Cobalt Blue* was consummate craftsmanship. At the time Brook talked of his interest 'in drones and perceptual psychology', specifically the way the mind changes 'when it listens to something that stays the same' – in effect classic Minimalism.

Cobalt Blue led to a successful solo tour in 1992 and work with David Sylvian and Robert Fripp on their world tour of 1993. Film work beckoned and though, on the surface, the gifted and handsome Brook seemed to be arcing on a typical Hollywood-beckoning career, he spent a good deal of time working at Peter Gabriel's Real World studio in England. In 1995 along came an astonishing album of new Ambience, *Dream*, a fertile collaboration between Brook and U. Srinivas, a Southern Indian raga master of the electric mandolin. A mixture of Brook's 'love of ornamentation of Indian and Arabic music and its linear development' with a greater interest in 'the vertical features such as harmony and melody', the album had a freshness of sound and a smoothness of approach which made it instantly accessible.

LISTENING

Hybrid (EG 1985) was remastered for CD in 1990 and is still critically acclaimed for its unconventional use of guitar and sound treatments courtesy of Brian Eno and Daniel Lanois. Its humid sound is derived in part from the use of sixteen-second digital delay and the sound of live crickets! In 1986 Brook teamed up with U2's The Edge for the Ambient soundtrack *Captive* (Virgin). Brook still maintains that the best-ever use of his Infinite Guitar was 'the high violin sound at the beginning of "I Still Haven't Found What I'm Looking For"' on U2's 1987 smash *The Joshua Tree*. On the prismatic *Cobalt Blue* (4AD 1992) Brook achieves a satiny guitar sound by putting his instrument through Neve pre-amps. Strings, bells and buzz-bass adorn a recording assisted by the Eno brothers, Roger on keyboards and Brian on treatments, string arrangements and computer mixing. *Live At The Aquarium* (4AD 1992) is a live document of the album, recorded at London Zoo. *Dream* (Real World 1995) is a wonderful recording of ensemble pieces by the Indian mandolinist U. Srinivas, Brook and a cast which includes the English violinist Nigel Kennedy and the Brazilian percussionist Nana Vasconcelos. More fascinating was Brook's use of sampling and mixed Ambiences, particularly on the deeply meditative 'Think'.

Working in Lanzarote with the Armenian duduk master Djivan Gasparayan in 1997, Brook recorded an exceptional album of cultural fusion called *Black Rock* (Real World 1999). Brook, who has always contended he 'wouldn't have had a career in music if it weren't for Brian Eno', has lent his sound and production skills to numerous ethnic albums in addition to the one with Gasparayan, working with Youssou N'Dour, Nusrat Fateh Ali Khan and Cheb Khaled, among others.

Brook's rhythmically entrancing music has easily transferred to film, starting with the post-Gulf War *Fires In Kuwait* (1992), then Michael Mann's *Heat* (1996) and on to Kevin Spacey's debut feature *Albino Alligator* (1997), the soundtrack of which was issued by 4AD.

U2

Beginning as an ecstatic 1980s rock band with an echo-laden guitar sound, U2 were very much seen as part of the 'big music' trend established by such earnest rockers as Echo And The Bunnymen, Simple Minds and The Waterboys. Over time they were to radically reinvent themselves as the Ambient rock group of the late twentieth century. More visionary than their contemporaries, they seized on the studio skills of Brian Eno and Daniel Lanois to create a series of rock masterpieces. *The Unforgettable Fire* (1984*)*, *The Joshua Tree* (1987) and *Achtung Baby* (1991) saw the most dazzling use of electronic and studio sounds since the era of The Beatles. Even after selling millions of records globally and becoming rock's premier live stadium draw, U2 were not interested in resting on their laurels. In 1995, working with Brian Eno under the name Passengers, they released a series of Ambient soundtracks, some of which went on to grace the film work of Michelangelo Antonioni and Wim Wenders.

All the members of U2 were born in the early 1960s. The band was founded in north Dublin in 1976 by fourteen-year-old drummer Larry Mullen. Amazingly, he had seriously studied various drum styles, including military and jazz. Initially a school band, U2 also comprised guitarist Dave 'The Edge' Evans (of Welsh extraction), Englishman Adam Clayton and the extrovert and charismatic singer Paul 'Bono' Hewson. The Edge took up the guitar when his family moved to Dublin at the age of eight. He had an academic approach to the instrument and by fifteen he had acquired a considerable facility. Clayton was a typical ex-boarding school middle-class bohemian who had a nice bass guitar and amp. Bono had approached the guitar when he was thirteen but it was his almost messianic lyrical vision, powered by a Christian idealism, which pushed the group forward.

Aided by 'fifth member', manager Paul McGuinness, the gutsy young group signed to the Island label in 1980. Island's boss, Chris Blackwell, considered U2 'the most important signing since King Crimson'. Were U2 progressive rock? They had gone through three years of punk gigs and were looking for new collaborators like famed Joy Division engineer Martin Hannett and producer Steve Lillywhite. Recorded at Windmill Lane Studios in Dublin, their debut album, *Boy* (1980), had an aquatic quality, contrasting anthemic rock songs with brooding instrumental passages of spray, fine drizzle and lapping waves. Lillywhite even added concrete sounds of milk bottles and scraped bicycle spokes to the hit song 'I Will Follow'. The Edge's unconventional approach to his semi-star-shaped Gibson Explorer electric guitar was to eschew blues influences for echoed chords and sustained harmonics. He used a system of two Vox amps coupled to two Memory Man echo units linked to a switchbox connected to his guitar. He also played a classic Fender Stratocaster.

The Edge was also an able keyboardist and pianist, as heard on *October* (1981), which, with its use of uillean pipes, was a more spiritually Irish affair than the first album. Extending his abilities, he played lap steel guitar and sang on *War* (1983), U2's first UK number-one album. Steve Lillywhite again produced, extending the sound palette with violin, saxophone and backing vocalists. 'New Year's Day' was a suitable showcase for The Edge's flawless keyboard and guitar skills. That year also saw him work with Holger Czukay and Jaki Liebezeit of the German experimental group Can. His interest in the European avant-garde was an important factor in pulling U2 out of a musical rut which endless touring had landed them in by the end of 1983.

In 1984 Brian Eno and Daniel Lanois left the Grant Avenue studio in Ontario, where they were busy creating Ambient gems, to go to Ireland and produce U2. Eno had accepted on the insistence of Bono but was viewed with suspicion by Chris Blackwell. The aim was to bring out the subtleties in U2's music and record in Slane Castle, a magical country location beside the River Boyne. Eno liked the large ballroom with its chandeliers and Lanois brought in a Stevens twenty-four-track portable recording system on wheels. Power was provided by a water-paddle system at the back of the castle. Eno was the man with notebooks and strategies to offer. Lanois actually captured whatever the band created, whether it was in the 'splashy-sounding' ballroom or out on the balcony which ran around the castle, where The Edge would often sound his guitar to the ancient burial grounds dappled with sunshine. Two months were spent there and another two in Dublin's Windmill Lane studios honing the results. The album was called *The Unforgettable Fire* and the lyrics dealt with subjects as diverse as the Japanese atomic holocaust, Martin Luther King and heroin addiction.

Blackwell was happy with the presence of such rock anthems as 'Pride' and 'Bad' but the overall sound of U2 had been pushed into new territory by Eno and Lanois. 'A Sort Of Homecoming' sounded as if it had absorbed all the nuances of the Irish climate. The title track mixed guitar Ambience with a lovely string arrangement. On '4th Of July' The Edge's guitar glided into the world of pure tones courtesy of Eno's treatments. Lanois contended that the 'deep, rubbery padded sound' of 'Elvis Presley And America' was in fact the backing track from 'A Sort Of Homecoming' slowed down and with a few compressor and echo effects added. Held-chord keyboard shimmers, as on 'MLK', were a direct result of Eno's presence. The album, which also used a Fairlight Computer Music Instrument, was U2's second successive UK number one in the autumn of 1984.

Touring aside, Bono's collaborative album with the much-loved Donegal folk group Clannad, 'In A Lifetime' (1985), saw him at ease with music where texture was as important as melodic surprises or impactful sonorities. The Edge also went the atmospheric route, recording the soundtrack album *Captive* (Virgin 1985) with the Canadian guitarist Michael Brook. There he gained an acquaintance with Brook's infinitely sustaining guitar and had one built for himself. The sessions for U2's fifth studio album, *The Joshua Tree*, took up most of 1986 and were conducted in the homes of both The Edge and Adam Clayton as well as at Windmill Lane. Lanois and Eno were in and out and the English engineer Flood was also on hand. Lanois himself also played guitars. With the emphasis on spirited performance and the concision of songs, Lanois recorded much of the material off the floor using wedges not headphones.

The opener, 'Where The Streets Have No Name', was full of Ambient keyboards and The Edge's ratcheting, reflecting guitar. 'I Still Haven't Found What I'm Looking For' was memorable for its dextrous interplay of guitar styles, even though at one stage Eno wanted to erase it. 'With Or Without You' was heavenly and used Yamaha Sequencer for the first third of the song. The high Yamaha DX7 synth sounds courtesy of Eno were a perfect complement to the emotional welling at the core of the piece. So far this was the finest mixture of Eno and U2 on record as the song exploded into a climax of The Edge's splintered electric guitar. Lanois recorded The Edge's pensive slide guitar on 'Running To Stand Still' using a humble portable radio-cassette machine at Windmill Lane. Early in 1987 the album was mixed at two locations – Lanois worked on a twenty-four-track set-up at The Edge's house in south Dublin, while old hand Steve Lillywhite came in to mix four songs at Windmill Lane, including 'With Or Without You'. The album was memorable for The Edge's assortment of textures on Michael Brook's Infinite Guitar, Fender, Gibson Explorer and Gibson ES Jazz guitars. According to Lanois, the 'grinding' guitar sound on 'Exit' was the result of using a reject plastic-necked guitar with no frets in a situation that was a good example of faith in the famous chance procedures of Cage and Eno.

By the spring of 1987 *The Joshua Tree* was the biggest rock album in the world, sitting comfortably at the top of the UK and US charts. U2 were proclaimed by *Time* magazine to be 'Rock's Hottest Ticket' and they had achieved this with a perfect blend of Ambient and rock styles. But by the beginning of the 1990s they were looking for another change. Thus a year was spent on their most ambitious album yet, *Achtung Baby*, released in the autumn of 1991. Lanois was the name producer, with Eno coming in for two- or three-week stretches to help out. Flood engineered, with Steve Lillywhite assisting at the crucial mixing stage in Dublin. The first significant feature of the album was its recording at Hansa in Berlin, the studios where Eno worked with David Bowie on *Low* and *'Heroes'* in 1977. Hansa's large dining hall provided the focus for an album of burning intensity, The Edge often routing his guitars through the filters of analogue synthesizers to get more distorted sounds. The incendiary 'Until The End Of The World' became the theme music for a Wim Wenders film, while the spangled nature of 'One', 'Trying To Throw Your Arms Around The World' and 'Love Is Blindness' was accentuated by Eno's shimmering keyboards.

Recorded in short bursts around the *Achtung Baby* tour (dubbed 'Zoo TV' as it featured material designed by Eno for Philips flat Vidiwall screens), *Zooroopa* (1993) was realized in various Dublin locations, with The Edge, Eno and Flood in the production chairs. The album began with the familiar Eno synth washes and progressed as a quirky selection of songs where Bono stretched his vocal abilities and Eno sang as well as adding strings, loops, synths and various keyboards. As a result the sparkle was still in U2. Proving the Eno chemistry was still in evidence, they formed a group with him called Passengers for the mostly instrumental outing *Original Soundtracks 1* (1995), where Eno is credited with sequences, synths, treatments, mixing and chorus vocals.

During the summer of 1995 U2 worked with the dance-music producer Nellee Hooper (producer of UK ensemble Massive Attack) on the genesis of a new album. By the autumn they had retired to an old warehouse in Dublin which featured some good old analogue recording and mixing equipment. There they were joined by the Scottish DJ Howie B, who created loops and grooves with his record decks. Production was credited to Flood, with Howie B and others handling computer sequencing. By 1996, when Larry Mullen had recovered from a back problem, the group were happily sampling themselves – The Edge even using the facility of Akai samplers to play guitar phrases on keyboards. Work was also done in Miami and the resultant *Pop* (1997) revealed a new U2 comfortable with the trance beats of Techno and Rave culture. Most instruments endured heavy processing, The Edge opting in this case to get away from the clean sun-bound guitar arrows of times past and route his instrument through vintage ARP synthesizer to radically alter its sound. *Pop* is famous for both its use of Ambient recording techniques and Flood's decision to work with analogue synthesizers such as the ARP and classic EMS VCS3.

LISTENING

U2 have always been Island recording artists, though from 1993 their music appeared as a product of Polygram International, which had purchased Island. The superbly produced *The Joshua Tree* (1987) is still one of the best-sounding rock albums of all time. Two fine examples of The Edge's crystal-clear guitar lines can be heard on 'Sweet Fire Of Love' from Robbie Robertson's eponymous solo album (Geffen 1987) and on 'Silver And Gold' from the live part of U2's *Rattle And Hum* (1988). *Original Soundtracks 1* (1995), released by the band under the name Passengers, is particularly recommended for its dazzling array of instrumental styles and Ambient vocal tracks, including 'Your Blue Room' and 'Beach Sequence' from Antonioni's comeback film with Wim Wenders *Beyond The Clouds* (1996). In 1998 Island released *Best Of U2 1980–1990*, which embraced, in limited quantity, a disc of 'b' sides, including some captivating work with Eno such as 'Bass Trap' and 'Walk To The Water'.

DANIEL LANOIS

With a high degree of commitment to sonic performance and the blending of acoustic elements, the Canadian musician and studio sorcerer Daniel Lanois was a vital source of some of the best Ambient rock of the late 1980s and early 90s. By 1987 he had helped midwife three number-one albums by U2 and Peter Gabriel which defined the sound of the decade. His rural background seemed to seep into his productions, so full were they of atmosphere and presence. As a guitarist, engineer and producer with an ability to read music, he symbolized the new breed of creative studio technician. Both Robbie Robertson of 1960s group The Band and Bob Dylan have benefited from his presence, making breakthrough comeback albums in the 1980s and 1990s where the Ambient sound was as vital as the songwriting skills.

　　Lanois was born in Ottawa in 1951. Exposed as a child to French and Irish folk music, he moved to English-speaking Ontario when he was ten, becoming bilingual. He took up the lap steel guitar after being offered lessons by a door-to-door salesman. Woodwind instruments followed. He ended up as a teenager playing in dance bands and revues, even 'backing up strippers in North Ontario for a year and a half in the 1960s'. He concluded the decade playing rhythm and blues before a fascination with tape recorders led him and his brother Bob to build a studio in the basement of their parents' house in Hamilton, Ontario. Using Roberts and Revox tape machines, the pair recorded a lot of Toronto Gospel music. It was with this limited technology that Lanois learned the value of 'making a commitment to a blend'.

Lanois felt he was part of 'the shift, which began in the late 1960s, of creative people getting into engineering'. In 1980 the studio was moved to Grant Avenue, Ontario and made into a twenty-four-track facility. Here every nook and cranny of a three-storey Victorian house was utilized, the entire structure turned into a vérité-recording environment. Lanois became Canadian producer of the year in the early 1980s for his work with Martha & The Muffins, his sister's new-wave band. Living in New York at the time, Brian Eno heard some of the 'off-balance' music coming out of the studio and arrived there in 1980. According to Lanois, meeting Eno 'rekindled the fire and passion he had for music as a youth'.

Before long the two fell into a working partnership, with Lanois quick to pick up on Eno's ideas and translate them into sound. His musical literacy meant that work could be done swiftly. Accordingly the house became 'a studio as sound-processing laboratory' for a host of classic Ambient albums by Harold Budd, Jon Hassell, Michael Brook, Roger Eno and the Lanois brothers themselves. The Grant Avenue sound was notorious for the extensive use of tape loops, washy harmonizer effects and, as early as 1981, one of the earliest uses of digital sampling – in the words of Lanois, 'an electronic network of effects and processes'. Eno recorded his densely organic album *On Land* (EG 1982) there and Lanois contributed many effective steel guitar sounds to the excellent *Apollo: Atmospheres And Soundtracks* (EG 1983).

The Grant Avenue sound was one of texture, nuance and treatments. This was transferred to mainstream rock when both Lanois and Eno recorded U2's *The Unforgettable Fire* (Island 1984) in and around Slane Castle in Ireland. Lanois would then spend a year with Peter Gabriel on his excellent high-fidelity recording *So* (Charisma 1986), where fabulous bass parts and vocal harmonies were augmented by tasteful use of polyphonic synthesizers and a computer music console. Its number-one chart position reinforced Lanois' reputation as an alchemical presence in the studio. His co-production with Eno of the multi-platinum U2 disc *The Joshua Tree* (Island 1987) saw him perform guitar, autoharp and background vocals.

Flush with success, Lanois bought a house in New Orleans and turned it into the exotic Kingsway Studio. Here he recorded the Neville Brothers' *Yellow Moon* (A&M) and his first solo disc, *Acadie* (Warner Bros.), both released in 1989, the latter full of rustic simplicity, acoustic folk leanings and watery translucent tones. Around the same time the Irish film-maker Philip King made a film about Lanois titled *Rocky World* (Warner Music Vision). In the 1990s the producer toured with his own band and continued to lend his Ambient wizardry to recordings by U2, Peter Gabriel and Bob Dylan.

LISTENING

As well as the aforementioned productions one should hear Lanois' touch on Robbie Robertson's debut solo album, *Robbie Robertson* (Geffen 1987), where the half-North American Indian guitarist wanders into a sound world of deep Everglades spiritual trance, rumbling thunder drums and, of course, U2. This humid Deep South production sound was also conjured up at Lanois' New Orleans studio for Bob Dylan's impressive *Oh Mercy* (CBS 1989) and The Neville Brothers' *Yellow Moon* (A&M 1989) – the latter merging soul and Gospel with Lanois' treated guitar sounds and some good keyboards and effects from Eno. With Peter Gabriel he also atmospherically mixed the soundtrack *Birdy* (Charisma 1985) and co-produced the award-winning *US* (Real World 1992).

Lanois' solo output deserves more attention. *Acadie* (Warner Bros. 1989) is dedicated to displaced French Canadians who settled in New Orleans in the eighteenth century. Sung in French and English, the album is full of soft grooves, Eno ambiences, treated guitars and a folkish quality not a million miles away from Nick Drake. *The Beauty Of Wynona* (Warner Bros. 1993), made with his own band, is more experimental rock. Lanois' filmic production of Bob Dylan's *Oh Mercy* included the addition of cricket sounds and sliding echoey swamp guitars. His return to the desk for Dylan's bluesily rich-sounding *Time Out Of Mind* (Sony 1997) was heralded as a stroke of genius. As well as playing Omnichord or auto-harp guitar and a Fender Jazzmaster, Lanois is famous for owning a version of Michael Brook's Infinite Guitar, one of only three in existence.

ENYA

The most successful female Irish composer of all time, Enya has made a million-selling career out of Ambient and electronic music. By combining the sonic layering techniques observed first-hand in the Cologne studio of the renowned German producer-engineer Conny Plank with the 'wall-of-sound' approach of Phil Spector, Enya zoomed to the top of the charts with the irresistibly catchy 'Orinoco Flow' in 1988. Since then it has been wave after wave of successes – Grammy awards, album sales of thirty-three million and a huge reputation as the maker of a unique Celtic mystical healing music, an aural balm to quieten the minds of the frenetic multitudes all over the world.

Enya became successful at a time when the average sound of records had leaped in quality. U2, Peter Gabriel and others had all defined a new form of Ambient fidelity. Also, Irish Rock had come of age, developing into a global phenomenon in the process. Thus Enya's particularly Irish mood music seemed right for the times. Enya had a strong background in atmospheric music, having once been a member of Clannad. Born in Gweedore, Donegal in 1961, she was the fifth child in a Catholic family of nine, and was brought up speaking fluent Irish. Her father was an Irish traditional music professional and her mother a singer. At twelve she attended boarding school and studied classical piano for six years with the aim of becoming a teacher. At the beginning of the 1980s she joined her brothers, sister Maire and uncles in Clannad, playing keyboards and singing.

Though she had worked with Clannad in Conny Plank's studio in 1981, Enya was not credited until the band's sixth album, *Fuaim* (Tara 1982), appearing under her Irish name, Eithne Ni Bhraonain. Tensions within the group led to Enya departing and living with Clannad's former managers, Nicky and Roma Ryan, in Dublin. There she worked within the confines of a sixteen-track studio on her own material, using a continuous overdubbing technique to enhance her choir-like vocals. Through Irish connections she met the English film producer David Puttnam and began writing a soundtrack for a French feature, *The Frog Prince*. Decisively, she changed her name to its English phonetic form, Enya.

In 1986 Enya worked in London and Dublin on the soundtrack to the BBC series *The Celts*. The resultant BBC album *Enya* (1986) was a highly impressive form of Ambient folk with Enya showing great skill at sound-painting with acoustic piano, voices and an array of DX7, Kurzweill, Juno and Emulator synthesizers. Harp lines were synthesized while her golden voice was over-dubbed up to 100 times in English, Welsh, Latin, French and Irish-Scots Gaelic. This electronic drift was punctuated at times by uillean pipes and acoustic guitar.

Back in Dublin Enya continued with her painstaking methods. Considered to be the slowest composer in the business, Enya is known to have taken up to a year to produce one track. Nevertheless Warner Bros., as they had done with The Grateful Dead in the 1960s, were prepared to give her great artistic freedom. With Nicky Ryan using his Phil Spector and Beach Boys influences as a producer-arranger, his wife writing all the lyrics and Enya concentrating on the music and electronics, a formidable working machine came into operation. No samplers or sequencers were used in the making of *Watermark* (WEA 1988), the album which shot Enya to fame and eventually sold eight million copies. Instead hundreds of vocal segments were recorded on a thirty-two-track digital tape machine and mixed to another. Enya played all her keyboards in real time, with most keyboard and synth sounds multi-layered to achieve the required effect. Analogue tape delays and low-pitched drum sounds were used to gain depth. 'Orinoco Flow' was developed from a pizzicato string pre-set on a Roland D50 synth – the familiar plucking effect at the beginning of the number-one hit single is that sound. The title came from the London studio where it was finished. The title track of *Watermark* was a radiant piece of Ambient keyboard work mindful of the original nocturnes of Irish composer John Field.

Three years would elapse between that album and her next effulgent offering, *Shepherd Moons* (WEA 1991), a number-one hit which would stay four years on the British charts and sell four million copies in the US. Again the mixture of folk, Irish church music, aerated multi-tracked vocal and a sort of lullaby simplicity guaranteed its success. Four more years would be given over to the recording of *The Memory Of Trees* (WEA 1995), which again mixed up-tempo vocal electronica with wonderful melancholic Ambiences, earning Enya another Grammy award. Around the same time she provided music for Martin Scorsese's *The Age Of Innocence*, starring Daniel Day Lewis and Michelle Pfeiffer. Many have attributed healing powers to Enya's form of sweet Celtic folk music. Though she is faithful to the power of the studio and the modern wonders of electronics, and is a truly international artist, the popular image of Enya is that of a berobed princess who lives in a castle on the Dublin coast.

LISTENING

By 1995 Enya had sold eighteen million copies worldwide of her first three albums; two years later the figure had jumped to thirty-three million. *Watermark* (WEA 1988) is a great place to start as the album features tracks like 'Orinoco Flow', the more atmospheric title track and the moving 'Bright Days Of My Youth'. Her multilingual fluency and mellifluous voice turn all words to beautiful sounds. *Shepherd Moons* (WEA 1991) is a gorgeous recording, its emotional climax 'Smaointe' ('thoughts'), a masterpiece in sound-painting as Enya's flawless Gaelic vocal is balanced by deft touches on keyboard and Liam O'Flynn's uillean pipes. In late 1997 WEA released the triple-disc set *Box Of Dreams*, a thematic summation of her career which emphasized the stately keyboard sound as much as the 'hits'. If you just want a taste, the wonderfully titled single-disc compilation *Paint The Sky With Stars* (WEA 1997) will do the trick perfectly.

BOOK FOUR

HOUSE, TECHNO AND TWENTY-FIRST-CENTURY AMBIENCE

IT'S TRUE TO say that House and Techno and the kaleidoscope of sub-genres gave birth to the most significant change in popular music since the 1960s heyday of psychedelic rock. Not only did they change the way people made music from the late 1980s onwards; they also radically altered the way people listened to and experienced music. The elongated repetition of beats moved the focus of the music away from its creators towards the listener, the old audience-subject divide dissolving as millions the world over danced and danced to the new electronica. As with Psychedelia, House and Techno were spurred on by a new drug, namely Ecstasy. The combination of this speedy hallucinogenic with the kinetic rhythms of the new dance music exploded into a phenomenon that seemed to have no end. As the music mutated, new forms were thrown up by the year. Ambient House and Ambient Techno were mind-balming responses to the intensity of club culture. Trip-Hop and Drum and Bass were UK black variations of what was originally an innovation by black Americans. Rock music absorbed House and Techno, and DJs and electronicists began to tour and act like rock stars. As one century tipped into another, dance music was still a primary source of interest and creativity as Trance, a futuristic blend of technology and House and Techno, became a chart-topping, globe-girdling sensation.

Our story starts in the Munich flat of Giorgio Moroder during the mid-1970s. It was here, with American singer Donna Summer and a bunch of analogue synthesizers, that Moroder came up with the extended disco mix. Perfect for the then superior-quality twelve-inch 45rpm record, the Summer-Moroder chemistry resulted in 1977 in the futuristic electronic fantasy of 'I Feel Love', a milestone release which merged Kraftwerk with soul dance music. The extended twelve-inch dance mix had been pioneered in New York two years earlier and it was in the Big Apple, during the 1970s, that the first DJs began to alter fundamentally the way recorded music was played. Kool Herc, Francis Grosso, Larry Levan and Frankie Knuckles all allied their twin-turntable record decks with mixers, drum machines and even keyboards to lengthen and spice up their performances.

At the same time the working-class ghettos of the South Bronx produced two extraordinary talents in Grandmaster Flash and Afrika Bambaataa. Flash would turn Hip-Hop, a form of music based on the scratching sound of records and the extension of the drum parts (the breakbeat) into late-twentieth-century America's most successful popular music. Multi-sampling and dance grooves were sophisticatedly enshrined by Afrika Bambaataa in his Electro music, thus named because it sampled the electronic pop of Kraftwerk. So by the early 1980s New York was a hotbed of new music activity, its club culture throwing up Garage, a form of ardent soul music bathed in drum claps and electronica.

Chicago House got its name from the electronic soul mixes of Frankie Knuckles's Warehouse parties, which played from 1977 to the early 1980s. Knuckles had moved from New York and was DJing for a gay audience who preferred psychedelics to alcohol. Hence the flavour of early Chicago House records was insistent bass figures, looping drums and a strong erotic content delivered by a male drag diva. As time passed and musicians like Larry Heard made the music both more instrumental and cerebrally stimulating, labels like Trax were willing to invest more in innovation. Trax's owner, Larry Sherman, encouraged his producer, Marshall Jefferson, to seek out new sounds and new artists. After they heard the work of Phuture, who used a squelchy Roland drum box in their music, Acid House was born. Both Sherman and Jefferson made an equation between their sound and the buzzing drones of 1960s Psychedelia. Ultra-Minimalist and simplistic, the squirting, repetitive noises of Phuture's 'Acid Tracks' (1987) would connect deeply with Ecstasy culture.

Over in Detroit the post-industrial landscape of an inner city still bearing the wounds of the 1967 race riots was captured by a different music. Detroit Techno didn't follow the disco roots of Chicago House but instead plugged into a futurist landscape – one outlined by the electronic beauty of Kraftwerk and the sadness of Vangelis's soundtrack for the classic 1982 sci-fi film *Blade Runner*. More introspective, Techno was instrumental electronica in which darting keyboards and impatient rattling drums were the order of the day. If Derrick May was the chief philosopher, eschewing soul disco roots for electronic masterpieces like 'Strings Of Life' (1986), then Kevin Saunderson was the pragmatist, lacing a Techno mix with female vocal for his multimillion-selling hit 'Big Fun' in 1988.

In Britain the 'cut 'n' splice' nature of Hip-Hop was adapted by Anne Dudley and The Art Of Noise for their 1984 debut album, *Who's Afraid Of The Art Of Noise*. An interest in synthesizers, sampling and Dudley's Classical education produced 'Moments In Love', a soothing piece of electronica which would inspire Ambient House. But the real impact of House and Techno was first felt in Manchester. Emboldened by Acid House, 808 State even named themselves after a Roland drum machine. One of their key members, Gerald Simpson, produced the first authentic UK House/Techno track in 'Voodoo Ray' (1988), a work so good it was remixed by Frankie Knuckles for heavy Chicago dance-floor rotation. While in 808 State, Simpson helped out with the making of 'Pacific State' (released in 1989, after he had gone solo), a delicate ride through a panorama of glistening samples which ushered in the 'Balearic' sound. For years clubbers had ventured to Ibiza for the experience of hearing eclectic club music played at open-air clubs like Amnesia. It was here that two Londoners, Danny Rampling and Paul Oakenfold, had their first Ecstasy experience. Returning to England they opened clubs and by 1988 UK Acid House had erupted. Imported records and home-grown talent like M/A/R/R/S, Bomb The Bass, S'Express and Andrew Weatherall all helped to shape the soundtrack to 1988's 'Second Summer Of Love' but its real hero was Ecstasy, or E.

Ecstasy was an energy psychedelic which was first invented in Darmstadt, Germany in 1912. Interestingly, one of the most important drugs of the twentieth century was discovered in the very place from which Stockhausen, in the 1950s, would launch his Electronic crusade. Ecstasy was reproduced by the chemist Alexander Schulgin in California during the late 1960s. From the West Coast neuro-consciousness frontier it spread outwards like an ocean, enticing anyone that came near with warm feelings of empathy. When combined with repetitive dance music Ecstasy, or E, produced spine-tingling highs and a long, comforting come-down. It induced a common 'love' experience not unlike the psychedelic drugs of the 1960s but when allied to the fractal properties of House and Techno made people want to dance all night long. The black gay discos of 1970s America were the first to experience Ecstasy in this context before it was taken up by white American student youth, English New Romantics and the colourful clubbers of Ibiza. By 1989 Raves – House and Techno events with lasers, huge sound systems and thousands of dancers – made Ecstasy an intrinsic part of UK music culture. The full impact of House and Techno was fully realized when a Manchester Indie band, The Stone Roses, released an eponymous debut album fully integrating great rock music with House grooves. The opening salvo of 'I Wanna Be Adored' was the most exciting and innovative sound (combining Ambient, House and heart-stopping rock guitar) heard in the UK since the days of The Beatles. Then the Scottish rock band Primal Scream made an album saturated in Ecstasy and psychedelics titled *Screamadelica* (1991). Despite the occasional death attributed to the drug, its popularity was unstoppable. By 1995 half a million people a week in the UK were taking Ecstasy and blissing out at dance parties. The popularity of Trance at the end of the century was put down to the return of really good Ecstasy which heightened the pleasure of this super-fractal chromium-polished sub-genre of House.

The intensity of Ecstasy dancing was always followed by a wish to wind down. Both The KLF and The Orb noticed that clubbers liked eclectic mixes of Ambient music. In London between 1989 and 1990 these DJs invented Chill Out or Ambient House. This was House music subtracted of its incessant thumping beats and filled with Ambient samples of nature, extraneous noises, vocal snippets and other people's music. The KLF's *Chill Out* (1990) and The Orb's *Adventures Beyond The Ultraworld* (1991) defined the genre. The chart-topping Orb were associated with ideas of outer space and inner journeys and in March 1993 were pictured on the cover of *Melody Maker* with Pink Floyd. The message was clear – Ambient House had widened out the music's stylistic template. House and Techno of the early to mid-1990s would now progress into many different and interesting areas. Orbital adopted Steve Reich's tape-loop experiments to make beautiful, lush Techno. Enigma used Gregorian chant to make a form of Spiritual House while both Mixmaster Morris and The Future Sound of London were influenced by the 1970s synthesizer tapestries of Tangerine Dream. In 1993, when the German DJ Sven Väth released a radiant album of Ambient Trance called *Accident In Paradise*, the term 'Progressive House' came into common parlance.

Intelligent or Ambient Techno was the Techno equivalent of Progressive House. In Germany it was led by the classically trained electronicist Pete Namlook, whose Fax label released Ambient recordings in huge quantities. Namlook believed that the new Ambient music would enjoy the same status in the future as baroque music had been given in the twentieth century. Ambient Techno produced its greatest artist in Britain under the name Aphex Twin. Richard James was a country boy who loved making his own instruments with the inventor's spirit of a Stockhausen or John Cage. Though he was inspired by the sounds of Chicago House and Detroit Techno, James had a compositional ability which leaned towards such giants of classical music as Mozart or Beethoven. Multi-timbral, harmonically sophisticated and sonically enriching, James's work as Aphex Twin was some of the finest Ambient Techno of its era. Playing with psychological states such as 'lucid dreaming', in 1994 James came up with the poignantly beautiful electronic chamber album *Selected Ambient Works Vol. 2*, a work of magnificent timbral inventiveness and masterly compositional skill. In New York fusion-bassist and producer Bill Laswell created considerable refinements of Ambient House and Techno by merging them with Ethnic, Dub, Jazz and Funk stylings. The technology-fixated, non-vocal nature of Ambient Techno meant that the music could be taken to real extremes. The term 'Isolationism' was used to describe a form of implosive music which laid bare its raw means of creation. In the UK Scanner utilized a mobile phone-skimming device to capture private conversations and fold them into his Ambient creations. In Norway Biosphere and in Germany Thomas Köner made Ambient music reflecting their love of Arctic climes with minimal electronic equipment. The Australian Paul Schütze combined environmental Ambiences à la Brian Eno with the discreet sounds of electro and acoustic instruments to make site-specific recordings rich in psychological nuance.

Trip-Hop was the Ambient extension of Hip-Hop, a form of slow-motion breakbeat music that blended Rap with Dub Reggae and noirish soundtrack samples. A calming response to the visceral highs of Ecstasy music, Trip-Hop was the product of post-club marijuana consumption. Sound loops and vinyl scratching were important ingredients but the overall effect was one of cool film music for the mind. The English city of Bristol was its focal point and threw up three outstanding talents in Massive Attack, Tricky and Portishead. Massive Attack came to prominence with the track 'Unfinished Sympathy' in 1991. A beautiful Trip-Hop reverie, it even included orchestrated strings. Successive recordings with Indie rock singers Tracey Thorn and Liz Fraser made Massive Attack international Trip-Hop stars. One of their members, Tricky, received huge critical acclaim for his solo album *Maxinquaye* (1995), an ingenious mixture of paranoid Rap, sampling, rock and Trip-Hop rhythms. As a black British underclass take on post-House culture Tricky's art would strike a deep resonance, particularly in the US. Portishead were a white trio who had studio associations with both Massive Attack and Tricky. An interest in turntables, keyboards, analogue synthesizers, soundtrack music and the blues resulted in Portishead's sensational debut album, *Dummy*, becoming a worldwide million-seller in 1995. Dramatic use of film samples, loud drum breaks, the shivery sound of an old Thereminvox and the pained vocal of singer Beth Gibbons made an irresistible sound cocktail which became a ubiquitous presence in TV advertising and movie music. Sampling and Hip-Hop elements would define the career of Coldcut, a studio and DJ duo from London who made 'sampladelia' their musical totem for the 1990s. In America sampled breakbeat music came into its own in 1996 with recorded releases from DJ Shadow and DJ Spooky. Shadow, a Californian, took the entire history of vinyl music and turned it into a form of Ambient Hop. His debut album, *Endtroducing. . .* (1996), dazzled with its fusion of record samples (opera, soundtrack, Tangerine Dream, narration, orchestration) and body-swerving Hip-Hop drum and percussion breaks. The New York-based black militant intellectual DJ Spooky made moody Ambient Hip-Hop which acknowledged African drum rhythms, Dub Reggae, cosmic jazz, sci-fi and German space-rock of the 1970s.

As time went on, black British youth wanted its very own music, a sound distinct from imported House and Techno and more energetic than Trip-Hop. During the early 1990s, at London's Rage club, the answer came in the form of Jungle – a jittery, high-speed amalgam of Reggae afterbeats, Hardcore Techno, Hip-Hop, soul and jazz. The fragmented drum-loop-driven music was perfect for taking cocaine and smoking marijuana. Though Jungle emerged from Ecstasy culture, its style was post-House and predominantly urban black. Soon its creators were digging deeper into the world of computer-morphed drum sounds and the term Drum and Bass began to replace Jungle. Drum and Bass was syncopated (offbeat) whereas House and Techno used common time signatures like 4/4. More importantly, the percussive thrust of the music was the melody, its instrumental parts more decorative. When the sound became more complex the term Intelligent Drum and Bass was used to describe the sophisticated early-1990s Ambient style of, say, LTJ Bukem.

But nobody could have predicted the arrival of Goldie, the undisputed king of Ambient Drum and Bass. Of mixed race, Goldie was a graffiti artist and Hip-Hop fanatic who had spent some time in America. His return to the UK coincided with the rise of Trip-Hop but his real inspiration was the Jungle played in clubs by DJs Fabio and Grooverider. Collaborating with London duo 4 Hero, Goldie spent months researching sampling techniques, coming up, in the process, with his unique concept of 'time-stretching'. His vision was a Drum and Bass music of symphonic proportions where the mental impression of time would be altered by a series of stretched or compressed musical samples. Goldie's obsession with contrasting fast and slow elements, orchestration and 3D soundspace was fully explored on *Timeless* (1995), his genre-defining Ambient Drum and Bass masterpiece. As well as the frenetically fast drum and percussion breaks, the listener was treated to a variety of other sounds such as strings, ethnic flutes, Fender Rhodes keyboards and soul–diva vocals.

Certainly the new black British dance music did much to open people's ears to what lay behind the evolution of House and Techno. LTJ Bukem, Goldie and 4 Hero all openly embraced jazz. Thus it wasn't surprising that Britain's leading jazz musician, Courtney Pine, should immerse himself in percussion loops, DJ mixing and whatnot for such ground-breaking Trip Jazz recordings as *Underground* (1997). Neither was it surprising that Dub Reggae experienced a renaissance, a critical reassessment as the original Drum and Bass. In Jamaica turntable DJs playing records through large amplified 'sound systems' had been popular since the 1940s. Special 'acetates' were cut for sound-system dances during the early 1960s and from these exclusive studio 'instrumentals' and 'versions' evolved. The version of the early 1970s was a mix–down of a popular song where the rhythmic element was boosted and spaces were left for the DJ to 'toast' (Rap) to during performance. Jamaican studio producers like King Tubby and Lee Perry became experts at making effects-laden versions and by the mid-1970s Dub Reggae was in the ascendant. It was King Tubby who originated the term 'Drum and Bass' and with Lee Perry he made Dub the most influential musical genre to come out of Jamaica. Surprisingly, it was all done on the most minimal of equipment – basic tape decks wired to old reverb and echo machines. Lee Perry, who became famous for such Dub albums as *Super Ape* (1976), started his legendary Black Ark studio with a used four-track mixing desk bought in London's Edgware Road for £35. Unsurprisingly, the Jamaican Reggae legacy was the root of US Hip-Hop and by definition all turntable-led musics. For it was from Jamaica that Kool Herc, New York's 1970s inventor of the breakbeat, originally came. He even taught his turntable skills to Grandmaster Flash, who himself was West Indian. Finally, Dub was also an element in the new Techno sound of young British Asian musicians. Electronic tabla supremo Talvin Singh espoused a meeting of Acid House, Dub Reggae, Drum and Bass and Indian classical musics on the 1997 album *Anokha – Soundz Of The Asian Underground*.

The diversification of dance-music culture in the 1990s did not signal the end of the original House and Techno blueprint, which returned, with a vengeance, at the close of the twentieth century in the form of Trance. The ultimate Acid House and Techno computer-sampling hybrid, Trance was a music tailor-made for club nirvana as millions the world over danced to slithery mixes full of synthesizer riffs, drum-machine rolls, long, suspenseful build–ups and even lengthier breakdowns. The whole Trance experience was that of the endless mix played in turbo-charged superclubs packed to the gills with Ecstasy-high ravers. The new sound was perfectly in tune with a younger generation *au fait* with mobile phones, personal computers and the Internet. Trance originated in Frankfurt and Berlin during the early 1990s with the likes of Jam & Spoon, Pete Namlook and Sven Väth. It became popular in Goa, in the south of India, during the mid-1990s, giving birth to the psychedelic form Goa Trance. Championed the world over by Paul Oakenfold, the original Ibiza Acid House kid, Trance would make him the world's most popular DJ by the end of the century. The late 1990s saw Euro Trance go mainstream as DJs like Paul Digweed and Sasha played to the throngs at superclubs like Gatecrasher in the UK and Space in Ibiza. Though much Trance was over-simplistic it did produce some brilliant music such as that by Berliner Paul Van Dyk, whose sheen-like 'For An Angel' (1998) was true twenty-first-century music for the head, heart and feet. Alongside the stabbing synths and relentless beats, Van Dyk was a maestro of subtle keyboard melodies, trickling electronic sounds and velvet-like production. Even the American pop queen Madonna was allured by the form when she employed the Ambient producer William Orbit to give her 1998 album *Ray Of Light* the Trance glow – a move which returned her to critical and commercial favour. Trance reached its zenith in late 1999 when Germany's Andre Tanneberger, as ATB, sold a million and hit the UK number-one spot with his naggingly addictive '9PM Till I Come', a track centred around a repeating guitar sample.

And the music just continued to mutate. Between 1997 and 1999 Big Beat emerged in Britain to become the fastest-selling dance music ever. Combining bone-crunching beats, synthesizer sounds, samples and an approach to Techno derived from the structures of rock music, The Chemical Brothers went on to sell millions of records. To them nothing was sacred: Hip-Hop, Acid House, Techno, 1960s Psychedelia and folk music were all there for the taking. Years were spent over individual tracks and albums such as *Surrender* (1999) were simply brilliant distillations of aural history into a new form of Rock Techno. In France, Air came from the world of Chill Out and Loungecore to fashion a floating music of analogue synthesizers, jazz keyboards, electric organs, vocoder, drums and guitars. Elements of Debussy, Stevie Wonder, Pink Floyd, French film music, Kraftwerk and Trip-Hop were all commingled on their million-selling debut album, *Moon Safari* (1998). They rightly saw themselves as 'retro-futurists', their highly sophisticated music earning them the description 'the Pink Floyd of dance music'.

What a long, strange trip it had been. After years of musicologists thinking that the barriers were up and should stay up between classical, jazz, rock and pop music, along came House and Techno to tear them down. House and Techno implied that the music itself was the most important thing, the makers of that music a vital but secondary issue. The mix, the sample, the club, and the audience were the crucial ingredients in the experience. As the music transformed like fractal geometry through a plethora of genres – Hip-Hop, Electro, Garage, Chicago House, Acid House, Disco House, Deep House, NU Chicago,

Balearic, Ambient House, Progressive House, Power House, Euro House, Italo House, NU House, Dutch House, German House, Pop House, Handbag House, Detroit Techno, German Techno, Belgium Techno, Dutch Techno, Euro Techno, Ambient Techno, Hardcore Techno, Gabba, Happy Hardcore, Stomping Hardcore, Bouncy Hardcore, Old Skool Hardcore, Hard Banging House, London Acid, Tech Step, Tech House, Megadog Ambient, Trip-Hop, Down Tempo, Breakbeat, Drum and Bass, Westcoast Sound, NU Skool Breakz, Acid Jazz, Jazz Step, Flava Funk, Post Rock, Lo-Fi, Chill Out, Loungecore, Asian Underground, Big Beat, Trance, Psychedelic Trance and Progressive Trance – a veritable sonic democracy had emerged: a truly Ambient sound for the twenty-first century.

DONNA SUMMER AND GIORGIO MORODER

During the mid to late 1970s, when Kraftwerk were beginning to have Techno hits in the US, Donna Summer was the biggest thing in disco music. Her breathy vocal style, which ranged from sensual groan to lofty aeration, was instantly recognizable on such brilliant creations as 'Love To Love You Baby' (1975) and 'I Feel Love' (1977). Moreover the context of her tingly space-fantasy voice was sleek electronic music driven by Giorgio Moroder's hypnotic drum-machine beats, tape loops and synthesizer sounds. Summer and Moroder popularized the extended twelve-inch single mix, a form within which they carved out an entire new genre: Eurodisco. With its emphasis on Minimalism, repetition, ersatz drama and synthetic rhythms, it's no wonder that the music of Donna Summer and Giorgio Moroder is perceived as a cornerstone of House and Techno as well as all other dance-related electronica.

Summer was born Donna Gaines in Boston in 1948. She sang Gospel music and showed a predilection for ballads and Broadway musicals. In 1970 she relocated to Munich, where she was a member of the German production of the hippie musical *Hair*. Her voice and statuesque beauty made an impression on an up-and-coming Italian producer named Giorgio Moroder. Born in northern Italy in 1940, Moroder had spent a lot of time in German nightclubs as a showband guitarist. In 1970 he met a musician in Munich who owned a Moog Series 3 synthesizer and he began to experiment with this. From there on he became a synthesizer obsessive, embracing the Buchla, MiniMoog, ARP and Prophet 5 before the dawn of the digital era. Moroder, with the help of guitarist Pete Bellotte, ran a small production studio called Music Land in the basement of a Munich flat. In 1974 he was even experimenting with the first drum machines.

Moroder and Bellotte suggested producing solo work for Summer, who quickly came up with 'Love To Love You Baby'. Originally recorded on twenty-four-track with a drum loop and Fender Rhodes electric piano accompaniment, 'Love To Love You Baby' (Oasis) was eventually extended to over sixteen and a half minutes and hit number two on the US singles chart in 1975. The song created controversy for its length, motor-driven sound and Summer's uncharacteristic erotic delivery. Yet it was a futuristic modern fantasy in sound; Summer the disco diva pulling all who heard her into her very own erotic dream world. In 1976 alone 'Love To Love You Baby' sold well over one million copies in America.

Yet the best was yet to come. Summer was a premier signee to Casablanca Records in America. During the late 1970s the marketing clout of this label plus Moroder and Bellotte's production skills, both in Germany and in California, would make her a US-chart-topping dance sensation with a string of number-one singles and albums. Summer was an original writer and her chosen vehicle was the double semi-autobiographical dance concept album. Such creations as *Once Upon A Time* (1977) and *Bad Girls* (1979) revealed that Summer was as aware of modern black American experience as she was of technology. And it was the technological brilliance of 1977's 'I Feel Love' that really paved her path to success.

'I Feel Love' stands as a pivotal moment in Western culture. As Kraftwerk were cutting up US dance floors with 'Trans-Europe Express', 'I Feel Love' merged Germanicity with black music's long history. Opening with the characteristic wash of synthesizer drone, 'I Feel Love' soon settled down to a mellifluous panorama of panning synth noises, motoric rhythms and dry, dunking drum machines. Summer seemed to sing from atop the clouds, her voice full of the nuances of soul and Gospel. Amazingly, Moroder and Bellotte filled its eight and a half minutes with creaking and clanky synth sounds and loads of sonic space. Much tonal change was applied to the bass synthesizer and the future trademark House sound of dry drum-machine resonations abounded. A UK number one, 'I Feel Love' was pure Trance, an electronic soul music which juddered forward on its own marvellous dynamic. About six minutes in there is almost no difference between its physical make-up and that of many House or Techno classics ten years down the line.

Summer and Moroder continued to make great singles. 'MacArthur Park' (1978) was nearly eighteen minutes, a sweeping epic which embraced *Star Wars*-type electronic sounds and dramatic electronic brass punctuations. 'Dim All The Lights' (1979) was great dance music which comprised treated Summer vocalization and an audacious drum-machine break which would become a House trademark. As Summer became a bona-fide platinum album American superstar, Moroder continued to explore electronics. His $E = MC^2$ (Oasis 1979) was one of the first digitally recorded albums. From then until the late 1980s he had his own digital studio in San Fernando Valley called Oasis, where he recorded many film soundtracks.

LISTENING

'Love To Love You Baby' was originally released on Moroder's own Oasis imprint before the US label Casablanca encouraged its expansion to almost seventeen minutes. The full twelve-inch sensation can be heard on the album *Love To Love You Baby* (Casablanca/Polygram 1975). In fact Donna Summer's music can be heard on dozens of Casablanca albums. One of her best selections is *The Dance Collection* (Casablanca/Polygram 1987), which includes the original twelve-inch mixes of 'I Feel Love', 'MacArthur Park' and 'Dim All The Lights'. Giorgio Moroder has his own lengthy discography, which includes the sound-tracks for *Midnight Express* (1978), *American Gigolo* (1980) and *Top Gun* (1986).

NEW YORK GARAGE AND ELECTRO

While many cite Chicago and Detroit as the main epicentres of House and Techno, the great New York melting pot also had its part to play in the evolution of a new electronic music. New York was certainly the birthplace of the DJ mixer. Moreover its Hip-Hop craze threw up such pioneers as Grand-master Flash and Afrika Bambaataa, two brilliant purveyors of a new sound which used samples and scratched beats, known as Electro. New York was where the twelve-inch dance mix was invented, its collision of black musics leading to the rise of the soul-based Garage music from the late 1970s to the late 1980s. Because Joey Beltram had worked through the New York Garage scene of the late 1980s, his cumulative experience was to unleash a more physically strident form of House in 1990 with his renowned single 'Energy Flash' (R&S).

At the beginning of the 1970s there was a retrenchment of New York's gay community in the face of discrimination. Such clubs as the Sanctuary were havens for black and Hispanic gays who wished to take drugs and listen to long improvised DJ sets which mixed music of a myriad styles together. Francis Grosso is credited as the DJ pioneer at the Sanctuary while such venues as the Loft, the Gallery and Galaxy 21 all expanded the idea of the DJ happening through tweaking equipment and sound for more energetic audiences wired on amphetamines, hallucinogenics and fruit juices. The French drummer François Kervorkian (later to remix U2) worked with a DJ named Walter Gibbons at Galaxy 21. Through this synergy Gibbons got the idea of extending a mix over a twelve-inch record to give more depth and quality to the sound. Hence in 1975 the Salsoul label put out the first twelve-inch single. The move would change dance music for good, paving the way for Donna Summer's mesmerizing 'I Feel Love' two years later.

Frankie Knuckles and Larry Levan evolved through this new club scene where non-stop dancing as celebration was preferred to the alcohol and cocaine haze of disco culture. Both played venues where keyboards and drum machines were linked to record decks, but in 1977 Knuckles was lured to Chicago to invent House, leaving Levan to open the legendary Paradise Garage, the huge SoHo club which gave New York's deep Soul House sound its name. Levan, Brooklyn-born in the mid-1950s, became a legend for his triple-deck mixes of every style of music which took his audiences higher and higher. Mescaline, LSD and Ecstasy were the hallucinogenics of choice by the early 1980s, when Levan was opening people's minds to the mind-warping groove of Manuel Göttsching's Trance masterpiece *E2–E4*.

Elsewhere in New York straight black working-class music was changing fast. The South Bronx threw up two outstanding talents in Grandmaster Flash and Afrika Bambaataa. Flash was born in 1958 in Barbados but was educated in New York. He got into DJing, specifically the art of the emphasized drum or 'break' beat utilizing two turntables. The precise stopping and flicking back of records earned him the nickname Flash. He formed a performance ensemble called The Furious Five. Though he was widely respected among New York's poorer black community, it wasn't until he made the incredible recording 'The Adventures Of Grandmaster Flash On The Wheels Of Steel' (Sugarhill 1981) that the world realized that something new had arrived in music – the sample.

'Wheels Of Steel' still stands as a pivotal recording in the history of electronic music. The main groove was provided by the bass riff from Chic's disco hit 'Good Times', with added ingredients from Blondie, Queen, the New Jersey rappers The Sugarhill Gang and, of course, the turntable genius of Flash himself. The backward 'scratch' movement of the records was integrated into a seven-minute mix which whipped Hip-Hop into a 'scratch 'n' mix' masterpiece so elegant that it deserved a new title: Electro. On this more than on any other record we can hear just how exciting New York DJ-led music was at the beginning of the 1980s.

Afrika Bambaataa, born in 1960, used his Zulu roots to show black New York youth that the way forward lay in creativity and not negativity. A giant on the Hip-Hop scene, he is also credited with innovating Electro. In 1982 he used parts of Kraftwerk's track 'Trans-Europe Express' (1977) and 'Numbers' (from their 1981 album *Computer World*) to create the electronic beat collage 'Planet Rock' (Tommy Boy). Again new black music producers were looking to Germany, in this case Düsseldorf, for inspiration. As the decade wore on Afrika Bambaataa continued to create a form of electronic funk with help from the likes of James Brown and producer Bill Laswell.

In tandem with this, Garage continued to thrive under the new 'mix' ethos, where people like Larry Levan and Shep Pettibone created slick electronic soulful song mixes. Levan's seven-minute remix of diva Gwen Guthrie's 'Seventh Heaven' (Island 1983), stuck out a mile for its gall as weird bass, drum claps and oscillating electronics vied with Guthrie's impassioned vocal for prominence. Pettibone's bubbling electronic mixes on the Prelude label were some of the best that Garage had to offer. D Train's 'You're The One For Me' (1982) swirled with glittering synthesizers matched to knife-edge bass riffing.

On the surface this was funk but as the track progressed the vocal emotion was matched to myriad synthesizer- and studio-generated sounds.

By 1987 the Paradise Garage had closed. The music itself was changing, with new labels catering for a different sound which matched jazz and funk to rough edits and heavy soundboard tweaking. One of these Garage labels, Nu Groove, emerged in 1988 and was soon championing the music of white Brooklynite Joey Beltram. From the age of thirteen Beltram had been a DJ and loved the Hip-Hop scene. He was a respected graffiti artist and was into playing with primitive tape-loop and cassette systems. His vision was a big sound which drew on Garage and Hip-Hop but went further. Turning to the Belgian label R&S, Beltram released 'Energy Flash' in 1990. With a beat like the sound of wooden crates being clonked around an echo chamber, 'Energy Flash' came complete with burbling synths, wonky drones, drum claps and a wispy electronic chorus. Beltram saw it as a fusion of Garage and Electro with a European edge. A disembodied voice chanted a mantra to LSD and Ecstasy, and Hardcore Techno was born.

LISTENING

Classic Mix Vol. 1 (Beechwood 1991) features a range of Garage classics, including Levan's inimitable Gwen Guthrie 'Seventh Heaven' mix and much Shep Pettibone stuff. *Classic Electro* (Beechwood 1994) contains the original 'Grandmaster Flash On The Wheels Of Steel' twelve-inch mix. Afrika Bambaataa's *Planet Rock – The Album* came out on a Tommy Boy CD in 1986.

CHICAGO HOUSE AND ACID HOUSE

The birth of Chicago House and its prodigal son Acid House is one of the most extraordinary occurrences of the late twentieth century. The combination of soul, disco and electronic pop made for endless grooves which became the prime black music of Chicago from the late 1970s to the late 80s. People like DJ Frankie Knuckles and producer Marshall Jefferson were doyens of the seamless mix which elevated mere clubbing into an all-weekend dance experience. Fuelled by marijuana, LSD and the new 'happy' drug Ecstasy, House became a phenomenon which exploded outwards from Chicago around the world. Due to a studio accident with a squelchy-sounding Roland rhythm box, black Chicago musicians even fathered Acid House, a sub-genre which made an enormous impact on British youth culture of the late 1980s.

The word 'House' owes its origins to a club called the Warehouse where Frankie Knuckles wove his extraordinary mixes in sound from 1977 to 1983. Knuckles had been born in New York's South Bronx district in 1955 and got involved in club happenings while still a teenager. He and New York DJ legend

Larry Levan started to deconstruct records in performance and observe the effect on LSD-high audiences. Knuckles got his biggest break when he was offered a DJ job at the Chicago Warehouse, where he began working in 1977. There he would incorporate a reel-to-reel tape machine into turntable grooves which mixed soul records with dance electronica like Donna Summer and Giorgio Moroder. When Knuckles played at the weekend it was primarily to a gay clientele in an alcohol-free zone. High on various hallucinogenics, thousands of followers danced until Sunday afternoons.

In 1983 Knuckles moved from the Warehouse to the Power Plant, where he perfected his luscious style. The Warehouse became the infamous Music Box and Knuckles's weekend slots were taken over by DJ Ron Hardy, who whipped his audiences up to levels of frenzy with deck mixes tied to Roland rhythm boxes. Psychedelics were the drugs of choice and the music simply became known as 'House'. In 1984 Knuckles bought a Roland 909 drum machine from Detroit's Derrick May, who was occasionally driving to Chicago to check out the new music with its pulse-like insistent four-on-the-floor dance beat. Record labels like Trax and DJ International sprung up to cater for artists like Larry 'Mr Fingers' Heard and Farley 'Jackmaster Funk' Williams.

Farley was a regular on Chicago's WBMX radio, where he specialized in dance mixes. In the autumn of 1986 he succeeded in breaking House internationally with the huge hit record 'Love Can't Turn Around' (DJ International). Full of exuberance, 'Love' was quintessential House, with its cheesy synth sounds, disembodied hollering vocal loops, synthetic whistles, clattering drums, dry cymbals, soul-diva samples, electronic tones, keyboard sprinkles, bright textures and seemingly boundless, undulating repetition. Larry Heard was a different kind of musician, a jazz drummer with a love of Miles Davis. From 1984 he began working with a Roland 707 drum machine and the speeded-up note device (arpeggiator) of a Roland Juno 6 synthesizer. His 1986 masterpiece 'Can You Feel It' (Trax), credited to Mr Fingers, merged Chicago House with Detroit Techno. The ear was assaulted with a myriad of crafted electronic percussion lines, including the familiar insistent bass figure, a House trademark. Over this Heard laid down occasional stabbing synths, facsimile handclaps, busy cymbals and a ghostly keyboard Ambience. The sweet, velvety sound was machine music made by a master craftsman.

Heard's label, Trax, had been set up by a white Vietnam War veteran called Larry Sherman after seeing how popular House music was at the Music Box. The runaway success of Trax encouraged Sherman to invest in black producers like Marshall Jefferson who worked in good Chicago studios like Universal which sported an up-to-date Neve mixing console. A former post-office employee, Jefferson made a typical celebratory House record in 'Move Your Body' (Trax 1986), a repetitive vocal and instrumental melisma to the form. Yet it was in 1987 that Jefferson made his grand impact when he midwifed the first Acid House recording.

In 1986 a group of Chicago friends, including DJ Pierre (Nathaniel Jones), were experimenting with the moist, sticky sound of the outmoded Roland 303 bassline. With its single-octave keyboard and various filter knobs, the small metal box from 1983 produced weird squirting and plopping sci-fi noises. When Pierre revealed the sound to Marshall Jefferson it reminded him of trippy LSD music. Jefferson produced the track, credited to Pierre and Co, as Phuture. When Larry Sherman heard the sound he saw an affinity between it and the burring Jimi Hendrix psychedelia he'd heard in Vietnam. Ron Hardy played the tape at the Music Box and the classic Phuture record 'Acid Tracks' (Trax 1987) was born.

Jefferson saw hundreds of Acid House records follow in its wake, many a reductionist take on House with the 303 wearily flaring up to no great effect. One of the finest, DJ Pierre's 'Dream Girl' (Trax 1988), brought the soul back into Acid House but by then the form was in decline in Chicago. Internationally Chicago House's biggest success was still in the offing. When Frankie Knuckles began DJing in the late 1970s, a young DJ named L'il Louis was specializing in cassette-deck mixes at a straight club called the Future. A drummer and bass player steeped in blues and Led Zeppelin, Louis turned professional DJ by the mid-1970s. Inspired by Knuckles, he switched to reel-to-reel tape mixes and by the early 1980s was studying engineering at Columbia records. His reputation grew to such an extent that he outdrew Frankie Knuckles as a DJ when up to 8,000 people attended his Bismarck Hotel sets. Playing exclusive 'hot-mixes', Louis debuted 'French Kiss' there in 1987, an insistent Roland 808 drum track with stabbing synth slowed down over time to make space for orgasmic female sighs. When first released in 1988 the track was met with thousands of orders, so much so that Louis licensed it through major labels (Columbia in the US, Phonogram in the UK). By 1989 'French Kiss' was a million-selling accolade to over a decade of Chicago innovation.

Though the close of the 1980s saw a scattering of the original pioneers – Frankie Knuckles back in New York, DJ Pierre heading for New Jersey with a more emotive Garage sound – the Minimalist character of both House and Acid House was to hotwire itself into a new global music. Its instrumental, repetitive and lengthy nature was the best musical prescription for a mind high on Ecstasy. It erupted in late-80s Britain with a vengeance and continued to spread and mutate throughout the world. Its very openness to sound dragged in other musics, old and new, and saw traditional barriers come crashing down. In truth House and Acid House were a revolution in sound which swept the way clear for a new awareness of Ambient music.

LISTENING

As most of House's greatest moments were on twelve-inch vinyl singles the best place to get a good overview is the CD compilations from companies like Beechwood Music UK. Their Mastercuts series is exemplary: *Classic House Vol. 1*, *Classic House Vol. 2* (both 1994) and *Classic House Vol. 3* (1996) cover all the major releases. *Classic Acid* (1996) contains the genre-bending work of Phuture and DJ Pierre which ushered in Acid House.

DERRICK MAY AND DETROIT TECHNO

If one individual is responsible for the purest aesthetic of Techno music, which revitalized Minimalist and Ambient instrumental musics during the late 1980s and the whole of the 90s, it is Derrick May. This Detroit-born intellectual rejected the sentimental blues and soul aspects of his black cultural heritage for European synthesizer music. In the motoric beats of late-70s Kraftwerk and the ornate futurism of Vangelis May found an emotional connection which would lead him to produce some of the most imitated and far-reaching music of his generation.

Born in 1964, May grew up in the affluent middle-class suburb of Belleville, west of Detroit. Blacks were in the minority there, but at high school in the late 1970s he met Juan Atkins and Kevin Saunderson, two aspirants who shared his love of UK electro-bop, Giorgio Moroder and Donna Summer and of course Kraftwerk. This music provided them with dreamscapes which were at odds with the post-industrial wasteland that inner Detroit had become.

Juan Atkins was older than May and began teaching him how to mix music. In 1981 May began tentatively DJing but he wasn't a success. Inspiration came from Atkins when the latter formed Cybotron at community college with a Vietnam veteran named Rick Davis who owned a lot of ARP synth gear. 'Alleys Of Your Mind', released on Atkins's own Deep Space label in 1981, was the spark for the birth of Techno. Keyboards and drum rhythms hit it off in exciting new patterns but Davis's Jimi Hendrix fixation was at odds with Atkins's chillier electronic vision. By 1985 Atkins had formed Model 500 and started another label, Metroplex.

Both May and Saunderson also had labels, Transmat and KMS, and offices near to Atkins's in Detroit. The Belleville Three, as they became known, were a new conduit for the hopes of Detroit's black intelligentsia. Inspired by Vangelis's painterly soundtrack to Ridley Scott's visionary 1982 sci-fi movie *Blade Runner* and frequent trips to the burgeoning Chicago House clubs, May began amassing equipment such as the economical Yamaha DX 100 digital synthesizer and the Ensoniq Mirage multi-sampling keyboard. Using these with Roland 808 and 909 drum machines and a four-track tape machine, he started creating his own music. Underground clubs provided a forum for May in the mid-1980s but the release of 'Strings Of Life' (1986), under his moniker Rhythim Is Rhythim, turned him into a star. Its busy keyboard stabs, sampled orchestral strings and pounding drum track made it a runaway success in the UK dance scene of 1987. By 1989 it was a Rave classic, a ubiquitous record on European turntables. In the interim Kevin Saunderson's Inner City label had a scored a two-million-selling hit with 'Big Fun' (1988).

If Detroit Techno could be commercial, its more cerebral output was fascinating. Such a 1986 track as 'The Dance' was more accurate of where Derrick May was coming from. Using Akai samplers, he overlaid different electronic rhythms which led to long sequences of ghostly keyboard tones. The sound was windowpane-clear, owing its lineage to the work of Eno, Tangerine Dream and of course Kraftwerk. Together with Saunderson, May played his form of 'pure' Techno at Detroit's revered Music Institute Club. Yet when May performed in the UK in 1989 he was horrified that his vision had been turned into a form of drug music for white youth. By 1990 the Music Institute was closed and personal problems in Detroit led him to decamp to Europe.

Coming round to the realization that his hothouse plant had grown into a wild flower, May began working with Steve Hillage, the 70s hippie guitarist who'd formed System 7 with his partner Miquette Giraudy. May contributed to several System 7 albums until 1995, when he signed a deal with Sony Japan for the CD issue of his illustrious Transmat catalogue. He was also consulted by Roland on synthesizer design.

May has always put the intellectual and social ambitions of his art before commercial concerns. As one of Techno's greatest inventors he saw the form as a future step for American black youth. Disgusted at the rise of 140bpm (beats per minute) Hardcore Techno in the UK during the early 1990s, he opted to release very little music. A disliker of studios and clinical sounds (his Rhythim Is Rhythim string sounds were sampled on basic cassette tape), he is nevertheless an inspiration to an entire generation of electronic musicians from all racial backgrounds. One of his acolytes, Carl Craig, born in 1969, worked with him on updating his club smash 'Strings Of Life' in 1989 before going on to become one of the hottest new stars of Detroit Techno, releasing beautiful widescreen recordings through Warner Bros. and remixing archetypal German electronica by Can.

LISTENING

In 1991 Network in the UK released the excellent Derrick May EP 'Innovator: Soundtrack For The Tenth Planet' - a clutch of six Techno classics released between 1986 and 1988, including 'Strings Of Life' and 'The Dance'. Sony Japan handled the first subsequent CD reissue of May's Transmat releases in 1995 before he signed a deal with R&S, who released *Innovator* (1998), a double-disc expanded version of the original Network title. Carl Craig's major label debut, *Landcruising* (Blanco 1995), was Techno writ large, a sleek sixty-minute voyage through an electronic landscape which acknowledged its debt to both Kraftwerk and Tangerine Dream while exploring pastures new. *Programmed* (Talkin' Loud 1999), credited to Craig's Innerzone Orchestra, was Techno as space-jazz fantasy, where Moog, Theremin, Rhodes and *Blade Runner* textures were as important as the Latin and accelerated Techno grooves.

ANNE DUDLEY AND THE ART OF NOISE

Formed in 1983, The Art Of Noise were one of the first British studio groups to embrace sampling and the afterglow effects of Ambient House. Their effervescent and humorous pop singles like 'Peter Gunn' (with Duane Eddy, 1986) and a version of Prince's 'Kiss' (with Tom Jones, 1988) were just the very visible aspect of a Dadaist sensibility which was both eclectic and learned. Spearheaded by academic and synthesizer expert Anne Dudley, The Art Of Noise reached their peak with *The Ambient Collection* (1990), a Minimalist masterpiece of sound and melody arrangement which spurred on the Ambient House explosion of the 1990s.

Anne Dudley was a 1960s London child who was brought up in a classical-music-loving family. The complex music of The Beatles was her first introduction to the pop world, which she immediately fell in love with. A talent for sight-reading and harmony led to outstanding results in her final exams at London's Royal College of Music. After taking a Master's degree at King's College she became a session keyboardist and arranger in the recording studios of early-80s London. At home she explored various synthesizers like the MiniMoog and the relatively new PPG Wave, the first digital synth with analogue characteristics, sequencing and sampling options. Teaming up with fellow session musicians JJ Jeczalik (Fairlight CMI, keyboards) and Gary Langan (instruments) in 1983, Dudley became a vital ingredient of The Art Of Noise, a studio band overseen by production mentor Trevor Horn, who immediately signed them to his ZTT label. Their debut creation, 'Close (To The Edit)' (a play on the title of a Yes album), was intensely percussive and featured samples. It appeared on their first album, *Who's Afraid Of The Art Of Noise* (1984), a recording which took the splice and scratch character of American Rap music and added it to a plethora of found sounds, choral vocal and drumming beats. The plush Ambience of 'Moments In Love' would become a perfect chill-out anthem for the Balearic Rave generation of the late 80s.

Wanting independence, Dudley and crew left ZTT and signed to China Records in 1985. Their 1986 album *Invisible Silence* included the wonderful 'Camilla', a hypnotic upright-bass figure sprinkled with gorgeous sounds and topped off with a treated vocal sample from 10cc's dreamy 1975 masterpiece 'I'm Not In Love'. More commercial recordings would follow, including the aforementioned hit with Tom Jones, before tapes were given to the renowned producer Youth (cohort of both The KLF and The Orb) to compile and mix *The Ambient Collection* in 1989. In fact The Orb's Alex Paterson was also involved.

Sitting neatly in time between The KLF's 1989 *Chill Out* and The Orb's 1991 *Adventures Beyond The Ultraworld*, *The Ambient Collection* laid out Ambient House's more fanciful preoccupations with perfectly produced sounds. Thus, after getting through some pleasant lounge muzak with choral voice samples,

Youth pressed the Pink Floyd button to reveal a motorbike starting up, a passing train, the overhead whizzing of a plane or helicopter, birdsong, punted water and river flow. A cool tune with some nice flute sampling and lush strings then emerged centre stage. Elsewhere horse hooves made a familiar stereophonic pan, people walked through rooms and closed doors loudly, church bells pealed and clocks ticked in familiar Floydian mode while Youth and Paterson injected proceedings with that bright sequenced shimmer which would soon make The Orb famous. Only the deep grooves of the closing track, 'Art Of Love', made any concession to the dance floor.

Feeling that The Art Of Noise had run its course, Dudley easily returned to freelance arranging, her reputation built upon 80s work with Paul McCartney and Phil Collins. Yet she was drawn back to the exotic when she teamed up with Jaz Coleman (ex-leader of early-80s punk group Killing Joke, which also included Youth) and made *Songs From The Victorious City* (China 1990). With his Indian–Persian ancestry and classical leanings towards string music, Coleman approached Dudley to help him with composition. The pair ended up recording with a thirty-piece string orchestra in Cairo. This dive into Arabic music was complemented by her 1995 album *Ancient And Modern*. Working on her Wurlitzer electric piano, vintage synths, Roland D70 polyphonic synthesizer, Atari-run computer sequencing software, a forty-channel desk and various digital and analogue tape systems, Dudley wrote a cycle of hymn-like tunes for a seventy-piece orchestral and choral ensemble. Though mindful of Bach and English pastoralism, Dudley's creation did import African percussion, drum loops and the Minimalism of Philip Glass and John Adams.

LISTENING

The Art Of Noise's early sampling innovations can be heard on the CD *Who's Afraid Of The Art Of Noise* (ZTT 1985). The Ambient wonders of Youth's compilation and remix *The Ambient Collection* (China 1990) still sound impressive. As well as writing many television theme tunes Dudley became a respected film-music composer after scoring Neil Jordan's *The Crying Game* in 1992. Her fresh-sounding 'classical album' *Ancient And Modern* came out on Echo in 1995. JJ Jeczalik kept himself busy as a remixer, releasing in 1993 the *Art Of Sampling*, a CD full of interesting sounds for the serious samplist. In 1996 he released his debut album, *artofsilence.co.uk* (Hit Records), a mélange of electronic dance and Ambient music. So respected were The Art Of Noise in Rave culture that two further remix albums followed *The Ambient Collection*. *The Fon Mixes* (China 1991), realized in a Sheffield studio, featured Carl Cox, The Prodigy and members of both Cabaret Voltaire and 808 State. *The Drum And Bass Collection* (China 1996) contained some excellent mixes. In 1999 the group re-formed and put out a new ZTT album, *The Seduction Of Claude Debussy*.

808 STATE

One of the major House groups to emerge from Manchester after Chicago House and Detroit Techno erupted in the UK in the late 1980s, 808 State set themselves the task of being a progressive albums band from the word go. In 1989 they scored a huge instrumental hit with the balmy 'Pacific State', a track which cascaded with Latino timbres, jazzy horns and twittering bird sounds. Inspired by Brian Eno and Minimalist trumpeter Jon Hassell, 808 State's sophistication pushed House way beyond its early clattering beat fixation, opening the way for the coming of Ambient House and Intelligent Techno musics.

808 State were originally founded by Graham Massey, Gerald Simpson and Martin Price in a dance-import record shop called Eastern Bloc in Manchester in 1987. Massey was in his late twenties, had begun playing Cuban and Brazilian music as a young teenager and had a passion for Miles Davis, Santana, tape music, Faust, Robert Fripp and Brian Eno. He played keyboards and wind instruments and hooked up with Gerald Simpson (in his early twenties and soon to become A Guy Called Gerald) because of a shared musical interest and the latter's proficiency with Roland drum machines. Price was in his early thirties, owned Eastern Bloc and urged Massey and Gerald on to make their own Acid House music once the records started to come through from Chicago in 1987. Massey and Simpson's cassette jams would make their way to the local Hacienda club's raves. Using mostly two-track tape and Roland rhythm boxes, 808 State were actually named after their beloved Roland TR-808 drum machine.

High on the Acid House sound of the Roland TB-303 bassline, the trio made *Newbuild* (Creed 1988) as a form of homage to the form. Working in a local sixteen-track studio, 808 State expanded to include two young DJs, Darren Partington and Andy Barker, who had come from an Electro music background. A Roland D50 synthesizer was added to their small array of Roland boxes and synths; in fact the group were a living endorsement of the Japanese electronic instrument company. They were keen on early sampling and sequencing ideas inspired by Derrick May's classic Techno anthem 'Strings Of Life' (Transmat 1986). Parallel chordings, ghost samples, tight compositions, guitar effects pedals and real instruments made 1989's *Quadrastate* (Creed) a lush instrumental ride. Its sonorous opening salvo, 'Pacific State', would become one of the great anthems of the Rave generation.

Yet by the time *Quadrastate* had appeared, Gerald was long gone to a life of innovation as A Guy Called Gerald. Though he had left 808 State in 1988, he still was given a publishing credit for 'Pacific State'. Massey's love of Jon Hassell meant that 808 State provided him with a series of remixes of 'Voiceprint' from his then current hybrid electronic album *City: Works Of Fiction* (Land 1990). Hassell's acoustic-electronic soundscapes were etched into 808 State's first album for the crossover label ZTT, simply titled *90*. By 1991's *Ex-El*

(ZTT), 'The State' were moving towards jazz fusion with help from the Icelandic singer Björk and New Order's Bernard Sumner.

The outspoken Martin Price, who saw House and Techno as a new beginning for UK music rather than another youth rebellion music, opted to leave in 1991, reducing 808 State to a trio of Massey, Barker and Partington. The dynamic of the group – Massey's early-thirties experience versus the computer-friendly enthusiasm of two early-twenties DJs who styled themselves The Spinmasters – pushed 808 State into intriguing remix areas and a willingness to make dance music as interesting and accessible as possible. *Gorgeous* (ZTT 1993) refined their sophisticated beat sound further, with elements of jazz and some gothic airiness from 4AD's This Mortal Coil. In 1994 they pushed deeper into technology by being one of the first groups to embrace the Internet with their computerized information service State to State. Even in 1996, on *Don Solaris* (ZTT), one could detect Drum and Bass elements among the polished lustre of sound.

LISTENING

Both *Quadrastate* (1989) and *90* (1990) are well worth hearing, as is the 808 State remix of Jon Hassell's 'Voiceprint' (Land 1990). The group are responsible for many 1992 remixes, including Afrika Bambaataa's 'Planet Rock' (Tommy Boy), the Yellow Magic Orchestra's 'Light In Darkness' (Eternal), The Art Of Noise's 'Legs' (China) and the avant-Techno of The Future Sound Of London's 'Papua New Guinea' (Jumpin' & Pumpin'). A remix of David Bowie and Brian Eno's 'Sound And Vision' was ranked as one of their all-time favourites. The State's Graham Massey also collaborated with Björk on her second album, *Post* (One Little Indian 1995). In 1998 ZTT released the 808 State CD compilation *808:88:98*. In 1999 Rephlex reissued the debut album, *Newbuild*, credited to Massey, Price and Simpson, on all formats.

A GUY CALLED GERALD

One of the first young black British electronicists to connect with the sounds emerging from Chicago and Detroit, Gerald put out the classic 'Voodoo Ray' in 1988, merging the blipping feel of Detroit Techno with the effortless dance rhythms of Chicago House. Filled with elements of soul, funk and African musics, the track had an almost devotional female vocal which conjured up a whole new sonic direction. Gerald's attention to detail and love for the purest sound world of Detroit's Derrick May paved the way for the coming of Ambient Techno.

Born in 1966, Gerald Simpson began his life in music in the early 1980s as a DJ around the Manchester suburbs playing Electro records. By the mid-1980s he had acquired two pieces of machinery which defined the entire House music explosion – the silver Roland TB 303 bassline box and the Roland TR 808 drum machine. (The Japanese modules with their on-board sequencers were responsible for producing the strange bubbly sounds and intricate accelerated beats typical of early Acid House.) Inspired by Chicago House, he became the third member of the Manchester group 808 State in 1988.

After working on their debut album, *Newbuild* (Creed 1988), and contributing to their rapturous 'Pacific State' (released in 1989 as a twelve-inch single), Gerald was sufficiently thrilled by the sound of Detroit Techno, particularly Derrick May, to leave 808 State in 1988 and record his own music. A sixteen-track Manchester studio became the focal point for sessions which merged the sound of the Roland boxes with the bass notes of a Roland SH-101 analogue mono synthesizer. He even used a sampler to get the aerial vocal effect. The result, 'Voodoo Ray', was a sparkling, uplifting, intelligent record which, when released by Rham, quickfired the whole Manchester dance explosion. Even Chicago House maestro Frankie Knuckles licensed the track for a whirlwind series of dance-floor remixes. By the summer of 1989 'Voodoo Ray' was a UK club sensation.

Beset by financial problems, Gerald continued to make records and even work with Cabaret Voltaire as a mixer. Though he lost the rights of 'Voodoo Ray' early on, his dedication to studio craft and creating new music resulted in the release of *Black Secret Technology* (Juice Box 1995), an album which defined the emerging Drum and Bass genre. Here Gerald used sampling, sequencing and analogue synths to create a sound which chattered with spliced drum beats underlined by soulful female vocal and endless interesting Ambient sounds plopped into the mix. His art was based on a thorough knowledge of MIDI (Musical Instrument Digital Interface) sequencing linked to a fondness for hands-on tape manipulation. In the Akai 950 he found a sampling unit whose capacity for processing and filtering looped sounds was capable of matching the ground-breaking rhythms of his musical imagination.

LISTENING

The original 'Voodoo Ray' can be found on *Classic House Mastercuts* (Beechwood 1994). Even as late as 1999 the six Frankie Knuckles remixes were still available on a Warlock twelve-inch. *Black Secret Technology* came out in 1995 and in a remastered edition on Juice Box in 1996.

ECSTASY AND THE NEW RAVE PSYCHEDELIA

Not since the LSD explosion of the 1960s had a drug made such an impact. Ecstasy literally changed the course of popular music at the end of the twentieth century, affecting the way it was made, listened to and enjoyed. The entire history of House, Techno and offshoot musics like Acid House, Ambient House and Drum and Bass would have been completely different without Ecstasy. After the three- or four-hour high Ecstasy had a slow, glowing come-down, perfect for listening to quieter music. Hence Ambient became popular and the phrase 'chill out' entered the popular lexicon.

In the UK Ecstasy triggered the most significant youth movement in history, leading to vast numbers attending 'Rave' events which lasted for days. The drug registered deep in the British consciousness, uniting generations of people and cutting across class and racial barriers. Around the world 'E culture' impacted in a variety of different ways and was inextricably bound up with new computer technology. 'Cyberdelia' was a term which described a new, forward-thinking philosophy which used the awareness derived from Ecstasy with the new tools of increasingly complex personal computers. For millions, Ecstasy was a doorway to the twenty-first century with its very own brand-new electronic soundtrack.

Ecstasy is not, as some have suggested, a mixture of LSD and amphetamine. Yet its effects are both mildly psychedelic and energy-releasing. Unsurprisingly, the drug has its popular roots in the work of a group of Californian scientists, psychologists, therapists and philosophers who believed that Timothy Leary's 1960s LSD idealism was not in vain. During the 1970s and 1980s investigations were done on a series of chemical analogues like Intellex, 2CB, Vitamin K and Entheogen. The latter would soon be called Empathy and eventually Ecstasy. Many therapists saw these drugs as benign facilitators to psychological recovery. Vitamin K, which can produce intense disassociative hallucinations, was seen as a key to a higher plane. The Berkeley ethno-biologist Terence McKenna did not put much faith in the new synthetics, instead opting for naturally occurring hallucinogens derived from 'magic' mushrooms (psilocybin), cactuses (mesca-line) and tree bark (DMT) which he had researched in South America. Yet his lectures and writings about man's evolution towards a higher consciousness dynamized a situation where Ecstasy, the easy-going empathogen, was begin-ning to take on the qualities of a psychotherapeutic wonder drug.

In fact Ecstasy dates back to well before the flurry of interest in the 1960s. MDMA, as it was known, was first synthesized in 1912 by the German company Merck in Darmstadt, the town that would later launch Stockhausen's electronic music revolution. Interest in the chemical was ended by the First World War. It was then heard of again in Poland in the late 1940s. By the early 1950s it was one of many drugs considered by the US Army as an interrogation aid but when several laboratory animals died after MDMA injections the idea was scrapped. It wasn't until an inquisitive psycho-pharmacologist named Alexander Schulgin rediscovered the drug in California in the 1960s that the cult of Ecstasy began to take hold. A Russian émigré and US Second World War veteran, Schulgin was born in the 1920s. He had a life-transforming experience on mescaline in 1960 and began synthesizing his own compounds. Between 1965 and 1967 he created several batches of MDMA and tested them on himself, his family and friends. Over the next three decades Schulgin would synthesize hundreds of new molecular combinations but none with the warm, airy effect of Ecstasy. By the late 1970s thousands of people around Schulgin had experienced the drug while around half a million doses had emanated from Californian labs.

It was in the gay black discos of 70s America that the spine-tingling nature of MDMA was first experienced. Allied to bright, loud, rhythmic dance music, its effect was pure euphoria. Boston, New York, Chicago and most famously Texas were breeding grounds for a new drug culture. MDMA or Empathy became known as XTC, Ecstasy or simply 'E'. Millions of doses were manufactured around America and the entire black House and Garage cultures of Chicago and New York were clued into the drug. Yet it was the massive consumption reported among the youth of Texas that alerted the US government, which set out to make Ecstasy illegal by the summer of 1985. But the genie was out of the bottle and nothing could ever be the same again.

In the UK in the early 1980s E had become the drug of choice among New Romantic musicians, who boasted a large gay fraternity. Many of these musicians took their first Ecstasy in New York gay clubs like the Paradise Garage and came back to the UK transformed. Soon London had its own scene among the fashion and music élite. And soon it spread to the intellectual bohemian set, the famous psychiatrist R. D. Laing praising its therapeutic properties. Yet it would take working-class experiences of Ecstasy on the Spanish holiday island of Ibiza to take it to the next level of becoming a mass cultural phenomenon in the UK.

Ibiza had long been a hippie haven frequented by Pink Floyd, along with famous artists, writers, film directors and so on. It had a tradition of great open-air parties hosted by the likes of José Padilla in San Antonio. Open-air discotheques like Amnesia, with its mixture of stars, gays, straights and out-rageously cool Spaniards, combined with Ecstasy to create a whole new European club experience. By the mid-1980s Amnesia's DJ Alfredo was mixing Chicago House into a new genre of European House music which became known as 'Balearic'. It was in this atmosphere that dozens of English working-class youth had their first Ecstasy pill. And it was at Amnesia in 1987 that two South London DJs, Danny Rampling and Paul Oakenfold, experienced how good House music sounded on E. Back in London they formed two clubs, Shoom and Future, which opened up the scene known as the 'UK Acid House Explosion'.

By early 1987 Chicago House was denting the UK charts, helped in no small way by future BBC dance guru and DJ Peter Tong, who facilitated the spread of Acid House in the UK through the ffrr imprint of London Records. During the summer of 1987 a strange bass-heavy dance tune made of scratches and multiple drum patterns soared to the top of the charts. M/A/R/R/S's 'Pump Up The Volume' (4AD) was a meeting of British DJs and musicians which drew much from recent black American music culture. It was a repetitive collage which seemed to herald an end to po-faced British rock bands. Others soon followed, Tim Simenon's Bomb The Bass and Mark Moore's S'Express scoring huge sampler-drum sequencer-House hits in early 1988. Moore's group even got to number one with 'Theme From S'Express'. A part-Oriental music night-tripper, Moore DJ'd at the London gay club Delirium and was a talent scout for Rhythm King records, which recorded UK Acid House artists featuring the notorious squirting Roland TB 303 bassline box. In 1988 Moore introduced Philip Glass to the new repetitive music coursing its way through London clubland, even getting him involved with a S'Express remix. Unashamedly supportive of the use of samplers and computer sequencing software, Moore would go on to work with the figureheads of Detroit Techno, Derrick May and Carl Craig.

Ecstasy had been illegal in the UK since 1977, when Midlands police found a huge laboratory store of MDMA and related compounds. Yet its criminalization as a Class A drug could do nothing to stop its lightning-fast dispersal through the country's club culture. The 'loved-up' and 'happy smiling people' vibe of Rampling's Shoom and Oakenfold's Spectrum was to be the theme of London's first Acid House 'Summer Of Love'. The new music and the happiness and touchy-feely glow of E seemed to transport clubbers back to their childhood, where lollipops, teddy bears and pastel shades reigned supreme. By the autumn of 1988 it wasn't surprising that Oakenfold's club night had a change of name to The Land Of Oz after the famous Judy Garland children's film.

That summer of 1988 was termed in some circles 'The Second Summer Of Love' as its neo-psychedelic trappings of tie-dye T-shirts and oil-wheel hallucinogenic club visuals harked back to the original Summer Of Love of 1967. Andrew Weatherall, a Windsor DJ who played at both Shoom and Spectrum, even exhorted the new club generation to 'drop acid'. This did not help matters when the UK tabloid media mistakenly confused Acid House with LSD. In fact references to Acid related to that particular form of House music while the real drug of choice was Ecstasy. The country's conservative Right was even more incensed when two twenty-one-year-olds mysteriously died after Ecstasy ingestion. Researchers in Baltimore realized that MDMA's toxicity level was a dose just a little over what was in the average pill! Later it would emerge that heat exhaustion, drug mixing and drinking too much water (to offset the drug's intense dehydration effect) could all cause death. Yet nothing seemed to deter thousands looking to E for the ultimate bliss-out.

The word 'Rave' had occasionally surfaced in the psychedelic music scene of the 1960s but was in more common parlance in black soul and jazz circles. The English writer Nicholas Saunders (the elder-statesman champion of the positive aspects of Ecstasy) best described Rave culture as 'a combination of the drug with music and dancing to produce an exhilarating trancelike state similar to that experienced in tribal rituals or religious ceremonies'. In 1989 Rave became the new religion. Warehouses filled with coloured dry-ice, lasers, visuals and various themed amusements were the setting for all-night House and Techno parties.

The famous orbital M25 motorway around London became a focal point for convoys of weekend ravers as they waited for their secret destination to be released via a telephone voicebank. The fact was that raves were illegal but the secretive strategies of such organizers as Sunrise just heightened the E rush. As the numbers rose, raves went outdoors and the UK Acid House scene hit its second peak at a 17,000-strong summer event in the Buckinghamshire country-side called Back To The Future. For all concerned the Second Summer Of Love had truly arrived.

Though reviled by the police and the Conservative government, House music and all its sub-genres had an unstoppable momentum in the UK. And the emerging music was getting better and better. The autumn of 1989 saw a series of recordings which perfectly encapsulated the blissed-out Rave vibe. A group of Italian DJs mixed Manuel Göttsching's timeless Trance-groove *E2–E4* into one of the greatest Balearic House tracks of all time in 'Sueno Latino'. A British indie group, The Beloved, made a rapturous Ecstasy anthem in 'Sun Rising', replete with choral overtones. But the most powerful music of the year came from Manchester, a city whose House movement had exploded around the nerve-centre of its Hacienda dance club. By the winter of 1989 the breezy 'Pacific State' by 808 State was a chart sensation and the new Ecstasy rock of The Stone Roses was drawing in tens of thousands with a revolutionary sound for 'head, heart and feet', exemplified in the walloping 'Fool's Gold'.

As The Stone Roses attracted 30,000 people to Spike Island in Cheshire in the spring of 1990, the UK was being transformed by Rave. New coalitions were growing up between travellers and DJs, hippies, punks, environmentalists, rock groups and New Age mystics. Psychedelic writer Fraser Clark dubbed it 'shamanarchy' and pointed to the new Techno tribal traveller as its epitome. Scottish group The Shamen worked with the likes of Mixmaster Morris on a new touring synergism of rock and Rave which converted thousands more to the Ecstasy experience in 1990. The Glastonbury Festival welcomed the growing number of travellers with their own sound systems. All over the UK autonomous groups of youth were forming their own communities around Rave culture, playing their own music, performing free and pulling in audiences in the thousands. In the autumn of 1990 a group of talented individualists who mixed art and music began throwing free Techno parties in London. By 1991 they were called Spiral Tribe and were travelling around the country with the intention of playing twenty-four-hour full-on dance music to anyone who would listen. Their raves weren't just about dancing but were a celebratory open-air communion as fire-eaters, jugglers and other artists joined their expanding troupe. They caused outrage when they were seen as the prime movers in a mega-Rave in Avon in the summer of 1992 which lasted for five days. By 1994, when the government outlawed free raves, Spiral Tribe had become a European touring sensation, dubbing their Techno-oriented DJ festivals 'Teknivals'.

In the UK Ecstasy culture spawned endless musical stylizations. In the

Ambient sphere Ambient House was the beginning of a whole slew of 'chill out' musics such as Intelligent Techno and Ambient Trance. 'Amberdelia' was a better term to describe a growing movement which blended traditional psychedelia with the new Ambience. Techno became Hardcore Techno while Hip-Hop interfaced with Techno to produce Jungle (Drum and Bass). Goldie became an Ambient Jungle superstar in 1995, the year when E culture was worth over £2 billion a year in the UK alone. Clubs continued to flourish and DJs were firmly ensconced in the national music industry. Then, in the winter of 1995, an Essex girl named Leah Betts died after taking one Ecstasy pill at her eighteenth-birthday party. The death made international headlines and many began to wonder whether MDMA was safe after all. Yet after an extensive inquiry it was revealed that Leah Betts had died of excessive water ingestion.

Regardless of this tragic event, Ecstasy consumption continued to rise. Half a million people a week were taking the drug in the UK by the mid-1990s but a real fact was that fatality was a rarity and the risk of this outcome was authoritatively estimated to be 0.00004 per cent. The Scottish writer Irvine Welsh dubbed users of Ecstasy 'the chemical generation'. The crucial interplay between Ecstasy and dance music was something that just couldn't be contained. It had spread like a virus throughout the world, establishing loci of activity in Amsterdam, Berlin, Paris, Tokyo and Frankfurt. America had its very own Rave culture, the 1990s featuring different scenes on the East Coast and West Coast, with indoor and outdoor events occurring spontaneously throughout the southern states, Washington, New England and the Pacific North-West. And if Los Angeles boasted outdoor Rave audiences of up to 17,000 then San Francisco had the most vibrant scene of all. A nexus of ideas ranging from biofeedback research to new computer possibilities had morphed into a new cyberdelic and amberdelic culture that integrated chip technology, Techno music, Eastern philosophy and the doctrines of 60s psychedelic gurus Ken Kesey and Timothy Leary. The Grateful Dead were worshipped as Rave ancestors and the Bay area became a cradle of outdoor Rave energy where Ecstasy was only one drug in a cornucopia of psychedelics (plant-derived and synthetic), all consumed with the intention to push at the consciousness envelope. In the end the combination of Ecstasy with House and Techno music was the spark which lit the flame of desire for an altered state of consciousness, one which was thrillingly enjoyed by millions as the millennium neared its end.

LISTENING

To gain an idea of the UK Ecstasy scene at its peak listen to the Irvine Welsh-compiled *Anthems For The Chemical Generation* (Virgin 1997), which features 808 State, The Beloved, The Stone Roses and The Shamen. The Balearic mood is perfectly captured on *Classic Balearic Mastercuts Volume 1* (Beechwood 1996), which features quintessential Trance tracks by Sueno Latino, BBG (the chugging 'Snappiness') and The Grid's resplendent 'Floatation'.

THE KLF

One of the most exciting outfits to emerge from the UK House music scene of the late 1980s, The KLF were two pop-cultural anarchists who went out of their way to subvert the corporate nature of the established music business. Initially called The JAMs (and inspired by the mix nature of US Hip-Hop), they made a form of sampled beat music which drew widely from rock, soul and pop history. They had a huge impact on the charts before making their first significant album, *Chill Out* (1990). The result of post-Rave studio jam sessions, *Chill Out* was the first important Ambient House long-player. A recording which cross-faded musical samples with natural and found sounds, it pushed the notion of Ambience into a new dimension. *Chill Out* made 1970s rock cool again, particularly that of Pink Floyd, while proving a perfect come-down album for the Ecstasy generation. More Ambient music, like *Space* (1990), showed that while evoking such 70s groups as Tangerine Dream, the new Ambience was firmly linked to the electronic styles of Chicago House and Detroit Techno.

Probably The KLF's greatest Ambient statement was the 1990 film *Waiting*, a documentary of a spring sojourn on a Scottish island whose magnificent soundtrack mixed the incendiary guitar of Jimi Hendrix with bird calls, sea sounds, crackling fires, liturgical chant and the relentless beat of House.

The KLF were Jimmy Cauty and Bill Drummond. Both had backgrounds in music and the arts. Cauty, born in 1957, was a London-based art bohemian, who'd had teenage success when he drew a best-selling decorative print based on Tolkien's *The Hobbit*. He then gravitated to music and nouveau-funk band Brilliant. Drummond, born in 1954, was a Scot who loved rural life but was also involved in the Liverpool new-wave scene of the early 1980s. He managed Echo And The Bunnymen and played guitar in another group, Big In Japan. Drummond then did some A&R work for Warner Bros., through which he met Cauty. Tired of the scene, the pair decided to confront the music business head-on as The Justified Ancients Of Mu Mu, better known as The JAMs. Their debut album, *1987 – What The Fuck Is Going On?* (Jams 1987), was a truly irreverent take on scratch mixing as The Beatles, The MC5, Samantha Fox, Acker Bilk, James Brown and Abba were all sampled in a concoction that was largely indebted to the Electro-Rap pioneers Afrika Bambaataa and Grand-master Flash. Recorded in five days and promoted by daubing prominent London buildings with the JAMs logo, *1987* became a *cause célèbre* when the Swedish superstars Abba took exception to the reworking of their hit 'Dancing Queen'. Cauty and Drummond were sued in the autumn of 1987 and had to destroy all remaining copies of their album, which they did by burning them in Sweden. Unfazed, they saw out 1987 by releasing a series of singles which celebrated Whitney Houston, Lalo Schifrin and Petula Clark. By the spring of 1988 they were lifting riffs, beats and melodies wholesale from Michael Jackson, Sly Stone and Jimi Hendrix records. Ace manipulators of the UK pop scene the duo decided to mix a Gary Glitter rock beat with the BBC Radiophonic Workshop's theme for *Dr Who* to make 'Doctorin' The Tardis', a joke record they pushed to number one in the UK charts by making out an American police car was the source of the song! For added mirth they dubbed themselves The Timelords and then penned a manual titled *How To Have A Number One The Easy Way*.

The close of 1988 saw Cauty and Drummond assume the permanent moniker of Kopyright Liberation Front, or KLF, and release a devastating Acid House anthem in 'What Time Is Love?'. Drummond saw House music as the perfect antidote to po-faced British indie-guitar rock. 'All you basically need is the Roland 909 bass and Roland 808 snare sounds and there you have it.' During 1989 The KLF embraced House with a vengeance, releasing the Trancey '3 A.M. Eternal' and the Techno-influenced 'Last Train To Trancentral'. In fact over the next two years 'What Time Is Love?' and '3 A.M. Eternal' would be released nine times apiece, in widely different versions. In the autumn of 1989, at an Oxfordshire Rave called Helter Skelter, they even distributed £1,000 in Scottish banknotes to the gathered throng from the back of a lorry.

As 1989 neared its end Jimmy Cauty got involved in Ambient music, DJing at the Chill Out room at London's The Land Of Oz. He was friendly with Alex Paterson, an A&R man at EG Records, a company which had released much of Brian Eno's Ambient work. Together they made a fantastic mix of soul vocal and Pink Floyd guitar chime titled 'Loving You' which was debuted on John Peel's BBC radio programme under the name The Orb. With the match lit, Ambient House required a bigger statement. In the early months of 1990 it duly arrived wrapped in a sleeve picture of bucolic sheep, a clever echo of Pink Floyd's 1970 opus *Atom Heart Mother*. The album, titled *Chill Out*, had a beautiful post-Rave lustre resulting from the use of steel guitar and the remarkable softness of Cauty's eight-voice Oberheim synthesizer. Within its gentle montage of cicadas, sheep, dogs, didgeridoo, passing planes, trains and cars, washing waves, bird calls and sonar blips one could discern strains of Elvis Presley, Fleetwood Mac, Acker Bilk and 808 State. It looked back to the work of Pierre Schaeffer in its celebration of sound for its own sake but placed it in the new context of House. Every once in a while the drifting tapestry parted a little to allow a House beat to be heard but the effect was only momentary. The lengthy 'Madrugada Eterna' replayed the crashing VCS3 synth noise from Pink Floyd's 'On The Run' on *Dark Side Of The Moon* before immersing itself in American broadcast soundbites. In short, *Chill Out* was a magnificent conceptual achievement.

The KLF contended that *Chill Out* was 'music that makes love with the wind and talks to the stars'. Drummond: '*Chill Out* was a live album made from lots of bits and pieces, some off tapes, others from LPs. It took two days to put together, bouncing things from DAT [digital audio tape] to DAT.' Cauty: 'It wasn't edited. Quite a few times we'd make a mistake and have to then go back to the beginning and start again. It was like spinning plates. We used the two DAT players, a record deck, a couple of cassette boxes and a twelve-track recorder all fed through a mixer.' In fact The KLF's famous Trancentral studio was a South London squat where Cauty parked his American police car. Instrumentation was minimal – an Akai S900 sampler, an Atari computer, a digital delay, the Oberheim eight-voice polyphonic synthesizer, a boom microphone and the above recording and mixing devices.

Then, in the spring of 1990, the pair took most of this gear to the Isle of Jura, off the west coast of Scotland, for an eight-day visit. With film-maker Bill Butt in attendance The KLF created the film *Waiting*, an atmospheric rendition of their trip. Images of Cauty and Drummond setting up their recording gear on a beach were interspersed with long takes of them warming themselves by a blazing fire, recording birds and insects and generally relaxing. Sonically the soundtrack was a mix of church hymn, Balkan liturgical chant, slices of *Chill Out*, nature sounds, excerpts from '3 A.M. Eternal' and 'Last Train To Trancentral', revolving around a continuous burst of Jimi Hendrix guitar. Visually, a large speaker stack represented Hendrix, every appearance heralding another blast of 'Voodoo Chile' or 'All Along The Watchtower'.

Released at the close of 1990, *Waiting* was a reminder of the earlier impressionistic film and music work of Pink Floyd in various exotic Mediterranean locations. Still fascinated with Ambient, The KLF filled the interval between *Chill Out* and *Waiting* with another great release – *Space*, credited to Jimmy Cauty. More spartan than *Chill Out*, the album began with many references to the NASA space programme and the usual nods to Pink Floyd's *Dark Side Of The Moon* before it settled down to something more substantial twelve and a half minutes in. Johann Strauss's *Blue Danube* (à la *2001: A Space Odyssey*) opened a section punctuated by a keyboard facsimile of Eric Stewart's piano melody from 10cc's 'I'm Not In Love', Tangerine Dream synth drones and opera singing. The second half of the thirty-eight-minute Ambient excursion was more beat-oriented, its finale a Pink Floyd heartbeat segued into the sound of crashing waves. Said Cauty about the results: 'It was all done on Oberheim keyboards. Loads of samples were chucked in, big-sounding classical loops and choral edits. Nothing was prepared, I started on a Monday morning and just jammed the whole thing. By Friday it was all done.'

At the beginning of 1991 Cauty and Drummond again reached number one in the UK with a seven-inch remix of '3 A.M. Eternal'. By early spring they had released their most commercial album, *The White Room* (Jams), a slick compendium of 'Stadium House' hits, Progressive House and Ambient Reggae tunes. In 1992 they were voted Best British Group by the UK industry, an accolade they responded to by dumping a dead sheep smeared with the letters 'KLF' at the awards ceremony. In 1993 Cauty and Drummond returned as The K Foundation, with an agenda to shake up the art world as much as they had the music scene. Their first move was to nail £40,000 to a canvas and chain it to the railings of London's Tate Gallery as an award for the worst British artist. Their second objective was to turn £1 million into some kind of art statement. After much thought they supposedly burned the money in a boathouse on Jura during the summer of 1994, a spectacularly Ambient gesture which seemed to conclude the duo's fascinating career.

LISTENING

In 1988 TVT in New York released an album titled *The History Of The Jams*, an excellent compilation of some of the highlights from The JAMs' short but eventful career. It goes without saying that *Chill Out* (Jams 1990) is an essential recording in the evolution of both Ambient and House music. If it can be found, Jimmy Cauty's *Space* (KLF 1990) has a lot to recommend it.

THE STONE ROSES AND PRIMAL SCREAM

Before the summer of 1989 the UK Acid House scene was still an underground phenomenon, albeit a rapidly expanding one. During that summer everything was changed by the release of the 'technicolour masterpiece' that was *The Stone Roses*. This was a debut album which pulled Indie guitar music into the candy-coloured world of Ecstasy as guitar riffs and careful song arrangements gave way to body-swerving beats. There were shades of LA psychedelia, The Beatles and Simon & Garfunkel, but the real meat was when the enormous rhythm section exploded in your ears, like on the opener, 'I Wanna Be Adored'. This was House music played by a rock band. It was the most innovative sound in UK rock since the heydays of Led Zeppelin. It spawned a new form, best described as Ravedelia, and hot-wired the spread of House and Techno all around the country. In the early 1990s the Scottish group Primal Scream picked up the mantle and made the most psychedelic album in the UK since the 1960s. They called it *Screamadelica*, a 1991 confection which was to become the glorious apex of Ecstasy rock.

The Stone Roses were officially formed in 1984 but it would take until 1987 for the classic line-up of singer Ian Brown, guitarist John Squire, bassist Gary 'Mani' Mounfield and drummer Alan 'Reni' Wren to gel. All were born in the early 1960s. Brown and Squire grew up together in the poorest parts of Manchester. Brown's earliest memories of Squire date back to the age of four. During their early teens they formed a strong bond at secondary school, sharing an interest in rock music. Brown, a convert to boxing and karate, championed punk heroes like The Clash while fine artist Squire favoured The Beatles. The extrovert Brown looked to Northern Soul all-night dance parties for inspiration while the introverted Squire seriously took up the guitar at fifteen. He formed one outfit with Mani Mounfield in 1982 before Brown was encouraged to join him as vocalist. The Stone Roses followed their punk ideals until the addition of drummer Reni Wren in 1985. The darkly exotic Reni made the group more rhythmically sophisticated. Legend has it that one day the trio of Brown, Squire and Wren bumped into Mani walking up a Manchester street just when they were looking for a new bassist. That was in 1987.

The Roses had already met Gareth Evans, who owned a number of Manchester clubs. He became their manager and allowed them writing and rehearsal space. Their local following, gained from playing warehouse parties, was in the thousands. For years they had organized their own gigs, now they were in serious demand. In early summer of 1988 The Roses signed an eight-album deal with the Silvertone label, which gave them much creative freedom, including the use of Squire's Abstract Expressionist paintings as cover art. A number of influences were now impinging on the group. Musically, John Squire acknowledged The Velvet Underground via the stripped-down rock sound of The Jesus & Mary Chain and early Primal Scream. He also loved Carlos Santana. Ian Brown advocated Reggae and 1960s psychedelia by Hendrix, Pink Floyd and Love. Reni and Mani were into heavy metal and funk. As far as stimulants were concerned the group had long forsaken amphetamines for LSD, marijuana and Ecstasy. Looking around for a suitable producer they were directed to John Leckie (producer of Be-Bop Deluxe) after enthusing about his results on the psychedelic mindfeast *Psonic Psunspot* (Virgin 1987) by XTC as The Dukes Of Stratosphear. Demos were passed, rehearsals attended. Leckie was convinced of their greatness and agreed to midwife their debut album.

The Stone Roses was recorded in London and South Wales. Emphasis was on the performance of songs, some of which had been written five years earlier. Leckie was mesmerized at the Mani-Reni rhythm machine, Squire's effortless funky lead guitar and Brown's messianic lead vocal presence. The May 1989 release of *The Stone Roses* was greeted with euphoria. Here was an album as fresh as mountain pine, shot through with classic pop references, full of futuristic possibilities for rock. Squire made no secret of his admiration for Jimi Hendrix's studio wizardry, especially on *Are You Experienced* (1967). *The Stone Roses* began with 'I Wanna Be Adored', a declamatory House-rock track that seemed to sweep away everything before it. Out of Ambient noise emerged a snaking bass melody over which was heard the gleaming sprinkled tones of Squire's Gibson electric. Then the shockingly beautiful juxtaposition of Reni's four-on-the-floor Chicago House beat before Brown's plea for universal love soared over the top. I challenge anyone not to be moved by this heavenly sound. The opening alone will send rivulets of pleasure up and down your spine. This was Ecstasy rock *in excelsis*.

If The Stone Roses were perceived as the new psychedelia, then 'Waterfall' and 'Don't Stop' were the reason. Trickling up-tempo guitar from Squire framed a tale of a young girl's voyage of hallucinogenic discovery as the rhythm section danced in the background. Three minutes in and Squire hit the wah-wah pedal, nodded in the direction of Hendrix, before the whole burst into a million shards of sonic light. 'Don't Stop' was the same track vamped through the mixing desk, an iridescent creation of backwards guitar solo (recalling Hendrix's 'Third Stone From The Song'), high-frequency percussive sounds simulating Indian sitar and Brown's Ecstasy-fuelled mantra about shining people. The backdrop of pristine House rhythms made this the stand-out track. The other jingle-jangle Byrds- and Beatles-styled songs plus the Simon & Garfunkel homage 'Elizabeth My Dear' did not detract from the album's achievement. The fact that the innovative material was framed by pleasing pop and rock made it all the more startling. The album's valedictory eight-minute 'I Am The Resurrection' was like a gauntlet thrown in the face of the UK music industry. A thumping beat ushered in more declamations from Brown about new youth energy and resurgence. Again Squire came up trumps with some lovingly cascading guitar work and three and a half minutes in the track became his. Funky riffing, feedback and slabs of noise backed to the hilt by a barnstorming rhythm section said it all. This was instrumentally astonishing rock music, as tonally elegant as anything by Led Zeppelin in their prime. When Squire finessed the end of a blistering blues riff, a chiming acoustic reprise of 'I Wanna Be Adored' came in before the whole combusted in one giant psychedelic crescendo.

The group toured to great acclaim, their independence amplified by an almost 'punk' defiance of authority and the media. Famously, they rejected a support slot with The Rolling Stones and had the plug pulled on them by the BBC for being too loud. Late in 1989 they released 'Fool's Gold', a defiant slice of Ravedelia. Drum loops, slivery bass work, circular percussion and Squire's ratchety, effects-laden guitar conjured up an anthem for the Ecstasy generation. This was pure Acid dance music played by brilliant rock instrumentalists. At this point The Stone Roses were on top of the world; photographed in the Swiss Alps, there seemed to be nothing to stop them becoming as big as The Beatles.

Then things started to go seriously awry. They began 1990 by trashing a former record company because of an unofficial video release. This landed the group in court and jail. A summer festival at Spike Island in the Mersey estuary saw 30,000 fans wait six hours, with no adequate refreshments, for The Roses to take the stage. Poor organization lost the group nearly £500,000. A US tour was cancelled but their summer 1990 single 'One Love' included a lengthy Ambient composition, 'Something's Burning' – shuffling drums, deft Squire licks, atmospheric production. This piece of gold did nothing to lift the spirits of a group bogged down in legal red tape. After deciding to leave Silvertone, they were prevented by a court injunction from releasing anything from the ongoing Welsh recording sessions with John Leckie. Also, John Squire was becoming obsessed with playing and acting like Jimmy Page. By the summer of 1991 Silvertone relinquished their hold and The Stone Roses signed to Geffen in the US for millions of dollars. Finally the group played live to huge American audiences on both coasts.

Artistic differences and cocaine use were said to be dividing the band. After a protracted period John Leckie opted out of the second album sessions, feeling the 'spark had gone stale'. After years of anticipation *Second Coming* was released near the end of 1994, to universal disappointment. Rumours of Squire's Jimmy Page obsession were no idle speculations – the pre-album single 'Love Spreads' was vintage mid-1970s blowsy Led Zeppelin blues-rock. The album's 'Driving South' was more Zepp, made worse by its blatant stealing of Hendrix's famous 1968 'Voodoo Chile' riff. There was more midnight-blues, Stones-Zeppelin pastiche but over time people began to appreciate the good songs. Certainly the productions in which Leckie was involved were better. 'Ten Storey Love Song' began with a psychedelic flourish, its declamatory style reminiscent of the 1989 album. 'Begging You' was fearsome House/Techno, a rolling firestorm of beats to a jerky blues guitar and wailing Brown vocal. 'How Do You Sleep' was another of their candy-coloured grooves. Elsewhere producer Simon Dawson birthed some great performances: 'Breaking Into Heaven' was wondrous spatial Ambience opening on to a dramatic rock vista; 'Daybreak', infectious, fast and celebratory; 'Your Star Will Shine', chunky acoustic Beatles-era psychedelia; 'Tightrope', tight acoustic-guitar rock; 'Tears', pastoral English folk meets typical Roses rock swagger.

Little did they know it at the time, but *Second Coming* would be The Stone Roses' swansong. Before the spring 1995 tour got underway, Reni Wren was out of the band. Personal injury to Squire (a broken collarbone) led to cancellation of the group's headlining slot at Glastonbury. By the end of the year it was sad to witness a divided Stone Roses on stage, Ian Brown on one side and Squire, with his Jimmy Page-slung Gibson and Marshall stack, on the other. By the spring of 1996 Squire had gone, having completed 180 shows on the 'Second Coming' world tour. Brown struggled on with Mani and other musicians but by the end of the summer the Stone Roses saga was over. As they had emerged from Acid House, the sudden glare and expectation of the world's media had catapulted them into overwhelming fame. The brilliance of their debut album notwithstanding, their entry into the world rock machine crucially cut them adrift from the very roots which vitalized their original music.

Primal Scream came from the opposite direction – from rock into Ecstasy Rave. In fact they were a traditional po-faced British independent guitar-clang group before they discovered the marvels of Ecstasy. Bobby Gillespie, born in Glasgow in 1964, met Velvet Underground-styled band The Jesus & Mary Chain in 1984. He then sent their demos to his friend Alan McGee at the London-based Creation label and facilitated a recording contract. In fact the same year he became their drummer and gained a live support slot for his own group, Primal Scream. Steeped in the bare rock 'n' roll sound of archetypal punk rockers The Clash and The Sex Pistols, Primal Scream eventually centred around Gillespie as vocalist and guitarists Robert Young and Andrew Innes. Their 1987 Creation debut, *Sonic Flower Groove*, entwined a US East and West Coast 60s influence with their indie guitar sound, while 1989's *Primal Scream* (Creation) had more than a touch of blues metal, notably Led Zeppelin. Though their early work was seen to influence The Stone Roses the latter album was uninspired. Primal Scream were well on their way to obscurity and then they discovered Acid House.

Gillespie and the band began hanging out at raves and were astonished by the sheer energy of the new Ecstasy culture. They met DJ Andrew Weatherall, who liked their musical taste and agreed to have a go at remixing part of their second album. Gillespie was impressed with the fact that it would be his first time in a proper recording studio and after some work 'Loaded' was unveiled to universal acclaim. Riding high in the UK charts, 'Loaded' began the 1990s with an affirmative yes for Rave rock. The track opened with an excerpt from a 60s Peter Fonda film where the iconic hippie actor talks about 'having a good time and getting loaded', presumably on drugs. Then Weatherall's Housey beat-driven production takes over as lazily in the background steel guitar, soul horns and Gospel diva vocals (reminiscent of the late-60s Rolling Stones) cruise along in one huge celebratory groove. With riffing electric guitar inserts the entire seven minutes of 'Loaded' was pure exhilaration.

Throughout 1990 and 1991, in various London studios, Primal Scream experimented with breakbeats, Ambient House and Techno in a glorious quest to create the perfect acid-trip rock. One Creation single after the other was released, each one pushing at the perimeters of rock and dance cultures. Yet the sheer genius of the music wouldn't be apparent until it was all available in one place, namely the classic *Screamadelica*, released near the end of 1991. *Screamadelica* was drenched in hallucinogenic drugs, an album where psychedelia, House, Techno, blues, rock, soul and electronica merged with the surrounding Ecstasy culture. 'Come Together' was Rap pushed into the stratosphere, a looping orgasm of drum beats, bass riffs, the soaring Gospel vocal of black Mancunian Denise Johnson and the sampled voice of the US politician the Reverend Jesse Jackson. 'Higher Than The Sun' merged Gillespie's laconic stoned intonation with a wonderfully rubbery production by The Orb which coursed through many fantastical variations on House and Techno beats. 'Higher Than The Sun' was perfect 'rock/Ravedelia', the very sonic consti-tuents and lyrics mirroring the 'never felt so fantastic in my life' quality of the initiate's first Ecstasy experience.

In fact 'Higher Than The Sun' appeared twice, its second spaced-out incarnation subtitled 'a Dub symphony', with Dub elements courtesy of Weatherall's drum mixing and Jah Wobble's bass. Yet nothing could touch the sheer blissed-outness of The Orb's version, then kings of Ambient House. Elsewhere there was a beat-laden, sitar-buzzing, a thickly laden version of Texas psychedelians The 13th Floor Elevators' 'Slip Inside This House' and a stomping, blipping, Chicago House-influenced Denise Johnson cut, 'Don't Fight It, Feel It'. The rotund, beautiful soul singer Johnson was an essential ingredient in the transformation of The Scream into bona-fide dance-floor rockers. The Weatherall-produced 'Inner Flight' and 'Shine Like Stars' were like early-morning lullabies for the post-Ecstasy come-down – all gossamer, dawn light and sea surf. And not to let you forget where they were really coming from, Primal Scream engaged Rolling Stones producer Jimmy Miller to give the early-70s Jagger-Richards touch to the Gospel rocker 'Movin' On Up' and the booming acoustic-electric ballad 'Damaged'.

Screamadelica was toured with great intensity, the gigs featuring support DJ sets from both The Orb and Andrew Weatherall. Gillespie and Denise Johnson were a magic vocal pairing, backed by two guitarists, bass, drums, keyboards and computer programmer. Gillespie urged the throngs 'to get their rocks off' in the sense of getting high on drugs. In fact the group made no effort to hide their love of drugs, Gillespie espousing the use of magic mushrooms, Ecstasy and hashish alongside harder drugs like cocaine and amphetamines. As the tour wound around the world The Scream (particularly Gillespie and guitarist Young) began living out a Rolling Stones fantasy. Recorded in Memphis and Hollywood in 1993, *Give Out, But Don't Give Up* (1994) replaced the scorching Ecstasy highs of *Screamadelica* with a rootsy American sound courtesy of the Atlantic label's producer Tom Dowd and famed psychedelic funkster George Clinton. Though it was fine funk-soul rock (Denise Johnson's diva vocals were particularly good), with the exception of the kaleidoscopic Declan Lynch mix of 'Struttin', *Give Out, But Don't Give Up* was a step backwards.

Andrew Innes, the guitarist-keyboardist (in whose London flat part of *Screamadelica* was recorded) decided to push the group back towards innovation. On holiday in Ibiza during the summer of 1995 trippy songs began to emanate from Gillespie's head. During 1996 Innes directed proceedings in London and by the end of the year Mani Mounfield had joined them from the ranks of the disintegrated Stone Roses. In Birmingham's Moseley Shoals studio things began to really move and by the summer of 1997 Primal Scream had another great album in the shops. *Vanishing Point* was a companion album to *Screamadelica*, more sepia-toned in its cool Dub Reggae sound and a veritable tribute to the 1971 road movie *Vanishing Point*, where a rebellious ex-cop decides to drive a Dodge Challenger from Denver to San Francisco, ignoring all speed limits along the way.

'Burning Wheel' opened the proceedings with a sound collage which swiftly moved into the organ-clouded, ratchety-electric-guitar era of Syd Barrett's Pink Floyd. Then the song was tugged up into a thumping House beat accompanied by Gillespie's strung-out vocal before returning to the autumnal sound of early Floyd. 'Get Duffy' was instrumental, a grooveride with bass clarinet for companionship. 'Kowalski' (the hero of *Vanishing Point*) included the film's DJ voice-overs and was a kind of homage to *Tago Mago*-era Can. Gillespie's voice mirrored Can singer Damo Suzuki, the electronic chaos of the track like that of Can's album. Incidentally, *Tago Mago* was released the same year (1971) as the Richard Sarafian film.

Producer Declan Lynch was credited with stereo panning, test tones and vintage synthesizers. Even Andrew Weatherall was back on board for the ebullient 'Trainspotting', a kicking Dub statement with echoing percussion, shimmering keyboards and a descending guitar figure lifted in part from Jack

Bruce's bass solo on Cream's 1967 hit 'Sunshine Of Your Love'. Reggae legend Augustus Pablo played melodica on the sublime Dub ballad 'Star', where Gillespie sings 'everybody is a star' in some kind of Ecstasy glow. Generally, though, *Vanishing Point* wasn't the 'Higher Than The Sun' vibe of *Screamadelica*. 'Into The Void' more than hinted at the darker corners of drug excess, its twilight guitar sound at odds with a mind-blowingly swooshy production sound. Squealing Octave Cat synth, pounding bass, vocodered vocals, echoing Dub Reggae grooves, garage rock and, of course, one Stones pastiche made up the rest of the album.

At the time of *Vanishing Point*'s release Gillespie talked of a love for the Trip-Hop of Tricky, 'the classical noise of Stockhausen' and the electronic explorations of the BBC Radiophonic Workshop. Denise Johnson was no longer with them but Primal Scream were again on the cutting edge. As if *Vanishing Point* wasn't dubby enough, the group handed over the tapes to Adrian Sherwood, who gave it a further Reggae boost in his renowned On–U Sound London studios. *Echo Dek* (1997) even featured Jamaican singer Prince Far I. Having reunited with dance culture, the Scream were happy to follow its lead. By the end of the 1990s they had readied more new music, this time with the help of Big Beat supremos The Chemical Brothers.

LISTENING

The Stone Roses (Silvertone 1989) was the most important rock album to be released during the UK Acid House music explosion. It united a generation and pointed the way forward for a new music which combined the repetitive rhythms of House and Techno with the melodic sophistication of great rock. The compilation *Turns Into Stone* (Silvertone 1992) contains full versions of the 1989 twelve-inch dance classic 'Fool's Gold' plus the Ambient sound-painting 'Something's Burning'. *Second Coming* (Geffen 1994) has some great sonic moments.

If there is only one Primal Scream album in your collection then it has to be *Screamadelica* (1991), a perfect historical prism on Rave music possibilities of the early 1990s. All relevant Primal Scream albums are on Creation. Both *Vanishing Point* (1997), with its widescreen instrumentalities, and the remix disc *Echo Dek* (1997) are well worth seeking out.

ORBITAL

One of the most sophisticated Techno groups to emerge from the UK in the 1990s, Orbital drew their inspiration from a myriad of sources. Their multi-dimensional sound embraced elements of Steve Reich, Philip Glass, Kraftwerk, Afrika Bambaataa, Grandmaster Flash, post-punk groups like New Order and

Cabaret Voltaire, early 1980s Electro-bop units like The Human League and of course the US House, Acid House and Techno scenes. Named after the London-encircling M25 motorway (meeting point for many legendary raves), Orbital saw themselves as 'garage electronicists'. Their name also conveyed their fondness for tape-loop systems à la Steve Reich. On record their talent was in assembling a diverse array of timbres and systematizing them into a polychromatic whole. Tracks such as the glowing 'Halcyon And On And On' (1992) were milestones of Ambient Techno music, deserving their own description 'soundtracks to the computer age'.

Brothers Phil and Paul Hartnoll were born in Kent, southern England, in the 1960s. Their earliest musical memories were creating drones on their father's organ. Both did labouring jobs on building sites and were inspired by punk rock to fiddle about with guitars. Paul, born 1968, the younger brother by four years, attended art classes at Hastings College before diving into a musical career. Pure electronica coming out of the BBC Radiophonic Workshop was an inspiration, as was the anarcho-politico expression of the punk and commune group Crass. Tired of dead-end jobs and inspired by Sheffield's Cabaret Voltaire, the duo bought a cheap Roland TR-909 drum machine and some economical Korg synthesizers.

Infected with the Acid House virus, Orbital officially came into existence in 1987. Buoyed by the dynamics of club and DJ culture, the Hartnolls eventually released their debut twelve-inch single on O-Zone, a label founded by a DJ on the then pirate radio station Kiss FM. 'Chime' was another Rave anthem – squelchy Roland 303 rhythm box with the added flair of finely drawn string synthesizers and bobbing rhythm sequences. They played live and were signed to London's ffrr imprint in the spring of 1990. When 'Chime' was reissued a month later it entered the Top Twenty of the UK singles charts.

In London Orbital were seen as 'just another dance act', but the duo had other ambitions. Live, they wanted to play their equipment like any other band, eschewing reliance on backing-tape systems. Their studio was a mobile array of synthesizer keyboards and modules, samplers, sequencing units and a small mixing desk. They took this set-up on the road, eventually touring the US, Australia and Europe several times.

'Halcyon And On And On' was released as part of an EP titled 'Radiccio' but soon topped the UK dance-floor charts as a track in its own right. Nearly ten minutes long, 'Halcyon' opened with slow, lush synth chords backing a foreground of tinkly piano loops. Then an ethereal voice floated into view (a sample of the aerated singer of pop group Opus III), to which was added a suspenseful descending bass-synth melody. Then more Opus vocal loops took up the chorus while underneath a chiming guitar sample could be heard. If this wasn't enough the track then transformed into a tight House drum-rhythm groove before returning to variations on the vocal samples. Synth drones filled in the far distance as if 'Halcyon' was an aural painting. The softness of its tones, coupled with Orbital's careful tracking, made for an ecstatic celebration in sound. Reputedly written in a single afternoon, 'Halcyon' functioned as both dance music and chill-out balm. It became the centrepiece of Orbital's second album, untitled like the first and released in the spring of 1993.

Though Orbital were now perfectly in tune with Rave culture and were in-demand remixers (The Shamen and Yellow Magic Orchestra had both benefited from their skills), they still saw themselves as Techno anarchists. They didn't rent expensive studios but opted instead to buy cheap electronic units and lease rehearsal spaces to record on the hoof. Their 1994 album *Snivilisation* was a left-field concept whose vocal samples were aimed squarely at the economic waste and runaway materialism of late-twentieth-century Western society. Orbital played new technology coupled with old synths (ARP, Oberheim, OSCar). Pushed along by a Technicolour array of rhythm tracks, *Snivilisation* possessed a powerful organic presence. The sudden appearance of squirty Acid House sounds reminded one that Orbital possessed not one but two silver Roland 303 drum boxes. At times the music sounded as if the machines were set up and let run by themselves. 'Philosophy By Numbers' even echoed Kraftwerk's 1981 album *Computer World*. Another vintage German electronic group, NEU!, were honoured by the inclusion of some thrash rock just as on *NEU! '75*. The album ended in a melisma of female vocals and gleaming electronic Ambience.

The year of *Snivilisation* saw Orbital become one of the main attractions at the annual Glastonbury Festival, a huge tradition which saw hippie, indie-rock and House/Techno cultures converge in one locale in the hundreds of thousands. By 1995 Orbital were voted the best live Techno act in the world. They used a Beckman Oscilloscope to create dazzling sine-wave images which were synched directly with their music. Using two sequencers and massive volume, Orbital were able to improvise new electronic creations right there in front of audiences in any location. At the end of the twentieth century their workmanlike approach, love of sound and lack of pretentiousness resulted in drawing the public closer to electronic music and its various processes.

LISTENING

'Chime' can be heard on Orbital's first untitled ffrr album from 1991, often referred to as the 'green' album. Relicensed to the London label's subsidiary Internal, Orbital's second untitled long-player (1993) featured 'Halcyon And On And On' and was known as the 'brown' album. *Snivilisation* (Internal 1994) is still their finest work, a sonic trip through electronic music history past and present. It reached number four in the UK charts. In 1996 Orbital wrote a four-movement suite for a film called *The Box*, which subsequently appeared on the double-disc *In Sides* (Internal 1996). A favourite among film and TV producers, Orbital busied themselves at the audiovisual console before returning with another chart success in *The Middle Of Nowhere* (ffrr 1999) – a disc which opened with Mexicana brass and worked its way through electronic noise, heavy-metal

Techno and Hispanic Trance before closing with the familiar synth sounds of early Kraftwerk.

ENIGMA AND SPIRITUAL HOUSE

During the autumn of 1990 a curious track emerged from Germany which mixed a European House beat with South American flute and Gregorian chant. A triumph of seamless sampling, 'Sadeness' went to number one in twenty-three countries and became a dance-floor sensation. Credited to Enigma, the track heralded a form of House music which had strong spiritual overtones. Given Ecstasy culture's will to communion and its celebratory nature, Enigma's music 'for body and soul' was a tailor-made soundtrack. In fact it was the most visible tip of a trend towards 'religiosity' exemplified by Sheffield's 'Nine O'Clock Service' Techno church and million-selling CD sets of Catholic chant by Spanish monks.

Michael Cretu, a Romanian, was born in Bucharest in 1957. A gifted classical musician since the age of nine, he graduated with distinction from the Frankfurt Conservatory in the late 1970s. Though he was heading towards a career as a pianist, his job as a successful arranger and producer of mainstream German pop and rock albums took off in the 1980s. Cretu signed to Virgin in 1983 and was producing Mike Oldfield by 1987. He married singer Sandra Lauer in 1988 and settled in Ibiza, where the pair built a recording studio.

Cretu's life was literally transformed by the island's dance-music boom. Delving into computer and sampling techniques, Cretu (with the help of his partner) came up with 'Sadeness', a ravishing House track which featured sensual female voice, Andean pipes and the trademark sound of Franciscan friars singing the centuries-old liturgy. By the end of 1990 'Sadeness' was a worldwide number-one smash. It was immediately followed up by the startling album *MCMXC A.D.* (Virgin 1990), which came with an image of a hooded figure emanating light in front of a cross. Female voices sang in French and English, there were Latin titles and Latin Gregorian chants, orgasmic groans, Eastern melismas, snatches of the alien theme from Spielberg's 1977 film *Close Encounters Of The Third Kind*, sparkling pianos, heartbeats, high-pitched guitars and the relentless House rhythms of programmed drums. Everywhere there were beautifully deployed tones as if Cretu had spent years painting the sound on to his computer screen. It was variously described as 'epiphanous dance-floor music', 'like new Pink Floyd', 'mood/trip music' and 'intoxicating sound scenery'.

Enigma weren't the only musicians to use Early Music in their mixes. In 1989 The Beloved had sampled the plainchant (or unison singing) compositions of the twelfth-century German abbess Hildegard of Bingen. Her evocation of celestial revelation chimed perfectly with the gushing Ecstasy feel of their hit

'Sun Rising'. Later the Australian classical composer Barrington Pheloung even went as far as dubbing a House track on to a new recording of Allegri's *Miserere*, an ethereal example of plainchant and polyphonic (multi-voiced) choral writing by an early-seventeenth-century priest of Rome's Sistine Chapel. Pheloung did this for a 1992 episode of the hit Central TV series *Inspector Morse* titled 'Cherubim and Seraphim' (a reference to child spirits and angels). Though a highly accomplished academic, Pheloung spoke of having 'roots in both soul and Eurodisco' and was a total convert to Akai sampling and Notator computer techniques. The famous *Morse* episode centred around Ecstasy culture and beatific visions, its use of a specially created 'spiritual House' soundtrack complementing its theme of chemically aided ecstatic revelation.

This 'spiritual' trend was taken to its furthest limit by a young Anglican vicar in Sheffield who founded the notorious 'Nine O'Clock Service'. Within an environment of glowing crosses, lasers and dancing, this new Techno church was said to be wooing young people back to God. In reality what was happening was that Ecstasy was fuelling the worship and the whole exercise was turning into just another hedonistic cult with the vicar as all-powerful figurehead. On a broader level Enigma's music opened up a market for plainchant exemplified by the success of a group of monks from the Santo Domingo de Silos monastery in Spain. In 1993 EMI released *Canto Gregoriano*, a two-CD set of Gregorian incantation which topped both the popular and classical charts in the UK and sold millions the world over.

Meanwhile the Cretus were still enjoying the long, balmy evenings of Ibiza. The second Enigma album, *Cross Of Changes* (1993), had a more ethnic feel and was another platinum-selling number one. A single from the recording, 'Return To Innocence', soared to the top of the charts in eight different countries. By 1996 Enigma had sold a total of twenty-five million records and were considered the most successful act ever to emerge from Germany. In fact Cretu's music was a ubiquitous international presence in film, advertising, fashion and sport. Album number three, 1996's *Le Roi Est Mort, Vive Le Roi* ('the king is dead, long live the king') sounded laboured compared to its predecessors, though it was immaculately crafted, with effective use of NASA spaceshot samples, widescreen Ambient keyboard and electronic washes plus a variety of rhythm tracks.

Enigma's fourth opus, *The Screen Behind The Mirror* (Virgin 2000), was a return to form, its multi-dimensional music made memorable by the use of samples from Carl Orff's dramatic 1937 choral and percussive masterpiece *Carmina Burana*.

LISTENING

Enigma have always been signed to Virgin Germany. *MCMXC A.D.* (1990) is the definitive album and an influential one at that. In 1991 Cretu assembled *MCMXC A.D. – The Limited Edition*, which replaced the original cover apparition with a 3D colour hologram. It included four extra mixes of 'Sadeness', 'Mea Culpa', 'Principles of Lust' and 'The Rivers of Belief' credited to Curly M.C., a Cretu pseudonym.

THE ORB AND AMBIENT HOUSE

Ambient House began its life as a form of post-Rave come-down music concocted in a South London squat during the late 1980s. Out of these DJ sessions emerged The Orb, a group who made extremely long House tracks filled with textural Ambience and space. Drawing on influences as diverse as Chicago House, Steve Reich, Brian Eno, Cluster, Dub Reggae and 70s rock (specifically that of Pink Floyd) The Orb made the idea of cool, spacey House enormously popular. Initially viewed with suspicion by the UK music press, The Orb's Ambient House music eventually reached number one in the UK album charts with the 1992 'Dubcore' classic *U.F.Orb*. Against all predictions, The Orb became a live sensation, a spectacular sound and light extravaganza which broke the US in 1995. Extremely important in the history of House and in late-twentieth-century music as a whole, The Orb opened all music to the liberating democracy of the sampler.

The dynamic of The Orb was always in the hands of its one constant member, Alex Paterson, who was born near Battersea, South London, in 1960. This fact may explain the use of Battersea's distinctive abandoned power station on the sleeves of early Orb albums. Paterson's father died at the age of three and he ended up at a local school for children from broken homes. An indifferent student, his only early passion was for chess, at which he excelled. At this school he met African-born Martin Glover, later to be called Youth when he played bass in the punk rock group Killing Joke. Paterson became the drum roadie for the band, whose lead singer, Jaz Coleman, would later work with Anne Dudley of The Art Of Noise.

An early moment of enlightenment came in 1979 when Paterson first heard Eno's then current Ambient album *Music For Films* on EG Records. He was on a Killing Joke tour and remembered taking LSD and listening to Eno's record over and over again in a tenth-floor room 'as I viewed the Ruhr steel works explode in the distance. The scene seemed to be taking place in the music as well.' When Killing Joke fell apart Paterson joined EG as an A&R man in 1986. He listened more and more closely to Eno and was impressed by the clarity of his music. Then Paterson heard the silken Chicago House of Larry 'Mr Fingers' Heard and was an instant convert. He began DJing with Jimmy Cauty of The KLF. When UK Acid House burst into the countryside in 1989, Paterson and Cauty would return, after a rave, to Cauty's South London Trancentral studio on Sunday morning and make long, winding experimental mixes minus the kicking drums. Paterson contends that out of these chill-out sessions emerged early versions of the KLF hits '3 A.M. Eternal' and 'What Time Is Love?' alongside the first fantastic Orb track, 'Loving You'.

The year 1989 also saw Paterson get a job as Ambient DJ at The Land Of Oz, based in London's Heaven club. Resident dance DJ Paul Oakenfold felt that Ambient music was a good way to clear the dance floor but the Chill Out Room caught on and developed its own subcultural popularity, complete with brain machines, guarana drinks and light shows. Paterson, Cauty and now Youth were the players in the evolution of Ambient House as multiple sources as diverse as Eno, hypnotherapy recordings, Manuel Göttsching's *E2–E4* and more were mixed into a seemingly endless sound continuum. Paterson remembers the Chill Out room as 'an eight-track mixer with four or five record decks where we'd loop the intro of 808 State's "Pacific State" minus the drums into parts of The Beloved's "Sun Rising". One night we even conceived a version of 10cc's "I'm Not In Love" which went on for two whole hours!' The culmination of all this activity came at the end of 1989 when Paterson and Cauty recorded 'Loving You' as a session for BBC Radio 1's John Peel. Over twenty minutes of bright, translucent sounds ticked by as waves lapped, voices harmonized in ecstasy, keyboards tinkled and the sky-high vocal of Minnie Ripperton's 1975 number-one song 'Loving You' floated on the airwaves. The track was even graced by a sample of David Gilmour's trademark guitar chime from Pink Floyd's 1975 masterwork 'Shine On You Crazy Diamond'. Now rechristened 'A Huge Ever Pulsating Brain That Rules From The Centre Of The Ultraworld (Loving You)', the track was an immediate classic. The Orb had arrived.

The year 1990 began with the release of The KLF's Ambient manifesto, *Chill Out*. Coming direct from the same Trancentral sessions that had produced 'Loving You', *Chill Out* featured no credit to Paterson and soon after its release Jimmy Cauty split from The Orb. Work in progress ended up as the Cauty solo album *Space* (KLF 1990) and Paterson carried on with the help of Youth. Mindful of independence, Paterson had long formed his own imprint, Wau! Mr Modo, which went through the dance label Big Life Records. 'Loving You' was re-released several times but the real coup was 'Little Fluffy Clouds', credited to Paterson and Youth and released in the winter of 1990, to become an instant House smash. The nine-minute twelve-inch original was framed around American singer Rickie Lee Jones's reminiscences about the natural beauty of Arizona, where she grew up. Heard over the introduction was the distinctive harmonica tone from Ennio Morricone's theme for the 1968 film *Once Upon A Time In The West*. Swooping plane engine sounds were also audible until the start-up of Steve Reich's 1987 Minimalist piece for guitarist Pat Metheny, *Electric Counterpoint*. Radio broadcast snippets, bells, various synth stabs and electronic whoops led the listener into the familiar thumping beat of House. Defined by a soft but deep production sound with crystal clarity and excellent separation, 'Little Fluffy Clouds' made the accelerated 130bpm of Hardcore Techno seem primitive by comparison.

Still holding down his A&R job at EG, Alex Paterson (now known as Dr Alex in clubs owing to his mind-tweaking Ambient mixes) was assembling a vast amount of musical ideas. Sound samples had been recorded in Barcelona, Berlin and New York. Youth was on board, his interest in Led Zeppelin, Can and Reggae of vital importance to Paterson's aims. Also, Paterson had met a young engineer named Kristian 'Thrash' Weston in a Battersea studio. Born in the early 1970s, 'Thrash' (who came from a metal-rock background) had a wondrous grasp of new technology. His world was Akai samplers, computer software, outboard sound processors and vintage synthesizers like the Moog and Prophet 5. Paterson had great ideas for sounds; Thrash could turn those ideas into luminous reality. At least half a dozen London studios were used and twenty outside musicians were involved in an intense two-month session which became The Orb's debut album, *Adventures Beyond The Ultraworld*, released in the spring of 1991.

A double-disc/LP affair wrapped in black and opening out to reveal a cover showing Battersea power station (obvious stylistic references to Pink Floyd), *Adventures Beyond The Ultraworld* was a gauntlet thrown down to all those who had sniffed at the idea of Ambient House. Bookended by 'Little Fluffy Clouds' and 'Loving You', the album's contents not only pushed House music into another dimension but set new standards for Ambient sound production. Thrash was reputed to have used a Cyclosonic panner to throw the music around the mix in three dimensions. Though only twenty-four-track recording was used, Thrash's treatments of found voices, news broadcasts and various musical styles from Reggae to space-rock were quite remarkable.

Disc One contained a virtual recreation in sound of the *Apollo 11* moonshot. Here Paterson and Thrash were ably assisted by the guitarist Steve Hillage and his partner Miquette Giraudy. Hillage, famous for his glissando, or sliding, style of electric guitar playing, had led the French hippie-rock group Gong in the early 1970s before working with the American studio ace Todd Rundgren. Hillage's interest in both electronic music and New Age concerns led to the recording of the astonishing *Rainbow Dome Musick* (Virgin 1979) for a London spiritual festival. Undramatic, tonal, Minimalist and beautiful in its mixture of Tibetan bells, soft keyboards and synthesizer timbres, *Rainbow Dome Musick* attracted the attention of Paterson, who described it as 'Ambient linear' and 'great to mix to'. In fact Paterson met Hillage while playing the album at The Land Of Oz. The *Adventures Beyond The Ultraworld* tracks 'Supernova At The End Of The Universe' and 'Back Side Of The Moon' were full of the essence of *Rainbow Dome Musick*. Discreet sounds of Giraudy's Moog modular synth were peppered with NASA-speak from the *Apollo 11* rocket launch and flight. Trickling electronica and splashy sounds conveyed weightless space as Dub rhythms vitalized 'Supernova'. If that wasn't Ambient enough the fourteen-minute 'Back Side Of The Moon' was a mystical evocation of the *Apollo 11* lunar landing. Drifting motion and spine-tingling Moog made for an hypnotic experience, a sampled astronaut repeating mantra-like the phrase 'I've been waiting for music like this all of my life.' Other *Apollo*-speak included 'trans-lunar injection burner' and 'on my lens cap'. This was definitive space music, Ambient psychedelia which spoke eloquently to the Ecstasy generation. Even Pink Floyd's then bass player, Guy Pratt, helped out on the slo-mo somnam-bulance of 'Spanish Castles In Space'.

Disc Two opened with the Ambient Reggae of 'Perpetual Dawn', which included genuine West Indian toasting and sampled laughter. Inspired by drum recording done in Conny Plank's Cologne studio with Killing Joke during the 1980s, Paterson and Thrash looped drum breaks for 'Into The Fourth Dimension', which included religious chorales and a string sample from Vivaldi as well as the familiar buzzing Roland 303 Acid House box. The pulsating 'Outlands' featured Berlin Techno musician Thomas Fehlmann. For the sublime 'Star 6 & 7, 8, 9', The Orb revisited such 1969 Pink Floyd pastoral sound sketches as 'Cirrus Minor' and 'Grantchester Meadows'. Paterson commented on this bright, tinkly instrumental: 'I was interested in natural sounds going through samples in a rhythmic way. Alongside the guitar played on a Yamaha DX7 synth you got a bumble bee, birds and a motorbike. The happy feeling was one of being in a big open space with that little harmony going off.'

The end of 1991 saw the release of an entire album of remixes, *Aubrey Mixes – Ultraworld Excursions*, with honours going to Youth for his Goa ethnic re-interpretation of 'Spanish Castles In Space'. By this stage The Orb were a phenomenon, having produced Primal Scream's Ecstasy anthem 'Higher Than The Sun'. Moreover Youth was getting awards for his 'Trance-dance' pop productions. Five months were spent producing the next Orb recording, the mega-single 'Blue Room', which ran for just under forty minutes. Steve Hillage played slide guitar, punk veteran Jah Wobble provided an earth-shattering bass, vocalist Aisha hummed like a heavenly angel, Miquette Giraudy played analogue synth and Paterson and Thrash tweaked knobs. Sirens, backwards guitars, sonar blips and whatnot oscillated around a pounding beat which was pure dance-floor throb. The title 'Blue Room' referred to a US Air Force base in Ohio which supposedly held downed UFOs and their alien occupants. In the summer of 1992 it made the UK Top Ten. Released soon afterwards, The Orb's second album proper, *U.F.Orb*, went to number one in the UK charts. Ambient House had made Paterson and Thrash pop stars!

U.F.Orb pushed the Ambient House idea totally in the direction of Dub Reggae. The core players were the same as on the first album, *Adventures Beyond The Ultraworld*, Youth producing one track in his own Butterfly studio. The new album had an even better sound, courtesy of the forty-eight-track SSL desk the group used for mixing in Fulham, London. Akai samplers, computers, analogue delays and the usual Oberheim twelve-voice, Prophet and Korg synthesizers were present. Sampled animal sniffs, plastic microphones used as reverbs, tape loops, deep breathing and Russian space programme recordings were some of the ingredients of *U.F.Orb*. The album opened in space as the sound field mimicked a moving spaceship, analogous to the alien-meeting soundtrack of Spielberg's 1977 film *Close Encounters Of The Third Kind*. Flute and velvet keyboards led into a rippling synth line backgrounded by splashing water which was then pushed forward by a Reggae bass riff. This Dub effect was at the heart of *U.F.Orb*, Thrash taking great pride in the way they recorded a track with drum and bass rhythms only to drop them out at key stages, thus allowing the surrounding instruments to carry the beat. This was freely adopted from Jamaican Reggae, whose artists had invented Dub in 1973.

The title track of *U.F.Orb* was straight down-to-the-dance-floor pumping House/Techno with plenty of drop-in samples. 'Blue Room' was present in a shorter seventeen-minute version! 'Towers Of Dub' (which had been remixed to mind-blowing effect by DJ friend Andrew Weatherall in 1991) demonstrated that The Orb were white Reggae's most proficient heads. There was plentiful use of synthesized bass keys and ethnic percussion on the rest of the album. Paterson made it clear that *U.F.Orb* was a 'very compact' statement. Amazingly for Ambient House's most successful act, The Orb's subsequent tour was about quaking bass sounds and laser lights all aimed at making the sold-out venues heave with dance excitement. Steve Hillage guested for his 'glissando' guitar parts and Paterson termed The Orb 'a non-centralized figure of amusement on stage'.

Humour and The Orb both went hand in hand. Offered the chance to remix Mike Oldfield's *Tubular Bells II*, the pair took the multi-tracks and erased most of the contents, coming up with 'Sentinel' (WEA 1992), a work filled with Acid House drum samples. At the beginning of 1993 they ventured to Morocco and Egypt to collect sound snippets for a projected concept album to rival anything by Pink Floyd titled *The Seven Wonders Of The World*. Thrash would spend six months working on 'a squishy bass run' of a track titled 'Plateau' for the projected release. More time was spent building a studio in Battersea and filling it with vintage equipment like ARP Odyssey, EMS Synthi and Mellotron. The Orb were even invited to remix U2. While Thrash lost himself in filters, effects boxes and wiring up analogue synths and Dr Alex dreamed of greater concepts, the financial independence underneath The Orb dissolved. Ending up in court, the duo had to unhook themselves from both production and record company and sign a new contract with Island. Their first release on the label came towards the close of 1993, a creditable live album, *Bro Evil '93*, a play on the title of Miles Davis's 1971 *Live Evil* (CBS).

The Orb were now working more closely with Swiss-German computer Techno musician Thomas Fehlmann, but their 1994 releases were disappointing. More metallic in character, *Pomme Fritz* boasted only one 'Ambient linear' track (the title) while the rest seemed to doodle in no particular direction. Strangely, this 'little album' garnered good Stateside reviews. Another project shared between Fehlmann, Weston, Paterson and guitarist Robert Fripp, *FFWD*, fell on the same stony ground of aimlessness. Fehlmann himself considered it 'an Orb track which became so long that it became a whole album!' Then, just as *FFWD* hit the store racks at the close of the summer of 1994, Thrash walked out in frustration. It seemed he hated touring and was a studio perfectionist. The Orb became Paterson, Fehlmann, engineer Andy Hughes and sundry drum and bass players.

Orbus Terrarum, released in the spring of 1995, was a substantial return to form. Intersecting sounds, dissolves, whirlpools of effects, clear vocal samples and distant rhythms brought The Orb back to their planar Trance excellence. Thrash was credited throughout, his Dub preferences intertwining perfectly with the harsher sound timbres produced by Fehlmann. Both 'Valley' and 'Plateau' featured pitch-shifted revolving sound loops. 'Oxbow Lakes' even saw Paterson play classical piano. Pedal-steel guitar, Dub, thrash metal and Detroit Techno were some of the sound highlights from the balance of *Orbus Terrarum*. The album was favoured in America, *Rolling Stone* magazine giving it its top review on release. As the 1990s evolved, The Orb continued to create. Jean–Michel Jarre's 'Oxygene Pt 8' was remixed as the trouncing Techno of 'Toxygene' in 1997 while in 1999 Paterson was even working with the German electronic pioneer Hans-Joachim Roedelius. In short, The Orb was a crucial part of House music's genesis, a unit who did more than any other to show that sampling technology could produce startlingly creative new music.

LISTENING

The Orb's first two Big Life albums, *Adventures Beyond The Ultraworld* (1991) and *U.F.Orb* (1992) (with their lavishly futuristic Designers Republic sleeves), catch Ambient House at its height. The 1991 Strange Fruit release *Peel Sessions* includes the definitive Pink Floyd-sampled mix of 'Loving You' as performed by Alex Paterson and Jimmy Cauty. *Orbus Terrarum* (Island 1995) is still great late-period Orb. In 1996 Deviant released an excellent double disc of Orb remixes, *Auntie Aubrey's Excursions Beyond The Call Of Duty*, which included the twelve-inch version of Primal Scream's 'Higher Than The Sun'. Other remix beneficiaries of The Orb have been Yello, The Art Of Noise and Bill Laswell, to name but a few. Island released *The Best Of The Orb* in 1998, a compilation of rare seven-inch edits, dance mixes, radio versions and alternate cuts in single and double-disc formats.

MIXMASTER MORRIS

Inspired by the new Minimalism of House and Techno, the 1990s saw Mixmaster Morris become the hardest-working DJ on the international Ambient scene. An ardent critic of hardcore dance music and the corporate record industry, Morris saw his role as a prophet of Intelligent Techno. A tireless global traveller (around 100 shows a year at his peak), Morris placed great emphasis on timbral variety in both the music he chose to DJ and his recorded works. Under the name The Irresistible Force he recorded three psychedelic Ambient albums and collaborated with the Frankfurt Techno guru Pete Namlook. Interestingly, Morris saw that the strength of the original Detroit Techno dwelled within its beautiful and Ambient textures and not in its beat. Morris catchphrases such as 'I Think Therefore I Ambient' and 'It's Time To Lie Down And Be Counted' displayed a humorous side to his quest for musical democracy.

Mixmaster Morris was born in Brighton, England, during the 1960s. He grew up in Lincolnshire in a literary household which showed indifference to music. At school in the 1970s he lost himself in computers, preferring to write programmes than hang out with the other boys. Energized by punk rock, Morris was inspired by the likes of Colin Newman's Wire and Cabaret Voltaire to create his own sounds. By the beginning of the 1980s Morris was living in London, working as a computer systems analyst and doing the odd one-man gig with a primitive synthesizer, drum machine and tape-echo set-up. He experimented with small on-board keyboard samplers, jammed with West London musicians and by 1985 had his own DJ radio slot, *The Mongolian Hip Hop Show*.

Fascinated by the emergent UK Acid House scene of the late 1980s, Morris set out to combine live sampled and sequenced music with a spectacular light show. His Brixton 'Madhouse' sessions, which he ran as The Irresistible Force, became the stuff of legend. He witnessed the birth of Ambient House one night at London's Heaven as members of The Orb and KLF began breaking dance records up with long instrumental interludes. In 1989 Morris was a key creator, alongside The Shamen, of Synergy, a band and House performance concept which toured Europe for two years. Supporting The Orb and reconstituted 1970s rock musicians such as Steve Hillage, Morris now saw Ambient House as part of a larger psychedelic revival and aligned himself with Fraser Clark's 'Evolution' movement towards a higher consciousness. When Clark invited the American ethno-biologist Terence McKenna to London to lecture, Morris soundtracked the performance.

Dressed in a silver suit and with the smiley air of a little pixie, Morris was a constant presence on the Spiral Tribe and Glastonbury Techno hippie scene. He then signed to the cutting-edge Ambient label Rising High and released *Flying High* (1992). Full of sampled music – Kraftwerk and Spacemen 3 were two of the more obvious edits – the album was a gushing dedication to Morris's own musical history. Brian Eno, Miles Davis, Tangerine Dream, Edgard Varèse and John Cage were all afforded 'Godlike Genius' status on the sleeve. Utilizing a sampling keyboard, a multi-timbral synth and cheap effects, Morris achieved a soft, glowing, vibey music of spatial textures, voice excerpts and entrancing rhythms. Even Terence McKenna appeared on the opening track, 'Spiritual High'. The frequency-shifting nature of Morris's sound (akin to turning a radio dial across some distant astral transmissions) was due to his obsession with the mixing desk. 'I love tweaking buttons. To me the mixing desk is the essence of my music making and I run the mixes through the desk over and over again, changing the sounds all the time with the faders and buttons.'

Morris then journeyed to Frankfurt to record *Dreamfish* (1993) with Germany's Ambient Techno king Pete Namlook. Though fascinated with Namlook's collection of analogue synthesizers, Morris completed the sublime disc of shifting electronic moods in just forty-eight hours. The energetic DJ was now part of a growing Ambient Techno scene which stretched across the world, taking in places as far-flung as Tokyo, St Petersburg, San Francisco and Goa. In 1994 alone, Morris performed his live DJ mixing in sixteen countries. What was refreshing about Morris was that at the same time as being open to the new Techno sounds of Ken Ishii, Tetsu Inoue, Aphex Twin and Orbital he showed complete respect for the classic German electronica of Harmonia, NEU!, Popol Vuh, Klaus Schulze, Tangerine Dream and Holger Czukay. He admired the work of La Monte Young, especially the pre-Velvet Underground drone experiments of The Dream Syndicate.

Global Chillage (1994) came with a hologrammic sleeve and saw Morris push the idea of 'multi-frequenced electronic mantra' to the limit. The Eastern-tinged 'Waveform', with its oscillating tones, arcing structure and bass beats, was Morris at his luxuriant best. At the time Morris became a big fan of the Internet, spending hours on his Apple Mac creating web pages which would communicate his passion for 1970s electronica, analogue synthesizers and new Techno artists to anyone who was interested. He was even keen on downloading virtual synthesizers and using them in his own music. The site was a perfect place to log on and find out about Morris's Ambient DJ duties, which, at the close of the 1990s, took him from the Mojave Desert to the Berlin Love Parade and onwards to Mount Fuji.

LISTENING

Mixmaster Morris released his best album in 1998. Credited as usual to The Irresistible Force, *It's Tomorrow Already* (Ninja Tune) was his most varied collection of electronic and acoustic music to date. Marshall McLuhan, Alan Watts, John Cage and Sun Ra were just some of the inspired vocal samples used, plus there was a more pronounced rhythmic cohesion. Morris's first two solo discs, *Flying High* (1992) and *Global Chillage* (1994) were released on Rising High, as was *Dreamfish* (1993). The second collaboration between Morris and Pete Namlook, *Dreamfish 2* (Fax 1995), was disappointing.

THE FUTURE SOUND OF LONDON

The wonderful thing about the House and Techno explosion was its potential for surprise. Both the UK and US music scenes were taken unawares by the arrival of The Future Sound of London in 1994. A duo who believed in the 'psychology of facelessness', their calling card was state-of-the-art computer and video imaging coupled with a form of Intelligent Techno music which considered sound itself to be at the very hub of creativity. They openly rejected musicianship and bravely stated that 'today a musician is someone who can operate technology'. Their music, as heard on *Lifeforms* (Virgin 1994), was a kaleidoscope of sampled exotica, held to earth by the faintest reference to House and Techno beats. They chose to use new digital data links to perform live around the world from their London studio. They remixed others, published new book concepts and generally enlivened the Ambient Techno music scene. In truth, FSOL, as they became known, showed that new computer and sampling technology, allied to the House and Techno aesthetic, could make the electronic dreamscapes of both Cage and Stockhausen a reality.

Gary Cobain and Brian Dougans met in Manchester in 1986. Dougans was from Glasgow and had been composing on his father's electronic equipment since the age of ten. His father worked for the Scottish BBC and was interested in electro-acoustics. Cobain hailed from Nottingham and had musical ambitions from the age of eight. He eventually gained a degree in music technology from the University of Manchester. Dougans studied studio technology at another Manchester college. At the famous Hacienda club they met the video artists Stakker, who included the Apple Macintosh wizard Mark MacLean. Hiring a Fairlight Computer Video Instrument, they made some landmark audiovisual material for MTV. 'Humanoid' (credited to Stakker) went on to become a UK Acid House classic when released by Westside in 1988. The 'Humanoid' twelve-incher utilized the Roland TB-303 bassline to its fullest, backed by a relentless beat and a cyber-vocal intoning the word 'humanoid'. The track was so authentically Acid House that it was re-released in Chicago by Trax, the originators of the form.

Industry incomprehension of their futuristic audiovisual music soon withered Cobain and Dougans's relationship with Stakker. The duo then concentrated on pure music, releasing a string of white-label twelve-inch singles under such monikers as Mental Cube, Smart Systems, Yage and The Future Sound of London. As the last they scored a huge hit with 'Papua New Guinea' (Jumpin' & Pumpin' 1992), an energy-up Rave anthem which liberally sampled the high-priestess voice of Lisa Gerrard from the neo-ethnic group Dead Can Dance. They then signed to Virgin and formed a new association with Mark MacLean, now rechristened Buggy G. Riphead. Their London-based Earthbeat studio was typical of the new mindset of musicians after House and Techno. Vintage synthesizers like the EMS Synthi, MiniMoog, OSCar and even the 1980s Oberheim Matrix vied for space with banks of Akai Samplers, Roland drum and synth boxes, synth modules like E-Mu vintage keys and outboard effects units. Atari and Apple Mac computers, with professional recording software, were also essentials, as was a thirty-six-channel mixing desk. More unusual was the presence of a complete Sony video-editing studio with cameras and monitors, financed by Sony. 'If you want to make technological music, you should be thinking of technological images to go with it,' said Cobain at the time.

The ambition of FSOL was clear – to blur the distinctions between audio and visual, performance and recording, absence and presence. They wanted to get away from what they saw as the simple 'graphic retinal stimulation' of music video and achieve a deeper imaging experience. At the time I described their images as 'hallucinogenic worlds of cracked eggs and organic shapes as if Salvador Dali had been born in the cybernetic era and had swapped canvas for computer graphics'. The cover of their first Virgin 'single' showed a tendrilled organism floating in space between two ovoid worlds. 'Cascade', released in the autumn of 1993, was over thirty-five minutes long – the average length of a 1960s album. Its contents was pure glistening electronica, its Techno beat well back in the mix as ethnic flutes, choral voices and a myriad other gorgeous sounds massaged your ears. Its most audacious sample was the nuclear bomb detonation intro from Can's classic 1971 album *Tago Mago*.

More experimental was the 1993 album *Tales of Ephidrina*, credited to Amorphous Androgynous. One track, 'A Study Of Six Guitars', could have come from an old scratched Robert Fripp album. In fact Fripp and David Sylvian approached FSOL to remix a tune from their collaborative album *The First Day* (1993). To make the track 'Darshana', FSOL had the audacity to take Sylvian and Fripp's entire album and empty it into their samplers, then whittle it down and top it off with some splashy keyboards from their E-Mu vintage keys unit. The duo admitted to endeavouring to create a '3-D Headspace' and in the latter stages of production, when all the samples had been overlaid and synchronized with the computers, they wrote 'live' on the faders, mixing sounds and effects as they went along. 'I'm obsessed with the spatial effect of our music,' said Dougans at the time.

Lifeforms, FSOL's debut album for Virgin, was released in the summer of 1994. A sprawling double-disc opus, it was both Ambient and avant-garde, its lush sound an open invitation for the listener to map on to the album his or her emotions or memories. *Lifeforms* was criticized for being 'amorphous' but that was its very point – to seamlessly link disconnected sounds into a unifying whole. Cobain commented: 'We are at the receiving end of sound, we cut up the history of sound.' Dougans wryly saw the work as 'an extreme personal experience, excellent in the background and even better on headphones'. Certainly it was true Ambient Techno, with an agenda to push forward into new territory. It had a beauty all of its own because it did not resort to beat instrumentals or melodic and harmonic devices to hook the listener. As FSOL said, the very sounds themselves were the stars. Robert Fripp, Talvin Singh and Klaus Schulze were three of the more obvious sampled musicians. On a near-forty-minute CD-single version of *Lifeforms*, Liz Fraser from The Cocteau Twins and Talvin Singh were the featured artists among the lush ethno-acoustics.

Equally valid during this period was FSOL's attitude to touring. Using the ISDN (integrated services digital network), they performed music through three British Telecom phone links. Famed for their Kiss FM radio broadcasts, they valued these 'live-studio' events because they allowed greater experimentation than on record. During the summer of 1994 they used radio stations in the UK, Europe and America to perform live, even dubbing a six-city American ISDN broadcast a 'tour'. The elasticity of these broadcasts allowed the duo to integrate more 'found' music into their flow, the London BBC Radio sessions including items from Eno and Fripp's *No Pussyfooting*, Miles Davis's *Kind Of Blue*, Pete Namlook's *Alien Community* and various KLF and Orb productions. FSOL made no secret of their sampled sources, openly showing any studio visitor their vinyl collection of Tangerine Dream and Klaus Schulze rarities, TV and musical soundtracks and the Indian vocalise of Sheila Chandra.

Buggy G. Riphead and FSOL had formed a triumvirate called EBV. Riphead spoke of a hyperreal scenario of 'synaesthetic visuals', mindscapes which could plug into the brain's Alpha waves. In fact it would take another two years for this concept to be realized. The much-spoken-about book *Psychology Of Facelessness*, in which, according to Cobain, 'the actual mental state of making electronic music would be revealed', was channelled into their second Virgin album, *Dead Cities* (Virgin 1996). The near-200-page book which accompanied the disc was a lavish mixture of text and morphed computer-generated images. It was interesting and lovely, dull and repetitive, all at the same time. *Dead Cities* credited Run DMC, Ozric Tentacles, Ennio Morricone, Vangelis and dozens of other sound sources. There was a greater rhythmic content than on previous Virgin releases and the track 'We Have Explosive' was even Hardcore Techno in character. Some tracks sounded identical to Aphex Twin, others sounded as if they were mangled Acid Jazz. Yet FSOL's ability to write, engineer and produce themselves was impressive – for example, their merging of Morricone's flute theme from *Once Upon A Time In America* (1983) with Vangelis's trademark vocal writing from *Blade Runner* (1982) was flawless.

LISTENING

Early Acid House items like 'Stakker Humanoid' may be found on such Ambient compilations as *Space 'N' Bass* (DTK 1998). The glowing textures of *Lifeforms* (Virgin 1994) succeed in linking Techno and Ambient music while pushing it into uncharted waters. But probably the best place to really experience FSOL is the 'live/studio' context represented on the 1994 Virgin recording *ISDN*, a compilation of broadcast excerpts of concerts given in Holland, the UK and New York in the same year.

APHEX TWIN

At the beginning of the 1990s appeared an artist who confounded everybody's expectations about what Techno music had to offer. His name was Richard D. James and he became famous under the moniker Aphex Twin. James was a restless maverick whose only interest in life was making original music. By the age of twenty-two he had an astonishing 1,000 tracks of unreleased material stacked up in his home studio. His creative ease was likened to that of Mozart, and classic releases such as *Selected Ambient Works 85–92* (1992) and *Selected Ambient Works Vol. 2* (1994) placed his inventions in sound right alongside the achievements of Stockhausen, Ligeti, Xenakis and Reich.

Aphex Twin's music was like an electronic symphony. Multi-layered with several coincident harmonic levels, it revelled both in melodic and timbral invention. Its percussive tug allied it to House, Techno and Rave, yet its other constituents – sound wash, playful keyboard tunes, ghostly electronic patterns and alien synthetic noise – pushed the music into new compositional territory. So satisfying were his early creations that they had a vaporous quality which seemed to snuggle around the brain like a warm glove. And so impressed was Philip Glass with his talent that in 1997 he allowed James to remix his orchestral version of the 1977 Bowie and Eno standard *'Heroes'*. Richard James was born in Limerick, Ireland, in 1971. Shortly afterwards his family moved to Cornwall, where he grew up in a small rural village. From an early age he began modifying the family piano's sound à la John Cage but with no knowledge of the American composer's 'prepared piano' technique. During puberty he experimented with tape recorders and as he got older he added circuits and amplification. His speciality was dismantling cheap synthesizers and keyboards to make something new out of them. His musical awakening occurred in 1986 when he heard a Chicago House track by Larry 'Mr Fingers' Heard. An instant convert to Acid House, he clubbed, then DJ'd and finally began including his own music in sets.

James continued to 'tweak' his equipment. Once he explained to me: 'I started off just tweaking pots and making ranges bigger. I took filters out, rebuilt them and made them more powerful. Then I began to improve the actual sound-generating properties of my synths by adding new elements. Then I added dozens of more controls which could activate parameters with voltages or via computer.' With no recognized qualifications, James went to London in the early 1990s to attend an interview for a sought-after course in Electronics and Micro-Computer Design. When he showed the interviewers his inventions he was admitted without pause.

Since 1985 he had been creating tracks. Friends began compiling tapes of his work into bootleg cassettes complete with sleeve inserts. His first 'official' release was 'Analogue Bubblebath' (1991) on the regional Mighty Force label. Characterized by a special aura, it began with an oscillating, rubbery synth noise accompanied by jittery drum sounds, a persistent keyed chord and a strange descending pitch. This was then lifted up by a dancing keyboard riff with the occasional addition of tambourine and other percussion. In fact the track's very title was indicative of its effect – hearing it was like aural immersion in a soft feathery bath.

James's favourite artists were the lords of Detroit Techno, May, Atkins and Saunderson, and Chicago's Acid House kings Phuture. During 1992 he flooded the market with a variety of tracks credited to aliases like Polygon Window, Diceman and Blue Calx. His most important statement though came in the autumn of 1992 in *Selected Ambient Works 85–92*, released by the Belgian R&S label and credited to Aphex Twin. The album was derived from his friends' famous car compilations, its nirvanic opening Ecstasy-high anthem 'Xtal' mastered from a version that had been played on 'thirty car stereos and sixty Walkmans!'.

From the very start, *Selected Ambient Works 85–92* was a classic. Bathed in effects, 'Xtal' possessed a thump shrouded in an angelic chorus of female voice and synth tone. 'Tha' reminded one of a sheet of board being flapped in the air over which a keyboard melody was heard coloured by a wispy Ambient synth and a distant taped conversation which could have occurred on a train platform. Tracks like 'Pulsewidth', 'Green Calx', 'Ptolemy' and 'Heliosphan' were all stamped with the label of good House, Acid House and Techno club music. 'Ageispolis' was beaty but with a forlorn atmosphere and the feeling of shimmering water. *i* was pure late 1970s Brian Eno Ambience. 'We Are The Music Makers' contained the line 'We are the music makers and we are the dreamers of dreams', followed by a pounding rhythmic section set to what sounded like Morse code. 'Delphium' was cerebral electronica best described by the term Intelligent Techno. The disc's finale, 'Actium', floated on its own dynamic, the beat maintained by synth keys as soft and sharp noises bobbed up and down in the mix to a tinkly background keyboard melody. With track titles reminiscent of ancient Greek and astronomical charts, James had invented his very own 'bathospheric' music whose seeming aim was to envelop the listener.

By the end of 1992 James was a Techno star. He was signed to Warp in Sheffield and Sire in the US. More experimental work came out in 1993 as the Polygon Window-credited *Surfing On Sine Waves*. Settling in a working-class area of North London, James began building another studio made up of old EMS, Moog and ARP synths reconfigured to his own specifications. He got to know the EMS's inventor Peter Zinovieff, who sold him various synthesizer units. 'I even put a sampler/playback unit in one synth, an Oberheim Matrix (a super-analogue 1980s American creation) in order to manipulate all my samples for my live shows. Then I started customizing my own effects, making phasers, flangers and loads of filters. I even made loads of spring reverbs and put them in cardboard boxes.' On a 1993 tour of the US James played venues coast to coast as Aphex Twin. His self-designed glyph, which cleverly combined the letters 'A' and 'T', looked like an ancient symbol. He began listening to other artists, admiring the works of David Sylvian, Holger Czukay, Xenakis, Tangerine Dream, Edgar Froese and especially Ligeti; the last for his close harmonic style.

With a pile of circuits without cases, an unconventional rural-hippie image and troughs of unreleased tapes, James seemed only in it for the music. He admitted to erasing tracks and releasing recordings only to give him money and time to create more music. Even the results themselves were of little interest to him. His real passion was the creative act itself, the very moment when his mind connected to the equipment and produced sound. As if to prove this, in the spring of 1994 Warp released *Selected Ambient Works Vol. 2*, a series of chilly soundscapes created in a state of semi-reverie. 'That was all done lucid dreaming. This was me basically going asleep, dreaming up a track in my studio or in an imaginary studio with imaginary equipment and then waking myself up and re-creating that track in my studio.' James worked live to tape, all his studio hardware at arm's reach. Sleep deprivation and marijuana lent *Selected Ambient Works Vol. 2* the quality of spectral music.

James was only twenty-two at the time, but *Selected Ambient Works Vol. 2* was so convincing that some writers were dubbing him a creator of 'genius'. Comparisons with Mozart were made and certainly some of its contents bring to mind older forms such as sonata and fugue. None of its twenty-four tracks had titles and all were represented by circular pictograms and indeterminate images. The overall aural effect evoked a sense of awe, some tracks sounding as if a boy genius was just passing a keyboard and decided to have a little tinkle. Other tracks were like waking dreams, replete with muffled cooing voices and phantom rhythms. Disc One opened just like that. Track Three seemed to emerge from dense fog. Track Five had a slow tribal beat and a kind of discreet Soviet atmosphere. The rest had a childlike quality, as if made in a very lofty and distant nursery. Disc Two was even more remote – the deep knocking sounds of Track One balanced by lengthy soft synthesizer tones. Track Two was perfect ghost music to humming electronics. Track Five was a lovely series of echoing keyboard splashes set to various sound frequencies. Track Seven came with a heavy beat but what was over it was almost Christmas music. Following that was a horn-like composition supported by a stately synth melody as finely resolved as anything by Chopin. In all, Aphex Twin's *Selected Ambient Works Vol. 2* just took the breath away.

Though much of the album was reminiscent of such Eno Ambiences as *Discreet Music* (1975), *Music For Airports* (1978), *On Land* (1982), *Apollo* (1983) and *Thursday Afternoon* (1985) James denied any intentional similarity. Much of the contents was post-Techno, the work of Derrick May and such pushed forward and organicized. James envisaged orchestral electronica and he admired Michael Nyman and Stockhausen. Unfortunately, that year BBC Radio 3 presented the German composer with James's music. Stockhausen poured scorn on environmental Ambience and saw Aphex Twin's music as 'emulating Philip Glass'.

Nevertheless, fêted by the music industry, James pushed forward, 'only making music for himself'. He remixed others' work, including English Pop House group Saint Etienne. In 1995 he came up with another album, *I Care Because You Do*, a more beat-friendly collection. Weird noises abounded but its Hip-Hop and breakbeat origins were to the fore. He even collaborated with Philip Glass on the repetitive frenzy of 'Icct Hedral', thus flying in the face of Stockhausen's stern advice. Drum and Bass plus vocals appeared on the more pop-friendly 1996 opus *Richard D. James* and as time progressed Aphex Twin was perceived as an original artist who was part of the rich tapestry of the contemporary music scene. His stated ambition was 'to make music till I drop and never to get a job'.

LISTENING

Though Richard James set up his own Rephlex record label during the 1990s, he is mostly identified with the Sheffield label Warp. He even appears on their first Ambient Techno compilation, *Artificial Intelligence* (1992) as The Dice Man. Above all, *Selected Ambient Works 85–92* (R&S 1992) and *Selected Ambient Works Vol. 2* (Warp 1994) are absolutely essential recordings – aesthetically enriching and, in terms of late-twentieth-century Techno, peerless.

PETE NAMLOOK AND AMBIENT TECHNO

In 1993 Frankfurt's Pete Namlook declared: 'Ambient Music is the most interesting music of the twentieth century. Ambient will be the classical music of the future.' As an independent record producer, Namlook had not only taken on the multi-national record industry but also the thriving German Hardcore Techno scene. In 1992 he had released Germany's first Ambient Techno CD, *Silence*, on his own Fax label. Astonishingly, in the course of a year he had put out 100 different recordings. Working from his own Sonic studios he could produce a dance track in a matter of hours, a complete Ambient album in a week. His beautifully packaged records became instant artefacts and, as his fame grew, he attracted some of the brightest names in new music. Mixmaster Morris, Bill Laswell and Klaus Schulze were all honoured to work with Namlook. Upcoming Techno musicians such as Japan's Tetsu Inoue and San Francisco's Jonah Sharp were given unprecedented creative freedom. As the 1990s evolved, Namlook recorded both classical musicians and synthesizer pioneers in an Ambient Techno context.

Namlook was born Peter Kuhlmann in Frankfurt in 1960. His mother was a laboratory photo technician who loved the black rock 'n' roll of Fats Domino and Chuck Berry. His father, a locksmith, favoured electronic music and was a fan of Wendy Carlos's *Switched-On Bach*. Namlook's earliest musical memories were those of sitting on his parents' floor and hearing the bossa-nova strains of

Antonio Carlos Jobim and the mellow jazz of Miles Davis. By the early 1970s he was spending all his pocket money on records, his favourites being Kraftwerk's debut album and Pink Floyd's *Meddle*. His upbringing was nomadic. He changed schools six times and lived for long periods in the Canaries and the Greek islands. His mother urged him to play guitar and once a cousin had shown him the chords of Led Zeppelin's 'Stairway To Heaven' he was off. By his mid-teens he was playing classical guitar and knew every Beatles song by heart. When he learned John Coltrane's *A Love Supreme*, Namlook knew his future lay in music.

Keenly interested in the relationship between science and music, Namlook enrolled in the Goethe Institute to begin serious study of music in his late teens. Using his father's new Revox tape machine, he made tape loops and recorded church bells. Inspired by Messiaen, he began recording birdsong and then transposed it to guitar. He said: 'My aim was then to combine music and nature.' Soon Namlook rejected his vocal counterpoint studies and left the Goethe Institute. He had been financing himself with a job in a bank and over the next eight years he became a top computer-based currency dealer, rising high enough to have the exclusive account of AEG. Every spare mark was invested in music equipment, every spare moment was spent recording. His aim was simple: 'to be able to live from music by the age of thirty'.

During the early 1980s Namlook listened attentively to the ECM catalogue and was inspired by Pat Metheny and Jan Garbarek. He bought a Roland guitar synthesizer and experimented with jazz-fusion. He invested in synthesizers, embracing the digitally advanced Yamaha DX7 as soon as it appeared in 1983. The early 1980s also saw some recording for the Frog label, but in 1986 he made a complete New Age-styled album as Romantic Warrior for the Stuttgart label Blue Flame. His synth music was then compiled with that of Tangerine Dream and Enya.

Privately Namlook was collecting vintage synthesizers like the EMS Synthi, the MiniMoog and the Prophets. He became a specialist in studio monitors and through this was invited to one of Frankfurt's leading Techno clubs, the Omen, in 1991. Inspired by the feeling of celebration in sound and light, Namlook began making Techno music with his friend DJ Criss. They called themselves Sequential and on the flips of their twelve-inchers they put Ambient music. Listening to Namlook's early Techno sides one can hear the first full rush of the music as skittering Roland drum machines drive translucent keyboard and synthesizers. Soon the names Sextant, 4 Voice and Crypt Corp (all pseudonyms for Namlook and various collaborators) would make waves in the Frankfurt Techno clubs. But Namlook was more ambitious. He wanted to put Ambient Techno on the map. During 1991, with the help of DJ Dr Atmo, he assembled *Silence*, 'the first full-length Ambient Techno album in Germany'.

Silence was divided into four movements. It opened slowly, grandiose background synth strings embellished by the sounds of rain and high-frequency synthesizer melodies. Then followed Ambient female vocal and long electronic tones with slow, ticking-clock percussion. Ethnic dulcimer, tweaked notes, fat keyboard sounds and a hypnotic structure described as 'Heart Trance' were its major qualities. Namlook wanted to release it in CD format (then risky as German production was expensive) but first tried majors like Sony, Warner Bros. and EMI. They considered it 'boring' and so in 1992 Namlook released his debut CD on his own Fax label. Limited to 600 copies, it was an immediate best-seller and was duly licensed to the UK label Rising High.

Namlook's Fax label was quickly becoming legendary. Each release used a coding system of a circle within a circle. Green was for House, yellow for Trance and blue for Ambient. Each recording was strictly limited in its original format (usually 1,000 copies) but further demand was met by foreign reissues. In 1993 Namlook enjoyed his most productive year up until then as Fax's Ambient output began to outsell everything else on the label.

On a mountain in the German countryside, he used DAT tape to record the acoustic sounds of percussion, rain stick and didgeridoo. Back in Frankfurt he transferred these to CUBASE on his Apple Mac computer to make the sublime *Air*, an electro-acoustic creation which played with ideas of space and the search for a loved one. The CD was released on Fax in the spring of 1993 and was another hit. Mixmaster Morris had dropped into Namlook's studio on his way to the fiftieth-birthday celebrations of the discovery of LSD in Basle. Within two days the duo had made *Dreamfish*. Morris was impressed with Namlook's Frankfurt studio, its compact design, its collection of vintage 1970s synthesizers such as two EMS Synthi AKSs (the suitcase version of the famous VCS3) and the Oberheim 4 Voice (a four-octave polyphonic synthesizer developed in the US) and its lack of mixing desk, Namlook preferring instead to line-mix direct to his then enormous Apple Quadra computer with its three-gigabyte hard disc.

Japan's Tetsu Inoue also collaborated with Namlook on the milestone 1993 release *2350 Broadway*. Inoue had left Japan for New York in 1988 seeking new outlets for his Ambient vision. Originally a jazz guitarist, and a pupil of the Brooklyn Conservatory of Music, Inoue was interested in pure sound tones stretched out across an aural space. Eastern travels led him to a form of spiritual Ambient Trance. In its double-disc format *2350 Broadway* (named after Inoue's New York apartment building) was the most accomplished Ambient recording on Fax of its day, deserving of the title Absolute Chill Out music. Other 1993 highlights were Namlook's work with Norway's king of stasis Geir Jenssen on *The Fires Of Ork*, the Technodelic splurging electronica of the Jonah Sharp collaboration *Alien Community* and the sumptuous Trance grooves of the second recording union with Tetsu Inoue, *Shades Of Orion*. The year ended with the release of Namlook's first Classical Ambient CD, *Passion*, with a cellist he met on a plane journey. Namlook said of his new direction: 'I love Bach and I love improvisation. I want to get to the limits of people's minds with my music.'

Namlook's incredible output of at least one new disc a week continued in 1994. *Air 2*, based on the notion of a telepathic astronaut drifting around the earth, was lovingly realized Ethnic Ambient Techno. There were more releases with Jonah Sharp, Tetsu Inoue and new synergies with the Canadian 'Technocian' Richie Hawtin (*From Within*) and New York Ambient Dub merchant Bill Laswell (*Psychonavigation*). In fact bassist Laswell would be a constant Fax presence, appearing on a dozen successive releases! In 1995 Namlook made a strong musical connection with Klaus Schulze when he recorded *The Dark Side Of The Moog* at the former Tangerine Dreamer's personal studio in Hambuhren. It would kick-start a series of releases over the next five years, all dedicated to the synthesizer inventor Bob Moog. Each included a playful reference to Pink Floyd – the second 1995 disc was subtitled 'A Saucerful Of Ambience'. Namlook's interest in analogue synthesizers saw him work with Ludwig Rehberg (one of the people behind the continued availability of the EMS range) and Oskar Sala, a veteran electronic musician and expert on the 1930s instrument the Trautonium. Namlook reissued his 1990 album *My Fascinating Instrument* in 1995. At the time he crusaded for more invention in modern instrument making, citing the Trautonium's ability to access subharmonic tones or an interactive scale (the inaudible notes between the black and white keys of a piano) as a key area for research and development. Namlook released a second Sala disc, *Subharmonic Mixtures*, in 1997.

As the 1990s wore on, Namlook kept releasing his tastefully designed blue and black CDs. Fruitful sessions with Tetsu Inoue, Richie Hawtin, Bill Laswell and Atom Heart continued to fill his release schedule. A third version of *Air* appeared in 1996 and *Silence 3* came out at the beginning of 1998. The 'Dark Side Of The Moog' series had reached its eighth instalment by 1999, a year when Namlook facilitated the release of two quiet Ambient works by the Swede Peter Benisch and the Dutchman Jochem Paap.

LISTENING

The catalogue of Namlook's label Fax +49-69/450464 (to give it its full title) is vast. Rising High records in London licensed two compilations, *Definitive Ambient Collection 1* and *Definitive Ambient Collection 2* in 1993 and 1994. For a wider overview track down the Fax compilations *The Ambient Cookbook* (1995) and *Genetic Drift* (1996), four and two CDs respectively. Worth a listen in any edition are the individual albums *Air*, *Silence*, *Escape* (which shows Namlook at his most early-90s Trance-heavy), *2350 Broadway*, *Alien Community*, *Shades Of Orion*, *Psychonavigation* and *From Within*.

BILL LASWELL AND COLLISION MUSIC

During the 1990s the American bass player and producer Bill Laswell emerged as one of the most significant international figures in Ambient music. Through his own independent Greenpoint Studio in New York and Island Records in the UK, he facilitated the release of over two dozen collaborative recordings which merged the worlds of acoustic Trance, Jimi Hendrix, The Orb, Dub Reggae, Hip-Hop, Indian music, jazz and more into one enormous Ambience. By 1993 alone, Laswell had been involved in over 200 albums, including recordings by Whitney Houston, Brian Eno, Laurie Anderson and Peter Gabriel. Yet his 1990s work, part inspired by Gurdjieff, part dynamized by William Burroughs, saw him build on the ideas of Cage, Stockhausen, Brian Jones, John McLaughlin, Can, Afrika Bambaataa and Pete Namlook. Critically lauded for *Panthalassa*, his 1998 reconstruction of work by Miles Davis, Laswell saw Ambient in terms of creating symphonic movements; the use of chance and improvisation to produce 'an endless space of creativity'.

Laswell was born in Illinois, near Lake Michigan, in 1950. His youth was itinerant and he played guitar and then bass in various school and church bands. From an early age he considered the groove made by electric bass to be a religion and during the mid-1960s he played the black R&B and chitlin circuit of the Deep South. James Brown was a major inspiration, as was the Free Jazz of John Coltrane and Ornette Coleman. He also encountered the famous funk bassist Bootsy Collins and during the early 1970s spent much time in Ann Arbor and Detroit, where he saw Iggy Pop and the MC5. He worked in the Michigan funk and rock scenes before gravitating to New York in the late 1970s.

In 1978 Laswell met Giorgio Gomelsky, a music business svengali who had connections with The Rolling Stones, Gong and the subversive English group Henry Cow. Gomelsky provided a loft where Laswell could experiment with new music. Material was born, a loose aggregation of musicians, including guitarists Sonny Sharrock and Nicky Skopelitis. Laswell also became New York House producer for the French label Celluloid, which openly embraced Ambient ideas and World Music. Associated with Manhattan's noisy Downtown scene, Laswell was also a member of Massacre and Deadline. In 1980 he met Rober Musso, a young string multi-instrumentalist and talented studio engineer from New Jersey. In a matter of hours they recorded a track for Material's debut album, which featured a nascent Whitney Houston on vocal. The same year Laswell appeared on Brian Eno and David Byrne's *My Life In The Bush Of Ghosts* (EG). A strong bond of experimentation was formed with Eno, who invited him to appear on the 1982 EG album *On Land*. His star clearly in the ascendant, Laswell would be famous within a year.

Herbie Hancock had risen to fame in the late 1960s through his electric keyboard work with Miles Davis. In 1983 Hancock and Laswell recorded 'Rockit', a state-of-the-art Electro single full of sampled scratched beats and groovy synth sounds which predicted the Techno future. 'Rockit' was a huge chart hit in the UK and the duo's follow-up Columbia recording, *Sound System* (1984), won a Grammy award for its fusion of the 'Rockit' sound with African rhythms. As an in-demand producer Laswell spent the rest of the 1980s overseeing albums by Laurie Anderson, Mick Jagger, Reggae duo Sly and Robbie, Motörhead, PIL, Ryuichi Sakamoto, Yoko Ono, Afrika Bambaataa,

Iggy Pop and The Ramones. This eclecticism was also reflected in his own work with the avant-funk group The Golden Palominos and with Material.

Moving closer to a new improvised Ambience, Laswell teamed up with the Indian musicians L. Shankar (violin) and Zakir Hussain (tabla) for *Hear No Evil* (Venture 1988). This recording mirrored John McLaughlin's 1970s acoustic-fusion group Shakti, which in fact contained the same Indian players. Yet *Hear No Evil* was more introspective and also featured the Bayou guitar style of Nicky Skopelitis. The latter also played on Material's fifth and most important album, *Seven Souls* (Virgin 1989). A veritable evocation of William Burroughs's 1987 novel *The Western Lands* (his personal vision of *The Egyptian Book Of The Dead*), this was another trance-inducing Ambient journey full of Arabic, African and Indian shadings. Burroughs narrated various segments from the book, the whole culminating in a wash of synthesizers and instrumental ambience as Burroughs's narcotic voice read from the last page of *The Western Lands*.

By 1990 Laswell was an exciting point of musical confluence. After a meeting with Chris Blackwell, he got the go-ahead to release a variety of 'pan-ethnic polyrhythmic' musics through Island records on a label titled Axiom. One of the first was a Moroccan field-recording of the Gnawa Musicians of Marrakesh, who originated from Guinea and played a highly intricate form of acoustic Trance music. Inspired by Brian Jones's innovative Moroccan recordings of the late 1960s, Laswell journeyed to the Rif Mountains in late 1991 to record *Apocalypse Across The Sky* by the Master Musicians of Jajouka in homage of Brian Jones and the writers Paul Bowles and Brion Gysin, who had originally exposed the West to this ancient form of modal repetitive music.

Laswell's studio complex and equipment situation in New York had grown considerably by 1992. He had a huge collection of bass guitars (including a Paul McCartney-like Hofner) and played eight-string, five-string and fretless models. He used these in conjunction with a multitude of outboard effects pedals such as wah-wah. His Greenpoint Studio complex in Brooklyn was 5,000 square feet with no separation between the twenty-four-track recording console and the performance spaces. He used Platinum Island in Manhattan to do all his mixes. In time Laswell would concede the importance of the digital revolution, and Akai samplers, forty-eight-track digital mixers and so on were all handled by his trusty engineers Robert Musso and Oz Fritz. Laswell continued to involve himself in recordings by guitarists Sonny Sharrock and Skopelitis. Still the best was yet to come.

The year 1994 was Laswell's most prolific to date, with over thirty releases on a variety of labels such as Black Arc, Subharmonic, Strata, Fax and Axiom. The Material album *Hallucination Engine* was electro-acoustic Trance music which featured a cast of twenty musicians drawn from all corners of the musical globe. That disc contained the Shankar co-authored cut 'Mantra', recorded in Madras, India, and a spoken-word contribution from Burroughs. Licensed through Tim Simenon's label Stoned Heights, *Divination Vols. 1 And 2* contained Laswell's most outré constructions in Ambient Trance music so far. At the time it was name-checked against Ambient House and Techno acts such as The Orb and Banco De Gaia and included a stellar performance from English bassist Jah Wobble. Laswell also began a strong association with Pete Namlook on *Psychonavigation*, a Deep Ambient venture whose opening track lasted thirty-eight minutes and was strangely monikered 'Psychic And UFO Revelations In The Last Days'. During the final month of 1994 appeared *Axiom Ambient – Lost In The Translation*, an overlapping and intertwining collage of eight symphonic Ambient movements containing some of the most impressive music from the Axiom catalogue. The Orb and Tetsu Inoue – Laswell particularly admired the latter for his sensitivity in the studio – were both represented. One track, 'Peace In Essaouria', was mixed for the late Eddie Hazel and Sonny Sharrock and featured the playing of both guitarists in a sublime dedication to Jimi Hendrix's 1967 ballad 'Little Wing'. The track concluded with the saxophonist Pharoah Sanders playing a haunting ballad for Sharrock in the coastal Moroccan town of Essaouria.

Laswell's extensive travels to Japan, Thailand, Korea, India, Africa, Mongolia, Uzbekistan and China had a considerable impact on the way he viewed sound. He saw himself as a locus of production which relied on 'intuition and instinct'. His interest was in 'real experience and real situations which create an atmosphere and environment for a flow of music'. And 'flow' was the right word as the late 1990s saw no end to Laswell's around-the-clock creativity. In 1995 he released *Axiom Funk*, an overt dedication to Hendrix and the jazz leanings of the twilight of his career, with contributions from funk legends Bootsy Collins, George Clinton and Maceo Parker. In 1996 came the beautiful Paul Bowles box *Baptism Of Solitude* on Meta (a label dedicated to Aural Ambience) which combines recordings of Bowles reading his own work with added Ambient treatments by Laswell and Robert Musso. That year Laswell revisited Pete Namlook, this time in conjunction with Klaus Schulze, to make two editions of the 'Dark Side Of The Moog' series. Another 1996 Axiom release, *Altered Beats*, sought a new syntax in Hip-Hop as Laswell repositioned his 1980s work with Herbie Hancock and Afrika Bambaataa as a new form of turntable 'Chamber Hop' with help from Tokyo's DJ Krush and the San Franciscan New Skool of Rob Swift. Asian opera and hypnotic breakbeat were just two of the many features on display. This was followed by a double *Axiom Dub* extravaganza, which, according to Laswell, 'doesn't specifically mean Reggae but an adding, subtracting and mutating music'. The Orb, Jah Wobble, Jaki Liebezeit and DJ Spooky were just some of the contributors to this intense and heavy Dub experience.

'Reconstruction', 'Remix Translation' and 'Sound Sculpture' were all descriptions applied to Laswell's way of making records. By the end of the century many leading record labels were keen to allow him access to the master tapes of famous musicians and see what he could come up with. Nineteen ninety-seven saw the release of Bob Marley's *Dreams Of Freedom* (Island), where, using ethnic and electronic sources, Laswell couched eleven Marley songs in what he described as 'Ambient Translations'. This led to *Panthalassa* (Columbia 1998), Laswell's ground-breaking 'reconstruction' of Miles Davis's late-1960s and early-1970s jazz-rock oeuvre. Taking twenty-five reels of two-inch tape from the original Teo Macero masters of the albums *In A Silent Way*, *On The Corner* and *Get Up With It*, Laswell added subtle synth Ambiences and bass loops. The results were spectacular, literally reinventing a period of Miles Davis's career which many had found too dense to assimilate. In fact Laswell had been inspired by the 'collision music' of *On The Corner* (1972) to follow his chosen path. At the time he told me: 'I wanted to re-envision the whole thing, the sound, the size of the low-end, the clarity of lines, the separation and the impact of rhythm which is a repetitive rhythm not so different from rock or Hip-Hop and not so much related to jazz.' After *Panthalassa* Laswell relocated his Greenpoint Studio to New Jersey, where he did further work on Davis's *On The Corner* for the DJ/Mix album *Panthalassa: The Remixes* (Columbia 1999).

LISTENING

Laswell has been involved in so many albums it's quite possible that anybody with a hint of an interest in modern music will have something by him, produced by him or with him as contributor. Relevant here are his excursions into Ambient, Techno and New Sampling/Mix musics. Of the Axiom compilations, *Manifestation* (1993) and *Axiom Ambient: Lost In The Translation* (1994) are recommended, particularly the latter, which serves as a stylish take on all of Laswell's Axiom releases, including a portion of his 1993 collaboration with The Orb, 'Praying Mantra'. Other Axiom releases worth seeking out are *Gnawa Music of Marrakesh* (1990), *The Master Musicians Of Jajouka* (1992), *Funkcronomicon* (1995) and *Altered Beats* (1996).

   Laswell's own work as bass player and ensemble player came to fruition on *Hear No Evil* (Venture 1988) and the two exceptional works in musical hybridization credited to Material: *Seven Souls* (Virgin 1989) and *Hallucination Engine* (Axiom 1994). The double-disc *Divination* set (Stoned Heights/4th & Broadway 1994) is Laswell's excellent voyage into Ambient Trance. Around that time he lent his bass and sound skills to a series of Fax recordings with Pete Namlook such as *Psychonavigation* (1994). The three-way symbiosis of Namlook, Laswell and Klaus Schulze produced the superb *Dark Side Of The Moog 5* (1996) introduced by the inventor himself Robert Moog. Among his extramural activities, the Ambient treatments of Paul Bowles's readings, *Baptism Of Solitude* (Meta 1996), and *Panthalassa* (Columbia 1998), an extraordinary clarification of Miles Davis's music from the late 1960s and early 1970s, stand as testaments to a remarkable sonic visionary.

WILLIAM ORBIT

Made famous by Acid House, William Orbit became one of the most in-demand remixers of the 1990s. Based in a small self-designed studio in North London, Orbit had a facility with timbre which resulted in many sparkling productions featuring some of the most renowned names in modern music. Prince, Sting, The Human League, Peter Gabriel and Kraftwerk all availed themselves of Orbit's magic ears – entire multi-track tapes were loaded into samplers and rearranged until the sounds flowed like a clear stream. So impressed was the American pop queen Madonna that Orbit provided her with much Ambient and Trance input for the award-winning 1998 album *Ray Of Light*, considered her finest achievement. Outside the mainstream Orbit has produced much instrumental electronica of value, particularly in the guise of Strange Cargo. During the mid-1990s he even created an Ambient cycle of his favourite composers, including works by Satie, Ravel, Part and Gorecki.

Born William Wainwright in the 1960s, Orbit entered the music business during the early 1980s as a wily independent. After secondary school he and a musician friend, Grant Gilbert, went to work on North Sea oil rigs. Returning with substantial amounts of cash, they built their own studio in the picturesque Little Venice district of London and began to record as Torch Song. Initially a guitarist, Orbit quickly mastered keyboards but found his real instrument was the mixing desk. A sophisticated pop and rock group, Torch Song were signed to IRS and released many records, including the twelve-inch single 'Ecstasy' in 1986. Recognition eluded them and Orbit began to record on his own under the pseudonym Strange Cargo. Mixing Ambient dreamscapes with Brazilian-inflected acoustic guitar instrumentals resulted in some stellar music reminiscent of Tangerine Dream and Vangelis at their best. IRS boss (and former manager of The Police) Miles Copeland wrote in the sleeve notes to *Strange Cargo* (No Speak 1987): 'not since Pink Floyd has an artist had such a sense of space combined with power and delicacy.'

Yet Orbit was bagged with the New Age trend of the time and seen as interesting rather than exciting. Fired by Acid House, he began to experiment with the snaky sound of the Roland 303 bass box. Teaming up with black singer Sharon Musgrave, Orbit formed the House combo Bass-O-Matic. They quickly signed to Virgin, and in 1990 had a UK Top Ten entry with the catchy single 'Fascinating Rhythm'. A follow-up album, *Set The Controls For The Heart Of The Bass* (a pun on an old Pink Floyd track) was pure sci-fi Acid House, brimful of bleeps, squelches, B-movie dialogue and a booming beat. Enthralled by the bass sounds of his Roland Juno 106 synthesizer and sampled sounds from such vintage equipment as the Prophet 5 synth, Orbit made a second Bass-O-Matic album, *Science And Melody* (Virgin 1991), again featuring Sharon Musgrave, along with added singers and rappers. Once more the results were state-of-the-art Techno dance music.

By this stage Orbit had moved his Guerilla studio to a small house near Muswell Hill in North London. It was also the home of Guerilla Records, a small Progressive House label whose releases, like *Dub House Disco Vol. 1*, would influence the development of 90s Trance. An Otari mixing desk, twenty-four-track recording, Akai samplers, a computer running CUBASE sequencing software, a pile of effects plus a few keyboards and synthesizers was all that Orbit required to work his particular brand of wizardry. He was particularly fond of the Roland Juno 106, an analogue synthesizer marketed in 1984 which had certain digital characteristics – namely a MIDI facility which allowed it to interface with other pieces of electronic equipment. Easy to use and producing 128 warm programmable voices, the Juno 106 was Orbit's favourite production aid. One prestigious job was the remixing of Peter Gabriel's 'Mercy Street' to promote the release of the 1990 Virgin compilation *Shaking The Tree*. In 1991 Orbit was paid his greatest compliment when Kraftwerk's Ralf Hütter emerged from his Düsseldorf seclusion and arrived at Guerilla, tape in hand, to oversee a new mix of 'Radioactivity'.

Despite the acclaim, Orbit continued his passion for Ambient music. *Strange Cargo 3* (1993) was another leap forward. Present were the familiar acoustic spacing, sleek dynamics and background brushstrokes of electronic colour. More apparent was a panoramic sense of depth which made it perfect music for TV and film soundtracks. 'Gringatcho Demento' chugged along on a riveting beat, treated electric guitar, dreamy keyed vocal samples and Spanish dialogue. 'Best Friend Paranoia' seemed to emerge from some funereal swamp of discreet organ sounds before delving into soft drum rhythms circulated by echoing acoustic guitars and nifty electro-tones. 'Monkey King' was sound stretched across tape – radio tones à la Stockhausen, ghostly washes, distant Arabic chant presaging a primordial jungle beat reminiscent of the 'Fourth World' music of Jon Hassell. The strangest cut on *Strange Cargo 3* was a reworking of 'Harry Flowers' (from the 1970 film *Performance*, starring Mick Jagger) which alternated between English whimsy and Dub Reggae. The album sold 100,000 copies with hardly a push from Virgin.

That year, 1993, Orbit took a second residence in Los Angeles, a beach house where he installed another studio. He also played orchestral music on a local radio station. He experimented with an album of reworked soundtracks by composers such as Nino Rota, Bernard Herrmann, Lalo Schifrin and Henry Mancini. Though it didn't work out it alerted the president of WEA (Bernard Dickens, the man who ignited Enya's career) to Orbit's talent and he was signed to a new deal which allowed him creative freedom through his own N-Gram imprint. First off Orbit revitalized old Torch Song material and released *Toward The Unknown Region* (1995), an Ambient House concoction with Laurie Mayer's vocals gliding over the top. More complex, with its combination of chamber and electronic textures plus the voices of Beth Orton, Sharon Musgrave and Laurie Mayer, was *Hinterland* (1995), the fourth Strange Cargo album. Again the emphasis was on rhythm and Dub, with lots of Orbit's trademark acoustic guitar chords.

A 1995 visit to Orbit's London studio revealed a fairly basic set-up. He still had the same old mixing desk, a load of valve amps, limiters and compressors, a huge graphic equalizer and customized racks with military-spec connectors for perfect sound. He'd upgraded his Akai samplers and computers but his keyboard and synthesizer stack was still the same. At the time he emphasized: 'It's not the equipment but the way I see sound and position it. It's all about dynamics, a real light and shade thing. It's the silences, the spaces. That's where the real melodies are. The instruments themselves are irrelevant, they could be anything.' As if to prove his love of 'profound melody', Orbit had sat down and re-recorded some of modern music's greatest Ambient compositions. Transplanting to tape his earlier passions as a classical DJ in LA, Orbit came up with *Pieces In A Modern Style*, an electronic celebration of the genius of Samuel Barber, Maurice Ravel, Erik Satie, Arvo Pärt and Henryk Gorecki.

If Orbit used samples and sequencers to recreate the sad hues of Barber's *Adagio For Strings* and Part's *Cantus in Memory Of Benjamin Britten*, then his House version of Ravel's *Pavane pour une infante défunte* was sheer inspiration, an audacious meeting of crystalline early-twentieth-century piano melody with the druggier rhythms of late-twentieth-century dance culture. Scheduled for release during the summer of 1995, the album was postponed when the publishers of both Pärt and Gorecki objected to the use of their clients' work in such a context. A performance with twenty-one musicians at London's Festival Hall was saved only by the interjection of Philip Glass, who allowed Orbit to replace the banned Pärt and Gorecki numbers with some of his music.

Though Orbit had reached his lowest ebb – he despaired over a future of endless remixes – salvation was at hand in the comely shape of Madonna. As far back as 1992 Orbit had remixed 'Erotica' for club consumption. He did more of the same in 1994 and in 1997 he was dumbstruck when she asked him to come to Larrabee Studios in California and oversee the album *Ray Of Light* (Maverick/Warner Bros. 1998). Universally acclaimed as Madonna's greatest-ever achievement, it relocated her from 80s pop to edgy 90s Techno/Trance. Of its thirteen tracks Orbit co-wrote seven with Madonna and co-produced twelve. Full of Orbit's sonic Ambiences, *Ray Of Light* was a fantastic listening experience. Orbit cushioned Madonna's new-mother spirituality in a bottomless sea of glinting surfaces. 'Drowned World'/'Substitute For Love' layered and layered sounds – multiple drum programmes, backwards guitar and panned cymbals were just some of the highlights. The title track began with some nifty guitar chords before dissolving into blipping Trance of a superior quality. 'Candy Perfume Girl' used a Trip-Hop drum sound while the clanking intro to 'Shanti'/'Ashtangi' would not have been out of place on a Tricky album. In retrospect no other producer would have had the experience and sonic knowledge to midwife such a dazzling collection of contemporary sounds. Deservedly, Orbit picked up a Grammy award for his skills. By 1999 *Ray Of Light* had garnered four such trophies.

LISTENING

All the Strange Cargo releases are worth hearing, especially *Strange Cargo 3* (Virgin 1993) and *Hinterland* (N-Gram 1995). Madonna's *Ray Of Light* (Maverick/Warner Bros. 1998) shows Orbit in full bloom as Ambient/Trance producer. His electronic classical suite *Pieces In A Modern Style*, featuring music by Barber, Satie, Ravel, Cage, Gorecki and even Beethoven, was finally given the green light by WEA in early 2000. A delightful Ambient creation, it closed a sonic circle between the early Ambient Minimalists and the realization of their ideas in the age of technology.

SCANNER, BIOSPHERE AND ISOLATIONISM

Around 1994 a new strain of Ambient music began to be heard. Introverted, often implosive, this new form took its inspiration from the avant-garde fringe and included ingredients of rock drone, 1970s synth music, strange sampling and unusual rhythms. Dubbed Isolationism, it seemed intended to push the world away rather than embrace it. Surprisingly, it began with rock groups using their instruments in an unconventional way. Textures and sampling were now the preserve of the new post-rock/lo-fi ensembles like America's Tortoise and Labradford or the numerous UK-based sound merchants such as Ultramarine, Global Communication, G. P. Hall, Main, Node and EAR.

Computers combined with samplers and sequencers were the new Isolationist tools. In 1994 Virgin released a double-CD compilation titled *Isolationism* which married the two sides of the musical coin. Zoviet France (from Newcastle) were fans of both Cabaret Voltaire and Ligeti and made strange, unsettling beatless loops. Main (who emerged from psychedelic band Loop) admired German synth groups like Popol Vuh and Ash Ra Tempel and traded in electronic drones and heartbeat guitar noise. Disco Inferno were Ambientizing rock by using guitars and drums to trigger keyboard samples of, say, Miles Davis or even classical music. A greater degree of self-absorption was evinced by those Isolationist musicians inspired by House and Techno artists such as Scanner, Biosphere, Thomas Köner, Paul Schütze and Jon Tye.

Scanner, aka Robin Rimbaud, came to prominence during the early to mid-1990s as an Isolationist *par excellence*. Working alone, he developed a brand of personal electronica that became highly controversial for its use of voyeuristic scanned cellphone conversations. Using a cheap scanner (hence his art name), Rimbaud examined the way late-twentieth-century technology had altered communication. Using minimal equipment, his recordings gave off a highly charged portrait of a society breaking up emotionally – where the strongest human feelings of sexual fantasy, jealousy and avarice were communicated via personal phones and answerphone messages. As his music developed, Rimbaud extended his vision to environmental and installation works. Always working at a distance from mainstream Techno and House culture, he was nevertheless an essential ingredient of the zeitgeist – appearing at international Ambient festivals like Sonar and running the Quiet Club of Brian Eno's dreams in the Electronic Lounge (at London's ICA) between 1994 and 1998. He became one of the few Techno musicians to be admired by Stockhausen.

Rimbaud was born in 1964 in Wandsworth, South London. He lost his father when he was very young and over the following years was fascinated by tape recorders and crossed telephone lines. He then took up serious piano lessons and confesses to 'being shocked into submission by John Cage' when he was eleven. He began putting things into the family piano to 'prepare' it and change its timbral range. Later Rimbaud did his A-levels, secured a modern art degree and studied literature. He played a modicum of guitar and was passable on keyboards. His second inspiration was the experimental electronic rock of Cabaret Voltaire and Test Dept of the early 1980s, when Rimbaud played in a number of 'industrial' bands. He even found common ground with Düsseldorf's NEU! But it was the purchase of a £90 scanner (with a frequency range of 0–1,000 megahertz) from a South London anarchist group that changed his music conclusively.

Working with a four-track recorder, a couple of reel-to-reel tape machines, an echo unit and a Yamaha keyboard and guitar set-up, Rimbaud made *Scanner 1* and *Scanner 2* between 1993 and 1994, releasing them on his own Ash label. He considered *Scanner 1* to be a 'rites of passage album, a summary of the previous fifteen years'. Ambient textures swam in the background while strange sounds were emphasized in the mix. Many of the foregrounds contained explicit pornographic conversations captured by the scanner. It was both unsettling and strangely fascinating. *Scanner 2* was more varied, with a greater emphasis on homogeneity as sound loops and voices merged. By the time of *Mass Observation* (1994), Scanner, as Rimbaud was now known, was working with others, extending his environmental Ambiences into areas of Dub House and Techno rhythm.

Yet Scanner found conventional clubs 'too loud and too late'. He was a self-confessed teetotaller uninterested in alcohol, tobacco, tea, caffeine or any other drugs. He was a practising vegetarian and hated television, his Battersea flat simply a functional place to create his work. At the ICA he founded the Electronic Lounge to cater for people interested in new electronica who wanted to converse. A great success, it attracted the interest of David Toop, DJ Spooky, Laurie Anderson, Paul Schütze and others and dynamized a stronger symbiosis among the diverse Ambient music community. In 1995, after hearing some of Scanner's work, Stockhausen declared: 'He has a good sense of atmosphere and is searching in a realm of sound that is not usually used for music.'

Scanner continued to record, his output increasingly reflecting the sound-morphing qualities of his Akai S1000 sampler. In 1997 he released *The Garden Is Full Of Metal* (Sub Rosa), an album of landscaped sound Polaroids created from location recordings of film-maker Derek Jarman made in London's Charing Cross and Dungeness in Kent. Scanner had met Jarman as far back as 1984 and even created music for his 1988 film *The Last Of England*. In 1998 Scanner was made Professor Of Sound at a Liverpool university. Since then he has extended his ideas to the theatre and performance art, as well as live DJing and improvisation. Much of his site work mixed text and electronic sound using the latest computer software and sound sensors to create feedback environments where the audience itself participated in the art. Scanner's 1999 album *Lauwarm Instrumentals* (Sulphur) was a return to the organic. Some tunes drifted on a haunting electronic Ambience. 'Ground Veil' revolved around the disembodied sound of a synthesized female lift announcer. 'Lithia Water' was simple Drum and Bass clothed in the ethereal theme music of David Lynch's famous 1990 TV series *Twin Peaks*. The album's closing seven minutes were purely orchestral as sampled strings and voices veered towards the operatic.

One could hardly find a more isolated place than Tromsö on the northern coast of Norway. Thirty miles inside the Arctic circle, the town experiences all the wonders of its geographical situation – tundra, fiords, mountains, the Aurora Borealis, three-month dark winters and three-month bright summers. It is here that Biosphere (Geir Jenssen) constructed a music permeated by space and a particularly Arctic chillness that was the very template of Isolationism. Yet the use of vocal samples and warm analogue synth textures gave his work a humanity that was missing from dozens of other European artists working in the Techno scene.

Jenssen was born in the mid-1960s and had a normal Norwegian upbringing with a keen interest in healthy pursuits like skiing and mountaineering. Inspired by the English post-punk music of Joy Division and Eno's Ambient records, Jenssen bought an analogue synthesizer in the early 1980s and experimented with cassette tape. By 1986 he was in a group, Bel Canto, who toured Europe, but after spending a hassly year in Brussels he returned to Tromsö for 'space and isolation'. Having already, as Bleep, recorded a solo album which mixed Acid House, Ambient and Belgian New Beat Techno, Jenssen decided to follow a purer Ambient vision. Coincidentally, in the Belgian city of Ghent Renaat Vandepepelière's label R&S had established itself as one of the best new Techno labels in the world. Early 1990s records such as Joey Beltram's classic Hardcore anthem 'Energy Flash' and Jam & Spoon's pioneering Trance of 'Stella', not forgetting R&S's discovery of Aphex Twin, made the label an essential New Music imprint. Its decision to push Ambient on a new offshoot, Apollo, coincided with the completion of Jenssen's first album as Biosphere. *Microgravity* (Apollo 1991) introduced the world to a music of strong environmental Ambience, distant walls of icy synthesizer, compelling filmic voice samples and subtle rhythmic undertows. Immediately one imagined lone elk in an icy forest or slowly drifting icebergs.

Patashnik (Apollo 1994) made the name Biosphere famous as it topped the UK indie chart and provided a soundtrack for a Levi's jeans commercial.

Suffused with the glowing lights of Tromsö's beautiful skies, *Patashnik* was Techno Ambience taken to a new level of excellence. Textures, sounds and ideas had a crystalline clarity, many tracks having the quality of aural films. 'Startoucher' included a girl's voice talking about touching the stars as 'sound' moved organically in the background. The title track was Detroit Techno recorded with a distant Northern European twist which worked well as both dance music and listening Ambience. Wind, radio voices, sonic plops and that cloudy, yearning synth sound drifted through 'Mir'. The album closed with the wonderful acoustic guitar and electronic tones of 'En-Trance'. Unsurprisingly, the third Biosphere album, *Substrata* (All Saints 1997), witnessed a huge jump in sound quality as Jenssen explored digital recording media. Inspired by a climbing trip to the Himalayas, *Substrata* was Biosphere's most complete expression – a beautiful but sparsely populated earscape which began with the distant sound of a plane over water and ended with strangely crackling flames.

Even more 'chilled' than Biosphere was the unique music of Dortmund's Thomas Köner. Born in 1965, Köner saw his 'sounds' as a total retreat from the outside world. His music had the immersive quality of silent decays and barely audible aural sightings. Equivalent to glimpsing the distant movement of a ship on a calm horizon, a Thomas Köner album combined the rumblings of early 1980s Eno albums with the dronal aesthetic of La Monte Young. Köner's means was to fix contact microphones to gongs and sample their vibrations. These were then stretched and treated to digital reverberations and delays. The results were as stunningly close to 'silence' as any Ambient music in history. *Nunatak Gongamur* (Barooni 1990) was a virtual recreation of the British explorer Robert Scott's final days in the icy Antarctic of 1912 and was full of deep desolation and glacial movement. Köner pushed deeper into subsonic and ultraharmonic textures on *Teimo* (Barooni 1992) as the manipulated gong sounds paralleled the effect of slow death due to freezing.

Yet Köner's music was as iridescent as it was foreboding. A trip to the Arctic provided nourishment for his impressive *Permafrost* (Barooni 1993). Here he was interested in 'combining the phenomena of timbre and light – a light that can define colour, atmosphere and the presence of music shining diffusely through the spectrum of sound'. *Permafrost* defined its musical presence through a glowing, gradually shifting surface. As with House and Techno music the more the listener stayed with it the more details were revealed. This was deeply spiritual Ambient music, created at the very frontiers of possibility. Köner was inspired by both the desolation of post-industrial Dortmund and the glistening textures of Techno. His sound world may be the very definition of Isolationism but by 1997 he was willing to collaborate with Sonic Boom's EAR. on *The Köner Experiment* (Mille Plateaux), where exotic electronica and unusual bowed acoustic sounds met his polar Ambiences.

Köner has worked with the Australian Paul Schütze, one of the most fêted Ambient and electronic composers of the 1990s. Though his music is warmer than that of either Köner or Biosphere, Schütze's exploration of psychological spaces has a potent Isolationist quality. Describing himself as a 'sound-designer', Schütze has done work that embraces the gamelan of Debussy, the fusion sound of early-70s Miles Davis, the organic Ambiences of David Sylvian and Holger Czukay, the Minimalism of Terry Riley and the more rarefied areas of Techno. Born in Melbourne in 1958, Schütze was interested as a boy in both progressive rock and ethnic classical music. Early groups concentrated on his use of electronics and soon he was playing keyboards and percussion. In 1979 he travelled the world and returned to Australia to play in the group Laughing Hands.

By 1982 Schütze was fed up with band activity and decided to DJ for three years. By chance he began composing for films in 1985, winning a prestigious Australian award in the process. Working on the fringe, Schütze wrote twenty film scores in five years but was frustrated by the medium. By 1989 he began to write music for installations, initially as sound collages, but as time went on he concentrated more on musical tapestries. A move to London during the early 1990s saw him work in the Ambient Techno area for R&S in Belgium. His first Virgin album, *Apart* (1994), was at least the tenth recording by this prolific artist. Its emotionally welling mixture of percussion, strings and slow, slow Ambiences was mindful of the late-1980s work of Sylvian and Czukay. Schütze talked of making one long track titled 'Sleep' so late in the night that his exhausted brain dictated the funereal pace of the music.

On *Driftworks* (Big Cat 1996) Schutze's energetic tones were not unlike those of Terry Riley on *A Rainbow In Curved Air* (1969) but with the emphasis on bass, percussion and 'noises'. Many critics noted how Schütze emphasized the extraneous sounds, with the music placed in the background. As if to retort, Schütze formed Phantom City, a live jazz improvisation group with Bill Laswell on bass. Their first recording, *Site Anubis* (Big Cat 1996), was based on a dream where a statue of the Egyptian god Anubis arrives to emit radiation in a city. The same year Schütze's second Virgin solo album, *Abysmal Evenings*, explored Debussyian Javanese gamelan in terms of tropical atmospheres. Hooked by the idea of location as a trigger for internal memories, Schütze created *Second Site* (Virgin 1997), based on photos of an eighteenth-century astrological garden in Jaipur, India. Over 100 minutes long, *Second Site* mixed percussion, reed flutes and spoken text and studio processing to an extraordinary level of realization. Amazingly, Schütze's interest in spatial music was pushed further through *Third Site* (Rykodisc 1999), an album of soundscapes, improvisation and jazzy Ambiences based on his own experiences of mountain-embedded thermal baths in a Swiss alpine village. This fascinating album, with its mixture of shakuhachi flutes, bowed guitars, gongs, vibraphone, electronics and the voice of Thomas Köner, revealed Schütze's enchantment with 'sense memory, sound mapping and the shaping of poetic narrative within designed spaces'.

Having worked with Schütze and Scanner, Jon Tye (aka MLO) became a respected curator of the strange and unpredictable. With a catalogue which embraces Ambient, electronica, Drum and Bass as well as the more fringe aspects of jazz improvisation, studio experiment and noise distortion, Tye inhabits an area which is so unique that it suits the tag Isolationist. As a DJ Tye could loop white noise with elements of musics as diverse as Ligeti and The Steve Miller Band. A catalyst for all kinds of 'chance musics', his own recording output and label fostered some of the late twentieth century's more unforeseen collaborations. Born in Kent, Tye moved to Devon in the 1960s before another move to London in his teens. His father was a keen music fan and over time the young Tye developed a passion for Mahler, Stockhausen, Ravi Shankar, The Velvet Underground and The Beatles – this latter interest perhaps pointing towards the constant melodicism which surfaces in his music. In his twenties he formed a group inspired by the American New Wave, then a trip to New York in 1985 converted him to Hip-Hop.

Soon Tye was invigorated by the slick sound of Chicago Acid House and Detroit Techno. Through various labels he had sonic connections to Derrick May, Orbital and The KLF. Then he formed the Music Of Life Orchestra (MLO) and recorded for R&S. The debut album, *IO*, (Rising High 1994) was one of the most sublime Ambient creations of its era, recalling Eno at his most inspired. Bored with the rise of Hardcore Techno, Tye formed his own label, LO Recordings, and began to push the sound envelope. *Extreme Possibilities 1* (LO 1995) was a highly accessible series of recordings which embraced Ambient Jungle, Space Jazz and marimba-based Techno. *Collaborations* (LO 1995) brought together interesting partnerships (Schütze with UK jazzer Lol Coxhill, Tye with schoolboy computer whizz Daniel Pemberton as 2 Player). Tye's own vehicle MLO released two gorgeous albums of Ambient House and Techno in *One Hour, One Minute, One Second* (ITP 1995) and the triple mix/remix concept *Plastic Apple* (Mo's 1996). Full of energy, Tye DJ'd, formed London clubs and even recorded more extreme (Stockhausen-influenced) noisescapes as Twisted Science, whose 1998 *Sharpest Tool In The Box* was a *Sunday Times* Record of the Week. A believer in tape loops and happy accidents, Tye undertook his most ambitious project with 1998's *Root*. Thirty different one-minute guitar pieces by Sonic Youth guitarist Thurston Moore were individually looped by Tye and then sent out to a range of other artists and musicians in vacuum-cleaner bags. People like David Bowie, Yoko Ono, Russell Mills and Scanner all responded with new audio or visual works which became both a successful exhibition and album. In effect the work of Jon Tye is a contradiction in terms. Through an 'Isolated' seeking out of the strange and unusual, he has on many occasions tipped over into the mainstream – in short, an Isolationist without being isolated.

LISTENING

Scanner's discography is quite large but listen to the moving Derek Jarman tribute *The Garden Is Full Of Metal* (Sub Rosa 1997) and the mature realization of *Lauwarm Instrumentals* (Sulphur 1999) to get a strong insight into his work.

Both *Patashnik* (Apollo 1994) and *Substrata* (All Saints 1997) are the essential albums to date of Biosphere. Anything by Thomas Köner on Barooni is representative, *Permafrost* (1993) being one of the greatest realizations of chilling Ambience on record. Paul Schütze's discography numbers well over twenty titles, with *Apart* (Virgin 1995) and *Third Site* (Virgin 1999) being two of his best works. Jon Tye's oeuvre is represented by *IO* (Rising High 1994), *Plastic Apple* (Mo's 1996) and the fascinating series of compilations on LO such as *Collaborations* (1995), *Further Mutations* (1997) and *Root* (1998).

Other recommended recordings are the gentle, lush, intelligent Techno of Global Communication's *76:14* (Dedicated 1994), the Moog synth drones of *Node* (Deviant 1995), the industrial soundscapes and treated guitar Ambiences of G. P. Hall's *Figments Of The Imagination* (FMR 1994), the Oriental dream worlds of Steve Jansen and Richard Barbieri on *Other Worlds In A Small Room* (Medium 1996), the analogue and instrumental washes of EAR's *Millennium Music* (Atavistic 1997) and finally the gorgeous Ambient compositions of Dutchman Mark Van Hoen on the masterly R&S/Apollo disc *Playing With Time* (1999), where Ligeti, Aphex Twin and Eno are all absorbed and reconstituted in a frosted futurescape.

MASSIVE ATTACK, TRICKY AND TRIP-HOP

UK House and Rave culture threw up many hybrids and in the long 1990s come-down from those first Ecstasy highs the music began to turn in on itself. Originating in Bristol, Trip-Hop was a slow, reflective blend of Rap/Hip-Hop, Dub Reggae, Rock, Slo-Mo Soul and film soundtrack. Its key was a brittle production sound which openly brandished the scratched-record sources of its samples. It relished the slow breakbeat, the strangely oscillating loop and inhabited a twilight world of late-night stoned reverie. Grass and hashish were its drugs and its output was a series of colour-noir aural documents resplendent in their various Ambiences. Emerging from the same late-80s Bristol collective, Massive Attack, Tricky and Portishead would all achieve worldwide fame with their own personalized takes on trippy Hip-Hop.

Massive Attack were the first out of the traps. Grant 'Daddy G' Marshall and Andrew 'Mushroom' Vowles were both members of a roving DJ/sound system group The Wild Bunch which included producer Nellee Hooper. Daddy G was born in the late 1950s while Mushroom was a late-60s child. Near the end of the 80s these two wanted a more group-like identity and recruited singer Robert '3D' Del Naja, born in 1966, to form Massive Attack. Contacts with the Rap artiste Neneh Cherry led to a recording situation. Nearly a year in production and using eight different studios in Bristol and London, *Blue Lines* (Wild Bunch/Circa 1991) was a *de facto* Trip-Hop document suffused with strings, smouldering Rap and dreamy hypnotic rhythms. Soul diva Shara Nelson was outstanding as the lead vocalist while veteran Reggae singer Horace Andy also made valuable contributions. Even Neneh Cherry herself turned up on the credits. Tricky, under his real name Adrian Thaws, rapped on two tracks but the clincher was the incredible 'Unfinished Sympathy', whose string section was recorded at Abbey Road studios. A locked-drum groove underpinned by a series of 'sound events' – sprinkled piano notes, shrieking diva, scratching, wavular string movement and ghost voices – 'Unfinished Sympathy' was topped off by Shara Nelson's spirited vocal performance.

Three years in the making and with Nellee Hooper back for production duties in Bristol and London, *Protection* (Wild Bunch/Circa 1994) was a brilliant record by anybody's standards. Tracey Thorn of jazz-tinged indie duo Everything But The Girl appeared on two cuts and Tricky on two others. Jazz pianist Craig Armstrong etched some beautiful sounds, Horace Andy was back on vocals and new black singer Nicolette cooed her way into one's subconscious. The overall production sound was a giant leap on from 1991. 'Protection', with its ricocheting guitar, trap-drum beat and synthesizer decoration, single-handedly restored Tracey Thorn's career as she proceeded to record a new Everything But The Girl album, *Walking Wounded* (Virgin 1996), in similar vein.

Tricky and 3D were writing more and more in the studio and the jumpy 'Karmacoma' was indicative of the twenty-six-year-old Tricky's future direction. 'Three' was a rolling beat full of velvet-like touches, soundtrack music for the imagination. 'Weather Storm' was purely instrumental – a shuffling bass figure to a background of light percussive rain and Craig Armstrong's deft after-dark piano. The album just swam in its own fog, the lilting beats seemingly permeated by the marijuana smoke the group blew in the cover photo. Fittingly the album closed with a sampled Rap version of The Doors' 'Light My Fire'.

A life-long love of Reggae saw Massive Attack do an entire album remix with the Mad Professor in 1995. Never in a hurry, it would be another three years before their third album proper, *Mezzanine* (Virgin 1998), appeared. Recorded in Bristol and mixed at Jimi Hendrix's old London studio Olympic, the album, right from the opening sound of 'Angel', had a darker mood, driven by a stronger leaning towards rock. 'Risingson' continued the rock grunge (though balanced by some lovely tweaked harmonized vocals) and even included a sample of The Velvet Underground. The entry of Liz Fraser (in her first outing since the disintegration of The Cocteau Twins) on 'Teardrop' pushed things into a new dimension, her floating voice almost created for Trip-Hop grooves. Elsewhere samples from The Cure and Isaac Hayes peppered a disquietening record. The mini-soundtrack 'Exchange' with its merging of Dub and filmy orchestration appeared in two versions. Fraser even guested on two further tracks and performed live on the subsequent 'Mezzanine' tour. Yet, after achieving stadium-level popularity, Massive Attack were reduced to a duo by the close of 1998 when 'Mushroom' Vowles quit the group. 3D and Daddy G promised to play no more concerts until 2001 while recruiting Fraser as star vocalist for a fourth album.

Tricky was to benefit enormously from his early contributions to Massive Attack. With money from the group he was able to invest in a four-track home studio and in 1992 put down the first of his amazingly lucid paranoid takes on Trip-Hop. The song was called 'Aftermath' and it would catapult Tricky to worldwide fame when Island re-released it in 1994. His featured singer was fifteen-year old Martina Topley-Bird, a schoolgirl and soul mate whose gently lullabying vocals perfectly matched his own sense of delirium. Tricky released the track himself in 1993 and to this day it stands as one of Trip-Hop's finest moments. Framed around a never-ending slow, thumping beat with a bottom-less bass, the song's quality was in the array of sounds and samples Tricky chose to employ. Flutes, voices and a fuzz guitar were the first instrumental impressions. The shrill sounds of wires and struck barrels were also in evidence. Two samples from David Sylvian and the *Blade Runner* soundtrack topped off a magical studio mix. At times the lyrics distinctly related to pain and mother-hood, at others they were lost in a haze of sound. It was this particular quality of indecipherability against the clarity of repetitive structure that would make Tricky a star.

Born Adrian Thaws in Bristol in 1968, Tricky came from a tough back-ground. His epileptic mother killed herself when he was three. He never really knew his father and, like the young Jimi Hendrix, was brought up by a series of relatives. Petty crime, murder and prison were the backdrop to his young life. Marijuana was a common escape and in his early teens he began to smoke in quantity. He admired the multi-racial aspect of Ska and showed a tendency to Jamaican Rap. He found refuge in Bristol's black clubs and slowly forged a relationship with Massive Attack. His stoned, mumbling reflections on life evinced what it was like to be a poor English black kid at the end of the twentieth century. He absorbed Acid Jazz (a form of jazz with House and Techno characteristics), Hip-Hop and Reggae but in particular the possibilities of new home-production technology. After the success of 'Aftermath', Tricky was signed to Island and in 1995 came the critically acclaimed album *Max-inquaye*, named after his mother.

Maxinquaye was a world in slow motion, perfectly balanced home recordings which threw in a slew of sampled riffs, sounds and colours from Tricky's Akai S1000 sampler. The main themes were sexuality, broken emotional ties and dope-fuelled paranoia. 'Overcome' had the quality of African dream, with its ghost rhythms and use of Ambient space. 'Black Steel' jumped out of the soup as it was a rock take on a Public Enemy rap drenched in Indian tabla. 'Hell Is Around The Corner' used an entrancing slow soul beat while 'Pumpkin' was Drum and Bass so light it fluttered in the ethereal air, its noirish feel as close to Portishead as Tricky would ever get. There was the brilliant descending guitar note of 'Suffocated Love' and 'Feed Me' was permeated with the feel of Bob Marley's redemptive Reggae.

Established, Tricky worked with singers Neneh Cherry and Björk while doing remixes for Stevie Wonder. He then travelled to Jamaica with Martina (who was the mother of his first child). Beginning as a live album but ending up a sampled one, *Pre-Millennium Tension* (1996) benefited from a superior production sound. Piano, violin, harmonica and guitar were also to the fore and mix-downs were done both in Spain and New York, where Tricky would begin a new life. Full of rage and self-absorption, *Pre-Millennium Tension* veered from Hip-Hop intensity to full-on ghetto Reggae. Yet among the grind were two brilliant creations. 'Makes Me Wanna Die' was supported by lovely jazz-guitar chords and an underwater drum beat over which Martina sang poetically about 'walking on the moon' and 'smoking hydroponic' (an incredibly strong home-grown marijuana hybrid). 'Christiansands' was quintessential Trip-Hop, its fleeting rhythm slowing down in front of your ears as Tricky and Martina duetted about religion.

Tricky's uncompromising 'ghetto politics', his preference for wearing dresses, his love of weed (he even called his own label Durban Poison) and asthmatic condition were all lapped up by the press. His third album, *Angels With Dirty Faces* (1998), was a claustrophobic mix of Gospel, Dub, rock, Hip-Hop and blues. The press turned, accusing Tricky of self-indulgence, and the esteemed critic Ian MacDonald trounced the record for lacking any real harmonic progression. *Angels* used rock instrumentation as a foundation with off-beat rhythms and guest musicians like guitarist Marc Ribot. Martina was again an outstanding foil for Tricky's sometimes demented rantings. The dirge-like character of the blues fitted an album partly recorded in New Orleans. 'Broken Homes' was full of Ambient space, spirited along by English vocalist Polly-Jean Harvey. 'Singing The Blues' saw Martina approximate Billie Holiday on a dirge about trying to make ends meet. On the almost-Ambient 'Carriage For Two' (about his baby girl) Tricky credits Holiday, while on the excessive 'Record Companies' he sang: 'My baby mamma kick it like Billie Holiday.'

No one could fault Tricky's rage. Even with record industry support he was still angry. 'Money Greedy' was an intense rock blues which sampled Public Enemy. It could have come off U2's 1997 *Pop*, an album which used Nellee Hooper, Howie B and Mike 'Spike' Stent, all of whom were involved with Tricky and Massive Attack. 'Analyse Me' had a light bell quality underscored by occasional shard guitar. On it Tricky sang about his mother and Martina's vocalise was perfectly aerial. 'Talk To Me (Angels With Dirty Faces)' was dark and dirge-like with a clicking hi-hat and dissonant drum plus a wisp of background flute. In terms of downer records, *Angels With Dirty Faces* was in a league of its own. Then Tricky went off to Los Angeles and came up with *Juxtapose* (1999), a far sunnier-sounding outing. Though its boom drums and up-front production with US Hip-Hop collaborators like DJ Muggs pulled it away from Trip-Hop towards mainstream popular music, elements like the piano or sitar-like acoustic guitar of 'For Real' and the classical guitar and Eastern strings of 'Wash My Soul' (which quoted Julie Andrews) displayed Tricky's continued fascination with Ambient sound veneers.

Both Massive Attack and Tricky played a part in the genesis of Portishead, named after an estuary town near Bristol and formed in 1993 by Geoff Barrow and Adrian Utley. With the addition of singer Beth Gibbons, Portishead's moody meeting of noir soundtrack, slow Hip-Hop breakbeats and heart-wrenching blues was to catapult them to worldwide fame when their debut album, *Dummy* (1994), sold a million copies. Barrow was born in the early 1970s and worked in Bristol's Coach House studios as a tape operator. There he met Massive Attack and assisted in the computer programming of *Blue Lines* in 1991. Also interested in turntables and keyboards, he even helped Tricky find his studio feet at the same time. Utley was born in Portishead in 1957 and had been a session musician for years, loved jazz, played with guitarist Jeff Beck and had an abiding passion for Mahler and Ennio Morricone. He played bass, guitar, Fender Rhodes electric keyboard, organ and loved analogue synthesizers like the ARP Odyssey and MiniMoog. Utley's enthusiasm for 1960s soundtrack music and Barrow's admiration for Afrika Bambaataa led to a spatial style of Ambient Hip-Hop. This detailed sound was topped off by the racked, aerated voice of Beth Gibbons, born in 1965, an aspiring singer who performed blues in local pubs.

Portishead's style gelled in 1994 after they decided to soundtrack a short film. Their approach was to perform live in various Bristol studios. They liked analogue and valve equipment, even going so far as to master on to vinyl to get a crackly quality. Looped beats and other segments were stored on Akai samplers. Individual instrumental sounds were added for effect – Hip-Hop scratches, Fender Rhodes piano, distorted sounds. The resulting instrumental mixes were then sent to Gibbons for her to improvise her usually tortured vocal over the top. Then more mixing was done. This painstaking approach was obvious from the dizzying array of samples and sounds on *Dummy* (Go! Beat 1994) and guaranteed its 1995 status as best new UK album.

Yet in retrospect *Dummy* has dated faster than either Massive Attack or Tricky's music of the same period. Its overuse in advertising and film is one reason but another was its nagging squawking bird scratches and Theremin-like ghost sounds. (Utley has always been a fan of famous film composer and Theremin-user Bernard Herrmann.) It also had a distinctly English sound, a music-hall or barrel-organ quality which sounded somehow parochial. There's certainly an air of cerebral contrivance to the music itself – an entire world away from the naturalistic black expression of Tricky. Yet, for all that, specific tracks on *Dummy* still hold their potency. 'Strangers' was built on a solid sliding beat backed by fuzz guitar, horns and bossa-nova rhythms. Gibbons's voice was mixed into the far distance and the whole stopped to allow for an Ambient sample from jazz group Weather Report. 'It Could Be Sweet' was light Acid Jazz with breakbeats, acoustic drums and cymbals where the Fender Rhodes piano conveyed the feeling of falling rain.

'Roads' was in fact a pun on the famous electric keyboard. Shimmering Rhodes with long-decaying notes began a track which featured looped drums, strings arranged by Utley and a marvellously creamy echoing guitar reminiscent of old US soul records. As a single 'live' performance this was the best the album had to offer. The closing track, 'Glory Box', was identical in style to Tricky's 'Hell Is Round The Corner' (from *Maxinquaye*) because it used the same sampled Isaac Hayes bass/beat figure. Gibbons's tale of failed Eros was heightened by a torturously mangled feedback-led guitar solo which rose to an explosive breakbeat climax topped off by her echo-laden, screaming vocal. After the success of *Dummy* Utley and Barrow 'retro-fitted' a Bristol studio and called it State Of The Art. Analogue synths and computers were combined while two agonizing years were spent on *Portishead* (Go! Beat 1997), an album of spectacular Russian-styled string blasts, oscillating electronic tones and giddy rhythms which continued exactly where *Dummy* had left off.

LISTENING

Massive Attack's early recordings are credited to Wild Bunch/Circa. The definitive *Protection* (1994) is a must for anyone interested in Trip-Hop, particularly for its contributions by singer Tracey Thorn and pianist Craig Armstrong. All of Tricky's material goes through Island records, the early albums routed through the 4th & Broadway subsidiary. *Maxinquaye* (1995) is outstanding but his subsequent albums right up to 1999's *Juxtapose* all possess originality. Portishead's *Dummy* (Go! Beat 1994) was an era-defining album for it brought the Ambience of Trip-Hop to a mass white audience. Honourable mention must go to Howie B's *Music For Babies* (Polydor 1996). Born in 1963, Howard Bernstein was raised in Scotland and studied psychology in Manchester. Inspired by the music of Santana, John McLaughlin and Brian Eno, he made a name for himself in 1980s London as a creative engineer. Through Nellee Hooper he gravitated to recording with Massive Attack and Tricky. His 'vibing' skills attracted the interest of U2 and Eno, who invited him to shape mixes for their Ambient album *Original Soundtracks 1* (Island 1995), released under the name Passengers. That same year Howie B made his debut solo album, *Music For Babies*, in Spain. The result was an album of warm electronic soundwashes, VCS3 bubbles, spatial Japanese vibes and sleepy Trip-Hop rhythms encompassing cool jazz. His subsequent programming and loop contributions to U2's Techno-rock album *Pop* (Island 1997) made him famous.

COLDCUT

If any outfit celebrated the new 'barriers are down' ethos that followed House and Techno culture it was Coldcut. Famed for their late-night weekend radio shows on London's Kiss FM during the 1990s, Coldcut took the philosophy of sampling to its logical extreme. Dubbed 'sampladelia', their mix transmissions were cornucopias of every musical style ever invented, occasionally hooked to the relentless beat of House. Huge tapestries of sound stretched in front of the listener as rock greats like Jimi Hendrix and U2 rubbed shoulders with James Brown, Philip Glass and Vangelis. Ethnic flutes and drums were as likely to crop us as the latest piece of Ambient Techno sheen. Beyond this Coldcut made CD albums and embraced every form of computer culture to make advances in areas like CD-Rom and video software. Their vision, conceived as 'zentertainment', used every conceivable tool to forge new musical experiences for the twenty-first century.

Coldcut comprised Matt Black and Jonathan More, who were inspired by US scratch and Hip-Hop music to become noted DJs in the House and Acid House-drenched London of 1987–8. Their first recording was *Beats And Pieces*, put together at home in 1987 on a cheap four-track cassette recording system, a work which made ample use of Led Zeppelin's famous big drum sound from 'When The Levee Breaks' (1971). They became in–demand Acid House mixers and recorded with popular singers like Yazz and Lisa Stansfield. They combined old analogue synthesizers like Moog and EMS with the typical Roland drum boxes of their day.

In 1989 they signed to Big Life, who released *What's That Noise*. This was followed in 1990 by *Some Like It Cold* and then in 1993 Arista put out *Philosophy*. All recordings took a cavalier attitude to tune, instead reinforcing the sampled texture and the timbre of individual and effects instruments. Mixing an independent streak with a strong sense of musical revolution, they had formed their own label, Ninja Tune, as early as 1990, which helped to cushion their fall from Arista in 1994.

Concentration on video led to the formation of Hex, a multi-media arm of Ninja Tune which embraced CD-Rom (a form Coldcut would excel in), club culture and the Internet. But the area which showcased their genius was the elongated and inspired mixes on London's Kiss FM, on a weekend radio slot called *Solid Steel*. This was a new form of mix 'n' match music which treated all sonic history as one giant meta-form to be sampled. Anything could happen, any form of music was ripe to be transplanted and recontextualized by virtue of new computer sampling technology. Yet More and Black did not lose sight of their listeners, bathing them in luxuriant electronic Ambience one minute, sliding some wonderful black soul diva into focus the next, until some mind-warping Pete Namlook Techno rhythm came into view. The very nature of their programming reminded one of Terry Riley's spiritual Minimalism and the linear expansiveness of Indian raga.

Working out of their London Ninja Tune headquarters, Coldcut continued to push their art to the limits. They manipulated old records, old analogue synthesizers, new digital sound tools and hard–disc computer recording to achieve astonishing results. They boasted of having nearly 15,000 samples at their disposal as well as banks of sound-processing equipment for effects like delay, echo, harmonizing and compression. In 1997 they released the acclaimed double CD *Let Us Play* on Ninja Tune. Ostensibly taking ten years to record, *Let Us Play* combined live playing with a digital/sampling ethos to create a textured futuristic jazz music. The package's second disc was a CD-Rom playable on both Apple Macintosh and PC systems and featured snazzy video and visuals, lots of Coldcut information and interactive software aids to help the user remix CD tracks and generate his or her own beat patterns. Always inventive and future-thinking, More and Black (in association with the Cambridge visual company CamArt) put together 'V Jamm' in 1999, a pioneering software tool which enabled users to voyage into a new world of video and TV sampling and image mixing.

LISTENING

As well as the recordings mentioned above, Coldcut (via Ninja Tune) released *Journeys By DJ* in 1995, a beat collage of various DJ recordings and *More Beats And Pieces* in 1997, a remixed version of their original 1987 recording after it was desk-tweaked by other musician-DJs. On the track of the continuous digestion and reabsorption of sound, Coldcut then put out *Let Us Replay* (1999), a remix of their 1995 album with such revered names as Grandmaster Flash, Mixmaster Morris and Carl Craig cropping up on the credit list.

DJ SHADOW AND DJ SPOOKY

Influenced by Dub Reggae and disco, DJ culture and Hip-Hop really took off when Grandmaster Flash created the classic 'Wheels Of Steel' in 1981. The combining and sampling of nine different sources 'live' on record decks was audacious. By 1990 in the UK the DJ was seen as culturally pivotal to the future of music, a player of diverse sounds, a breaker of boundaries and prejudices, a harbinger of a new form of symphony. Initially many were sceptical of the DJ's powers of transformation but by the mid-1990s two American individuals emerged to push the art form into entirely new areas. Both DJ Shadow and DJ Spooky collaged music's entire history into shifting 'electronic hybrids' where the musicality was in the assembly of edits, samples and beats. Shadow's Hip-Hop roots led to a form of Ambient Hop. Spooky's intellectual basis and Dub-informed mixes resulted in a form of Space-Hop. Listening to their output was akin to taking a ride on the rollercoaster of twentieth-century aural history.

DJ Shadow came from Davis, California and was inspired by Grandmaster Flash's 1982 international hit 'The Message' to pursue a career in Hip-Hop music. Fascinated by the plastic nature of edited sounds and breakbeats, Shadow wished to combine them with a wider canvas of sources, including film soundtracks and jazz. He worked on West Coast radio, made cassette mixes on a home four-track and dreamed of transfiguring the Rap-oriented nature of the then current Hip-Hop into a broader canvas of tones and sounds. A thirteen-minute mix titled 'In/Flux' (1994) saw the white DJ heralded as the progressive successor to Grandmaster Flash. But it was his monumental 1996 album *Endtroducing* . . . (Mo Wax) which really made his name as a master of 'the displaced context of sounds juxtaposed with music'.

Endtroducing . . . was sleeved with images of record buying and record covers. Shadow pronounced on the album's copious credits that 'it reflected a lifetime of vinyl culture'. In its double vinyl version, Side One constituted a plethora of recorded skips and weird percussive loops. Yet acoustic piano, scratches, narrative segments, funky electric guitar and ghost arias littered the soundscape. On Side Two Shadow sampled Tangerine Dream's 'Invisible Limits' from their 1976 *Stratosfear* album and mixed it with some wonderfully skimming percussion. For 'Stem/Long Stem', Shadow chose the orchestral textures of harp, cor anglais and strings, placed alongside a slew of different drum sounds plus an excerpt of Elliot Gould's voice from the 1973 film *The Long Goodbye*. What ostensibly began as a wedging of classical chamber music right up against Hip-Hop militancy ended with a sublimely beautiful acoustic-guitar coda.

Shadow was one DJ credited with inventing Trip-Hop, a term which described trippy Hip-Hop. Yet *Endtroducing* . . . possessed none of the druggy aura of, say, Tricky. Shadow's creations possessed more cerebral clarity. Ambient Hip-Hop or Ambient Hop was a better description of a music dizzying in its panoply of samples, majestic in its forward motion. Vinyl disc two featured the resonant ballad 'Midnight In A Perfect World' alongside rhythmic tracks derived from Can and James Brown, and ended in a jazzy mood. Recorded in San Francisco, *Endtroducing* . . . listed James Brown, Coldcut and The Art Of Noise among its many dedications.

DJ Spooky was black, from a middle-class Washington family and multi-talented. Born in 1971, he had an Ivy League education (in French Literature and Philosophy) and loved Hendrix, Hip-Hop, European cinema, painting, sculpture and serious writing. His real name was Paul Miller but he termed himself DJ Spooky, The Subliminal Kid, after a character in a William Burroughs novel. He rigged up various sound emitters and began DJing at college in the late 1980s. One night in Washington he was playing records on LSD and perceived the cursive nature of sound, its ability to create in his words 'mood sculptures'. His relocation to New York found the dreadlocked thinker carving out new spaces for Ambient music. Spooky saw the Mix as the most important element, the creation of something new 'between abstraction and cacophony'. He saw Rap as a dead end and, like DJ Shadow, wanted to extend the possibilities of Hip-Hop. He called his creations 'recombinations'. I would term them Spacey Hip-Hop or simply Space-Hop.

Spooky's debut disc, *Songs Of A Dead Dreamer* (1996), had a darker edge than Shadow's beauteous sampling. Shifting blocks of sound and African/Reggae rhythms clouded the foreground while indeterminate noises hovered behind. It took a long time for a groove to emerge from this dense forest and when it did it was of the cosmic Bootsy-Collins-meets-Sun-Ra variety. Elsewhere there were sonic references to the writer H. G. Wells, the famous sci-fi film *Forbidden*

Planet, Erik Satie and Klaus Schulze. With much use of echo boxes, Spooky's seventy-four-minute debut was one huge dubscape. Its booklet set out Spooky's musical philosophy and discussed how Thomas Edison set in motion the Ambient nature of imperfect recordings; flowing assemblages of sound; and the kinetic nature of Spooky's musical 'objectiles'. Spooky saw the Mix as 'the electronic equivalent of blank canvas', a 'communal art structure', and the role of the DJ as one 'reconfiguring ethnic, national and sexual identity'.

LISTENING

DJ Shadow's *Endtroducing . . .* (Mo Wax 1996) is simply one of the finest Ambient albums to emerge from American Hip-Hop, an essential experience in sound from start to finish. Its cover sticker even proclaimed him the 'Jimi Hendrix of the sampler'. DJ Spooky's *Songs Of A Dead Dreamer* (Asphodel 1996) places Dub Reggae and Hip-Hop in a new context of dense cosmic hubbub. His *Riddim Warfare* album (Outpost 1998) was more Hip-Hop or Rap in character but with blues-guitar interludes, female vocal samples and found voices screaming for your attention. Only the Dub/World Music Ambiences of its final seven minutes offered the listener any real respite.

GOLDIE AND AMBIENT DRUM AND BASS

Ambient Drum and Bass was really the intersecting of two different musical currents of the UK dance scene of the early 1990s. The first was the mixing of Acid House music with flavours of Reggae Dub, black rock, jazz and the breakbeats of Hip-Hop. The second was an increase in beats per minute owing to Hardcore's obsession with speedier drugs. If the average House track was 120bpm then Hardcore revelled in 160bpm upwards. As the beats accelerated Hardcore sounded sillier but the net effect was one that Brian Eno had predicted long before, that the more events in a piece of music the more uniform that music. All of this was adapted by DJs and musicians to forge the first truly black British music: Jungle, better known as Drum and Bass.

Its origins are credited to two black scenesters named Fabio and Grooverider, whose London club Rage pioneered the web of reggae, soul, jazz, Hip-Hop, House, Hardcore Techno and Ambient sounds. From the late 1980s to 1993 Rage birthed Jungle and transformed the life of its most famous exponent, Goldie. Fabio and Grooverider's style was speeded-up breakbeats and deep, deep bass sounds. Within black culture the new sound had to compete with imported Digital Reggae from Jamaica (Ragga) but the potential of fragmented drum loops plus the club scene proved too much of a pull for sophisticated black British youth, who rejected Ecstasy for cocaine and marijuana. Jungle harnessed new developments in sampling and sequencing to push the House revolution to its logical zenith, Drum and Bass. If 1960s rock led to treble-heavy, guitar-focused music, 1980s House was all about beat and rhythm. Nineteen-nineties Jungle stripped the dressings back until the popular term Drum and Bass became the moniker for a music entirely made up of electronically morphed drum and bass sounds.

What's really fascinating about Jungle is that it was the Ambient form of the music which proved most successful. It lent itself to albums, even highly ambitious double CDs. Ambient Jungle or Intelligent Drum and Bass was not just the preserve of Goldie. Before him practitioners such as LTJ Bukem, DJ Rap and 4 Hero were all doing wonderful things with breakbeats and Ambience. LTJ Bukem is perceived rightly as the cool professor of 'pure' Drum and Bass. Hailing from the South London suburb of Croydon, Bukem (Danny Williamson) was classically educated with an ear which bent towards the warm jazz sound of the Fender Rhodes electric piano. DJing through the Rave scene, he arrived at the beginning of the 1990s with his sound already honed. Kinetic drums were surrounded by a smooth jazz Ambience which immediately lulled the listener into a state of wanting more. Establishing his own Good Looking label, Bukem released the genre-defining 'Atlantis' (1992) with its bass figure, bell timbres, sparkling surfaces and soul singer ululating nothing but tones. In places it had an Acid House quality and the elongated synth washes of an Eno or Carl Craig but its defining feature were its jittery, speeded-up drum breaks which possessed a strange calming quality. 'Music' (1993) was even better. Oriental bell motifs floated over a belting Gospel breakbeat as held synth chords floated up and down, not unlike a vintage Klaus Schulze performance. This went on unerringly for a whole nine minutes. His reputation established' Bukem founded Speed, a club in London's West End with Jungle pioneer Fabio which oozed Ambient Jazz sophistication. Bukem's Good Looking label became one of the cornerstones of Intelligent Drum and Bass, acts like Aquarius and Artemis pointing to a return to the purity of original Detroit Techno.

Dego McFarlane and Mark Mac, better known as 4 Hero, started their own label, Reinforced, in a North-west London flat in 1989. Hell-bent on absorbing all the trends into a new interpretation of Hip-Hop instrumentality, they initially reflected the dynamic and enervating impact of Hardcore Techno. The duo's (non-drug) take on the state of Hardcore could be heard on 1993's *Journey From The Light*, whose 'Elements' combined bits of 808 State, helium angel choirs and pitch-bent Don McLean. Obviously tired of Rave culture, 4 Hero spent much time in their Internal Affairs studio with Goldie, working on samples and pushing the art of the breakbeat so that it could become a super-malleable form. Moving towards a fusion of jazz-rock, German synthesizer and super-breakbeat, *Parallel Universe* (1994) was thoughtful stuff indeed, its analogue synth sounds reminiscent in places of mid-1970s Marvin Gaye. As time progressed 4 Hero soaked up Trip-Hop and Ambient with ease, and their Talkin' Loud album *Two Pages* (1998; released 1999 as *Two Pages Reinterpreta-*

tions) merged strings, vibraphones, soul lyric, lush jazz keyboard/synth and upright bass with a rainbow collection of fascinating breakbeats.

Which brings us neatly to Goldie, the man who grabbed the furies of Hardcore and turned them into something beautifully sensual. Goldie, born Clifford Price in Wolverhampton in 1965, was the product of a mixed marriage and a broken home. His painful childhood was spent drifting from foster families to children's homes around the English Midlands. Inspired by New York graffiti culture and the Northern Soul dance scene which blended hard funk with beautiful melody, Goldie became a convert to Hip-Hop. In 1984 Birmingham Council commissioned a large mural from him, his eye-catching graphic comic-strip style a reminder of the Pop art of the 1960s but with a more streetwise edge. Two years later Channel Four TV took him to America to make a film about graffiti art and in New York's South Bronx he met his hero Afrika Bambaataa. Soon he was living there, later transiting to Miami, where a penchant for making and wearing gold jewellery resulted in his catchy moniker. Back in the UK in the late 1980s he painted for Soul II Soul and immersed himself in the emergent Trip-Hop scene of Massive Attack, Nellee Hooper and Howie B. By the early 1990s Goldie was a successful artist in his own right.

4 Hero hired him to do artist and A&R work for their Reinforced label. One night in 1991 he went to Rage and took Ecstasy, his mind dancing to the sharding drums and deep booming bass of Fabio and Grooverider's mixes. Now obsessed by Breakbeat, Goldie kept going into the studio and working on his sound – something that floated upwards from Hardcore, that retained the 150bpm acceleration but went somewhere else. Days were spent with 4 Hero researching sampled sounds, one session filling fifteen DATS with new sonic material. By 1993 Goldie had found his musical identity with 'Terminator', an eerie breakbeat track which used a new pioneering technique known as 'time-stretching' whereby samples could be stretched over any beat structure without altering their pitches. This led to a vertiginous alternation of fast and slow within a music whose actual linear time passage was difficult to gauge.

More significant was 'Angel' (1993), which introduced Northern Soul singer Diane Charlemagne to the world at large. Her vocal soared over a panoply of crashing beat loops, textured synths, bone-crushing rhythms, backwards tape samples and Hardcore Techno synth stabs until the very breakbeats themselves became melodic components. The track was co-produced by 4 Hero in their own studio. Goldie then began remixing, which brought him into contact with software engineer Rob Playford, who owned Moving Shadow, a label dedicated to pushing the envelope of Breakbeat. Originally a 1980s soul and Acid House DJ, he graduated to making home music with a Yamaha DX7, Atari computer and Akai S950 sampler. During the early 90s Playford made records where breakbeat loops were repeated over and over. He learned to speed up the sound and thicken it by cutting up the loops and overlapping them. After 'Angel' Goldie teamed up with Playford and worked at the latter's home for over four months in 1993–4. Using Notator software and armfuls of Goldie's research DATs, the duo set to work to make a classic Drum and Bass track using everything they knew. Three different string parts were produced on an E-mu vintage keys module which flew up and down the sound field. Drum breaks were split to give a circular space feel and extra heavy basslines were added. Originally intended to be forty minutes, the resultant 'Timeless' came in at twenty-one minutes. Breathtakingly multi-dimensional, at times ethnic in its flute and Japanese textures, the track was symphonic in its ambition. On the strength of this alone Goldie was snapped up by ffrr and it was released as a single in the winter of 1994.

Nearly a year later the album *Timeless* (ffrr 1995) made Goldie a star. Quickly selling over 100,000 copies, it brought Ambient Jungle/Drum and Bass to the mainstream, its title track, with Diane Charlemagne singing about 'Inner City Life', mesmerizing all who heard it. The album combined kicking rhythms and futuristic synth noises with a widescreen Ambience that had never been heard before. Playford was now using an Apple Macintosh running new software and loads of enhancers, expanders and modulators. Tracks like 'State Of Mind' were lush Acid Jazz while the mind-boggling 'Sensual' stretched time, pitch and whatnot into an orb of tweaked sounds which ranged from Acid House to drifting Ambience. The overall effect of *Timeless* was reassurance, the feeling that out of the darkness of Hardcore could come beauty and light.

Goldie's Metalheadz label and club quickly dominated the scene. Both Brian Eno and David Bowie showed interest as Goldie grew rich on his celebrity. Meanwhile Playford fitted out London's old Trident studios with all manner of analogue and digital equipment. Working upwards of fifteen hours a day, Goldie spent much time recording *Saturnz Return*, a double CD released in early 1998 which many felt was over-ambitious. Disc One contained a sixty-minute dedication to his mother where the huge Drum and Bass middle section was surrounded by a twenty-six-piece string orchestra. The disc ended with a haunting David Bowie Ambient vocal and a hidden classical environmental track, 'Dream Within'. Disc Two was bristling with 'loud' sounds – Noel Gallagher's guitar and KSR-1's rap to name but two, and again lush, enveloping Ambiences – the wonderful Diane Charlemagne floater 'Believe', the cool ethno-jazz Drum and Bass of 'Dragonfly' and, in 'Letter Of Fate', the haunting electro-strings of a reminiscence of attempted suicide. Interestingly, *Saturnz Return* closed with a Goldie meets Miles Davis scenario as an impatient horn blasted over the drum breaks. (By 1999 Columbia were commissioning Goldie's Metalheadz protégé Doc Scott to give Miles Davis the Drum and Bass treatment.) Television crews then rushed to the UK to film Goldie, the man who did most to prove that Drum and Bass music could go way beyond its initial underground status.

And finally, in a field mostly dominated by male artists, we must mention the brilliant DJ Rap. Born Charissa Saveiro in Singapore in the early 1970s, she arrived in the UK while still young and ended up a teenage runaway. Finding a natural home within the Rave scene, she quickly began making her own music.

Intriguingly, her debut track was titled 'Ambience – The Adored', and here she proved herself a good vocalist. She worked the scene hard, constantly DJing, and in 1993 made the noted Ambient Jungle track 'Spiritual Aura', whose strings and belting rhythms were up there with anything by Goldie. She formed her own imprint and evolved her personal style of quaking bass and steel-hard beats. After a slew of releases her major-label debut, *Learning Curve* (Epic 1998), confirmed her talent as a great pop star who could cut it rough with the best of them. Spiritual Ambiences floated all around the floor-thudding breaks, Rap even acknowledging the maestro influence of Derrick May as 'Ordinary Day' borrowed the opening melody of his classic 1986 Detroit Techno anthem 'Strings Of Life'.

LISTENING

LTJ Bukem's music came out on his own Good Looking label. Such mellifluous Drum and Bass tracks as 'Music', 'Atlantis', 'Moodswings' and 'Cosmic Interlude' can be found on the 1996–9 collections *Logical Progression* and *Points In Time*. His twenty-first-century debut album, *Journey Inwards*, was even more accomplished. 4 Hero's work dominates the entire Jungle and Drum and Bass oeuvre. Their futuristic *Parallel Universe* (Reinforced 1995) is often name-checked but the Talkin' Loud albums *Two Pages* (1998) and *Two Pages Reinterpretations* (1999) embrace much black music history with strong leanings towards cosmic jazz.

Of course 4 Hero are all over Goldie's iconic debut album *Timeless* (ffrr 1995), which mixes sensuality with a huge Drum and Bass ambition. The trilogy of 'Inner City Life'/'Pressure'/'Jah' which makes up the opening twenty-one minutes still possesses the power to sonically surprise. *Saturnz Return* (ffrr 1998) was heavily criticized for its length (150 minutes 35 seconds) and its orchestrated hour-long paean 'Mother', but in places it was truly ravishing, not least on the drifting Soul Ambience of 'Believe'. Mindful of criticism, Goldie even released a slimmed-down version of the album in *Ring Of Saturn* (ffrr) late in 1998. Highly recommended is the Epic Japan edition of DJ Rap's *Learning Curve* (1998) which has a different track order and listing from the UK original and includes a new version of her totemic 'Spiritual Aura'.

COURTNEY PINE AND TRIP JAZZ

Courtney Pine arrived in the mid-1980s as the most visible face of UK jazz. Black, committed and with a mellifluous tone on bass clarinet, tenor and soprano saxophones, Pine embraced all that was best in post-war jazz, then absorbed and reinterpreted it in terms of melodic and often sensuous compositions. Astonishingly, he easily digested the achievement of John Coltrane, whose tumbling note technique and mysticism became key ingredients of Pine's art. As time went by Pine's music became more spiritual and expansive, culminating in the rich tableau of *To The Eyes Of Creation* (Island 1992). Evolving at breakneck speed, Pine immersed himself in New York Hip-Hop, performing with DJs and Rappers like Gang Starr before recording a pair of late-1990s albums featuring sequenced loops, scratches and breakbeats. Almost a missionary in his faith in acoustic Jazz, he nevertheless performed this music with DJs and technicians handling sequencers and samplers around the world. So impressive was Pine's 'Trip Jazz' that even the Drum and Bass giants 4 Hero ended up remixing his music.

Courtney Pine was born in London in 1964 of Jamaican parents. A bright child, he took thoroughgoing music lessons while at school, achieving high grades in theory, arranging and counterpoint. He seriously studied piano and clarinet in his teens. Even during his schooldays he was sessioning for Reggae bands. Once out of school in 1981, Pine learned much about musical discipline and performance while on the road with various soul, reggae and funk groups. In south London he worked hard to promote jazz throughout the black communities, forming the Jazz Warriors big band in 1985, which included the talents of tenor player Steve Williamson and vocalist Cleveland Watkiss. Pine was soon working with famous jazz drummers Elvin Jones and Art Blakey. A chance appearance on television led to a contract with the Island label.

Rehearsed in two days and recorded in three, *Journey To The Urge Within* (Island 1986) rapidly sold 100,000 copies and charted. A simple amalgam of jazz standards, Coltrane sax stylings and soul blues, the album was authentic British jazz made by a black jazzer who spoke in eloquent terms. Only twenty-two at the time, Pine could draw a line through 'the Trad Jazz of Sidney Bechet, the Swing Jazz of Coleman Hawkins/Lester Young, the Be-Bop of Charlie Parker/Dexter Gordon, the Hard Bop of Sonny Rollins and John Coltrane, the Free Jazz of Pharoah Sanders/Albert Ayler/Ornette Coleman and the Fusions of Weather Report and The Mahavishnu Orchestra'. Pine was particularly fond of the mystical Free Jazz of John Coltrane's 1960's recordings *Om* and *Ascension* and he was already studying Chinese and African music.

As Pine adopted a Coltrane-like quest, his subsequent recordings, like *Destiny's Song And The Image of Pursuance* (1988), *The Vision's Tale* (1989) and *Within The Realms Of Our Dreams* (1991), revealed an artist whose musical thirst seemed unquenchable. His search reached a climax on *To The Eyes Of Creation* (1992). The sleeve notes cited such sources as *The Tibetan Book Of The Dead*, the Koran, the Bible, the *Bhagavad Gita*, Rastafarianism and various Afro-centric philosophies as inspirational, while on the technical level Pine was now using Wavestation and Prophet synthesizers. The album's expansive music was as impressive as its dedications and at times majestic, by turns taking in Gospel, luminous Indian raga and African Ambiences.

By 1996 Pine was working with digital mixers, samplers and tape. He was writing everything on an Apple Macintosh and generating such things as sound loops, flute and saxophone lines in his own home studio. Impressed with the skills of DJs, he transferred acoustic drum loops to acetates for spinning in the studio. He played EWI digital wind controllers and used his evolving high-tech sensibility to process, filter, pitch-shift, time-stretch and fine-tune his sounds. Now his saxophone technique was so advanced that he was using technology to generate multiple lines à la Roland Kirk or play in microtones or place a traditional sax style in a detuned environment. Arriving in New York with a bunch of tapes and an Apple Powerbook, he achieved a real synthesis of DJ culture and jazz on *Modern Day Jazz Stories* (Talkin' Loud/Antilles 1996).

The New York sessions involved a flexible jazz group on Hammond organ, double bass, saxes, trumpet, guitar and vocals. In the studio they were constantly thrown looped drum beats and scratches to respond to by championship DJ Pogo. Other sound manipulations were handled by a technician friend known as Sparkii. (Both had come up through the UK live sound-system scene.) Pine felt the duality of acoustic music versus technology produced better results and from the outset of *Modern Day Jazz Stories* the effect was of Hip-Hop combined with jazz-fusion, best described as Trip Jazz. The effect is more Bill Laswell than anything Pine had attempted up to then. After a strange Ambient opening the loops and scratches of Hip-Hop appeared before Pine coasted in with a sonorous soprano melody. The music floated along to a breakbeat groove in a fusion which was confidently authentic. Voice samples, acoustic guitar loops, dirty-sounding vinyl manoeuvres, block beats, tabla drums, vocalizing and Coltrane pyrotechnics defined an album that pushed at the very definition of jazz.

On stage Pine was now playing with four musicians, a vocalist and two DJs. It was no mere borrowing or sampling but hardcore jazz right up against hardcore black dance culture. Pine's aim was to reflect the climate he lived in. 4 Hero and he were already trading sounds, for Ambient Drum and Bass to him was a music which facilitated space and creativity. Even his live upright-bass player performed with Jungle and jazz artists. Pine considered his 1997 project *Underground* (Talkin' Loud) to be a mixture of black traditional music (blues, be-bop, soul, jazz, avant-garde) and modern black forms (Hip-Hop, Drum and Bass, Acid Jazz, Trip-Hop). Recorded in New York and London, the album credited DJ Pogo and Sparkii as co-producers. Its inspiration was a bunch of breaks and loops from Pine's own record collection which were then duplicated by live musicians and the results fed back into the technology for further tweaking. Opening with 'Intro – Inhale', a clever summary of the eleven tracks, the album had a gritty street Hip-Hop feel. Here the fusion was complete as attractive reed and woodwind solos collided with killer Technics record-deck breaks. Jazz guitar, organ and electric piano added lustre. Pine reined in his more overt Coltranisms for a more considered blend of light and shade. In terms of feel, groove and general character, *Underground* was no different from albums like 4 Hero's *Two Pages* (1998).

LISTENING

On a purely jazz level all of Courtney Pine's albums are interesting. In terms of the developments covered by this book his music expanded considerably after the excellent *To The Eyes Of Creation* (Island 1992). His absorption of modern technology and DJ culture resulted in the trailblazing *Modern Day Jazz Stories* (Antilles/Talkin' Loud 1996). But it's with the superbly fluid *Underground* (Talkin' Loud 1997) that Pine made Trip Jazz a true hybrid.

TALVIN SINGH AND ANOKHA

When Techno and Drum and Bass were absorbed by British Asian musicians a whole new revolution occurred. People like Asian Dub Foundation and most visibly Talvin Singh created genuine fusions of Indian classical music and breakbeat electronics. Inspired by Ambient Junglist LTJ Bukem, John Coltrane, Shakti, UK Electro and Ska, plus his own rich Indian heritage, Singh produced the award-winning panoramic soundscape *OK* (Island) in 1998. Of equal importance was his London club Anokha (meaning 'unique'), which attracted young Asians and a multicultural audience to hear barrier-breaking blends of East and West. Black and white, Asian and Oriental thrilled to the sounds of pure Carnatic string and vocal music beefed up by quaking, floor-filling beats. The effect of this was to open London's club spaces to a new synergy where it wasn't uncommon to experience Jamaican Rap, Asian Techno and English string music all at the same time.

Talvin Singh was born in Leytonstone, East London in 1970. His otherwise normal urban upbringing ended at fifteen when he left England for India with £100 in his pocket. He ventured to the Punjab in the north-west to steep himself in the manifold beat cycles of classical Indian tablas. He stayed for eighteen months under the tutelage of Pandit Singh, a master musician who had studied under the same tabla guru as Alla Rakha, the great virtuoso percussionist who accompanied Ravi Shankar during the 1960s and 1970s. Rakha's son, Zakir Hussain, was simultaneously beginning a musical journey in the US with guitarist John McLaughlin which would result in Shakti, one of the greatest Indo-fusion groups of all time. Hussain would eventually champion the cross-cultural work of Singh.

After his first Indian odyssey, Singh was gripped with a passion for the tablas. He studied hard for four years and returned every year to the subcontinent for ever more musical and cultural nourishment. In the UK of the 1980s Singh was puzzled by the popularity and growing commerciality of Bhangra (the loping, swing-based percussion and vocal music of the Punjab) as his own serious musical interest pointed towards classical and jazz forms. He soon came into contact with the New Jazz firmament, especially the music of the renowned saxophonist Courtney Pine. What was interesting was that Singh saw the combination of sitar and tablas as unrepresentative of Indian music. More than once he outspokenly declared that 'there was no tonal relationship between the sitar and the tablas'.

Singh loved the purer Carnatic music of Southern India – the use of voice, violins and the fretted veena (like a flat guitar). He adored the long tradition of string music in Madras but still couldn't help have affection for the intense film music of the Bombay movie industry, known as Bollywood. Inspired by Acid House and Dub Reggae, he saw a huge future for electronicized tablas (where the two drums were connected to mixing boards and effects units before amplification and recording). A constant traveller, he was ready by the 1990s to branch out. One of his first collaborations was concerts in 1990 with the astral jazz legend Sun Ra. He then worked with the Icelandic pop star Björk on her first two albums, appeared on The Future Sound Of London's *Lifeforms* (1994), played the best Ambient Raves and club spaces and toured with Massive Attack. By 1996 he was ready to go out on his own.

In love with club culture and realizing that Drum and Bass was not just a fad but the resurrection of percussion as the core of musical evolution, Singh founded his ground-breaking London club space Anokha in 1996. Here Techno and Drum and Bass beat cycles were meshed with Indian music which had a Carnatic purity. A magnet for young Asians as well as a culturally diverse audience, Anokha was a huge success. An album, *Anokha – Soundz Of The Asian Underground*, (Omni/Island 1997) went on to sell in six-figure quantities on both sides of the Atlantic. Not only did it mesh the latest computer-driven Drum and Bass sounds with a diverse range of characteristic Indian timbres, it also painted a very broad canvas. Acid Jazz, flute ballads, emotive vocalizing and beautiful string sounds were all in evidence. The contrast between, say, State Of Bengal's Ambient New Break part-Rap masterpiece 'Chittagong Chill' and A. Rahman's vistavision flute and string Madras soundtrack 'Mumbai Theme' was both audacious and perfectly judged.

His confidence growing, Singh then took Anokha on a world tour and used the opportunity to crystallize ideas for his first solo album, *OK* (Island 1998), the title deriving from wartime slang for 'zero killed' according to Singh. Over nine months he visited different musicians and recorded parts in different studios. In New York he worked in Bill Laswell's Greenpoint complex, his famous bass appearing on both 'Mombasstic' and 'Soni'. Moreover Laswell's Ambient atmospheres, so readily available on his Axiom imprint, could be heard on 'Disser/Point'. Singh also recorded all over India, Japan and London before assembling all the pieces in his Brick Lane basement in London's East End. The eleven-minute Ambient tour de force 'Traveller', with its bamboo flutes and Madras strings, was absolutely brilliant music whose finale owed much to Ryuichi Sakamoto's filmic string writing. In fact Sakamoto played modular flute on the album.

Twenty-two individual musicians were credited with input to *OK*, while additional credit was given to the Madras Philharmonic and the Nenes Choir, a troupe of traditional Okinawan singers recorded in Japan. Singh himself handled all tablas, drums, key sequencing triggers, computers, pianos, gongs, atmospherics, sonics and other noises. Highlights of the album were the aforementioned 'Traveller'; the floating Drum and Bass veena–and–flute Ambience of 'Butterfly'; the Oriental strangeness of the title track, with its Chinese lute and Okinawan choir; the breezy piano and flute Trancedelia of 'Light'; and the dubbed–out Indian choral of 'Soni'.

Though Singh provided a performance key with the album, many reviewers still showed much ignorance of Indian music. When *OK* was released in the late winter of 1998, the *Sunday Times* made the grievous error of discussing the album in terms of sitars and tablas. Given Singh's known antipathy towards the sitar and the fact that the instrument did not appear on the credits, the review demonstrated a typical ignorance that was widespread. During the 1960s the sitarist Ananda Shankar had made dismal orchestral recordings of rock hits for EMI which were pure pastiche. Singh railed against this kind of thing, *OK* being one of the most militant flagships for a true Indo-fusion music ever recorded. This music leaned more heavily towards the South of India than the North. Its use of voice, strings and veena followed the Carnatic tradition of the South. While its use of bansuri flute, sarangi (or box cello) and, of course, tablas drew on the Vedic tradition of the North, *OK* bypassed the region's most famous instrument – the sitar.

Almost a year to the day after the release of his panoramic debut, Talvin Singh became the first British Asian to scoop the coveted Mercury Music Award for the most outstanding contribution to new music. Given that The Chemical Brothers' slick Rock Techno album *Surrender* (Virgin 1999) was also in competition, this was no mean feat. Having remixed Madonna and played with David Sylvian, Singh was happy to welcome in the twenty-first century with concert presentations of *OK* featuring Bill Laswell and Ryuichi Sakamoto and a brand-new Anokha compilation.

LISTENING

Anyone interested in how Drum and Bass triggered a new form of British Asian music has to hear *Anokha – Soundz Of The Asian Underground* (Omni/Island 1997), with its great contributions by Osmani Soundz, The Milky Bar Kid, A. Rahman and of course Singh himself. *OK* (Omni/Island 1998) shows an artist at the height of his powers, a perfect distillation of Indian classical music, Western Techno, Drum and Bass and other ethno and rock influences which are fully composed but fluent. During the late 1990s Singh worked at Peter Gabriel's Real World studio. There he produced the percussion album *One World, One Drum* (Real World 1997) and also recorded valuable sessions for David Sylvian's comeback solo album, *Dead Bees On A Cake* (Virgin 1999).

DUB REGGAE

The significance of Jamaican Reggae in the evolution of House, Techno and related musics is often overlooked. Years before the dance explosion of the 1980s in America and the UK, Jamaican DJs, engineers and producers were creating music which depended on record decks and large sound systems for its deployment. From the late 1940s onwards the DJ and his sound system dominated Jamaican music. From imported American R&B of the 1950s through Ska and Rocksteady in the 1960s to Roots and Dub in the 1970s, Jamaican music was always record-led. Producer-engineers like King Tubby and Lee Perry made huge careers out of their ability to strip a record down to its rhythmic basis and rebuild it using studio effects. 'Dub Reggae', as it became known, was hugely influential and in truth was the original Drum and Bass. Mixing, sampling and rapping all owe their origins to Dub Reggae. New York's pioneering Hip-Hop DJ of the 1970s, Kool Herc, was actually born in Kingston, Jamaica. And if famous turntablists like The Orb and DJ Spooky openly acknowledged the influence of Dub, the whole style of late-twentieth-century dance music owes Reggae a huge debt of gratitude.

The distinctiveness of Jamaican Reggae derives from its assimilation of African, Scottish, English, Irish and Hispanic folk musics as well as American R&B and jazz. The slowing down of the beat was a characteristic of Reggae from the Rocksteady of the late 1960s onwards, the slo-mo rhythm given its ultimate expression via Dub. The term derives from 'dub acetate', meaning an exclusive recorded mix of a song made to be previewed by a DJ at a sound-system dance. These unique records originated in the mid-1950s and by the early 1960s Jamaican DJs prided themselves on getting them to play for the public. During the late 1960s the 'instrumental' became popular. Basically a mix of a hit song without the singing, the instrumental was dynamized by Spanish Town DJ Ruddy Redwood when he began playing them at dances in 1967. By 1970 the 'version' had taken over. This was basically the rhythmic element of an original track with enough space left for DJ 'toasting' (rapping) and/or instrumental embellishment. Moreover all single record releases now carried a 'version' of the main track on the 'b' side with various producers, engineers and DJs adding novel elements to the mix. But the full-blown studio-enhanced 'Dub' effect, which used all sorts of studio gizmos, arrived during the early 1970s with the rise of King Tubby.

Osbourne 'Tubby' Ruddock was born in Kingston, Jamaica in 1941. He became an electronics engineer, worked in the famous Treasure Isle studio and started his own sound system. Inspired by the instrumentals at Ruddy Redwood dances in 1968, Tubby set out to have the biggest sound system in Kingston. Helped by the DJ and toaster U-Roy Beckford, Tubby became a hit on the dance floor and in the record shops by virtually inventing Rap. By 1972 he was King Tubby, with his own tiny studio in the poor Waterhouse district. He cut his own acetates using a primitive two-track tape machine, a mixer and a reverb unit. In 1972 he acquired a good four-track tape unit and began customizing his mixing console to achieve interesting effects. From the following year he had a second four-track, making his studio *the* place for producers to get their tracks mixed into Dub. Tubby's 1973 album with Lee Perry, *Blackboard Jungle Dub*, showcased his considerable talents as it was one of the first stereo Dub albums involving three separate mixes woven into one huge aural extravaganza. Singles began to appear with the words 'Drum and Bass by King Tubby' printed on them. Tubby's style was to use lots of equalization and reverb and drop instruments or vocals in and out of the mix.

Tubby worked extensively with Augustus Pablo, born Horace Swaby in Kingston in 1952, a classically trained session musician who excelled at organ, keyboards and the melodica. Pablo became a legend on the latter instrument, its refined harmonica-like sound gracing many finely etched minor-key instrumentals of the early 1970s. He also had his own Rockers record label and sound system. A collaboration with singer Jacob Miller, 'Baby I Love You', was given the King Tubby mix in 1974. Heard by Chris Blackwell, Island's founder, it was released in the UK on that label in 1975 as 'King Tubby Meets Rockers Uptown', the 'Uptown' of the title being Tubby's studio. This was a sensational track, the defining moment of Jamaican Dub Reggae as a quaking, propulsive drum and bass line was offset by echoing Pablo melodica and deft vocal drop-outs. In 1976 the pair released an album of Dubs, *King Tubbys Meets Rockers Uptown*, to universal critical acclaim. Tubby continued to drench his mixes in reverb and delay effects and worked effectively throughout the remainder of the 1970s with artists like Yabby You Jackson and producer Bunny Lee. Tubby's engineers, Prince Jammy and Scientist Brown, became famous in their own right and in 1985 Tubby opened a new, proper recording studio. Unfortunately, this giant of sonic history was shot dead in 1989 near his home, leaving a wealth of brilliant music behind him.

King Tubby's innovations of the early 1970s led to a Dub inferno. Mikey Dread, Tapa Zukie and dozens of others became famous for their Dub albums and by the late 1970s it was *de rigueur* for any self-respecting Reggae artist to have their music 'Dubbed up'. One of the most influential of Tubby's collaborators was Lee 'Scratch' Perry, a mystic-religious Roots Rastafarian. Born in 1936 in Hanover country, Perry grew up in rural poverty. Leaving school early, he sustained himself with manual work, dance and dominoes competitions before arriving in Kingston in 1961. Having written plenty of songs, he hooked up with various sound systems and landed a job at Studio One as a talent scout. Staying there for most of the Ska years, he recorded extensively, even taping early sessions with Bob Marley And The Wailers. Perry became a freelance producer in 1966 and two years later founded his Upsetters record label. Recording all over Kingston, he had UK chart success in 1969 with a sax instrumental. His interest in drum/bass rhythm tracks and wide-ranging love of James Brown, Ennio Morricone and The Beatles, overlaid by his near-messianic devotion to Rastafari, made his music truly unique.

Unsurprisingly, Perry and Bob Marley became very close and from 1969 to 1971 Perry midwifed The Wailers' career, recording early Roots songs and mixing entire Dub albums. In fact Wailers' songs are included on Perry's 1973 *Blackboard Jungle Dub*, a collaboration with King Tubby. His work with Tubby convinced him to build his own studio. Buying a house in Washington Gardens, he spent considerable money on his Black Ark backyard studio. This wasn't a primitive set-up but involved a Teac four-track, a Soundcraft mixing board, Echoplex delay, Mutron phaser and two-track mix-down tape machine. Some describe the sound he achieved with this equipment as 'sub-aqua'. From 1974 he began recording with a vengeance, the limitations of his set-up leading him to have Moog synth lines overdubbed in London. Signed to Island, Perry had huge success with productions like Max Romeo's 'War In A Babylon' and Junior Murvin's 'Police And Thieves' in 1976, the same year he released his multi-layered reverb and delay ultra-slow masterpiece *Super Ape*. Famous for its limpid sound, Black Ark did not survive into the 1980s. Rejections from Island and a split with his girlfriend led to the studios being burned down. During the 1980s Perry travelled and in 1989 settled in Switzerland, married and continued to record.

The influence of Reggae in the UK reached its peak in the 1980s when groups like Steel Pulse, Misty In Roots and Aswad all became famous for their mind-warping Dub sets. In fact the connection between punk and Reggae initiated by The Clash's version of 'Police And Thieves' in 1977 was a crucial precedent in the evolution of House, Techno, Jungle and Drum and Bass in the UK. Moreover two UK-based Dub producers, Adrian Sherwood and The Mad Professor, were crucial points of contact for Lee Perry in the 1980s and 90s. Born in London in 1958, Sherwood had typically Northern white English parents. He was DJing in his teens, had a sound system and even organized some of Bob Marley's early UK gigs. He started a label in the late 1970s and worked with Jamaica's Prince Far I, dubbing live off the mixing desk for a series of albums titled 'Cry Tuff Dub Encounters'. Sherwood's obsession with Dub led in the 1980s to the creation of the East London label On U Sound, for which Perry made an album in 1986 titled *Time Boom*. Perry also worked extensively with The Mad Professor, a London-based Guyanese Dub expert. From the age of ten, Fraser (The Mad Professor's real name) made his own electronics and was inspired by both Tubby and Perry to go into Dub. This he did in the 1980s and with the setting up of his Ariwa label he eventually recorded over 100 albums. His collaboration with Perry, *Black Ark Experryments* (1995), was one of Scratch's most intricate recordings.

If pure rhythm and electronics became more important to Jamaican Reggae during its 'Dancehall' and 'Ragga' phases from the late 1970s to the late 1990s, people like Sherwood and The Mad Professor were expanding the palette of UK Reggae to embrace Indian music, Trip-Hop and Drum and Bass. In retrospect one could trace the entire history of House and Techno to Jamaica, for it was in Kingston that New York's original DJ, Clive 'Kool Herc' Campbell was born in 1955. Moving to New York's notorious South Bronx district in the late 1960s, Herc brought with him a cultural appreciation of the sound system. He built his first one in 1971, using two turntables for uninterrupted funk music parties. Noticing how excited his black audience would get during the instrumental breaks of James Brown records, Herc created a veritable merry-go-round of instrumental breaks. Hence the creation of the word 'breakbeat' and the lionization of Herc as DJ during the early and mid-1970s. He taught some of his DJing techniques to Grandmaster Flash and terms like 'B Boy' (someone who dances on breaks) and 'Hip-Hop' came out of his 1970s parties. In a nutshell, the whole US DJing and Rap phenomenon could be traced to a Jamaican infused with a sound-system heritage which stretched back decades.

LISTENING

As outlined in Steve Barrow and Peter Dalton's superb 400-page *Reggae – The Rough Guide* (1997), many Reggae albums have been issued over and over on a dizzying variety of labels. Anything by King Tubby is interesting but the best can be heard on *King Tubbys Meets Rockers Uptown* (with Augustus Pablo) (Clocktower 1976) and *Dub Gone Crazy: The Evolution Of Dub At King Tubby's 1975–1979* (Blood & Fire 1992). The Augustus Pablo CD compilation *Original Rockers* (Greensleeves 1987) catches some of the best 'Far Eastern' mixes put down by Pablo and Tubby between 1972 and 1975. A focus on King Tubby-Lee Perry collaboration *Blackboard Jungle Dub* (Clocktower 1973) is a neat way into the vast catalogue of Scratch. *Super Ape* (Island 1976) reveals an imagination at the height of its powers. Yet the definitive Lee Perry set has to be *Lee Scratch Perry: Arkology* (Island 1997), a triple-disc set of hits, mixes, Dubs and unreleased cuts from the heydays of his Black Ark studio between 1976 and 1979. On the UK side, check out any African Headcharge/Dub Syndicate releases on On U Sound, while The Mad Professor's *No Protection* (Wild Bunch 1995), a remix of Massive Attack's *Protection* (Wild Bunch 1994), is a fascinating exercise in Trip-Hop Dub. But no round-up of Jamaican Reggae can ignore the legendary Bob Marley, whose hugely successful Island catalogue, from *Catch A Fire* (1973) to *Survival* (1978), was given the Ambient treatment by Bill Laswell in 1997. *Dreams Of Freedom: Ambient Translations Of Bob Marley In Dub* (Island) is a trancey, liquid take on Marley's wonderfully fresh sound with additional studio atmospherics added by Laswell and Tetsu Inoue in New York.

TRANCE

The ultimate hybrid of slick Techno, Ambience and House was Trance, a form responsible for the re-explosion of global club culture as the twentieth century drew to a close. Put simply, Trance was an ultra-smooth computer-generated music which revelled in repetition. Synthesizer and keyboard arpeggios were repeated and repeated, rising in pitch until an entire track seemed to explode in a nirvana of snare drum rolls and crescendos. Its tendency to octave-leap and pitch-shift emerged from highly sophisticated sequencing software. Its penchant for four-on-the-floor beat pulsations, slight instrumental and vocal decoration, mammoth drum breaks, rising suspense and seamless mixes made it a huge global phenomenon by 1999. Primarily a German creation, (ATB's '9PM (Till I Come)' sold one million copies in the UK alone), Trance had enormous input from UK DJs like Paul Oakenfold and European labels like Belgium's R&S. In a nutshell Trance was responsible for the rebirth of House and the ideal of one long trip through the subtleties of electronic dance music.

The unfolding of Trance can be traced from the Hi-NRG New York dance scene of the late 1970s and early 80s, through the German Progressive House outcrop of the early 1990s and the UK's Goa Trance/Epic House offshoots of the mid-1990s to the neo-psychedelic sensation of Euro Trance in the late 1990s. In the New York gay clubs of the late 1970s a new type of music began to take over from staid disco. It was called Hi-NRG and consisted of impassioned diva vocals, throbbing beats, synth stabs and fairly basic electronic percussion. Hi-NRG went through a second phase during the early 1980s when the Electro sounds of New Order were adopted by American pop acts like Madonna. In fact New Order's 'Blue Monday' (1983) contained many elements (such as snare rolls and intense sequenced drum repetitions) which would later become Trance staples. But it was in Germany that Trance really came into its own. Artists like Hardfloor, Jam & Spoon, Sven Väth, Pete Namlook, and Paul Van Dyk all emerged during the early 1990s with epic sounds that would make them famous.

Hardfloor started it all with the 1992 release 'Hardtrance Acperience', a phantasmagoria of Roland 303 Acid boxes, stepped percussion and a huge, heart-stopping build-up to detonation. Hailing from Düsseldorf, Oliver Bonzio and Ramon Zenker were inspired by the original Acid House. Born in the 1960s, they heard Phuture's twelve-inch single 'Acid Tracks' in a Düsseldorf club and vowed to seek out the machine responsible for the spurting Chicago sound. After some years of searching they finally procured three Roland TB-303 Basslines. Forming Hardfloor, in 1991 they signed to the Frankfurt Trance label Harthouse with an agenda to make a huge Techno/House beat accompanied by a wiggling Acid line which built so slowly to a climax that clubbers would be gasping with frustration. They did this admirably with 'Hardtrance Acperience'.

The Frankfurt duo Jam & Spoon were also inspirational in the early German Trance scene. Their 1992 masterpiece 'Stella' was all squishy synthesizers, light, unsyncopated drums, acoustic guitar samples, female angel vocal and piano Minimalism. It appeared on an R&S EP titled 'Tales From A Danceographic Ocean', a reference to Yes's truly awful 1973 album *Tales From Topographic Oceans* (Atlantic) and to the Progressive Rock era as a whole. Hence the use of the term 'Progressive House' to describe the new German sound. The implication was that the original House of the 1980s was now undergoing a similar transformation to that which rock had experienced in the early 1970s. Yet, contrary to the idea that House would lose its impact and become over-complex, in reality Progressive House/Trance made it more streamlined and accessible, as demonstrated by the infectious 'Stella'. Jam El Mar (Rolf Ellmer) was a classically trained musician, concert guitarist, producer and remixer. Spoon (Markus Löffel) was originally a cook who, in the late 1980s and early 1990s, worked with German Technopop sensation Snap. Promoting and A&R led to the opening of the famous Frankfurt Techno club XS. Inspired by the energized Frankfurt scene, the pair formed Jam & Spoon and recorded 'Stella'. Their fame was cemented by the 1992 remix of Belgian act Age Of Love. The React single 'Age Of Love' was a huge seller in the UK; its throbbing motion, jigsaw details, burbling pitch-ascending synth lines, girlie invitation to dance and climactic drum rolls were future Trance blueprints. Two Jam & Spoon albums, *Triptomatic Fairytales 2001* and *Triptomatic Fairytales 2002*, were released simul-taneously by R&S in 1993 and the duo went on to remix music by Enigma, New Order, Mike Oldfield and Giorgio Moroder.

Both Jam & Spoon and Hardfloor had fruitful contact with Sven Väth (pronounced 'fate'), the undisputed king of German Ambient Trance in the early 1990s. Frankfurt-born Väth loved the use of poignant euphoric synthe-sized strings to make emotional Trancedelia. His DJ sessions at Club Omen became legendary, sometimes lasting up to fifteen hours. In 1991 he founded the Eye Q label and in 1992 Harthouse Records. With studio partner Ralph Hildenbeutal he formed Barbarella and made inter-galactic Trance records. Travels to India and Tibet widened his horizons and in 1993 he released the stunning Progressive House/Ambient Trance album *Accident In Paradise* (Eye Q). Tracks like the Ambient meditation 'Caravan Of Emotions' seemed to take their cue from the multi-layered keyboard music of Vangelis. Väth used natural samples picked up in Goa and Nepal but the overall effect was the beautiful sound of multi-layered synths and keyboards. The soft percussion and crystalline nature of the floating 'L'Esperanca' was Väth at his most elated.

Väth was an inspiration to many, including Canada's Richie Hawtin, future Trance star Paul Van Dyk and Frankfurt's Ambient guru Pete Namlook. In fact, after hearing Väth DJ at Club Omen, Namlook began making Trance records and releasing them with their customary yellow-circled sleeves on his own Fax label. His early 1990s Sequential releases with Craig Rock and DJ Criss are spirited but basic Trance recordings featuring a pounding beat with swooshing synths and tweety percussion. In 1993 Namlook made his best Trance sides with Dr Atmo as Escape. All Joey Beltram hardbeats with skittering synth attacks and whooshy apocalyptic strings, some releases like 'Escape To Neptune' were hyperspatial in their urgency. The peak of this Trance period came with 'Escape To Polaris' – a fabulous darting keyboard line underpinned by huge synth chords and kinetic percussion.

Paul Van Dyk was signed to Väth's Harthouse as Cosmic Baby during the early 1990s. Born in the late 1960s in East Germany, Van Dyk (pronounced 'dook') did not let the DDR's austere socialism stand in the way of his love for English Electro, particularly the Manchester sound of New Order, which he heard via Western radio stations. He taught himself DJing with two clapped-out turntables and a semi-functioning mixer. When the Berlin Wall fell in 1989 he arrived in the West with a bag of tapes. He was soon playing at Club Trésor. His drug-free happy/sad vibe got him signed to the Berlin Techno label MFS in 1992. Continually DJing, within a year he was Berlin's top Trance DJ with a residency at E. Werk. Van Dyk was a firm believer in optimistic, uplifting Trance, and his 1992–3 work as Cosmic Baby (with a pianist from Nuremberg) was like a Ferrari of the genre. Ultra-slick drum pads surrounded by finely decorous synth sounds and the breath of female vocal, as heard on Cosmic Baby's 'Space Track' (1993), would define the future of Trance. In the same year Van Dyk remixed New Order's 'Spooky' and Sven Väth's aforementioned 'L'Esperanca', beginning a successful career which would culminate in late-1990s stardom.

The Trance rush of the early 1990s diffused as the decade wore on. In the UK Orbital, Leftfield, Underworld and William Orbit all made Trance tracks but the rise of Drum and Bass sidelined the form. Yet there was Goa Trance, a form of Technodelia which had its roots on the beaches of Southern India. During the late 1980s Goa had become a Rave mecca, famous for its lax attitudes to drugs and loud dance music. As in San Francisco in the 1960s, this atmosphere imbued a preference for psychedelics like LSD and mescaline. Hence the music was more psychedelicized, with greater emphasis on instrumental detail and exotica. Goa Trance was an amalgam of kinetic beats with whirling synths and bright instrumental textures. After a trip to Goa, DJ Mark Allen started to play this music in 1994 at a new club called Return To The Source – a truly psychedelic happening which moved between Manchester and London. Open to all and steeped in hippie accoutrements (mandalas, stalls, light shows, incense, healing, meditation, Eastern mysticism, UFOs, New Age philosophy and so on), Return To The Source attracted a huge following right across the music-loving spectrum. By 1996 Goa Trance was a real phenomenon, with releases by Madra Gora, Prana and former Orb producer Youth via his Dragonfly label. Return To The Source attracted Acid House veterans like Danny Rampling and Paul Oakenfold and by 1998 it was hosting Trance parties globally. Goa Trance may have seemed hopelessly naive to many but some of the music by Alien Mutation, Dr Psychedelic, Transequence, Celestius and Trance Twin Quartet was Ambient Trance of a highly sophisticated and good-humoured quality.

Trance music's most fervent campaigner was Paul Oakenfold, who promoted the music right through the 1990s. By the end of the century he was considered the world's most famous and most important DJ. Born in Mile End, London, in 1961, Oakenfold had a colourful career that stretched right back to the birth of

Acid House. He had trained as a chef and the end of the 1970s saw him working in a Covent Garden bar with DJ friend Trevor Fung. A visit to New York in 1984 brought him into contact with clubs such as Studio 54 and the Paradise Garage. Determined to make it in the music business, he lived for a year in Harlem and became a record poller for Def Jam. Inspired by Hip-Hop, he returned to London and became an A&R man for Champion records, signing a fledgling Will Smith to their roster. He took up remixing and on the advice of Trevor Fung started to check out Ibiza.

After seeing how club music was changing in Spain in 1985, Oakenfold returned to London and started a club in Purley, south of the capital, based on his Balearic experience. A mixture of rock, Rap and dance records did not go down at all with the crowds. His Funhouse club was a damp squib, its failure partly attributed to the lack of Ecstasy. Yet another trip to Ibiza in 1987 with DJ Danny Rampling and others proved to be a pivotal experience. Oakenfold returned and started mixing it up at clubs like The Project and Future. His 1988 Spectrum club at London's Heaven birthed the 'Acieed' chant and attracted everyone interested in Acid House, including The KLF, The Orb, The Stone Roses and Happy Mondays. Oakenfold then produced (with Steve Osbourne) the latter's Madchester classic *Pills 'N' Thrills And Bellyaches* (Factory 1990). That same year he began 'Movement 98' for slower beats, aimed against hurtling Hardcore. His production duties won him a Brit Award in 1991 and he went on to remix The Shamen, New Order and Massive Attack.

Oakenfold's approach as a DJ was subtle, tasteful and smooth. During the early 1990s he was chosen by U2 to accompany them on their 'Zoo TV' world tour and he pushed the band towards club music with a dance-floor mix of 'Real Thing'. In 1993 he mixed the seminal Trance cut by Grace 'Not Over Yet'. Soon he was a champion of Goa Trance and began touring the world, playing his choice of 'tasteful Trance' to larger and larger audiences. He could bewitch a 100,000-strong crowd at Glastonbury and played globally (New York, Bombay and Havana to name some) to ecstatic audiences. Through A&R work at East West (part of Warner Bros.), working at BBC Radio 1 and performing his delicious sets at UK superclubs such as Cream, Gatecrasher and Home, he pushed Trance into the mainstream by 1999. His Global Underground mix *Paul Oakenfold – New York* (Boxed 1998) was liquefying, plasmatic and mix-perfect Trance which justified his claim that it was the music of the twenty-first century.

To choose a point where Trance went mainstream is difficult. Some say it was when UK DJs Sasha & John Digweed's compilation *Renaissance* was released on Network in 1994. Others would point to the release of French combo BBE's 'Seven Days And One Week' (Positiva) (trippy, echoing keyboard riff to cream-thick bass rhythm), which became an Ibiza anthem in 1997. In some quarters it was all put down to the arrival of high-quality Mitsubishi Ecstasy, which returned clubbers to the imaginary nirvana of 1988. Certainly in 1997 clubs the world over began to switch to Trance nights. Sheffield's Gatecrasher, for example, became a Trance mecca as clubbers returned to the childishness of early Acid House. Cuddly toys, lightsticks, headgear and other psychedelic kitsch were now the in thing. By 1998–9 superclubs like Gatecrasher, Cream, Ministry Of Sound and Renaissance in the UK and Manumission, Amnesia and Pacha in Ibiza had all succumbed to the allure of high-velocity Trance.

And what of the music? The optimistic Berlin-based Paul Van Dyk was unstoppable, his up-sound straddling the globe in the late 1990s. Already a German star, he went truly international with the hypnotic Trance anthem 'For An Angel' (Deviant 1998), all feather-light keyboard tinkles and chugging beat similar to New Order at their best. That same year Deviant released a triple-disc set of Dyk mixes, *Vorsprung Dyk Technik* (a play on the Audi car ad), which were considered state-of-the-art. By 1999 his emotionally charged six-hour DJ sets at Gatecrasher made him a Trance supremo. And then, of course, there was Sasha and Digweed.

Sasha, the Ibiza Trance star of 1999, was born Alexander Coe in Wales in 1970. His family moved to Manchester in 1988, where he frequented the Hacienda and was inspired by C. C. Rogers's seminal Chicago House classic 'Someday'. He became a DJ and worked at a pirate radio station for years before leaving the UK for Australia and the US. His style was Progressive House and Deep Trance sets which sometimes lasted all night. His friendship with John Digweed led to the establishment of the New York Twilo Trance club in late 1997. The mainstream success of Sasha, with his interest in The Beatles, Bob Marley, Goldie and Paul Oakenfold, was confirmed by his 1999 single 'Xpander' (Deconstruction) – a rippling, oscillating classic which remained true to original Acid House while forwarding the motoric drive of Trance – and the Global Underground album *Sasha – Ibiza* (Boxed 1999).

John Digweed was born in southern England in the late 1960s. By his early teens he was obsessed with records and equipment. By hanging around a DJ in his local club he got a chance to spin. Eventually he landed his own slot in a Hastings pier venue. By the mid-1990s he was playing the Renaissance club in Derby and with Sasha co-mixed the *Renaissance* album in 1994, which went on to sell 200,000 copies, thus beginning the club-mix CD phenomenon. Considered to be the James Brown of DJing, Digweed made his name with Fabio and Grooverider at Heaven before endlessly touring the world with his Trance mixes of grooves, breakbeats and hushed percussion. A twelve-hour session at the Twilo club in New York with Sasha caused huge block-long queues on New Year's Day 1998. By 1999 his Northern Exposure and Global Underground compilations had sold half a million copies.

Both Sasha and Digweed were disenchanted by the idea of pop Trance but in 1999 ATB's '9PM (Till I Come)' (Ministry) sold millions worldwide, becoming the UK's first Trance number one. Pulsing, gatecrashing percussion, a niggling guitar sample which crept up on you, simple synth stabs and repetition were the ingredients which twenty-eight-year-old Andre Tanneberger combined to make him an instant star. Amazingly, the track was completed in a single day and was a ubiquitous 1999 airwave presence. Often criticized for its Eurocentricity and its simplistic, ultra-Minimalist take on House and Techno, Trance was the supercharged chrome-finished manna for a mass dance audience entering the twenty-first century – the perfection of computer music and Rave's promise of endless bliss-out.

LISTENING

For the early Progressive House scene there is no better place to start than Sven Väth's 1993 opus *Accident In Paradise* (Eye Q), which stills sounds impressive, moving from Ambient to Trance with ease. Also worth searching for is Pete Namlook's double-CD *Escape* (Fax 1994), which captures the rush of early Frankfurt Trance. The blue-sleeved Volume compilations *Trance Europe Express 1* (1993) and *Trance Europe Express 2* (1994) cover the early evolution of the form and feature seminal tracks by Paul Van Dyk, Speedy J, Hardfloor and Sven Väth.

For both enervating and Ambient styles of Goa Trance hear the 1998 Rumour compilations *Psychedelic Flashbacks*. The Global Underground series on Boxed (1997–9) featured some of world's most famous Trance DJs, including Paul Oakenfold, John Digweed and Sasha. The double CD *Paul Oakenfold – New York* (1998) (mixed by the DJ in New York) is recommended for its velvet mix of delicate Trance, floaty Jungle, breakbeats and House. The real Ambient side of Trance is represented by *Return To The Source – Ambient Meditations Vol. 1* (1998) and *Return To The Source – Ambient Meditations Vol. 2* (1999), reflective slow Trance with strong whiffs of Eastern promise. The later CD was actually mixed by The Orb's Alex Paterson. Latter-day Trance is well served by compilations, of which *The Best Trance Anthems . . . Ever!* (Circa 1999) is recommended as it features a good historical overview, from the early Trance of Jam & Spoon and Age Of Love through that of Grace, Underworld, BBE and Chicane and on to the Euro Trance of Robert Miles, Paul Van Dyk and Energy 52. Virgin's thirty-seven-track *Trance Mix '99*, subtitled 'A Spiritual Journey Through Time And Space', sums up the ecstatic feel of Millennium-end Trance over two CDs and includes famous mixes of Sasha's 'Xpander' and ATB's '9PM (Till I Come)'.

THE CHEMICAL BROTHERS AND ROCK TECHNO

Approaching the twenty-first century like a steam locomotive without brakes, The Chemical Brothers invented a music of thunderous beats, instrumental twists, psychedelic flourishes and electronic riffs. The form became known as Big Beat – a quaking form of House/Techno which was laced with all the fun elements of rock and pop and had its most successful exponent in Brighton's

Fatboy Slim. Yet The Chemicals' music was far more complex than the Big Beat genre they spawned. Taking years over individual tracks, the duo used analogue synthesizers, digital sequencers, samplers, computers and a mountain of studio effects to create unique experiences in sound. Inspired by early Hip-Hop, Acid House, Techno and The Beatles, they gave to Techno the dynamics of rock. Tracks built up, changed and went to places that were deliciously unpredictable. The Chemical Brothers closed the loop started by The Stone Roses. Where the latter dynamized rock with House influences, The Chemicals sold millions of albums by mastering a form of post-Rave Rock Techno.

Ed Simons and Tom Rowlands were both born in southern England during the very early 1970s. Simons, a Londoner, attended public school and was all set for a legal career when his head was turned by Acid House. He got into Public Enemy, danced at House clubs and bought his first sampler when he was only sixteen. He decided to attend Manchester Polytechnic so that he could live in the city that had produced his musical heroes New Order.

Rowlands grew up in leafy Henley-on-Thames. Cabaret Voltaire and Ska were his first musical loves. In 1987 he heard The JAMs' (later The KLF) samplamania album *1987: What The Fuck Is Going On?*, which prompted him to buy a sampler. While at school he was a member of many bands; one of them, Ariel, would embrace Balearic House culture and eventually land themselves an Indie record deal with the Deconstruction label. After school Rowlands headed for Manchester to study and be near the famous Hacienda club. Since Simons and Rowlands were both reading history at the Polytechnic they inevitably met in 1989, became House converts and began buying records together.

By 1990 they were DJing at a Manchester club called Naked Under Leather, named after a 1960s erotic film starring Marianne Faithfull and Alain Delon. Soon they changed their name to The Dust Brothers and built up a small audience playing a mixture of Hip-Hop, Acid House and rock. They graduated and with the help of a domestic hi-fi, a keyboard, plus sampler and computer, they made their first track, 'Song To The Siren' (1992). Named after the famous Tim Buckley song but sampling the early 1980s cover by The Cocteau Twins as This Mortal Coil, the track was full of Hip-Hop breaks, booming Techno, earthquake bass and of course sirens. After sending loads of copies to legendary DJ and Primal Scream producer Andrew Weatherall The Dust Brothers were signed to his Junior Boys Own label and 'Song To The Siren' was released in 1993.

In 1994 things really fell into place for Simons and Rowlands. Their first EP on Junior Boys Own, '14th Century Sky', featured the funky electronic clamour of 'Chemical Beats' and joyously sampled The Beatles and The Beach Boys. They became in-demand mixers and performed live with Andrew Weatherall. Firmly established in London, they started a three-month residency at Robin Turner's Heavenly Social Club which became legendary. Performing on Sunday nights in a central London basement, they mixed up everything from Hip-Hop, The Beatles, Traffic, LTJ Bukem and Chic to underpinned squelchy

Acid House, big bass riffs and relentless beats. Alcohol and amyl nitrite were the drugs of choice as the club celebrated eclecticism and drunken celebration. Soon the likes of Primal Scream and Tricky were checking out The Dust Brothers' very human electronica. Their sets always included the mantra-like cacophony of The Beatles' 1966 psychedelic masterpiece 'Tomorrow Never Knows', a song that would soon become pivotal in their recording career.

By 1995 The Dust Brothers had become The Chemical Brothers. They signed to Virgin and introduced electric guitars on the 'Leave Home' EP. Aimed firmly at a rock audience, their debut album, *Exit Planet Dust*, took three weeks to make and was released in the summer of 1995. Aided by the vocals of rock singer Tim Burgess and folkie Beth Orton, the album sold 250,000 copies in the UK and eventually one million copies worldwide. Over a year was spent in The Chemical Brothers' Orinoco studios in South London on their most important album, *Dig Your Own Hole*. Perfectionists and sound prospectors, their approach in the studio was to work their Akai samplers and Apple Mac computer all the time. Up to a dozen drum samples would be used to create one huge beat. CUBASE sequencing software plus add-ons created loops and beats over which other sounds were added. These derived mostly from analogue synthesizers like the vintage Synthi AKS, ARP 2600 and the famous House monosynth the Roland SH101. The Chemical Brothers liked to mix live, sometimes recording up to an hour of passes on DAT before editing them down to four minutes of music. One track, 'Setting Sun', had been boiling away for a year. After they met Oasis founder Noel Gallagher at a Glastonbury Festival he agreed to record a vocal for the track in early 1996. Released in the autumn of 1996, 'Setting Sun', with its pummelling 'Tomorrow Never Knows' drums, squealing sitars and dirty, raucous production, went straight to the top of the UK charts. The Chemical Brothers had arrived.

The release of *Dig Your Own Hole* in the spring of 1997 caused a furore. Ed Simons described it as 'a widescreen Technicolour version of their first album'. This was sulphuric Techno with piles of phenomenal breakbeats which mixed up disco, psychedelia, rock, folk, Hip-Hop and Acid House. Its Grammy-winning opener, 'Block Rockin' Beats', contained an Old Skool Hip-Hop sample from Schooly D and was New York Rap ripped through the raw insides of technology. 'Electro Bank' included voice snatches of the original Hip-Hop DJ, Kool Herc. 'It Doesn't Matter' sampled US 1960s experimentalists Lothar And The Hand People. In fact there was a strong texture of early American electronica to the album, especially the work of the late-1960s New York synthesizer duo Silver Apples.

'It Doesn't Matter' also featured a booming bass riff, a Chemicals Brothers trademark. 'Don't Stop The Rock' returned to the squelchy repetition of Chicago Acid House. 'Lost In The K-Hole' (a reference to the weightless, catatonic experience of taking too much Ketamine aka Vitamin K aka Special K as experienced by thousands of American ravers) was rock funk sprinkled with electronic dust. 'Where Do I Begin' was psychedelicized electronic folk and the album's finale was the vertigo-inducing 'Private Psychedelic Reel'. It began with low-pass fibrillating electronic tones and, just half a minute in, the defining tri-note sitar riff appeared. Then timbral changes were followed by sliding Fender guitar, the repetition leading to massive exploding drums at two minutes. The sitar and drum repetition was pushed to the limits of distortion as wave after wave of sounds were added – synth swoops, stereo dissolves and pans, sampled high-pitched flute at four minutes, oscillating synth at five minutes, more guitar, stop-starts; all ending in a maelstrom of psychedelia that Pink Floyd's Syd Barrett would have been proud of. This track got the most attention from rock critics basking in reveries of nostalgia for the candy-coloured 1960s. The Chemical Brothers did admit their love of the vintage UK psychedelia of Kaleidoscope and Tintern Abbey and 'Private Psychedelic Reel' was simply nine minutes of outrageous 60s-style hallucinatory music played by Techno geniuses of the 1990s.

Dig Your Own Hole went to the top of the UK album charts and by the end of 1997 had achieved over a million and a half sales. The Chemicals avidly toured the US, Europe and Japan. Live they were an exciting experience, building mountains of sonic suspense before letting the audience have another of their shuddering breaks. Simons was always positioned in front of a wall of synthesizers and behind two keyboards used to trigger samples. Usually to his right stood Rowlands, tall with blond, lanky hair, vibing up the crowds at the front with his mixing desk, sequencer and effects units. These effects – Sherman filter bank, tone bender, Alesis Quadraverb, Ibanez analogue delay and Space drum – were part of the magic of The Chemical Brothers. The American leg of the 1997 tour resulted in one million US sales for *Dig Your Own Hole*.

Fourteen months were spent in the Orinoco studio perfecting the next album. Originally titled *Here Come The Warm Arts* (after an old Eno record), *Surrender*, released in the summer of 1999, was simply a modern masterpiece. Simons described it as 'acoustic Trance' or 'organitronic'. Trance, Techno, Hip-Hop, Electro and Ambience were all treated to the glossiest sheen The Chemical Brothers could muster. Brimful of confidence, Simons and Rowlands displayed an uncanny ability to absorb everything around them and still make it sound startling. 'Music: Response' opened the disc and was a Big Beat version of the sound of Kraftwerk's influential 1981 album *Computer World*, including vocodered vocals. 'Under The Influence' was Trance with organic scratching fully integrated into the melody and rhythm of the track. 'Out Of Control' took a year to write and included vocal and guitar performances from New Order's Bernard Sumner and Primal Scream's Bobby Gillespie. Recorded in one torturous forty-eight-hour session, 'Out Of Control' was The Chemical Brothers meets Hi-NRG as relentless beats and synth and sample swoops built up to a perfect New Order guitar clang, a sound which derived from forty different Sumner guitar parts.

The title of *Surrender* came from the Timothy Leary lyric of The Chemicals' favourite song, John Lennon's 'Tomorrow Never Knows'. In fact Noel

Gallagher was brought back in to work on 'Let Forever Be', another psychedelic rocker whose military drum pattern owed much to the above Beatles classic. But the first real glory of the album had to be 'Sunshine Underground' – a cineramic epic of keyboard lullaby, glowing flute, antique psychedelia, furious percussion and accelerating tempo that burst into glorious Techno life at nearly four minutes. This was followed by 'Asleep From Day', which featured the sleepy vocals of American singer Hope Sandoval. Blue-tinted and reminiscent of The Velvet Underground at their most fragile, 'Asleep' had touches of classic 1960s pop, Brian Eno's DX7 washes for U2 and tinkly music boxes. 'Got Glint?' was immaculate House/Techno resulting from processing with an ARP synthesizer and playing Roland Digital Octopad drums. 'Hey Boy Hey Girl' was pure Rock Techno, a screaming celebration of voice, guitars, beats and effects. The title track sampled Kraftwerk from their early 1970s 'Ananas Symphonie' period, a crystalline sound laid on a bedrock of drums and echoing electronica.

The finale of *Surrender*, 'Dream On', owed much to the voice, acoustic guitar, piano and French horn of Jonathan Donahue, another American friend and a member of the dream-pop group Mercury Rev. With its ululating vocals, optimistic arrangement and feeling of bliss-out (especially in the flute passages), 'Dream On' was a joyous celebration of Ecstasy culture and all that it had produced. It even had a false ending, a short instrumental reprise which mixed electronic texture with American country nuance. *Surrender* sold one million copies in the first month of release and proved that The Chemical Brothers' aim 'to find new sounds and push music into fresher and more exciting territories' was no idle boast. Put simply, The Chemical Brothers proved that what House and Techno had started in the 1980s had a mature and interesting life extending into the twenty-first century.

LISTENING

Of the albums mentioned above, *Dig Your Own Hole* (Virgin 1997) and *Surrender* (Virgin 1999) are thoroughly recommended, the former for its dizzy-busting electronic inventiveness, the latter for its pristine post-Rave Ambience. The Chemical Brothers are also the authors of a number of mix albums of which *Brothers Gonna Work It* (Freestyle Dust 1998) – a mix of Chemicals music with DJ faves from the likes of Renegade Soundwave, Unique 3 and Spiritualized – is by far the best.

AIR

With an ambition to be 'deep, strange, original and extreme', Air floated out of Paris in the late 1990s on a weightless sea of analogue synthesizers. Their soaring, gentle optimism was perfectly captured on the 1998 album *Moon Safari*, which sold a million copies worldwide. Synonymous with blissful Ambient, Chill Out and Lounge music, Air were self-confessed dreamers of 'retro-futurism'. Like Eno's classic Ambient music, Air summoned up a vision of the future by recombining elements of the past. Aspects of Debussy, Ravel, The Beatles, Stevie Wonder and 1960s French pop music laced their compositions. As more recordings were released a similarity to Pink Floyd emerged, a comparison which only heightened their reputation as makers of beautiful Ambient electronic rock for the twenty-first century.

Jean-Benoît Dunckel and Nicolas Godin were both born in 1970 in the Paris suburb Versailles. Quiet, leafy and Catholic, the place made the pair long for escape. At fifteen they formed a college rock quartet called Orange with others and spent six years as Versailles' leading indie band. Dunckel was a gifted pianist and ended up at the Paris Conservatoire. He also taught maths for a living. Godin followed a career path into architecture and settled in the cobbled, hilly streets of Montmartre in northern Paris. Meanwhile Dunckel hooked up with Anglo-Parisian Patrick Woodcock and made psychedelic soundtrack music. Soon Godin joined and Air came into being in 1994.

When Orange were together they were road-managed by Etienne de Crécy. After their demise in the early 1990s de Crécy moved to Paris and became entranced by the early House and Techno import records being played in clubs. He started making his own House records and in 1995 formed the Solid label, whose release of Air's debut track, 'Modular Mix' (1995), exploded the French New Beat and Down Tempo scene. Vibrating electronic sounds, harp-like guitar, soft breakbeats, orbiting rain-like Fender Rhodes keyboard, brass injections and luminous production made this an edifying chill-out experience. Licensed to Mo Wax in the UK in 1996, 'Modular Mix', made Air hip among the DJ set. Their next single, 'Casanova 70' (Solid 1996), was more smooch Ambience than 'Modular Mix' as the influence of French pop icons like Serge Gainsbourg and Françoise Hardy could be heard in its swimming synthesized strings, filmic brass and vibrating Rhodes. 'Les Professionnels' was part of the same release but further expanded Air's arsenal of sonic effects as Lounge transmuted into widescreen experimental Ambience. Rhodes, Hammond organ, MiniMoog synthesizer, computer sequencing, echo delay and mellifluous editing all chimed together to make a glorious classic. The entrance of a plucked acoustic guitar about a minute from the end was as delicious as any moment in musical history.

When turned into a huge full-out Dub sampled dance affair by Etienne de Crécy, 'Les Professionnels' became 'Solidissimo' in 1997 and Air were adopted as UK Trip-Hop darlings. Yet Dunckel and Godin were as interested in 'the harmonies and emotions of the chords and melodies' as the energy-led dance scene. Another 1997 single (now credited to their new label Source) included beaty material but its title cut, 'Le Soleil Est Près De Moi' ('The Sun Is Near To Me'), was Air at their most sublime. Recorded over days and nights in Godin's cramped Montmartre apartment, with neighbours complaining about the sound of the Rhodes, 'Le Soleil' was achingly slow with the vocal delivered Kraftwerk-style through a vocoder. Rapturous, sprinkled with sonic diamonds and a wonderful church organ, the single was great enough to land Air a major recording contract with Virgin.

With their advance Air bought more equipment and relocated to an eighteenth-century stone barn in Versailles. With only eight-track tape recording, one microphone and a pile of keyboards and effects boxes Air spent 1997 recording *Moon Safari*. The array of instrumentation was impressive. Added to the MiniMoog, Hammond, Rhodes, electric organ, vocoder, drums and guitars were Solina Strings, Wurlitzer organ, Korg MS20 synthesizer, Mellotron, harmonica, glockenspiel, clavinet and various effects. Both 'Sexy Boy' and 'Kelly Watch The Stars' were Electro-pop firmly aimed at the charts. 'All I Need' was a pure electro-acoustic ballad with Beth Hirsch on vocals. Both 'Talisman' and 'Ce Matin Là' ('That Morning') were undiluted Euro film soundtrack. 'Remember' recalled the vocodered synthesizer work of Tonto's Expanding Headband from the early 1970s. In fact Tonto provided many synthesizer sounds for Stevie Wonder, an artist who had a great influence on Air's music. The Moog solos on 'Remember' may have been credited to seventy-year-old French synthesist Jean-Jacques Perrey but their phrasing and that of 'Le Voyage De Penelope' ('Penelope's Journey') were pure Tonto. The best track on *Moon Safari* was its opening seven-minute 'La Femme D'Argent' ('Silver Lady'), a bass-driven slow-beat jewel of kaleidoscopic texture which could be likened to an astronaut skiing on the moon after taking LSD!

On its release, at the beginning of 1998, *Moon Safari* shot Air to worldwide fame. They quoted Debussy, John Barry and Ennio Morricone as influences on the album and were immediately adopted as crossover sensations among the trendy intelligentsia. They toured the world and gave many interviews. Their philosophy was pure Art and they spoke eloquently about the colour, shape and form of music. Dunckel even talked about his love of the piano and discovering 'new styles of classical music'. Though *Moon Safari* was a highly literate mélange of synth rock, psychedelia, French café muzak and Trip-Hop, Air were dissatisfied with it and wanted to dig deeper and become more original.

After hearing the album, Sofia Coppola, daughter of the American director Francis Ford Coppola (*The Godfather*, *Apocalypse Now*) commissioned Air to soundtrack her directorial debut, *The Virgin Suicides*. Still working in Versailles, Air temporarily dumped the Moog, vocoder and Rhodes and spent the first five months of 1999 watching the film and improvising to live drums. Having been dubbed 'the Pink Floyd of dance music', it was on *The Virgin Suicides* that Air came closest to the supremos of Ambient rock. There were many stylistic similarities: slow tempos, unison voicings, choral backdrops, minor-to-major chordal harmony, lagging drums, funereal organs, slide-guitar fills, mellifluous saxophones, dramatic build-ups. The album could be compared to middle-period Pink Floyd recordings like *More* (1969), itself a continental soundtrack. Even the finale to *The Virgin Suicides*, 'Suicide Underground' with its oscillating organ, stepped slo-mo drums and sustained guitar licks, could have been Air's version of the climax from Pink Floyd's 1968 *A Saucerful Of Secrets*.

Air attended the Cannes Film Festival in the summer of 1999 and allowed Virgin to reissue their early singles on the excellent *Premiers Symptomes* that autumn. They returned to Paris to make more music and at the beginning of the new century presided over the release of *The Virgin Suicides* album. Accusations of similarities to Pink Floyd were greeted with enthusiasm by Dunckel and Godin, who saw the conceptual, melodic and progressive nature of the Floyd's music as a positive inspiration. Attentive listeners could detect homages to Pink Floyd on old cuts like 'Casanova 70', with its *Wish You Were Here*-styled funky keyboard solo. But given all the UK rock groups who'd been likened to the Floyd (cue Radiohead) but weren't, it was ironic that Air, a French band, had most in common with them. Both were middle-class and grew up in rural idylls. Both had backgrounds in architecture. Both were inspired by psychedelia. Both used electric organs, Moog synthesizer and Fender Rhodes with rock instrumentation. Both spent a long time framing their compositions for maximum sonic effect. Both recorded more instrumental than vocal music. And both were interested in lunar movements and recorded an album with the word 'moon' in its title. So, in a nutshell, Air's achievement was to have innovated French hi-fidelity Lounge music and become the Pink Floyd of the twenty-first century.

LISTENING

The seamless segue of dream music which begins with the Etienne de Crécy mixes of 'Modular Mix'/'Les Professionnels' and ends with the incredible 'Le Soleil Est Près de Moi' on the album *Premiers Symptomes* (Virgin 1999) is peerless Ambient electronica from the closing years of the twentieth century. *Moon Safari* (Virgin 1998) was the album that made Air and is recommended for its infectious up-vibe futurism. *The Virgin Suicides* (Virgin 2000) mostly jettisoned the lush sound for an exquisite set of mood instrumentals which came out all Floydian.

Twentieth-century Ambience – the Essential 100 Recordings

Stuck on a desert island or just lost in space? If you are in possession of the following you'll get a widescreen view of just what sonic delights the modern age had to offer.

1. Mahler – *Symphonic Movements* (Rickenbacker) (Virgin 1989)
2. Satie – *The Early Piano Works* (De Leeuw) (Philips 1998)
3. Debussy – *The Complete Works For Piano* (Gieseking) (EMI 1995)
4. Ravel – *Orchestral Works* (Martinon) (EMI 1995)
5. Delius – *Beecham Conducts Delius* (Beecham) (EMI 1987)
6. Villa Lobos – *Complete Works For Guitar Vol. 2* (Korhonen) (Ondine 1995)
7. Messiaen – *Quartet For The End Of Time* (Delos 1986)
8. Paul Bowles – *Black Star At The Point Of Darkness* (Sub Rosa 1991)
9. John Cage – *In A Landscape* (Drury) (Catalyst, 1994)
10. Stockhausen – *Electronic Music 1952–1960* (Stockhausen 1991)
11. Miles Davis – *Sketches Of Spain* (Columbia 1960)
12. *2001: A Space Odyssey* (original soundtrack) (MGM 1968)
13. Wendy Carlos – *Switched-On Bach 2000* (Telarc 1992)
14. La Monte Young – *The Well-Tuned Piano* (Gramavision 1994)
15. Terry Riley – *A Rainbow In Curved Air* (Columbia 1969)
16. Steve Reich – *Music For 18 Musicians* (ECM 1978)
17. Brian Eno – *Discreet Music* (Obscure 1975)
18. Philip Glass – *Glassworks* (CBS Masterworks 1982)
19. Keith Jarrett – *The Köln Concert* (ECM 1975)
20. Harold Budd – *The Pavilion Of Dreams* (Obscure 1978)
21. Jon Hassell – *Aka-Darbari-Java (Magic Realism)* (EG 1983)
22. Michael Nyman – *The Draughtsman's Contract* (Charisma 1982)
23. John Adams – *The Chairman Dances* (Nonesuch 1986)
24. Arvo Pärt – *Tabula Rasa* (ECM 1984)
25. Henryk Gorecki – *Symphony No. 3* (Nonesuch 1992)
26. Gavin Bryars – *The Sinking Of The Titanic* (Obscure 1975)
27. The Beatles – *Magical Mystery Tour* (Parlophone 1967)
28. Bob Dylan – *Pat Garrett And Billy The Kid* (Columbia 1973)
29. The Beach Boys – *Smiley Smile* (Capitol 1967)
30. Jimi Hendrix – *Electric Ladyland* (Reprise 1968)

31. Ravi Shankar – *Improvisations* (World Pacific 1962)
32. The Velvet Underground – *The Velvet Underground & Nico* (Verve 1967)
33. Simon & Garfunkel – *Bridge Over Troubled Water* (Columbia 1970)
34. Brian Jones – *Brian Jones Presents The Pipes Of Pan At Jajouka* (Rolling Stones 1971)
35. Van Morrison – *Astral Weeks* (Warner Bros. 1968)
36. Marvin Gaye – *What's Going On* (Tamla Motown 1971)
37. David Bowie – *Low* (RCA 1977)
38. The Byrds – *The Notorious Byrd Brothers* (Columbia 1968)
39. Love – *Forever Changes* (Elektra 1967)
40. Neil Young – *Decade* (Reprise 1977)
41. Tim Buckley – *Happy Sad* (Elektra 1968)
42. The Grateful Dead – *Live/Dead* (Warner Bros. 1969)
43. Quicksilver Messenger Service – *Happy Trails* (Capitol 1969)
44. Fairport Convention – *What We Did On Our Holidays* (Island 1969)
45. John Martyn – *Solid Air* (Island 1973)
46. Clannad – *Magical Ring* (RCA 1983)
47. Pink Floyd – *Wish You Were Here* (Harvest 1975)
48. Led Zeppelin – *Led Zeppelin IV* (Atlantic 1971)
49. Mike Oldfield – *Tubular Bells* (Virgin 1973)
50. Can – *Future Days* (Spoon 1973)
51. Tangerine Dream – *Stratosfear* (Virgin 1976)
52. Popol Vuh – *Aguirre, Wrath Of God* (original soundtrack) (Cosmic Music 1976)
53. Manuel Göttsching – *E2–E4* (Inteam 1984)
54. Kraftwerk – *Trans-Europe Express* (Capitol 1977)
55. Klaus Schulze – *Mirage* (Island 1977)
56. Jean-Michel Jarre – *Oxygene* (Polydor 1977)
57. Vangelis – *Blade Runner* (original soundtrack) (East West 1994)
58. Joy Division – *Closer* (Factory 1980)
59. The Durutti Column – *The Return Of The Durutti Column* (Factory 1980)
60. New Order – *Power, Corruption And Lies* (Factory 1983)
61. This Mortal Coil – *It'll End In Tears* (4AD 1984)
62. Sonic Youth – *Daydream Nation* (Blast First 1988)
63. Spacemen 3 – *The Perfect Prescription* (Glass 1987)
64. Ennio Morricone – *Film Music* (Virgin 1993)
65. Todd Rundgren – *Todd* (Bearsville 1974)
66. John McLaughlin – *My Goal's Beyond* (Douglas 1971)
67. Robert Fripp (with Eno) – *Evening Star* (EG 1975)
68. Peter Gabriel – *So* (Charisma 1986)
69. Bill Nelson – *Chance Encounters In The Garden Of Lights* (Cocteau 1988)
70. Laurie Anderson – *Big Science* (Warner Bros. 1982)
71. Ryuichi Sakamoto – *The Sheltering Sky* (original soundtrack) (Virgin 1990)

72. David Sylvian (with Holger Czukay) – *Plight & Premonition* (Venture 1988)
73. Michael Brook – *Hybrid* (EG 1985)
74. U2 – *The Joshua Tree* (Island 1987)
75. Donna Summer – *The Dance Collection* (Casablanca 1987)
76. Afrika Bambaataa – *Planet Rock* (Tommy Boy 1986)
77. *Classic House – Vol. 1* (Beechwood 1994)
78. *Classic Acid House – Vol. 1* (Beechwood 1996)
79. *Classic Balearic – Vol. 1* (Beechwood 1996)
80. The KLF – *Chill Out* (KLF 1990)
81. The Stone Roses – *The Stone Roses* (Silvertone 1989)
82. Primal Scream – *Screamadelica* (Creation 1991)
83. Enigma – *MCMXC A.D.* (Virgin 1990)
84. The Orb – *Adventures Beyond The Ultraworld* (Big Life 1991)
85. Mixmaster Morris – *Flying High* (Rising High 1992)
86. The Future Sound Of London – *Lifeforms* (Virgin 1994)
87. Aphex Twin – *Selected Ambient Works Vol. 2* (Warp 1994)
88. Pete Namlook – *Air* (Fax 1993)
89. Bill Laswell – *Panthalassa* (Miles Davis 1969–1974) (Sony 1998)
90. William Orbit – *Pieces In A Modern Style* (WEA 2000)
91. Massive Attack – *Protection* (Circa 1994)
92. DJ Shadow – *Endtroducing . . .* (Mo Wax 1996)
93. Goldie – *Timeless* (ffrr 1995)
94. Talvin Singh – *OK* (Omni 1998)
95. Scratch & The Upsetters – *Super Ape* (Island 1976)
96. Augustus Pablo – *Original Rockers* (Greensleeves 1979)
97. Paul Oakenfold – *Paul Oakenfold – New York* (Boxed 1998)
98. Paul Van Dyk – *Vorsprung Dyk Technik* (Deviant 1998)
99. The Chemical Brothers – *Surrender* (Virgin 1999)
100. Air – *Premiers Symptomes* (Virgin 1999)

Bibliography

Since the core of this book was written from primary sources – the fifty or so in-depth interviews done with musicians for *Sound On Sound* from 1986 to 1996 were invaluable research – the bibliography is made up of books and features which I found inspirational. Robert Hughes's *The Shock of the New* is of particular import, for it focused my mind, at an early age, on the sheer vitality of twentieth-century innovation. Books on art and ideas and certain works of literature are essential to understanding the drift of artistic change from the nineteenth century to the twentieth. Many of the features I found simply delightful, their authors full of passion and brio for their subject. I've also included a short list of my own essays as they were crucial points of progress on the way to the book you are now holding. The year of publication refers to the edition I've used.

Ades, Dawn, *Dada and Surrealism* (Thames and Hudson, 1974)
——*Dali* (Thames and Hudson, 1988)
——*Photomontage* (Thames and Hudson, 1986)
Aftel, Mandy, *Death of a Rolling Stone – The Brian Jones Story* (Sidgwick & Jackson, 1983)
Alexander, John, 'Terry Riley' (*Strange Things*, July 1989)
Alexandrian, Sarane, *Surrealist Art* (Thames and Hudson, 1989)
Antonia, Nina, 'Jimmy Miller – The Stones' Greatest Producer' *(Record Collector*, November 1993)
Antonioni, Michelangelo, *That Bowling Alley on the Tiber* (Oxford, 1986)
Ballard, J. G., *The Terminal Beach* (Penguin, 1966)
Barkass, Lin and Norman-Taylor, Anthea (eds.) 'Opal Information' (*Opal*, 1988–96)
Barrow, Steve and Dalton, Peter, *Reggae – The Rough Guide* (Rough Guides, 1997)
Baudelaire, Charles, *Intimate Journals* (Panther, 1969)
——*Les Fleurs du Mal* (Dover, 1992)
Berger, John, *The Success and Failure of Picasso* (Writers & Readers, 1980)
Bergman, Billy and Horn, Richard, *Experimental Pop – Frontiers of the Rock Era* (Blandford, 1985)
Bigazzi, Giampiero (ed.), *John Cage* (Sonora, 1993)
Bockris, Victor, *A Report from the Bunker – With William Burroughs* (Vermilion, 1982)
——*Lou Reed – The Biography* (Vintage, 1995)
——*The Life and Death of Andy Warhol* (Hutchinson, 1989)
Bockris, Victor and Malanga, Gerard, *Up-Tight – The Velvet Underground Story* (Omnibus, 1983)
Bogarde, Dirk, *An Orderly Man* (Triad, 1984)
Booth, Stanley, *The True Adventures of The Rolling Stones* (Heinemann, 1985)
Borges, Jorge Luis, *Labyrinths* (Penguin, 1970)

Bowles, Paul, *Call At Corazon* (Abacus, 1989)

——*Pages From Cold Point* (Arena, 1986)

——*The Sheltering Sky* (Grafton, 1986)

——*Their Heads Are Green* (Abacus, 1990)

Brosnan, John, *Future Tense – The Cinema of Science Fiction* (MacDonald & James, 1978)

Brown, Peter and Gaines, Steven, *The Love You Make – An Insider's Story of The Beatles* (Pan, 1984)

Burroughs, William, *Cities of the Red Night* (Picador, 1982)

——*Letters to Allen Ginsberg 1953–1957* (Full Court, 1982)

——*The Western Lands* (Picador, 1988)

Burroughs, William and Ginsberg, Allen, *The Yage Letters* (City Lights, 1986)

Buskin, Richard, 'Giorgio Moroder – Electric Dreams' (*Sound On Sound*, March 1998)

Bussy, Pascal, *Kraftwerk – Man, Machine and Music* (SAF, 1993)

Bussy, Pascal and Hall, Andy, *The Can Book* (Tago Mago, 1987)

Calder, John (ed.), *A Henry Miller Reader* (Picador, 1985)

Cardwell, Donald (Prof.), *History of Technology* (Picador, 1994)

Carr, Ian, *Miles Davis* (Paladin, 1988)

Carroll, Lewis, *Alice In Wonderland* (Random House, 1927)

Castañeda, Carlos, *A Separate Reality* (Penguin, 1973)

—— *Journey to Ixtlan* (Penguin, 1974)

Chapman, Seymour, *Antonioni or The Surface of the World* (UCLA, 1985)

Chusid, Irwin, *Raymond Scott – The Man Who Made Cartoons Swing* (Columbia, 1998)

Clews, Richard, 'Inside the Synth Lab – Recording Vangelis' (*Sound On Sound*, November 1997)

Cocteau, Jean, *Opium – An Illustrated Diary of His Cure* (Peter Owen, 1993)

Cocteau, Jean and Phelps, Martin (ed.), *Professional Secrets – An Autobiography of Jean Cocteau* (Vision, 1972)

Collin, Matthew, *Altered State – The Story of Ecstasy Culture and Acid House* (Serpent's Tail, 1997)

Cott, Jonathan, *Stockhausen – Conversations with the Composer* (Picador, 1974)

Cutler, Chris, *File Under Popular – Theoretical and Critical Writings On Music* (November Books, 1985)

De Quincey, Thomas, *The Pleasures and Pains of Opium* (Penguin, 1995)

De Monfried, Henry, *Hashish* (Penguin, 1985)

DeRogatis, Jim, *Kaleidoscope Eyes – Psychedelic Music from the 1960s to the 1990s* (4th Estate)

Dickson, E. Jane, 'Schlock of the New – Are You Ready for the Consciousness Craze?' (*Sunday Times*, March 1990)

Doerschuk, Robert L., 'Eno' (*Keyboard*, March 1995)

——'Wendy Carlos – The Magic in the Machine: Reflections from the First Great Modern Synthesist' (*Keyboard*, August 1995)

Doggett, Peter, 'Neil Young Retrospective' (Parts 1–3) (*Record Collector*, July–September 1991)

Downing, David, *Future Rock* (Panther, 1976)

Dudfield, Simon, 'The 3rd Summer of Love' (*The Face*, July 1990)

Duncan, Alastair, *Art Nouveau* (Thames and Hudson, 1994)

Edwards, Gwynne, *The Discreet Art of Luis Buñuel* (Marion Boyars, 1982)

Einarson, John and Furay, Richie, *For What It's Worth – The Buffalo Springfield Story* (Rogan House, 1997)

Eliot, T. S., *Collected Poems 1909–1962* (Faber, 1980)

Ellen, Mark, 'Never Trust A Hippy – The Incredible String Band' (*Q*, June 1993)

Eno, Brian, 'Bringing Up Baby – The Making of U2's Achtung Baby' (*Rolling Stone*, November 1991)

Ethridge, David, 'The Mellotron – The Rime of the Ancient Sampler' *(Sound On Sound*, June 1993)

Everett, Anthony, *Abstract Expressionism* (Thames and Hudson, 1975)

Fiedler, Leslie A., *Love and Death in the American Novel* (Stein & Day, 1975)

Fish, M. and Hallbery, D., *Cabaret Voltaire – The Art of the Sixth Sense* (SAF, 1985)

Fisher, Paul, 'Philip Glass – Record Breaking Glass' (*Classic CD*, September 1991)

Flaubert, Gustave, *Madame Bovary* (Penguin, 1950)

Fricke, David, 'Velvet Underground – Peel Slowly and See' (Polydor, 1995)

Fuller, Sophie, *Guide to Women Composers* (Pandora, 1994)

Furlong, Monica, *Genuine Fake – A Biography of Alan Watts* (Unwin, 1987)

Garratt, Sheryl, 'New Age Clubbing – Welcome to the Hippydrome' (The Face, February 1990)

Gaunt, William, *The Aesthetic Adventure* (Sphere, 1988)

——*The Pre-Raphaelite Tragedy* (Sphere, 1988)

George, Nelson, *The Death of Rhythm and Blues* (Pantheon, 1988)

Gill, Andy, 'Electronic Music and Synthesized Sound' (*NME*, January 1980)

——'We Can Be Heroes – Krautrock Special' (*Mojo*, April 1997)

Glass, Philip, *Opera on the Beach* (Faber, 1988)

Gleason, Ralph J., *The Jefferson Airplane and the San Franciscan Sound* (Ballantine, 1968)

Goldman, William, *Adventures in the Screen Trade* (Futura, 1985)

Good, Timothy, *Above Top Secret – The Worldwide UFO Cover-Up* (HarperCollins, 1993)

Gray, Louise, 'Detroit Techno – The Great Bleep Forwards' (*The Wire*, February 1992)

——'Orbital – Loop Gurus' (*The Wire*, June 1993)

Griffiths, Paul, *A Guide to Electronic Music* (Thames and Hudson, 1979)

——*Modern Music – A Concise History From Debussy to Boulez* (Thames and Hudson, 1979)

Gurdjieff, G. I., *Meetings with Remarkable Men* (Arkana, 1988)

Gysin, Brion, *The Process* (Paladin, 1988)

Gysin, Brion and Wilson, Terry*, Here to Go – Planet R-101* (Quartet, 1985)

Heath, Chris, 'New Order' (*UK Mix*, October 1986)

Heylin, Clinton, *Dylan – Behind Closed Doors (The Recording Sessions 1960–1994)* (Penguin, 1996)

Hilton, Timothy, *The Pre-Raphaelites* (Thames and Hudson, 1989)

Hogg, Brian, 'Psych-Out: Psychedelia on Film' (*Record Collector*, November 1990)

Holmes, Paul, *Debussy* (Omnibus, 1989)

Honan, Park (ed.), *The Beats – An Anthology of Beat Writing* (Dent, 1987)

Hoskyns, Barney, *Beneath the Diamond Sky – Haight Ashbury 1965–1970* (Bloomsbury, 1997)

——*Waiting for the Sun – The Story of the Los Angeles Music Scene* (Viking, 1996)

——'Love – Through the Keyhole' (*Mojo*, June 1997)

Hounsome, Terry, *New Rock Record* (Blandford, 1983)

Hoyle, Martin, 'Györgi Ligeti – Orchestral Manoeuvres' (*Time Out*, October 1989)

Hughes, Robert, *The Shock of the New – Art and the Century of Change* (BBC, 1980)

——*Nothing If Not Critical* (Harvill, 1991)

Humphries, Patrick, *Nick Drake – The Biography* (Bloomsbury, 1997)

Huxley, Aldous, *The Doors of Perception* (Penguin, 1961)

Huysmans, J. K., *Against Nature* (Penguin, 1959)

Jackson, Blair*, Grateful Dead – The Music Never Stopped* (Plexus, 1983)

James, Martin, 'French Air' (*Flipside*, November 1999)

Jarman, Derek, *Dancing Ledge* (Quartet,1984)

Joyce, James, *Ulysses* (Penguin, 1969)

Joynson, Vernon, *The Acid Trip – A Complete Guide to Psychedelic Music* (Babylon, 1984)

——*The Flashback – The Ultimate Psychedelic Music Guide* (Borderline, 1988)

Kempster, Chris (ed.), *History of House* (Sanctuary, 1996)

Kent, Nick, 'Stone Roses/Happy Mondays – Mancunian Candidates' (*The Face*, December 1989)

Kerouac, Jack, *The Dharma Bums* (Granada, 1972)

——*Satori in Paris* (Quartet, 1973)

Kozinn, Allan, *The Beatles* (Phaidon, 1995)

Kundera, Milan, *The Unbearable Lightness of Being* (Faber, 1985)

——*The Book of Laughter and Forgetting* (Penguin, 1987)

Kurtz, Michael, *Stockhausen – A Biography* (Faber, 1992)

Landau, Jon, 'Paul Simon 1972' (*Rolling Stone*, 1981)

Lanza, Joseph, *Elevator Music – A Surreal History of Muzak* (Quartet, 1995)

Lebrecht, Norman, *The Companion to 20th Century Music* (Simon & Schuster, 1992)

Le Fanu, Mark, *The Cinema of Andrei Tarkovsky* (BFI, 1987)

Le Fanu, J. Sheridan, *In A Glass Darkly* (Alan Sutton, 1990)

Lewis, Dave, *Led Zeppelin – A Celebration* (Omnibus, 1991)

Lincoln Collier, James, *The Making of Jazz – A Comprehensive History* (Papermac, 1981)

Lloyd, Ann (ed.), *Movies of the Sixties* (Orbis, 1983)

——*Movies of the Seventies* (Orbis, 1984)

Logan, Nick and Woffinden, Bob, *The Illustrated NME Encylopedia of Rock* (Salamander, 1978)

Lovecraft, H. P., *At the Mountains of Madness* (Panther, 1975)

Lucie-Smith, Edward, *Eroticism in Western Art* (Thames and Hudson, 1972)

——*Symbolist Art* (Thames and Hudson, 1988)

MacDonald, Bruno, *Pink Floyd – Through the Eyes of . . .* (Sidgwick & Jackson, 1996)

MacDonald, Ian, 'Germany Calling' (Parts 1–3) (*NME*, December 1972)

——*Revolution in the Head – The Beatles' Records and the Sixties* (Pimlico, 1995)

Mackintosh, Alastair, *Symbolism and Art Nouveau* (Thames and Hudson, 1975)

McCann, Ian, 'Call For An Ambience' (*Vox*, November 1992)

McDermott, John, *Jimi Hendrix – The Complete Studio Recording Sessions 1963–1970* (Little Brown, 1995)

McDermott, John and Kramer, Eddie, *Hendrix – Setting the Record Straight* (Warner, 1992)

McKenna, Terence, *Food of the Gods – The Search for the Original Tree of Knowledge* (Rider, 1992)

Machlis, Joseph, *Introduction to Contemporary Music* (Dent, 1980)

Mackay, Andy, *Electronic Music* (Phaidon, 1981)

Manning, Peter, *Electronic and Computer Music* (Oxford, 1993)

Márquez, Gabriel García, *One Hundred Years of Solitude* (Picador, 1978)

Martin, Gavin, 'I Am a Cyber Thinker – William Gibson' (*NME*, October 1993)

Martin, Kevin, 'The Lonely Crowd – Isolationist Music' (*The Wire*, September 1993)

Mertens, Wim, *American Minimal Music* (Kahn & Averill, 1988)

Miller, Jim, *The Illustrated Rolling Stone History of Rock and Roll* (Salamander, 1978)

Mueller, Klaus D., *Klaus Schulze – The Works* (P.O.E.M., 1991)

Nash, J. M., *Cubism, Futurism and Constructivism* (Thames and Hudson, 1974)

Neal, Charles, *Tape Delay* (SAF, 1987)

Needs, Kris, 'Pete Namlook – With Ambient Everything Is Possible' (*NME*, June 1993)

Nelson, Thomas Allen, *Kubrick – Inside a Film Artist's Maze* (Indiana, 1982)

Nyman, Michael, *Experimental Music – Cage and Beyond* (Studio Vista, 1974)

Paytress, Mark and Reed, John, 'The Beatles and Psychedelia' (*Record Collector*, June 1993)

Pichois Claude and Ziegler, Jean, *Baudelaire* (Vintage, 1991)

Poe, Edgar Allan, *The Fall of the House of Usher and Other Stories* (Marshall Cavendish, 1992)

Potash, Chris (ed.), *The Jimi Hendrix Companion – Three Decades of Commentary* (Schirmer, 1996)

Povey, Glenn and Russell, Ian, *Pink Floyd in the Flesh – The Complete Performance History* (Bloomsbury, 1997)

Poynor, Rick, *Eno and Mills – More Dark Than Shark* (Faber, 1986)

Prendergast, Mark, *Irish Rock: Roots, Personalities and Directions* (O'Brien, 1987)

——'Ambient Music' (*Record Collector*, June 1994)

——'Ambient Noises, Ambient Techno' (*Sound On Sound*, March 1995)

——'Background Story – The Rise of Ambient Music' (*New Statesman*, October 1993)

——'Breaking Free – The Technological Revolution' (*Music & Musicians International*, August 1989)

——'Brian Eno – Art, Contingency and Catholicism' (*Variant*, Spring 1993)

——'Future Perfect – Holger Czukay and David Sylvian' (*Music & Musicians International*, June 1988)

——'Jimi Hendrix – Racial Rehabilitation' (*New Statesman*, 1995)

——'New Electronic and Instrumental Music' (*Sound On Sound* April 1989)

——'Stockhausen – Pop's Unsung Random Pioneer' (*Observer*, May 1992)

——*Tangents – Tangerine Dream 1973–1983 (Virgin, 1994)*

——'Tangerine Dream – The Dream Roots Collection' (Castle, 1996)

——'The New Age Music Conundrum' (*Sound On Sound*, January 1987)

Proust, Marcel, *Remembrance of Things Past Vol. 1* (Chatto & Windus, 1966)

Repsch, John, 'Joe Meek' (*Record Collector*, October 1990)

Reynolds, Simon, *Energy Flash – A Journey through Rave Music and Dance Culture* (Picador, 1998)

——'Shaking the Rock Narcotic – Post Rock' (*The Wire*, September 1993)

Rhode, Eric, *A History of the Cinema – From its Origins to 1970* (Pelican, 1978)

Rimbaud, Arthur, *Illuminations* (New Directions, 1957)

Rogan, Johnny, *Neil Young – The Definitive Story of His Musical Career* (Proteus, 1982)

——*Timeless Flight – The Definitive Biography of The Byrds* (Square One, 1990)

——*Van Morrison – A Portrait of the Artist* (Elm Tree, 1984)

Roud, Richard, *Godard* (Secker & Warburg, 1967)

Rushkoff, Douglas, *Cyberia – Life in the Trenches of Hyperspace* (Flamingo, 1994)

Rycroft, Charles, *Psychoanalysis Observed* (Pelican, 1968)

Sandford, Christopher, *Bowie – Loving the Alien* (Little Brown, 1996)

Saunders, Nicholas, *E is for Ecstasy* (Nicholas Saunders, 1993)

Sawyer-Lauçanno, Christopher, *An Invisible Spectator – A Biography of Paul Bowles* (Paladin, 1990)

Scaduto, Anthony, *Bob Dylan* (Abacus, 1973)

Schaeffer, John, *New Sounds – The Virgin Guide to New Music* (Virgin, 1990)

Schaffner, Nicholas, *Saucerful of Secrets – The Pink Floyd Odyssey* (Sidgwick & Jackson, 1991)

Schwarz, K. Robert, *Minimalists* (Phaidon, 1996)

Searson, Charles, 'Mahler's Final Enigma' (*Classic CD*, March 1993)

Secrest, Meryle, *Salvador Dali – The Surrealist Jester* (Paladin, 1988)

Selvin, Joel, *Summer of Love – The Inside Story of LSD. . .* (Plume, 1995)

Shaar Murray, Charles, *Crosstown Traffic – Jimi Hendrix and Post-War Pop* (Faber, 1989)

Shapiro, Harry, *Waiting for the Man – The Story of Drugs and Popular Music* (Quartet, 1988)

Shapiro, Harry and Glebbeek, Caesar, *Jimi Hendrix – Electric Gypsy* (Heinemann, 1990)

Singer, Caroline, 'Ravi Shankar' (*Record Collector*, September 1998)

Sinker, Mark, 'Altered States – The Chemistry of Sound, Drug and Dream' (*The Wire*, November 1992)

Sinyard, Neil, *The Films of Nicolas Roeg* (Letts, 1991)

Smith, Andrew, 'R&S (Renaat & Sabine in Ghent)' (*Volume*, TEE1 1993)

Stableford, Brian (ed.), *The Dedalus Book of Decadence (Moral Ruins)* (Dedalus, 1990)

——*The Second Dedalus Book of Decadence (The Black Feast)* (Dedalus, 1992)

Stevens, Jay, *Storming Heaven – LSD and the American Dream* (Heinemann, 1988)

Steward, Sue, 'Laurie Anderson – Angel In A Hardhat' (*20/20*, November 1990)

Stockhausen, Karlheinz, *Towards a Cosmic Music* (Element, 1989)

Sylvian, David, *Trophies – The Lyrics of David Sylvian* (Opium Arts, 1981)

Tamm, Eric, *Brian Eno – His Music and the Vertical Colour of Sound* (Faber, 1989)

——*Robert Fripp – From King Crimson to Guitar Craft* (Faber, 1990)

Tarkovsky, Andrei, *Sculpting in Time* (Bodley Head, 1986)

Taylor, Derek, 'Inside The Byrds – Personal Reflections' (*Sony*, January 1990)

Thomas, Adrian, 'Gorecki – A Place at the Top' (*Classic CD*, December 1992)

Thompson, Hunter S., *Fear and Loathing in Las Vegas* (Paladin, 1972)

Tingen, Paul, 'John Adams – Crossing Borders' (*Sound On Sound*, February 1997)

——'Miles into the Future – Bill Laswell Reshapes the Music of Miles Davis' (*Sound On Sound*, May 1998)

Tobler, John, 'Captain in the Quest for Arthur Lee' –*Love Masters* (Elektra, 1973)

Toop, David, 'Ambient Music In Sensurround Sound' (*The Wire*, May 1992)

——'Aphex Twin – Lost In Space' (*The Face*, March 1994)

Trask, Simon, 'Can – The Right Time' (*Music Technology*, November 1989)

Troy, Sandy, *One More Saturday Night – Reflections with The Grateful Dead* (St Martin's Press, 1991)

Turner, Steve, *Van Morrison – It's Too Late to Stop Now* (Bloomsbury, 1993)

Vail, Mark (ed.), *Vintage Synthesizers* (GPI, 1993)

Vale, V. and Juno, Andrea, *J. G. Ballard* (Re/Search, 1988)

Walker, John A., *Art Since Pop* (Thames and Hudson, 1975)

Watts, Alan, *The Essential Alan Watts* (Celestial Arts, 1977)

Wenders, Wim, *Emotion Pictures* (Faber, 1989)

White, Paul, 'Alan Parsons – Twenty Years of Pink Floyd's Dark Side of The Moon' (*Sound On Sound*, November 1993)

Wilde, Oscar, *The Picture of Dorian Gray* (Marshall Cavendish, 1991)

Williams, Nicholas, 'Toru Takemitsu – Out of the East' (*Classic CD*, October 1994)

Wilson, Colin, *C. G. Jung – Lord of the Underworld* (Aquarian, 1988)

——*G. I. Gurdjieff – The War Against Sleep* (Aquarian, 1986)

——*The Occult* (Mayflower, 1973)

Wilson, Simon, *Pop* (Thames and Hudson, 1975)

Witts, Richard, *Nico – The Life and Lies of an Icon* (Virgin, 1993)

Wolfe, Tom, *The Electric Kool-Aid Acid Test* (Bantam, 1980)

Yorke, Ritchie, *Van Morrison – Into the Music* (Charisma, 1975)

Young, La Monte, Zazeela, Marian, and Furneth, David, 'The Well-Tuned Piano' (Gramavision, 1987)

Zimmer, Dave and Diltz, Henry, *Crosby, Stills & Nash – The Authorized Biography* (Omnibus, 1984)

Index

A NOTE ON THE AUTHOR

 Mark Prendergast, born in Dublin, is the author of more than one million words on New & Electronic music. He has written about classical music and rock for newspapers, journals and magazines worldwide and authored the first definitive history of Irish rock. Now resident in London his *Ambient Century* is the culmination of two decades listening with 'all gates open'.

A NOTE ON THE TYPE

The text of this book is set in Bembo. This type was first used in 1495 by the Venetian printer Aldus Manutius for Cardinal Bembo's *De Aetna*, and was cut for Manutius by Francesco Griffo. It was one of the types used by Claude Garamond (1480–1561) as a model for his Romain de L'Université, and so it was the forerunner of what became standard European type for the following two centuries. Its modern form follows the original types and was designed for Monotype in 1929.